Warman's AMERICAN POTTERY AND PORCELAIN

Volumes in the Encyclopedia of Antiques and Collectibles

Harry L. Rinker, Series Editor

Warman's Americana & Collectibles, 6th Edition,
edited by Harry L. Rinker

Warman's American Pottery & Porcelain,
by Susan and Al Bagdade

Warman's Country Antiques & Collectibles, 2nd Edition,
by Dana Gehman Morykan and Harry L. Rinker

Warman's English & Continental Pottery & Porcelain, 2nd Edition,
by Susan and Al Bagdade

Warman's Furniture,
edited by Harry L. Rinker

Warman's Glass,
by Ellen Tischbein Schroy

Warman's Oriental Antiques,
by Gloria and Robert Mascarelli

Warman's Paper,
by Norman E. Martinus and Harry L. Rinker

Warman's
American Pottery and Porcelain

SUSAN and AL BAGDADE

Wallace-Homestead Book Company

Radnor, Pennsylvania

Published in Radnor, Pennsylvania 19089, by Wallace-Homestead,
a division of Chilton Book Company.

Library of Congress Cataloging in Publication Data
Bagdade, Susan D.
Warman's American pottery and porcelain / Susan and Al Bagdade.
p.   cm.—(Encyclopedia of antiques and collectibles)
Includes bibliographical references and index.
ISBN 0-87069-693-9
1. Pottery, American—Collectors and collecting.
2. Porcelain, American—Collectors and collecting.
I. Bagdade, Allen D.   II. Title.   III. Series.
NK4005.A1B35   1994
738'.0973'075—dc20   94-3191
CIP

Cover photos, *clockwise from top right:*
Comport, 12", Fiesta Ware, Homer Laughlin, **$80.00;**
Pillow Vase, 7$\frac{1}{2}$", "LOUWELSA WELLER" mark, **$2,000.00;**
Cookie Jar, Little Red Riding Hood, Hull, **$325.00;**
Teapot, 5$\frac{3}{4}$", Shell and Seaweed pattern, "Etruscan Majolica" mark, **$1,500.00;**
Plate, 10", Currier and Ives pattern, Royal China, **$5.00.**

1 2 3 4 5 6 7 8 9 0   3 2 1 0 9 8 7 6 5 4

CONTENTS

PART I / INTRODUCTION

PART II / MANUFACTURERS AND LISTINGS

PREFACE

Since our *Warman's English & Continental Pottery & Porcelain* price guide was so well received by everyone associated with the antiques field, we decided to turn our attention to the arena of American pottery and porcelain. Once again, we found that there really was not one comprehensive volume dealing with all aspects of American pottery and porcelain.

We feel that by providing helpful materials such as reference books, museums, collectors' clubs, periodicals, and marks along with a concise history of the manufactory, we have made our book different from any other American price guide. It definitely fills a void for antiques dealers and collectors.

As with our earlier tome, this volume was a true division of labor. Al was once again in charge of the nearly eleven thousand listing entries and their prices along with taking the three

hundred photographs. Susan wrote the histories for the nearly one hundred fifty manufactories which were divided into four headings: Art Pottery, Dinnerware, General, and Utilitarian.

Everywhere we sought information, whether at auction houses, antiques shows, antiques shops or malls, flea markets, museums, or pottery factories, we found encouragement and enthusiasm for this much needed project.

As with our other books, we invite readers to send their comments to us in care of our publisher, Wallace-Homestead Book Company, 201 King of Prussia Road, Radnor, Pennsylvania, 19089. We hope our readers are pleased with this new effort.

Susan and Al Bagdade
September, 1994

ACKNOWLEDGMENTS

Harry L. Rinker has guided us through every step of planning and preparing this book. Without his help, advice, prodding, and encouragement, this book would not have been possible.

Ellen Schroy at Rinker Enterprises has helped us in many ways with suggestions and resources.

A special debt of thanks must go to Rich Kleinhardt for drawing, on a very tight schedule, all the American pottery and porcelain marks required for this manuscript.

We must thank the auction houses for providing complimentary subscriptions to their extensive catalogues and access to their photographs. The authors express grateful appreciation to auctioneers Leslie Hindman of Chicago and Terry Dunning of Elgin, Illinois who allowed us to photograph auction properties.

David Rago, Harmer Rooke, and John Toomey were kind enough to send photographs from their auction catalogues for items we had trouble locating.

Additional thanks to Randi Schwartz, John Stein and Nancy Rosenbaum, Ruby Edelman, and Mercedes Di Renzo for lending us pieces from their collections to photograph for the cover of this book. An extra special thanks to Charles Bagdade for taking the cover photographs.

We would also like to thank Troy Vozzella, our editor at Chilton, and all the many Chilton personnel who worked to make this American pottery and porcelain book a reality.

Special Credits

Our gratitude must go to the following people for their exceptional help with either data for this book and/or photographs. Without their generous help, we would have been unable to write this book: Randi Schwartz, Ruby Edelman, Jazz 'e Junque, John Stein, Nancy Rosenbaum, Betty Blair, Dunning Auction Service, Leslie Hindman Auctioneers, David Rago, John Toomey, Don Treadway, Gerald Schultz, Harmer Rooke, Garth's Auction, Inc., and Skinner Auction Gallery.

Warman's AMERICAN POTTERY AND PORCELAIN

Part I / Introduction

ORGANIZATION OF THE PRICE GUIDE

Nearly one hundred and fifty companies/categories dealing with American pottery and porcelain are divided into four sections: Art Pottery, Dinnerware, General, and Utilitarian Ware. Companies/categories are listed alphabetically within these four divisions.

Companies that produced more than one type of ware, such as Roseville, were placed where collectors would be most likely to look for them first (for example, Roseville is in the Art Pottery section). Companies whose products were diverse and produced in large quantities were placed in the various sections according to what they made, such as Art Pottery and General for Buffalo and Hull. Histories for these companies were not repeated. Readers should check the cross referenced notes for the location of the history.

Companies that produced all types of products, without any one predominating, were placed in the General Manufacturers section.

Utilitarian categories list items that are collected as a group, such as yellowware, cookie jars, redware, railroad china, etc., even though they were made by many different companies. Readers should rely on the index to find where all products of a specific company are listed.

History: Every category has a history that details the founding of the company, its location, dates of existence, nature of the wares, and general information. Notes about marks are included in the history. Some company dates may not be exact since the reference materials available do not always agree about opening and closing dates of manufactories.

References: Reference books are listed whenever possible to encourage the collector to learn more about the category. Books are listed only if there is a substantial section on the specific category being considered, or if it is a complete book on that category. Included in references are author, title, publisher, (if published by a small firm or individual, we have indicated "privately printed"), and date of publication or most recent edition.

Some of the books listed may be out of print and no longer available from the publisher; these will usually be available in public libraries or through inter-library loan. Readers also may find antiques book dealers at antiques shows, flea markets, and advertising in trade papers and journals. Many book dealers provide mail order services. Additional general reference books on American pottery and porcelain are listed in the bibliography.

Periodicals: In addition to publications of collectors' clubs, there are numerous general interest newspapers and magazines that devote attention to American ceramics. A sampling includes the following:

Antique Monthly, 2100 Powers Ferry Rd., Atlanta, GA 30339
Antique Review, P.O. Box 538, Worthington, OH 43085
Antique Trader Weekly, P.O. Box 1050, Dubuque, IA 52001
Antique Week, P.O. Box 90, Knightstown, IN 46148
Antiques and Auction News, P.O. Box 500, Mount Joy, PA 17552
Antiques and Collecting Hobbies, 1006 S. Michigan Ave., Chicago, IL 60650
Antiques and The Arts Weekly, 5 Church Hill Rd., Newtown, CT 06470
Antiques (The Magazine Antiques), 575 Broadway, New York, NY 10012
Collector Magazine and Price Guide, P.O. Box 4333, Charlottesville, VA 22905
Collector News, Box 156, Grundy Center, IA 50638
Maine Antique Digest, 911 Main St., Waldboro, ME 04572
Mid Atlantic Antiques Monthly, P.O. Box 908, Henderson, NC 27536
New York-Pennsylvania Collector, Drawer C, Fishers, NY 14453
The Daze, 10271 State Rd., Box 57, Otisville, MI 48463
West Coast Peddler, P.O. Box 5134, Whittier, CA 90607
Yesteryear, P.O. Box 2, Princeton, WI 54968

Museums: Museums are listed if significant collections pertaining to the category are on display. Many museums have large collections of American ceramics but did not provide a detailed listing for inclusion in this book. If the name of the museum and the city where it is located are the same, only the state is listed for the location of the museum. A listing of museums with significant American ceramics is located in the Appendix.

1

Collectors' Clubs: All collectors' clubs have been verified to be active. The most recent address is listed for membership information.

Additional Listings: When the category/company is covered in more than one listing, other listings are added to help the reader find additional information. Be sure to check the index to locate all the data.

Marks: When wares are marked, we have included representative marks for that manufactory. Readers should realize that there is some variation in the marks within the same manufactory. However, to see the full range of marks used by a firm, one must consult one of the marks books listed in the Bibliography.

DERIVATION OF PRICES USED

Prices for listed items were derived from a variety of sources. Field work involving antiques shows, flea markets, antiques shops, and antiques malls were a major source for pricing. The prices listed are the actual retail prices of an item, i.e. what the collector would have to pay to purchase the piece.

General ceramics and specialized auctions were another important source for pricing. These items are identified in the guide with an (A) prior to the listed price. The price reflects the hammer price plus whatever buyer's premium was charged.

Another important source of pricing came from antiques trade papers, journals, antiques magazines, and price lists solicited from antiques dealers. These were important for determining what pieces were actually available, what their condition was, as well as what price was required to obtain the piece.

Dinnerware pieces are listed individually. However, the collector can often find the best value when purchasing a complete dinner service. Many more partial sets are available on the marketplace than complete sets. With this in mind, the collector can fill out a partial set with some diligent searching using the pricing found in this guide as a reference point. This also holds true for those who wish to replace or add additional pieces to a complete service.

For the most part, quotation marks are not used with pattern names in the listings or histories.

THE ROLE OF CONDITION
IN PRICING AMERICAN CERAMICS

Condition is one of the major factors that dictates price. In a very few instances, where an item is extremely rare, or is a true one-of-a-kind piece, condition may not be the deciding factor in determining if a piece is worth purchasing.

The term "mint" should mean just that: factory fresh without any sign of wear or damage. "Flea bites, dings, and nicks" are just terms for damage. The same holds true for such overused words as "age cracks and hairlines" which actually indicate damaged goods.

The collector should strive to purchase the best possible examples. Due to the large quantity of material produced by the major companies, this can be accomplished with diligent shopping.

The frequent use of over-the-glaze transfers and decals on American ceramics makes them vulnerable to damage. Fading, splitting, and loss of body are fairly common; examples with these defects should be avoided. Since early American ceramic glazes tended to be heavy, cracking and staining of the surface and underbody are fairly common and detract from the appearance of the piece as well as its value.

Knife scratches on the surface, if minimal, are acceptable, but if the scratches pierce the glaze or design, they attract and retain dirt which is difficult to remove. By holding a plate on the horizontal and gently tilting it towards the light, the depth of scratching can usually be ascertained.

Broken or repaired pieces should be avoided unless the piece is of such merit that it belongs in a collection. However, the price should reflect the degree of damage and repair. Slight variations in color, surface texture, and glaze often indicate a repair. Examine carefully knobs, handles, and spouts which are easily damaged. The use of a black light can often detect repairs and should be used when a question exists.

The key element is to purchase the best example that fits comfortably within your pocketbook.

STATE OF THE MARKET

Over the past few decades, interest in American ceramics has been on a steady climb, and this appears to be the case going into the next century. The bright colors, simple decorations, availability, and relatively low prices are all factors contributing to this popularity. Once overlooked as unsophisticated compared with their English, European, and Oriental cousins, it is precisely this naivete that works in its favor in the eyes of collectors.

During the past year, art pottery has had its share of highs and lows. Unusual examples of Arts and Crafts, Art Nouveau, and Art Deco are selling very well at auction, antiques shows, and shops. A few highlights included an organic form Teco vase which reached $22,550, and a volcanic glazed Dedham vase which sold for $44,100. Well-painted examples of Rookwood pottery are also doing very well, but the scarcity of these contributes to the high selling price. The majority of the pieces in this grouping are pretty sluggish. This is due partly to the large amount of rather undistinguished material being offered to collectors. The antiquer who is just venturing into the American art pottery field should do quite well since prices are fairly competitive.

Several of the lesser-known companies have caught the eye of purchasers, and examples from these potteries should be watched for future movement. Walley, Pillin, California Faience, and Scheier, to name a few, are doing well at auction; good examples can be secured for reasonable prices. They appear to be at the take off point.

The "darlings" for the American ceramics collector are dinnerware and accessory pieces. Collectors taking their first tentative steps into the antiques market are active in this arena. Examples are sought after for display and use. There is an abundance of dinnerware in complete and partial sets, and most are priced well within the range of the majority of collectors. Patterns from Red Wing, Hall, Syracuse, and Russel Wright are among those that have caught the eye of novices as well as experienced collectors.

This dinnerware arena appears very muddled since no distinct collecting patterns have emerged. This may change, but at the present, collectors jump from one pattern to another with-

out a favorite or two emerging. With the large number of patterns on the market, this will remain true for the near future.

This is not the case for Homer Laughlin's Fiesta, however. This design has been around since 1936 and Fiesta collectors are well-schooled in the prices they must pay for this dinnerware. Rare shapes have all but disappeared from the market, and when they do surface, prices are very high. Ordinary shapes are plentiful, and collectors should shop for the best price and condition with an eye on their pocketbook.

Going hand-in-hand with dinnerware is the popular category called kitchenware. Manufacturers such as Hall, Regal, and Watt have become "hot," and prices have risen accordingly. Popular patterns have been pushed to artificial highs compared to the amount of material available, but prices should come back to earth in the not-too-distant future. Collectors who are storing kitchenware to watch the price trends may find that these pieces will trail off and then drop in price as collections are returned to the marketplace.

Ceramics produced by West Coast potteries such as Vernon Kilns, Bauer, Wallace, and Catalina Island are actively sought after. Better pieces such as bookends, candlesticks, and the like are soaring. The Western theme found on Wallace china is presently pricey and desired by collectors. Some of the lesser-known makers such as Winfield and Brayton Laguna are beginning to have a following and prices should rise for these up-and-coming potteries.

A similar picture emerges in the American Indian pottery field. Fine early examples, unique pieces, and those potted by known artists are selling well. Contemporary pieces are also doing well, but there is a large amount of material available.

The bloom is off the cookie jar market. This was one of the glamour collecting categories, but there are so many jars on the market, that it becomes quite confusing to try and assemble a theme collection. The rarer items are falling short of pre-auction estimates. This trend will likely continue as more and more jars flood the market, including the reissues of rarer jars. This market appears to be saturated.

The Harmer Rooke Galleries' auction of the large Georgeanna Greer stoneware collection is a microcosm of this entire field. Artistically decorated pieces are selling at very high prices, but the majority of the more common shapes and decorations are struggling. This is also a field that has a wealth of material, and antiquers have become selective when purchasing pieces for their collections.

SEEING AMERICA'S CERAMICS INDUSTRY

The collector of American ceramics is in a fortunate position. Many fine museums specializing in ceramic products of the United States are within easy reach. Several top quality museums maintain extensive collections of work native to the region and provide a wealth of educational materials.

One such museum we visited while traveling around the country seeking material for this book is the East Liverpool Museum of Ceramics located in East Liverpool, Ohio. Situated in one of the major United States pottery and porcelain centers from the late 1800s to well into the 20th

Placing dishes in saggers prior to the firing process. Courtesy of the East Liverpool Museum of Ceramics, OH.

East Liverpool Museum of Ceramics, East Liverpool, OH.

century, the museum offers a glimpse into the technology and economics of this period. It is a must stop for any serious collector of American ceramics. Museums such as this one can be found in many parts of the United States.

In addition, several working porcelain and pottery factories offer tours of their facilities. The great Homer Laughlin factory in Newell, West Virginia (across the river from East Liverpool), Hall China, and the Robinson Ransbottom concern offer walking tours complete with demonstrations of the art of the commercial potter.

ABBREVIATIONS USED IN THE LISTINGS

A.D.	after dinner		K	karat
adv	advertising		l	length
C	Century		med	medium
c	circa		mkd	marked
circ	circular		mtd	mounted
cov	cover, covered		mts	mounts
d	diameter or depth		NE	New England
dbl	double		oct	octagonal
dtd	dated		opal	opalescent
emb	embossed		orig	original
ext	exterior		pr	pair
ftd	footed		prs	pairs
ground	background		rect	rectangular
h	height		sgd	signed
hex	hexagonal		SP	silver plated
H-H	handle to handle		SS	sterling silver
horiz	horizontal		sq	square
hp	hand painted		vert	vertical
imp	impressed		w	width
int	interior		yr	year
irid	iridescent		#	numbered
irreg	irregular			

Part II / Manufacturers and Listings

ART POTTERY

The potteries listed under this heading specialized in art and decorative pottery utilizing innovative forms, techniques, and glazes. Many of the potteries were fairly large, while others were quite small and can be classified as studio potteries.

In a few instances, large manufacturers, such as Red Wing, Buffalo, and Hull, created some art pottery lines in addition to their more extensive general lines. Listings are included in each appropriate section.

1911

AREQUIPA POTTERY
Fairfax, California
1911–1918

History: Arequipa Pottery was started in 1911 in a tuberculosis sanatorium at Arequipa as a project for the female patients. Frederick Rhead, art director at Roseville, and Agnes, his wife, served as instructors, using the native California clays.

After an attempt to incorporate Arequipa and Roseville, the Rheads left, and Albert Solon became pottery director in 1913. He had trained in England as a ceramic engineer and worked in a tile factory before coming to the United States. A variety of works was made by hand at the pottery. Patients were responsible for much of the decorating and hand finishing, while Solon experimented with a variety of glazes. Works exhibited at the Panama-Pacific Exposition in 1915 won several awards.

F.H. Wilde replaced Solon in 1915 and continued the work with glazes. With the constant turnover of patients and the frequent changes in directors during the years of its existence, no specific style developed at Arequipa. Handmade Spanish-type tiles were introduced by Wilde before the pottery was forced to close due to the war in Europe in 1918.

Most pieces were marked with the jug-under-a-tree mark along with the company name either painted, incised, or impressed. Some have the date added to the mark. Paper labels also were used.

Museums: National Museum of History and Technology, Smithsonian Institution, Washington, DC; New Orleans Museum of Art, LA.

Bowl
  4½" d
    Incised leaves, shaded brown gloss glaze 495.00
    Rounded sides, matte light gray-blue mottled glaze, mkd(A) 200.00
  7½" d, white and blue incised lilies of the valley on blue-gray ground, incised "AA, 1911" mark(A).......... 385.00
  10" d, center w/slip trail relief of green and yellow peacock and purple and yellow rose, yellow and green garland on inner border, white rim and ext, "AREQUIPA CALIFORNIA, 190" mark(A) 1980.00
  11" d, mauve glaze 200.00
  12" d, dark brown glaze................. 450.00
Vase
  3¼" h, bulbous shape, modeled stylized flowers, gloss black glaze, imp "3/ps3/24" mark 350.00
  3½" h, matte tan ground, teal blue shoulder(A)................................ 193.00
  4" h, light blue matte glaze 250.00
  4½" h, squat shape, incised flowers under matte feathered blue-gray glaze, imp "AREQUIPA/CALIFORNIA/532/16/EMI" mark 400.00
  5" h, matte rose glaze, dtd 1912...... 550.00
  5½" h, carved black stylized blossoms on sinewy stems, feathered brown ground, stamped "AREQUIPA/CALIFORNIA/301," incised "NN 11" mark 850.00
  6" h
    Arts and Crafts squeeze-bag de-

sign at top, matte purple glaze, imp mark(A) 935.00

Inverted baluster shape w/dbl ribbing, scalloped rim, matte plum glaze, mkd 700.00

Rust and black squeeze-bag curlicues and arabesques, light green excised and incised lotus blossoms, light blue-green ground, Frederick Rhead, rim restored, incised "Arequipa" mark(A) 4400.00

6⅛" h, shouldered ovoid shape, glazed pink and yellow vine on mouth, matte green glazed ground, imp tree, vase, and "AREQUIPA CALIFORNIA, 2084" mark(A) .. 1045.00

6¼" h, squeeze-bag white, cobalt, and brown stylized vines on shoulder, flowing green ground(A) 1650.00

6¾" h, carved tall grasses under raspberry pink and light green matte glaze, stamped "AREQUIPA, CALIFORNIA, 206-5" mark(A) 825.00

7½" h, bulbous shape, incised grasses and flowers, curdled matte blue glaze, mkd(A) 495.00

7¾" h, swollen cylinder shape, incised and molded scattered blossoms on shoulder, matte plum glaze(A) 288.00

8" h

Green lava glaze 550.00

Relief of florals and leaves, pink-brown semi-gloss glaze w/brown flecks, incised "Arequipa, CA, GG, #256, MS 111" marks(A) 990.00

11¼" h, reticulated, raised wisteria blossoms, irid green glaze, unmkd(A) 1980.00

Vessel, 2½" h, 5" d, narrow opening, applied leaves on rim, blue and white flambe glaze, mkd(A) 1210.00

made by Henry Chapman Mercer in Doylestown, Pennsylvania. Batchelder became partners with Frederick Brown, while sculptors Charles and Emma Ingels made master molds for him.

The early tiles were designed in low relief and hand pressed from plaster molds. Some had medieval heraldic subjects or views of California landscapes. The relief tiles made from California clays were sprayed with slip in a variety of colors. Each tile was signed.

With Lucian Wilson as a new partner, the factory moved to Los Angeles in 1916 and became a full-service tile factory making glazed faience tiles in numerous designs. Architectural panels, moldings, corbels, fireplace facings, and fountains also were made, along with architectural terra-cotta, garden pots, and bookends. Batchelder was able to supply a large quantity of tiles in a variety of colored glazes during the building boom of the 1920s.

In 1930 the full effect of the Depression hit the company, and it went bankrupt in 1932. The stock was sold to Bauer Pottery. By 1936 Batchelder started over in Pasadena as Batchelder Ceramics. Using high-quality glazes, he made slip-cast earthenware bowls and vases in modern adaptations of the classical Chinese forms. This was a small operation and Batchelder hand incised his name on most pieces. Batchelder ceramics were sold through department stores and gift shops until Batchelder retired in 1951.

Reference: Jack Chipman, *Collector's Encyclopedia of California Pottery*, Collector Books, 1992.

Ashtray, 4½" d, hex shape, relief "BATCHELDER," light blue glaze, nicks(A) 165.00

Bookend, 4½" h, seated boy and girl in Dutch costumes, dark brown glaze w/blue and green accents, imp "BATCHELDER LOS ANGELES, 20808x" mark, pr(A) 200.00

BATCHELDER LOS ANGELES

BATCHELDER POTTERY COMPANY
Pasadena and Los Angeles, California
1910–1932
1936–1951

History: Ernest Batchelder started making tiles in his studio in Pasadena, California, in 1910. He was influenced by the Moravian tiles

Tile, 2¾" sq, tan w/dark gray leaves, imp "O.E. BATCHELDER" mark, $30.00

Vase

3" h, pot shape, cobalt glaze, "O.E. Batchelder" mark	**100.00**
5" h, mustard, brown, and gray flambe glaze(A)	**165.00**
5¾" h, flared shape w/closed rim, mottled cobalt gloss glaze on brown ground(A)	**275.00**
6" h, sphere shape, mottled cobalt and black gloss glaze(A)	**220.00**
6¼" h	
Bell shape, rolled rim, mirror brown, black, and gray glaze, cipher mark(A)	**192.00**
Flared shape w/curled-in rim, textured orange bisque ext, brown int(A)	**165.00**
6½" h, bulbous body, 3 loop handles, semi-gloss black glaze(A)	**330.00**
7½" h, cylinder shape, closed rim, irid speckled brown glaze(A)	**247.00**
8¼" h, bulging shoulder, narrow neck, clear to opaque olive green glaze(A)	**192.00**

DELDARE WARE
UNDERGLAZE

BUFFALO POTTERY
Buffalo, New York
1903–1983

History: The Buffalo Pottery was established in 1903 by the Larkin Soap Company to produce premiums for its mail-order business. Louis H. Brown, who came from Crescent Pottery in Trenton, New Jersey, was the first manager, and he brought artists and craftsmen with him to Buffalo. William Rea was the first superintendent. Although most wares were made for the Larkin Company, products also were sold to outlets throughout the country.

The first wares were semi-vitreous china dinner sets that were given away with the soap products. Commemorative, historical, and advertising examples also were made, along with the first American underglaze Blue Willow pattern. From 1905–1909 Buffalo Pottery made a series of semi-vitreous china pitchers in twenty-nine patterns. The decorations were transfer printed and often hand decorated. Many were edged in gold.

William Rea brought Buffalo Pottery into the art pottery arena with his Deldare Ware in 1908. Pieces had a solid olive green ground with a high gloss glaze. Goldsmith's *Vicar of Wakefield* provided the design ideas for the transfer-printed scenes. Artists decorated the pieces by hand according to rigid patterns and signed each piece. Dinner sets, tea sets, dresser sets with trays, vases, drinking sets, pitchers, chocolate sets, and other pieces were made in Deldare.

The Fallowfield Hunt featured English foxhunting scenes with borders of hunters on horseback. A title was written on the face of each piece. A second pattern, Ye Olden Days, had a continuous border of old two-story houses and local scenes of English life, both indoors and out. This pattern was made from 1908–1909 and then reissued from 1924–1925. It was discontinued both times because of high production costs.

Emerald Deldare, made with olive clay in 1911, depicted Dr. Syntax scenes, as well as Art Nouveau motifs, geometric designs, stylized flowers and butterflies, and scenes of lakes and mountains. These limited-production pieces are sought after due to their superior design and decoration. In 1912 Albino Ware, featuring hand-decorated sailing scenes, rural Dutch windmills, and other pastoral designs, was made on the same shapes as Deldare.

The change from semi-vitreous ware to vitrified china took place in 1915, and the stamped mark changed from "Buffalo Pottery" to "Buffalo China." Lines included Luna Ware, Cafe-au-Lait, and Ivory Ware in soft colors. During World War I, Buffalo Pottery produced extensively for the government.

After the war, production resumed on commercial dinnerwares for hotels, institutions, steamship lines, etc., as well as on Larkin premiums and items sold directly to the public. The last time that Buffalo pottery was offered as a Larkin premium was in 1923. After that, Larkin imported china pieces for their premiums since that was cheaper than producing their own. The body color of institutional ware was added to the "Buffalo China" mark after 1930.

In 1940 Buffalo Pottery was reorganized under the name Buffalo Pottery, Inc. During World War II, production was again dominated by dinnerware for the armed forces. In 1950 the first Christmas plates were made, and they were manufactured until 1962. Buffalo continued to mass produce hotel and industrial wares for firms such as the Chesapeake and Ohio Railroad, one of its major clients. In 1983 Buffalo China, Inc., was acquired by Oneida Ltd. of Oneida, New York.

Reference: Violet and Seymour Altman, *The Book of Buffalo Pottery,* Schiffer Publishing, Ltd., 1987.

Museum: Historical Society Museum, Buffalo, NY.

DELDARE WARE
The Fallowfield Hunt
Berry Bowl, 6¼" d, "The Start," sgd, dtd 1908, set of 6 (A)...................... **1100.00**
Bowl, 9⅛" d, 4" h, "The Death," sgd "A. Steiner," dtd 1908(A)................. **880.00**
Card Tray, 7¾" d, men at breakfast, dtd 1909(A)................................... **660.00**
Chop Plate
   12¼" d, "Breakfast at The Three Pigeons," pierced for hanging, dtd 1908(A) **605.00**
   13¾" d, "The Start," dtd 1908(A) **770.00**
Creamer, 2¼" h, "Breaking Cover," sgd "H. Ford," dtd 1908(A)............. **185.00**
Mug, 3¾" h, "Breaking Cover," sgd "L. Palmer," dtd 1908(A) **357.00**
Pitcher
   7¼" h, "Breaking Cover," sgd "L. Newman," dtd 1909(A) **770.00**
   8" h, oct, "The Return," sgd "L. Streissel," dtd 1909(A) **880.00**
Plaque, 12" d, "Breakfast at the Three Pigeons".. **555.00**
Plate
   7¼" d, "Breaking Cover," sgd "L. Newman," dtd 1909(A) **275.00**
   8½" d, "The Death," sgd "L. Wil/L. Wit.," dtd 1908(A) **275.00**
   9⅜" d, "The Start," sgd "L. Streissel," dtd 1909(A) **253.00**
   10" d, "Breaking Cover," sgd "W. Foster," dtd 1909(A) **232.00**
Tankard
   4½" h, sgd "G. Bero," dtd 1908(A).. **495.00**
   12½" h, "The Hunt Supper," sgd "W. Foster," dtd 1909................. **950.00**
Teapot, 4½" h, "Breaking Cover," hairlines, sgd "S. Palmey," dtd 1908(A) **275.00**
Tea Tile, 6" sq, dtd 1908.................... **325.00**
Ye Olden Days
Bowl, 9" d, 3½" h, "Ye Village Tavern," sgd "Stiller," dtd 1908 .... **315.00**
Calendar Plate, 9⅜" d, sgd "E. Van Host," dtd 1910 .... **975.00**
Candlestick, 9¼" h, untitled, drilled at factory for lamp, (A) **165.00**
Card Tray, 7¾" d
   "Mr Pickwick Addresses The Club," sgd "L. Newman," dtd 1909 "Brush and Brickell limited Pittsburgh" on base(A)...................... **825.00**
   "Ye Lion Inn," sgd "M. Vogt," dtd 1908(A).................................... **385.00**
Charger, 13½" d, "Ye Evening at Ye Lion Inn" **350.00**
Chocolate Set, pot, 3 cups and saucers, "Ye Village Street," dtd 1909 .... **2800.00**
Chop Plate, 13¾" d, "An Evening at Ye Lion Inn," sgd "A. Steiner," dtd 1908(A)..................................... **467.00**

Cream and Sugar, "Scenes of Village Life in Ye Olden Years".................. **350.00**
Cup and Saucer, "Ye Olden Days" **200.00**
Dresser Tray, 9" w, 12" l, "Dancing Ye Minuet"..................................... **650.00**
Fruit Bowl, 9⅛" d, 3¾" h, "Village Tavern," sgd "L. Wit," dtd 1908(A).. **302.00**
Jardiniere, 8" d, 6" h, "Ye Village Street," dtd 1909(A)......................... **990.00**
Mug, 4½" h, "Ye Lion Inn" **250.00**
Pitcher
   6⅛" h, "Their Manner of Telling Stories—Which He Returned With a Curtsey," sgd "E. Dawlman," dtd 1908(A)...................... **462.00**
   7⅝" h, "To Spare an Old Broken Soldier,—To Advise Me in a Whisper" sgd "K. Caird," dtd 1909(A) **325.00**
   8" h
      Oct, "To Spare an Old Broken Soldier—To Advise Me in a Whisper," sgd "K. Caird," dtd 1909(A)..................................... **467.00**
      "Welcome Me With Most Cordial Hospitality," dtd 1924.............. **675.00**
   9" h, oct, "This Amazed Me—With a Cane Superior Air," dtd 1909(A) **450.00**
   10¼" h, "Ye Olde English Village— Ye Lion Inn," sgd "H. Ball," dtd 1908(A)..................................... **630.00**
   12½" h, tankard type, "The Great Controversy/All You Have To Do Is Teach Dutchmen English," sgd "A. Steiner," dtd 1908(A) **770.00**
Plaque, 12¼" d, "Ye Lion Inn," sgd "K. Caird," dtd 1909(A)......................... **210.00**
Plate
   6¼" d
      "At Ye Lion Inn," sgd "H. Ford," dtd 1908(A)............................... **155.00**
      Salesman's sample, "Hand Painted—Deldare Ware—Underglaze" on face(A) **1210.00**
   7⅜" d, "Village Street" **90.00**
   8½" d, "Ye Town Crier" **175.00**
   9¼" d, "Ye Olden Times" **173.00**
   10" d, "Ye Village Gossips," sgd "M. Delany," dtd 1909(A)................. **187.00**
Relish Dish, 12" l, "Ye Olden Times," rim chip, sgd "H. Sheenen," dtd 1908(A).. **231.00**
Soup Plate, 9" d, "Ye Village Street" ... **240.00**
Sugar Bowl, 4½" h, "Scenes of Ye Village Life in Ye Olden Days," sgd "A.B.," dtd 1924(A) **245.00**
Tankard
   4¼" h, "Ye Lion Inn," sgd "A. Wade," dtd 1909(A) **260.00**
   12½" h, "Great Controversy— Teach Dutchman English" **895.00**
Teapot, 4½" h, "Village Life in Ye Olden Days" **375.00**

Tea Set, pot, 5½" h, creamer, 3" h, sugar bowl, 4½" h, "Scenes of Village Life in Ye Olden Days" 1000.00

Tea Tile, 6⅛" d, "Traveling in Ye Olden Days," sgd "M. Broel," dtd 1909(A).. 550.00

Tea Tray, 12⅛" l, 9⅛" w, "Dancing Ye Minuet," sgd "L. Winter," dtd 1908(A).. 630.00

Tray, 13¾" l, 10¼" w, "Heirlooms" ... 595.00

EMERALD DELDARE WARE

Card Tray, 7¾" l, "Dr. Syntax Robbed of His Property," dtd 1911 .... 550.00

Charger, 13½" d, "Lost," flock of sheep in white fog, stylized floral border, printed "1911, Buffalo Pottery, Emerald Deldare Ware" mark(A) 1870.00

Chocolate Pot, 10⅝" h, hex, geometric and floral design, stylized dragonfly border on neck(A) 1870.00

Cup and Saucer, "Dr. Syntax at Liverpool," dtd 1911.............................. 650.00

Cup and Saucer, A. D., 3⅛" h, geometric and floral design, stylized dragonfly rims(A)............................ 660.00

Pitcher, 10" h, oct, "Dr Syntax—A Noble Hunting Party—He Canter'd By My Lady's Side—Who Undertook to be His Guide"(A) 1870.00

Plate

6¼" d, "Syntax Floral Offering"....... 450.00

8½" d, "Misfortune at Tulip Hall" ... 560.00

9¼" d

"Dr Syntax—The Donkie's Bray'd and Lo the Sound—Awak'd Him from His Thought Profound—and as He Stad'd and Look'd Around—He said or Else He Seem'd to Say—I Find I Have Lost My Way," restored rim chip(A)............................... 148.00

Garden Trio 600.00

10" d

"Dr Syntax Making a Discovery" . 500.00

"Yankee Doodle" 1350.00

Deldare Ware, Ye Olden Days, tray, 13¾" l × 10¼" w, "Heirlooms," olive, sgd "Foster," dtd 1908, $595.00

Sugar Bowl, "Dr Syntax in the Wrong Lodging House," dtd 1911 .... 375.00

Tray

12" l, 9¼" w, "Dr Syntax—Rural Sports," dtd 1911 .... 1050.00

13¾" l, 10½" w, "Dr. Syntax Mistakes a Gentleman's House for an Inn," chips, dtd 1911(A) 395.00

Vase, 8" h, kingfisher w/iris pattern..... 1500.00

BYBEE POTTERY

Bybee, Kentucky

1809–Present

History: Webster Cornelison started a pottery using his own name in 1809 in Bybee, Kentucky. James Eli, his son, began keeping company records in 1845. The firm, known as Bybee Pottery since 1954, is now owned by Walter Cornelison II—a sixth-generation descendent of the original founder.

In the early years, the company made salt-glazed stoneware. During the 1920s and 1930s, it used the rich clay that came from the area to produce fine artwares in heavy matte finish glazes. These pieces—primarily vases, candlesticks, and bowls—were shaped on the potter's wheel.

Utilitarian wares are now made in approximately a dozen glazes. One of the marks used is the stamped or impressed map of Kentucky with the words "Genuine Bybee." "Cornelison Pottery" was stamped on pieces from the 1930s and 1940s, and sometimes gold paper stickers were used.

Creamer, Cov, 5" h, blue-green glaze, mkd 20.00

Pitcher, 5" h, matte green glaze 19.00

Vase

5" h, 3 molded rings on neck, matte rose finish, mkd 40.00

6" h, ringed, shaded blue glaze, "Seldon Bybee" mark................... 15.00

6½" h, blue-green glaze................. 80.00

6¾" h, dbl handles, matte olive green glaze, map of Kentucky and "Bybee" mark 70.00

7" h

Dark red glaze, "Seldon Bybee" mark 32.00

Dbl handles, matte green feathered glaze 150.00

10¾" h, 3 handles, irid khaki green glaze w/mint green streaks........... 150.00

*Vase, 4³/₄" h, matte green glazed ext,
gloss green int, $35.00*

*Vase, 10¹/₂" h, olive green shaded
glaze, "Seldon Bybee, B.B." in globe
mark, $165.00*

11" h, 3 handles, cobalt glaze,
#569, "Seldon Bybee" mark **165.00**

had monochrome matte glaze finishes, although
some examples were done in high gloss. Tiles
and inserts were made in plaster molds and then
polychrome decorated. Florist ware was also
made, and for a short time in the mid 1920s, art
porcelain molds were made for West Coast
porcelain manufacturers.

No artwares were made during the Depression years, although some tiles were made for the
1932 World's Fair. Bragdon bought out Thomas
in the late 1930s and continued to operate the
firm, but no commercial artware was made. He
sold the factory in the early 1950s and worked
for the new owners until he died in 1959.

Artwares have the incised "California
Faience" mark; tiles were marked with a hand
stamp.

Museums: National Museum of History and
Technology, Smithsonian Institution, Washing-
ton, DC; The Newark Museum, NJ; The Oakland
Museum, CA.

Bookend, 6¹/₂" h, figural eagle in
   flight, wax matte blue glaze, mkd,
   pr(A) **357.00**
Bowl
   5³/₄" d, matte black int, gloss
    turquoise ext, mkd **220.00**
   6" d, fluted, blue on turquoise ext,
    turquoise int **200.00**
   6³/₄" d, lobed body, gloss sea green
    glaze, incised "California
    Faience" mark **800.00**
   9" d, turquoise ext, yellow int **115.00**
   12" d
    Blue ext, aqua int, wear on int **65.00**
    Gloss black ext, turquoise int **425.00**
Flower Holder, 6" h, 2 figural peli-
   cans, turquoise glaze(A) **125.00**
Tea Tile, Persian flowers, cobalt,
   white, and yellow **295.00**
Trivet
   5¹/₄" d, cloisonné-style blue pea-
    cock on matte ochre ground, in-
    cised mark(A) **385.00**
   5¹/₂" d, squeeze-bag style yellow

$\mathcal{C}aliforni\alpha$
$\mathcal{F}aience$

CALIFORNIA FAIENCE
Berkeley, California
1916–1950s

History: William Bragdon and Chauncey
Thomas began making art pottery and tiles in
1916. They adopted the name California Faience
in 1924.

The art pottery pieces were mostly cast and

*Bowl, 7" d, 3" h, gloss light blue
glaze(A), $99.00*

Vase, 4 1/2" h, gloss turquoise glaze, red clay body(A), $176.00

CHICAGO CRUCIBLE COMPANY
Chicago, Illinois
c1920–c1932

History: The Northwestern Terra-Cotta Company discontinued its Norweta line after acquiring the Chicago Crucible Company in 1920. The expanded facilities made decorative pottery vases, lamp bases, and ashtrays with mottled glazes in shades of blue and green. Additional production included wall plaques with relief portraits and whimsical open-mouthed frogs, but these lines were discontinued after a few years. A raised in mold mark was used. Some architectural terra-cotta also was made.

Reference: Sharon S. Darling, *Chicago Ceramics and Glass: An Illustrated History from 1871–1933*, Chicago Historical Society, 1979.

Vase
  4 3/4" h, rolled rim, green and yellow
    glaze, mkd.................................. 375.00
  5" h, 4 lobes, feathered green and
    ochre glaze, stamped mark(A) 387.00
  7" h, bulbous body, stepped neck, 2
    angular handles, bubbly green
    over brown glaze, imp mark(A).... 247.00
  8" h, matte green and caramel
    glaze, unmkd(A) 121.00
  9" h
    Bulging top, swirling raised stems
    w/elongated stylized leaves,
    matte green glaze, imp mark(A) 715.00
    Four openings at middle w/2
    open handles to top, matte
    green glaze w/light green and
    ground suspensions................. 600.00

poppies in turquoise ground, black base, imp "California Faience" mark(A) 880.00
Vase
  3" h, multicolored floral band, blue
    ground....................................... 895.00
  3 1/4" h, bulbous shape w/closed rim,
    dark blue gloss glaze 125.00
  3 3/4" h, matte turquoise glaze 105.00
  5 1/2" h
    Bulbous shape, gloss turquoise
    glaze....................................... 225.00
    Collar neck, textured blue-green
    glaze, mkd(A).......................... 825.00
  6" h
    Doves and arrows in relief,
    turquoise glaze 750.00
    Semi-matte yellow glaze............. 325.00
  6 3/4" h, trumpet shape, mustard
    glaze, chips on base, mkd(A) 302.00
  8" h, band of squeeze-bag stylized
    red, green, blue, pink flowers on
    turquoise ground, mottled yellow
    body, incised "California
    Faience" mark(A) 1650.00
  8 1/2" h, bulbous shape, matte green
    crystalline glaze(A) 247.00
  9" h, 8" d, maroon glaze 525.00
  13" h, gloss violet glaze 425.00
Vessel, 5 1/2" h, gourd shape, closed rim, ridged body, matte pumpkin and dull green glaze, incised "California Faience" mark 500.00

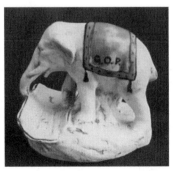

Figure, 4" h, pink and green blanket, ivory ground w/brown wash, $175.00

9¾" h, organic shape, multiple openings, strap handles, matte dark green glaze **1650.00**

CLEWELL
Canton O.

CLEWELL ART WARE
Canton, Ohio
1906–1966

History: Charles Walter Clewell founded a studio in 1906 and it continued operating until he died in 1966. He was a metal worker, not a potter, who covered ceramic bodies with a tight covering of copper, silver, or burnished copper to make ornamental and utilitarian pieces. He purchased pottery blanks for his covered works from Weller, Cambridge, Owens, and Knowles, Taylor, and Knowles.

Clewell worked by himself and won a medal for his covered artware at the Paris International Exposition in 1937. He made vases, lamps, complete stein sets, and pitchers in various shapes and sizes with this metal-over-pottery technique. He studied the oxidation of copper and experimented with methods of reproducing the corrosion until he eventually developed the matte green or blue-green colors he used for his artware.

Wares were usually marked with an incised or impressed "Clewell" along with numbers.
Museum: The Canton Art Institute, OH.

Bowl, 3" h, 7" d, geometric design on lip, 4 buttresses(A) **495.00**
Bud Vase
  7½" h, green and brown patina **460.00**
  8" h, bulbous base, tapered stick neck w/flared rim, red to green patina, incised "Clewell" mark(A) **412.00**
Candlestick, 9½" h, bulbous shaft on circ base, brown to green patina, incised "Clewell 415-2-6" mark, pr(A) **550.00**
Cider Set, pitcher, 11" h, 5 mugs, 4" h, mkd(A) **467.00**
Humidor, 7" h, barrel shape, riveted sides, hammered trim(A) **250.00**

Jardiniere, 9" h, 12" w, unmkd(A) **495.00**
Jug, 17½" h, angular handles, horiz ribbing, light to dark green patina, restored base hole **600.00**
Vase
  3½" h, green patina, Weller blank .. **255.00**
  5" h
    Blue and green patina, #339-6 .... **300.00**
    Flared form on pedestal, dark orange to green patina, "Clewell #120-2-6" mark(A) **470.00**
    Green and rust swirled patina, mkd **410.00**
    Thick green patina **275.00**
  6" h
    Dark green and rust brown patina, #254-2-6 .... **450.00**
    Faceted, raised curlicue design, brown and green patina, unmkd(A) **495.00**
  6½" h, incised floral and leaf design, #837(A) **770.00**
  6¾" h, green patina w/brown accents **350.00**
  7" h
    Art Nouveau floral design **495.00**
    Bulbous base, cylinder body, dark blue-green patina, #325-2-6(A) **295.00**
    Cattail and dragonfly design, dark green patina on copper-clad pottery body **475.00**
  7½" h, ovoid shape w/rolled rim, brown and green patina, "Clewell, 317" mark(A) **412.00**
  8" h
    Ovoid shape, green patina **575.00**
    Trumpet shape, green patina, mkd **450.00**

Vase, 9" h, blue-green patina on copper-clad pottery body, drilled base(A), $500.00

Vase, 9³/₄" h, brown patina, Weller blank, $1875.00

Vase, 14¹/₂" h, green and blue patina on copper-clad pottery body, incised "#378-25" and signature mark(A), $2310.00

8¹/₂" h, shouldered, green patina	**625.00**
10" h	
Dark green patina w/blue accents, #292-6	**750.00**
Green to brown patina, stress lines	**600.00**
11" h, incised and tooled poppies on copper-clad pottery body, "Clewell Metal Art, Canton, Ohio, #1118" mark	**1200.00**
12" h, narrow base, bulbous top, green to orange patina	**1850.00**
12¹/₂" h, green and black mottled patina	**1200.00**
13" h, brown to green patina, #313-224(A)	**2530.00**

17" h, carved irises and leaves accented w/gold patina, dark copper patina ground, paper label(A)	**2860.00**
21¹/₂" h, milk-can shape, red-brown and green patina, incised "Clewell/450-26" mark(A)	**2750.00**

1905

CLIFTON ART POTTERY
Newark, New Jersey
1905–1914

History: Fred Tschirner and William A. Long established a factory in 1905 and made art pottery there until 1911. Crystal Patina, the first product, had a porcelain-like dense body that was decorated with a pale green crystalline glaze. Later semi-matte colors included green, yellow, and tan.

In 1906 the company introduced Clifton Indian Ware, an adaptation of American Indian pottery made from unglazed New Jersey red clay. The interiors of the pieces were covered with a high gloss black glaze so water could not penetrate. The wide variety of pieces made included candlesticks, vases, mugs, jardinieres, pedestals, and umbrella stands which were copied by Owens and Weller. Souvenir and cooking utensils also were made.

Other Clifton lines included Robin's Egg Blue, which used the same dense body as Crystal Patina with a matte blue glaze. Tirrube had a matte finish background with flowers covered in a light slip.

After 1911 the focus of the firm shifted to wall and floor tiles made with leadless glazes developed by Charles Stegmeyer. In 1914 the name of the company was changed to the Clifton Porcelain Tile Company.

Marks were incised on Crystal Patina and impressed on the Indian Ware. Crystal Patina pieces were marked with series numbers in the 100s, Indian Ware with 200s. Some early pieces were dated.

Museums: National Museum of History and Technology, Smithsonian Institution, Washington, DC; The Newark Museum, NJ.

*Pitcher, 7¹/₂" h, matte terra-cotta and
brick red, gloss black int, mkd, $215.00*

Bud Vase, 5¹/₂" h, bulbous base,
faceted neck, crystalline celadon
glaze, "Clifton 181, 1905" mark(A) .   247.00
Humidor, Indian Ware, black and
terra-cotta geometric design 75.00
Jar, 2¹/₂" h, sphere shape w/3 feet,
emb stylized lily pads, matte green
glaze, incised "Clifton/146" mark(A)   385.00
Mug, 4" h, Indian Ware design in col-
ors..   95.00
Oil Lamp Base, 12" h, bulbous shape,
earth tone geometric designs,
mkd(A) 770.00
Pitcher, 6¹/₂" h, bulbous top, tapered
body, matte olive green glaze, miss-
ing top(A) 33.00
Plate, 8" d, majolica, black raspberry
design, sponged cream ground,
mkd(A) 66.00
Teapot, 8" h, matte green glaze 120.00
Vase
  5" h
    Bulbous shape, earth tone band
    of Indian-style geometrics,
    bisque clay, stamped "226, Lit-
    tle Colorado, Ariz." mark(A).....   247.00
    Squat base, short cylinder neck,
    earth tone Indian geometrics,
    imp "CLIFTON" mark 225.00
  6³/₄" h, emb large poppies from
  neck, matte streaked light green
  glaze(A) 525.00
  8" h, Tirrube................................   125.00
  8¹/₂" h
    Bottle shape, squat base, green-
    gold speckled glaze w/green
    drips, "Clifton 1906, 166"
    mark(A) 250.00
    Indian Ware, bulbous base,
    straight neck, rolled rim, white-
    outlined brown flying birds,

brick red clay body, cream
stripe on neck 440.00
Squat base, long neck, Crystal
Patina, drip crystalline celadon
glaze, shape #166, dtd 1906(A)   165.00
8³/₄" h, bulbous base, trumpet neck,
green crystalline glaze, #104, dtd
1905(A) 292.00
9" h, baluster shape, flared foot, yellow-green flambe over metallic
crystalline flambe, incised
"Clifton" mark(A)........................   220.00
10" h, cylinder neck, wide shoulder,
crystalline celadon glaze, dtd
1906, incised mark(A) 385.00
12" h
  Dark brown and cream semi-
  matte intaglio geometric designs, red earthenware,
  "Clifton, #227" mark(A) 385.00
  Squat base, slender neck, white
  mums, gray leaves, bisque
  terra-cotta ground, mkd(A) 440.00
Vessel, 4³/₄" h, 8" d, squat shape
w/small neck, matte green flambe
over crystalline apple green glaze,
"Clifton 1906, AP, 160" mark(A) 605.00

COWAN POTTERY

COWAN POTTERY
Cleveland, Ohio
Rocky River, Ohio
1912–1931

1912 – 1931

History: R. Guy Cowan, who came from an
East Liverpool, Ohio, family of potters studied ceramics under Charles Binns at Alfred University.
In 1912, with the encouragement of the Cleveland Chamber of Commerce, he opened a pottery studio incorporated as the Cleveland Pottery
and Tile Company. For several years he made
both tiles and artwares with heavy glazes and
lusters to cover the red clay body.

In 1917 Cowan won first prize for his art pottery at the International Show at The Art Institute
of Chicago. He closed his studio and joined the
army in that same year.

When he returned in 1919, the studio did not
meet his needs, and he opened a new one in
Rocky River, Ohio, in 1920 with Wendell G.
Wilcox as the manager. A high-fired porcelain
body made from English clays replaced the redware body previously used. Ceramic sculpture

became Cowan's focus, and numerous awards were won. Figures, the most popular of these molded porcelain pieces, were often made in limited editions of fifty to one hundred, after which the molds were destroyed. Waylande Gregory was the leading figure artist, but many other artists worked for Cowan, including Richard Hummel, who formulated an oriental red glaze which was used on art pottery vases. Inexpensive items, such as lamp bases, jars, and decorative figures, also were made, and there was always a struggle to maintain a balance between the art pottery lines and the more commercial pieces.

Console sets with flower bowls and figural flower frogs, candlesticks, vases, compotes, and nut and candy dishes were made in various sizes and shapes for the general public. The soft-finished ivory glaze and interior pastel shades became a Cowan trademark. Tiles also were made.

Various pastel shades were used for tablewares in the Colonial and Federal patterns. Lusterware and crackleware glazes were popular during the 1920s and Cowan Pottery examples were sold all over the country.

In 1927 an inexpensive line of flower containers called "Lakeware" was developed in four colors: oriental red, peacock green-blue, Flemish gray-blue, and olive green. These were used mostly by florists. Cowan Potters, Inc., was formed in 1929 with plans for new lines, including paperweights, ceramic bookends, desk sets, and other accessories made for the Wahl Pen Company. Due to financial problems caused by the Depression, the firm went into receivership in 1930 and remained in business for only one more year, using materials already on hand. When it closed in 1931, Cowan became art director of Onondaga Pottery Company in Syracuse, New York.

Cowan examples were marked in a variety of ways. From 1912–1917 the redware was incised with "Cowan Pottery" and sometimes initialed. On porcelain bodies, "Cowan" was impressed and imprinted. Later examples had the semicircular Cowan mark with the initials "R.G."

Reference: Tim and Jamie Saloff, *The Collector's Encyclopedia of Cowan Pottery,* Collector Books, 1993.

Museums: Cleveland Museum of Art, OH; Cowan Pottery Museum at Rocky River Public Library, OH; Everson Museum of Art, Syracuse, NY; New Orleans Museum of Art, LA; The Western Reserve Historical Society, Cleveland, OH.

Bowl
6" d, cream ext, green int	**30.00**
9" d, 5½" h, copper luster finish	**58.00**
9¼" d, ftd, cream ext, green int	**35.00**
10¼" d, mother-of-pearl glaze, c1930–31	**75.00**

Candlesticks, 2⅛" h, matte white glaze, pr, $29.00

10¾" d, 3 feet, white ext, frosted gloss pink int w/lily pad flower frog	**95.00**
12" d, orange luster glaze	**175.00**
Bucket, 6" h, ftd, purple metallic luster finish	**250.00**
Bud Vase, 6½" h, orange luster glaze	**25.00**
Candlestick	
1½" h, sq step shape, Clair de Lune glaze, pr	**75.00**
4" h, pleated, black glaze, pr	**165.00**
8" h, twisted stems, raised geometrics on base, matte green finish, pr	**140.00**
Charger, 11½" d, light blue emb fish, seaweed, and creatures, dark blue ground(A)	**495.00**
Comport, 7" l, diamond shape, tan lined w/green	**27.00**
Console Bowl	
16" l, canoe shape w/sea horses, blue spotted glaze	**110.00**
17" l, pink ext, cream int	**50.00**
Decanter, Alice in Wonderland Queen, oriental glaze	**450.00**
Figure, 9" h	
"Radio Woman," black on cream	**4500.00**
Semidraped nude, white glaze	**175.00**
Flower Holder	
6½" h, nude dancer w/scarf, white glaze	**135.00**
8" h, Heavenbound, woman standing on toe, hand on hip, white glaze, c1925	**250.00**
11¼" h, figural standing flamingo, white glaze, mkd(A)	**302.00**
Strawberry Jar, 7¾" h, w/underplate, mint green	**125.00**
Tea Service, Federal Line, pot, creamer, sugar bowl, 4 cups and saucers	**295.00**
Trivet, 6¾" sq, hex shape, ftd, raised leaves and vines, turquoise finish	**225.00**
Urn, Cov, 13" h, 2 flared horiz handles, 2 emb rams' heads, sq base,	

Vase, 3³/₄" h, deer, archer, and birds design, tan, imp mark, $85.00

C
K   A
W

1875 - 1889

REGISTERED

CHELSEA KERAMIC ART WORKS ROBERTSON & SONS.

gloss turquoise ground, imp
"COWAN" mark(A) 440.00
Vase
  4" h
    Flared lip, irid orange glaze 50.00
    Stick shape, ivory glaze 15.00
  5" h
    Baluster shape, olive green w/oil-
      spot crystals 90.00
    Fan shape, apple green w/gold
      speckles 100.00
    Four feet, blue luster glaze.......... 45.00
  5¹/₂" h, ftd, fluted body, blue luster
      finish 100.00
  6" h, hp portrait medallion of
      woman, floral ground, gold han-
      dles and trim, sgd "Postgate" 170.00
  6¹/₂" h, pink ground w/yellow
      speckles.................................. 110.00
  6³/₄" h, ball shape w/small opening,
      orange crackle finish, c1930–31 .. 195.00
  7" h
    Bulbous shape w/small opening,
      Egyptian Blue glaze.................. 165.00
    Green drip over pearl luster
      glaze, hairline........................... 75.00
  7¹/₈" h, fan shape w/sea horses, yel-
      low glaze.................................. 55.00
  7¹/₂" h
    Classic shape, blue luster finish ... 50.00
    Metallic purple glaze 80.00
  8" h, bulbous base, flared rim, red-
      orange glaze.............................. 250.00
  8¹/₄" h, sq flat shape w/flared rim, 2
      small scroll handles, Antique
      Green, hairline 45.00
  11" h, flared pillow shape, exotic
      bird design, gloss green and
      turquoise glaze, imp "COWAN"
      mark(A) 440.00
  11³/₄" h, scalloped, blue w/aqua iri-
      descence 68.00

CHELSEA KERAMIC ART WORKS
Chelsea, Massachusetts
1866–1894

DEDHAM POTTERY
Dedham, Massachusetts   1893+
1895–1943

Chelsea History: The Chelsea Keramic Art Works was established by Alexander W. Robertson in 1866 and Hugh, his brother, joined him two years later. Bean pots, flowerpots and simple vases were made. James, their father, joined them in 1872, and the pottery started to produce more decorative pieces, such as ornate redwares.

After seeing the oriental art works at the 1876 Philadelphia Centennial Exposition, Hugh perfected oxblood (sang de bouef) and craquelle glazes similar to those used in the Orient. Other colored glazes also were developed, and Chelsea won several awards at three World's Fairs.

After James died in 1880 and Alexander went to California in 1884, Hugh continued to perfect his costly glazes until 1889 when he was forced to close the unprofitable operation. Several years later Hugh was hired to reopen the pottery and manage it. After several more years, the pottery was moved to Dedham, Massachusetts, and renamed Dedham Pottery.

Works produced before 1875 were not marked. Chelsea faience, introduced in 1877, made use of the many glazes developed by the family.

Dedham History: In 1895 when Chelsea Keramic moved to more favorable conditions in Dedham, Massachusetts, the company name was changed to Dedham Pottery. Hugh Robertson perfected the craquelle glaze he developed at Chelsea, and Dedham became famous for this glaze which was used on about fifty patterns.

The tableware pieces had blue in-glaze border decoration and gray background and pictured rabbits, ducks, elephants, swans, lions, owls, birds, turtles, irises, clover, magnolias, grapes, poppies, water lilies, azalea, and other animals and flowers. The rabbit, designed by Joseph L. Smith, was the most popular pattern and was adopted as the company trademark. The elephant, designed by Charles Davenport, head of decorating, was the second most popular pattern.

All of the work was done freehand, without the use of stencils or decals, and each piece had the company name on it. Some of the patterns were done for special orders. The spider-web veining of the craquelle glaze was produced by rubbing the rapidly cooled piece with Cabot's lamp black powder.

William Robertson took over the pottery in 1908 after Hugh died. There were problems with supplies during World War I, but by 1925 the operation was back to normal. When William died in 1929, J. Milton Robertson took over until 1943 when the pottery was forced to close due to increased costs and a shortage of skilled personnel.

The only other product made at Dedham was hand-thrown vases with high-fired glazes on a high-fired base. The effect of one glaze running down over the other was called Volcanic Ware, but these pieces were not popular.

Reference: *The Dedham Pottery and the Earlier Robertson's Chelsea Potteries,* Dedham Historical Society, 1968.

Collectors' Club: Dedham Pottery Collectors Society, 248 Highland St., Dedham, MA 02026, $18 per year for quarterly newsletter.

Museums: Brooklyn Museum, NY; Chrysler Museum, Norfolk, VA; Dedham Historical Society, MA; Museum of Fine Arts, Boston, MA; National Museum of History and Technology, Smithsonian Institution, Washington, DC; New Orleans Museum of Art, LA; Wadsworth Atheneum, Hartford, CT; Worcester Art Museum, MA.

CHELSEA

Bowl, 8³⁄₄" d, scalloped border, hp blue flowers, white crackle ground(A) 660.00
Charger, 11" d, applied lovebirds on cherry blossom branch, gloss olive green glaze, "CHELSEA KERAMIC/ROBERTSON & SONS" mark(A). 1650.00
Ewer, 10" h, bulbous base, slender neck, brown drip over gray-green ground, imp "CKAW" mark 350.00
Pilgrim Flask, 10¹⁄₂" h, dolphin feet
    Oil painting of classical-style woman on side, "HCR" and "CKAW" mark(A) 1370.00
    Relief of French blue glazed roses on gloss olive body, chips, stamped "CHELSEA KERAMIC ART

WORKS/Robertson & Sons/J.D." mark(A) 1370.00
Pitcher, sphere shape
    5¹⁄₄" h, raised floral design under gray-green crackle glaze, mkd(A). 302.00
    5¹⁄₂" h, glossy, feathered blue-green glaze, "CKAW" mark(A) 165.00
Plaque, 13¹⁄₂" d, painted and slip-decorated portrait of Lincoln, red clay body, "CKAW/Robertson & Sons" mark(A) 660.00
Plate, Rabbit pattern
    8¹⁄₂" d, raised design, dark blue, imp "CPUS" in clover and rabbit mark(A) 198.00
    10" d, raised design, med blue, imp "CPUS" in clover mark(A) 250.00
Teapot, 7" h, flattened form, slip-painted landscape in natural colors on sides, Hugh C. Robertson(A) 1650.00
Vase
    2¹⁄₂" h, sphere shape, gloss yellow, sea green, and brown glaze, stamped "CKAW" mark(A) 330.00
    4" h, oxblood glaze w/irid accents(A) 467.00
    4¹⁄₄" h, bulbous body, crimped rim, olive glaze w/brown streaks, chips, imp "CKAW" mark(A) 220.00
    5³⁄₄" h, narrow base, wide shoulder, white lava flowing from shoulder on lustered buff body, stamped "CKAW" mark(A) 357.00
    6" h, narrow neck on protruding shoulder, oxblood glaze, stamped "CKAW" mark(A) 3410.00
    6¹⁄₂" h, oct, applied elephant's-head handles, brown and blue-green mottled glaze, imp mark(A) 495.00
    6⁵⁄₈" h, bulbous body w/4 small vert cylinders, cylindrical neck, mustard glaze(A) 907.00

Vase, Chelsea, 5" h, yellow flowers, olive green shaded to black ground, imp "CKAW" flame mark, $750.00

6³/₄" h, 4 sides, w/two small elephant's-head handles, blue
crackle glaze, mkd(A) **330.00**
7¹/₄" h, long neck, protruding shoul-
der, mottled oxblood glaze, restored neck, stamped "CKAW"
mark(A) **770.00**
8" h, Chinese form, oxblood glaze,
"CKAW" mark.............................. **1850.00**
12³/₄" h, oval body, rect foot and
neck, lion's head handles, yellow, red, pink, and green painted
roses and butterflies on gloss dark
green and brown ground,
stamped "CHELSEA KERAMIC ART
WORKS, ROBERTSON & SONS"
mark(A) **220.00**

DEDHAM
Ashtray, 4" d, Rabbit pattern, med
blue, blue band on inside hollow,
"DEDHAM POTTERY" mark(A).............. **220.00**
Bowl
4¹/₂" d, Grapes pattern, dark blue **350.00**
5" d, Lotus pattern, raised design on
ext(A)... **440.00**
5¹/₂" d, Lotus pattern, raised fluted
emb design, blue embellishments **695.00**
6" d, Grape pattern, stamped mark,
incised "DP" on base **475.00**
7" d, Grape pattern border, crack-
led glaze, "DEDHAM POTTERY"
mark(A) **220.00**
8¹/₂" sq, Rabbit pattern on int, "DED-
HAM POTTERY" mark,(A) **800.00**
9" d, Swan pattern, dark blue on
ext, "DEDHAM POTTERY REGISTERED"
mark(A) **522.00**
9¹/₄" d, cut edge, Azalea pattern on
inner border, fine crackling, "DED-
HAM POTTERY REGISTERED" and 2
imp rabbits mark(A) **935.00**
Bowl, Cov, 9¹/₄" d, Horsechestnut pattern, med blue, blue stamped
mark(A) **175.00**
Butter Pat
3¹/₂" d
Pansy pattern, stamped mark **350.00**

*Bacon Rasher, Dedham, 9⁷/₈" l, 6¹/₄" w,
med blue, $425.00*

Wild Rose pattern, registered
mark **310.00**
Candlestick, 3¹/₂" h, Rabbit pattern on
base, med blue, blue bands on center, "DEDHAM POTTERY REGISTERED"
mark, pr(A) **350.00**
Charger, 12" d, Horsechestnut pattern,
dark blue, blue band on rim, "DED-
HAM POTTERY REGISTERED, Tercentenary 1636–1936" and 2 imp rabbits
mark(A) **495.00**
Chocolate Pot, 8³/₄" h, Rabbit pattern,
dark blue outer band on base, blue
band on rim and lid, "DEDHAM POT-
TERY REGISTERED" mark(A) **3850.00**
Coaster, 4" d, elephant in center, dark
blue ground, blue bands on rim,
"DEDHAM POTTERY REGISTERED, DEDHAM
TERCENTENARY 1636–1936" mark(A).. **660.00**
Creamer, 3¹/₄" h, Rabbit pattern, dark
blue, blue stamped mark(A) **165.00**
Cup and Saucer, A.D., Rabbit pattern,
dark blue, "DEDHAM POTTERY REGIS-
TERED" and 2 imp rabbits mark(A) **330.00**
Eggcup, 2¹/₂" h
Grape pattern, dark blue, 2 blue
bands above design, "D.P."
mark(A) **253.00**
Baby Elephant pattern, one with
raised trunk, med blue, "DEDHAM
POTTERY" mark(A) **440.00**
Rabbit pattern, med blue, "DEDHAM
POTTERY" mark(A) **187.00**
Flower Frog, 6¹/₂" h, figural standing
rabbit, "DEDHAM POTTERY REGISTERED"
mark(A) **2750.00**
Humidor, 7" h, 2 walking elephants,
inscribed "Dedham Pottery/May
1917/#79" mark(A) **1980.00**
Mustard Jar, 3" h, Azalea pattern, dark
blue, blue band on lid, "DEDHAM
POTTERY" mark(A) **550.00**
Pitcher
2³/₄" h, blue Rabbit pattern border,
blue line on rim and base, blue
"DEDHAM POTTERY REGISTERED"
mark(A) **1045.00**
4¹/₂" h, blue standing rabbit on side,
white crackle glaze(A) **1850.00**
5" h, Elephant pattern, one small
elephant w/raised trunk, dark
blue, "DEDHAM POTTERY REGISTERED"
mark(A) **770.00**
5¹/₈" h, blue crowing rooster on one
side, reverse w/owl on log,
crackle finish, "DEDHAM POTTERY
REGISTERED" mark(A) **1040.00**
5¹/₄" h
Grape pattern, dark blue, "DED-
HAM POTTERY REGISTERED"
mark(A) **440.00**
Rabbit pattern, dark blue, band

Pitcher, Dedham, 5¹/₄" h, blue Morning and Evening design, $1250.00

on rim, "DEDHAM POTTERY REGISTERED" mark(A) **715.00**

Plate

6" d, dark blue

Cherry pattern, raised, "DEDHAM POTTERY" and imp rabbit mark(A) **3190.00**

Crab pattern with seaweed, sgd "Maude Davenport" **1200.00**

Elephant pattern, "DEDHAM POTTERY REGISTERED" and 2 imp rabbits mark **1050.00**

Horsechestnut pattern, raised design, blue band on rim, "DEDHAM POTTERY" and imp rabbit mark(A) **160.00**

Moth and Flower pattern, "DEDHAM POTTERY" and imp rabbit mark **1050.00**

Turtle pattern, med blue, "DEDHAM POTTERY" and imp rabbit mark(A) **4950.00**

6¹/₂" d, Rabbit pattern, dark blue **135.00**

8¹/₂" d

Azalea pattern, dark blue, "DEDHAM POTTERY" and 2 imp rabbits mark(A) **247.00**

Horsechestnut pattern, dark blue, raised design, sgd "Maude Davenport," "DEDHAM POTTERY" and imp rabbit mark(A) **550.00**

Iris pattern, med crackling, "DEDHAM POTTERY" and imp rabbit mark(A) **155.00**

Pine Cone pattern, dark blue, "DEDHAM POTTERY" and imp rabbit mark(A) **1870.00**

Poppy pattern on border, poppy in center, dark blue, sgd "Hugh Robertson," "DEDHAM POTTERY" mark(A) **880.00**

Rabbit pattern, dark blue **275.00**

Tapestry Lion border design, Kings Crown design on inner

border, "O" rebus in border, blue "DEDHAM POTTERY" and imp rabbit mark(A) **2200.00**

10" d, dark blue

Birds in a Potted Orange Tree pattern on border, raised design, "DEDHAM POTTERY" and imp rabbit mark(A) **1320.00**

Butterfly and Flower pattern, raised design, dark blue, "DEDHAM POTTERY" and imp rabbit mark(A) **2200.00**

Iris pattern, fine crackle, sgd "Maude Davenport," "DEDHAM POTTERY" and imp rabbit mark(A) **302.00**

Lobster pattern w/waves over plate, blue banded rim, "DEDHAM POTTERY" mark(A) **1045.00**

Magnolia pattern, raised design, "DEDHAM POTTERY" and imp rabbit mark(A) **88.00**

Polar Bear pattern, raised design, sgd "Maude Davenport" **1200.00**

Pond Lily pattern, raised design, blue band on rim, sgd "Maude Davenport," "DEDHAM POTTERY" and imp rabbit mark(A) **1430.00**

Tufted Duck pattern, crackle glaze, foot chip, "DEDHAM POTTERY" and imp rabbit mark(A) ... **198.00**

Turkey pattern, "O" rebus in border, crackle glaze, "DEDHAM POTTERY" and imp rabbit mark(A) **180.00**

Wolf Chasing Owl pattern, pink-gray glaze, "DEDHAM POTTERY," imp rabbit, and "2–12" mark(A) **11,000.00**

Salt, 1⁵/₈" h, 3¹/₄" l, figural walnut on leaf, glazed bisque, imp "CKAW" mark, pr(A) **1540.00**

Salt and Pepper, 2³/₄" h, Rabbit pattern on base, dark blue, floral pattern on shoulder, "DP" mark(A) **231.00**

Soup Bowl, 8¹/₂" d, Pond Lily pattern .. **310.00**

Soup Plate, 9" d, flared rim, Rabbit pattern, dark blue, "DEDHAM POTTERY" mark(A) **265.00**

Stein, 5³/₄" h, Rabbit pattern on base, dark blue, sgd "Maude Davenport," "DEDHAM POTTERY" mark(A) **495.00**

Sugar Bowl, 3" h, 4¹/₂" w, Rabbit pattern, dark blue, blue band on rim, "DEDHAM POTTERY" mark(A) **282.00**

Teapot, 6" h, rabbit band on middle, blue line on rim, crackle glaze, blue "DEDHAM POTTERY" mark(A) **1870.00**

Tea Tile, 7" d, Rabbit pattern border, med blue, "DEDHAM POTTERY REGISTERED" and imp rabbit mark(A) **715.00**

Toothpick, 2¹/₈" h, boot shape, blue

band and bow, crackle glaze, "DED-
HAM POTTERY" mark(A) **1760.00**
Trivet, 7" d, Rabbit pattern, dark blue,
"REGISTERED" mark **265.00**
Vase
 5" h, ovoid shape, red, turquoise,
 and green volcanic glaze **3100.00**
 7¼" h
  Moss green and brown glaze
  w/blue flecks, hairlines, "DED-
  HAM POTTERY" mark(A) **165.00**
  White crackle w/stylized blue
  branches and blossoms, imp
  rabbit mark **1800.00**
 7¾" h, ovoid shape, volcanic
 green, blue, and red mottled
 glaze w/craters, incised "Dedham
 Pottery, HCR" mark(A) **1100.00**
 11¾" h, lustered red, green, and
 cobalt volcanic glaze, "Ded-
 ham/Pottery/HCR" mark(A) **41,000.00**

GRIFFEN, SMITH AND HILL
Phoenixville, Pennsylvania
1879–1889

History: In 1879 Beerbower and Griffen became Griffen, Smith and Hill and specialized in
majolica. The two Griffen brothers were techni-
cians, Smith did designs and glazes, and Hill was
the master potter. The following year the factory
closed for a short time due to a worker's strike,
and Hill left. Although the name changed to Griffen, Smith and Company, the GSH monogram
was still used to mark the wares.

Many European artisans were employed and
at the World's Industrial and Cotton Centennial
Exposition in New Orleans in 1884–1885, the
company exhibited approximately one hundred
fifty examples of Etruscan majolica. Success at
the exposition led to numerous new orders and
operations were expanded. When George Hartford decided to give majolica as a premium with
purchases of baking powder, the Great Atlantic
and Pacific Tea Company became GSH's largest
customer. Another firm gave GSH products with
the purchase of tea.

By 1886 the financial picture had changed.
The high cost of hand decorating and the low
bulk prices charged for the premiums caused a
drop in profits. There also was less demand for

majolica. In 1889 Smith withdrew from the concern and J. Stuart Love became a partner in the
newly named Griffen, Love and Company.

Griffen, Smith and Hill's Etruscan majolica
designs reflected the Victorian interest in marine
and plant life. Begonia, maple, and oak leaves,
ferns, vegetables, fruits, and a wide assortment of
flowers all appeared on majolica pieces. The famous Shell and Seaweed pattern was done in
shades of pink, brown, gray, and blue with green
seaweed accents. Shells and dolphins, oriental
motifs, including thorns, bamboo and bird designs, and human and mythological figures also
were used.

All sorts of shapes were made, including butter pats, compotes, napkin plates, bowls, humidors, cheese bells, paperweights, sardine boxes,
syrup jugs, cuspidors, umbrella stands, and
pitchers. Interiors of hollowware pieces usually
were pink, but some were pale blue or green.
Dinner, tea, and coffee services were made in
Cauliflower, Bamboo, and Shell and Seaweed
patterns.

"GSH" was the earliest mark used. By 1880
some pieces were marked with two concentric
circles between "GSH" and "Etruscan Majolica."
Other marks also were used.

References: Marilyn G. Karmason with Joan
B. Stacke, *Majolica*, Harry N. Abrams, 1989; M.
Charles Rebert, *American Majolica, 1850–1900*,
Wallace-Homestead, 1981.

Museums: Chester County Historical Society,
West Chester, PA; Historical Society of
Phoenixville, PA; Philadelphia Museum of Art,
PA.

Bowl
 8¼" d, majolica, Shell and Seaweed
 pattern, mkd(A) **330.00**
 9¾" d, majolica, center w/cherub
 on lion, leaf border, dusty rose
 ground, mkd **100.00**
Bread Tray, majolica, Oak Leaf pattern **225.00**
Butter Pat, majolica
 Leaf pattern **25.00**
 Shell and Seaweed pattern **195.00**
Cake Stand, 5" h, 9" d, majolica,
 Maple Leaf pattern, green, yellow,
 and brown, mkd **150.00**
Coffeepot, majolica, Shell and Sea-
 weed pattern **950.00**
Compote, 9¼" d, majolica, Daisy pat-
 tern, yellow and pink flowers, green
 leaves, imp "GSH" mark **325.00**
Creamer, majolica
 3¼" h,
  Corn pattern **200.00**
  Shell and Seaweed pattern(A) **247.00**
 3½" h, Begonia pattern **75.00**
 4¼" h, Bamboo pattern, hairline(A) . **195.00**
Cup and Saucer, majolica
 Bamboo pattern **300.00**

Cauliflower pattern **325.00**
Shell and Seaweed pattern(A) **209.00**
Dish, 13" l, majolica
Begonia leaf shape, green and
brown, mkd................................ **95.00**
Oak Leaf pattern, "GSH" mark **180.00**
Ice Cream Tray, majolica, Shell and
Seaweed pattern........................... **950.00**
Oyster Plate, 14½" d, majolica, Shell
and Seaweed pattern...................... **250.00**
Pickle Dish, 9" l, majolica, begonia
leaf shape, "GSH Majolica" mark...... **75.00**
Pitcher
5" h, majolica
Hawthorne pattern, pink flowers
on bark ground **125.00**
Shell and Seaweed pattern, al-
bino(A)..................................... **50.00**
5⅜" h, majolica, Bark and Leaf pat-
tern, natural colors(A) **45.00**
5½" h, majolica, Rose design,
cobalt ground **185.00**
6¾" h, majolica, Shell and Sea-
weed pattern(A) **210.00**
7¼" h, light green leaves and flow-
ers, beige ground, pink int, imp
"ETRUSCAN" mark **245.00**
7½" h, majolica, Fern pattern, mkd . **75.00**
8" h, majolica, Wild Rose and But-
terfly pattern **225.00**
8½" h, majolica, Corn design.......... **170.00**
Plate
7" d, majolica, Shell and Seaweed
pattern....................................... **150.00**
8" d, majolica
Bamboo pattern **125.00**
Emb scene of mythological fig-
ures in center, basket-weave
border, mauve glaze, imp mark **55.00**
Shell and Seaweed pattern, imp
"GSH Etruscan" mark................. **285.00**
9" d, majolica, Cauliflower pattern,
imp "GSH Etruscan" mark **125.00**
9¼" d, majolica

*Plate, 8" d, majolica, mauve glaze, imp
mark, $55.00*

*Plate, 8⅞" d, majolica, pink and green
leaf design w/yellow accents, pink
basketweave border, imp mark,
c1879–90, $75.00*

Apple and Strawberry design,
pink berries, yellow apples,
green leaves, blue border,
cream ground, imp "GSH"
mark(A)..................................... **154.00**
Shell and Seaweed pattern(A) **440.00**
Platter, 11¾" l, 9" w, majolica, Oak
Leaf pattern, natural colors, chip,
mkd(A) **385.00**
Shaker, 4" h, majolica, Coral pattern,
pink and turquoise, mkd(A) **467.00**
Spittoon, 6¼" h, majolica, Shell and
Seaweed pattern, pink int(A) **1100.00**
Sugar Bowl, Cov, majolica
Shell and Seaweed pattern(A) **225.00**
Wild Rose pattern, cream ground,
mkd.. **100.00**
Syrup Pitcher, majolica
6¾" h, Shell and Seaweed pattern,
silver lid **495.00**
8" h
Bamboo pattern, green, blue,
brown, and pink, mkd(A) **385.00**
Sunflower pattern, pink ground,
mkd(A)................................... **550.00**
Tazza, 9½" d, majolica, molded leaf
design, tree trunk base, natural col-
ors, c1885, imp "GSH" mark(A) **137.00**
Teapot
Shell and Seaweed pattern
4½" h **465.00**
5" h **585.00**
8⅜" w, majolica, Cauliflower pat-
tern, natural colors, pink accents,
imp "GSH" mark(A) **550.00**
Tea Set, pot, creamer, sugar bowl, majolica
Bamboo pattern **495.00**
Cauliflower pattern **695.00**
Tobacco Jar, 6¾" h, Shell and Sea-
weed pattern, repaired shell finial,
imp "GSH" mark.............................. **1800.00**

GRUEBY POTTERY
BOSTON.U.S.A.

1907-1911

GRUEBY POTTERY
Boston, Massachusetts
1897–1921

History: W.H. Grueby worked at Low Art Tile Works from 1880 until 1890 when he started a plant in Revere, Massachusetts to make architectural faience. In 1894 Grueby-Faience Company was formed to make glazed bricks, tiles, and architectural terra-cotta.

In 1897 Grueby-Faience was incorporated to make art pottery. Grueby made the glazes and was general manager, William Graves was the business manager, and George Kendrick the designer and craftsman of the early artware designs. The thrown artwares had excellent shapes and unique glazes and earned medals for the company in Paris, St. Petersburg, and St. Louis.

Hand-modeled pieces were decorated with freehand flower and leaf designs on which the veining was actually an additional thin piece of clay. Cucumber Grueby green was the most successful of the matte glazes, but blue, yellow, brown, gray, and ivory also were used. The Grueby green was copied by Van Briggle, Rookwood, Hampshire, Teco, and Pewabic, to name a few imitators. Grueby also made lamp bases for other companies.

The business was divided into architectural faience and art pottery. In 1907 the Grueby Pottery Company was incorporated in Massachusetts as a marketing company for Grueby-Faience. After bankruptcy proceedings, the Grueby Faience and Tile Company was organized in 1909 for production of architectural wares utilizing Grueby's glazes and methods. Graves became head of Grueby and the last artwares were made in 1911.

After the pottery burned in 1913, Grueby Faience and Tile was rebuilt to continue architectural faience. James Curley joined the firm in 1919 and improved its economic position. The company was sold to C. Pardee Works of Perth Amboy, New Jersey, and Pardee moved Grueby to New Jersey in 1921.

Grueby's artwares were marked, but sometimes the marks were obscured by the heavy glaze. Paper labels were used with the compa-

ny's lotus trademark. Pieces after 1905 were marked "Grueby Pottery."

Reference: Dr. Susan Montgomery, *The Ceramics of William H. Grueby,* The Arts and Crafts Quarterly Press, 1993.

Museums: Museum of Fine Arts, Boston, MA: New Orleans Museum of Art, LA; The Newark Museum, NJ.

Chamberstick, 2" h, 6" d, dbl handled, dark matte blue glaze, imp mark(A)	357.00
Paperweight, 2³/₄" d, matte yellow raised scarab, blue ground, imp mark(A)	248.00
Pot	
2¹/₂" h, 10" d, molded coiled gloss green int, matte green ext, hairline(A)	200.00
4" h, squat body, raised rim, matte crackled green glaze(A)	210.00
Vase	
2" h, 3" w, matte dark green glaze, paper label(A)	262.00
3" h, feathered matte yellow glaze on defined leaf design, chips(A)	605.00
5" h, organic shape, sculpted leaves, matte light green glaze on shoulder, dark green on base(A)	1870.00
7" h	
Gourd shape, matte green crackle glaze	1395.00
Jardiniere shape, leaf-carved body, dark yellow textured glaze, 8 white matte enamelled buds on shoulder, imp mark(A)	4400.00
Matte green glaze over 5 carved and applied leaves	1000.00
Sculptured blue irises w/green leaves, matte dark yellow glaze, imp "Grueby" and "J.E." mark(A)	11,000
8" h, flared shape, alternating leaves and buds, matte green glaze, imp mark(A)	1760.00
8¹/₂" h, lotus bulb, sphere shape w/small vert neck, 7 green broad	

Bowl, 4" h, 9¹/₂" d, matte green glaze, imp circ mark and #143(A), $1650.00.
Photograph courtesy of Don Treadway and John Toomey, Oak Park, IL

Vase, 8" h, matte green feathered glaze,
sgd "W.P.,' imp circ mark(A), $5500.00.
Photograph courtesy of Don Treadway
and John Toomey, Oak Park, IL

leaves, light blue matte neck,
shoulder, and raised vert bands,
chips(A) 3190.00
9" h
  4" w, red water lilies, med green
  lily pads, dark green ground,
  carved buds on rim, #134(A).... 1100.00
  Squat melon ribbed organic
  shape, matte dark yellow fin-
  ish, mkd(A) 2310.00
11½" h
  Organic leaf-shaped arches on
  base in matte black glaze
  w/blue accents, matte green
  ridged body(A) 1760.00
  Ovoid shape w/star rim, 3 yellow
  jonquils on spiked green stems

Vase, 10½" h, molded lotus
leaves, mottled green glaze,
c1905(A), $1450.00

and leaves, matte green
  glaze(A) 3025.00
12" h
  Cylinder shape, hand thrown,
  thick matte green glaze 650.00
  Yellow flower buds, tooled and
  applied leaves, veined matte
  green glaze, mkd(A) 3850.00
  13" h, bulbous base, cylindrical
  neck, thick matte green glaze,
  imp mark(A) 1430.00
  16" h, compressed ovoid body,
  long cylindrical neck, molded
  vert leaves from base, yellow
  flowers and long stems from
  neck, thick avocado green
  crackle glaze, imp blossom and
  "GRUEBY POTTERY BOSTON U.S.A."
  mark(A) 16,500.00
Vessel
  4¾" h, sphere shape, matte feathered green glaze, "GRUEBY POT-
  TERY, BOSTON, U.S.A." mark(A) 660.00
  6½" h, 9" d, flared rim, vert ribbing,
  organic matte yellow glaze,
  "GRUEBY FAIENCE CO. BOSTON U.S.A.
  KI" mark(A) 1980.00

J.S.T. & CO.
KEENE.NH.
c.1874

Hampshire
Pottery

HAMPSHIRE POTTERY
Keene, New Hampshire
1871–1923

History: James Taft and James Burnap established a pottery to make flowerpots, but before
they started production, there was a fire, and
they had to rebuild. In 1874, they acquired another pottery that was used to make redware.
One pottery was used to make jugs, pitchers,
churns, cuspidors, water kegs, and such, while
the other made earthenware hanging vases, flowerpots, cuspidors, florist ware, and Rockingham
teapots.
  Thomas Stanley, an Englishman, joined the
pottery in 1879 and introduced a majolica-type
ware for pitchers, tea sets, mugs, and vases. The
corn pattern was one of the most popular. Under
the direction of Wallace King in 1882, the company produced a line of Royal Worcester type
ware with a muted ivory ground for souvenir and
specialty pieces, such as plates, rose bowls,
pitchers, and bonbon dishes. Some items were

decorated in the underglaze technique used for Rookwood's Standard ware.

Cadmon Robertson joined Hampshire in 1904 and was responsible for a huge variety of matte glazes, including a green matte glaze used on art pottery vases, bowls, flower holders, candlesticks, clock cases, and lamp bases.

Taft stopped production in 1914, after King retired and Robertson died, and in 1916 he sold the firm to George Morton from Grueby. Morton expanded the business, then closed it due to the war, and returned to Grueby in 1917. After the war Morton reopened the firm to make white china for hotels and restaurants. From 1919–1921 mosaic floor tiles also were made. Due to competition, the pottery closed in 1923.

Some Hampshire pieces were marked, and some paper labels were used.

References: Marilyn G. Karmason with Joan B. Stacke, *Majolica,* Harry Abrams, 1989; Joan Pappas and Kendall Harold, *Hampshire Pottery Manufactured by J.S. Taft and Company, Keene, New Hampshire,* Crown Publishers, 1971.

Museums: Chrysler Museum, Norfolk, VA; Colony House Museum, Keene, NH; National Museum of History and Technology, Smithsonian Institution, Washington, DC; New Orleans Museum of Art, LA.

Bowl
  4" d, 2¹/₄" h, artichoke-style panels, scalloped cut rim, matte green finish, imp "HAMPSHIRE POTTERY," circled M, and "109" mark(A) **121.00**
  7" d, swastika decoration **285.00**
  9" d, raised tulips and leaves, half matte and half gloss green glaze, inscribed "HAMPSHIRE POTTERY," circled M, and "57" mark(A) **220.00**
  10" d, raised water lilies and pads, matte green glaze **90.00**
Bud Vase, 6¹/₄" h, slender neck, bulbous base, 2 serpent handles, matte green glaze(A) **440.00**
Candleholder, 6¹/₂" h, handled, shield back, matte green finish, #29 .... **175.00**
Chamberstick, 3¹/₄" h, 7¹/₄" w, leaf shape w/rolled edges, loop handle, matte green glaze w/light green mottling, inscribed "HAMPSHIRE POTTERY," circled M, and "31" mark(A).. **275.00**
Chocolate Pot, 9" h, mint green, cream, and peach Royal Worcester finish, gold trim, crimped base, crackle glaze, stamped "HAMPSHIRE POTTERY, KEENE, N.H." mark(A) **110.00**
Chocolate Set, pot, 6 cups and saucers, Royal Worcester finish **210.00**
Cider Set, pitcher, 12" h, 5 mugs, 5" h, sq handles, raised striped design at rim and base, gloss mahogany

glaze, imp "JST & CO. KEENE N.H." mark(A) **275.00**
Creamer
  2¹/₄" h, 3¹/₂" d, mint green top, shaded brown base, heavy matte crackle finish, imp "JST & CO. KEENE N.H." and stamped number mark(A) **121.00**
  3¹/₄" h, 7" w, matte green glaze, inscribed "HAMPSHIRE POTTERY" and circled M mark(A)....................... **121.00**
Ewer
  6" h, transfer of "Log Chapel, Saranac Inn" **35.00**
  11" h, matte green finish, glaze flake **130.00**
  11¹/₄" h
    Matte dark aqua mottled finish w/gray and black flecks, scalloped cut base, imp "HAMPSHIRE" and "3" mark(A) **385.00**
    Royal Worcester finish, yellow flowers, brown stems, green leaves, ivory ground................ **175.00**
Fairy Oil Lamp, 4" h, 7" w, ftd, large loop handle, matte green finish w/dark green flecks on base, inscribed "HAMPSHIRE POTTERY" and "79" mark(A) **165.00**
Inkwell, 3" h, 4" d, 3 holes on top, center well, matte green glaze w/dark green flecks, inscribed "HAMPSHIRE POTTERY" and "26" mark(A).. **143.00**
Mug, 5³/₈" h, brown ship silhouette on gold ground, gloss green lower band, imp "J.S.T. & Co., Keene, N.H." mark(A) **225.00**
Pitcher
  4" h, side pouring spout, matte green glaze w/black speckles **250.00**
  4¹/₂" h, bulbous shape, emb white blackberry sprays, blue ground, twig handle, hairline................... **45.00**
  5³/₄" h, part mahogany and part mustard-orange glaze, crackle finish, raised "JST & CO. KEENE N.H." mark(A) **66.00**
  7" h, bulbous body, shaped rim, tapered base, shaped handle, matte green finish, drippings, imp "JST & CO KEENE N.H." mark(A) **121.00**
  9¹/₂" h, ewer shape, matte green finish **175.00**
Shaving Mug, 3³/₄" h, Royal Worcester finish, gold-trimmed flower motif, stamped "HAMPSHIRE POTTERY" mark(A) **88.00**
Stein, 7" h, white vert drip designs on matte dark green glaze, raised circ design on neck, imp "HAMPSHIRE" mark(A) **88.00**

Sugar Bowl, 3" h, 6" H-H, crimped design on perimeter, imp vert lines on neck, matte green finish, raised "HAMPSHIRE POTTERY" mark(A)........... **110.00**

Tea Set, pot, 4" h, cov sugar bowl, 3½" h, creamer, 2¼" h, gloss dark green glaze, imp "JST & CO. KEENE N.H." mark(A) **143.00**

Urn, 11" h, architectural handles, matte green glaze............................ **432.00**

Vase
   2¼" d, 4½" h, raised half-moon panels, white, dark and med green mottled matte glaze, inscribed "HAMPSHIRE POTTERY," circled M, and number mark(A) **412.00**

   2¾" h, 4" d, bowl shape, raised landscape of trees on perimeter, matte green glaze, imp "HAMPSHIRE" mark(A)............................ **132.00**

   3½" h
      Aspen leaf motif, matte green glaze... **175.00**
      Conical shape, blue volcanic glaze on white clay................. **250.00**

   4" h
      Green raised tree trunk w/berries and leaves, light green ground, serrated rim............................ **200.00**
      Three-ftd, rolled crimped rim, gold "Mt. Washington" on face, gloss dark green glaze, unmkd(A) **88.00**

   4½" h
      Bulbous base, cylinder neck, 2 scrolled handles, gloss brown glaze, imp "J.S.T. & CO." mark(A) **225.00**
      Matte green finish **85.00**

   4¾" h, raised light green, brown, and dark green mottled glaze, "HAMPSHIRE POTTERY," circled M, and "54/1" mark(A) **198.00**

Vase, 5" h, three handles, mottled matte green glaze, light green int, imp "Hampshire 27" mark, $250.00

5" h
   Bulbous base, pinched neck, flared rim, med and dark blue mottled matte glaze on top, light blue base w/vert drip design, inscribed "HAMPSHIRE POTTERY" and "118" mark(A) **385.00**

   Squat shape, light green matte glaze w/brown highlights, #118(A)..................................... **176.00**

5¼" h, bulbous body, dark aqua mottled matte glaze w/raised black, gray, and light aqua mottled glaze, inscribed "HAMPSHIRE POTTERY" and circled M mark(A) ... **198.00**

6" h, squat shape, light blue drip at top over matte blue glazed body, imp mark(A) **385.00**

7" h, raised leaflike panels, 6 protruding flower heads, cocoa-red crackle glaze, matte finish, "HAMPSHIRE POTTERY" and circled M mark(A) **522.00**

7¼" h, raised vert leaflike panels, dark blue and aqua matte glaze w/black and blue mottling and gray flecks, inscribed "HAMPSHIRE POTTERY," circled M, and "98" mark(A) **440.00**

7½" h
   Aqua mottled matte glaze w/flecks of black and gray, light aqua on rim, "HAMPSHIRE POTTERY," circled M, and "38" mark(A)..................................... **330.00**

   Cylinder shape, cobalt gloss glaze, inscribed "HAMPSHIRE POTTERY" and circled M mark(A) **242.00**

7¾" h
   Bulbous body, wide, tapered neck, scattered buds on body, matte green finish w/dark green flecks, "HAMPSHIRE POTTERY," circled M, and "130" mark(A) **385.00**

   Flared rim, raised bladelike panels, matte green finish w/cream vert flecks on neck, "HAMPSHIRE POTTERY," circled M, and "11" mark(A)..................................... **275.00**

8" h
   Incised geometric design, cream drip on teal blue ground **425.00**

   Raised lightning designs, 2 twig handles, shaded matte green glaze, imp "HAMPSHIRE" and circled M mark(A) **660.00**

8¼" h, 5 imp vert panels, mottled light blue around rim, aqua crackle finish, inscribed "HAMPSHIRE POTTERY" and "#814325" mark(A) **715.00**

8½" h, bulbous shape, dark brown and pink crackled and mottled matte finish, imp "HAMPSHIRE," circled M, and "55" mark(A)............ 412.00

8¾" h, 6 raised pr of lily pads on perimeter, gloss cobalt glaze, inscribed "HAMPSHIRE POTTERY" circled M, and "72" mark(A)............ 232.00

9¼" h
Raised vert bladelike designs outlined in white, matte green glaze, inscribed "HAMPSHIRE POTTERY," circled M, and "11/1" mark(A)................................... 440.00

Trumpet neck, bulbous base, raised leaflike panels, matte oatmeal glaze, inscribed "HAMPSHIRE POTTERY," circled M, and "124" mark(A)................... 660.00

9½" h, bulbous base, vert neck, flared rim, light gray crackle matte glaze, inscribed "HAMPSHIRE POTTERY," circled M, and "107" mark(A) 357.00

10" h, molded leaves at bulbous base, cylinder neck, matte green glaze, imp "HAMPSHIRE POTTERY," circled M, and "#124" mark(A).... 467.00

10¾" h, Grecian urn style, squared handles, matte dark green glaze w/gray flecks, imp "JST & CO. KEENE N.H." and "8" mark(A).................. 440.00

Violet Holder, 2¼" h, raised floral designs, matte green glaze, inscribed "HAMPSHIRE POTTERY" and circled M mark(A) 132.00

Water Pitcher, 6½" h, dbl spouts, center overhead handle, matte green glaze w/green flecked crackle finish, inscribed "HAMPSHIRE," circled M, and "36" mark(A) 209.00

HILL/FULPER
Flemington, New Jersey
1805–1929

STANGL
1929–1978

(See General Manufacturers' section for history)

History: The Fulper factory, founded by Samuel Hill in 1805, manufactured drain tile and farm items using the red clays native to Flemington, New Jersey. Abraham Fulper purchased the factory in 1860, and working with his three sons, expanded the business to include water, vinegar,

and pickling jars, butter churns, ginger beer bottles, and mugs. One of the best-selling items was the Fulper Germ Proof Filter—cobalt-blue-decorated stoneware jars made to hold drinking water in public places. After several name changes, the factory was incorporated in 1899 as the Fulper Pottery Company.

Martin Stangl came to New Jersey from Germany in 1910 as a chemist and plant superintendent for William Fulper. After a short stay developing an industrial artware line for Haeger Potteries of Dundee, Illinois, Stangl returned to Fulper as general manager and helped invent a group of famille rose glazes, including ashes of roses, deep rose, peach bloom, old rose, and true rose. He was also responsible for some of the clay shapes. John Kunsman was Fulper's master potter, although other potters also worked for the company.

Vasekraft, an art pottery line using classical and oriental shapes, was first produced in 1909. Pieces often were made in unusual shapes and the line included jardinieres, vases, bowls, bookends, cigarette boxes, candleholders, cooking ware, lamp bases, and mugs made of heavy stoneware with a variety of glazes, such as the expensive famille rose, "Mission Matte," "Mirror Glaze," cat's-eye, rouge, mustard matte, bronze, cucumber green, cafe au lait, and mulberry. Crystalline glazes also were used. The Vasekraft lamp bases were made in many shapes, sizes, and glazes, and ceramic shades also were produced. The toadstool and mushroom bases are particularly noteworthy.

In response to import shortages due to World War I, Fulper produced bisque dolls and dolls' heads from 1918–1921. These usually were marked with the Fulper name. The now-famous Fulper dolls' heads are the porcelain ones created by Stangl. Solid-color green dinnerware, the first of the colored dinnerware lines made in the United States, was introduced by Stangl to bolster the output of the Fulper Pottery. Other colors were added to the line. From 1920–1928 high-quality porcelains were made under Stangl's direction. Perfume dolls in the shape of ballerinas, powder and candy boxes, bookends, candleholders, and baskets were hand decorated.

Many marks were used on the various Fulper products. Some pieces were artist signed along with a raised, incised, or ink-stamped company name. Some Vasecraft pieces had paper labels and often a vertical ink-stamped "FULPER" within a rectangle. The 1920s porcelains were marked with oriental-style letters within an outlined rectangle. Dolls and dolls' heads were usually marked with the Fulper name.

References: Harvey Duke, *Stangl Pottery*, Wallace-Homestead, 1993; John Hibel, Carole Hibel, Robert DeFalco, *The Fulper Book*, text by David Rago, the Arts and Crafts Quarterly Press, 1992.

Museums: Chrysler Museum, Norfolk, VA;

F
U
L
P
E
R

New Jersey State Museum, Trenton, NJ; Newark Museum, NJ; New Orleans Museum of Art, LA; Philadelphia Museum of Art, PA.

Bookend, 6³/₄" h, Gothic style w/top forming candleholders, matte green Mission Verte glaze, unmkd, pr **300.00**

Bowl
  8" d, fluted body, gloss black glaze w/silver crystals, #654 .... **550.00**
  9" d
    Applied diagonal bands forming feet, celadon green over orange-skin surface, yellow, rust, and green streaked int, stamped vert "FULPER" mark **1000.00**
    Chinese Blue flambe over matte blue ground, #422 .... **325.00**
    Ten sides, ivory over mustard glaze **55.00**
  10" d
    7" h, effigy, 3-figure support, brown and gray flambe over green crystalline glaze(A) **605.00**
    Four small feet, wide flaring rim, blue flambe ext, yellow int, #447, black vert mark(A).......... **187.00**
  11¹/₂" d, blue, ivory, and brown flambe glaze, #559(A) **206.00**
  11³/₄" H-H, 2 small handles, vert scalloped body, matte rose and green flambe glaze, stamped mark(A) **210.00**
  12" d, oyster scalloped, attached flower holder, blue and ivory flambe **350.00**
  13" d, 3¹/₂" h, gray drip over green .. **275.00**

Bud Vase
  5¹/₂" h, blue and brown flambe on blue speckled ground, pr **250.00**
  9" h, trumpet shape, leopard-skin finish **300.00**

Candleholder, 7³/₄" h, shield back w/handle, dark tan w/black streaks.. **195.00**

Candlestick
  10" h, sq shaft, thick blue glaze over ivory at top, pr **650.00**
  11" h
    Dark green to tan gloss glaze **135.00**
    Twisted shape w/fluted edge, green crystalline glaze, black vert mark, pr(A) **330.00**

Cider Mug, green leopard-spot glaze .. **75.00**

Console Set, bowl, 9" d, 2 candleholders, 3¹/₂" h, green glaze over pink ground w/turquoise accents..... **295.00**

Dish, 7" d, jade green crystalline glaze **125.00**

Dresser Box, 8¹/₂" h, Art Deco style, kneeling Egyptian-revival woman finial, multicolored(A) **302.00**

Figure, cat, 5" h, 9" l, blue, brown, and cream flambe glaze, repaired chip, vert mark(A) **715.00**

Flask, 10" h, Pilgrim style, 2 small scroll handles, apple green and gunmetal brown flambe glaze(A) **440.00**

Flower Frog, 10¹/₂" h, deer on slanted base, matte blue glaze(A) **124.00**

Fruit Bowl, 11" d, 6¹/₂" h, ftd, vert ribbing on bowl, green and caramel splotched semi-matte glaze, incised vert mark(A) **302.00**

Jar
  4¹/₂" h, mahogany brown and dark blue on tan **250.00**
  12" h, gloss periwinkle blue and gunmetal brown flambe glaze, raised vert mark(A)...................... **1430.00**

Jug
  9¹/₂" h, musical, green crystalline glaze **150.00**
  12¹/₄" h, upright vert handle, copper dust glaze, raised vert mark, paper label(A) **2310.00**

Lamp
  12" h, perfume, Cytharia **950.00**
  14¹/₄" h, figural ballerina, yellow tiered skirt, black mask, white bodice **1495.00**
  18" h, mushroom, gunmetal and cream brown crystalline flambe glaze, leaded glass inserts in shade, stamped vert mark(A)........ **9900.00**

Lamp Base, 10¹/₂" h, tapered shape w/3 angular arms, matte green glaze, repaired chips, vert mark(A) .. **357.00**

Pitcher, 4" h, green flambe on rose **90.00**

Urn
  3" h, blue and green glaze **75.00**

Lamp, 16¹/₂" h, 10" d, Germanic, mottled metallic brown matte glaze, green, blue, and white slag glass, black vert "FULPER" mark(A), $7700.00. Photograph courtesy of Don Treadway and John Toomey, Oak Park, IL

6½" h, 3 small handles on neck, leopard-skin green and gunmetal crystalline glaze(A) **4677.00**

Vase

4" h, shades of green w/burgundy, rose semi-matte flambe **80.00**

5½" h, 5" d, gloss green glaze w/gold crystals on rim, #577 .... **275.00**

6" h

9" w, bowl shape, blue flambe glaze w/black at rim over geometric design(A) **715.00**

Relief-molded green rose, med blue ground **180.00**

Two small handles at shoulder, famille rose over green and brown crystalline drip, raised vert "FULPER" mark(A) **550.00**

6¼" h, 3 handles, dark green drip glaze, #530 .... **375.00**

6½" h

Dbl handles, med gray w/blue flambe and crystals **325.00**

Fan shape, blue crystalline glaze, pr **400.00**

Three strap handles, black crystalline glaze over butterscotch flambe ground, stamped vert mark **225.00**

7" h, 3 handles

Blue crystalline drip over blue-green semi-gloss ground w/light green streaks and brown clay highlights **285.00**

Blue flambe glaze w/crystals(A) ... **308.00**

Bulbous shape, green drips over plum ground **250.00**

Green crystalline glaze **165.00**

Med gray and blue ground w/dark blue crystals **225.00**

7¼" h

Barrel shape, tiger's-eye flambe glaze, sq vert ink mark(A) **385.00**

Urn shape, 2 small side handles, dark blue-green drip on brown   **170.00**

7½" h

Dark brown streaks from top, tan ground, gloss finish, black stamped "FULPER" mark **150.00**

Dbl buttressed handles, green crystalline glaze, vert oval mark(A) **412.00**

7¾" h, dbl handles, splashed mauve to green luster glaze, imp "FULPER" mark **295.00**

8" h, 10" w, brown and blue crystalline drip over cream to mustard base, dark brown flecks(A) **990.00**

9" h

Matte green glaze over matte rose glaze **195.00**

Round shape w/wide loop handles, matte green glaze w/brown accents, textured surface, raised vert mark(A) **715.00**

9½" h

Dark blue over green glaze **245.00**

Urn shape w/handles, blue glaze . **250.00**

9¾" h, molded mushrooms at base, tan ground w/dark brown accents, 2 rect openings on neck, gloss finish **1250.00**

10" h, urn shape, dbl handles, blue crystalline glaze **150.00**

11" h

Bulbous shape, 2 small handles at middle, green flambe w/yellow crystalline drip at top, #517, raised vert "FULPER" mark(A) **1045.00**

Oct shape, matte purple glaze w/blue streaks and dots, c1920   **365.00**

Pinched neck, wide lip, 2 small handles on shoulder, blue and cream flambe crystalline glaze, black vert mark(A) **467.00**

Vase, 7⅞" h, splashed caramel glaze, imp vert "FULPER" mark, $295.00

Vase, 9½" h, drip brown glaze over mottled green ground, imp vert "FULPER" mark(A), $220.00

Vase, 13" h, twelve cutouts, Flemington green glaze, Fulper paper label and vert stamp mark(A), $6600.00. Photograph courtesy of Don Treadway and John Toomey, Oak Park, IL

12" h
Bulbous shape, 2 side loop handles, thick blue-green textured glaze, imp vert "FULPER" mark(A) 990.00
Famille rose over dark gray, bits of suspended famille rose, raised vert "FULPER" mark(A) 935.00
13" h, everted rim, thick green crystalline glaze(A) 660.00
13½" h, baluster shape, flared rim, black to pumpkin orange flambe glaze, vert oval mark(A) 660.00
15" h, baluster shape, blue to matte gray flambe glaze, raised vert mark(A) 1320.00
16⅛" h, ovoid shape, light green crystalline glaze at mouth, dark crystalline glaze on shoulder, matte green glaze on body, vert "FULPER" mark(A) 1320.00

HULL POTTERY COMPANY
Crooksville, Ohio

(See General Manufacturers section for Hull Pottery history.)

Basket, Blossom Flite pattern, 6" h, #T2, $45.00

BLOSSOM FLITE
Basket, 6" h, #T-2 .... 45.00
Console Bowl, 16½" l, pink and black, #T-10.................................. 80.00
Cornucopia, 10½" w, gloss pink, #T-6 50.00
Creamer, #T-15 .... 16.00
Ewer, 9" h, floral design, gold trim, #T-3 .... 50.00
Sugar Bowl, Cov, #T-16 .... 16.00
Tea Set, pot, creamer, and sugar bowl 115.00
Vase
  10½" h.. 50.00
  19½" h, pink and black, #T-7 .... 110.00
BOW-KNOT
Basket
  6½" h, blue, #B-25 .... 185.00
  10½" h, blue and pink, #B-12......... 685.00
  12" h, #B-29 .... 1500.00
Candlesticks, 3½" h, #B-17, pr 175.00
Console Bowl, 13½" d, pink, #B-16 ... 250.00
Cornucopia, 7½" h, #B-5.................. 85.00
Ewer, 5½" h, #B-1 .... 120.00
Flowerpot, 6½" h, #B-6 .... 135.00
Jardiniere, 5¾" h, #B-18 .... 185.00
Vase
  5" h, #B-2 .... 105.00
  6½" h.. 75.00
  8½" h
    Blue
      #B-7... 155.00
      #B-8... 210.00
      #B-9... 155.00
  12½" h, #B-14 .... 995.00
Wall Plate, 10" d, #B-28 .... 925.00
BUTTERFLY
Ewer, 13½" h, #B-15 .... 125.00
Jardiniere, 6" h, ivory matte ground, gold trim, #B-5 .... 50.00
Lavabo, pebble finish......................... 100.00
Vase, 9" h, ftd, white and blue, #B-9 .. 75.00
CALLA LILY
Ewer, 10" h, #506/33 .... 325.00
Vase, 8" h, #520/33 .... 135.00

CONTINENTAL
Basket, 12½" h, persimmon glaze,
#C55 ....   75.00
Candleholder, 4" sq, orange, pr 50.00
Pitcher, 12½" h, #C56 ....   50.00
Planter, 8½" l, 4½" w, rect, orange,
#C68 ....   40.00
Vase, 12" h, orange, #C29 ....   50.00

CRAB APPLE
Vase, 8" h, turquoise..........................   120.00

DOGWOOD
Basket, 7½" h, pink, #501 ....   200.00
Ewer
7" h, #505-7 ....   250.00
8½" h 180.00
11½" h, #506-11½ 350.00
Vase
4¾" h, #516...................................   60.00
6½" h, #502...................................   100.00

EBB TIDE
Candleholder, #E-13, pr....................   60.00
Console Bowl, 15¾" l, snail, gold and
burgundy, #E-12 ....   125.00
Cornucopia
7½" h, turquoise gloss glaze, #E-3 ..   45.00
11¾" h, pink, #E-9 ....   135.00
Tea Set, pot, creamer, sugar bowl, red
w/gold trim 195.00

FANTASY
Candleholder, 6½" h, blue w/white,
#78, pr 45.00
Vase, 10" h, #F-30 ....   25.00

FIESTA
Planter, 10" d, 4" h, yellow and green,
#403 ....   12.00

GRANADA-MARDI GRAS
Basket, 8" h, #65 ....   85.00
Ewer, 10" h, #66................................   80.00
Teapot, 8" h, raised flowers, shaded
matte pink ground..........................   285.00
Vase, 9" h, #48 ....   45.00

IRIS
Basket, 7" h, #408 ....   295.00

*Cornucopia, Dogwood pattern, 3¾" h,
pink flowers, cream top, pale blue-green
base, #522, $32.00*

Floor Vase, 16" h, #414-16 ....   420.00
Pitcher, 13½" h, #401 ....   300.00
Vase
4¾" h, #403.....................................   60.00
7" h, #407..   90.00
8½" h, #406.....................................   145.00
16" h, rose and peach, #414 ....   450.00

MAGNOLIA
Glossy
Compote, 13" d, #H-23..................   70.00
Cornucopia, 8½" h, #H-10 ....   49.00
Teapot, 6½" h, pink, #H-20 ....   60.00
Vase
5½" h, gold trim, #H-1 ....   25.00
12½" h
Blue flowers, pink ground, #H-
16 ....   70.00
Green-brown irid ext, white
int, #H-22 ....   85.00
White flowers, pink ground,
#H-17 ....   70.00
Matte
Ewer
4¾" h, #14 ....   16.00
13½" h, pink and blue, #18.........   165.00
Teapot, 6¾" h, 9¼" l, raised yellow
flower w/green leaves, matte pink
ground......................................   160.00
Vase
6¼" h, #11 ....   45.00
6½" h, #16 ....   45.00
8½" h, #7 ....   68.00
10½" h, pink and blue, #9..........   80.00

NOVELTY
Bottle, Leeds, 7½" h
Elephant, pink 50.00
Pig, blue...   50.00
Lamp, kitten 75.00
Planter
Deer, gold trim, #57........................   30.00
Kitten and basket, #61 ....   20.00
St. Francis, white, #89 ....   35.00
Wall Pocket, figural flying duck, #540   55.00

OPEN ROSE
Candleholder, 6½" h, figural dove,
pink and blue, #117-6½, pr 250.00
Cornucopia, 8½" h
#101 ....   55.00
#141 ....   150.00
Hanging Basket, 7" h, #132 ....   225.00
Jardiniere, 8½" d, #114 ....   395.00
Lamp Base, 10½" h, #139 ....   295.00
Vase
4¾" h, #127....................................   60.00
6¼" h
#122, single loop handles...........   50.00
#136, dbl loop handles...............   50.00
8½" h, pink and green, #102 ....   75.00

ORCHID
Bookend, 7" h, #316, pr 750.00
Ewer, 13" h, cream and rose 550.00
Lamp, 10" h, beige 550.00

Vase

4³/₄" h, #307................................... 75.00

6" h

#303.................................... 125.00

#310.................................... 200.00

6³/₄" h, #306.............................. 140.00

8" h, #301-8............................. 110.00

PARCHMENT AND PINE

Basket, 6" h, #S-3 .... 45.00

Cornucopia

8" h, green, #S-2-L 32.00

12" h, #S-6, pr........................... 200.00

Ewer, 14" h 65.00

Pitcher, 13¹/₂" h, green........................ 125.00

Tea Set, green 135.00

Vase, 10" h, #S-4 .... 70.00

POPPY

Basket, 12" h, pink and cream, #601 .. 1195.00

Cornucopia, 8" l, pink and blue, #604 250.00

Pitcher, 4³/₄" h 85.00

Vase, 10¹/₂" h, pink and blue, #606 .... 275.00

ROSELLA

Cornucopia, 8¹/₂" l, #R-13................... 50.00

Vase

5" h, #R-2, pr 50.00

8¹/₂" h.. 40.00

SERENADE

Ashtray, yellow, #S23 .... 85.00

Candlestick, 6¹/₂" h, #S16, pr 60.00

Pitcher, 13¹/₂" h, pink, #S13 .... 195.00

Teapot, 6-cup, pink, #S17 .... 125.00

SUENO TULIP

Basket, 6" h, #102-33 .... 225.00

Ewer, 8" h, pink and light blue, #109-

33 .... 125.00

Flowerpot and Saucer, 4³/₄" h, #116-

33 .... 95.00

Jardiniere

5" h, pink.. 35.00

7" h, #115-33.............................. 195.00

Vase

6" h

#104-33 .... 85.00

#107-33 .... 80.00

8" h, #107-33............................ 65.00

9" h, white 50.00

SUN GLOW

Basket, 6¹/₂" h, pink, #84 .... 35.00

Bell, yellow 75.00

Beverage Pitcher, 7¹/₂" h, yellow, #55 . 40.00

Bowl, 5¹/₂" d, pink, #50 .... 15.00

Casserole, Cov, 8¹/₄" d, #51-7¹/₂.......... 42.00

Cup and Saucer 28.00

Grease Jar, 6" h, #53......................... 95.00

Vase, 8" h, #94 .... 35.00

Wall Pocket

6" h, w/gold trim 45.00

8¹/₄" h, whisk-broom shape, ribbed

pink ground w/yellow and green

butterfly and raised florals 65.00

THISTLE

Vase, 6¹/₂" h, blue 35.00

TOKAY

Basket, 10¹/₂" h

green and white, #11 .... 70.00

moon shape, green and pink, #11 ... 70.00

Consolette, 15³/₄" l, #14..................... 90.00

Ewer, 12" h, pink, white, and green,

#13 .... 150.00

Vase, 12" h, pink, white, and green,

#12 .... 55.00

TROPICANA

Vase, 8¹/₂" h, #53.............................. 325.00

TULIP

Bud Vase, 6" h, #104-44.................... 65.00

WATER LILY

Console Bowl, 13¹/₂" d, #L-21............ 120.00

Jardiniere

5¹/₂" h, #L-23................................. 85.00

6¹/₂" h, 8¹/₂" w, matte pink w/raised

yellow flower w/pink center and

green base, #L-24-8¹/₂..................... 275.00

Teapot, tan and cream 125.00

Vase

5¹/₂" h, #L-1................................. 25.00

9¹/₂" h, shaded pink, #L-11 .... 95.00

12" h, dbl, gloss pink, #L-27 .... 79.00

WILDFLOWER

Basket, 10¹/₂" h 155.00

Cornucopia, 8¹/₂" h, #W-10-8¹/₂......... 55.00

Pitcher, 8¹/₂" h, tan, #W-11 .... 90.00

Vase

6¹/₂" h, pink and brown, #W-54 ...... 150.00

9¹/₂" h, pink and blue, #W-13 .... 65.00

12¹/₂" h, #W-18-12¹/₂ 250.00

WOODLAND

Glossy

Bud Vase, dbl, 8¹/₂" h, #W-15 .... 40.00

Console Bowl, 14" d, glossy pink 50.00

Cornucopia

5¹/₂" l, #W-2 .... 55.00

11" h, #W-10 .... 115.00

Ewer, 13¹/₂" h, two-tone gloss, #W-

24... 275.00

Vase

7" h, pink w/green and gold trim,

#W-4 .... 55.00

8¹/₂" h, #W-16 .... 45.00

*Window Box, Woodland pattern,
10" l, matte finish, hairline,
"#W-14-10," $20.00*

Wall Pocket, 8" h, rose flower, pink
  ground w/olive handle **95.00**
Cornucopia, 11" l, #W-10 .... **35.00**
Pitcher, 5½" h, #W-3
  Pink **55.00**
  Yellow and green **45.00**
Window Box, 10" l, #W-14 .... **58.00**

JUGTOWN POTTERY
Seagrove, North Carolina
Early 1920s–Present

History: Jugtown Pottery was established by
Jacques and Juliana Busbee in Moore County,
near Seagrove, North Carolina, about 1921. Early
wares were sold in their tea and sales room in
Greenwich Village in New York City.

From 1922–1947 Jugtown wares were produced by Ben Owen and supervised by Jacques.
All types of traditional utilitarian pottery pieces
were made, including vases, candlesticks, flower
bowls, and table accessories in an assortment of
glazes, from salt glaze to heavy glazes. Chinese-
style pieces also were made, with Chinese Blue
being the most popular color. Other colors included cream, orange, white, black, green, and
brownish orange with black areas.

When Jacques died in 1947, Juliana continued to operate the pottery with Owen until she
became ill in 1958. When she signed two deeds
of sale for two different companies, there were
complications and the pottery closed but reopened the next year after the legal problems
were resolved. Ben Owen established his own
pottery close by and made similar wares. He
marked his pieces "Ben Owen, Master Potter."

John Mare managed Jugtown from 1960 until
the nonprofit corporation Country Road, Inc.,
purchased it in 1968, and Nancy Sweezy operated it for the new owner. Vernon Owens, who
had been chief potter since 1960, purchased the
pottery in 1982. Through all these years the same
shapes and glazes were made.

The pieces were marked "Jugtown Ware" in a
circular die-stamped mark impressed in the clay.
The same mark was used all through the company's history.

Museums: Chrysler Museum, Norfolk, VA;
Cleveland Museum of Art, OH; National Mu-
seum of History and Technology, Smithsonian
Institution, Washington, DC; St. Johns Art
Gallery, Wilmington, NC.

Bean Pot, 5¾" h, dark brown glaze,
  applied closed handles, imp "JUG-
  TOWN WARE" mark **75.00**
Bowl
  3" h, 5" d, green frog-skin glaze **45.00**
  4½" h, 6¾" d, ext w/blue, red, and
    white mottled glaze, int w/mot-
    tled turquoise and red Chinese
    Blue glaze, mkd **250.00**
  5½" d, tea bowl shape, mottled
    ochre glaze **75.00**
  7¼" d, ext w/Chinese Blue glaze,
    turquoise int, circ mark(A) **165.00**
  8" d, Chinese Blue glaze **149.00**
  11" d, flared shape, light gray mot-
    tled glaze(A) **82.00**
  15" d, open handles, orange glaze,
    redware body **35.00**
Candlestick, 15" h, Chinese White
  glaze, pr **350.00**
Creamer, 3⅓" h, intertwined incised
  linear design, salt-glaze finish
  w/cobalt accents on handle and
  rim, imp "JUGTOWN WARE" mark(A) ... **60.00**
Jar
  4½" h, redware w/amber-orange
    glaze, mkd(A) **15.00**
  6" h, 2 small handles on shoulder,
    Chinese Blue glaze, circ mark(A) . **357.00**
  8" h, 4 small handles, frog-skin
    glaze, circ mark(A) **495.00**
  8¼" h, dbl handles at middle, Chi-
    nese Blue mottled turquoise and
    red glaze, mkd(A) **467.00**
  12½" h, dbl handles, mirror black
    glaze on red clay body, mkd(A) ... **687.00**
Jug, 4¾" h, stoneware, gray glaze(A) .. **105.00**
Mug, 5" h, applied handle, med
  brown glaze, imp "JUGTOWN WARE"
  mark(A) **30.00**
Pitcher, 8" h, 3 concentric rings on
  upper body, incised design on neck
  and   spout,   sandstone   glaze
  w/turquoise accents, imp "JUGTOWN
  WARE 1977" mark(A) **55.00**
Plate
  6" d, orange glaze **40.00**
  10½" d, redware body, mkd(A) **28.00**
Pot, 3½" h, 2 handles, burnt orange
  glaze **65.00**
Sugar Bowl, Cov, 5" h, clear glaze on
  orange clay body, imp "JUGTOWN
  WARE" mark(A) **44.00**
Tea Set, pot, creamer, sugar bowl,
  brown stoneware, mkd **85.00**
Vase
  4" h
    Chinese White flowing glaze **70.00**
    Mottled turquoise and dark red
      glaze, pr(A) **330.00**
  4½" h, Chinese Blue splashed
    glaze **195.00**

Vase, 4" h, white glaze(A), $125.00

5" h
Chinese Blue glossy red and
turquoise glaze, imp "JUGTOWN
WARE" mark(A)........................... 467.00
Closed neck, cobalt glaze, circ
mark(A).................................... 467.00
5½" h, protruding shoulder, dark
red mottled glaze w/turquoise
spots(A) 415.00
5¾" h, mottled opaque celadon
glaze(A).................................... 66.00
6" h
Beehive shape, turquoise glaze.... 185.00
Brown and green glaze............... 90.00
Bulbous shape, Chinese White
glaze....................................... 125.00
6½" h, ovoid shape w/narrow neck,
white crackle drip glaze on
bisque body(A) 165.00
7" h, 2 applied medallions, Chinese
Blue, mottled oxblood, green,
white, and turquoise glaze,
stamped circ "JUGTOWN POTTERY"
mark(A) 550.00

Vase, 7" h, mottled red, blue, and gray
glaze, imp mark(A), $220.00

7¼" h, closed-in neck, Chinese
Blue glaze, circ mark(A).............. 440.00
7¾" h
Corset shape, Chinese Blue, mottled turquoise and red glaze on
shoulder and neck, clear glaze
on gray stone body, circ "JUG-
TOWN POTTERY" mark(A) 385.00
Splashed turquoise and mauve
glaze, imp mark 475.00
9" h, bulbous body, flared neck,
mottled red glaze, mkd(A) 935.00
11" h, bulbous base w/flared neck,
Chinese Blue, mottled turquoise
and red glaze, circ "JUGTOWN POT-
TERY" mark(A)............................. 825.00
Vessel, 8¾" h, bulbous shape, 2 small
handles, mottled turquoise glaze
over red underglaze, imp mark(A) ... 550.00

c.1904-1936

MARBLEHEAD POTTERY
Marblehead, Massachusetts
1904–1936

History: Marblehead Pottery was actually
started as part of a group industry called Hand-
craft Shops, which were therapeutic workshops
for recovering sanitarium patients. The pottery
work proved too difficult and Marblehead separated itself from the sanitarium after the first year.

The pottery was founded by Herbert Hall, but
was really controlled by supervisor Arthur Baggs.
By 1908 the company was making vases, jardinieres, lampstands, and tiles in simple shapes
with gray, brown, blue, and yellow matte glazes.

In 1912 Marblehead introduced a small line
of tin-enameled faience in the form of teapots,
mugs, children's sets, and small breakfast and
luncheon sets. These were done in soft colors on
cream, white, or gray grounds. When Baggs became owner of the pottery in 1915, the mainstay
of the operation was the matte-glazed wares
made in Marblehead blue, gray, wisteria, rose,
yellow, and tobacco brown. Decorative jars,
lamps, sculpture, and garden ornaments were
added to the general line. Flowers, fruits, animals
and sea motifs were used on the hand-thrown
pieces. Molds were used only for bookends and
tiles. Baggs became a professor of ceramics at
Ohio State University in 1928. He returned to

work at Marblehead every summer until the pottery closed in 1936.

Marblehead won a series of awards for its pottery. Most examples were marked with a ship and "MP" cipher.

Museums: National Museum of History and Technology, Smithsonian Institution, Washington, DC; New Orleans Museum of Art, LA; The Newark Museum, NJ.

Bookend, 5½" h, carved decoration of
  Egyptian, blue and semi-gloss matte
  glaze, mkd, pr 575.00
Bowl
  3" d, yellow semi-matte glaze 375.00
  4" d, matte purple glaze, mkd(A) 187.00
  6" d, 3" h, matte brown glaze
    w/yellow and dark brown
    specks(A) 198.00
  6¼" h, tapered ovoid shape w/wide
    mouth, matte wisteria glaze on
    ext, violet int, imp ship and "M.P."
    mark(A) 550.00
  8" d, 3" h, blue, green, and brown
    feathered matte glaze, imp
    mark(A) 357.00
  9" d
    2" h, mottled green, pink, and
      gray semi-gloss glaze(A) 121.00
    4" h, dark blue ext, light blue
      gloss int, imp mark(A) 465.00
    5" h, tapered shape, matte gray
      glaze(A) 176.00
    Band of brown, yellow, blue, and
      green stylized leaves and
      grapes(A) 1870.00
Bud Vase, 7" h, gray glaze 275.00
Chamberstick, 4" h, 4" d, matte pink
  glaze w/gray accents, mkd(A) 275.00
Cider Cup, 4" h, dark blue designs
  w/dark green band 185.00
Pitcher
  5" h, narrow base, wide top, light
    yellow band w/people and
    camels, cream ground, blue han-
    dle, hairline, c1910(A) 110.00
  8¼" h, matte green body, black
    handle, incised black band at rim,
    repaired spout, c1904(A) 247.00
Rose Bowl, 5" d, dark purple glaze 195.00
Vase
  3" h, squat shape, 2 loop handles,
    matte blue glaze(A) 230.00
  3½" h
    Flared shape, blue ext, light blue
      int 300.00
    Incised and painted brown leaves
      and yellow berry design,
      brown ground w/dark brown
      border top and base 650.00
  3¾" h, green glaze 225.00

4" h
  Cylinder shape, matte yellow and
    green glaze w/brown accents,
    imp mark(A) 522.00
  Flared shape, matte dark blue ext,
    gloss light blue int, imp mark ... 150.00
  4½" h, hourglass shape, matte navy
    blue glaze(A) 282.00
  4¾" h, stylized yellow berries and
    blue-green leaves on matte gray
    speckled ground, ship mark(A) 1430.00
  5" h, purple and blue mottled glaze 450.00
  5½" h
    Black leaves and berries on blue
      ground 1100.00
    Bulbous shape w/flared rim, blue-
      gray stylized blossoms on
      leaves, light mauve speckled
      ground, ship mark(A) 2090.00
  6" h
    Broad tapered shape, narrow
      neck, matte blue glaze(A) 330.00
    Fan shape, blue glaze, mkd 295.00
    Tapered form w/bulbous base,
      matte blue ground w/maroon
      accents, imp mark and paper
      label(A) 825.00
    Thick blue and green matte glaze
      ext, green int(A) 385.00
    6¾" h, black-outlined stylized trees
      w/green leaves, red berries,
      brown trunks, blue ground(A) 1100.00
  7" h
    Blue, yellow, orange, and brown
      macaws on brown and yellow
      leafy branches, matte yellow
      ground(A) 2530.00
    Dark brown acorns, oak leaves,
      and vert lines, green ground,
      sgd "H. Tutt," imp mark(A) 2860.00
    Green to dark yellow feathered
      glaze, imp mark(A) 715.00

***Vase, 8" h, purple design, matte blue
ground(A), $935.00***

Vase, 15" h, painted 2 tone stylized trees, slate gray ground, imp mark(A), $17,600.00. Photograph Courtesy of Don Treadway and John Toomey, Oak Park, IL

7¹/₄" h, blue speckles on matte gray surface, "MH" and sailing ship mark... **525.00**
9" h
 Gray painted Arts and Crafts design, matte gray glaze w/specks of gray and brown, sgd "H.T."... **3500.00**
 Narrow body, wide top and base, dark green and yellow checkerboards top and base, dark green vert lines, green ground, sgd "H. Tutt," imp mark(A)....... **1050.00**
9³/₄" h, hand-thrown cylinder shape, 5 clusters of green, brown, and gray-black trees on blue-gray ground, imp mark(A) **5500.00**
Wall Pocket, 5" h, 7" w, flared top, matte green glaze............................ **300.00**

MERRIMAC POTTERY COMPANY
Newburyport, Massachusetts
1897–1908

History: Thomas Nickerson formed Merrimac Ceramic Company in 1897 to make florist ware

and enameled tile. When W.G. Fisher joined a year later, they expanded the company.

In 1900 the focus was shifted to hand-thrown decorative and glazed artwares—the first of which were vases and flower containers in matte green and yellow glazes. The name was changed to Merrimac Pottery Company in 1902.

By 1903 the range of glazes was expanded to include metallic luster, iridescence, and crackle. Garden pottery also was added to the product line along with Arrhelian ware, based on redware from the Roman times. The artwares won a silver medal at the St. Louis Exposition in 1904.

In 1908, shortly after Nickerson had sold the pottery to Frank Bray, it was destroyed by fire. Early wares were not marked. From 1900–1901 a paper label was used. After that the mark was impressed or incised.

Museums: Boston Museum, MA; Worcester Art Museum, MA.

Bowl
 5" d, 2¹/₄" h, squat shape, closed rim, crackled pink mottled glaze(A) **192.00**
 8¹/₂" d, 5¹/₄" h, rolled rim, carved, stylized blossoms and lily pads, feathered matte green glaze, unmkd(A) **1540.00**
Bud Vase, 4" h, wide base, narrow neck, 2 loop handles on base, organic matte green glaze, unmkd...... **200.00**
Vase
 3³/₄" h, globular shape, matte blue glaze, imp mark(A) **125.00**
 4" h, cylinder shape w/closed rim, blue and green speckled glaze drips on dark green feathered body, paper label(A) **425.00**
 4¹/₄" h, squared rim, dimpled shoulder, horiz ribbing, matte green glaze(A) **125.00**
 6" h, bulbous shape, modeled stylized leaves and buds, feathered matte green glaze, unmkd(A) **880.00**
 7" h, bulbous shape w/tapered base, rolled rim, carved stylized leaves and buds, matte green glaze, paper label **1500.00**
 7¹/₄" h, cylinder shape w/turned-in rim, tooled and applied quatrefoils and leaves on long stems, textured dark green glaze, paper label(A)....................................... **3630.00**
 7¹/₂" h
  Applied leaves, matte green glaze, hairline, unmkd(A) **1980.00**
  Bulbous cylinder shape, carved long-stemmed 4-leaf flowers, leaf-shaped base, semi-matte

Vase, 7¹/₂" h, semi-matte vegetable green finish(A), $2000.00. Photograph courtesy of David Rago Arts and Crafts, Lambertville, NJ

med green glaze, stamped
"MERRIMAC" mark(A) **4675.00**
White streaks on matte gray-
brown glaze, red clay, imp fish
and "Merrimac" mark(A) **330.00**
11³/₈" h, green feathered glaze **1250.00**
14" h, dark green glaze **3500.00**
Vessel, 10¹/₂" h, bulbous body, ta-
pered base, semi-matte dark green
mottled glaze, paper label(A) **522.00**

c.1895

NEWCOMB POTTERY
New Orleans, Louisiana
1895–1940

History: In 1894 Mary Given Sheerer went to New Orleans, Louisiana, to teach pottery and china decoration at H. Sophie Newcomb Memorial College for Women. Ellsworth Woodward, the founding Dean, supervised the pottery making operation "to provide useful and appropriate employment" for Southern women.

Joseph Mayer worked at Newcomb from the early 1890s until 1927. Using the womens' drawings, he shaped all the pots for the decorators. The bronze medal awarded to Newcomb Pottery at the Paris International Exposition in 1900 demonstrated European recognition of the American art pottery movement and was the first

of many medals won by the company. In 1901 Tulane University provided a building for the pottery enterprise.

Both the English design schools and the Arts and Crafts movement influenced the designs on Newcomb Pottery. No two pieces were alike since each piece was hand thrown and then individually decorated by the artist/decorators working at the pottery. Southern flora and fauna were popular decorative motifs. A range of cobalt blues and sage greens was the hallmark of Newcomb Pottery. Approximately ten to fifteen young women graduates of the college worked each year on the pottery designs.

Potters experimented with slip decoration and used underglaze painting into the 1930s. Some of the finest examples were made before 1910 and were awarded numerous prizes at the various expositions. From 1903–1907 pottery designs were deeply indented designs on the wet clay. A red glaze was used from 1903–1905, and yellow and orange were added from 1905–1908.

Many fine designers worked at Newcomb over the years, but the mainstays were Sadie Irvine, Henrietta Bailey, and Anna Francis Simpson. When Paul Cox, who had studied under Professor Binns at Alfred University, became technical director of Newcomb in 1910, matte glazes were developed. From 1910–1915 modeled designs largely replaced the incised ones, and the florals changed from stylized to more naturalistic. Sadie Irvine fashioned pieces with scenic oak trees, hanging moss, and a shining moon. During this period the designs shifted away from the simplicity of the Arts and Crafts movement to a more romantic appearance. Blues and greens were still the main colors used, but matte glazes predominated.

In 1918 Paul Cox left Newcomb and the pottery moved from the Garden District to an area adjacent to Tulane's campus. Kenneth Smith took over Cox's job as ceramist and became manager in 1929. During the 1920s, the wares became fairly standardized and bowls and vases were decorated with naturalistic flowers or the trees-with-moss designs. Some experimental works were still produced. After Sheerer visited the Paris Exposition in 1925, some Art Deco designs were used at Newcomb Pottery. Espanol, a new design motif influenced by a Spanish mantel, appeared in many variations throughout the 1930s.

The retirement of two long-standing employees in 1931 marked the end of an era for Newcomb Pottery—Ellsworth Woodward left after 46 years and Mary Sheerer after 37. Though the wares were being sold in many parts of the country, the stock was reduced because the three main decorators were spending more time teaching at the college than making pottery. During the 1930s, the trees-and-moss scenes were continued along with newer abstract designs. By

1935 only Smith and Irvine were left to carry on the pottery making and even during the Depression, pieces were entered in exhibitions.

In 1939, it was decided to continue the pottery school, but no longer conduct a commercial enterprise. The Newcomb Guild was established in 1941 to sell, on a limited basis, the works of interested students and alumnae. A utilitarian line of simple vases, bowls, and ashtrays in muted colors or glazes was introduced in 1944, but the Guild closed down when Sadie Irvine retired in 1952.

Various marks were impressed, incised, or painted on Newcomb Pottery. In 1901 a registration system was introduced, and in 1910 a number was assigned to different shapes. Unacceptable pieces had an emery wheel through the mark.

Museums: Howard-Tilton Library, Tulane University, New Orleans, LA; Louisiana State Museum, New Orleans, LA; Metropolitan Museum of Art, New York City; Museum of Fine Arts, Boston, MA; National Museum of History and Technology, Smithsonian Institution, Washington, DC; New Orleans Museum of Art, LA; The Newark Museum, NJ.

Mug, 5" h, band of white and yellow flowers w/yellow and blue leaves, green and blue bands, med blue ground, "BG28 & Q" mark(A), $1430.00

Pitcher, 8" h, oranges on trees, streaked light blue to cream ground, dark blue rim, spout, and handle, "A.B.K., N.C.' mark(A), $2200.00

Bowl
  4" h
    8" d, carved light pink flowers and stems on shoulder, dark blue ground, Sadie Irvine, "SI, TD54, 68" mark(A) **165.00**
    8³/₈" d, flared shape, incised beige bands on rim, mauve ground, mkd(A) **275.00**
Bud Vase, 5¹/₂" h, spherical base, stick neck, lustered oxblood glaze, incised "NC/JM" mark(A) **715.00**
Chamberstick, 4" h, blue, green, and cream stylized flowers, dark blue ground, #TG37(A) **1100.00**
Cup and Saucer, 4" h, cup w/red and cream pinecones w/green foliage on blue ground, saucers w/green swirls on blue ground, H. Bailey, set of 4(A) **4750.00**
Jar, 4¹/₂" h, 5" d, spherical shape, carved blue and green oak trees w/light blue sky and white moon, "NC, SI, JH, 75, SW27" mark(A) **1320.00**
Jar, Cov, 7³/₄" h, carved band of light blue sweet peas, gloss dark blue ground, cov w/center blossom and "Here are sweet peas on the tip toe of flight," "NC, MTR, W, JM SS64" mark(A) **10,450.00**
Match Holder, 2" h, bell shape, carved blue oak trees and moss on pink and gray matte ground, "NC, SI, JH, SV14, 12" mark(A) **770.00**
Mug, 3" h, flared base, incised gloss

stylized ivory flowers on green stems, cobalt band and handle, Leona Nicholson, dtd 1906, "NC, LN, BC95, JM, Q" mark(A) **1870.00**
Pitcher, 6" h, slender, flared shape, incised and painted white jonquils on shoulder, carved green leaves and stems, gloss finish, Ada Lonnegan, "WW27 Q, J.M." mark(A) **1800.00**
Plaque, 6" d, blue and green trees w/moss and pink sky, dark blue ground, Sadie Irvine, #PP91(A)........ **1210.00**
Plate
  7¹/₂" d, incised border of stylized blue, yellow, and green flowers, gloss glaze, hairline, imp "NC, LN, JM, W, BV17" mark(A) **1320.00**
  12" d, carved and painted pink and

cream pinecones w/green foliage, dark blue ground, H. Bailey, #NS86(A).................................... **1540.00**

Trivet, 6″ d, incised and painted white flowers w/yellow centers and green leaves and stems, dark matte blue glaze, Sadie Irvine, #S784 .... **875.00**

Vase

2½″ h, carved white blossoms and large blue leaves on shoulder, matte dark blue glaze, "NC/HB/PV13/2″ mark(A) **880.00**

3″ h

  2″ w, red rose design on dark blue ground, purple vines at top, purple band at base, Sadie Irvine **550.00**

  3″ w, white jonquils at shoulder w/carved green leaves, matte blue ground, Anna Francis, #ME28 .... **750.00**

  4″ w, bulbous shape, short neck, green to blue gloss glaze on red clay.. **375.00**

3⅓″ h, spherical shape, gloss green curved leaves, light blue ground, dtd 1901, "NC, JM, D71, U″ mark(A) **2200.00**

4″ h

  Dark blue, light green, yellow, and pink geometric leaves at top, med blue matte glaze w/specks of dark blue, incised vert lines, "#67 OG73, C.M. Xharlaron, J. Meyer″ mark(A) ... **1200.00**

  Ivory painted and carved poppies, dark green whiplash stems and leaves, dark green top and base borders, A. Roman, c1895–99, block mark(A) **14,300.00**

4¼″ h, ovoid shape, band of carved purple flowers on shoulder, matte dark red glaze, hairline, "NC, SI, JM, 25, PS44″ mark(A).................. **1100.00**

4⅞″ h

  Compressed ovoid shape w/short neck, light blue, yellow, and green molded daffodils, blue streaked ground, imp "NC," circled C, and "205″ mark(A)....... **1320.00**

  Squat shape, pink gardenia, matte blue ground, "JM, AM″ mark **1200.00**

5½″ h, matte blue and white arched curtains, blue ground, mkd.......... **1250.00**

6″ h

  Bottle shape w/4 small loop handles on neck, thick light green glaze w/yellow and dark green drip, imp "NC″ mark **550.00**

Vase, 6″ h, blue and green trees and Spanish moss, light pink sky, Sadie Irvine, "#327 & 5793″ mark(A), $2420.00

  Ovoid shape, pale blue, green, and gray ethereal landscape w/3 southern pines, imp "NC J-262 R.M.″ mark(A) **880.00**

6¾″ h, band of white and yellow gardenias w/green foliage on shoulder, matte blue glaze, incised "NC, SI, 100, SY30″ mark(A) . **1045.00**

7″ h

  Cylinder shape, moonlit landscape w/moss-draped oak trees, dtd 1925, "CN, JM, AFS O266 318″ mark(A) **1320.00**

  Pink and blue flowers w/yellow centers on shoulder, matte blue glaze, red-pink overglaze, Sadie Irvine, #194(A) **1500.00**

7½″ h, bulbous base, tapered cylinder neck, molded light gray-green, yellow, and green 3-petal flowers and stalks, Sarah Irvine, imp "NC, HP75″ mark(A).............. **1100.00**

8″ h, bulbous base w/long tapered neck, light blue, yellow, and green molded jonquils, dark blue ground, imp "NC, 179 KH32″ mark(A) **1650.00**

8½″ h

  Carved purple swamp scene with moss, moon, and trees, Sadie Irvine, dtd 1927, hairline(A) **3960.00**

  Cylinder shape, light blue, yellow, and green molded jonquils, dark blue ground, tan int, imp "NC″ incised circled B, and "M250A.M. Gd40″ mark(A) **2090.00**

9″ h

  Incised band of dark blue oak leaves, light blue ground, gloss light blue body, sgd "Marie de Hoa Le Blanc and Irene Borden Keep"(A) 5220.00

Red and cream flowers w/green leaves, med blue ground, Sadie Irvine(A) 935.00

10" h, white jonquils, green stems, light blue ground, Anna F. Simpson, 1924 .... 3800.00

10½" h, carved pink pinecones and green needles, matte blue ground, H. Bailey, c1919, "NC, HB, JM, KI42, 268" mark(A)............ 3960.00

12" h, elongated cylinder shape w/flared rim and base, incised green, blue, and white iris blossoms, buds, and spiked leaves in paneled border, imp "NC LN Cp-63 JM and W" mark(A) 3850.00

12½" h

Blue carved irises, blue and green vert stems and ground, Leona Nicholson, "NC" mark 4500.00

Orchids on neck, blue vert ribbing, blue and green semimatte glaze, buff body, "NC" mark 2500.00

13" h, slender tapered form, carved and painted blue iris design, blue and green incised vert lines, blue-green ground, sgd "Sadie Irvine," dtd 1912 "EX19" mark(A) 2640.00

Vessel

3¼" h, squat shape, dbl handles, incised gloss white quatrefoils w/yellow centers, blue-green,

Vase, 16" h, carved blue trunks, green pine needles, light blue sky, green trees and ground, Anna Simpson, "#HC55, 142" mark(A), $9900.00. Photograph courtesy of Don Treadway and John Toomey, Oak Park, IL

blue, and white ground, "NC, JM, Q, BS76" mark(A)......................... 2090.00

6" h, carved band of pink flowers and green leaves on shoulder, dark blue ground, H. Bailey, dtd 1927, "NC, QE81, 61, HB" mark(A) 2370.00

Vase, 14" h, light green and blue carved cypress trees, dark blue band at top, Sadie Irvine, "FU49, B" in circle mark(A), $7700.00

NILOAK

NILOAK POTTERY COMPANY
Benton, Arkansas
1910–1947

History: Charles Dean Hyten of Hyten Pottery, later known as Eagle Pottery, formed Niloak Pottery with a group of investors in 1911. At first he made ordinary stoneware crocks, churns, and jugs, as his family had before him, but when demand decreased for these wares, Hyten set out to create a unique art pottery.

He swirled together two or more colors of the native Arkansas clay and placed the marbleized results on the potter's wheel to form the vases and bowls called "Mission Swirl." These were marketed under the name "Niloak"—kaolin spelled backwards. Pieces were usually brown, blue, or cream, but green, pink, and white also were used. Early swirl pieces had a rough texture, dull exterior, and clear interior glaze that made the pieces waterproof. The pottery was quite successful, due to a good distribution system, and as the result of its popularity, other shapes were made, including lamps, umbrella stands, pitchers, tankards, candlesticks, and clock cases. By the 1920s pieces were mass-produced to meet the demand and shapes became more standardized.

Hyten frequently demonstrated and exhibited the Niloak technique. In 1925 he obtained a trademark for his wares, and in 1928 he received a patent on the swirl pottery technique. That same year the company was incorporated as the Niloak Pottery and Tile Company.

By 1929 there was a large, new showroom on Military Road, but with the Depression looming, there were heavy expenses and decreased sales. In 1931 Hyten developed a line of molded wares in matte, semi-matte, gloss, and dip glazes called Hywood Art Pottery. M. Stoin from Weller worked on this line before the fire of 1932. Howard Lewis, who joined the company in 1932, referred to this new glazed ware as Hywood by Niloak, capitalizing on the Niloak name. Some hand-thrown pieces were made but when Rudy Ganz designed molds for the cast pieces, the technique changed to this less expensive and easier method of production. In 1933 Niloak exhibited at the Chicago Century of Progress Exposition. Ganz left in 1933 and Lewis left in 1934.

In 1934 a group of Little Rock businessmen purchased Niloak, and the company concentrated on industrial castwares in an attempt to increase sales. By 1937 castware was called simply Niloak. At the end of the 1930s sales improved in all aspects of the pottery: stonewares, castware, and some swirl pieces. Winburn was in total control, and Hyten, who had become a castware salesman, resigned in 1940 and moved on to Camark Pottery.

Just prior to World War II, Niloak was quite prosperous. The company continued to produce an abundance of castwares, in addition to stonewares, flowerpots, a new line of novelties, and a small number of swirl pieces. However, by 1942 the facility was mostly converted to war production, especially the manufacture of clay pigeons for military training.

After a fire in 1945, the company continued to fill numerous back orders for castwares, but there were few new sales. Postwar glazes were primarily glossy. By 1947, Niloak was no longer functioning as a pottery and Winborn formed the Winborn Tile Company with his brother.

A variety of impressed die-stamped marks was used on the Mission Swirl pieces. Raised mold marks were used on later pieces and ink-stamped markings on Hywood Art Pottery were introduced in 1931.

Reference: David Edwin Gifford, *Collector's Encyclopedia of Niloak,* Collector Books, 1993.
Museum: Chrysler Museum, Norfolk, VA.

Bowl	
4¼" d, Mission Swirl	65.00
7½" h, rolled scalloped rim, figure of Peter Pan on rim, blue glaze	145.00
10" d	
Melon ribbed, blue glaze	25.00
Mission Swirl	200.00
Bud Vase	
4" h, Ozark Dawn II glaze	22.00
7" h, Mission Swirl	50.00
Candlestick, 10" h, stepped shaft, brown, blue, and ivory Mission Swirl, mkd, pr(A)	247.00
Candy Jar, Cov, 8½" h, hand thrown, Mission Swirl	2550.00
Cigarette Jar, 4¾" h, Mission Swirl	150.00
Cornucopia, 6" h, cream glaze	15.00
Creamer, 3½" h, green	45.00
Cup and Saucer, castware, imp bouquet design, rose glaze, set of 6	48.00
Ewer	
7" h, matte rose glaze	20.00
9" h, rose ext, gray int, matte, pr	100.00
10" h, matte blue emb cameos on sides	38.00
Floor Vase, 18" h, Mission Swirl	1400.00
Humidor, 5" h, Mission Swirl	450.00
Jug, 5½" h, Mission Swirl	750.00
Lamp Base, 9¾" h, vase shape, Mission Swirl	350.00
Novelty Ware, figure	
3¼" h, cannon, matte rose glaze	35.00
4" h, horse, nose up, ears down, gloss rust glaze w/drips	45.00
5" h, standing pig, dark red glaze	35.00
8" l, canoe, brown	30.00
Pitcher	
4" h, Ozark Dawn, imp "NILOAK" mark	12.00
5" h, light pink glaze	75.00
6" h, matte blue glaze	25.00
7" h, Bouquet pattern, blue glaze	25.00
7½" h, imp flowers, pink gloss glaze	32.00
7¾" h, ball shape, Ozark Dawn II	125.00

Planter
  3½" h, polar bear and basket, tan
    glaze 30.00
  3¾" h, seated camel, blue glaze 45.00
  5" h, boxing kangaroo, tan glaze..... 28.00
  5½" h, figural pelican, red and
    white 35.00
  6" h
    Circus elephant, Ozark Dawn II .. 48.00
    Figural squirrel, tan glaze 25.00
  6½" h, figural swan, pink glaze....... 30.00
  7" h, bust of woman w/bonnet, blue
    glaze, Hywood castware 20.00
  7½" h, figural swan, white glaze..... 35.00
  8" h, deer in grass, blue glaze 30.00
  8½" h, wishing well, blue glaze 30.00
Pot, 2¾" h, Mission Swirl 110.00
Strawberry Jar/Planter, 7" h
  Med blue 15.00
  Ozark Dawn II 35.00
Toothpick, 2¼" h, Mission Swirl......... 60.00
Tumbler, 4" h, Mission Swirl............... 60.00
Vase
  2½" h, figural shoe, med blue glaze 20.00
  3½" h, Mission Swirl....................... 50.00

Vase, 3⅝" h, Ozark Dawn glaze, imp
"NILOAK" mark, $30.00

4" h
  Mission Swirl 60.00
  Urn shape, molded floral swags,
    chartreuse glaze....................... 15.00
4½" h, Mission Swirl....................... 65.00
5" h, Mission Swirl 75.00
5¼" h, corset shape, Mission Swirl.. 50.00
6" h
  Mission Swirl 90.00
  Two handles
    Blue glaze............................... 18.00
    Ozark Dawn 30.00
  Wing handles, green glaze 25.00
6½" h, molded swirl shape, 2 small
  handles on rim, matte med green
  glaze 30.00
7" h
  5½" d, Mission Swirl 120.00
  Overlapping leaves, Ozark Dawn
    II 39.00
7½" h
  5 holes at top, blue glaze............. 20.00
  Ribbed, 2 handles top to base,
    matte green glaze.................... 35.00
  Rolled rim, Mission Swirl, cream,
    blue, and brown swirls............. 165.00
  8" h, Mission Swirl, 5 colors............ 165.00
  8¾" h, oviform w/flared rim, Mis-
    sion Swirl, blue, brown, and
    ivory, stamped "Niloak"(A) 165.00
  9" h, cone shape, Mission Swirl 200.00
  9¾" h, Mission Swirl....................... 250.00
  10" h, Mission Swirl
    Dark brown, blue, and cream...... 250.00
    Rolled rim, buff and red-brown
      swirls 185.00
    Tapered body, wide rim(A) 220.00
  10½" h, Mission Swirl design in 5
    colors 235.00
  11" h, Mission Swirl 265.00

Vase, 3¾" h, mottled matte blue finish,
imp "Niloak' mark, $35.00

Vase, 9" h, Mission Swirl, blue, cream,
and brown, imp mark(A), $176.00

NORTH DAKOTA SCHOOL OF MINES
University of North Dakota
Grand Forks, North Dakota
1910–1963

History: In 1910, Earle Babcock persuaded the University of North Dakota to establish a Ceramics Department to work with North Dakota clay. Margaret Cable, who studied with Charles Binns and Frederick H. Rhead, taught at the North Dakota School of Mines in Grand Forks from 1910–1949.

Pottery examples made at the school included vases, figurines, cookie jars, lamp bases, ashtrays, tea sets, and plaques. Almost all of the pieces were made from molds, although a few were hand thrown by Margaret Cable. Pottery was sometimes decorated with designs carved in low relief or was hand painted with colored glazes. Native themes included flowers and animals. Some pieces were done in Art Nouveau and Art Deco styles.

Other artists working with the native clays at the facility were Flora Huckfield, Agnes Dollahan, Frieda Hammers, Margaret Pachl, and Julia E. Mattson. Only a limited number of pieces were sold to the general public. Some pottery was marked "U.N.D., Grand Forks, N.D." On other pieces the incised and underglaze cobalt blue mark was a circle formed by the words "University of North Dakota Grand Forks, N.D. Made at School of Mines of N.D. Clay."

Reference: Margaret Barr, Donald Miller, and Robert Barr, *University of North Dakota Pottery, The Cable Years,* Knight Publishing Company, 1977.

Collectors' Club: North Dakota Pottery Collectors' Society, Sandy Short, Box 14, Beach, North Dakota 58621, $10 per year.

Bowl
4" h, shaded green glaze, mkd	**30.00**
4½" h, band of excised poppies on rim, olive green glaze, mkd	**450.00**
5" d, shaded blue glaze, sgd "Huck"	**210.00**
5½" d, 3¼" h, matte green glaze, sgd "Cable"	**425.00**

6" d, incised flower design, shaded lime green to sand brown ground	**225.00**
7" d, sky blue glaze, sgd "Mattson".	**85.00**
Ginger Jar, burgundy glaze, sgd "Middleton"	**70.00**

Jar
3½" h, bulbous body, excised cream glazed coyotes on rim, ochre base(A)	**330.00**
7½" h, bulbous body, vert neck, matte blue-gray excised stylized lamb and wreath of flowers, peach ground, Van Camp	**950.00**
Jardiniere, 6" h, 6½" d, incised Arts and Crafts blue and green stylized flowers, matte green ground(A)	**1870.00**

Lamp
7" h, blue and violet glaze, sgd "Smith," dtd 1936	**195.00**
10½" h, tapered shape, shaded matte blue, green, and rust glaze, factory drilled base, die-stamped mark(A)	**330.00**

Paperweight
3" d, raised 4-H design, gloss green glaze	**75.00**
3⅜" d	
Brown raised "R" and chain, matte finish	**125.00**
Open flower head, lime green to yellow shading, mkd	**85.00**

Pitcher
6" h, painted floral design, sgd "Mattson"	**275.00**
6¼" h, emb viking ship on sides, med blue glaze, mkd	**1495.00**
Plate, 9" d, painted stylized Indian decoration, c1933	**225.00**

Vase, 4½" h, 6" d, brick red, brown, and yellow native American birds, sgd "Jacobson"(A), $357.00

Pot
  2" h, red geometric band, buff
    ground, mkd(A) 100.00
  3¹/₄" d, mint green carved wheat,
    cream ground, sgd "Huckfield" ... 175.00
  4" h, brown ext, mint green int, sgd
    "Julia Mattson" 135.00
Sugar Bowl, Cov, 3¹/₂" h, cobalt trim,
  cream ground, ink stamp on side 480.00
Tea Tile, 5" d, matte green incised
  oxen and wagon, brown glaze(A).... 248.00
Tray, 6" d, leaf shape, blue and green
  shades, artist sgd 150.00
Vase
  2³/₄" h
    Band of incised flowers, mauve
      glaze, incised "G, H8-Huck-
      1376" mark(A) 250.00
    Bowl shape, aqua glaze, sgd
      "Mattson" 28.00
  3" h, squat shape, blue glaze.......... 100.00
  3¹/₄" h, bowl shape, sand-colored
    glaze, sgd "Mattson".................... 32.00
  3¹/₂" h, excised band of coyotes on
    ivory ground, matte blue body,
    stamped "934, JM" mark(A) 550.00
  4" h
    Bulbous shape, shaded blue
      ground, sgd "Huck" 215.00
    Carved tulips, gloss blue glaze(A) 147.00
    Incised lotus blossoms under
      satin green glaze, mkd 200.00
  4¹/₄" h, 5" w, pear shape, teal blue
    gloss glaze.................................. 195.00
  4¹/₂" h
    Gloss lilac blue glaze, Julie Matt-
      son, dtd 1927.......................... 135.00
    Light bulb shape, screw rings on
      neck, shaded irid blue-green
      glaze, stamped mark 130.00
  4³/₄" h, bulbous base, straight neck,
    carved band of wheat stacks,
    brown shades, sgd "Huck" 375.00
  5" h
    Cobalt and taupe slip on tan
      ground, artist sgd 185.00
    Rings on neck, light green glaze .. 235.00
  5¹/₄" h, red gloss excised Viking ship
    design on dark brown ground, red
    gloss glaze body, mkd(A)............ 660.00
  5¹/₂" h
    Matte green glaze, 3 dark brown
      rings on neck 175.00
    Turquoise to aqua flambe glaze ... 165.00
  5³/₄" h, carved cowboy and lasso
    and "WhyNotMinot," gloss blue
    glaze, stamped "JTT 175" mark(A) 302.00
  6" h
    Bulbous shape, dark green carved
      band of holly berries, matte

Vase, 6" h, Gingerbread Girl, brown, mkd, $575.00

      light green ground, stamped
      mark(A).................................... 880.00
    Green incised ivy shoulder band,
      buff ground, mkd 375.00
    Wheat design, green glaze........... 395.00
  6³/₄" h, imp rings on shoulder, matte
    green glaze................................. 315.00
  7" h
    Bulbous shape, band of carved
      stylized flowers, matte ivory to
      turquoise, mkd(A) 275.00
    Wood texture, light and dark
      brown matte glaze w/incised
      circle and curl design w/tex-
      tured black ground, mkd(A) 296.00
  7¹/₄" h, cylinder shape, green,
    brown, and blue abstract flowers,
    mkd.. 350.00
  8¹/₄" h, Apple Blossom design, in-
    cised and painted pink apple
    blossoms, cream to pink ground,
    mkd.. 850.00
  8¹/₂" h
    Bulbous body, flaring neck, green
      incised swimming fish, gun-
      metal ground, incised
      "Marie"(A) 1430.00
    Cylinder shape w/small flared
      rim, Apple Blossom design,
      dark pink and green incised flo-
      rals and leaves, gloss pink and
      cream ground, incised "Huck
      #5087 Apple Blossoms"
      mark(A).................................... 1045.00
  8³/₄" h, band of carved flowers on
    shoulder, gloss prairie rose glaze,
    stamped mark(A) 470.00
  9" h
    Olive and gray glaze, sgd "Pachl" 175.00
    Sgraffito iris blossoms and leaves

in brown, med green ground, circ ink and incised "L.M. Barlow 1-11-50" mark(A) **467.00**

9½" h, incised stylized tulips under apple green glaze, Elizabeth Bradley, c1933 .... **600.00**

11" h, brown glaze, sgd "Hovelson" **195.00**

Vessel

2½" h, 5½" d, tapered shape, carved ring of girls holding hands, matte light and dark brown glaze, M. Knutson, dtd 1946(A) **275.00**

2¾" h, 3¾" d, band of pink flowers and green leaves on shoulder, pink ground, Margaret Cable, dtd 1930(A) **495.00**

4" h, barrel shape, incised long-beaked birds on branch over tall grass, matte green glaze, stamped "UNIVERSITY OF NORTH DAKOTA GRAND FORKS, N.D./MADE AT SCHOOL OF MINES/N.D. CLAY" mark(A).......... **825.00**

GEOH
Biloxi art
Pottery
961

G. E, OHR,
BILOXI.

GEORGE OHR/
BILOXI ART POTTERY
Biloxi, Mississippi
1883–1906

History: George Ohr began making pottery in Biloxi, Mississippi, in 1883. His first products—pitchers, cooking pots, water coolers, and chimney pots—were sold at local and regional fairs. By the late 1880s, he discontinued molded wares and started throwing his pottery.

Known as "the mad potter of Biloxi," Ohr's technique involved twisting, denting, folding, pinching, squeezing, and generally "torturing" the white- and red-burning local clays into extremely thin-walled pieces. He made a tremen-

dous variety of pieces, including vases, teapots, jugs, bowls, and pitchers—no two of which were alike in shape or decoration. Many pieces showed Art Nouveau influences; some were made with marbleized clay or were decorated with modeled snakes and lizards; and vases often had ruffles or applied loop handles.

Ohr did outstanding work with glazes in bright, luster, and matte finishes. He used tortoise shell, mottled, metallic, monochromatic, and transparent lead glazes and also made some unglazed pieces. He won a medal at the St. Louis Exposition in 1904.

Although Ohr's son Leo helped with the clays, his was essentially a one-man operation. The pottery closed in 1906. His pieces were usually signed and "Biloxi" was most often incised or impressed.

References: Robert W. Blasberg, *The Unknown Ohr,* Peaceable Press, 1986; Garth Clark, Robert A. Ellison, Jr., Dr. Eugene Hecht, *The Mad Potter of Biloxi: The Art and Life of George E. Ohr,* Abbeyville Press, 1989; *The Biloxi Art Pottery of George E. Ohr,* Mississippi State Historical Museum, 1978.

Museums: Mississippi Museum of Art/Gulf Coast, Biloxi, MS; National Museum of History and Technology, Smithsonian Institution, Washington, DC; State Historical Society, Madison, WI.

Bowl

3½" d, crimped body, streaked brown and gold gloss glaze, stamped "G.E. OHR, BILOXI" mark(A) **770.00**

9" d, folded and crimped sides, green, purple, and gunmetal drip glaze, restored rim and base, unmkd(A) **2200.00**

Bud Vase, 4" h, bulbous base, yellow speckled glaze, mkd....................... **210.00**

Figure, 3¼" h, ivory and brown speckled panther head on dark brown plaque, mkd.................................. **650.00**

Inkwell, 2⅞" h, 3½" l, figural log cabin, circ opening in roof, green glaze, imp "G.E. OHR, BILOXI" mark(A) **1035.00**

Mug

4½" h, 2 applied asymmetrical ear handles, applied plaited snake, speckled brown and green glaze, script mark **4800.00**

5" h, g-clef handle, streaked gunmetal glaze on yellow-green glaze, incised "G.E. Ohr" mark(A) **715.00**

Pitcher

3" h, twisted and crimped middle, dark brown metallic glaze, imp "G.E. Ohr, Biloxi, Miss." mark **1200.00**

4" h, 2 spouts and handles, clear glaze w/green and dark blue

Puzzle Mug, 4" h, yellow, green, and brown speckled glaze, gunmetal accents, script "GE Ohr' mark(A), $467.00

Vase, 6" h, black, red, brown, and caramel volcanic glaze, imp "G.E. Ohr, Biloxi, Miss." mark(A), $3500.00

sponged pattern and brown drips, die-stamped mark 2800.00

4¹/₄" h, scalloped and folded rim, cutout handle, gunmetal gray glaze on mottled green base, mkd(A) 1760.00

7" h
 Incised geometric design on neck, fisherman in boat, mountains, butterflies, and flowers on body, folded handle w/leaf design, gloss green glaze, incised "G.E. Ohr, Biloxi, 1896" mark(A) 880.00
 Paneled, molded design of children, women, and florals, dark red w/black accents, imp "George E. Ohr, Biloxi, Miss." mark(A) 3080.00

Teapot, 5³/₄" h, green, dark blue, and clear pigeon-feathered glaze on orange clay body, reglazed cov, mkd(A) 1540.00

Vase
 3³/₄" h, flaring body, folded base, white bisque, script mark(A) 880.00
 4¹/₄" h, squat base, twisted middle, speckled green and dark blue glaze on splotchy rose and cream ground, stamped "G.E. OHR, BILOXI" mark(A)............................ 1980.00
 5" h
  7" w, twisted base, cylindrical neck, 2 shaped handles, gunmetal and brown glaze, "GE Ohr" mark(A) 1980.00
  Green crystalline glaze, "G.E. Ohr, Biloxi, Miss." mark(A) 880.00
 6¹/₂" h, ruffled and folded rim, pink glaze w/sponged band of blue-green and gunmetal, int w/ochre and brown speckles, rim chip(A) . 4950.00
 6³/₄" h, pinched middle, rose-pink gunmetal glaze w/green sponged and dripped glaze, mkd(A) 3300.00
 7¹/₄" h
  Bulbous top, narrow waist, spread circ black mottled foot, volcanic red glaze w/gray blisters, incised "G.E. Ohr" mark(A)................................... 9380.00
  Ruffled rim, dimpled base, green gunmetal and mahogany glaze w/clear drip glaze, mkd(A) 1870.00
 8¹/₂" h, squat base, cylinder neck, 2 applied ring handles, speckled dark and olive green glaze w/gunmetal glaze drip on neck, stamped "G.E. Ohr, Biloxi, Miss." mark(A) 7700.00

Vessel, 4¹/₂" h, 5¹/₄" d, folded rim, bright green glaze w/red and gunmetal drips, mkd(A) 4675.00

Water Vessel, 9" h, ring handle at top, buff bisque body, stamped "G.E. OHR/Biloxi, Miss." mark(A)............. 355.00

Vase, 4" h, 4" d, brown speckled gloss glaze, imp "G.E. Ohr, Biloxi, Miss." mark(A), $990.00

1911

Vase, 3" h, 3" d, white carved geometrics, matte blue ground(A), $1045.00

OVERBECK POTTERY
Cambridge City, Indiana
1911–1955

History: Overbeck Pottery was established by four sisters—Margaret, Hannah, Elizabeth, and Mary Francis—in the family home in Cambridge City, Indiana, in 1911. Margaret died during the first year of operation; Hannah, an invalid, supplied designs for decorations of the pottery until her death in 1931; and Elizabeth developed the glazes and clay mixtures and threw the pieces until she died in 1937. Mary Francis, who was involved with the artistic side of the works, continued to make pottery by herself until she died in 1955, at which time the pottery closed.

Two methods of decoration were used on the thrown pottery examples: glaze inlay and carving. In the beginning, the vases, bowls, candlesticks, flower frogs, tea sets, and tiles were glazed with matte finishes in colors such as hyacinth, turquoise, and creamy yellow. Brighter glaze colors were added later. Most designs were based on nature and pictured insects or flowers. Small ceramic figurines and other ceramic sculptures were introduced in 1936. Molds were used for some dinnerwares and the figurines.

The mark usually was the "OBK" cipher. Before 1937 it also included the initial of the sister who decorated and/or made the piece. Studio pieces were marked "MF."

Reference: Kathleen R. Postle, *The Chronicle of the Overbeck Pottery,* Indiana Historical Society, 1978.

Museums: Art Association of Richmond, IN; Art Gallery, Ball State University, Muncie, IN; Indianapolis Museum of Art, IN; Postle Collection, Cambridge City Library, IN; Wayne County Historical Society Museum, Richmond, IN.

Figure
  2" h, bluebird standing on flower
    bed, incised "OBK" mark **250.00**
  4" l, dachshund, black, blue, and
    pink, mkd(A) **220.00**
  4¼" h, southern man in pink coat
    and light blue pants, holding hat,
    mkd(A) **225.00**
Pin, 2" d, blond woman, purple, pink,
  and white skirt w/green spots, scalloped edge, imp "Overbeck"
  mark(A) **275.00**

Tumbler, 4" h, band of green stylized grasshoppers, light yellow ground, set of 4(A) **1540.00**
Vase
  5" h
    Bulbous shape, matte blue styl-
    ized fir trees, brown under-
    glaze, incised "OBK, E, H" mark. **1200.00**
    Rolled rim w/raised shoulder, 3
    excised panels of matte green
    stylized birds w/branches,
    matte French blue ground, imp
    "OBK/EH" mark(A)..................... **3080.00**
    Three panels of incised geometric
    designs, matte blue and brown
    glaze, "E.H. and O.B.K."
    mark(A) **1540.00**
  6" h, matte white excised stylized
    birds on powder blue ground,
    "OBK, E.H." mark(A) **2860.00**
  8" h, white carved stylized birds,
    matte raspberry red ground,
    stamped "OBK/E" mark(A) **6325.00**
  8¾" h, cylinder shape w/small

Vase, 11" h, incised butterscotch glazed
stylized little girls, bows, cats, and
circles, teal blue ground, imp
mark(A), $5500.00

neck, band of incised stylized clouds and rain, matte speckled brown glaze, incised "OBK/E F." mark(A) **4600.00**

Owens Utopian

J.B. OWENS POTTERY
Zanesville, Ohio
1891–c1928

History: John B. Owens incorporated J.B. Owens Pottery Company in 1891 and moved to Zanesville, Ohio, the following year. At first he made flowerpots, and then jardinieres and teapots with a Rockingham-type glaze.

In 1897 he introduced his slip-painted underglaze-decorated artwares. Utopian, the first of his famous lines, was decorated with flowers, animals, and human figures in both high gloss and matte finishes. During the decade in which he made art pottery, Owens employed many talented artists several of whom went on to open their own potteries at later dates.

A rivalry existed among the Zanesville potteries. Owens, Weller, and Roseville each offered a large number of lines, many of which were imitations of each other's works. Owens, which had more new lines than either of the other potteries, introduced within a short period of time Lotus, Alpine, Henri Deux, Corona, Cyrano, Venetian, Feroza Faience, Gun Metal, Mission, Wedgwood Jasper, Rustic, Opalesce, Utopian Opalesce, Art Vellum, Red Flame, Aborigine, and Sunburst. In 1905 Owens won four gold medals for artwares at the Lewis and Clark Exposition in Portland, Oregon.

In addition to the tremendous amount of art pottery, Owens had a commercial line by 1902. Over the years, he made continuous additions to his plant to accommodate all the work being done. In 1902 the plant was destroyed by a huge fire, but it was rebuilt quickly. In 1905 Owens expanded the plant to accommodate his interest in tile production, calling this portion of his business the Zanesville Tile Company. The less expensive, mass-produced lines were discontinued and Owens concentrated on the high quality artwares called Owensart. When F. Ferrel joined with Owens, additional lines were introduced, such as Soudanese, Aqua Verdi, and three new versions of Lotus.

The Tile Manufacturers Association took over the Zanesville Tile Company and closed it in 1920, and Owens ceased producing art pottery

soon after that. Several years later he began tile work again at a new Zanesville location.

Several different ciphers were used as marks on Owens' pottery, and some pieces were artist signed.

Museums: National Museum of History and Technology, Smithsonian Institution, Washington, DC; Zane Grey Museum of Ohio Historical Society, Zanesville, OH; Zanesville Art Center, OH.

Bowl, 5½" d, Lotus, 5-color berry design **225.00**
Bud Vase
   3¾" h, Utopian, small orange flowers, brown-green stems and leaves, dark brown ground **220.00**
   10" h, Standard glaze, cherries w/leaves, artist sgd...................... **275.00**
Ewer
   6" h, Utopian, pansies, #1056, sgd "Steele" **155.00**
   12¼" h, matte floral design **175.00**
Loving Cup, 6¾" h, 3 handles, Utopian, matte brown w/strawberries, artist sgd **495.00**
Mug, 4½" h, Utopian, cherries, brown ground, artist sgd........................... **150.00**
Umbrella Stand, 20" h, Utopian, orange irises, brown glaze, sgd "Pillsbury"... **525.00**
Vase
   4" h
     Aborigine **95.00**
     Triangle shape w/pinched sides, shaded green leaves, med to dark brown shaded ground, mold #116, pr......................... **200.00**
     Utopian, paneled, pansies, matte finish, sgd "MC" **190.00**
   4½" h, Utopian, triangle shape, yellow roses, dark brown ground(A). **75.00**
   4¾" h, Utopian, twisted bottle shape, orange and yellow wildflowers, shaded brown ground(A) **110.00**
   5" h, Utopian, bulbous shape, flared rim, slip-decorated floral design, brown ground(A) **125.00**
   5¼" h, Feroza, gold luster irid metallic oxides **395.00**
   6" h
     Ovoid shape w/4 buttresses to base, 4 small feet, slender neck, bright green glaze, imp torch, banner, and "OWENSART" mark(A).................................... **412.00**
     Utopian, pillow shape, 4 small curved feet, green ivy leaves, dark brown-green ground **195.00**
     Verdi, aqua glaze **175.00**
   6½" h, Utopian, cylinder shape, yellow and green narcissus blossoms, brown ground, mkd(A)....... **220.00**

7" h, Utopian, 2 handles, slip-decorated grapes and vines **250.00**
7¼" h, ovoid shape, everted mouth,
4 flared feet, loop handles, green
glaze, imp "OWENSART MATT"
mark(A) **302.00**
8" h, emb enameled rose spray on
matte pastel brown and blue
ground, sgd "Tot Steele" **250.00**
8½" h
Henri Deux, Art Nouveau style
woman **495.00**
Utopian, baluster shape, floral
design **165.00**
9" h
Stork design on shaded gray to
pink crazed ground, Owensart. **290.00**
Utopian, bottle shape, orange
and yellow wildflowers,
shaded brown ground(A) **120.00**
10½" h
Henri Deux, 2 handles on neck,
brown and blue Art Nouveau
carved bust of woman, matte
ground, gold emb stylized
band, unmkd(A) **660.00**
Utopian, ovoid shape, wild roses. **220.00**
White lotus flowers, shaded pink
ground **195.00**
10¾" h, bottle shape, yellow roses
on dark brown ground(A) **75.00**
11¾" h, Utopian, slip-decorated
thistle design **230.00**
12" h
Standard glaze, floral design on
front, Indian profile on reverse . **400.00**
Utopian, wide middle, narrow
neck and base, slip-decorated
floral design, brown glaze(A) ... **145.00**

*Vase, 10¼" h, green berries, rust
leaves, light turquoise to shaded green
ground, cream int, imp "Owens 1243"
mark, $685.00*

12½" h, Utopian, tapered shape,
poppies mkd(A) **90.00**
13½" h, bulbous shape, gray and
brown slip-decorated Santa Barbara mission, "Mission Pottery"
on base(A) **990.00**
18½" h, tapered, 2 small handles
from shoulder to rim, incised dbl
curved lines, cobalt bands, and
spots, salt glaze, c1930, imp "J.B.
OWEN" in circle mark **450.00**

PAULINE
POTTERY

1888-1909

PAULINE POTTERY
Chicago, Illinois
1882–1888
Edgerton, Wisconsin
1888–1909

History: Pauline Pottery was established by
Pauline Jacobus in Chicago, Illinois. At first she
did china painting in her home; later she studied
art pottery with Maria Nichols of Rookwood.

By 1883 Pauline Pottery began to utilize Ohio
clays for its yellow earthenware pieces that were
finished with monochrome glazes or underglaze
decorations. Redwares also were made. By 1886
a second plant was needed due to the company's
success, and in 1888 a new pottery was built in
Edgerton, Wisconsin, close to a new source for
clay. An assortment of wares, including vases,
tea sets, candlesticks, fireplace tiles, and ewers,
were made—most of them brush-decorated with
clear glazes on cream ground. Pauline often
drew the floral and geometric patterns.

Oscar Jacobus, Pauline's husband, had
founded a separate plant for commercial wares,
but when he died in 1893 it closed. In 1894
Pauline sold her business, and the pottery became known as Edgerton Pottery. This new company failed in 1902.

Pauline started working at home again after
reassembling her kiln and established herself as a
studio potter. Students formed pieces in summer
workshops, and during the winter months,
Pauline and her daughter decorated them, often
with designs outlined with a thin black line. The
pottery experimented with a variety of glazes and

also produced a majolica-type ware. After 1902 the women used a blending of glazes, notably a peacock color that merged deep blue and dark green. Some wares had three color combinations. Pieces often were crazed and were not always waterproof. A sale to close the pottery was held in 1909, and the home and studio were destroyed by fire in 1911.

Not all pieces were marked. Early marks were either incised or impressed, while later ones were incised or imprinted in blue or green beneath the glaze. The Pauline name and trademark were used from 1902–1909. The most common mark was a crown with a "P" on one side and a reverse P on the other.

Reference: Sharon S. Darling, *Chicago Ceramics and Glass: An Illustrated History from 1871 to 1933,* Chicago Historical Society, 1979.

Museums: City Art Museum, St. Louis, MO; Neville Public Museum, Green Bay, WI; State Historical Society, Madison, WI.

Jar, Cov
  5" h, blue-gray quatrefoils on gilded ivory ground, brown sponged base, bisque lid, restored rim chip, mkd(A) 270.00
  5¼" h, barrel shape w/figural gnome on lid, tan, brown, and green, stoneware, mkd 1500.00
Pitcher, 12" h, multicolored Art Nouveau design 350.00
Teapot, 8¾" h, 4-sided w/ruffled rim, black-outlined yellow and green painted flowers, ivory ground, rim chip, mkd...................................... 500.00
Vase
  6¼" h, yellow buttercups w/blue trailing leaves, light yellow ground, applied ribbon neck, imp mark... 475.00
  6½" h, cylinder shape, closed rim, 3 long sprays of pine needles

Plate, 10" d, gold-outlined blueberries on brown vines w/green, brown, and cream leaves, cream to yellow ground, rust wash, gold rim(A), $350.00

from dark blue band, clear glazed buff clay body, hairline(A) 275.00
11¾" h, corseted shoulder, w/gold incised design, painted lady in blue gown in field, bouquet of white flowers, clear-glazed red clay body, hairline, incised "Pauline Pottery/Chicago" mark .. 3000.00
Vessel, 7" h, gourd shape, painted cascading ivory wisteria and green foliage, dark green to red clay body, glaze flakes and chips, mkd(A) 1320.00

S.E.G.

PAUL REVERE POTTERY/ SATURDAY EVENING GIRLS
Boston, Massachusetts
1906–1915
Brighton, Massachusetts
1915–1942

History: In 1906 the Saturday Evening Girls Club was started to improve conditions for underprivileged working girls by providing craft and ceramic activities. Mrs. James Storrow was the patron and Edith Brown was hired to supervise the pottery projects. The group moved to the Library Club House near the Old North Church and the new location provided the inspiration for the Paul Revere name. The undertaking was also called the "Bowl Shop" until 1915 at which time it moved to a new building in Brighton.

All sorts of tablewares and accessories were made, including plain and decorated vases, dinner services, breakfast and tea sets, bookends, inkwells, paperweights, and tiles detailing the story of Paul Revere's ride. Most popular were the children's breakfast sets which consisted of a pitcher, bowl, and plate decorated with chicks, rabbits, roosters, ducks, nursery rhymes, and so forth. Paul Revere Pottery pieces were also decorated with flowers, trees, boats, and the famous horse and rider for which the company was named.

The women hand-decorated pottery using mineral colors. Some utilized the incised technique outlining the design in black and painting with flat colors. The matte glaze palette included blue, green, gray, white, brown, and yellow, and some high glaze pieces also were made.

Paul Revere Pottery was never a successful monetary venture and always required additional financial backing from supporters. Edith Brown died in 1932, and the pottery closed in 1941.

Prior to 1915, some paper labels were used with "Bowl Shop" in addition to the impressed or imprinted mark showing Paul Revere on horseback. Some pieces had "P.R.P." or "S.E.G." painted on the base.

Museum: Society for the Preservation of New England Antiquities, Boston, MA.

PAUL REVERE

Boston Pot, 4¼" h, matte gold glaze, artist sgd, imp mark **175.00**
Box, 5" d, black-outlined green and brown landscape on cov, ochre ground, "EM 6/1" mark(A) **75.00**
Cup and Saucer, light blue band w/narrow black band, med blue ground **50.00**
Dinner Service, dinner plates, 10" d, bread and butter plates, 6¼" d, salad plates, 8" d, cups and saucers, semi-matte blue gray glaze, service for 6(A) **750.00**
Pitcher, 7⅛" h, matte yellow glaze, mkd **375.00**
Plate
  6¼" d, yellow glaze, "P.R.P." mark(A) **165.00**
  7½" d
    Center medallion of duck on white ground, "Monroe His Plate" on front, blue border(A) . **275.00**
    Light blue, black, and med blue bands **35.00**
    Mustard glaze, imp mark **65.00**
  8" d
    Border w/green trees, brown trunks, light blue ground, mkd(A) **264.00**
    Landscape in center circle, two-tone blue border(A) **200.00**
Tankard, 5" d, snow-capped mountains on rim, blue-green glaze **300.00**
Urn, 4½" h, mustard glaze.................. **165.00**
Vase
  2½" h, narrow base, wide body, narrow neck, green-yellow ground, "ER" mark **65.00**
  3½" h
    Flared top, slate blue gloss glaze on ext, rust int **175.00**
    Pot shape, gloss blue-gray glaze w/dark blue specks, #924(A) **104.00**
  3¾" h, green, blue, and red blended glaze w/silver crystals, light green ground **185.00**
  4" h, dark blue drip over gray ground...................................... **200.00**

4¼" h, continuous band of green trees and hills and blue sky, semi-gloss dark blue body(A) **660.00**
4½" h, gray and brown stylized flowers outlined in black, dark blue ground, sgd "FCN-LY," restored **285.00**
5" h, blue, green, lilac, and pink flambe w/pink crystals, blue-green ground **260.00**
6½" h
  Bulbous shape, light and dark blue flambe on matte black ground **225.00**
  Teardrop shape, dark red drip on blue-green ground, chips **275.00**
7" h, bulbous shape, mottled aqua glaze on green ground................. **155.00**
8" h, slender, tapered form, gloss blue glaze, mkd(A) **104.00**
8⅜" h, black-outlined shoulder band of flying ducks on green land w/yellow and blue sky, light blue body, paper label(A) **1320.00**
9" h, yellow tulips, mottled dark, light, and teal blue glaze, "P.R.P./11-26/JMD" mark(A)........ **2200.00**
10½" h, gloss blue to teal blue drip glaze, imp circ "Paul Revere Pottery/6-24-M" mark(A).................. **385.00**

SATURDAY EVENING GIRLS

Berry Bowl, 5" d, underplate, 6½" d, incised white band of flowers on matte blue ground, "S.E.G./40/10/10" marks(A) **425.00**
Bookend, 4¼" h, 5" w, landscape of green trees and lake, matte blue ground, "S.E.G., 4-21, EGT" mark, pr(A)... **495.00**
Bowl
  6" d, band of incised off-white flowers and green leaves on orange ground, blue speckled body(A) **1650.00**
  7½" d, 3¼" h, flared shape, incised black-outlined "Midnight Ride of Paul Revere," blue shades, in-

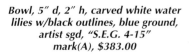

Bowl, 5" d, 2" h, carved white water lilies w/black outlines, blue ground, artist sgd, "S.E.G. 4-15" mark(A), $383.00

scribed int, "FR 144-4-09 S.E.G." mark **4500.00**

8" d, rolled rim, continuous band of incised green leaves on blue and tan ground, grayish base, "S.E.G. 9.13" mark(A) **880.00**

9" d, 3" h, int band of green trees and blue sky, ivory ground, "S.E.G. 3-4-14" mark **1100.00**

11¾" d, band of incised green and brown trees and hills w/blue sky, med green ground and int, "S.E.G, SG" mark(A) **2200.00**

Bowl, Cov, 4¼" h, 5½" d, blue-green glaze(A) **137.00**

Box, 2½" h, 4" d, cylinder shape w/domed lid, dark blue semi-gloss glaze, "S.E.G. 11-22" mark(A) **154.00**

Candlestick, 7" h, blue luster glaze, "S.E.G, J.G. 21, M" mark, pr **200.00**

Cup and Saucer, rabbit medallion, blue bands, "S.E.G. 11-21 SG" mark .. **200.00**

Cup and Saucer, A.D., stylized white blossoms w/yellow and black wavy lines, white ground, set of 8(A) **880.00**

Dessert Set, bowl, 8½" d, plate, 10" d, 5 small bowls, white stylized rim band, semi-matte blue ground **1250.00**

Dinnerware, coffeepot, trivet, cov sugar bowl, 8 bowls, 12 salad plates, 6 cups and saucers, dark blue glaze(A) **357.00**

Fruit Bowl, 4" d, blue band on yellow ground **45.00**

Luncheon Set, 5 cups, 5 dessert plates, 5 luncheon plates, green and blue band of trees and sky on rim, black outline, cream center(A) **1650.00**

Mug

3" h, rim band inscribed "John Fisk/Zueblin," matte brown and blue strolling rabbit on cream ground, blue shoulder band, hairline, inscribed "Xmas/1914/ S.E.G." mark(A) **385.00**

4" h, incised trees and landscape w/nightingale, motto "In the forest must always be a nightingale and in the soul a faith so faithful that it comes back even after it has been slain," green, blue, brown, cream, and yellow glazes, c1915, artist mark(A) **1430.00**

Pitcher, 7¾" h, black-outlined incised yellow tulips w/brown leaves, yellow ground, white ring below spout, hairline, "S.E.G./AM" mark(A) **660.00**

Plate

3½" d, center monogram, brown, yellow, and green border band of running pigs, artist's mark and "S.E.G." mark(A) **1595.00**

6¼" d, 3-color floral design **165.00**

Paperweight, 2" sq, black-outlined incised white swan, blue ground, "S.E.G. 3-15" mark(A), $220.00

Vase, 6" h, black-outlined band of yellow tulips and green leaves, med blue semi-gloss glaze(A), $770.00

Tankard, 5" h, snow-capped mountains around top, shades of blue and green **475.00**

Teapot, 5" h, black and white stripes, teal blue ground **195.00**

Tea Set, pot 7½" h, creamer, cov sugar bowl, incised band of blue iris blossoms and green leaves on light blue and tan ground w/white border, dark blue bases, "S.E.G., AM" mark, dtd July 8, 1912(A) **2640.00**

Tea Tile, 5¾" d, black-outlined green, brown, white, and orange center lake scene, light blue ground(A) **412.00**

Vase

5" h

Caramel and rust mottled glaze, mkd(A) **125.00**

Tapered base, wide, closed top, black glaze **120.00**

6" h

Silver crystals on brown speckles. **250.00**

Yellow glaze **195.00**

7¼" h, cylinder shape, black-out-lined stylized trees, gray-green glaze w/brown accents, "S.E.G." mark(A) **440.00**

8¼" h, band of olive trees, blue desert, tan ground, med brown gloss glaze body, "S.E.G., FL" mark(A) **4250.00**

9" h, stylized brown, green, and yellow flowers on matte yellow ground, hairlines, "9-26 S.E.G." mark.. **450.00**

10" h, blue luster glaze, "S.E.G, A.G., 12-16" mark **450.00**

12½" h, wide shoulder, corseted neck, matte mottled gray and blue-green drip over black base(A) **220.00**

13" h, gloss black glaze over bleeding blue ground, mkd **425.00**

Vegetable Dish, Cov, 10¼" d, band of blue, green, and orange landscape on ivory ground, mkd(A) **935.00**

ZANE WARE
MADE IN USA
c.1921

PETERS AND REED POTTERY/ ZANE POTTERY COMPANY
Zanesville, Ohio
1898–1941

History: John Peters and Adam Reed started a pottery in Zanesville, Ohio, in 1898 to make red earthenware flowerpots and garden wares. From 1903–1906 they also made cooking wares with a white lining. When the plant was enlarged in 1907, additional garden wares and some inexpensive hand-painted jardinieres in matte and high gloss glazes were produced.

The company began producing artware lines in 1912 when Frank Ferrel left Weller and joined Peters and Reed. Ferrel recreated many aspects of patterns such as Pine Cone that he had developed at Weller. The resulting line, called Moss Aztec, had molded relief designs sprayed with green. Other Peters and Reed artware lines included Pereco, Landsun, Chromal, Persian, and Montene.

With Peters' retirement, Reed became president and changed the pottery's name to Zane Pottery Company in 1921. Reed retired one year later, and Harry McClelland, who had worked at

Peters and Reed since 1903, took over. He continued the current lines and added Sheen, Powder Blue, Crystalline, and Drip. The clay body was changed from reddish brown to white in 1926.

McClelland died in 1931 and his family carried on until 1941 when they sold to Gonder Ceramic Art Pottery Company. Peters and Reed examples were usually not marked, while Zane Pottery had an impressed mark.

Reference: Jeffrey, Sherrie, and Barry Hershone, *The Peters and Reed and Zane Pottery Experience,* privately printed, 1990.

Basket, 6" d, 3" h, Moss Aztec design . **28.00**
Bowl
  5" d, 2" h, brown w/green accents .. **25.00**
  8" d, Pereco, shaded blue twigs, sgd "Ferrell"...................................... **100.00**
  8½" d, dark blue berries................. **50.00**
  9" d, 3" h, copper dust glaze........... **55.00**
  10" d, Landsun, blue shades............ **80.00**
Bud Vase, 6" h, imp leaves and berries, matte cream glaze w/brushed gold, "Zane Ware" mark **35.00**
Candlestick, 10¼" h, speckled blue semi-matte glaze, "Zane Ware" mark, pr **125.00**
Floor Vase
  14", marbleized glaze **375.00**
  22¾" h, olive-jar shape, vert ribbing, matte green glaze, unmkd(A) **110.00**
Jardiniere, 10" w, Moss Aztec, emb flowers **75.00**
Jug
  6" h, Cavalier, sprigged florals......... **89.00**
  6½" h, bulbous shape, raised purple grapes w/green leaves, streaked brown glaze................... **40.00**
Pitcher, 4" h, green and yellow raised fern leaves, gloss dark brown ground **54.00**
Spittoon, Moss Aztec, stylized rose design **45.00**
Tankard, 16" h, grapes design............. **275.00**
Umbrella Stand, 17" h, marbleized finish... **300.00**
Vase
  3" h, yellow and blue speckled finish **20.00**
  3½" h, Sheen ware.......................... **50.00**
  4" h
    Landsun, squat shape **50.00**
    Three legs, caramel glaze, floral design **65.00**
  5" h
    Brown drip glaze, "Zane Ware" mark **35.00**
    Underglaze rose decoration, "Zane Ware" mark **40.00**
    Zane Landsun flame **42.00**

Vase, 6" h, blue crystalline glaze, imp "Zane" mark, $48.00

Vase, 6" h, blue, brown, and yellow drip, beige ground, imp mark(A), $75.00

6" h
Black mirror finish	**40.00**
Chromal	**125.00**
Landsun, brown w/black	**55.00**

6¼" h, 2 handles, rose and green sprigs under rim, shaded brown ground...................................... **130.00**

6½" h, urn shape w/flared rim, matte dark blue glaze **90.00**

7½" h, Moss Aztec, leaves and berries **45.00**

7¾" h, Chromal, 3-color landscape scene **185.00**

8" h
Green and black drip glaze, "Zane Ware" mark	**55.00**
Moss Aztec, daisies design	**40.00**

8½" h, rust, black, blue, and yellow swirl **45.00**

9" h, Shadow ware, white and green drip on tan ground...................... **85.00**

9¼" h, hex shape, marbleized finish **80.00**

9½" h, chromolithograph of trees, bridge, and cloudy sky, mkd........ **395.00**

Tankard, 5½" h, Cavalier, yellow bust, gloss dark brown ground, $65.00

10" h
Blended gray shades	**35.00**
Landsun.......................................	**350.00**

10¼" h, sewer tile type, molded flowers, matte green glaze on red brick body(A).............................. **85.00**

10½" h, emb open flowers, leaves, and stems, terra-cotta **125.00**

12" h
Moss Aztec, grapes in relief, mkd	**55.00**
Yellow drip glaze	**55.00**

14" h, Chromal, scenic................... **185.00**

Wall Pocket
8" h, Aztec, relief grape design........ **65.00**

9" h
Aztec, moth design	**85.00**
Egyptian	**63.00**

PEWABIC POTTERY
Detroit, Michigan
1903–Present

History: Mary Chase Perry, a china decorator, and James Caulkins started Pewabic Pottery in 1903 in Detroit, Michigan. "Pewabic" in Chippewa means "clay with copper color." Mary developed the forms and glazes, and James worked with the clay.

Early artwares had a dark matte green glaze on bowls, jars, and vases. Sometimes these pieces had carved or applied stylized leaf or floral designs on simple thrown shapes. At the St. Louis Exposition in 1904, yellow, buff, and brown matte-glazed pieces were shown.

A new English Tudor pottery building was constructed for Pewabic in 1907, and at age 51

Mary Perry married the architect, William Stratton. Mary continued working with many glazes and added iridescent and luster glazes to the line. Her Egyptian blue glaze was perfected in 1911.

Pewabic also became famous for its decorative tiles and murals used in large churches throughout the country. The company made extensive ceramic mosaics for the Detroit Library, The Detroit Institute of Arts, and buildings in New York City, Omaha, and San Francisco. Tiles were made for churches in Detroit, Pittsburgh, Evanston, St. Paul, Philadelphia, and Washington, D.C.

Despite hardships during the 1930s, the firm continued and survived, making artwares until the death of Mary Perry Stratton in 1961 at age 94. In 1968 the Pewabic name was used by Michigan State University when it reopened the pottery as a school and studio. The building was placed on the National Register as a historic site in 1971. In 1981 the Pewabic Society bought the building from Michigan State University and operated it as a nonprofit ceramics learning center and gallery. Today the Pewabic Society is producing architectural tiles, vases, and small vessels.

Pewabic art pottery was marked, but heavy glazes sometimes covered the impressed backstamp. Paper labels also were used.

Reference: Lillian Myers Pear, *The Pewabic Pottery: A History of the Products and Its People,* Wallace-Homestead, 1976.

Museums: Detroit Institute of Art, MI; Fine Arts Gallery of San Diego, CA; Freer Gallery of Art, Smithsonian Institution, Washington, DC; Henry Ford Museum and Greenfield Village, Dearborn, MI; Pewabic Society, Detroit, MI.

Ashtray, oct, irid silver over gold glazed ground, Egyptian blue rim **325.00**
Bowl
  3" d
    Four incised hearts on bulbous base, irid pink to green glaze, imp "Pewabic" mark(A) **220.00**
    Metallic lustered turquoise green drip on irid blue and light brown ext, crazed turquoise int(A) **80.00**
  4" h, 6" d, green and gold drip irid glaze, "PEWABIC DETROIT" mark **350.00**
  4¼" d
    Flared shape, irid mauve, gold, and orange hammered glaze(A)   **220.00**
    Irid blue and mauve glaze **125.00**
  5½" d, 3 small feet, clear glaze on yellow-brown clay **275.00**
  5¾" d, carved leaves, golden glaze, chipped, mkd(A) **110.00**
  6¼" d, 4 lobes w/large raised leaves, matte green glaze, imp

    "Pewabic" and maple leaves mark(A) **1540.00**
  8" d, 3" h, black to green irid ext, imp circ mark(A) **320.00**
  8¾" d, 3¼" d, flared shape, rolled rim, metallic brown-rose luster ext, turquoise int, mkd(A) **330.00**
Box, 5" l, 2" h, incised gold fish on cov, irid gold and green glaze, turquoise ground **350.00**
Bud Vase, 6" h, blue drip glaze on neck, matte black ground(A) **605.00**
Candlestick
  7" h, brown drip over brown and green ground, incised mark(A) **165.00**
  9½" h, crazed orange luster glaze, base chips(A) **55.00**
Cup and Saucer, cup w/blue irid accents on light green ribbed body, heart-shaped handle, saucer w/gold, green, and purple metallic luster drip on light green ground, mkd(A) .   **88.00**
Jar, 5" h, bulbous middle, flared rim, mottled blue-gray and gold irid glaze, imp "PEWABIC/DETROIT" mark(A) **715.00**
Plate
  7¾" d, metallic olive green ground, mauve sections, irid turquoise border streaks **325.00**
  8" d, purple-blue irid luster spiral designs on light green ground(A) .   **80.00**
  11" d, dragonfly pattern **800.00**
  12" d, 3 round feet, raised overlapping leaves, dark burgundy metallic glaze, paper label(A) **285.00**
Pot, 3¾" h, bulbous middle w/flared rim, dark gray-green glaze w/red lustered patches, imp "PEWABIC/DETROIT" mark(A) **440.00**

Lamp, 8¾" h, olive overlay, mottled green finish, imp "Pewabic" mark(A), $100.00

Plate, 8" d, green and brown irid drip glaze, imp mark(A), $75.00

Vase, 3 1/2" h, navy blue glaze on top, unglazed clay base, imp mark(A), $170.00

Tray, 4 1/2" d, metallic lustered turquoise green drip on irid blue and light green ground, undulating rim, imp mark(A) 40.00
Vase
 2" h, 3" d, light green drips on brown glaze(A) 285.00
 2 1/2" h, gray irid w/turquoise drip glaze 275.00
 3" h, bulbous shape, irid blue and turquoise glaze(A)....................... 82.00
 3 1/2" h, matte brown drips on white luster ground w/purple irid accents, imp mark(A) 330.00
 3 3/4" h, turquoise streaks on neck, orange touches, metallic gray body, paper sticker 450.00
 4" h
  Blue metallic glaze w/pink and gold accents(A) 770.00
  Cylinder shape, metallic blue drip over dull silver glaze, imp mark(A) 495.00

Light gray luster w/irid blue flared rim, imp mark(A) 253.00
4 1/2" h
Bulbous body, rolled and flared rim, dark golden pink metallic glaze w/blue and silver drip, incised "Glazed by EJP" mark(A). 527.00
Dark brown and beige drips on light brown glaze, "PEWABIC" and maple leaves mark(A) 285.00
5" h
Cylinder shape, closed rim, thick matte brown glaze, maple leaf mark(A) 247.00
Wide base, narrow tapered neck w/small flared rim, green and purple metallic glaze w/gold and pink accents, circ mark(A). 660.00
5 1/4" h, baluster shape w/rolled rim, gold luster glaze(A) 512.00
5 1/2" h, corset top, flared neck, irid mottled beige to red glaze, raised circ mark(A)................................. 715.00
6" h
Bulbous shape, gloss turquoise glaze w/crystals and brown speckles 400.00
Gourd shape, beige drips over brown glaze, incised mark(A)... 330.00
Tumbler shape, wide top, narrow base, pink and yellow metallic glaze w/bright blue drip, imp mark(A) 1045.00
6 1/2" h
Flared rim, tapered foot, irid gold, purple, green, and blue splashed glaze, "PEWABIC DETROIT" mark 750.00
Gourd shape, cutout stylized jonquils on long stems, matte green glaze, mkd(A) 1760.00
6 3/4" h, irid blue glaze, imp mark..... 400.00
7" h, tapered base, irid cobalt glaze, imp mark(A) 440.00
8 1/2" h, bulbous body, straight neck, dark blue metallic glaze w/gold drip and pink and green accents, restored rim, paper label(A) 2530.00
9 1/2" h, ovoid shape, mottled turquoise glaze over lustered silvered gray to mauve base, imp circ "PEWABIC/DETROIT" mark(A)..... 4400.00
9 3/4" h, bulbous middle, flared rim, orange and cream luster glaze(A). 660.00
11 1/2" h, globular shape, cylinder neck, flared rim, feathered blue and gold luster glaze over blue ground, drilled base(A) 1980.00
12" h, silver-green metallic glaze w/pink and purple accents, circ mark(A) 1320.00
13 1/4" h, gloss black glaze

w/spotches of blue and irid gold,
chips on base, c1910(A) **715.00**
15½" h, gold metallic and irid
glaze, c1910, imp mark(A) **1045.00**

Pitcher, 3¼" h, painted white flower
blossom on dark brown clay body .. **12.00**
Tea Set, pot, creamer, sugar bowl,
brown ground **35.00**
Vase, 3½" h, gloss blue spatter on
black ground **25.00**

*The
Pigeon Forge
POTTERY
Pigeon Forge
Tenn.*

PIGEON FORGE POTTERY
Pigeon Forge, Tennessee
1946–Present

History: Douglas Ferguson started the Pigeon Forge Pottery with Ernest Wilson, his father-in-law, in an old tobacco barn in Tennessee. They used red or gray clay found in the area to make high fired stoneware. They built a new building in 1957.

Functional and decorative shapes were used for vases, bowls, pitchers, teapots, wall pockets, and such. Delicate and subdued glazes were utilized on the hard stoneware pieces, many of which were sculpted.

Jane Ferguson, Douglas' daughter, currently works at the pottery making one-of-a-kind hand-thrown utilitarian and architectural forms in high-fired stoneware and porcelain.

Most pieces were marked with the full name either stamped or incised on the base.

Ashtray, 8¾" d, owl design, green **15.00**
Bowl, 13" d, volcanic green glaze,
mkd **150.00**
Figure, bear 6" h, 2 cubs, 4" h, Art
Deco style, gunmetal black, set of 3 **125.00**
Jar, Cov, 3¼" h, painted white flower
blossom on dark brown clay body .. **14.00**
Oil Bottle, 4" h, painted white flower
blossom on dark brown clay body .. **12.00**

Wedding Vase, 7¾" h, matte terra-cotta finish, "The Pigeon Forge Pottery, Pigeon Forge, Tenn." mark, $18.00

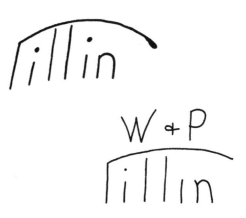

POLIA PILLIN
Los Angeles, California
1948–1992

History: Polia Pillin came to the United States from Poland in 1924. She studied painting and sculpture at the Jewish People's Institute and studied pottery for only six weeks at Hull House in Chicago. She was mostly self-taught in ceramics and was influenced by oriental pottery.

Polia and William, her husband, established a pottery studio in their garage in Los Angeles, California. William prepared the clay and glazes, and was responsible for the casting and firing. Polia was primarily a painter and she used color heavily on her ceramics, painting pieces with colored slips to which she added various oxides to derive pigments diverse in tone and intensity. She also used sponging, sgraffito, and banding techniques to achieve a variety of textures. Many of her painting styles carried over to her pottery, for example, some pieces exhibit the Byzantine quality of her paintings.

Pillin's works were signed "Pillin," "W & P Pillin," or "Polia Pillin." She died in 1992.

Museums: Dallas Art Museum, TX; Everson Museum of Art, Syracuse, NY; Long Beach Museum, CA; Otis Art Institute, Los Angeles, CA.

Bowl
3¾" h, 5" d, woman w/trees design,
multicolored **325.00**
4½" h, flared shape, white, brown,
and gray mottled gloss glaze(A) ... **82.00**
Charger, 13⅓" d, 3 standing women
in pastel colors, dark blue ground,
mkd **950.00**

Bowl, 6¹/₂" h, 9¹/₂" w, earth-tone
woman on horse on front, man on horse
on reverse, mottled yellow-brown
ground, brown rim, $695.00

Cup, 3" h, spherical, fish design, mot-
tled blue ground(A) **110.00**
Tumbler, 4³/₄" h, tapered cylinder
shape, pair of painted horses(A) **175.00**
Vase
  4" h, abstract design of girl, multicolored, "Polia Pillin" mark **125.00**
  4³/₄" h, girl w/rooster design, multicolored, hairline **95.00**
  5⁵/₈" h, flattened oval shape,
  woman holding book on front,
  woman w/bird on wrist on reverse in pastel colors, mottled
  gray ground **445.00**
  6" h, bottle shape, women's por-
  traits and birds, green striated
  ground, script mark(A) **302.00**
  6¹/₂" h, squat shape, women's por-
  traits and birds, sky blue
  ground(A) **440.00**
  7" h, cylinder shape, busts of 2
  women, multicolored **250.00**
  9¹/₄" h, white horse and 2 ladies,
  peacock green and red-brown
  ground, "Pillin" mark(A) **935.00**
  9¹/₂" h, bulbous shape w/corseted
  neck, feathered green and purple
  gloss glaze(A) **275.00**

olina, to continue the work he had started at
Nonconnah Pottery in Skylark, North Carolina.
  His best pieces were the cameo ware scenes
of American pioneer life that were done using
the pate-sur-pate technique in white on dark blue
matte, dark green, brown, and other colors. Crystalline glazes, in colors such as turquoise, ivory,
pink, and wine, were developed in the mid
1920s, and often two or three colors were used.
Vases, teapots, mugs, pitchers, candlesticks, cups
and saucers, creamers and sugar bowls, and
miniature pieces were made.
  Every piece of Pisgah Forest was handmade.
Most pieces were marked with the impressed
words "Pisgah Forest" or "Stephen." The date
was included on the mark from 1926–1961.
  Stephen died in 1961 and the pottery was
taken over by Tom Case and Grady Ledbetter
who continued to use the colored glazes. Cameo
ware and crystalline glazes were discontinued.
  Museum: Chrysler Museum, Norfolk, VA.

Beaker
  4" h, pink and gray **40.00**
  6" h, brown ext and green int glaze. **40.00**
Bowl, 4" h, 5¹/₂" d, ivory to green crystalline flambe glaze, mkd, dtd
1946(A) **330.00**
Cup and Saucer, cream ext, mauve int,
dtd 1937 .... **24.00**
Ewer, 8" h, green glaze **35.00**
Humidor, 4" h, streaked green glaze ... **75.00**
Jug, 8" h, plum ext, cream int, 1942 ... **70.00**
Mug, 4" h, cameo of fiddle player,
med blue ground, c1951(A) **198.00**
Pitcher
  3¹/₄" h, turquoise ext, cream int **20.00**
  3¹/₂" h
    Cameo of wagon train on med
    blue ground, mottled blue
    base, W. Stephen(A) **275.00**
    Turquoise glaze **45.00**
  4" h, blue and maroon crackle
  glaze, sgd "Stephen" **35.00**

PISGAH FOREST POTTERY
Arden, North Carolina
1920s–Present

  History: Walter B. Stephen founded Pisgah
Forest Pottery in the 1920s in Arden, North Car-

Pitcher, 7" h, white cameo on matte
green band, mottled blue body, sgd
"Stephen"(A), $460.00

Vase, 3³/4" h, crystalline turquoise ext, pink int, $65.00

4³/4" h, gloss aqua glaze over matte green border w/white jasper wagon train frieze, pink int, sgd "W.B. Stephen"(A) **192.00**
6¹/4" h, cameo on neck of riding Indians, brown ground, mottled gloss turquoise glaze, emb mark(A) **302.00**
Pot, 4" h, bulbous shape, blue crystalline ext, pink int, dtd 1938 .... **50.00**
Teapot, 6" h, gloss green glaze **50.00**
Vase
  3" h, forest purple crackle glaze **62.00**
  3¹/2" h, turquoise crackle ext, pink int, c1934 .... **65.00**
  4" h
    Blended gray, pink, and blue glaze, emb logo **38.00**
    Green swirl glaze, dtd 1921 .... **65.00**
    Maroon crackle ext, cream crackle int **55.00**
  5" h
    Blue and maroon high gloss glaze **55.00**
    Purple crackle glaze **64.00**
  5¹/2" h, corseted shape, clear, crazed oxblood glaze(A) **75.00**
  5³/4" h
    Bulbous shape, mottled med green glaze, dtd 1930 .... **125.00**
    Green and plum luster glaze, mkd **25.00**
  6" h
    Dbl handle, turquoise ext, pink int, sgd "Aunt Nancy" **250.00**
    Mottled green glaze, dtd 1930 ..... **100.00**
  6¹/2" h
    Forest green ext, pink int **85.00**
    White crystalline glaze **235.00**
  6³/4" h
    Gloss brown glaze, dtd 1941 .... **75.00**
    Turquoise glaze ext, pink int........ **75.00**
  7" h
    Cameo of Indian village, dark green ground, white crystalline glaze, pink int(A)...................... **1210.00**

Striated cream to brown, dtd 1941 .... **65.00**
7¹/4" h, baluster shape, white, blue, and blue-green crystals, pink int, sgd "Stephen," dtd 1941(A) **440.00**
8" h, sprigged white scene of "The Christmas Dinner," med blue ground, Chinese blue glaze on base, mkd(A) **550.00**
8¹/4" h
  Cameo of Indian hunting scene on neck, gloss green glaze on body(A)................................... **770.00**
  Turquoise and brown volcanic glaze, dtd 1928(A) **330.00**
8¹/2" h, turquoise crystalline glaze, c1936 .... **175.00**
9" h, blue crystalline glaze, mkd(A). **825.00**
9¹/2" h
  Cameo of Indian village, dark green ground, mottled turquoise base, dtd 1931(A) **1210.00**
  Gloss blue glaze **88.00**
10" h,
  Bulbous shape, aqua glaze, sgd "Stephen," dtd 1937 .... **260.00**
  Tiger's-eye flambe ext, rose-pink int(A)...................................... **82.00**
10¹/4" h, cobalt and gold crystalline glaze, dtd 1938(A) **1100.00**
13¹/4" h, white cameo of pioneer scene w/ox cart, matte dark green ground, body covered w/periwinkle blue crystalline glaze, sgd "W.B. Stephen," dtd 1939(A) **1430.00**

RED WING POTTERY/ RUM RILL POTTERY

Red Wing, Minnesota, and Little Rock, Arkansas

1930s–1942

See Red Wing Pottery in General Section for early history

History: Red Wing introduced a line of fine art pottery about 1930. Vases, figural flower holders, and figurines were made with smooth glazes and classical forms.

Belle Kogan was one of the artists who designed figures such as Bird, Oriental Man, Oriental Goddess, Cowboy, Cowgirl, Dancing Girl, Man Playing Accordion, and Tom Sawyer Lad. Some of her pieces have the letter "B" before the Red Wing mark.

Red Wing also made ashtrays, cookie jars, jardinieres, mugs, candlesticks, trays, bowls, and other items in a variety of glazes, including soft velvety matte, matte, and gloss. Different colored glazes were used on the outside and the inside of pieces. One popular line in a soft ivory matte glaze had brown color sprayed on and then lightly rubbed off.

The Rum Rill Pottery Company was originally founded in 1930 in Little Rock, Arkansas, as the Arkansas Products Company—a distributing and sales company for Camark. In the early 1930s George Rumrill contracted with Red Wing Pottery to produce Rum Rill pottery. The pieces, which were sold and distributed through the Rum Rill Pottery Company, were often called "RumRill by Red Wing."

George Rumrill discontinued his contract with Red Wing in 1938. Production of Rum Rill was moved to Florence Pottery in Mt. Gilead, Ohio, after a short association with the Bates Company in Chicago. Flower containers and vases were the main products, and some pieces were designed by Rumrill family members. By 1939 Florence Pottery made the entire Rum Rill line. Between 1939 and 1943, George Rumrill and Lawton Gonder, who was general manager at Florence, had a marketing relationship. Wares were also made at Shawnee Pottery Company in Zanesville, Ohio, after the Florence partnership.

Rum Rill's entire stock and molds were destroyed in a fire at the Florence Pottery in 1941. With no inventory, no factory, and the start of World War II restricting access to raw materials, the Rum Rill Pottery closed in 1943.

Some pieces were ink stamped "RumRill," and many pieces made at Red Wing had paper labels. Often examples were unmarked. Pieces made at factories other than Red Wing usually had "Made in USA" in the mark. Impressed marks and silver paper labels were used on artwares.

Reference: Dolores Simon, *Red Wing Pottery with Rumrill*, Collector Books, 1980.

RED WING

Ash Receiver, figural fish standing on tail, brown glaze	45.00
Ashtray, wing shape, red glaze, 75th anniversary issue	35.00
Bowl	
10" d, 7" h, tapered shape, yellow, orange, green, white, and tan horiz stripes, orange int, raised "RED WING USA 676" mark	20.00
11" d, red and pink accented raised florals and dancing people, nat-	

ural ground, imp "RED WING USA" mark **30.00**
Box, Magnolia ware, matte ivory, imp "RED WING USA 1018" mark **25.00**
Bud Vase, 7½" h, yellow speckles, gray ground, #433 .... **12.00**
Candleholder
3" h, leaf shape, matte white glaze w/brown accents, pr **24.00**
5" h, 7" l, figural dove, black **26.00**
Compote
5" h, bowl shape, ftd, lt green speckle ext, yellow int, imp "RED WING USA" mark **16.00**
7" h, paneled bowl, light brown ext, gloss yellow int, "RED WING USA M5008" mark **16.00**
Dish, 8" d, folded rim
Cherries in center, chartreuse ext, #103 .... **12.00**
Orange pear in center, gray ext, #103 .... **10.00**
Red apple in center, chartreuse ext . **10.00**
Ewer
7" h, Magnolia ware, light red flower w/green leaves, beige gloss ground, imp "RED WING USA" mark **30.00**
10½" h, serpent handle, serpents and face on base, ivory matte glaze **65.00**
Figure, 10" h, woman w/tambourine, cinnamon brown glaze **175.00**
Flowerpot
3¾" h, wide mouth, matte white w/band of geometrics, imp "RED WING U.S.A." mark **11.00**
4½" h, wide mouth, matte pink glaze, unmkd **11.00**
Pitcher
8⅛" h, vert ribbing on neck, med blue, #771 .... **38.00**
9" h, gray drip to burgundy base, imp "RED WING USA 2313" mark.... **30.00**
10½" h, ewer shape, molded scroll design on base, fluted neck, figural animal's-head handle, mint green ext w/brown spatter, yellow int, imp "RED WING USA 220" mark **60.00**
Planter
4" h, figural swan, matte green glaze, #259 .... **16.00**
5" h
Flared shape w/flutes, ftd, semi-gloss black glaze, "RED WING USA M5004" mark **14.00**
Rect form, matte green ext, gloss yellow int, raised "RED WING USA M 5009" mark **10.00**
6½" h, figural pear, lavender, imp "RED WING 913" mark **20.00**
7" l, rect w/vert ribbing in center,

gray ext, pink int, imp "RED WING
USA B1391" mark **11.00**
8" l, rect, matte white glaze, raised
"RED WING USA 1551" mark **13.00**
10" d, band of circles on rim, matte
white glaze, raised "RED WING USA
445" mark **10.00**
12" l, scalloped dish shape, char-
treuse ext, semi-gloss gray int,
imp "RED WING USA 1268" mark.... **12.00**
Bowl w/standing deer flower frog,
ivory, #526 .... **35.00**
Urn, ftd, Art Deco style, matte royal
blue finish, #753 .... **75.00**
Vase
4" h
Cornucopia shape, green semi-
matte finish **12.00**
Pear shape, white glaze, imp "RED
WING USA 983" mark **28.00**
4½" h, indented sides, gloss yellow
glaze, blue "RED WING ART POTTERY
175" mark **40.00**
5" h, figural overlapping leaves,
turquoise ext, dark brown int,
#1281 .... **10.00**
5½" h, 2 handles, green, tan, and
shaded brown glaze, #262 .... **125.00**
6" h
Cornucopia shape, matte white
ext, gloss light green int, imp
"RED WING USA 1097" mark **12.00**
Magnolia ware, matte ivory
glaze, imp "RED WING 975"
mark **30.00**
Paneled body w/stiff leaf base,
blue speckled ext, brown and
yellow int, imp "RED WING USA
M-1438" mark **25.00**
6¼" h, fan shape, vert ribbing, 2
small scroll handles on rim, aqua
glaze, "950 RED WING USA" mark... **25.00**
7" h
Brushware, 2 loop handles, open
flower head w/leaves, green..... **45.00**
Comma shape, smooth and tex-
tured orange ext, light green
int, imp "RED WING USA B 2113"
mark **20.00**
Fan shape w/conc ribbing, matte
brown speckled ground **30.00**
Olive flambe finish **45.00**
Ribbed fan shape, brown speck-
led matte ext, ochre gloss glaze
int **50.00**
Rect form w/center flutes, scroll
handles, stippled golden brown
glaze, imp "RED WING 751"
mark **22.00**
Wide base, narrow waist w/2
handles, flared top, yellow
speckle, imp "RED WING USA
505" mark.............................. **15.00**

7½" h
Applied leaves, vert ribbing, teal
blue ext, yellow int, imp "RED
WING U.S.A. 1362" mark **22.00**
Narrow base tapered to wide
shoulder, narrow rim, horiz ribbing, pale blue ground
w/brown spattering, raised "RED
WING USA 1583" mark **38.00**
7¾" h, 2 handles, white ext, green
int, #763 .... **25.00**
8" h
Ball shape, gloss green glaze,
#178 .... **85.00**
Birch bark finish **50.00**
Bulbous shape, narrow neck,
open handle, pink speckled
glaze, raised "M 1631 RED WING
U.S.A." mark **11.00**
Bulbous shape, relief of magnolia
blossom and leaves w/brown
wash, ivory ground, #1221 ...... **30.00**
Cornucopia shape, matte white
ext, light green gloss int, imp
"RED WING USA 1098" mark **18.00**
Flat sides, applied leaf on corner,
matte white ext, green int, imp
"RED WING USA 1105" mark **18.00**
Magnolia ware, matte ivory
glaze, imp "1215 RED WING
USA" mark.............................. **35.00**
Raised leaves on sides, light gray
ext w/purple accents, yellow
int, imp "RED WING U.S.A.
1103" mark............................. **28.00**
Rect, grapes and leaves in panel,
chartreuse ext, dark green int,
"RED WING USA B 2001" mark **16.00**
Shell form w/scrolled base, or-
ange speckle ext, white int, imp
"1365 RED WING USA" mark **20.00A**
Urn shape, dbl handles, bur-
gundy glaze, "RED WING ART
POTTERY" mark **75.00**

Vase, 8¼" h, mottled orange trial glaze,
#663, $95.00

8¼" h, jug shape, semi-matte white glaze, #1622 .... **25.00**

8½" h, vert ribbing, med blue, irid yellow int, #1171 .... **27.50**

9" h

Cylinder shape w/2 rect handles from neck to shoulder, blue ext, green int, blue stamped circ "155 RED WING WARE" mark **45.00**

Oval shape, raised scales, pink ground, white int, #1157 .... **15.00**

Paneled body, 2 small handles on shoulder, gloss blue ext, black int, stamped "154 RED WING WARE" mark **45.00**

9½" h, Art Deco style, semi-gloss orange glaze, #412 .... **30.00**

10" h

Bird of paradise, chartreuse ext, dark green int, imp "RED WING USA B2003" mark...................... **18.00**

Chinese shape, dark turquoise glaze w/black crackles, black int **75.00**

Vase, 9½" h, dancing maidens in forest, yellow glaze(A), $44.00

Vase, 9½" h, tan ground, brown leaves, aqua int, imp "RED WING 1162" mark, $25.00

Molded vert streaks, light green speckled ext, yellow int, imp "RED WING USA M1461" mark..... **18.00**

Textured dark green ext, char- treuse int, imp "RED WING USA B2104" mark **18.00**

10½" h, raised diagonal stripes, black, imp "RED WING USA M-1448" mark **19.00**

11" h

Bulbous shape, 2 handles from shoulder to rim, vert ribbing, light green glaze, blue stamped "RED WING ART POTTERY 226" mark **40.00**

Raised vert oak leaves, dbl spiral handles, dark brown ext, caramel int.............................. **20.00**

12" h

Egypto, dbl handles, cream and white **40.00**

Finger style, brown glaze............ **75.00**

13" h, terra-cotta geometric design, mkd.. **45.00**

Wall Pocket

7½" h, floral relief, white glaze, #1831... **70.00**

8½" h, dbl-cone shape, blue speckle ext, yellow int, imp "RED WING USA B1428" mark................ **19.00**

RUMRILL

Ball Pitcher, orange ext, white int, #547 .... **25.00**

Bowl, 6½" l, oval, raised overlapping lily pads on sides, dark blue glaze, #F-40 .... **27.00**

Bud Vase, 6½" h, circ base, sq ta- pered body, flower-shaped rim, seafoam green, #329 .... **24.00**

Cornucopia, 8" h, aqua glaze **45.00**

Flower Holder, 6½" h, figural ele- phant, mottled blue glaze, "Red wing Rumrill" mark........................ **50.00**

Planter

6" h

Hat shape, quilted body, aqua glaze, imp "RUMRILL H-36" mark **22.00**

Sq pleated body, turquoise ext,

Planter, 7" d, three small handles, cream and brown, "Rumrill, Made by Red Wing" mark, $45.00

white int, imp "RUMRILL 500"
mark 25.00
10½" H-H, figural swan handles,
turquoise glaze, imp "RUMRILL
441" mark 35.00
Urn
5¼" h, narrow base, flared body,
rolled rim, 2 handles, white ext,
green int 50.00
7¼" h, 2 handles, matte mottled
blue glaze.................................... 43.00
Urn, Cov, 13" h, 2 flat handles, raised
beaded waist, emb geometric
medallions on front and reverse,
turquoise ext glaze, cream int,
#948 .... 45.00
Vase
5¼" h, oct base, tapered neck,
seafoam green base, cream neck,
imp "RUMRILL 297" mark 35.00
6" h
Ball shape w/3 cylinder openings,
blue marble finish, #601 .... 85.00
Raised beaded neck, stiff leaves
from base, mint green glaze,
imp "RUMRILL 305" mark.......... 22.00
8" h, urn shape w/2 handles, tan
glaze, brown pedestal base.......... 40.00
9" h, 2 handles, swirl design, matte
pink glaze, paper label 37.00
15" h, Art Deco shape w/vert beading on sides, fluted neck w/circ
designs on shoulder, orange
glaze(A) 247.00

ROOKWOOD 1882

ROOKWOOD POTTERY COMPANY
Cincinnati, Ohio
1880–1967

History: Maria Longworth Nichols founded
her pottery in an old school house and named it
"Rookwood" after her father's estate. She designed the first art pottery wares. From
1880–1884, the company used a variety of
glazes and clay bodies with decorations that
were carved, printed, or painted underglaze. A
lot of gold was used over the glaze and numerous shapes were made, with new ones added to
the line each year.

Albert Valentien was employed in 1881 as
the first full-time decorator at Rookwood and he
worked with Laura Fry and many others. W.W.
Taylor became manager in 1883 and introduced
the *Rookwood Shape Record Book.* Mrs.
Nichol's husband died in 1885 and she married
Bellamy Storer the next year. When she retired in
1890, Taylor became president and took over her
interests in the pottery.

Standard Ware, which was introduced in
1883, was made by applying an underglaze slip
painting to a white or yellow body, and then
adding a glossy, yellow-tinted glaze which had
been combined with atomized grounds. The
glaze was perfected and patented by Laura Fry in
1889. Pieces often were decorated with fish,
fruit, portraits, or native flowers. Background colors included dark browns, reds, orange, and yellow under the yellow-tinted glaze. Standard
Ware characterized much of Rookwood's production through the 1890s.

The Tiger Eye glaze was developed by acci-
dent in 1884 and was the first of the crystalline
glazes. In 1889 Rookwood won a Gold Medal at
the Exposition Universelle in Paris for Tiger Eye
and dark wares. The Rookwood pottery continued to grow and expand. The Japanese artist
Kataro Shirayamadani brought a strong Japanese
influence to Rookwood pottery in 1887. He
worked for the company until 1948, except for a
ten-year period spent in Japan. A new plant was
built in 1892 and enlarged several times after
that. New shapes were also added every year.

In 1894 the Iris line was created by changing
the dark background colors to soft pastels decorated with slip painting and a gloss glaze. Sea
Green, introduced in the same year, had aquatic
decorations on a white body with a high gloss
lead glaze. Aerial Blue—a design with light
ground, blue decorations, and a gloss glaze—
was developed but never produced.

By 1900 Rookwood was experiencing competition from J.B. Owens, Roseville, Weller, and
other area potteries that were imitating Rookwood's Standard glaze on their pottery. Rookwood sent many of its artists to study in Europe to
improve their techniques. By 1904 Rookwood's
high-glazed wares were being phased out in
favor of a variety of matte finishes with stylized
decorations. Pieces were made with floral subjects decorated in reds, yellows, greens, and
blues, black-outlined designs with flat decorations, incised geometric designs, and sculpted
subjects in high relief.

Vellum ware was developed by Stanley Burt
in 1904 as a cross between a transparent glaze
and a matte finish. The glaze was developed in
the kiln at the same time as the decoration, thus

affording a greater variety of decorating themes, including scenes, plants, fish, birds, and landscape subjects. Vellum also accepted tints such as Green Vellum and Yellow Vellum.

Large architectural projects were undertaken about 1907 when Rookwood produced murals consisting of faience and wall plaques. Tiles were made for theatres, railroad stations, clubs, restaurants, homes, schools, and office buildings.

For its 30th anniversary in 1910, Rookwood introduced a matte-glazed line called Ombroso which was used on molded objects, such as bookends and paperweights. When Taylor died in 1913, Joseph Gest became president.

In 1915 Rookwood introduced a soft porcelain line with both gloss and matte glazes on flower bowls, vases, paperweights, and flower frogs. Jewel porcelain, which followed in 1920, was made until the closing days of the pottery. During the 1920s Rookwood used a wide variety of finishes. Ornamental wares were cast in molds—a less-expensive production method. Vases, paperweights, bookends, candlesticks, bowls, ashtrays, and tea sets were made in this way. Some were artist signed in the master mold, not individually signed.

John D. Wareham became president in 1934 when the company was experiencing financial difficulties. Many decorators had been laid off, the Depression had taken its toll, and equipment was outdated. Very little pottery was made in 1935, and production of architectural wares ceased in 1936. When the company filed for bankruptcy in 1941, it was purchased by a group consisting of Walter Schott, his wife Marge, and others.

When the United States entered World War II, Rookwood was forced to curtail production due to lack of supplies. Part of the plant was used for war work, and pottery was made on a limited scale. In 1941 the Schott group transferred ownership to the Institution Divi Thomae Foundation under the jurisdiction of the Roman Catholic Archdiocese of Cincinnati. The commercial operations were transferred to Sperti, Inc., with Wareham guiding the pottery production. Expansion was anticipated after World War II, but sales did not improve. By 1948 most of the decorators were laid off and production of signed, decorated pieces decreased.

Edgar Heltman took over direction of Rookwood in 1954, and they made simply shaped accessory pieces and commercial wares. In 1955 production all but stopped, and Sperti sold the company to James Smith in 1956. By 1960 Herschede Hall Clock Company bought Rookwood, moved it to Starksville, Missouri, and continued to make pottery in about sixty different shapes and nine glazes. Sales were modest and production was suspended by 1967.

The Rookwood marking system was based on numbers, letters, and symbols. Hand-decorated pieces were signed by the artist. Systematic dating began in 1886, and pieces made after that time were dated. The letter "P" with the reversed "R" was used in 1886. Until 1900 a flame point was added to this monogram each year. In 1901 Roman numerals were added below the monogram. This system was used until the pottery closed. In all, there were more than 120 artists or decorators who worked at Rookwood Pottery in its 87 years of operation.

References: Cincinnati Art Galleries, *The Glover Collection of Rookwood Pottery,* L-W Books, 1993; Virginia Raymond Cummins, *Rookwood Pottery Potpourri,* published by author, 1979; Anita J. Ellis, *Rookwood Pottery: The Glorious Gamble,* Rizzoli International Publications, Inc., 1992; Herbert Peck, *The Book of Rookwood Pottery,* Crown Publishers, Inc., 1968; ———, *The Second Book of Rookwood Pottery,* published by author, 1985; Kenneth R. Trapp, *Ode to Nature: Flowers and Landscapes of the Rookwood Pottery 1880–1940,* Jordan-Volpe Gallery, 1980; ———, *Toward the Modern Style Rookwood Pottery: The Later Years 1915–1950,* Jordan-Volpe Gallery, 1983; Neil Wood, editor, *A Price Guide to Rookwood,* L-W Books, 1993.

Museums: Brooklyn Museum, NY; Chrysler Museum, Norfolk, VA; Cincinnati Art Gallery, OH; Cincinnati Art Museum, OH; Cooper-Hewitt Museum, New York, NY; J.B. Speed Art Museum, Louisville, KY; Milwaukee Public Museum, WI; Museum of Fine Arts, Boston, MA; Museum of History and Technology, Smithsonian Institution, Washington, DC; Newark Museum, NJ; New Orleans Museum of Art, LA; Philadelphia Museum of Art, PA; St. Louis Art Museum, MO; Western Reserve Historical Society, Cleveland, OH.

Basket, 6" l, 3½" w, 4½" h, pinched int, applied handle, gold flowers w/brown centers, gloss brown glaze, sgd "Harriette R. Strafer," dtd 1890 .... **375.00**
Bookend
   5" h, figural elephant, matte dark blue glaze, flame, "XXIX, 2444D" mark, pr(A) **330.00**
   6½" h, standing rook in open book, gloss taupe and dark blue glaze, pr(A) **220.00**
   8" h, Art Deco Oriental figure, gloss blue body, dark blue headpiece, black comb w/red accents, #2362, dtd 1922, pr(A) **825.00**
Bowl, 9" d, imp Greek key design, seafoam to aqua shading, tan splashes, matte glaze, #214A **350.00**
Box, 4" l, 2⅝" w, rect, molded head, animals, scrolls, flowers, and leaves, matte green glaze, dtd 1929 **135.00**

Bowl, 9" d, med green glaze, flame, "II" and "16C Z" marks, c1902(A), $100.00

Bowl, 9¹/₂" d, 3⁵/₈" h, med blue w/char-coal gray splashes, flame, "XXVII," and "2163B" marks, c1927(A), $110.00

Dish, 6³/₈" l, 4¹/₂" w, rose glaze w/green shading, flame, "VI," and "1136" marks, c1906(A), $20.00

Humidor, 9¹/₄" h, maroon glaze, gray, black, and white cov and foot rim, "#2622" mark, dtd 1923, $950.00

Charger, 12¹/₂" d, center w/mauve and ochre galleon, light blue splashed border, John Wareham, dtd 1905(A) ... **1430.00**

Cider Set, pitcher, 8¹/₂" h, 4 mugs, 5" h, carved burgundy and green leaves, Sallie Coyne, dtd 1905(A).... **930.00**

Chocolate Pot, 12" h, Limoges style design of frogs jumping in water on side, 4 spiders and web on reverse, brown ground w/white and gold accents, sgd "M.L.N.," raised anchor and "Rookwood 1882" mark(A) **1320.00**

Coffeepot, 9" h, dark blue flower blossoms, Standard glaze, Amelia Sprague, #772, dtd 1898(A) **522.00**

Decanter, 10" h, grapes and leaves design, dark green to yellow shaded ground, sgd "ED," #673, dtd 1900 ... **995.00**

Dinnerware, blue sailing-ships design
  Cream and Sugar, 2¹/₂" h, hex, dtd 1896... **175.00**
  Cup and Saucer............................. **55.00**
  Fruit Bowl, 5¹/₂" d........................... **45.00**
  Plate, 6¹/₂" d **35.00**

Ewer, 7¹/₂" h, gold and green honeysuckle blossoms, dark brown ground, Elizabeth Lincoln(A) **440.00**

Figure, 5¹/₄" h, rook seated on branch,

gloss dark red, green, and brown, #6837, c1920 .... **150.00**

Humidor, 5¹/₂" h, scattered cigars in holly, Standard glaze, Sallie Coyne, dtd 1900(A)..................................... **231.00**

Jar, Cov, 8" h, carved palm fronds, yellow bisque ground, #142(A) **330.00**

Jug, Cov, 13" h, 4 ears of corn, Standard glaze, Sallie Toohey, #512X, dtd 1896(A)..................................... **1210.00**

Loving Cup
  4³/₄" h, 3 handles, dark blue gooseberries, brown, green, and orange shaded ground, Standard glaze, flame mark(A) **467.00**
  8" h, 3 handles, red incised circle and sq design, matte brown glaze, #330B, dtd 1907(A).......... **357.00**

Mug
  5¹/₄" h, band of half circles on rim, shaded green glaze, #1071, dtd 1906... **125.00**
  6" h, stylized incised leaves, matte green glaze, #587B, Sallie Coyne, dtd 1905..................................... **450.00**

Lamp Vase, 7" h, 10" d, gray and black owls and bats, dark green and terracotta shaded ground, raised gold design w/gold splashes, sgd "Albert Valentien," #923, dtd 1882, $2350.00

Pot, 3¹/₄" h, 4" d, matte dusty rose glaze, flame, "XVII" mark, c1917(A), $80.00

Paperweight
  3¹/₄" d, emb bull on top, light brown, reverse with "Boss, Chas. G. Schmidt Cincinnati Butcher's Supply Co., Cin., Oh".................. 100.00
  4" h, figural elephant, matte olive finish, dtd 1930 .... 250.00
Pitcher
  3¹/₂" h, autumn leaves design, orange to dark brown ground, Standard glaze, Carrie Steinle, #692, dtd 1898..................................... 425.00
  7" h, Art Deco design, dark blue, #7716, dtd 1909......................... 225.00
  9" h, loop handle, carved oak leaves, gray bisque ground, Nettie Wenderoth, c1883(A) 330.00
  10¹/₂" h, dark red-brown cherries, green leaves, Standard glaze, Lenore Asbury, dtd 1902 .... 950.00
Plaque
  8" l, 6" h, evening scene at riverbank, green sky, Vellum glaze, sgd "E. Diers", dtd 1913 .... 2500.00

9³/₈" l, 7⁷/₈" h, "The Top of the Hill," snow covered landscape w/gray mountains, light blue sky, Sara Sax, dtd 1916, imp marks(A)....... 4070.00
9³/₄" l, 7³/₄" h, blue, pink, yellow, and peach sailboats in harbor, Edward Hurley, dtd 1942(A)........... 5500.00
13" sq, green trees, blue lake, purple mountains, oak frame(A)........ 2750.00
Tankard, 7" h, carved and blue painted dragonflies, green ground, Sara Toohey, #784Z, dtd 1904(A) ... 990.00
Teapot, autumn leaves in shades of brown and orange, Standard glaze, restorations to lip, #555, E.T.H. Minor.. 1100.00
Trivet, 5¹/₂" sq, Southern lady in hoop skirt w/parasol, pastel colors, dtd 1921 .... 225.00
Vase
  4" h, incised geometric Arts and Crafts design, matte green glaze, #942F, dtd 1904(A) 286.00
  4³/₄" h, crow at base, carved branches at top, blue drip matte glaze, #1795, dtd 1923 .... 325.00
  5" h
    Dbl handles, vert fluting, blue-green matte finish, #6150, dtd 1930 .... 125.00
    Poppy design, Iris glaze, Carl Schmidt(A) 12,100.00
    Sq body, w/indentations at top, matte green glaze over orange, #2003, dtd 1914(A)................. 412.00
    Yellow matte and green accented swirled leaves, Arts and Crafts, dtd 1914(A)............................. 385.00
  5¹/₄" h
    Clover on green and peach ground, Iris glaze, Sallie Coyne, dtd 1904 .... 985.00

Tile, 4" sq, blue and rose glaze, flame "XXI & 2054" mark, c1921, pr(A), $90.00

Vase, 6" h, peach, yellow, and white dogwood blossoms, cream to peach to light blue shaded ground, crackle glaze, flame, "950F, LNL" mark, c1921(A), $375.00

Yellow daffodils w/green leaves and stems, light green, blue, yellow, and red mottled ground, mkd(A) 1235.00

5½" h, imp flowers, shaded mauve matte finish, #1902, dtd 1921 ...... 200.00

5¾" h, mint green and peach water lilies, Vellum glaze, Lorinda Epply, dtd 1893 .... 585.00

5⅞" h, blue, green, and purple forest scene, Sallie Coyne, dtd 1915 1450.00

6" h

Bowling-pin shape, green leaves, red berries, gloss brown ground, sgd "Gracie Hall," dtd 1904 .... 350.00

Fluted top, holly branches, leaves, and berries, burnt orange to dark brown ground, Standard glaze, Edith Felton, #551 .... 800.00

Multicolored daisies, Vellum glaze, #402, Lenore Asbury, dtd 1928 .... 1250.00

Straight narrow neck, bulbous base, painted flowers, Standard glaze, John D. Wareham, dtd 1895 .... 495.00

6½" h

Blue lilies on gray ground, Iris glaze, Edward Hurley, dtd 1900 .... 1375.00

Matte speckled light blue glaze, #6456, dtd 1939 .... 115.00

6⅝" h, ovoid shape w/4-lobed neck and mouth, black glazed ext, yellow int, #6953, dtd 1948 .... 225.00

6¾" h, Aerial Blue, sinking sailing schooner in whitecapped sea, #732, Sallie Toohey, dtd 1894 ..... 17,500.00

7" h

Carved spider design, burgundy, green, and blue metallic glaze, #1369E, William Hentschel, dtd 1913 .... 850.00

Iris glaze, Lindeman, dtd 1903 .... 950.00

Peaches and leaves, Standard glaze, #922D, Leona Van Briggle, dtd 1903 .... 800.00

7¼" h, ferns over stylized hills, matte blue and cobalt shading, William Hentschel, dtd 1926 .... 985.00

8" h

Autumn leaf design, Standard glaze, sgd "Coyne," dtd 1902 .. 695.00

Incised geometric design, green and brown wax matte finish, #900C, dtd 1907(A) 495.00

Poppy decoration w/whiplash stems, brown to white, Iris glaze, #905, Frederick Rothenbusch, dtd 1903(A) 1430.00

Sculpted and incised daffodils, matte green and yellow glaze, Albert Pons, dtd 1907(A) 880.00

Winter landscape, Vellum glaze, #1921, Kataro Shirayamadani, dtd 1912 .... 3000.00

8¼" h, 4 cream daffodils w/white petals, green stalks, light tan to olive ground, Iris glaze, Edward Diers, #922C 3000.00

9" h

Blue and green leaf design outlined in brown on matte yellow ground, #614E, Elizabeth Barrett, dtd 1925(A) 55.00

Corset shape, gray-purple boats on green ocean, Vellum glaze,

Vase, 9" h, Butterfat glaze, blue, pink, and brown flowers and leaves, shaded blue ground, "S. Sax, #304D" mark, dtd 1930(A), $1210.00

flame imp "XII/1358D/V/SEC"
mark(A) 1650.00
Floral design, Butter Fat glaze,
Kataro Shirayamadani, dtd
1943 .... 1000.00
Lavender-brown crystalline matte
glaze, #1358D, 1925 .... 425.00
Red and purple wax matte glaze,
floral design at top w/blue and
yellow drip, Vera Tischler,
#614E, dtd 1924(A) 825.00
9¼" h
Brown, yellow, and green portrait
bust of young man w/flowing
hair and hat, shaded brown
ground, Standard glaze, mkd(A) 1760.00
Turquoise and apricot scene of
snow-covered ground and
riverbank at sunset, Vellum
glaze, Frederick Rothenbusch,
dtd 1905 .... 2685.00
10¼" h, 3 purple irises w/green
grass, light green, cream, and
mauve shaded ground, Iris glaze,
Sallie Coyne, #951C, dtd 1910 .... 4000.00
10½" h, orange chrysanthemums
w/green leaves, Standard glaze,
sgd "Rose Fechheimer," dtd 1899   895.00
11" h
Bulbous base, wide mouth,
painted roses, Standard glaze,
Sallie Toohey, dtd 1894 .... 595.00
Painted poppies, Standard glaze,
sgd "Sturgis Laurence" 950.00
Wisteria, Iris glaze, Carl
Schmidt(A) 8800.00
11½" h, waterfront scene w/4 white
birds, Vellum glaze, Lenore As-
bury, #1663C, dtd 1918(A) 2200.00
12" h, 3 ladies in relief, brown drip
matte glaze, #2221 .... 400.00
13" h
Art Nouveau style carved and
painted orange poppies, Standard glaze, Sturgis Laurence,
#905BB, dtd 1903 .... 4000.00
Floral vellum, Edward Hurley(A).. 8800.00
Four maidens with hands joined,
purple ext, aqua int, #2543,
Louise Abel, c1922 .... 395.00
14" h, carved water lilies and leaves
at base, matte green glaze, hole in
base, Sallie Toohey, #6302, dtd
1903(A) 770.00
14¾" h, trumpet shape, speckled
brown on tan ground, jack-in-the-
pulpit design on base, #2020, dtd
1922.. 475.00
16½" h, painted green holly leaves
and orange berries, light orange
ground, Standard glaze, Kataro
Shirayamadani, #560A, dtd 1890   3000.00

ROSEVILLE POTTERY COMPANY
Zanesville, Ohio
1892–1954

History: George Young, a stoneware maker, purchased the J.B. Owens Pottery in Roseville, Ohio, and renamed it Roseville Pottery Company in 1892. He served as the general manager, and the company made flowerpots, cuspidors, cooking utensils, and umbrella stands. The firm purchased the Midland Pottery plant in Roseville in 1898, moved the main office to Zanesville, bought the Peters and Reed plant, and acquired the Muskingum Stoneware plant in 1901.

George Young hired Ross Purdy to develop Roseville's first artware line to compete with the other art potteries, such as Weller, Owens, and Rookwood. The first line was called Rozane, a term which also became the general name for all the artwares or prestige lines. The original Rozane had a high-gloss glaze of dark, blended colors decorated with underglaze slip painting. Nature studies, florals, animals, portraits, and American Indians were pictured on vases, bowls, floor vases, and such.

In 1902 Roseville introduced the Azurean line—blue and white underglaze decorations on blue ground—and the renamed Rozane Royal—pastel grays, blues, greens, rose shades, and ivory with underglaze slip painting. Rozane Egypto was a 1904 design featuring a soft green matte glaze. New lines were always in competition with products being introduced at Weller. In 1904 John Herold created Rozane Mongol—a high-gloss oxblood line that used typical Chinese vase forms—and Rozane Mara—embossed designs in metallic luster shading from deep magenta to rose.

The Japanese artist Gazo Fudji introduced oriental decorations on the 1905 line of Rozane Woodland. Outlined naturalistic flowers and leaves were incised in the clay and colored with a glossy enamel, while the ground was left in a bisque state. A crystalline glaze was used for Rozane Crystalis in 1906. The most famous Roseville art line was Della Robbia, designed in 1906 by Frederick Hurten Rhead who was art director at Roseville from 1904–1908. Seventy-two different forms of vases, tankards, bowls, and urns were made with the sgraffito process in 1906. The motifs were both naturalistic and stylized and featured such subjects as fruits, flowers, geometrics, animals, warriors, and gladiators. Rozane Olympic, introduced in 1905, was decorated with black-outlined white Grecian figures on a dark red background. Artwares continued to be made until 1919, but interest had started to decline before that date.

John Herold established the commercial artware department in 1903. Stein sets, smoker sets, dresser sets, tea sets, juvenile wares, banks, pitchers, and such were made with decalcomania transfers in a large number of patterns.

In 1908 Harry Rhead replaced his brother Frederick as art director. In 1914 Harry introduced the Pauleo line that consisted of luster and marbleized effects on eighteen different shapes. His 1915 Aztec design was a slipware line; and Donatello, from the same year, featured one hundred different shapes.

Two Roseville locations closed in 1910, and one plant had a fire in 1917. The one remaining plant was expanded in 1918. When George Young retired that year, his son Russell took over and Harry Rhead was replaced by Frank Ferrel, who remained art director until the pottery closed in 1954. With Ferrel's arrival in 1918, Roseville shifted its attention to industrial artwares—more than eighty lines were introduced during his tenure, with at least two new lines each year. Sylvan, his first design, used enameled leaves, foxes, owls, and grapes on a bisque ground that resembled tree bark. Dogwood had matte-glazed floral designs. Pine Cone, made from 1935–1950, became Roseville's most popular line—seventy-five different shapes were made in brown, blue, and green. Ferrel had utilized a similar design at other potteries where he had worked.

In 1932 the firm became Roseville Pottery, Inc. After World War II sales declined due to inexpensive imports and the growing interest in plastics. Several additional utilitarian lines were introduced by Roseville, such as high-gloss Mayfair and Artwood. The 1952 oven-to-tableware dinnerware, called Raymor, was not successful. In 1954 the Roseville plant was sold to the Mosaic Tile Company.

A wide variety of marks was used during the long years of operation. Some pieces originally had paper labels, while some were not marked at all.

References: Sharon and Bob Huxford, *The Collector's Encyclopedia of Roseville Pottery*, Collector Books, 1976, 1993 value update; ———, *The Collector's Encyclopedia of Roseville Pottery*, Second Series, 1980, 1993 value update.

Collectors' Club: Roseville's of the Past Pottery Club, Jack and Nancy Bomm, P.O. Box 68117, Orlando, FL 32868-1117, $19.95, six newsletters per year.

Museums: American Ceramic Society, Columbus, OH; Chrysler Museum, Norfolk, VA; National Museum of History and Technology, Smithsonian Institution, Washington, DC; National Road, Norwich, OH; New Orleans Museum of Art, LA; Zanesville Art Center, OH.

APPLE BLOSSOM
Basket, 10″ h, pink, #310	150.00
Candlestick, 4½″ h, pink, pr	95.00
Ewer	
6″ h, green	115.00
15″ h, pink	375.00
Jardiniere and Pedestal, 24½″ h, #302-8, #305-8	695.00
Tea Set, pot, creamer, sugar bowl, rose	235.00
Vase	
9″ h, pink, #387-9	150.00
12½″ h	245.00
Wall Pocket, 8½″ h, green	135.00
Window Box, 12″ l, #369	138.00

ARTWOOD
Planter, 6½″ h, 8½″ l, #1054	30.00

AZTEC
Vase	
9″ h, brown, blue, and cream	425.00
10″ h, blue	350.00

AZUREAN
Vase, 4″ h	450.00

BANEDA
Vase	
7″ h, green, #605-7	350.00
9″ h, green	475.00
10″ h, pink	495.00
12″ h, handle, green	900.00

BITTERSWEET
Basket, 10″ h, green	130.00
Candleholder, 3″ h, gray and rose, pr .	93.00
Console Bowl, 12″ d, tan ground, #829-12	120.00
Flowerpot, 5″ h, #856-5	90.00
Vase	
6″ h, yellow	75.00
10″ h, green	135.00

BLACKBERRY
Floor Vase, 15″ h	750.00
Hanging Basket, 4½″ h	650.00
Jardiniere, 12¼″ h, 16½″ d, unmkd(A)	357.00
Vase, 4″ h	225.00
Wall Pocket, 8½″ h	1100.00

BLEEDING HEART
Basket, 10″ h, blue, #360	325.00
Bowl, 11½″ l, 4½″ h	185.00
Ewer, 6″ h, pink	165.00
Vase	
4″ h	40.00
15″ h, blue	685.00

BURMESE
Wall Pocket, 7½″ h	200.00

BUSHBERRY
Basket, 10″ h, green, #371-10	145.00
Console Bowl, 13″ d, green	75.00
Cornucopia, 6″ h, blue	85.00
Ewer, 15″ h, blue, #3-15	375.00
Floor Vase, 18″ h	450.00

Jardiniere and Pedestal, 30" h, brown . **1200.00**
Mug, 3½" h, brown **55.00**
Vase
    6" h, blue, #156-6 .... **65.00**
    14" h, blue, #39-14 .... **325.00**
Water Set, ice lip pitcher, 4 mugs, blue **550.00**

CAPRI
Bowl, 7" d, red **35.00**

CARNELIAN I
Vase
    5¼" h, dbl...................................... **100.00**
    10" h, light green **125.00**
Wall Pocket, 8" h, green **150.00**

CARNELIAN II
Urn
    5" h, rose **130.00**
    8" h... **150.00**
Vase
    5½" h, pillow shape, pink and pur-
      ple.. **120.00**
    10" h, handle, lavender and green .. **250.00**
Wall Pocket, 8" h, green **150.00**

CHERRY BLOSSOM
Jug Vase, 4" h, pink and blue.............. **200.00**
Urn, 5" h, blue and pink **375.00**
Vase
    7" h, brown................................... **215.00**
    7½" h, pink and blue **415.00**
    10" h... **400.00**

CHLORON
Jardiniere and Pedestal, 42½" h, matte
    green glaze, chip on base(A) **880.00**
Umbrella Stand, 23¼" h, raised floral
    design, matte green glaze, c1907(A) **275.00**
Vase, 8" h, thick engraved silver on
    emb grapes and leaves, matte green
    crackle glaze, "TRP CO. CHLORON"
    mark **8500.00**

CLEMANA
Urn, 8½" h, green, #754-8 .... **375.00**
Vase, 6" h, tan
    #746-6 .... **120.00**
    #756 .... **300.00**

CLEMATIS
Bowl, 4" h, #445 .... **50.00**
Ewer
    6" h, brown, #16............................ **130.00**
    15" h, blue, #18-15 .... **285.00**
Hanging Planter, 8¼" h **199.00**
Jardiniere and Pedestal, 25" h, brown . **475.00**
Vase
    7" h, handled, brown, #188 .... **79.00**
    10" h, handled, green, #110............ **135.00**
Wall Pocket, 6" h, green, #1295 .... **185.00**

COLUMBINE
Basket, 12" h, tan, shape #368............ **175.00**
Bowl, 8" d, blue................................. **50.00**
Ewer
    7" h
      Blue, #18-7 .... **145.00**
      Pink... **140.00**

Floor Vase, 16" h, brown **375.00**
Vase
    7½" h, brown, #17-7 .... **65.00**
    9" h, #21-9.................................... **160.00**

CORINTHIAN
Vase, 10½" h, flowered rim, "Rv"
    mark **125.00**
Wall Pocket, 9" h................................ **125.00**

COSMOS
Basket, 8" h **90.00**
Bud Vase, 4" h, blue, #944-4.............. **55.00**
Vase
    4" h, handle, brown, #944 .... **69.00**
    6" h, tan, #947-6........................... **75.00**
    7" h, handle, green, #949............... **165.00**

CREMONA
Candlestick, 4" h, pink, experimental,
    pr **75.00**
Console bowl, 11" d, pink **97.00**
Fan Vase, 5" h, pink........................... **50.00**
Flower Holder, 4" h, green **95.00**
Vase
    7½" h, green **65.00**
    10½" h, green **195.00**

CROCUS
Tea Set, pot, 4" h, creamer, cov sugar
    bowl, yellow crocus w/green Arts
    and Crafts designs(A)....................... **605.00**
Vase, 11" h, raised white flowers
    w/yellow centers, orange stems,
    light blue ground(A) **187.00**

DAHLROSE
Bud Vase, 8" h................................... **75.00**
Console Bowl, 10" d, green and
    brown **135.00**
Vase
    6" h **65.00**
    8" h, 2 handles............................. **125.00**
Wall Pocket
    8" h.. **150.00**
    10" h... **175.00**

DELLA ROBBIA
Teapot, 5¼" h, sgraffito stylized roses
    under caramel and brown glaze,
    chip on lid, wafer mark(A).............. **495.00**

DOGWOOD
Tub, 4" h, 7" d................................... **75.00**
Umbrella Stand, 20" h(A)................... **385.00**

DONATELLO
Ashtray **65.00**
Cuspidor, 5½" h **295.00**
Flowerpot, 3" h.................................. **45.00**
Jardiniere and Pedestal
    22½" h.. **650.00**
    27½" h.. **975.00**
Pitcher, 6½" h **225.00**
Plaque, 8" d...................................... **365.00**
Vase, 10" h, green over gray **295.00**
Wall Pocket, 11½" h **200.00**

DUTCH
Pitcher, 9" h....................................... **135.00**

Candlestick, Donatello, 6¹/₄" h, $145.00

Tea Set, pot, creamer, cov sugar bowl,
   hairline on pot(A) 330.00
EARLAM
Candlestick, 3¹/₂" h 35.00
Urn, 6" h 200.00
FALLINE
Vase
  6" h
    Slender shape, brown base 280.00
    Squat shape, green base 240.00
  12¹/₂" h, brown.............................. 735.00
FERELLA
Bowl, 9¹/₂" d, w/flower frog, reticu-
  lated rim, red, unmkd(A) 357.00
Vase, 4" h 125.00
FLORENTINE
Bowl, 7" d 85.00
Bud Vase, Dbl, 9" h, brown 40.00
Vase, 6" h, handle, brown 40.00
Wall Pocket, 8" h.............................. 125.00
FOXGLOVE
Basket, 12" h, blue............................ 225.00
Candlestick, 2¹/₂" h, blue 65.00
Floor Vase, 16" h, green ground, pink
  and cream flowers, c1942 .... 375.00
Jardiniere and Pedestal, 24¹/₂" h, med
  blue ground, pink and yellow flow-
  ers... 950.00
Tray
  8¹/₂" d, blue.................................. 115.00
  16" l, blue 125.00
Vase
  4" h, blue 60.00
  6" h, handle, pink, #46 .... 165.00
  14" h, blue 450.00
FREESIA
Basket, 7¹/₂" h, brown 70.00
Bowl, 4" h, green ground, #669-4..... 70.00
Candleholder, 2" h, blue, #1160........ 45.00
Console Set, bowl, 10" d, #466, 2
  candlesticks, 4¹/₂" h, #1161, brown. 345.00
Ewer
  6" h, blue 75.00
  10" h, brown, #20.......................... 175.00
  15" h, green, #21 .... 395.00

Jar, 4" h, handle, blue, #669 .... 79.00
Pitcher, 10" h, brown, #20-10 .... 150.00
Vase
  4" h, handle, blue, #387 .... 75.00
  7" h, fan shape, #200 .... 85.00
  8¹/₂" h, brown............................... 48.00
Wall Pocket, 8¹/₂" h, green................. 135.00
FUCHSIA
Bowl Vase, 3" h, blue, shape #645 ..... 65.00
Vase
  6" h, blue 115.00
  7¹/₂" h, blue 135.00
Wall Pocket, 8¹/₂" h, turquoise 400.00
FUTURA
Jardiniere and Pedestal, 28" h 1950.00
Pillow Vase, 5" h, 6" l........................ 395.00
Vase
  6" h, fan shape 285.00
  6¹/₂" h, twisted, pink and blue-green 225.00
  7" h
    Pink and blue-green 220.00
    Trophy-cup shape, green leaves
     on base, unmkd(A) 935.00
  7¹/₂" h
    Egg shape, peach and lavender.... 425.00
    Sq shape, blue shades................. 325.00
  9¹/₂" h.. 850.00
  12¹/₄" h, 4 flaring sides, 4 sphere
    base, orange and brown glaze,
    unmkd(A) 275.00
  14" h, 2 handles at base, #411-14 ... 1150.00
Window Box, 5" h, 15¹/₂" l 825.00
GARDENIA
Candleholder, 5" h, brown, pr 45.00
Console Bowl, 12" d, tan 80.00
Ewer
  10" h, white, #617 .... 375.00
  15" h, brown.............................. 200.00
Pitcher, 6" h, brown........................... 60.00
Vase
  8" h, gray 55.00
  10" h, handle, brown 155.00

*Vase, Futura, 6³/₄" h, lime green, gun-
metal, green/gray, $300.00*

Vase, Gardenia, 9" h, brown, $85.00

HOLLAND
Chamber Set, pitcher, cov waste pot, child's potty, dish, 2 cov soap dishes, small pitcher, toothbrush holder, drinking mug, chips(A) 192.00
Stein Set, pitcher, 6 mugs, Dutch children, multicolored 300.00

HUDSON
Candlestick, 9" h
   Butterflies design 650.00
   Moths design 650.00

HYDE PARK
Ashtray 20.00
Chip and Dip Bowl 30.00

IMPERIAL I
Basket
   8" h 145.00
   13" h 250.00
Console Bowl, 10" d, brown 100.00
Jardiniere and Pedestal, 27" h 650.00
Vase, 10" h 135.00

IMPERIAL II
Vase
   7¹/₂" h, gloss blue and yellow 345.00
   9" h, blue and yellow lava glaze, #475-9 .... 385.00
Wall Pocket, 6¹/₂" h, brown and green 295.00

IRIS
Vase
   5" h, blue, #915-5 .... 75.00
   8" h, pillow shape, brown-orange color 135.00

IXIA
Console Bowl, 9" d, green 115.00
Vase
   6" h 40.00
   9" h, green, #860 .... 95.00
   10" h, green, #810-10 .... 95.00

JONQUIL
Bowl
   4" h 60.00
   5¹/₂" h 125.00
Urn, 4" h 125.00
Vase
   4¹/₂" h 185.00
   7" h, 2 narrow handles 140.00
   8" h 150.00

LAROSE
Wall Pocket, 7¹/₂" h 150.00

LAUREL
Bowl, 7" d, green 75.00
Vase
   6" h, red 128.00
   8" h, gold and black 150.00

LOTUS
Bowl, 9" d, blue and tan 150.00
Vase, 10" h, maroon 95.00

LUFFA
Jardiniere and Pedestal, 28" h 1700.00
Vase, 6¹/₂" h, brown 75.00

MAGNOLIA
Basket, 12¹/₂" h, green ground, pink and white magnolia, green leaves .. 160.00
Console Bowl, 14" d, green 90.00
Jardiniere and Pedestal, 25" h, pink 425.00
Pitcher, ice lip 150.00
Tea Set, pot, creamer, sugar bowl, brown 250.00
Vase
   8" h, #91-8 .... 115.00
   9" h, bulbous, brown, #94-9 .... 95.00
   14" h, tan, #97-14 .... 225.00

MAYFAIR
Tankard, 10" h, green 135.00
Vase, 10" h, green, #C1004 .... 90.00

MEDALLION
Planter, 4¹/₂" h, 7¹/₄" l, ftd, green medallion, silver wreaths, cream crackle ground 75.00

MING TREE
Ash Tray, 6" d, #599 .... 75.00
Basket, 12" h, green, #509 .... 190.00
Bookend, green, pr 175.00
Floor Vase, 14¹/₂" h, blue 550.00
Hanging Basket, 6" h, green 235.00
Vase
   8" h, white 55.00
   12" h, green, #584-12 .... 175.00
Window Box, 11" l, blue 65.00

MOCK ORANGE
Vase, 6" h, yellow 55.00

MODERNE
Vase, 10" h, blue-green, #800-10 .... 125.00

MONTACELLO
Basket, 6¹/₂" h 425.00
Vase
   4" h, brown 145.00
   8¹/₂" h, blue 450.00

*Vase, Mock Orange, 7" h, matte green
base, white and green flowers, rose top,
#983-7, $90.00*

*Planter, Peony, 8¹/₄" H-H, brown,
#386-6, $55.00*

MORNING GLORY

Candleholder, 5" h, green	245.00
Urn, 11³/₄" h, dbl handles, white, silver label(A)	302.00
Vase	
6" h, green	395.00
7" h, white	290.00
10" h, green	695.00
14" h, handle	1400.00

MOSS

Vase, 6¹/₄" h, blue ground	105.00

MOSTIQUE

Jardiniere, 9¹/₄" h(A)	100.00
Vase, 8" h, #164	60.00
Wall Pocket, 10" h	140.00

NOVELTY LINE

Stein	
4¹/₂" h, "This is so sudden" decal	260.00
5" h, "Better Late than Never" decal	265.00
Stein Set	
Indian, tankard, 11¹/₂" h, 6 mugs, Indian decals(A)	165.00
Quaker Men, tankard, 12" h, 5 mugs, 5" h, jar, 4¹/₂" h	2000.00

ORIAN

Candlestick, 4¹/₂" h, yellow and blue	175.00
Vase	
7¹/₂" h, yellow ext, blue int	195.00
8¹/₂" h, tan ext, blue int	95.00
10¹/₂" h, pr, rose and turquoise	275.00

PANEL

Jar, Cov, 10" h	175.00
Pillow Vase, 6¹/₄" h, brown	140.00
Vase, 8¹/₂" h, bulbous, brown	355.00

PEONY

Basket, 10" h, gold	125.00
Candlestick, 4¹/₂" h, yellow	95.00
Console Bowl, 12" d, pink	75.00
Ewer	
6" h, blue, shape #7	75.00
10" h, gold, shape #8	155.00
Jardiniere and Pedestal, 24" h	450.00

Vase	
7" h, handle	
Pink	60.00
Yellow	80.00
14" h, green and gold, #68-14	215.00

PERSIAN

Jardiniere, 9¹/₄" h, purple flowers, cream ground(A)	275.00

PINE CONE

Ashtray, 4¹/₂" d, green	145.00
Basket, 10" h, blue	425.00
Bowl, 9¹/₂" d, green	135.00
Candleholder	
4¹/₂" h, brown, #1099	85.00
5¹/₂" h, triple, green, #1106	300.00
Ewer	
10" h, blue	355.00
15" h, brown, #851	950.00
Floor Vase, 20" h, green, #777	2300.00
Pitcher, ice lip, 8" h, green	335.00
Planter, 8" l, brown, #468	175.00
Plate, 7³/₄" d, blue	800.00
Vase	
6" h	
Blue	175.00
Green, #748-6	95.00
7" h, brown, #112-7	115.00
8" h, blue ground, paper label	250.00
10¹/₂" h, blue, #711-10	395.00
12" h, brown, #806-12	295.00
15" h, blue, #807-15	665.00
Wall Pocket, 8¹/₂" l, triple, green	395.00

POPPY

Ewer	
10" h, gray	135.00
18" h, pink	395.00
Jardiniere and Pedestal, 32" h, yellow blossoms, stress hairlines(A)	825.00
Vase, 8" h, green	140.00

PRIMROSE

Jardiniere, 6" h, brown	70.00
Vase	
7" h, pink, #762-7	105.00
7¹/₂" h, #763-7	135.00
9" h, blue, #769-9	175.00

Vase, Pine Cone, 10" h, brown,
#709-10, $395.00

RAYMOR DINNERWARE
Autumn Brown
Coffee Mug 75.00
Corn Server, individual 32.00
Cup and Saucer 16.00
Plate
    6" d 12.00
    10" d 12.00
Ramekin, cov 25.00
Soup Bowl 18.00
Blue
Bread and Butter Plate, oval redesign,
    set of 6 .... 120.00
Charcoal
Plate, 8" d 22.00
Chocolate Brown
Bread and Butter Plate 6.00
Dinner Plate 8.00
Salad Plate 16.00
Vegetable Bowl 39.00
Dark Green
Bread and Butter Plate 8.00
Coffeepot 395.00
Dinner Plate 12.00
Gray
Bread and Butter Plate 8.00
Cruet, pr 100.00
Dinner Plate, 10" d 24.00
Ramekin, Cov 25.00
Mottled Green
Butter Dish, Cov 95.00
Corn Server 48.00
Dinner Plate 28.00
Ramekin, Cov 20.00
Terra-Cotta
Bread and Butter Plate 6.00
Corn Server, individual 28.00
Cream and Sugar, w/tray 165.00
Cup and Saucer 10.00
Gravy Boat 24.00
Ramekin, Cov 22.00

White
Bread and Butter Plate 6.00
Cup and Saucer 20.00
Dinner Plate 12.00
Pickle Dish 20.00
Vegetable Bowl 24.00
ROSECRAFT
Vase, 13½" h, bulbous shape, blue 155.00
ROSECRAFT HEXAGON
Bowl, 7½" d, "Rv" mark 120.00
ROSECRAFT VINTAGE
Jardiniere and Pedestal, 30" h, dark
    brown 500.00
Wall Pocket, 9" h 250.00
ROZANE
Jardiniere
    6½" h, 10" d, slip-decorated flying
        geese and stylized trees(A) 357.00
    7" h, yellow roses 150.00
Pitcher, 7¾" h, Royal Dark, yellow
    flowers, undulating rim 100.00
Vase
    5¼" h, 3½" w, narrow flared neck,
        painted daisy, shaded brown
        gloss glaze, "Rozane, RPC 809"
        mark 225.00
    8¼" h, Woodland, orange poppies
        and green stems, bisque
        ground(A) 1540.00
    8½"
        Della Robbia, sphere shape, 5
        concentric rings of excised
        white and yellow daisies
        w/green stems, sky blue base,
        "ROZANE WARE" mark(A) 9275.00

Vase, Rozane, Della Robbia, 15½" h,
tan outside panels, white and tan pop-
pies, dark green stems and leaves, dark
brown ground(A), $28,600.00. Photo-
graph courtesy of Don Treadway and
John Toomey, Oak Park, IL

Ovoid shape, 2 handles, ruffled
lip, dog and pheasant design(A) 330.00
9" h, pillow, dogs on table design,
#882 .... 275.00
10" h, sq twist shape, Woodland, incised and yellow, green, and
white painted mistletoe, tan
bisque ground w/cream to light
cream shading, "RV" wafer
mark(A) 825.00
12" h, Royal Dark Indian portrait,
Arthur Williams(A) 660.00

RUSSCO
Urn, 8½" h, yellow and green 140.00
Vase, 8" h
Green 100.00
Tan ext, bronze int 65.00

SILHOUETTE
Ashtray, white and aqua, #799 .... 85.00
Basket, 8" h, turquoise 110.00
Bowl, 6" d, turquoise, nude, #742 ...... 325.00
Ewer, 6" h, green, #716 .... 75.00
Urn, 8" h, white and aqua 245.00
Vase
7" h, fan shape
Red 255.00
White and aqua nude, #783 .... 200.00
8" h, green leaves, #721 .... 30.00
Wall Pocket, 8" h 160.00

SNOWBERRY
Basket, 8" h, pink, #1BK 129.00
Bowl, 6" d, blue, #1BL1-6 .... 45.00
Bud Vase, 7" h, green, #1BV 68.00
Console bowl
8" d, pink 90.00
10" d, raised colored flowers, med
blue ground, #1BL2-10 .... 95.00
12" d, green 95.00
14" d, green 90.00
Ewer
6" h, green 70.00
10" h, pink 150.00
15" h, green 250.00
Flowerpot and Saucer, green 95.00
Pillow Vase, 7" h, green, #1FH-7 .... 80.00
Tea Set, pot, creamer, sugar bowl 250.00
Vase
6" h
Green 40.00
Pink, #1V-6 .... 75.00
7" h, handle blue, #1V2-7 .... 60.00
Wall Pocket, 8" h, pink, #1WP-8 .... 125.00

SUNFLOWER
Vase, 5" h 200.00
Wall Pocket, 7½" h 525.00

SYLVAN
Jardiniere and Pedestal, 31" h, maple
leaves and hunting dog, hairline 550.00

TEASEL
Bowl, 4" h, pink 40.00

Urn, 6" h, rust and cream 75.00
Vase, 6" h, brown #881 .... 68.00

THORNAPPLE
Bud Vase, 7" h, #813 .... 75.00
Vase, 8½" h, pink and green, #816 ..... 135.00

TOPEO
Console set, bowl, 13" l, 2 dbl candleholders, 5" h 575.00
Vase
6" h, blue 195.00
7¼" h, red 140.00
12" h, blue 600.00

TOURMALINE
Ginger Jar, 10" h, peach 165.00
Urn, 5½" h, turquoise 37.00
Vase
6" h 65.00
7" h 55.00
10" h, blue, #616 .... 85.00

TUSCANY
Vase, 8" h, matte gray 135.00
Wall Pocket
7" h, pink 165.00
8" h, gray 165.00

VELMOSS
Vase
5" h 115.00
7" h, blue ground, green leaves 130.00

VISTA
Basket, 6½" h 325.00
Vase
10" h 525.00
12" h, tapered 300.00

WATER LILY
Basket, 8" h, #380 .... 135.00
Bowl, 10" d, brown 77.00
Vase, 8" h, #77 .... 45.00

WHITE ROSE
Basket, 11" h, 10" w, #363-10 .... 125.00
Ewer, 15" h, pink 475.00
Vase, 4" h
Blue 30.00
Green 30.00

Vase, Zephyr Lily, 7½" h, brown,
#206-7, $65.00

WINCRAFT

Bookend, green, #259, pr	**80.00**
Console Bowl, 12" d, turquoise, #1062	**79.00**
Tea Set, pot, creamer, sugar bowl, brown	**185.00**
Vase	
6" h, brown, pine cone design, #272..	**69.00**
14" h, green apple blossom, branch handles, step base, #263-14	**155.00**
Wall Pocket, 5" h, tan, #267-5............	**120.00**

WINDSOR

Vase, 6" h, rust, #547-6	**175.00**

WINDSOR II

Vase, 7³/₄" h, 2 handles, green leaves, dark rose ground(A).........................	**275.00**

WISTERIA

Bowl, 4" h	**155.00**
Jardiniere, 5" h..................................	**235.00**
Vase	
7" h, blue, handles on neck.............	**475.00**
9" h, brown, handles at base	**750.00**
10" h, brown....................................	**365.00**

ZEPHYR LILY

Ashtray, blue	**85.00**
Basket, 7" h, green.............................	**50.00**
Bowl, 4" h, 4" d, blue, #671-4	**65.00**
Bud Vase, 7" h....................................	**95.00**
Candleholder, 2" h, green, #1162, pr..	**93.00**
Ewer, 15¹/₂" h, green ground, #24	**250.00**
Tea Set, pot, creamer, sugar bowl, green..	**285.00**
Vase	
7" h, pillow shape, blue	**120.00**
8" h, green, #202-8	**95.00**
8¹/₂" h, blue.....................................	**95.00**
18" h, green	**375.00**
Wall Pocket, 8" h, blue, #1297	**190.00**

They moved to Oaxaca, Mexico, in 1950 and operated a pottery there. They returned to the states in 1978 and are currently making pottery in Green Valley, Arizona. The Scheier name is incised on the pieces.

Museum: Everson Museum of Art, Syracuse, NY

Bottle, 8" h, incised fish-people, gloss blue-beige ground, incised "Scheier" mark(A)...........................	**440.00**
Bowl	
5¹/₄" d, 4" h, ftd, incised horiz figures and swimming fish, dark sea blue ground, gloss glaze, incised "Scheier" mark(A).......................	**467.00**
6" d, semi-spherical shape, matte beige and brown glaze(A)............	**110.00**
6³/₄" d, 3⁷/₈" h, 4 hand-modeled fish on ext, brown glaze(A)	**605.00**
7" d, 3³/₄" h, speckled blue gloss glaze(A)	**300.00**
8¹/₂" d, ftd, grayish gold w/gloss brown glaze	**250.00**
8³/₄" d, white incised fish and children, gloss green ground, incised "Sheier" mark(A)........................	**550.00**
11" d, flared shape, turquoise blue glaze(A)	**440.00**
14" h, 13¹/₂" d, ftd, primitive style band of incised woman-fish figures, matte ochre glaze, incised script mark(A)	**2750.00**
Casserole, Cov, 13" H-H, feathered brown satin glaze, mkd(A)..............	**110.00**
Charger	
12¹/₄" d, primitive figure of woman holding child, infant in stomach, matte brown glaze on satin gray base, mkd.....................................	**900.00**
14¹/₂" d, hand thrown, central geo-	

Scheier

EDWIN AND MARY SCHEIER
University of New Hampshire
1938–1950
Green Valley, Arizona
At Present Time

History: Edwin and Mary Scheier are studio potters who taught at the University of New Hampshire from 1938–1950. They made both utilitarian and expressive, wheel-thrown pottery. Their sculptural bowls, vases, jars, and platters were influenced by African and pre-Columbian motifs and contemporary painters of the 1940s.

Charger, 10" d, yellow bisque matte glaze(A), $3300.00. Photograph courtesy of David Rago Arts and Crafts, Lambertville, NJ

Floor Vase, 21" h, black glaze(A),
$6600.00. Photograph courtesy of David
Rago Arts and Crafts, Lambertville, NJ

metric panels w/faces and bodies,
mauve and brown glaze(A) **880.00**
Plate, 9½" d, stylized Adam and Eve
w/snake and apple, gloss brown,
blue, and taupe glaze, incised script
mark(A) **300.00**
Vase
 7½" h, bulbous shape, semi-matte
 gray and oxblood glaze, incised
 mark(A) **385.00**
 8" h, incised abstract line drawing
 on dark brown glaze, mkd(A) **660.00**
 8¾" h, bottle shape, brown incised
 figure of half-man/half-fish, matte
 blue ground, incised mark(A)....... **660.00**
 10¼" h, wide band of stylized fish,
 matte light gray-beige ground **1200.00**
Vessel, 5" h, egg shape, band of incised fish-people, tan to dark blue
 shaded ground, incised "Scheier"
 mark(A) **440.00**

SEWER PIPE ART
Indiana, Ohio, Pennsylvania, West
Virginia
1880s–1930s

History: The same clay that was used to make
sewer tile was also utilized to make an assortment of folk art objects. In their spare time, workers in the various factories made planters, vases,
figurines, and such for their own use. Some
pieces were molded, while others were made
freehand. These pieces were not sold for profit
and are now called "sewer tile art" or "sewer
pipe art."

In addition to being made at sewer tile factories, these pieces were made at any factory that

used low-grade fireclay, places such as roofing-
tile and chimney-top factories, many of which
were located in Ohio. Additional clay works
were located in Indiana, West Virginia, and
Pennsylvania.

The first clay works factory was started in
1883 by James and Frank Maurio. From
1900–1925 many factories of this type opened
and prospered. The Depression and the introduction of plastic caused many of them to close.

Most of the sewer pipe art was made during
the 1920s and 1930s. Tree-stump planters, used
for planters and headstones, were the most com-
monly produced item. Some were quite ornate,
and others were more simple in design. Figures,
such as dogs, lions, and frogs, and lamps, ashtrays, dog dishes, plaques, pipes, and yard ornaments also were made. Freehand pieces are more
desirable than those made from molds.

References: Jack E. Adamson, *Illustrated
Handbook of Ohio Sewer Pipe Folk Art,* privately
printed, 1973; Susan Mellish, "Factory Workers
Formed Fireclay into Folk Art," *Antique Week,*
September 14, 1992.

Bank
 9" h, seated figural pig, chips(A)...... **247.00**
 10½" l, seated figural rabbit(A)........ **412.00**
Birdhouse
 7½" h, bark finish(A) **110.00**
 8½" h, circ base and roof, wood
 base(A) **330.00**
Bookend
 4½" h, tooled surface, chips(A) **72.00**
 5⅝" h, figural owl, sq tooled base,
 pr(A) **470.00**
Brick
 8¼" l, 4" w, relief bust of Lincoln,
 unglazed(A) **182.00**
 9" l, rounded top, imp "Nawell's
 Patent Foot Warmer" on base(A).. **12.00**
Desk Organizer, 10" l, 3 raised tree
 stumps, boat-shaped base, chips(A). **30.00**

Bank, 10" h, brown, sgd "Green's Bank"
on front, c1900, $1400.00

Desk Set
  5½" h, standing pig w/tree stump,
    tan glaze, chips(A) **28.00**
  8¼" w, figural fireplace(A) **72.00**
Doorstop, 9½" h, book shape, in-
  scribed "Richard, Irene, Daniel,
  Glenda, Richie, Vera, Mickey"(A) ... **247.00**
Figure
  3" h, man in shoe, tooled(A)............ **192.00**
  3¾" l, standing Scottie dog(A) **20.00**
  4¼" l, frog, "Made from our famous
    Lehigh Shale, strongest and best
    pipe on the market" on base(A) ... **104.00**
  5" h
    Lady's high-top shoe, tooled(A) ... **138.00**
    Seated cat, blue painted eyes....... **65.00**
  5" l
    Seated lion, rect base(A) **450.00**
    Shoe, daisy and button w/cat de-
      sign(A) **25.00**
  7" h, horse's head, hand molded
    and tooled(A)............................. **236.00**
  7½" l, crawling turtle(A).................. **302.00**
  7¾" l, reclining dog, rect base,
    chips on base(A) **126.00**
  9" h, seated bulldog, incised "S"(A) . **250.00**
  10" l, seated lion, rect scalloped
    edge base(A)............................... **385.00**
  11" h, seated squirrel w/nut, green
    painted eyes(A) **302.00**
  11¼" h
    Seated spaniel, firing cracks(A) **82.00**
    Standing collie, rect base(A) **550.00**
  12¼" h, owl seated on stump, in-
    cised "Ross Clay Plant"(A) **77.00**
  13½" h, seated flat-headed dog,
    tooled detail, chip on circ base,
    Ohio(A) **550.00**
  13½" l, standing pig, olive brown
    glaze, imp "National Sewer Pipe
    Co. Akron, Oh." on side,
    chipped(A).................................. **3630.00**
  14" l, crouching lion, rect base
    w/rounded ends, dark glaze(A) **275.00**
  14¼" h, owl on tree stump, incised
    "E.J.E."(A)..................................... **1000.00**
Flowerpot, 8½" h, w/saucer, tooled
  figural tree stump(A) **104.00**
Lamp, 8½" h, figural tree trunk, tooled
  detail, pr(A) **185.00**
Paperweight, 4" h, figural seated bull-
  dog, incised "Nobody Loves Me"(A) **95.00**
Pitcher, 12" h, tannish amber glaze,
  imp "U.S. Stoneware Co. Akron,
  Oh. 1G"(A) **40.00**
Planter
  6" h, figural tree stump(A) **20.00**
  13" h, elf w/pointed hat, hairline..... **150.00**
Plaque, 11" h, 6¼" w, polychrome
  embossed crane and reeds,(A) **125.00**
Umbrella Stand, 33" h, figural tree
  stump(A) **110.00**

SHEARWATER POTTERY
Ocean Springs, Mississippi
1928–Present

History: Peter Anderson established Shearwater Pottery in 1928 and worked there with his
son Jim and his brother Walter, who was an expert with glazes. Both wheel-thrown and molded
figurines, utilitarian pieces, and decorative articles were made. After Walter died, other family
members assisted at the pottery. The wares are
sold in Shearwater's own showroom.

Bowl
  4" d, green w/black accents **45.00**
  6" d, metallic glaze **25.00**
  8" d
    4" h, closed rim, emb lily pad de-
      sign w/reticulations, light green
      and gunmetal glaze, mkd(A) **850.00**
    4½" h, relief band of morning
      glory blossoms on shoulder,
      satin black glaze, mkd(A) **1210.00**
Candleholder
  5" h, figural duck w/spread wings,
    aqua glaze.................................. **95.00**
  11" h, figural peasant woman
    w/basket on head, hand on hip,
    cream glaze **110.00**
Figure
  4" h, seated black woman in brown
    and tan striped blouse, green and
    yellow circle band on head,
    green pants, tan tray in lap **25.00**
  5¾" h, black man w/mauve and
    purple shirt, light blue pants, gray
    spotted beard, tan sack on shoul-
    der... **35.00**

*Figure, 7" h, 8" l, black lady on yellow
horse(A), $200.00*

7" h, duck, blue glaze, pr **125.00**
8" h, bust of African youth, metallic
black glaze **225.00**
Jar, 7½" d, 5¾" h, bulbous, mottled
turquoise glaze, imp mark **300.00**
Pot, 2¼" d, 5" d, hand thrown, metal-
lic green glaze **50.00**
Vase
2½" h, 5" d, hat shape, metallic
olive green glaze, mkd **150.00**
5" h, blue glaze over rose ground,
imp mark **135.00**
6" h, bulbous shape, matte green
glaze **68.00**
6½" h, incised yellow ducks, gloss
turquoise accents at top and base,
mkd(A) **1100.00**
7" h, bulbous base, short neck
w/horiz rings, gunmetal and
green glaze **110.00**
7½" h, brown and blue mottled fin-
ish **75.00**
11½" h, tapered shape, stylized an-
imals and figures, blue shades
w/gold dust and crystals **650.00**
Vessel, 6" h, 5½" d, ridged body,
matte green and gunmetal glaze,
mkd(A) **165.00**

1900

TECO/AMERICAN TERRA-COTTA AND CERAMIC COMPANY
Terra Cotta, Illinois
1886–1930

History: William Gates established the American Terra Cotta and Ceramic Company in Terra
Cotta, Illinois, in 1886 to make sewer pipe, drain
tiles, and brick and terra-cotta decorative architectural items. The name was shortened to Teco,
an abbreviated form of terra-cotta. Many
Chicago landmarks feature architectural terra-
cotta pieces made by Gates' company.

"Teco Art Pottery might very appropriately be
called the art ideal of Mr. William D. Gates, its
creator. Desiring to produce an art ware that
would harmonize with all its surroundings,
which, while adding to the beauty of the flower

or leaf placed in the vase, at the same time en-
hanced the beauty of the vase itself, he has de-
voted a lifetime to experimenting with different
combinations to produce his ideal art pottery."
(From *Hints for Gifts and Home Decoration*,
Copyright 1905 by The Gates Potteries.)

Gates started experimenting with pottery
along with Elmer Gordon and two of Gates' sons,
William Paul and Ellis Day. Gates designed
many of the shapes that were eventually used for
Teco pieces, although many other artists and ar-
chitects also worked for the company. Though a
few pieces were thrown, Teco pieces were usually sculpted in clay, cast in molds, and sprayed
with glaze. Some shapes were made in a variety
of sizes. Nearly twelve hundred designs were
made and were identified with pattern numbers.
Window boxes, large urns and vases, fireplace
mantels, fountains, vases, pitchers, bulb pots,
low bowls, ashtrays, wall pockets, mugs, steins,
and lamp bases were made. The marbled or mottled surfaces were mostly smooth with graceful
lines and soft curves.

The first Teco wares were glazed in shades of
red, then buffs and browns. Teco is best known
for its matte green glaze, "Teco green," that was
used exclusively for nearly a decade and was the
hallmark of the pottery. Often the green had a silver blush or gunmetal frosting to the finish due to
excess copper colorant that floated to the surface
of the glaze during firing. This created a layer of
black copper crystals that resulted in a "charcoal-
ing" effect, especially where the glaze was
thickly applied near the lip, shoulder, and base
of a piece.

At the 1904 St. Louis Exposition, Teco won
two gold medals for its innovative crystalline artwares. In addition to matte green, new glaze colors introduced about 1910 included shades of
brown, gray, blue, rose, purple, and yellow. Designs were influenced by the Prairie School,
aquatic plants, leaves, and flowers.

Faience tiles were first manufactured in 1912.
Teco also made ten terra-cotta panels depicting
the life of Abraham Lincoln. Architectural terra-
cotta and art pottery were made at the same time.

Production of art pottery stopped during
World War I, but was resumed shortly after the
war when the terra-cotta business also was expanded. With the approaching Depression, Teco
ceased to be made. The pottery was sold to
George A. Berry, Jr., in 1930. He changed the
company's name to The American Terra Cotta
Corporation. The mark used on Teco was an impressed long-stemmed "T." Model numbers also
were used.

References: Sharon S. Darling, *Chicago Ceramics and Glass: An Illustrated History from
1871–1933*, Chicago Historical Society, 1979;
———, *Teco: Art Pottery of the Prairie School*,
Erie Art Museum, 1989.

Museums: Chicago Historical Society, IL; National Museum of History and Technology, Smithsonian Institution, Washington, DC; New Orleans Museum of Art, LA; Western Reserve Historical Society, Cleveland, OH; Worcester Art Museum, MA.

Ashtray, 4" d, matte green applied frog on rim, matte cream glaze on body(A) 165.00

Bowl
  3" d, 2" h, matte green glaze w/charcoaling............................. 150.00
  6" d, 2" h, matte green glaze 395.00
  8" d, scalloped rim, matte green and black glaze, imp "Teco" mark(A) 467.00
  12" d, Lotus, matte green glaze, #136(A) 522.00

Bud Vase, 4½" h, ovoid shape w/closed rim, matte veined green glaze, imp "Teco/61" mark(A) 467.00

Candlestick, 9" h, 5" d, matte green glaze, #325(A)............................... 522.00

Dish, 10⅛" d, molded cross-foot, green mottled glaze, #340, imp "TECO" mark 650.00

Floor Vase, 20⅝" h, rolled rim, 4 squared strap handles, matte green glaze w/charcoaling, imp "TECO" mark(A) 7150.00

Mug, 6" h, molded woven design in center, matte green glaze w/charcoaling, #298.............................. 375.00

Strawberry Jar, 17" h, buff finish, #G35(A) 282.00

Vase
  3½" h
    Bulbous, 3 feet, black, orange, and yellow crystalline glaze, mkd(A) 385.00
    Light brown crystalline glaze over white body, unmkd.................. 200.00
  4" h, horiz ribbing at neck, matte green glaze, #359(A) 385.00
  5" h
    Horiz ribbing, matte green glaze w/charcoaling, #363 .... 365.00
    Matte brown glaze, #233, imp mark(A) 357.00
  6" h, 2 small handles, matte green glaze, W. Gates, #427, imp "TECO" mark............................... 900.00
  6½" h, 3 handles, horiz ribbing, matte green glaze w/charcoaling, #278.. 1300.00
  7" h
    Four buttress handles
      Dbl gourd shape, matte green glaze, #287(A) 2200.00
      Everted rim, matte green glaze, #405, imp "TECO" mark........ 1200.00
    Two buttress handles, urn shape,

matte green glaze, repaired handle, #435(A) 825.00
  8" h, 4 squared-off buttress handles extending to base, matte green glaze, W. Gates, #433, imp "TECO" mark................................. 2100.00
  9" h
    Four slab sides, 4 small loop handles on shoulder, matte green glaze, Fritz Albert, #184(A) 1870.00
    Mottled brown ext, green int, #283 .... 1275.00
    Two slim loop handles, matte green glaze w/charcoaling, Fritz Albert, #283(A) 1045.00
  9½" h, amphora shape w/2 round buttressed handles, mottled matte green glaze, stamped "TECO" mark(A) 825.00
  10" h
    Arts and Crafts shape, woven border w/stylized tulips, light matte green glaze w/charcoaling, W.L.B. Jenney, #154(A) 1210.00
    Wide triangular base, narrow neck, matte green glaze, #198A(A) 660.00
  11" d, triangle shape, w/liner, lion's paw feet, green glaze, stress cracks...................................... 475.00
  11" h, Arts and Crafts style molded leaves and flowers, beige-mauve ground...................................... 550.00
  11¼" h, mottled gloss moss green glaze over metallic burgundy, shape #64B, unmkd..................... 325.00
  12¼" h, dark blue metallic and orange crystalline Aventurine glaze, "TECO" mark(A) 13,200.00
  13" h
    Art Nouveau form, thick matte ivory glaze, Moreau, #420(A)... 1870.00
    Relief-molded tulips, matte green glaze w/heavy charcoaling #134 .... 1100.00

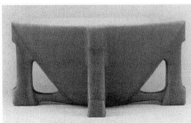

Vase, 12" w, matte green glaze w/charcoaling(A), $6600.00. Photograph courtesy of Don Treadway and John Toomey, Oak Park, IL

Vase, 12" h, matte green glaze over tan clay, #423, imp "TECO" mark(A), $2640.00

Vase, 13" h, raised florals, matte green w/charcoaling, imp mark, $795.00

Vase, 13¹/₄" h, mottled green surface, imp "TECO" mark(A), $440.00

Tall shape w/flared lip, matte green glaze, #410(A) **467.00**

18" h, short neck, cylinder body w/open swirling leaf base, matte green and grayish glaze, "TECO #310" mark(A) **22,500.00**

Wall Pocket

6¹/₂" h, 6¹/₂" w, geometric design, matte green glaze w/charcoaling, #443(A) **605.00**

14¹/₂" h, 7" w, tapered form, long and bent leaves, matte green glaze w/charcoaling, chip on reverse, "TECO" mark(A) **935.00**

TIFFANY STUDIOS
Corona, New York
1898–c1920   c.1906

History: Louis Comfort Tiffany started experimenting with pottery at his studio in Corona, New York, in 1898. Tiffany Furnaces' Favrile was first shown at the Louisiana Purchase Exposition in St. Louis in 1904, but by the next year the pottery was available for sale to the general public.

At first, Tiffany purchased ceramic lamp bases from other art potteries, but eventually made its own individually designed and handmade lamp bases, vases, and bowls. Art Nouveau influences were obvious in the designs, along with all sorts of native flora. The original Favrile pottery, a light yellow-green shading to darker tones, was called old ivory. By 1906 the company used other shades of green. Matte, crystalline, and iridescent glazes were used, and some pieces were biscuit-finished without glaze. Painted decorations were not used on Tiffany pottery.

In 1911 Bronze Pottery pieces were made with an interior gloss glaze and an exterior bronze plating. Tiffany stopped producing pottery sometime before 1920.

All Tiffany pottery was marked. Most often the "L.C.T." cipher was incised. Some examples had "L.C. Tiffany," "Favrile Pottery," or "Bronze Pottery" etched into the base. Pieces were not artist signed since all wares were attributed to the studio.

Museum: Chrysler Museum, Norfolk, VA.

Jug, 10¹/₂" h, figural ear of corn, ivory bisque ext, gloss ivory int, incised "LCT" mark(A) **1210.00**

Vase, 9" h, bronze clad w/silver
wash, incised "LCT, #BP237, LC Tiffany
Favrile Bronze Pottery"
mark(A), $1210.00

Pitcher, 10¹/₂" h, emb fruit design,
clear green glaze, restored foot,
"L.C.T." mark(A) 525.00
Vase
  6¹/₄" h, relief of 3 leaves, 3 molded
  curved handles, matte white
  glaze, incised "L.C.T." mark 2200.00
  6³/₄" h, molded branch and fruit on
  rim to body, peacock blue and
  gold dust glaze, incised "L.C.T."
  mark(A) 6600.00
  7" h, raised water lilies, clear
  celadon glaze, incised "L.C.T.,"
  ink "L.C. Tiffany-Favrile Pottery"
  mark(A) 1650.00
  8¹/₄" h, deep vert grooves, leaves at
  base, white bisque, green int, incised "L.C.T." mark(A).................. 990.00
  9" h, silvered-bronze poppy pods
  and leaves, "L.C.T.,#BP3M" and
  "L.C. Tiffany Favrile Bronze Pot-
  tery" mark(A) 4670.00
  10" h, relief of fruit on branches,
  pinched handles, white bisque,
  green int, incised "L.C.T." mark(A) 990.00
  11" h, carved peony and leaf design, green crystalline glaze, repaired chip, imp "L.C.T., #P960,"
  and "L.C. Tiffany Favrile Pottery"
  mark(A) 3080.00
  14" h
    Bronze Pottery, textured surface
    w/raised leaves and vines, dark
    brown patina, "L.C. Tiffany-
    Favrile, Bronze Pottery, E-72"
    mark(A)..................................... 4400.00
    Corset shape, raised white lilies,
    pea green luster glaze, restored

rim damage, incised "LCT"
  mark(A) 1100.00
16" h, ovoid shape, lobed sides,
  green and brown streaked glaze,
  c1900(A) 2645.00

1914

UNIVERSITY CITY POTTERY
University City, Missouri
1908–1915

History: Edward Gardner Lewis founded the
American Woman's League in 1907 to provide
more opportunities for women. Superior students
were invited to study at University City and the
Art Institute. An excellent group of potters
worked at University City, though it was only in
existence for a short time. The school was
headed by Taxile Doat who brought his extensive ceramic collection from France and used
many of the shapes at University City. Frederick
Rhead, Adelaide Robineau, and Julian Zolnay
were just a few of the fine artists who worked
with Doat on the low-fired earthenware, porcelain, and art porcelain. This notable group of ceramic artists won the grand prize at the 1911 International Exposition in Turin, Italy.

The pottery used superior-quality bodies, and
colored and colorless glazes in both matte and
gloss finishes. Many matte green pieces had various textures, such as alligator skin, crystalline,
and oriental crackle; a matte white similar to
Rookwood's Vellum finish also was used.

In 1911 both Rhead and Robineau left University City, and Doat continued to work with
other potters. The pottery was reorganized in
1912 and continued production until 1915. A variety of different marks was used but not all
pieces were marked. The earliest mark was an
impressed "U-P," and some wares had a "U-C"
backstamp.

Museums: Atascadero Library, CA; University
City Library, MO.

Jar, Cov, 2" h, ridged body, carved
cov, gloss white glaze, dtd 1914,
mkd(A) 165.00
Plaque, 9" d, pate-sur-pate design of
pale pink Virginia creepers on white
ground, "UNIVERSITY CITY, MO/1914/
PORCELAIN WORK/TD." mark(A) 3850.00

Vase, 6" d, 4" h, matte rose glaze, painted mark(A), $121.00

Vase
   3½" h, flattened oval shape, white snowflake crystals on white ground, "U-C, 1912" mark(A) **935.00**
   4¼" h, bulbous shape, brown to tan flambe glaze, incised "UC" mark(A) **302.00**
   7½" h, cylinder shape, cream glaze w/large gold crystals, "UC/1914/TD." mark(A) **4400.00**

VAN BriggLE
1904

ANNA
Van Briggle
original
♂

VAN BRIGGLE
COLO. SPGS.

VAN BRIGGLE POTTERY COMPANY
Colorado Springs, Colorado
1900–Present

History: Artus Van Briggle joined Rookwood in 1886 and was a senior designer by 1891. Rookwood sent him to Paris to study in 1893 and when he returned to Rookwood three years later, he worked to perfect the Ming dynasty matte glaze on his pottery. He finally succeeded in 1898. Due to severe tuberculosis, Van Briggle was forced to leave Rookwood and relocate to Colorado Springs, Colorado, where he established the Van Briggle Pottery Company in 1900.

Upon arrival in Colorado, he continued his glaze experiments at Colorado College. With Rookwood's help, his pottery was immediately successful, and his first exhibition was sold out. Van Briggle's low relief decorations on Colorado-clay pieces attracted a lot of interest. Although he was already quite ill, he married Anne Gregory, an artist, and she worked with him. Numerous medals and awards came from the 1903 Paris Exposition and from other expositions. When Van Briggle died in 1904, Anne became president and reorganized the company as the Van Briggle Company. Construction was started in 1908 on the Memorial Pottery to honor her husband's memory.

The Van Briggle Company produced all sorts of tiles for utilitarian purposes, plus decorated tiles for indoor and outdoor use. Garden pottery, as well as nearly three hundred designs in the art pottery line, were made. Novelty pieces included bookends, paperweights, flower frogs, letter holders, and the like.

Pieces produced from 1901–1912 exhibited some of the finest designs and glazes utilized by the company. One of the most famous designs by Artus Van Briggle, the Lorelei, portrayed a mermaid wrapped around the top rim of a vase. Glazes used by the company ranged from a semi-matte to pebbled and curdled effects to slightly glossy. Glazes were applied with an atomizer run by compressed air and sometimes a second glaze was used as an overspray to highlight certain parts of the design. Greens, blues, browns, and reds were the first colors used. Glaze colors reflected the Colorado landscape and designs were influenced by the wildflowers and fauna of the region. At first most vases were small, but by 1908 larger ones with Art Nouveau and dramatic shapes were made.

Anne remarried in 1908. The pottery was reorganized as Van Briggle Pottery and Tile Company in 1910 and by 1912, when it was leased to Edwin DeForest Curtis, Anne was no longer involved. In 1915 Curtis sold the company to Charles B. Lansing who continued to expand until a fire in 1919. He sold to I.F. and J.H. Lewis in 1920 and in 1931 they renamed the company Van Briggle Art Pottery Company. There was a major flood in 1935. In 1953 the Midland Terminal Railroad roundhouse was purchased and used as an auxiliary plant until 1968 when Memorial Pottery was sold to Colorado College and all operations moved to Midland. Kenneth Stevenson became the owner in 1969 and continued to produce art pottery with new glazes and designs. When he died in 1990, Bertha, his wife, and Craig, their son, continued the operation and produce art pottery to this day.

From 1912 until the 1920s turquoise blue or Ming turquoise, Mulberry, and Mountain Craig brown glazes were used. Persian rose, a lighter maroon than Mulberry, was used from 1946–1968. Other colors included Moonglo, Honey gold, Jet black, and Trout Lake green, to name a few. In 1970 Ming turquoise was reintroduced and is still in use, along with variations of Moonglo, Russet, Midnight and other colors.

The logo for Van Briggle pottery was a double "A" (for Artus and Anne) enclosed in a square. Pieces can be dated by the various back stamps. Up until 1920 the mark usually included the date or a particular pattern name.

References: Scott H. Nelson, Lois K. Crouch, Euphemia B. Demmin, and Robert Wyman Newton, *A Collector's Guide to Van Briggle Pottery,* Holldin Publishing Company, Inc, 1986; Richard Sasicki and Josie Fania, *Collectors' Encyclopedia of Van Briggle Art Pottery,* Collector Books, 1993.

Museums: Chrysler Museum, Norfolk, VA; Colorado State Historical Society Museum, Denver, CO; Everson Museum of Art, Syracuse, NY; National Museum of History and Technology, Smithsonian Institution, Washington, DC; New Orleans Museum of Art, LA; Newark Museum, NJ; Pioneer Museum, Colorado Springs, CO.

Bookend, 5" h, vert molded peacocks, matte maroon glaze **200.00**
Bowl
  4" d, Ming turquoise with dark blue drips, #685, c1919–20 .... **65.00**
  5¼" d, 3½" h, emb oak leaves and acorns, blue-green crystalline glaze, "AA, VAN BRIGGLE, Colo. Spgs., 670" mark(A) **385.00**
  5½" d, 3" h, oak leaves and acorns, Mountain Craig brown **60.00**
  6" d, 3" h, raised leaves and pods, matte blue ground, c1920s(A) **231.00**
  6¼" d, tapered shape, emb heart-shaped leaves, mottled matte brown glaze, "AA 1914" mark(A) **495.00**
  7" d, 3½" h, emb stylized blossoms on rim, matte robin's egg blue and purple glaze, #513, "AA, VAN BRIGGLE Colorado Springs 1906, 513" mark(A) **467.00**
  8½" d, 4¾" h, Persian rose leaf pattern... **125.00**

Bowl, 5½" d, raised acorn and oak leaf design, slate blue glaze, dtd 1920, $295.00

Chamberstick, 3¼" h, matte maroon glaze, dtd 1917(A), $110.00

  12" d, dragonfly design, blue on turquoise **200.00**
Candlestick, 4" h, bud shape, blue glaze, mkd, pr(A)............................. **90.00**
Cup and Saucer, Ming Turquoise **140.00**
Jar, 11" h, 2 side handles, vert ribbing w/flower heads, robin's-egg blue to dark blue glaze, incised "AA/191(7)" mark(A) **440.00**
Lamp
  7" h, squirrel, turquoise glaze.......... **105.00**
  19" h, figural kneeling Indian maiden, urn on shoulder, purple and lavender **275.00**
Mug, 5" h, tapered form, architectural handle, matte green glaze, #28B, dtd 1905 .... **450.00**
Pitcher
  3" h, gold ore glaze..................... **65.00**
  5¾" h, tapered shape w/buttress handle, matte blue glaze(A) **82.00**
Planter, 9" l, figural conch shell, turquoise glaze, sq "AA Van Briggle Colo. Springs" mark **55.00**
Plate
  6" d, emb swirled birds' heads and feet, matte robin's-egg blue glaze, "11, AA VAN BRIGGLE Colo. Spgs 10" mark(A) **385.00**
  8½" d, large poppy w/leaves, apple green glaze, #20, c1908–11 .... **975.00**
Pot
  3¼" h, lime green, #424, dtd 1906 . **350.00**
  4" h, dark green moth design, #688, dtd 1915..................................... **240.00**
Vase
  3¾" h, cylinder shape, molded relief band of large lily pads w/scrolling stems to flower under lip, matte mustard glaze, incised "Van Briggle/Colo./l/648" mark(A) **230.00**
  4" h, mistletoe, mottled turquoise on cream, #743, c1907–11 .... **750.00**
  4½" h, bulbous shape, band of emb

flowers, leathery burgundy glaze on matte green body, "AA, (2)86, 1905, VX" mark(A) 385.00

5" h

Raised spider on side, lime green matte glaze, #15, dtd 1902, mkd 1000.00

White matte glaze w/green accents over floral design, hairlines, dtd 1906(A) 275.00

5¼" h

Greek urn shape, Persian rose, c1930s.................................... 60.00

Molded floral heads on shoulder, incised stems to base, matte green glaze, incised "AA VAN BRIGGLE 382 1906" mark(A) 385.00

Ovoid shape, molded stylized lilies on shoulder, stems to base, matte yellow glaze on top over matte azure blue glaze, incised conjoined "AA VAN BRIGGLE COLO. SPGS, 443" mark(A).... 330.00

6¼" h, vert channels, blue glaze, dtd 1909..................................... 400.00

6¾" h, bottle shape, molded brown-eyed Susans under matte robin's-egg blue glaze, dtd 1916(A) 250.00

7" h

Blue and lavender over carved tulips, matte green glaze, #372, dtd 1906, mkd(A) 880.00

Molded poppies on whiplash stems, blue and green matte glaze, c1908–12(A) 770.00

8" h

Green shaded to brown crystals, #864, dtd 1916 .... 900.00

Mustard glaze w/crystals, #661, c1907–11 .... 995.00

9" h, bulbous base, tall neck, emb leaves, apple green glaze, #797(A) 605.00

9¼" h, corset shape, stylized spiderwort blossoms on tall stems, matte burgundy glaze, "AA, VAN BRIGGLE, 381 1906" mark 450.00

9½" h

Baluster form, molded Lorelei face inside rim, Persian rose finish, imp "AA/Van Briggle/Colo. Spgs" mark(A) 467.00

Flared shape, 6 molded long-stemmed flowers, matte aqua finish, mkd(A) 220.00

10" h

Cylinder shape w/flared shoulder, lilies design on whiplash stems, tobacco brown glaze w/yellow mottling and green accents,

"Van Briggle #289," circled "5, XX and 1905" mark(A) 3570.00

Calla lily and leaves, mustard w/blue 250.00

Dbl handles, emb small flowers and large leaves, mottled purple and green matte glaze, dtd 1903, mkd(A) 1760.00

11" h, bottle shape, emb stylized leaves, curdled matte green glaze, "AA 7, VAN BRIGGLE, Colo. Spgs" mark(A) 705.00

11½" h, 3 molded Indian heads, maroon glaze 495.00

12" h

Defined blue matte and maroon peacock feathers, suspended blue matte glaze, #386, dtd 1905(A)................................... 990.00

Ming turquoise, 2 molded flying sea gulls................................... 375.00

12½" h, emb trefoil flower heads on stems, robin's-egg blue matte glaze, "AA VAN BRIGGLE COLORADO SPRINGS 1906 (4)40" mark(A) 1650.00

13" h

Tapered body, bulbous neck, thick matte green glaze, brown clay body, rose overcast accents, #277(A)........................ 990.00

Tapered cylinder shape, burgundy ground w/blue sprayed yucca leaves, dtd 1916 .... 425.00

Two handles, yucca leaves design, dark teal blue glaze, "AA #774" mark(A) 550.00

13¼" h, bulbous base, tapered cylinder neck, 2 small handles on base, emb irises on long leaves, matte green to brown shaded

Vase, 16½" h, sculpted egrets, matte blue glaze(A), $592.00

ground, hairline, incised "AA/VAN
BRIGGLE/COLO. SPGS" mark(A) **247.00**
14" h
Despondency design, Persian
rose glaze, "VB USA" mark **950.00**
Two handles from shoulder to
rim, emb yucca leaves, dark
rose and matte blue glaze, incised "AA/Van Briggle/Colo.
Spgs" mark(A) **330.00**
14½" h, bulbous shape w/short
neck, feathered matte green
and purple glaze, #378, dtd
1905(A)................................. **1100.00**
15" h, tapered cylinder shape,
raised lily pads and vines, feathered dark purple matte glaze,
restoration to base, #106, dtd
1903(A) **2970.00**
16¼" h, tapered shape, molded
yucca plants, matte dark blue and
purple glaze, incised "Van Brig-
gle" mark(A) **467.00**

c.1913

VANCE/AVON FAIENCE
Tiltonville, Ohio
Wheeling, West Virginia
1900–1908

History: The Vance Faience Company was
incorporated in West Virginia in 1900 by Nelson
Vance, J.D. Culbertson, and Charles W.
Franzheim, founder of Wheeling Pottery Company in 1879. Vance operated a plant in
Tiltonville, Ohio, and experimented with both
utilitarian and ornamental lines.

Artwares were designed and made by
William P. Jervis who became manager in 1902.
The company name was changed to Avon
Faience Company. Jervis worked with Frederick
Hurten Rhead who was hired in 1903 to make
artwares. Pieces were decorated with underglaze
Art Nouveau motifs in a wide range of colors.
Sometimes designs were outlined in squeezed
white slip—the forerunner of the Jap Birdimal
line introduced by Rhead at Weller and also
made at Roseville. High relief molded decorations were used by Rhead and other artists who
worked at Avon.

In 1902 Wheeling Potteries Company absorbed Avon Faience, and it was operated as a

department of Wheeling. Avon continued to
make artware with a heavy body and to experi-
ment with decorative techniques, leaning more
towards utilitarian objects. Vases, jardinieres,
umbrella racks, steins, tobacco bowls, and
teapots were made. Jervis and Rhead left in
1903.

All art work was stopped at Tiltonville in
1905, and the Avon line was moved to Wheeling. The ceramic body changed from earthenware to semi-porcelain, thus ending the production of artwares. The Ohio plant was retained for
the manufacture of sanitary ware.

In 1908 the firm stopped making general
wares and made only sanitary wares until enter-
ing into receivership. The first art pottery examples had the Vance Faience marks. Some pieces
were incised "Avon" after 1902 or were marked
"W.Pts. Co."—an abbreviation for Wheeling Potteries Company.

Pitcher, 5½" h, figural grotesque face,
arms form handles, shaded gloss
burnt orange glaze, "A" and waves
mark(A) **110.00**
Vase
4" h
Globular shape, applied florals,
green shaded to cream ground,
mkd **350.00**
HP flowers, shaded brown top
and base **575.00**
Tapered base, incised stylized
trees w/brown trunks and green
leaves, burnt orange ground,
hole in base(A) **1870.00**
5½" h, bulbous shape, pinched rim,
squeeze-bag stylized brown trees,
orange to dark green ground,
unmkd **300.00**
6" h, squat base, elongated tapered

Pitcher, 7" h, white-outlined rust florals
and green leaves, shaded blue-green
to blue ground, Frederick Rhead,
mkd, $495.00

Tankard, 5³/₄" h, multicolored monk, brown handle and rims, "Avon" and waves mark, $125.00

neck, orange, green, and blue-green stylized landscape, black ground, c1903(A) **220.00**
7½" h, tapered body, button neck, squeeze-bag abstract beige and brown flowers w/black leaves, incised golden abstract design, restored chip on neck, incised "Avon/Z165/100S" mark(A) **990.00**
8" h, bottle shape, green, brown, and orange incised landscape design, unmkd(A) **330.00**
9" h, triangular shape, squeeze-bag yellow stylized roses w/green foliage, blue-green ground, center panels w/inscriptions, mkd(A) **1760.00**
11" h, tapered shape, stepped shoulder, teal blue, brown, and burnt orange incised landscape design(A) **705.00**
11½" h, narrow base, bulbous body, 4 holes at sides and center hole, raised curlicue design, olive base, brown middle, olive top **295.00**

Artwares, tiles, panels, and plaques were made in simple shapes and were covered with a variety of excellent glazes. Vases and bowls had a dark gray, green, pink, blue, or dark red-brown matte finish. The company won a bronze medal at the St. Louis Exposition in 1904.

After 1905 the firm made porcelain objects. Charles and Leon worked together until 1911, when Leon left. Charles remained at the company until his death in 1914.

The mark used most often was the incised stylized "V." An incised "Volkmar" mark also was used.

Museum: The Newark Museum, NJ.

Candleholder, 14½" h, 3-sided shape w/floral design at top, matte green glaze over white clay, incised mark, pr(A)... **467.00**
Lamp Base, 11¼" h, yellow chrysanthemums, dark brown ground, gloss glaze, drilled, stamped "v" mark **375.00**
Mug, 4" h, Arts and Crafts style, matte green glaze **85.00**
Pitcher, 7½" h, brown, yellow, and green streaked glaze...................... **270.00**
Vase
6" h
  Corset shape, thick crackled yellow glaze, mkd(A)................... **330.00**
  Incised geometric design, matte gray-green glaze..................... **485.00**
  Sphere shape, heart-shaped carved green leaves, yellow-green ground, incised mark(A) . **1870.00**
7" h
  6" w, 3 sq handles on shoulder, dark blue suspended matte glaze, hand thrown, incised "v" mark(A)................................. **408.00**
  Incised leaves, thick matte green glaze, hand thrown, mkd(A)..... **357.00**
10¼" h, tapered shape w/bulging

VOLKMAR KILNS
Metuchen, New Jersey
1903–1914

1879-1888

History: Charles Volkmar and his son Leon established Volkmar Kilns in Metuchen, New Jersey, in 1903 after Charles closed his pottery in Corona, New York. Both the high-gloss and semi-matte glazes that had been previously developed at Volkmar Pottery were used at the new facility.

Vase, 5" h, 7" d, cloverleaf top, matte blue-green glaze, incised mark(A), $176.00

shoulder, mottled green glaze, brown ground, incised "V" mark(A) **302.00**

13" h, bulbous shape, 2 handles, curdled and volcanic opaque celadon glaze, drilled base, "V" mark(A) **265.00**

W ꝺ W

WALLEY POTTERY
West Sterling, Massachusetts
1898–1919

History: Joseph William Walley made pottery in Portland, Maine, from 1873–1885. In 1898 he bought Wachusett Pottery in West Sterling, Massachusetts, and operated it until his death in 1919. He used the local red clay and was responsible for most of the handmade art pottery, although the company also made cast or hand-thrown pieces such as vases, planters, candlesticks, lamp bases, tea tiles, bowls, mugs, hair receivers, and powder jars. Walley's matte and gloss finishes were usually green, although brown was also used. Pieces were marked with an impressed "W J W."

Ashtray, 7¼" d, ftd, thick matte green and gunmetal glaze, red clay body(A) **55.00**

Bowl
6" d, green flambe glaze, red clay body, "W" mark(A) **220.00**
8" d, closed rim, applied large leaves, drip organic matte green glaze, imp mark(A) **1210.00**

Bowl, 7" h, 10" d, brown and rust carved leaves(A), $2420.00. *Photograph courtesy of David Rago Arts and Crafts, Lambertville, NJ*

Mug, 5½" h, sculpted grotesque face on side, flowing matte brown to green glaze, imp mark(A) **467.00**

Spirit Lamp, 5¾" h, 7¾" w, gloss brown glaze w/green streaks, imp "W.J.W." mark(A) **145.00**

Vase
3¼" h, squat base, rolled rim, gloss brown over blue-green drip glaze, imp "WJW" mark(A) **220.00**
3¾" h, squat base, cylinder neck w/rolled rim, matte blue glaze, imp "WJW" mark(A) **358.00**
5½" h, moss green glaze, mottled rim band, imp "W.J.W." mark(A) ... **135.00**
7" h, bulbous shape, collar rim, carved and applied leaves in brown w/green edges(A) **1430.00**

Vessel, 5½" h, tooled and applied round leaves w/curled edges, matte olive green glaze(A) **2200.00**

LONHUDA

LOUWELSA
WELLER

We𝓁𝓁er Pottery

WELLER POTTERY COMPANY
Zanesville, Ohio
1872–1948

History: Samuel Weller founded the Weller Pottery Company in 1872 in Fultonham, Ohio. He worked by himself making flowerpots, vases, cuspidors, crocks, and milk pans. Ten years later he moved his operation to Zanesville, Ohio, and over the years added several new sites. By 1890 he built a new plant and experimented with a variety of glazes in the production of jardinieres, pedestals, hanging baskets, vases, and umbrella stands.

He was very impressed with William Long's Lonhuda ware, shown at the 1893 Chicago World's Fair. The following year Weller bought Lonhuda Pottery and William Long came to Zanesville to supervise production. Weller's version of Lonhuda, called Louwelsa, was decorated with fruits, flowers, dogs, American Indians, Dutch cavaliers, portraits, and such, originally in the standard brown glaze. To compete with Rookwood's Standard Glaze, Weller hired fine artists to work on Louwelsa and it eventually became one of Weller's best-selling designs. The number of glazes was expanded to include high-glaze green and blue, red, Matte Louwelsa with pastel grounds, and Louwelsa Perfecto, a 1905 series that had delicate shades of sea green with pink and salmon matte finishes. From 1896–1920 more than five hundred different Louwelsa items were made, such as vases, jars, umbrella stands, oil and electric lamps, tobacco jars, and ashtrays. Some rare pieces had silver overlays.

Charles Upjohn, head of decorating from 1895–1904, was responsible for the Dickens Ware lines in matte, semi-gloss, and high-gloss glazes. The first Dickens Ware resembled a solid-colored Louwelsa; Dickens Ware II was sgraffito decorated, predominately in browns. Subjects included Dickens characters, as well as Indian portraits, tavern scenes, monks, and natural subjects. The third Dickens Ware, similar to Eocean, was created by Frederick Hurten Rhead. The front of each piece showed figures from Dickens' novels in relief, the back had a raised black disk with the name of the scene.

In 1899 Weller purchased the old American Encaustic Tiling Company plant and used it to make cooking utensils, flowerpots, and toilet articles. Between 1899 and 1905, plaster of paris molds replaced the potter's wheel, allowing hundreds of identical pieces to be produced using molds and the jiggering process.

Jacques Sicard, who had trained with Clement Massier in France, joined the firm in 1902 and made metallic-luster-glazed Sicardo pottery for about seven years. Vases, umbrella stands, jars, jewel boxes, candy dishes, plaques, candlesticks, figurines, and lamp bases were made in magenta, green, gold, silver, and purple and were decorated with flowers, stars, sea horses, and dolphins. Karl Kappes replaced Charles Upjohn in 1904 as head of decorating. By 1905 the company was producing about fourteen artware lines, including Aurelian and Eocean, introduced in 1898, Turada, an 1897 design with applied ornaments—lacy, pierced work on a high gloss, dark background—and Jap Birdimal, created by Frederick Rhead in 1904. Rhead used incised Japanese designs, animals, and birds inlaid with slip and covered with a high gloss glaze on blue, sea green, or brown grounds. He also introduced L'Art Nouveau which had flowing figures in high-gloss pastels or dark brown. Weller, Owens, Roseville, and Rookwood copied one another's designs and many artists worked at more than one of these Zanesville potteries.

By 1910 competition from the Japanese potters began to interfere with Weller's business, since the Japanese were able to make near-perfect copies at about half the cost. However, new lines continued to be introduced, including Fairfield, a 1916 series designed to compete with

Roseville's Donatello, and Weller Hudson made in a variety of ways from 1917–1934.

Samuel Weller purchased Zanesville Art Pottery in 1920, incorporated as S.A. Weller, and had three plants operating by 1922. His was always a family business, and when he died in 1925 Harry Weller, his nephew, became president. John Lessell, who was head of Weller decorating from 1920–1924 and creator of luster lines and designs such as LaSa and Lamar, left when Sam died and art pottery was replaced by industrial artwares. Modeler Rudolph Lorber came to Weller after World War I and was responsible for many less-expensive molded lines. With a big reduction in profits during the Depression, the three Weller plants were consolidated into one in 1931, and freehand decoration was terminated. Some new lines continued to be made, but only in molded wares.

Throughout its history, Weller made a wide assortment of brown and white cooking ware, such as mug sets, teapots, tumblers, mixing bowls, and bean pots. During World War II the company continued to make inexpensive lines, but after the war the foreign competition from Europe and Japan increased, interfering with Weller's business. Essex Wire took over the pottery in 1947 and closed it in 1948. Many different marks were used for each Weller line.

References: Sharon and Bob Huxford, *The Collectors Encyclopedia of Weller Pottery*, Collector Books, 1979, value update 1992; Ann Gilbert McDonald, *All About Weller: A History and Collectors Guide to Weller Pottery*, Antique Publications, 1989.

Museums: Chrysler Museum, Norfolk, VA; Museum of History and Technology, Smithsonian Institution, Washington, DC; National Road, Norwich, OH; New Orleans Museum of Art, LA; Zanesville Art Center, OH.

ALVIN
Bud Vase, dbl, 6" h **225.00**
APPLE BLOSSOM
Vase, 10" h **45.00**
ARDSLEY
Bud Vase, 7" h **35.00**
Vase, 9" h, fan shape, dbl **65.00**
ATLANTIC
Vase, 9" h, white **75.00**
AURELIAN
Jug
   5½" h, 3 feet, gold open rose, branches, and green leaves, orange accents, dark brown glossy ground **245.00**
   6" h, bulbous w/handle, painted blackberries **225.00**
BALDWIN
Jardiniere and Pedestal, 34" h **450.00**

Vase, Barcelona, 6¹/₄" h, blue and magenta flowers and leaves, mustard and tan ground, matte finish, $150.00

BARCELONA
Chamberstick, pr 260.00
Floor Vase, 17¹/₂" h............................. 675.00
Vase, 10" h, 3 handles 140.00
BLUE DRAPERY
Vase, 6" h 65.00
BLUEWARE
Vase, 11" h 150.00
BONITA
Vase
   5¹/₄" h, scroll handles 85.00
   6¹/₄" h, ruffled top........................... 95.00
   7¹/₂" h.. 120.00
   9¹/₄" h
      Orange tiger lily 160.00
      Small blue and lavender flowers.. 160.00
   10" h... 185.00
   10¹/₄" h, bluebells........................... 185.00
BRIGHTON
Figure, 7¹/₂" h, parrot, natural colors ... 600.00
BURNTWOOD
Vase, 10" h, Egyptians plowing
   w/oxen.. 150.00
CAMEO
Basket, 7¹/₂" h, beige.......................... 30.00
Vase, 6¹/₂" h, blue and white.............. 25.00
CHENGTU
Ginger Jar, 12" h................................ 150.00
Urn, 4" h, Chinese red 60.00
Vase, 12" h 125.00
CLAREMONT
Candlestick, 8" h, florals, pr................ 175.00
CLAYCRAFT
Jardiniere, 8" h, white Spanish missions with names on dark brown
   ground 575.00
CLAYWOOD
Vase, 3¹/₂" h....................................... 125.00
CLOUDBURST
Vase, 10" h, yellow luster 80.00

COPPERTONE
Console Bowl, 10¹/₂" d, w/frog on rim,
   flower frog in center 295.00
Vase, 8¹/₂" h.. 180.00
CORNISH
Vase, 7" h, handle, brown 98.00
CRETONE
Vase, 5³/₄" h, black antelopes, flowers,
   and leaves, ivory ground(A)............. 257.00
DARSIE
Pot, 3" h 28.00
DELSA
Tankard, 11³/₄" h, green 145.00
DENTON
Umbrella Stand, 22¹/₂" h..................... 1100.00
DICKENS WARE
Jardiniere, 9" h, 9" d, leaf design......... 375.00
Vase, 11" h, stag design 375.00
DICKENS WARE II
Mug
   5¹/₂" h
      Monk drinking ale 295.00
      Stag design 265.00
   6³/₄" h, Blue Hawk Indian............... 525.00
Pitcher, 5" h, grotesque fish 325.00
Vase
   4¹/₂" h, dbl handles, grotesque fish,
      sgd "Hunter" 325.00
   6" h, pillow shape, friar design........ 300.00
   9" h, blue, green, and brown incised golfer, tree bkd, "DICKENS
      WARE/WELLER" mark(A).................. 1100.00
   9¹/₂" h, multicolored football players 1250.00
   10" h
      Indian chief, sgd "A. Vaughan".... 875.00
      Multicolored monk...................... 525.00
DICKENS WARE III
Mug, 5" h, "Master Belling" 350.00
Vase, 12¹/₂" h, 6 handles at base, "Mr. Pecksniff," sgd "LS" 595.00
DUPONT
Wall Pocket, 9" h............................... 90.00
DYNASTY
Vase, 6" h 45.00
ELBERTA
Vase, 5" h, green 39.00
EOCEAN
Console Set, bowl, 10" l, 3¹/₂" h, 2 candlesticks, 8" h, painted cherries,
   gray to light blue shading 425.00
Mug, 5³/₄" h, mushrooms design 145.00
Vase
   7" h, floral design........................... 175.00
   9" h, large orchids.......................... 325.00
   10" h, wild rose decoration, sgd
      "Levi J. Burgess" 595.00
   13" h, gray w/pink flowers, sgd
      "L.B." 475.00

14" h, hp raspberries and vines, gray, blue, pink, and beige shades, Levi Burgess 775.00

ETNA
Mug, 5¹/₂" h, grape pattern.................. 165.00
Pillow Vase, 5¹/₂" h, floral 175.00
Tankard, 13¹/₂" h, grape and floral 350.00
Vase
    4¹/₂" h, braided handles, hy-drangeas...................................... 150.00
    10" h, pink thistles, shaded gray ground.. 145.00

FLEMISH WARE
Jardiniere and Pedestal, parrots and flowers design 1600.00

FLORENZO
Vase, 5¹/₂" h.. 30.00

FLORETTA
Ewer, 12¹/₂" h, floral........................... 325.00
Mug, 5" h 90.00

FLOWER FROGS
5" h, woodpecker 215.00
9" h, bluebird 450.00

FOREST
Jardiniere and Pedestal, 29" h, hair-lines(A)... 715.00
Pitcher, 5¹/₂" h 165.00
Teapot, 5¹/₄" h, woodland scene, imp "WELLER" mark.............................. 185.00
Vase, 4¹/₂" h.. 90.00

GLENDALE
Vase
    6" h.. 195.00
    6¹/₂" h, bird w/eggs in nest.............. 215.00
    9" h, birds design 375.00
Wall Pocket, 9" h............................... 250.00

Vase, Hudson, 12¹/₂" h, black-outlined blue, green, and cream heron, tan crackle ground, cattails on reverse, sgd "Timberlake," $1500.00

GOLDEN GLOW
Bud Vase, 8¹/₂" h................................. 85.00
Vase, 15" h, dbl handles 125.00

HOBART
Flower Frog, 8¹/₂" h, standing nude, ivory 125.00

HUDSON
Vase
  8" h
    Ball shape, 2 small handles, bluish to pink florals, sgd "McLauglin" 650.00
    Lilies of the valley design, sgd "Pillsbury" 575.00
    Scene of forest, trees, grasses, and ships w/mountains in back-ground, sgd "H. Pillsbury" 2800.00

IVORIS
Vase, 6" h 15.00

JAP BIRDIMAL
Pitcher, 4" h, sgd "L.P. & Rhead" 500.00
Urn, 9" h 475.00
Vase, 5¹/₂" h, 5³/₄" w, pillow shape, black and yellow Viking ship, blue-gray ground, "WELLER, X352" mark(A) 305.00

KENOVA
Vase, 6¹/₂" l, lizard handles, gray 235.00

KLYRO
Bud Vase, 7" h 65.00

KNIFEWOOD
Vase
    5" h, bird design............................. 250.00
    7" h, daisy and butterflies............... 120.00

L'ART NOUVEAU
Vase
    14³/₄" h, sq shape, ebb poppies, fruit, and woman w/flowing hair, matte salmon on celadon ground, "L'ART NOUVEAU MAT WELLER" mark(A) 440.00
    15" h, blond woman, matte pastels . 295.00

LASA
Bud Vase, 7¹/₂" h, pine trees and clouds, green, rose, and gold irid 275.00
Vase
    5¹/₂" h, pine tree, mountains, and clouds, rose and gold irid 250.00
    6" h.. 235.00
    6³/₄" h, tree landscape scene(A) 660.00
    11¹/₂" h, sunset over water w/trees... 500.00

LAVONIA
Bud Vase, 9" h, purple....................... 95.00
Candleholder, 4" h, purple 15.00

LEBANON
Vase, 10" h, men driving oxen, Chengtu glaze 225.00

LEMAR
Vase, 7¹/₂" h.. 80.00

Ewer, Louwelsa, 12" h, multicolored monk, dark brown ground, imp "Louwelsa-Weller, 580-6" mark, c1910(A), $220.00

LIDO
Cornucopia, 7¼" h, turquoise, pr 50.00
LORBEEK
Console Set, 3 piece, lavender............ 275.00
Vase, 7" h, pink 135.00
LOUWELSA
Bowl, 7¼" d, gold flower, brown glaze 175.00
Ewer
  4" h, 3 spouts, carnations design, sgd "HW" 155.00
  6" h, yellow daffodil w/green leaves, Standard glaze, sgd "M.P." 135.00
  8" h, 4 birds in flight 425.00
Tankard, 11½" h, long-stemmed flowers 275.00
Vase
  4" h, pillow shape, chrysanthemums design 250.00
  11" h, dalmatian portrait, sgd "A. Wilson" 1400.00
  17½" h, shouldered ovoid shape w/narrow neck and flared rim, brown, black, and green poppies, sgd "A. Haubrich," imp "LOUWELSA55WE." mark(A) 1430.00
MALVERN
Vase, 13½" h, burgundy and yellow... 120.00
MANHATTAN
Vase
  6½" h.. 40.00
  8" h, artichoke base, raised vert lines 75.00
MUSKOTA
Figure, 6½" h, fishing boy.................. 215.00
NOVELTY LINE
Figure, 4½" h, 8½" l, dachshund, brown 70.00

OAK LEAF
Basket, 9" h, blue............................... 50.00
Ewer, 8½" h, blue............................... 45.00
Vase
  8" h, brown.................................... 40.00
  10" h, green 45.00
PANELLA
Vase, 5½" h, dbl handles, turquoise ... 25.00
PARAGON
Vase, 7" h.. 135.00
PATRICIA
Vase, 7" h, white 60.00
PEARL
Vase, 10" h 225.00
PERFECTO
Vase
  8½" h, apple blossoms, green shading to lavender 295.00
  16" h, water lily design 1100.00
PIERRE
Casserole, Cov, pink 10.00
Dinner Plate, pink.............................. 8.00
Tea Set, pot, 8½" h, creamer, 2" h, sugar bowl, 2" h, lavender basket weave 70.00
PUMILA
Bowl, 10" d 65.00
ROBIA
Basket, 6" h, white and aqua flowers, tan and brown swirls..................... 55.00
ROCHELLE
Vase, 10½" h...................................... 495.00
ROMA
Bowl, 13" d, brown stripes, yellowware body 65.00
Bud Vase, 7½" h, triple...................... 80.00
Wall Pocket, 10" h............................. 125.00
ROSELLA
Dbl Vase, 5" h 65.00
SABRINIAN
Bowl, 9" l 110.00
Planter, 7" d, sea horse handles 295.00
Vase
  6" h.. 200.00
  10" h.. 300.00
SICARD
Center Bowl, 4½" h, 6" d, lobes, irid green clover and dots, irid copper ground(A)..................................... 660.00
Vase
  3" h, gold to green irid clover design on dark red ground, glaze flakes(A) 467.00
  5" h, 2 small handles, gold and green peacock feathers, dark purple to blue w/green, gold, and pink accents, "Sicard, Weller" mark(A) 1210.00
  6½" h, flower motif, metallic green w/red and gold accents............... 625.00

*Vase, Sicard, 11³/₄″ h, green, magenta,
and gold flowers and leaves, irid
blue-purple ground, imp "Weller"
mark, $1800.00*

7″ h, pillow shape, scalloped foot
and lip, thistle and floral design
on irid rose, blue, and green
ground, "Weller Sicard" mark(A) . 1100.00
9″ h, tapered cylinder body, bulbous top, gold-green irid spider
chrysanthemum on silver-green
to red ground(A) 880.00
11″ h, blown-out sections on base
and top, overall florals, gold dots
on green, gold, and red-purple
ground, #39 .... 1850.00

SILVERTONE
Basket, 13″ h 75.00
Vase
6¹/₂″ h, swirl pattern 150.00
8″ h, fan shape 165.00
12″ h 275.00
Wall Pocket, 10″ h 350.00

*Vase, 6³/₈″ h, blue, purple, and cream
berries, rust leaves, blue to green shaded
ground, $375.00*

SOFTONE
Console Bowl, 10″ d, blue 20.00
Cornucopia, 8¹/₂″ h, pink 18.00
SOUEVO
Pitcher, 12″ h 350.00
SYDONIA
Ewer, 9¹/₂″ h, sea horse handles 265.00
TURKIS
Vase, 5″ h 28.00
VOILE
Vase, 8¹/₂″ h, fan shape, artist sgd 75.00
WARWICK
Vase, 10″ h, handle 185.00
Window Box, 12¹/₂″ l 225.00
WILD ROSE
Basket, 5¹/₂″ h, green 50.00
Candleholder, 6″ h, triple 28.00
WOODCRAFT
Bowl, 3¹/₂″ h, white squirrels 65.00
Bud Vase, 10″ h 65.00
Vase
9″ h 95.00
12″ h, plums design 125.00
13³/₄″ h, owl peeking out of tree
trunk, unmkd(A) 247.00
18″ h, owl and squirrel 1050.00
WOODROSE
Vase
7″ h 95.00
9″ h 95.00
Wall Pocket, 6¹/₂″ h 75.00
ZONA
Pitcher, 8″ h, kingfisher pattern 115.00

T.J. WHEATLEY AND COMPANY
1880–1882
Wheatley Pottery Company
1903–1936
Cincinnati, Ohio

History: T.J. Wheatley was first associated
with the Coultry Works and taught a decorating
class there for other potters. In 1880 he opened
his own pottery in Cincinnati, Ohio, doing all the
pottery work by himself at first. Soon other artists
were working for him on his Cincinnati faience
in the Limoges style.

Wheatley patented a slip-painted underglaze
decoration method, but the patent did not hold
up in court. The Cincinnati Art Pottery that was
formed in 1879 provided some outside financial
support for Wheatley. Even though he sold an extensive line to Tiffany and Company in New
York, he left his pottery in 1882.

Wheatley built a pottery in Kentucky in 1882, but it was destroyed by fire in 1884. By 1897 he was working for Weller Pottery in Zanesville, Ohio.

In 1903 T.J. Wheatley and Isaac Kahn established Wheatley Pottery Company back in Cincinnati, Ohio, and made artwares called Wheatley ware, which used colored matte glazes over dark relief designs. Gardenware and architectural items also were made. Some pieces only had paper labels.

Kahn took over after Wheatley died in 1917. Garden pottery was expanded to include pedestals, fountains, jardinieres, flower boxes, and lawn sets. Wheatley's Plymouth gray ware in blended ivory and buff tones was a specialty.

In 1927 the company was purchased by the Cambridge Tile Manufacturing Company of Covington, Kentucky, and renamed the Wheatley Tile and Pottery Company. In 1930 the pottery was moved from Cincinnati to Hartwell, Ohio, where all operations ceased by 1936.

Early wares were incised "T.J.W. & Co." or "T.J. Wheatley" and some also were marked with a date. Many pieces from the Wheatley Pottery Company were unmarked except for a paper label with the words "Wheatley/Cincinnati Ohio" and the firm's cipher.

Museum: Cincinnati Art Museum, OH.

Tankard, 7¹/₄" h, matte green glaze, $185.00

Bowl, 2¹/₂" h, 8" d, water plant design, streaked green glaze, mkd **795.00**

Charger, 15³/₄" h, 10" w, slip-decorated scene of snow-covered church, gray and white, incised "N267/TWCo., 1880" mark **1000.00**

Oil Lamp Base, 7¹/₄" h, 4 sq buttressed feet, organic curdled matte green glaze(A) **880.00**

Vase
  8" h
    6" w, architectural shape, 4 buttressed tapered sides, middle band, suspended matte green glaze(A) **1540.00**
    7" w, pillow shape, ftd, painted landscape scene on each side, sgd and dtd "1879"(A) **1430.00**
    9¹/₄" h, squat base, cylinder neck, relief of ridged leaves and buds on stems, textured matte green glaze(A) **1210.00**

11¹/₂" h, bulbous base, raised collar on shoulder, thick matte cumbumber green glaze, chip on base(A) **302.00**

12" h, oval shape, multicolored painted scene of sailing ship in ocean on front, gloss dark blue body, glaze chips, incised "50, T.J.W. & Co., 1880" mark(A) **1760.00**

13" h, Japanese style applied purple and white flowers w/green leaves, shaded blue ground, mkd **2200.00**

13¹/₄" h, applied brown, green, and pink seaweed, shells, crayfish, and mussels, shaded green ground, mkd(A) **17,600.00**

13¹/₂" h, bulbous base, trumpet neck, slip-painted pink and white daisies and butterfly in landscape, cloudy blue sky, incised "T.J. Wheatley, 1879" mark **350.00**

14" h, organic shape, 4 vert handles w/webbed ends, undulating rim, matte green glaze, incised "615, WP" mark(A) **1540.00**

14¹/₂" h, applied pink poppy blossoms and buds w/green leaves, cobalt ground **500.00**

17" h, baluster shape, rounded panels, raised buds and stems w/carved leaves, matte green glaze **850.00**

19¹/₂" h, ribbed leaves and buds, matte ochre glaze, drilled base(A) **2310.00**

DINNERWARE MANUFACTURERS

Companies listed under this heading are best known for the extensive lines of dinnerware and table accessories that they produced over fairly long periods of time. Many of these companies merged, separated, or evolved from other companies. Listings are for the peak years of production.

MADE IN AMERICA

AMERICAN HAVILAND COMPANY
New York, New York
1940–1960s

History: In 1940 when import duties, increasing costs in Europe, and the start of World War II made it impossible for French producers to continue exporting Haviland China to the United States, Theodore Haviland opened a factory in New York.

Approximately fifty Haviland patterns were made in the United States. The first wares were marked "THEODORE HAVILAND New York," while later wares had the words "Made in America" and "New York." Prior to 1950 the firm was called Theodore Haviland & Co., Inc. After 1950 it was called Haviland and Co., Inc.

Collectors' Club: Haviland Collectors Internationale Foundation, P.O. Box 11632, Milwaukee, WI, 53211.

APPLE BLOSSOM PATTERN
Bread and Butter Plate, 6½" d	**11.00**
Cream and Sugar	**48.00**
Cup and Saucer	**20.00**
Dinner Plate, 10½" d	**16.00**
Platter, 14" l	**35.00**
Vegetable Bowl, 9¾" l, oval	**35.00**

CLIFTON PATTERN
Plate, 8¾" d, "Theodore Haviland Made in New York" mark	**18.50**

CONCORDE PATTERN
Platter, 14" l	**60.00**
Salad Plate	**16.00**

DELAWARE PATTERN
Cream and Sugar	**95.00**
Platter, 11½" l	**28.00**

FRONTENAC PATTERN
Cream Soup	**35.00**
Cup and Saucer	**25.00**
Dinner Plate	**25.00**
Fruit Dish	**20.00**
Gravy Boat	**65.00**
Soup Bowl	**12.00**
Vegetable Bowl, Cov	**95.00**

GOTHAM PATTERN
Gravy Boat	**45.00**

HELENE PATTERN
Cup and Saucer	**12.00**
Dinner Plate	**10.00**

KENMORE PATTERN
Bread and Butter Plate	**4.00**
Cup and Saucer	**6.00**
Cream Soup, w/underplate, "Theodore Haviland, Made in New York" mark	**10.00**
Dinner Plate, "Theodore Haviland, Made in New York" mark	**11.00**
Fruit Bowl, "Theodore Haviland, Made in New York" mark	**7.00**
Salad Plate	**6.00**
Soup Plate	**8.00**

LEEDS PATTERN
Platter, 14" l, "Theodore Haviland, Made in New York" mark	**50.00**

NORMANDIE'S GARDEN PATTERN
Vegetable Bowl, Cov, "Theodore Haviland, Made in New York" mark	**65.00**

PASADENA PATTERN
Cup and Saucer, "Theodore Haviland, Made in New York" mark	**30.00**

PINK SPRAY PATTERN
Cream and Sugar	**75.00**
Cup and Saucer, "T. Haviland, New York" mark	**25.00**
Dinner Plate	**35.00**

POSEY SHOP PATTERN
Cup and Saucer	**8.00**
Dessert Plate	**4.00**
Dinner Plate	**8.00**

REGENTS PARK ROSE PATTERN
Cup and Saucer, "Theodore Haviland, Made in New York" mark	**30.00**

Platter, 14" l, Springtime pattern, "Theodore Haviland, Made in New York" mark, $60.00

lain dinner sets, toilet sets, odd dishes, and hotel wares were made. In 1909 it was purchased by Canonsburg Pottery Company. John George was the first president, followed by his son in 1920, and succession continued in the George family.

In the early years of dinnerware production, all operations were done by hand. When Steubenville Pottery Company closed in 1959, Canonsburg bought its molds and equipment, and continued to produce "Rose Point by Steubenville." In 1960 the company employed a new underglaze technique for applying decals.

Wares were sold through department stores, chain stores, and mail order houses. Some form of a little cannon was used as the mark for long periods of time.

In 1976 the factory was sold to Angelo Falconi. There was a bankruptcy sale in 1978, but the plant had been idle since a fire in 1975.

ROSALINDE PATTERN

Bread and Butter Plate	20.00
Creamer	20.00
Cup and Saucer, "T. Haviland" mark	40.00
Dinner Plate, "T. Haviland" mark	35.00
Fruit Dish	14.00
Gravy Boat	50.00
Platter	
11½" d	100.00
14½" d	125.00
Salad Plate	22.00
Soup Bowl	18.00
Sugar Bowl, Cov	30.00
Vegetable Bowl, Cov	75.00

SHELTON PATTERN

Cup and Saucer, "Theodore Haviland, Made in New York" mark	50.00

SPRINGTIME PATTERN

Cream and Sugar	115.00
Cup and Saucer, "Theodore Haviland, Made in New York" mark	30.00
Platter, 11⅝" l	40.00
Soup Plate	28.00
Teapot	135.00
Vegetable Bowl, 9⅝" l	35.00

KEYSTONE

MADE IN USA

CANONSBURG POTTERY CO.

CANONSBURG POTTERY

Canonsburg, Pennsylvania
1901–1978

SIMPLICITY

THE HALLMARK

CANONSBURG

OF QUALITY

WARRANTED 22 KT. GOLD MADE IN U. S. A.

Temptation

History: The Canonsburg China Company was started in Canonsburg, Pennsylvania, in 1901 with the help of W.S. George. Semi-porce-

BERMUDA ROSE PATTERN

Berry Bowl	2.00
Cup and Saucer	3.00
Dinner Plate	6.00
Platter, 11½" l	7.00
Vegetable Bowl, 8¾" d	6.00

BLUEBIRD PATTERN

Plate, 9" d, 3 groups of blue and red flowers w/bluebird	5.00

CLOVER PATTERN

Bread and Butter Plate	2.00
Creamer	4.00
Cup and Saucer	3.00
Dinner Plate	6.00
Luncheon Plate	3.00
Sugar Bowl	6.00

GEORGELYN SUNSET PATTERN

Creamer	5.00
Sugar Bowl	8.00

KEYSTONE SHAPE

Plate	
7½" d, multicolored floral center, lacy gold border, scalloped edge	6.00
10¼" d, center w/multicolored garden flowers, raised border design	8.00
Platter, 11½" l, floral center w/roses, gilt border, scalloped edge, "Canonsburg Pottery Co." mark	5.00

ROYAL ROSE PATTERN

Platter, 14" l	6.00

STRAWFLOWER-ALLEGHENY WARE

Cup and Saucer	5.00
Dinner Plate	5.00

WASHINGTON COLONIAL PATTERN

Berry Dish	2.00
Cup and Saucer	4.00
Dinner Plate	7.00
Salad Plate	4.00

MISCELLANEOUS

Pitcher, 6¾" h, multicolored florals, band of gold	28.00
Plate, 11¼" d, 3 sections, multicol-	

Dinner Plate, 9¹/₄″ d, Simplicity pattern, pink roses, pale green border w/gold overlay, $8.00

Calendar Plate, 8¹/₂″ d, maroon 1909 calendar, multicolored scenes, black bird, crown and "Carrollton Pottery Co." mark, $10.00

ored pheasant in one, scattered florals in others, zigzag border w/green striped rim **10.00**
Relish Tray, 9¹/₄″ l, 2 purple and black Dutch harbor scenes on border, blue-line rim **5.00**

1920s

c.1910-1920

CARROLLTON POTTERY
Carrollton, Ohio
1903–late 1930s

History: The Carrollton Pottery Company, built by E.L. Henderson and his brother-in-law in 1903 in Carrollton, Ohio, made semi-vitreous porcelain wares. After a fire in 1914, the factory was rebuilt and in 1929 the company merged with seven others to form America China Corporation. Semi-porcelain dinner sets, tea wares, and toilet sets were made with an assortment of marks. The company operated until c1937 and then closed. Its building was used to refine beryllium until a fire in 1955.

Bowl, 9″ d, Flow Blue border w/gold accents, vert ridged border, bird and "Carrollton China" mark **45.00**
Fish Platter, 15¹/₄″ l, 11⁵/₈″ w, multicolored leaping trout in green water in center, gold rim, "Carrollton China" mark.................................. **45.00**

Plate
9¹/₄″ sq, curved clipped corners, ivory ground, gold-outlined rim ... **2.00**
9¹/₂″ d, 3 different multicolored busts of Gibson-type woman, shaped brown rim, set of 6 .... **300.00**
10″ d, center w/orange and green parrot on perch, 3 flower sprays on border, tan and dark brown geometric rim band, "Carrollton China" mark **10.00**
Platter, 12″ l, rect, small band of multicolored flowers on rim, "Carrollton China" mark.................................. **10.00**

CRESCENT POTTERY/ LEIGH POTTERS, INC.
Alliance, Ohio
1920–1926/1926–1931

History: F.A. Sebring built a pottery in Alliance, Ohio, in 1920 and operated it as the Crescent China Company until 1926. From 1926–1931 it operated as the Leigh Potters, Inc. and was run by Charles Sebring, son of F.A. Sebring.

Products made were similar to those being made at the other Sebring potteries and included dinnerware, kitchenware, and Leigh Art Ware, a semi-porcelain line decorated with decals.

The Depression affected the pottery business, and the plant closed in 1931.

EASTER TULIP PATTERN
Casserole, Cov	8.00
Dinner Plate	6.00
Luncheon Plate	5.00

GARDEN FLOWERS W/VERT FLUTED RIM AND GOLD ICICLES
Berry Dish	2.00
Bread and Butter Plate	2.00
Creamer	4.00
Cup and Saucer	2.00
Dinner Plate	5.00
Platter	
11½" l	10.00
13½" l	13.00
Salad Plate	3.00
Shakers, pr	4.00
Sugar Bowl, Cov	8.00
Vegetable Bowl, 9" d	10.00

MEISSEN ROSE PATTERN
Cup and Saucer	6.00

Plate, 9½" d, Meissen Rose pattern, multicolored garden flowers, maroon border w/gold overlay, "Leigh Ware-Meissen Rose-Maroon Emperor" mark, $6.00

Plate 8¾" sq, multicolored garden flowers, tan ground, gold rim, "Sienna Ware, The Crescent China Co." mark, $4.00

Sauce Dish	6.00
Vegetable Bowl, 9¼" l, maroon border w/gold overlay, "Maroon-Emperor, Leigh" mark	8.00

WILD FLOWER PATTERN
Dinner Plate	5.00

MISCELLANEOUS
Bowl, 10½" d, pink and white florals in center, ribbed int, raised design on border, scalloped rim w/green and gold edge, Crescent	37.00

COIORAMA

CRONIN CHINA COMPANY
Minerva, Ohio
1934–1956

History: The Cronin China Company, founded in 1934 in Minerva, Ohio, made semi-porcelain dinnerwares until 1956 when U.S. Ceramic Tile Company acquired all the stock and used the facilities to make wall and floor tile.

During the 1930s and 1940s, Cronin made hand-painted pitchers, platters, and bowls marked "Pottery Guild for the Block China Company." Colorama was a Fiesta-type ware made by Cronin, and Bake Oven was decaled baking dishes.

BLACK ART DECO STYLE FLOWER HEADS W/RED CENTERS, LEAVES, AND BORDER BANDS
Baker, 9" d	10.00
Dessert Plate	3.00
Dinner Plate	2.00
Mixing Bowl, 5" d	10.00
Pie Baker, handleless	3.00
Platter, 11¼" l	6.00

Individual Baker, 7" H-H, red and black Art Deco flowers, "The Cronin China Co., Minerva, Ohio" mark, $4.00

Salad Plate 2.00
Serving Bowl, 9½″ d 8.00
Soup Bowl 4.00

COURTING COUPLE PATTERN
Cake Plate, 10½″ H-H 14.00

FRUITS PATTERN
Berry Bowl 6.00
Bowl, 8½″ d 12.00
Bowl, Cov
    5½″ d 15.00
    8½″ d 25.00
Bread and Butter Plate 5.00
Cake Plate, 10¾″ d, tab handles 17.00
Creamer 10.00
Dinner Plate 7.00
Shakers, pr 25.00
Sugar Bowl 20.00
Water Jug, Cov, 7″ h 35.00

PETIT POINT, BLUE, FLOWERS, SILVER RIM
Pie Baker, individual 4.00
Plate, 7¼″ d 4.00

ROYAL RAJAH MAROON PATTERN
Plate, 9¼″ d 8.00

MISCELLANEOUS
Plate, 8″ d, New York World's Fair,
    1939–40 decal 80.00

CROOKSVILLE CHINA COMPANY
Crooksville, Ohio
1902–1959

History: The Crooksville China Company was established in Crooksville, Ohio, in 1902 and made semi-porcelain dinnerwares and toilet sets with old-country-type decorations.

"Pantry-Bak-in" was made with many different decals on waffle sets, bowls, teapots, covered jugs, fruit juice sets, coffeepots, baking dishes, cookies jars, spice jars, and such. Stinthal China was a thin semi-porcelain dinnerware. There were usually no pattern names on the dinner-

wares. Competition from Japanese imports and the introduction of plastic dinnerwares forced the company to close in 1959.

BLOSSOMS PATTERN
Dinner Plate 8.00
Salad Plate 6.00

BORDER ROSE PATTERN
Gravy Boat, attached undertray 24.00

GOLD GEOMETRIC OVERLAY BORDER, IVORY GROUND
Bread and Butter Plate 2.00
Creamer 4.00
Cup and Saucer 2.00
Dinner Plate 4.00
Sauce Dish 2.00
Soup Bowl 4.00
Sugar Bowl, Cov 5.00

PANTRY BAK-IN
Bowl, 8″ d, scattered bouquets of mul-
    ticolored flowers on ext, raised fruit
    band on rim 15.00
Pie Baker
    9″ d, scattered bouquets of multi-
    colored flowers on int, raised
    band of fruit on ext 12.00
    10″ d, Silhouette pattern, yellow
    ground 30.00
Teapot, 8¼″ h, brown-orange tulips
    on sides, raised fruit on shoulder 28.00

PETIT POINT HOUSE PATTERN
Mixing Bowl, 9″ d 40.00
Plate
    7¼″ d 4.00
    9¾″ d 5.00
Serving Plate, 12¾″ d 8.00

QUEEN ROSE PATTERN
Bowl,
    5″ d 4.00
    tab handle, 6″ d 6.00
Cup and Saucer 3.00
Dinner Plate, 10″ d 5.00
Platter, 11¾″ l 8.00
Salad Plate, 6″ d 4.00
Serving Dish, 11″ l, divided 7.00
Vegetable Bowl
    8″ d 7.00
    9½″ l 8.00

RUST BOUQUET PATTERN
Casserole, Cov 22.00
Creamer 6.00
Dinner Plate 6.00

SPRING BLOSSOM PATTERN
Bread and Butter Plate 2.00
Creamer and Cov Sugar Bowl 10.00
Cup and Saucer 3.00
Dinner Plate 3.00
Gravy Boat 5.00
Salad Plate 2.00

Soup Plate, 8″ d, Iva-Lure pattern, two-tone red flowers, shaded green leaves, $5.00

MISCELLANEOUS

Bowl, 10¼″ d, 5″ h, stoneware, heart design, blue and white 45.00

Cup and Saucer, oversized, shaded light blue border, white ground w/raised curlicues, bird and pennant mark.. 16.00

Plate, 9¼″ d

Center decal of dog watching bird in brown, white, and tan, green grass, gold raised rim 6.00

Multicolored decals of fish swimming in natural water setting, inner gold overlay band, shaped rim w/gold-outlined curlicues, pr. 10.00

Soup Bowl, 7¼″ d, dog silhouette....... 15.00

C.P.Co.

WARRANTED
SEMI-PORCELAIN
c.1910

CROWN POTTERY
Evansville, Indiana
1891–c1955

History: The Flentke family organized the Crown Pottery in 1891 in Evansville, Indiana. After taking over the Peoria Pottery Company in 1902, the firm became known as Crown Potteries Company.

Plain and decorated ironstone china, Crown

Porcelain dinnerware, toilet ware, and semi-porcelain items were made using various china decorating methods. The company went out of business in 1955 due to competition from Japanese imports.

CROYDON PATTERN
Pie Baker, 9¾″ d................................. 7.00
GARDEN FLOWERS IN CENTER
Light blue banded border
Creamer.. 3.00
Cup and Saucer 4.00
Dinner Plate 3.00
Platter, 13″ l....................................... 12.00
Soup Bowl 3.00
Sugar Bowl 6.00
Vegetable Bowl, 8¾″ d...................... 12.00
Yellow banded border
Cereal Bowl....................................... 3.00
Cup and Saucer 2.00
Dinner Plate 3.00
Gravy Boat 4.00
Platter, 13¼″ l 10.00
Salad Plate... 2.00
Vegetable Bowl, 9½″ d...................... 8.00
ORANGE LOGANBERRIES W/CHECKERBOARD DESIGN
Berry Dish 2.00
Creamer.. 3.00
Cup and Saucer 3.00
Vegetable Bowl, 9″ d........................ 10.00
SILVER BAND W/RED STRIPES DESIGN
Berry Dish 2.00
Cereal Bowl....................................... 3.00
Cup and Saucer 3.00
Dinner Plate 4.00
Gravy Boat 5.00
Platter
   11″ l.. 10.00
   15″ l.. 10.00
Salad Plate... 3.00
SWEDISH PATTERN, BLUE BORDER
Berry Dish 2.00
Creamer.. 3.00
Cup and Saucer 3.00
Dinner Plate 4.00
Platter, 11″ l....................................... 8.00
Salad Plate... 2.00
Sugar Bowl, Cov 4.00
Vegetable Bowl, Cov, 9″ d................. 8.00
THE MODE PATTERN
Dinnerware
Platter, 10¾″ l, oval.......................... 10.00
Kitchen Ware
Pie Baker 12.00
Shakers, range top, pr 12.00
WILD ROSE PATTERN
Bread and Butter Plate 2.00
Cup and Saucer 2.00

Dinner Plate 5.00
Gravy Boat, w/attached undertray 5.00

MISCELLANEOUS

Bowl
9¼" d, multicolored decal of garden
flowers in center, shaded med
green border w/raised panels,
green "Crown Pottery, Made in
U.S.A." mark 8.00
9½" d, orange tulips in center, or-
ange luster border 18.00
10" d, "Compliments of F.J. Corn-
well & Co., Plainview, Minn." in
center, border of pink roses and
white hydrangeas, maple leaf
shadow on orange ground, green
luster rim w/raised design 25.00
Casserole, Cov, 11¼" H-H, yellow
band of small pink roses on border . 20.00
Cup and Saucer, gray center band
w/red and black stripes, red-out-
lined handle 7.00
Gravy Boat w/undertray, Bluebird de-
sign 24.00
Pitcher
4¼" h, white opaque body, raised
branch design from handle termi-
nal 5.00
9" h, w/ice lip, white opaque body
w/raised curlicues 45.00
Plate
6⅝" d, yellow roses in border, light
tan border, "Souvenir of Decatur,
Michigan" on front, crown and
"C.P. China" mark 15.00
9¼" d, border decal of pink roses
and green leaves between blue
flower head w/pink center alter-
nating w/oval of pink roses, light
pink ground, gold and black half-
circle rim, crown and "C.P. Co."
mark 2.00

*Bowl, 10⅝" d, pink roses w/green
leaves, shaded pink border, "CROWN"
and crown in ribbon mark, $5.00*

10" d, decal of pear and purple and
green grapes and leaves, gold
overlay geometric border, gold
"HERREIR LUMBER AND HRWR CO. THE
PLACE WHERE EVERYONE LIKES TO BUY"
on reverse 22.00

UNION MADE
U.S.A.
WARRANTED
22 KT. GOLD
DUSTY ROSE

FRENCH CHINA COMPANY
East Liverpool and Sebring, Ohio
1898–1929

SAXON CHINA COMPANY
Sebring, Ohio
1911–1929

FRENCH-SAXON CHINA COMPANY
Sebring, Ohio
1935–1964

History: The Sebring brothers organized the
French China Company in 1898 in East Liverpool, Ohio, and made semi-porcelain dinnerware, tea sets, toilet wares, and novelties. The
company moved to a new plant in Sebring,
Ohio, in 1901 and continued to make semi-
porcelains. Saxon China Company was formed
in 1911 to make plain and decorated semi-vitreous dinnerwares.

In 1916 the Sebrings created Sebring Manufacturing Corporation, a holding company for
French China Company, Strong Manufacturing
Company, and Saxon China Company. Each firm
continued to operate separately until 1929 when
the holding company joined with American Chinaware Corporation. This merger failed two
years later and Saxon China Company reopened
as the French-Saxon China Company in 1935. It
produced semi-porcelain dinnerware, tea sets,
and various accessory pieces. In 1964 the
French-Saxon China Company was purchased by
Royal China Company of Sebring, Ohio.

Reference: William C. Gates, Jr. and Dana E.
Ormerod, *The East Liverpool, Ohio, Pottery Dis-*

trict: *Identification of Manufacturers and Marks,*
The Society for Historical Archaeology, 1982.

Berry Bowl, Flow Blue border w/gold
   overlay 2.00
Cake Plate, 11½" H-H, brown flowers
   w/lavender centers, green stems 3.00
Cereal Bowl, blue, pink, and yellow
   cosmos w/green leaves, wavy gold
   inner border, shaded shaped cobalt
   rim w/gold band 4.00
Creamer
   Blue, pink, and yellow cosmos
   w/green leaves, wavy gold inner
   border, shaded shaped cobalt rim
   w/gold band 3.00
   Flow Blue border w/gold overlay 5.00
   Maroon band w/gold overlay on
   shoulder 6.00
Cup and Saucer
   Blue, pink, and yellow cosmos
   w/green leaves, wavy gold inner
   border, shaded shaped cobalt rim
   w/gold band 3.00
   Cherries design, Flow Blue border
   w/raised design and gold floral
   overlay, "La Francaise" mark 20.00
Dinner Plate
   Blue, pink, and yellow cosmos in
   center, wavy gold inner border,
   shaded shaped cobalt rim w/gold
   band 6.00
   Bouquet of garden flowers in center,
   inner gold chain design, cobalt
   border w/gold overlay 4.00
   Flowing blue border w/gold overlay 3.00
   Yellow, blue, and pink florals w/col-
   ored leaves in center, rose colored scalloped border w/inner
   gold floral border 10.00

*Dinner Plate, 9" d, pink roses w/blue
and yellow flowers, gold border, "The
French Saxon China Co., Sebring, Ohio,
22 K gold USA" mark, $3.00*

*Platter, 15½" l, blue Dutch scene,
cobalt border w/raised design, gold
overlay, "LaFrancaise," fleur-de-lys and
"Semi-Vitreous" mark, $95.00*

Luncheon Plate, blue, pink, and yellow cosmos w/green leaves, wavy
   gold inner border, shaded shaped
   cobalt rim w/gold band 4.00
Pie Plate, 9½" d, dark pink and tan
   floral center, 22K gold border 12.00
Relish Dish, 7¼" l, blue, pink, and
   yellow cosmos w/green leaves,
   wavy gold inner border, shaded
   shaped cobalt rim w/gold band 5.00
Salad Plate
   Bouquet of garden flowers in center,
   inner gold chain design, cobalt
   border w/gold overlay 3.00
   Flow Blue border w/gold overlay 2.00
Soup Bowl
   Blue, pink, and yellow cosmos
   w/green leaves, wavy gold inner
   border, shaded shaped cobalt rim
   w/gold band 5.00
   Bouquet of garden flowers in center,
   inner gold chain design, cobalt
   border w/gold overlay 5.00
   Flow Blue border w/gold overlay 4.00
Sugar Bowl, Cov
   Blue, pink, and yellow cosmos
   w/green leaves, wavy gold inner
   border, shaded shaped cobalt rim
   w/gold band 4.00
   Bouquet of garden flowers, cobalt
   border w/gold overlay 5.00
   Flow Blue border w/gold overlay 5.00
   Maroon band w/gold overlay on
   shoulder 9.00
   Molded ridged handles, multicol-
   ored florals w/lacy gold trim 8.00
Tray, 13¼" H-H, small bouquet of
   multicolored florals in center,
   stepped border w/formal gold over-
   lay 15.00
Vegetable Bowl, Cov, 11½" H-H,
   Bluebird pattern 65.00

W.S. GEORGE
Queen
c.1920

Platter, 12" H-H, Dogwood pattern,
Bolero shape, "W.S. George Bolero"
mark, $10.00

W.S. GEORGE POTTERY COMPANY
East Palestine, Ohio
1909–1955

History: W.S. George bought a controlling interest in the East Palestine Pottery Company in 1904 and added a new plant called the Continental China Company. In 1909 he changed the name to W.S. George Pottery Company.

He made semi-porcelain dinnerware, plain and decorated table and toilet ware, hotel ware, and an assortment of white and decorated articles. Dinnerware was made in a great variety of shapes and designs, including Argosy from the late 1920s, Bolero, Lido, and Rainbow from the 1930s, and Del Rio Ochre from 1934.

Though W.S. George died in 1925, his family maintained the company. A wide variety of marks was used. Due to competition from less-expensive foreign imports, the company went bankrupt in 1955. In 1960 it was reorganized and operated by the Royal China Company of Sebring, Ohio.

ASTER PATTERN
Vegetable Bowl, 9" d	8.00

BLUEBIRD PATTERN
Cup and Saucer, A.D., set of 4	36.00
Dinner Plate, 9" d	5.00
Sugar Bowl	25.00

BLUSHING ROSE PATTERN
Plate, 9¼" d	8.00
Platter, 13¼" l	15.00

BREAKFAST NOOK PATTERN
Dessert Plate, 6½" d	2.00
Dinner Plate, 9½" d	4.00
Platter, 11½" l	10.00
Salad Plate, 7½" d	3.00

CANARY TONE, BAND OF ORANGE POPPIES
Creamer	8.00
Sugar Bowl, Cov	8.00

DOGWOOD PATTERN, BOLERO SHAPE
Plate, 10¼" d	3.00
Vegetable Bowl, 9" d	12.00

FORSYTHIA PATTERN
Bread and Butter Plate	2.00
Cereal Bowl	3.00
Cup and Saucer	3.00
Dinner Plate	3.00
Salad Plate	2.00

GASCON PATTERN
Gravy Boat	15.00

HOPALONG CASSIDY DESIGN
Cereal Bowl, 5¼" d	25.00
Plate, 9⅜" d, black decal of Cassidy on horse, beaded border	30.00

IROQUOIS PATTERN
Casserole, Cov, 10¼" H-H	23.00
Creamer	9.00

MEXI-LIDO PATTERN
Plate	
8" d	8.00
9" d	9.00
10" d	12.00

PEACH BLOSSOM PATTERN
Cereal Bowl	3.00
Creamer	3.00
Cup and Saucer	2.00
Dinner Plate	3.00
Gravy Boat, dbl spout	5.00
Platter, 12" H-H	7.00
Salad Plate	2.00
Sauce Dish	2.00
Sugar Bowl, Cov	4.00
Vegetable Bowl, 9¼" d	10.00

PETALWARE PATTERN
Eggcup	2.00
Plate	
7½" d, maroon	3.00
9" d, maroon	5.00
Sugar Bowl, pink	12.00

PRIMAVERA PATTERN, BOLERO SHAPE
Cov Creamer and Sugar Bowl	20.00

PUSSY WILLOW PATTERN

Berry Dish	2.00
Butter Dish, Cov	15.00
Cereal Bowl	3.00
Creamer	4.00
Dinner Plate	3.00
Platter, 13½" l	9.00
Shakers, pr	5.00
Sugar Bowl, Cov	5.00
Teapot, 9¼" h	23.00

RAINBOW PATTERN, GREEN

Cereal Bowl	2.00
Cup and Saucer	2.00
Dinner Plate	2.00
Salad Plate	1.00
Vegetable Bowl, 9" l	5.00

RUST FLORAL PATTERN

Bread and Butter Plate	3.00
Cup and Saucer	5.00
Dinner Plate	5.00
Salad Plate	4.00
Sauce Dish	4.00
Soup Plate	8.00

SHORTCAKE PATTERN

Berry Dish	5.00
Bowl, 9½" l, rect	12.00
Casserole, Cov	25.00
Dinner Plate	8.00
Gravy Boat	15.00
Luncheon Plate	7.00
Platter, 13¼" l	32.50
Soup Bowl	6.00

WAMPUM PATTERN, RANCHERO SHAPE

Bowl, 9" d	12.00
Bread and Butter Plate	6.00
Butter Dish, Cov	8.00
Cream and Sugar	15.00
Cup and Saucer	12.00
Dinner Plate	8.00
Gravy Boat	9.00

Salad Plate, 7" d, Shortcake pattern, $5.00

Platter	
11" d	15.00
13" d	18.00
Relish Dish, 9" l	8.00
Salt and Pepper	10.00
Teapot	25.00

MISCELLANEOUS

Teapot, 4¾" h, raised rings on neck, turquoise ground, "W.S. George East Palestine Oh. U.S.A." mark	24.00

PEACH BLOSSOM
MADE IN
U.S.A.

HALL CHINA COMPANY
East Liverpool, Ohio
1903–Present

History: Robert Hall established the Hall China Company in 1903 when the East Liverpool Potteries Company was dissolved. Robert Taggert Hall, his son, took over when Hall died one year later. Mostly toilet sets, whiteware, and jugs were made.

Robert Hall continuously experimented with ways to economically use a single-fire process to produce lead-free glaze. He finally was successful in 1911 when he developed whiteware that was strong, non-porous, and craze-proof. At first the new product was used for institutional wares, then eventually for the Gold Decorated teapot line.

By 1930 Hall acquired a new plant which was expanded many times during the 1930s and 1940s. Hall manufactured dinnerwares, kitchenwares, refrigerator wares, teapots, and coffeepots. Pieces were either hand painted or decorated by transferring decals or prints. Most pieces had identifying backstamps, although a wide variety of marks was used by the company.

Autumn Leaf, developed in 1933 as a premium line for the Jewel Tea Company, was used first on mixing bowls and other kitchenwares. In 1936 it became Hall's first decal-decorated dinnerware when it was offered as a breakfast set.

The line eventually included many different patterns, several shapes, and a large assortment of kitchenwares, accessories, and even clocks. New items were added and older pieces discontinued until 1976. Other companies used Autumn Leaf decals, including Columbia, Crown, Harker, American Limoges, Paden City, and Vernon.

Other Hall dinnerware patterns included Blue Bonnet, made for Standard Coffee Company from the early 1950s until the mid 1950s; Crocus (mid 1930s); Mums (late 1930s); Orange Poppy, made for the Great American Tea Company (1933–1950s); Pastel Morning Glory (late 1930s); Red Poppy, a Grand Union Tea Company premium (mid 1930s to mid 1950s); and Silhouette, made with an all-black decal for Cook Coffee and Standard Coffee (1930s). Taylor, Smith, and Taylor and Harker also used the Silhouette decals. Monticello and Mount Vernon, designed by J. Palin Thorley, were made with the Sears, Roebuck and Company Harmony House label from 1941–1959. Eva Zeisel designed the Hallcraft line in the early 1950s, and she also designed kitchenwares.

The Medallion kitchenware line was introduced in 1932 in ivory and lettuce. Other colors and shapes were added, as were decals. Hall continued to introduce numerous kitchenware lines over the next twenty years. Refrigerator Ware was made for general retail sales, as well as in exclusive designs for General Electric, Sears, Roebuck and Company, Hotpoint, Montgomery Ward, and Westinghouse. This line included water bottles or servers, leftovers or refrigerator boxes, and covered butters.

A wide assortment of figural teapots was part of the Gold Decorated line. Novelty teapots from 1938 were shaped like automobiles, baskets, birdcages, donuts, footballs, and basketballs. Aladdin dates from 1939. Coffeepots also were made in numerous shapes and some were sold to Enterprise, Tricolator, and Westinghouse. Hall made the coffeepot bodies for the Drip-o-lator sold by the Enterprise Aluminum Company.

Additional wares included beer sets, punch sets, Tom and Jerry sets, watering cans, advertising and promotional items, some items for hotels and restaurants, and china bodies for lamps.

References: Jo Cunningham, *The Autumn Leaf Story,* Haf-a-Production, 1976; Harvey Duke, *Superior Quality Hall China,* ELO Books, 1977; ———, *Hall 2,* ELO Books, 1985; Margaret and Kenn Whitmyer, *The Collector's Encyclopedia of Hall China,* Collector Books, 1989, 1992 value update.

Collectors' Club: National Autumn Leaf Collectors Club, Beverly Robbins, 7346 Shamrock Drive, Indianapolis IN, 46217, $20 per year, monthly newsletter.

Newsletters: Hall China Connection, P.O. Box 401, Pollock Pines, CA 95726; *Hall China Encore,* quarterly, Kim Boss, editor, 317 North Pleasant Street, No. YP, Oberlin, OH 44074-1113.

ARLINGTON PATTERN

Bread and Butter Plate	2.00
Cream and Sugar, E-line	27.00
Dinner Plate	4.00
Luncheon Plate	3.00

AUTUMN LEAF

Bowl	
5½" d	6.00
6" d, Radiance	5.00
7½" d, Radiance	20.00
9" d, Radiance	20.00
Butter	
¼ lb	195.00
1 lb, Cov	375.00
Cake Plate, 9¼" d, metal stand	110.00
Canister, 8¼" h	25.00
Casserole, Cov, 8½" d	35.00
Coffee Mug	38.00
Coffeepot	
Electric	300.00
Rayed, 9 cup, w/metal insert	90.00
Cookie Jar, tab handles	140.00
Cream and Sugar, early style	50.00
French Baker, 4" d	15.00
Fruit Dish	5.00
Gravy Boat	15.00
Pitcher	
6" h	15.00
8" h	62.00
Plate	
7¼" d	7.00
9" d	11.00
Platter, 13½" l, oval	22.00
Shakers, ruffled, pr	16.00
Sifter	200.00
Souffle, 10 oz	35.00
Soup Plate, 8½" d	12.00
Teapot, Aladdin	100.00
Teapot Infuser	8.00
Vegetable Bowl, Cov, oval	35.00

Chamberstick, 3" h, Autumn Leaf pattern, manufactured for National Autumn Leaf Collector Club, pr, $135.00

Dinner Plate, 9" d, Autumn Leaf pattern, $11.00

BLUE BLOSSOM PATTERN
Bean Pot, New England 185.00
BLUE BOUQUET PATTERN
Bowl, 8" d 45.00
Casserole, Sunshine 60.00
Creamer
    Boston... 15.00
    Mary Lou 15.00
Cup and Saucer 2.00
Plate
    7" d.. 10.00
    9¼" d.. 15.00
Platter, 11¼" l 22.00
Salad Bowl, 8¾" d............................. 16.00
Sugar Bowl 18.00
BLUE GARDEN PATTERN
Batter Jug 145.00
Casserole, Sundial, #1
    Blue trim 60.00
    Red trim 60.00
CAMEO ROSE
Bowl, 5¼" d 4.00
Cream and Sugar 22.00
Gravy Boat 15.00
Plate
    7¼" d.. 5.00
    9⅛" d.. 6.00
Platter
    11½" l... 22.00
    13½" l... 44.00
Teapot 35.00
Vegetable Bowl, 9" l 18.00
Vegetable Server, Cov......................... 65.00
CLOVER
Shakers, handled 45.00
CROCUS PATTERN
Ball Jug, #3 .... 75.00
Bowl, Radiance
    6" d.. 12.00
    9" d.. 20.00
Butter Dish, 1 lb 575.00
Casserole, Radiance............................ 40.00

Cup and Saucer 13.00
Fruit Bowl, 5½" d 6.00
Plate
    6" d.. 3.00
    7¼" d.. 3.00
    9" d.. 9.00
Platter
    11½" l... 18.00
    13½" l... 17.00
Pretzel Jar 95.00
Teapot
    Medallion 110.00
    New York.. 150.00
    Terrace... 100.00
Vegetable Bowl, oval 20.00
EVA ZEISEL DESIGNS, TOMORROW'S CLASSICS
Bouquet pattern
Vegetable Bowl
    Sq 16.00
    Tab 15.00
Caprice pattern
Gravy Boat 15.00
Fantasy pattern
Bowl
    8¾" sq 28.00
    9" d.. 40.00
Cup and Saucer 15.00
Plate
    6" d.. 6.00
    11" d.. 15.00
Platter
    15" d.. 50.00
    17½" d.. 60.00
Frost Flowers pattern
Service for 8 w/5 serving pieces 275.00
Harlequin pattern
Cream and Sugar 20.00
Gravy Boat 18.00
Jug, 1¼ qt 20.00
Mulberry pattern
Platter, 15" l..................................... 14.00
Vegetable Bowl, 8¾" sq 15.00
Spring pattern
Gravy Boat 20.00
GOLDEN CLOVER PATTERN
Casserole, #65 .... 30.00
GOLDEN GLO PATTERN
Teapot, Aladdin shape, metallic gold.. 45.00
HEATHER ROSE PATTERN
Plate, 7¼" d...................................... 4.00
Soup Bowl 4.00
KITCHEN WARE
Blue Garden pattern
Batter Bowl, Saf-handle 195.00
Casserole, #4 Saf-handle..................... 35.00
Leftover, loop handle.......................... 110.00
Five Band shape
Jug, 5" h, green 20.00
Gold Polka Dot pattern
Casserole, Cov, 8¾" d 22.00

Royal Rose pattern

Mixing Bowl 13.00

Shaggy Tulip pattern

Coffeepot, Drip-o-lator 50.00

Sundial shape

Creamer, brown............................... 20.00
Dish, Cov, yellow 20.00

MONTICELLO PATTERN

Plate

6½" d.. 3.00
8" d.. 4.00

MORNING GLORY PATTERN

Bowl

6¼" d.. 12.00
7½" d.. 13.00
Pretzel Jar 55.00

MT. VERNON PATTERN

Bread and Butter Plate 4.00
Cereal Bowl.................................... 6.00
Cream and Sugar 12.00
Cup and Saucer 12.00
Dinner Plate 8.00
Platter, 11¼" l 10.00
Salad Plate..................................... 4.00

ORANGE POPPY PATTERN

Bean Pot, New England 70.00
Casserole, oval, 8" l 30.00
Creamer.. 6.00
French Baker 18.00
Pitcher

5½" h.. 19.00
6½" h.. 28.00
Pretzel Jar 95.00
Salad Bowl, 9" d............................... 15.00
Shakers, loop, pr 45.00
Sugar Bowl 12.00
Teapot

Great American shape.................... 125.00
Melody shape 110.00
Streamline shape.......................... 200.00

RADIANCE PATTERN

Bowl, 7½" d, red, #4 .... 9.00
Salad Bowl, 9" d, red, #5 .... 14.00

RED POPPY PATTERN

Baker, French flute............................ 20.00
Bowl, 9" d 16.00
Cake Plate 25.00
Cereal Dish..................................... 12.00
Coffeepot, Daniel 35.00
Cream and Sugar 25.00
Cup and Saucer 7.50
Milk Jug 35.00
Plate

6½" d.. 5.00
7½" d.. 7.00
9¼" d.. 12.00
Platter

11¼" l.. 25.00
13¼" l.. 30.00

Salad Bowl 14.00
Shakers

Handle.. 30.00
Teardrop 35.00
Soup Plate 24.00

REFRIGERATOR WARE

General Electric

Casserole, Cov, 8½" d, gray w/yellow
lid 20.00
Leftover, gray w/yellow lid

4" d.. 8.00
6" d.. 15.00
6¾" d.. 15.00
Water Server, gray body, yellow
top 45.00

Hotpoint

Leftover

4¾" sq

Gray 40.00
Orange 15.00
Red... 15.00
5¾" sq

Dark green 20.00
Gray 20.00
6¾" d, dark green 25.00
6¾" sq, dark green 25.00
7¾" d, maroon.............................. 30.00
8" sq

Light yellow.................................. 25.00
Maroon 35.00
9¼" sq, warm yellow 25.00
Water Server, blue w/original cork
stopper... 85.00

Montgomery Ward

Leftover, large rect, ivory 60.00

Sears

Leftover, 3 sections, cadet blue and
white.. 50.00

Westinghouse

ADONIS

Leftover, round, blue and yellow 40.00
Water Pitcher, 7¼" h, blue w/yellow
lid and int 38.00

GENERAL

Butter Dish

Blue 15.00
Dark green 40.00
Leftover, rect

Orange 30.00
Yellow 30.00

HERCULES

Butter Dish, yellow 40.00
Leftover, rect

Green 30.00
Ivory 30.00
Water server, tan............................. 65.00
Leftover Jar, rect, delphinium 15.00
Phoenix water server, delphinium....... 35.00

RICHMOND PATTERN

Platter, 11½" l, Harmony House......... 18.00

ROSE PARADE PATTERN

Bean Pot	35.00
Bowl, straight sides	
7½" d, #1259	12.00
9" d	30.00
Casserole, 2 handles	35.00
Pitcher, 6½" h, #1259	18.00
Shakers, 5" h, handled, blue, pr	50.00
Teapot	48.00

ROYAL ROSE PATTERN

Casserole, Cov	35.00
Shakers, pr	22.00

SERENADE PATTERN

Cream and Sugar	16.00

SILHOUETTE PATTERN

Baker, French, fluted	20.00
Beverage Mug	35.00
Bowl	
8" d	24.00
9" d	30.00
Casserole, Cov., Medallion	30.00
Cream and Sugar, Medallion	45.00
Pepper Shaker, Medallion	15.00
Pretzel Jar	90.00
Salad Bowl, 9" d	25.00
Shakers, teardrop, pr	50.00
Teapot, Five Band	50.00

SPRINGTIME PATTERN

Bread and Butter Plate	5.00
Cake Plate	18.00
Cereal Bowl	5.00
Creamer	10.00
Cup and Saucer	5.00
Dinner Plate	6.00
Fruit Dish	6.00
Gravy Boat	12.00
Platter, 11¾" l	12.00
Salad Plate	5.00
Soup Plate	8.00
Sugar Bowl, Cov	15.00

TEAPOTS

Airflow

Black and gold	65.00
Canary	60.00
Cobalt	60.00
Daffodil and gold, 8 cup	55.00
Maroon	60.00
Turquoise and gold	50.00

Albany

6 cup, mahogany and gold	45.00

Aladdin

Oval opening	
Black and gold	60.00
Matte black w/white top and handle, gold trim	75.00
Round opening, 6 cup w/infuser	
Black and gold	60.00
Canary and gold	50.00
Chartreuse and gold	50.00

Cobalt and gold	60.00
Med blue and gold	50.00

Automobile

Black	850.00
Canary	775.00
Daffodil	775.00
Red	475.00

Basketball

Cadet blue	375.00
Red	800.00
Yellow w/gold trim	495.00

Boston, 6 cup

Pink	40.00
White w/blue flowers	139.00

Bowknot

Pink	45.00

Bowling Ball

Turquoise	1200.00

Cleveland

Green and gold	75.00

Coverlet

Yellow w/silver cov	40.00
White w/gold cov	40.00

Cube, 2 cup

Brown	45.00
Emerald	60.00

Donut

Red	389.00

Flare Ware

Autumn leaf	45.00
Matte chestnut brown	35.00

Football

Blue	550.00
Yellow	650.00

French

Cadet blue and gold, 6 cup	35.00
Cobalt and gold, 4 cup	65.00
Matte black and gold	55.00
Yellow gold w/floral design	45.00

Globe

6 cup Addison gold, dripless, #0823	35.00

Hollywood

Chartreuse and gold	40.00
Maroon	35.00
Red	75.00

Hook Cover

Light blue and gold	40.00

Kansas

Yellow w/gold trim	189.00

Los Angeles

Canary and gold	40.00
Cobalt	35.00
Cobalt and gold	65.00
Yellow	35.00

Manhattan

Green	40.00

McCormick, w/infuser

Maroon	30.00
Turquoise	20.00

Melody, 6 cup

Cobalt and gold	400.00
Emerald	400.00
Red	400.00
Yellow and gold	400.00

Moderne

Canary and gold	40.00
Yellow	20.00

Nautilus

Daffodil and gold	240.00

New York

Blue turquoise ground w/gold accents, 2 cup, 0689	27.50

Ohio

Brown w/gold	80.00

Parade

Canary w/gold trim	32.00

Pert

6 cup, yellow	65.00

Philadelphia, 5 cup

Cobalt	65.00
Ivory	30.00

Rhythm

Canary	90.00
Red	60.00

Star

Yellow and gold	79.00

Streamline

Yellow	23.00

Sundial

Canary	55.00
Pink and gold	90.00

T Ball

Canary, sq	60.00

Thorley

Apple, white w/pheasant decal	179.00
Grape, white w/rhinestone	225.00

Twin Spouts

Cobalt	115.00
Cobalt and gold	105.00
Green	60.00

Victorian Style

Birch, light blue	45.00
Connie, light green	45.00
Plume, pink	45.00

Windshield

Maroon	35.00
White w/gold polka dots	60.00

TEA TILES

5" d, maroon	30.00

6" d

Canary and gold	30.00
Ivory w/red border	30.00
Marine blue	25.00
Matte black and gold	30.00
Old rose and gold	30.00

TULIP

Coffeepot, Deca-plain	35.00
Platter, 13½" l	20.00

Tea Tile, 6" d, Silhouette pattern, $90.00

WHITE ROSE PATTERN

Creamer, blue and white	20.00
Mixing Bowl, blue and white	
7½" d	35.00
8½" d	45.00
Salt and Pepper, blue and white	12.00
Sugar Bowl, blue and white	28.00

WILD POPPY PATTERN

Jug, Cov, Radiance, #3	40.00
Tea Tile, 6" d	70.00

MISCELLANEOUS

Coffeepots

Basketweave, white	50.00

Drip-o-lator

Bricks and Ivy, white	45.00
Sash, white and red	95.00
Waverly, white	60.00
Ritz, black w/green lid	65.00
Sanka	20.00

Terrace

Red and white	65.00
Red, white, and blue	65.00

Tricolator

Buchanan, green	60.00
Diver, right pour, white w/floral pattern	50.00
Ritz, black w/red top	75.00
Washington, 7" h, green and gold	50.00
Punch Set, bowl, ladle, 12 cups, "Old Crow"	175.00

Coffeepot, 8½" h, Meltdown, orange-red, silver, and white, $55.00

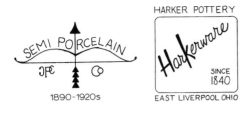

HARKER POTTERY

SINCE
1840

EAST LIVERPOOL OHIO

1890-1920s

HOTOVEN

HARKER
THE OLDEST
POTTERY IN
AMERICA
COOKINGWARE

HARKER POTTERY COMPANY
East Liverpool, Ohio
1840–1930
Chester, West Virginia
1931–1972

History: When Benjamin Harker, Sr., came to the United States from England, he sold clay to James Bennett and other potteries, then decided in 1840 to use the materials to make his own wares. That was the beginning of Harker Pottery, the oldest continually run pottery in the United States. For more than one hundred years, the Harker and Boyce families were involved with pottery in East Liverpool, Ohio, and much later, in Chester, West Virginia.

John Goodwin was hired to run the pottery and teach Harker's sons, George S. and Benjamin, Jr., the pottery business. When Ben Sr. retired, he sold the property to his sons. Over the years, many American potters worked at Harker before eventually opening their own establishments.

From 1840–1946, there was no recorded name for the firm. It made yellowwares and Rockingham pieces. From 1846 until 1851, when James Taylor was in partnership with the Harker sons, the firm made yellowwares and Rockingham ware pieces. The firm name was Harker, Taylor, and Company although for a time it was called Etruria Pottery. Pieces were impressed or embossed with those names.

From 1851–1877, there was a confusing collection of partners and firm names when the brothers split up and then rejoined. Artisans continued to come from England to work at the factory. When George died in 1864, David Boyce,

his brother-in-law, ran the pottery until George's sons were old enough to take over. During this period the company continued to manufacture utilitarian yellowwares that were either glazed or decorated with colored bands or sponging. Mugs, bowls, nappies, milk and baking pans, plates, and such were made. Rockingham products included hound-handled pitchers, Toby jugs, spaniel dogs, ewers, spittoons, mugs, and basins.

In 1877 W.W. Harker and his brother Hal sold their interest in the firm to George's sons. By 1881 the company began to make whiteware table, cooking, and sanitary pieces with clay imported from other areas instead of yellowwares and Rockingham made with buff-burning clay.

Utilitarian, everyday wares continued to be Harker's strong point. Early shapes were given names such as Bedford, Dixie, Cable, Waverly, Lorain, and Fairfax. Sanitary wares consisted of ewers, basins, toothbrush holders, shaving mugs, feeders for invalids and infants, and such. Transfer printing was used to decorate the early whitewares, while colored and metallic embellishments followed later.

The George S. Harker Company was incorporated as Harker Pottery in 1898. Before this time there had been a series of floods when the Ohio River was too high and transportation problems when the river was too low. When Harker needed to expand, it purchased the National China plant and a Homer Laughlin factory. When more room was needed, it followed other East Liverpool factories across the river to Chester, West Virginia, where conditions were better since that area was safe from floods and had room for expansion. In 1930 Harker formed the Columbia China Company, using the Statue of Liberty in color or monochrome as its trademark. A year later Harker purchased the old Knowles pottery but retained the East Liverpool address and mark.

During the Depression years, Harker tried to keep its workers busy as best it could. Its wares were sold in department stores and used as premiums for other businesses. Columbia survived until 1955, and made its most famous pattern, Autumn Leaf, for the Jewel Tea Company.

Harker usually applied decals over the glaze. Since the best decals came from Germany and were sold through catalogs, other potteries sometimes duplicated Harker patterns, although some decals were exclusive to Harker.

A tremendous number of souvenir pieces, as well as advertising giveaways, were made at Harker. Ashtrays were among the favorite souvenir pieces. Plates were frequently advertising pieces, as were pitchers, refrigerator jugs, jars, and plaques. Numerous giftwares also were made.

Harker kitchenwares, including HotOven (introduced in 1926), Bakerite (1935), and Sun-Glow (1937), are very popular with collectors. The company expanded its dinnerware production with floral-decorated lines and Colonial Lady, a silhouette pattern. Harker's Gadroon (1949), its most versatile and best-recognized shape, had a ropelike pattern on the edge of each piece.

However, Harker is best known for the intaglio line called Cameoware, which features a white pattern that appears to be carved out of the colored surface. George Bauer brought this design with him from Europe in 1939 and the process was patented in 1941. The first Cameoware pieces were made in the Dainty Blue pattern, but the line was expanded to include other patterns, a variety of shapes and dinnerwares, and pink and yellow colors. Other intaglio lines included Dainty Flower, which was made in almost every Harker shape, White Rose, made for Montgomery Ward and marked "Carv-Kraft," Wild Rice, Vine, Wheat, Engraved Rooster, and Cock O'Morn. Paul Pinney worked at Harker from 1940 until its closing and he supervised the colors for Cameoware and the other intaglio patterns.

During the 1950s Russel Wright made his first patterned dinnerware line for Harker called White Clover. It came in four colors. Stone china was introduced in the 1950s and 1960s. Pieces made from the heavy gray stoneware were decorated with the intaglio process or with decals or were dipped in white or solid-colored pastels.

Harker continued to expand and introduced new shapes after World War II. Sales were excellent in the early 1950s, but it was possible to see problems ahead. Production and personnel costs continued to rise, plastics were increasingly popular, and cheaper imports were forcing American potteries to struggle for market share. Harker Pottery was sold to the Jeanette Glass Company in 1969. To stimulate sales, Jeanette revived the Rockingham wares and made hound-handle pitchers, Rebekah-at-the-Well teapots, and Toby jugs.

In 1972, Harker Pottery closed. For a time before it burned down in 1975, the plant was used by Ohio Valley Stoneware.

References: Neva W. Colbert, *The Collector's Guide to Harker Pottery U.S.A.*, Collector Books, 1993; William C. Gates and Dana E. Ormerod, *The East Liverpool Ohio Pottery District: Identification of Manufacturers and Marks*, The Society for Historical Archaeology, 1982.

Museum: Museum of Ceramics, East Liverpool, OH.

AMY PATTERN
Cake Plate, 10½" H-H **8.00**

Casserole, Cov	**12.00**
Pie Plate	**18.00**
Pie Lifter	**15.00**
Rolling Pin	**95.00**
Salad Fork and Spoon	**35.00**
Shakers, pr	**12.00**
Sugar Scoop	**35.00**
Teapot	**22.00**

BLACK-EYED SUSAN PATTERN
Bread and Butter Plate	**3.00**
Dinner Plate	**5.00**

CAMEOWARE
Cock O'Morn pattern
Cup and Saucer	**4.00**
Dinner Plate	**6.00**
Luncheon Plate	**4.00**
Platter, 11½" l	**10.00**

Daisy pattern
Syrup Jug, yellow and white daisy	**15.00**

Dogwood pattern
Bread and Butter Plate, pink cocoa	**2.00**
Dinner Plate, pink cocoa	**3.00**

Bowl, 7³/₈" d, white, Cameoware, Dainty Flower pattern on blue ground, "Harker Pottery Co., Patented USA" mark, $28.00

Plate, 7¼" d, white, Cameoware, Dogwood pattern on pink cocoa ground, $3.00

Everglades pattern

Cup and Saucer, Harmony House label	7.00
Dinner Plate	5.00
Luncheon Plate	4.00
Salad Plate	4.00

Ivy Wreath pattern

Creamer	6.00
Cup and Saucer	3.00
Dinner Plate	4.00
Luncheon Plate	4.00

Provincial Tulip pattern

Cup and Saucer	3.00
Dinner Plate	4.00
Luncheon Plate	5.00
Platter	8.00

Rose pattern

Bread and Butter Plate, blue and white rose	5.00
Casserole, Cov, blue and white rose	28.00
Coffeepot, drip type, white rose, pink ground	60.00
Grease Jar, blue and white rose	18.00
Jug, Cov, blue and white rose	40.00
Pie Baker, blue and white rose	25.00
Plate, 10" d, blue and white rose	10.00
Platter, 11¾" l, rect, blue and white rose	18.00
Rolling Pin, pink and white rose	65.00
Shakers, pink and white rose, pr	8.00
Teapot, pink and white rose	45.00
Tea Tile, blue and white rose	25.00

Springtime pattern

Cup and Saucer	3.00
Dinner Plate	5.00
Platter, 11½" l, rect	10.00
Salad Plate	4.00

CHERRY BLOSSOM PATTERN

Dinner Plate	8.50

CHESTERTON PATTERN

Berry Bowl, gray	3.00
Bowl, 9" d	8.00
Bread and Butter Plate, gray	2.00
Cream and Sugar, gray	13.00
Cup and Saucer, gray	5.00
Dinner Plate, gray	5.00
Platter, 13½" d, gray	12.00
Soup Plate, gray	8.00

COLONIAL LADY PATTERN

Cake Lifter	22.00
Casserole, Cov	30.00
Cereal Bowl, tab	5.00
Condiment Set w/wire rack	50.00
Cup and Saucer	5.00
Custard Cup	2.00
Dinner Plate	5.00
Lunch Plate	4.00
Pie Plate	20.00
Salad Plate	3.00

COLUMBIAN PATTERN

Pie Lifter	18.00

CORINTHIAN PATTERN

Bread and Butter Plate	2.00
Cream and Sugar	6.00
Cup and Saucer	3.00
Dinner Plate	4.00
Gravy Boat, w/undertray	6.00
Salad Plate	3.00
Soup Bowl	5.00
Vegetable Bowl, 9½" l	6.00

CURRIER AND IVES PATTERN

Cake Set, cake plate, lifter, 6 dessert plates	35.00

DECO DAHLIA PATTERN

Cake Plate, 11½" H-H	15.00
Casserole, Cov, 5¼" h, 6½" d	20.00
Hot Plate, 6½" d, oct	20.00
Platter, 11" l	10.00
Teapot, 6¼" h	30.00

DRESDEN DUCHESS PATTERN

Cake Set, cake plate, 4 dessert plates, 7¼" d, Royal Gadroon shape	15.00

EARLY AMERICAN PATTERN

Cup and Saucer	3.00
Dinner Plate	6.00
Salad Plate	4.00
Tray, 12" H-H	12.00

IVY PATTERN

Cup and Saucer	4.00
Dinner Plate	3.00
Serving Bowl	6.00

LAURELTON PATTERN

Cake Plate, gray	5.00
Cup and Saucer, green	3.00
Dinner Plate, green	5.00
Luncheon Plate, green	4.00

MALLOW PATTERN

Berry Bowl	4.00
Bowl, 7¼" d	8.00
Bread and Butter Plate	5.00
Cup and Saucer	7.00

Dinner Plate, Mallow pattern, $5.00

Custard Cup..	6.00
Mixing Bowl	8.00
Pie Plate	9.00
Platter, 12" H-H	25.00
Salad Plate	6.00
Shakers, pr	20.00
Soup Bowl	7.00
Teapot	25.00

MODERN AGE SHAPE, ASSORTED DECALS

Cake Plate, 10¾" d............................	22.00
Mixing Bowl, 8½" d	10.00

MODERN TULIP PATTERN

Bowl

4¼" d...	3.00
5¼" d...	4.00
6" d...	6.00
Creamer...	7.00
Custard Cup......................................	2.00
Mixing Bowl, 9" d.............................	15.00
Pie Lifter	15.00
Shakers, pr	6.00
Sugar Bowl	7.00

MONTEREY ZEPHYR PATTERN

Casserole, Cov	8.00

Platter

9½" d..	9.00
11¼" d..	10.00

PASTEL TULIP PATTERN

Pie Baker, 9" d	12.00

PETIT FLEUR PATTERN

Cup and Saucer	6.00
Dinner Plate	10.00

PETIT POINT ROSE PATTERN

Cake Plate	4.00
Casserole, Cov, dbl	10.00
Pie Baker, 9" d	20.00
Pie Plate	6.00

Plate

8" d...	4.00
9" d...	10.00
Teapot	30.00

RED APPLE II PATTERN

Bowl, 8¾" d	18.00
Cup and Saucer, oversized	14.00
Platter, 14" l, Modern Age shape	22.00
Teapot	30.00
Utility Plate, 12" H-H, Virginia shape .	14.00

ROCKINGHAM

Mug, Davy Crockett, "Rockingham Harker Pottery #1840" mark............	25.00
Pitcher, hound handle, lg size.............	25.00
Teapot, 9½" h, Rebekah-at-the-Well design	275.00

ROLLING PIN

Calico Tulip pattern	85.00
Columbian pattern	100.00
Kelvinator	95.00
Lovelace pattern	75.00
Mallow pattern	110.00
Morning Glory pattern	95.00
Petit Point I pattern	95.00

Plaid Tulips pattern	80.00
Red Apple pattern	40.00
Seated Mexican decal	68.00

ROYAL DRESDEN PATTERN

Cake Plate, 12" H-H	8.00

TULIP PATTERN

Pie Baker	5.00

TULIP PATTERN, ORANGE

Bread and Butter Plate	2.00

Cake Plate

Round	5.00
Square...	5.00
Cake Lifter	5.00
Casserole, Cov, 8" d	35.00
Cereal Bowl	3.00
Chop Plate, 11½" d	8.00
Cream and Sugar	8.00
Cup and Saucer	3.00
Salad Plate	2.00
Salt and Pepper.................................	4.00
Soup Bowl	3.00
Teapot	10.00

WATER LILY PATTERN

Dinner Plate	5.00
Luncheon Plate	3.00

WILD ROSE PATTERN

Cake Lifter	10.00
Cake Plate	25.00

MISCELLANEOUS

Bowl

9" d, pale purple grapes w/red-brown and green leaves and shaded blue ground, luster finish, bow and arrow mark	10.00
9⅛" d, decal of child and puppy w/"Stop, Look, and Listen, Compliments of Mackey State Bank, Mackey, Indiana," vert fluted border, green rim, bow and "HP & Co." mark	14.00
Pitcher and Bowl, pitcher, 11" h, bowl, 17" d, Klondike pattern, rose-colored florals, gold trim, semi-vitrous ware	75.00

Plate

9" d, decal of 3 ocean fish in center, shaded green border and rim, bow mark	17.00

9¼" d

Gold 1907 calendar in center, multicolored Santa at top, holly leaves and berries on border, gold "Seasons Greetings, Utica, N.Y." on front	29.00
Stag on right side, shaded yellow, green, and brown on left, bow mark	6.00
9½" d, 2 groups of cherries hanging from branch, cream-yellow ground shaded to turquoise border, gold rim, bow mark	5.00

IROQUOIS CHINA COMPANY
Syracuse, New York
1905–1969

History: From 1905–1939 George Bowman controlled the Iroquois China Company where semi-porcelains were made. In 1939 the firm was sold by the bank to Earl Crane who made hotel wares until 1946 when Casual China, designed by Russel Wright, was introduced in a wide assortment of colors. In 1953 a mottled glaze effect called "Raindrop" was added to Casual China. Primarily floral decorations were added in 1959 and cookwares also were made. Two other important lines were Informal and Impromptu, designed by Ben Seibel. During the late 1950s or early 1960s, Iroquois dropped hotel wares and concentrated on these three popular lines.

In 1947 Iroquois built a plant in Puerto Rico and manufactured under the name Crane China Company. The plant was acquired by the Sterling China Company in the early 1950s, and the name was changed to Caribe China. This plant closed in 1977.

Financial problems during the late 1960s caused Iroquois to go in and out of production, but nothing was made after 1969. The plant was sold to a wood-working company in 1971. A wide variety of marks was used by Iroquois.

AUTUMN PATTERN

Cream and Sugar **12.00**

Soup Bowl, 7³/₄" d, Informal pattern, turquoise and mint green flowers, brown stems, white ground, yellow back, $12.00

Cup and Saucer	10.00
Dinner Plate	8.00
Platter, 12" d....................................	18.00
Salad Plate.......................................	5.00
Salt and Pepper..................................	6.00
Vegetable Bowl, 10½" d.....................	16.00

IMPROMPTU PATTERN

Bowl, 7⅛" l, 6⅛" w...........................	8.00
Butter Dish, Cov, white.......................	22.00
Coffeepot, 10" h, white w/rose decal ..	12.00
Cruet Set, 4 piece, white.....................	45.00
Platter, 14" l, white w/green ends	20.00

INFORMAL PATTERN

Coffee Server, geometric design	28.00
Creamer, 6" h, Harvest Time decal	8.00
Cup and Saucer, blue and white	15.00
Gravy Boat, w/stand, blue and white ..	25.00
Sugar Bowl, avocado and white w/white lid	12.00

INTERPLAY PATTERN

Casserole, Cov, 17" H-H, oval	34.00

EDWIN M.KNOWLES
CHINA CO.
15 1 11
1915

THE EDWIN M. KNOWLES CHINA-CO
MADE IN U.S.A.
36-4

EDWIN M. KNOWLES CHINA COMPANY
Chester and Newell, West Virginia
1900–1963

History: Edwin Knowles and several others started the Knowles China Company in Chester, West Virginia, in 1900. By 1913, the company offices were located in East Liverpool, Ohio, and a second plant was built in Newell, West Virginia. Both plants operated until 1931 when the Chester plant was sold to the Harker Pottery Company, and all operations moved to the Newell plant.

Semi-vitreous dinner services, toilet wares, cuspidors, and covered jars were made in a tremendous variety of shapes and patterns. By 1940 Edwin M. Knowles was the third-largest china company in the United States. A series of marks was used during the long history of the company.

The company closed in 1963 due to competition from inexpensive foreign imports.

ANN ANNCRAME PATTERN

Vegetable Bowl, oval, w/undertray	**27.00**

BLUEBELL PATTERN

Bowl	
8³/₄" d...	**10.00**
10" d..	**12.00**
Bread and Butter Plate	**2.00**
Creamer...	**3.00**
Cup and Saucer	**4.00**
Dinner Plate	**4.00**
Gravy Boat	**3.00**
Shakers, pr..	**8.00**
Sugar Bowl, Cov	**5.00**

BUTTERCUP PATTERN

Cereal Bowl.......................................	**4.00**
Dinner Plate	**12.00**
Salad Plate..	**6.00**
Sauce Dish	**5.00**
Vegetable Bowl, oval	**10.00**

CARLTON PATTERN

Bread and Butter Plate	**4.00**
Cup and Saucer	**5.00**
Dinner Plate	**6.00**

CLASSIC SATIN PATTERN, YELLOW BORDER W/GOLD OVERLAY

Berry Dish	**1.00**
Creamer...	**5.00**
Cup and Saucer	**2.00**
Dinner Plate	**6.00**
Gravy Boat, w/attached undertray.......	**8.00**
Platter, 15¹/₂" l	**15.00**
Soup Bowl	**3.00**
Sugar Bowl, Cov	**8.00**
Vegetable Bowl, 8³/₄" d......................	**10.00**

COUNTRY LIFE PATTERN, BLUE

Bread and Butter plate	**3.00**
Cup and Saucer	**5.00**
Custard Cup.......................................	**3.00**
Dinner Plate	**4.00**
Soup Plate	**4.00**

DAMASK ROSE PATTERN

Bread and Butter Plate	**1.00**
Cup and Saucer	**3.00**
Dinner Plate	**3.00**
Salad Plate..	**2.00**
Soup Bowl	**3.00**

DEANNA PATTERN

Platter	**20.00**
Sugar Bowl	**8.00**

FRUIT PATTERN

Bowl	
8" d, 4¹/₂" h	**25.00**
9" d, 3¹/₄" h	**25.00**
Casserole, Cov, 8" d	**15.00**

Platter, 13¹/₂" l, Deanna shape, orange glaze, "Edwin Knowles Semi-Vitreous China Co., Made in USA" mark, $20.00

Cream and Sugar	**20.00**
Cup and Saucer	**5.00**
Jug, Cov, 8" h, Utility Ware	**35.00**
Leftover, round, 4" d...........................	**10.00**
Salt and Pepper..................................	**25.00**
Water Server......................................	**30.00**

GOLDEN WHEAT PATTERN, YORKTOWN SHAPE

Creamer...	**4.00**
Dinner Plate	**3.00**
Sugar Bowl, Cov	**6.00**

GRAPEVINE PATTERN

Bread and Butter Plate	**2.00**
Creamer...	**3.00**
Cup and Saucer	**2.00**
Dinner Plate	**4.00**
Platter, 13¹/₄" l	**8.00**
Sugar Bowl, Cov	**4.00**

GRAY LURE PATTERN

Dinner Plate	**2.00**
Tray, 11³/₄" H-H.................................	**3.00**
Vegetable Bowl	**4.00**

HOSTESS PATTERN

Bowl, 6¹/₄" d......................................	**3.00**
Creamer...	**3.00**
Dessert Plate, 6¹/₄" d...........................	**3.00**
Dinner Plate, 9¹/₄" d...........................	**5.00**
Platter, 11¹/₂" l	**10.00**
Sugar Bowl	**5.00**

MAGNOLIA PATTERN

Bowl, Cov...	**25.00**
Bread and Butter Plate	**4.00**
Dinner Plate	**8.00**
Gravy Boat, w/attached undertray.......	**15.00**
Platter, 15" l, 11¹/₂" w, yellow and white magnolias, green trim	**20.00**
Salad Plate, 7" d	**6.00**
Soup Bowl	**6.00**

MODERN PLAID PATTERN

Bread and Butter Plate	**5.00**
Dinner Plate	**6.00**
Salad Plate..	**5.00**

PENTHOUSE PATTERN

Chop Plate	13.00
Dinner Plate	3.00

PICKET FENCE PATTERN

Creamer	10.00
Gravy Boat	10.00
Sugar Bowl, Cov	10.00

PRISCILLA PATTERN

Bowl

8" d, ftd	12.00
10" d	12.00
Chop Plate, 12" d	20.00
Platter, 11½" l	15.00

SEQUOIA PATTERN

Refrigerator Set, cov bowl, 4", 5", 6" d, set of 3	50.00

STARFLOWER PATTERN

Dinner Plate	8.00

TIA JUANA PATTERN

Cup and Saucer	4.00
Dinner Plate	4.00
Salad Plate	3.00
Serving Tray, Utility Ware	10.00

TULIP PATTERN, UTILITY WARE

Bowl, 10¼" d	22.00

WHEAT PATTERN

Berry Bowl	2.00
Cup and Saucer	2.00
Dessert Plate	2.00
Dinner Plate	3.00
Platter, 13" H-H	8.00
Soup Plate	3.00

MISCELLANEOUS

Biscuit Jar, 10¼" h, white ground w/raised floral design, mauve, green, and yellow scattered flowers w/brown leaves and stems, gold streaks, semi-porcelain	45.00
Bone Dish, border band of groups of 3 small pink roses from gold rope swags, light yellow ground, gold rim, set of 4	25.00
Pitcher, 9¾" h, opaque white stoneware	45.00
Plate, 8¼" d, decal of river boat w/"S.S. Admiral on the Mississippi—St. Louis, Mo.," white ground	3.00
Platter, 16" l, 4 groups of purple and yellow irises on border, semi-vitreous body, "Ed. Knowles Ivory" mark	16.00

Wash Set

2 piece, pitcher, 10½" h, bowl, 15½" d, white ironstone	100.00
5 piece, pitcher, 11¾" h, bowl, 16" d, shaving mug, cov slop jar, soap dish w/drain, wide gold band w/narrow gold bands	375.00

GENUINE

H·L·C USA

THE HOMER LAUGHLIN CHINA COMPANY

East Liverpool, Ohio
1871–1929
Newell, West Virginia
1929–Present

History: The Homer Laughlin China Company was founded by Homer and Shakespeare Laughlin in East Liverpool, Ohio, in 1871. Homer bought out Shakespeare in 1877 and continued manufacturing until he sold the company in 1897 to a group headed by Louis Aaron, Aaron's sons, Marcus and Charles, and W.E. Wells. The company still operates with these two families in control.

White granite ware was made as early as 1872, and Laughlin's whiteware won an award at the Centennial Exposition in 1876. Dinnerwares and commercial china became the mainstays of the company, and eventually it became the largest pottery in the world. Expansion was continuous; new plants were added in Newell in 1907, and by 1929 the entire operation had moved across the river to Newell, West Virginia.

Dr. Albert Bleininger, who joined the company in 1920 as ceramics engineer, was responsible for the clays and glazes. Frederick Rhead became art director in 1927 and introduced many new original designs before his death in 1942. Shapes created by Rhead included Liberty which had a gadroon edge on all pieces and was introduced in 1928, Virginia Rose (1929), Century (1931), Fiesta (1936), Nautilus (1935) with a sculptured-shell motif, Harlequin (1936), Brittany (1936), Eggshell Nautilus and Eggshell Georgian (1937), Swing (1938), and Theme made to commemorate the World's Fair in 1939. Don Schreckengost became art director in 1945 and was responsible for modern-looking shapes such as Jubilee, Debutante, Rhythm, and Cavalier.

In 1959 the company diversified into hotel, restaurant, and institutional china, and by the 1970s it was producing more of these wares than china for home use. It is still the largest china manufacturer in the United States.

Homer Laughlin wares were sold through large mail-order firms and department stores, given away as premiums with soaps, breakfast foods, and other household products, and distributed through coupon programs by grocery stores. The company used a tremendous number of shapes over the years and gave each one a name. However, only some patterns were identified by the manufacturer since most were given names by the distributors.

Virginia Rose, the most popular shape, was made from 1929 until the early 1970s and was used for more than a dozen dinnerware patterns that were either decaled or embossed, usually with pale pink roses. After the shape was discontinued for home use, it was adopted by the hotel china division for institutional wares.

Lightweight Eggshell wares came in a diverse assortment of patterns; the solid colored Jubilee was made to commemorate the 75th anniversary of the company; and Rhythm, from the late 1940s, was the first shape to be made on automatic jigger equipment.

Fiesta, in vivid colors with a simple design motif, was designed by Frederick Rhead and introduced in 1936. Concentric bands of rings were the only decorative elements aside from the bright colors—red, dark blue, light green, yellow, and ivory at first. Turquoise was added one year later. Numerous pieces were made in all of these colors until 1943 when "Fiesta red went to war"—the uranium oxide for the red glaze being no longer available. In 1944 turquoise, light green, dark blue, yellow, and old ivory were used, and the 1946 and 1948 price lists indicated the same colors. In 1951 light green, dark blue, and old ivory were retired and replaced by forest green, rose, chartreuse, and gray. These colors, along with the original turquoise and yellow, continued in production until 1959, when Fiesta red returned and rose, gray, chartreuse, and dark green were discontinued. In 1969 Fiesta was restyled, named Fiesta Ironstone, and made in antique gold, turf green, and red, retitled mango red. The red color was discontinued in 1972 and one year later all Fiesta dinnerware production ended.

Fiesta Kitchen Kraft, a bake-and-serve line in production from 1939 until World War II, consisted of utilitarian items in red, yellow, green, and blue. Fiesta was reintroduced in 1986 after a thirteen-year absence and made in cobalt blue, rose, white, apricot, and black with additions of gray and yellow. The "new" Fiesta was made on a vitrified body that was denser and did not absorb moisture. This Fiesta was more appealing to the restaurant trade, although it was still used in private homes. Turquoise, pale yellow, periwinkle blue, and sea mist green were added to the color line.

Harlequin was a less-expensive dinnerware designed by Rhead to be sold through Woolworth's without a trademark. Yellow, green, red, and blue were used along with bands of rings for decoration. Styling was similar to the Art Deco look of Fiesta and additional Fiesta colors were used. Harlequin was discontinued in 1964, reissued at Woolworth's request in 1979, and made for a few additional years. Harlequin animals in six forms and four colors also were sold at Woolworth's from the late 1930s into the early 1940s.

In 1938 Riviera was introduced and sold by the Murphy Company. It was lighter and less expensive than the other colored dinnerwares. Mauve blue, red, yellow, light green, and ivory were the colors used until the line was discontinued prior to 1950.

From 1900 to the present, Homer Laughlin coded almost all of its wares with the month, year, and plant in which the piece was manufactured.

References: Sharon and Bob Huxford, *The Collector's Encyclopedia of Fiesta,* Seventh Edition, Collector Books, 1992; Joanne Jasper, *The Collector's Encyclopedia of Homer Laughlin China,* Collector Books, 1993; Darlene Nossaman, *Homer Laughlin China: An Identification Guide,* privately published, 1992.

Collectors' Clubs: Fiesta Club of America, P.O. Box 15383, Loves Park, IL 61132-5383, quarterly newsletter, $20 per year; The Fiesta Collector's Quarterly, 19238 Dorchester Circle, Strongsville, OH 44136, $12 per year.

Museum: Museum of Ceramics, East Liverpool, OH.

Advertising Plate, 9" d, single rose w/green leaves in center, gold "Compliments of Brekke & Bakken, Faribault, Minn.," gold swag and ribbon border, "Homer Laughlin Hudson" mark **18.00**

AMBERSTONE PATTERN

Bread and Butter Plate	**2.00**
Cup and Saucer	**5.00**
Dinner Plate	**5.00**
Water Pitcher, disc	**25.00**

AMERICANA PATTERN

Bread and Butter Plate	**8.00**
Casserole, Cov	**95.00**
Creamer..	**20.00**
Cup and Saucer	**12.00**
Gravy Boat	**45.00**

Dinner Plate, Apple Blossom pattern, $3.00

Plate

9" d	12.00
10" d	13.00
Soup Bowl	20.00
Sugar Bowl	25.00

AMERICAN PROVINCIAL PATTERN

Cup and Saucer	4.00
Dinner Plate	4.00
Platter, 11½" l	13.00
Salad Plate	3.00
Spoon Rest	75.00

APPLE BLOSSOM PATTERN

Bread and Butter Plate	2.00
Cup and Saucer	5.00
Dinner Plate	3.00
Gravy Boat	4.00
Platter, 13½" l	10.00
Soup Bowl	4.00

ARISTOCRAT PATTERN

Bread and Butter plate	5.00
Creamer and Cov Sugar Bowl	12.00
Cup and Saucer	6.00
Dinner Plate	6.00
Salt and Pepper	8.00
Soup Bowl	5.00

ART CHINA

Ewer, 15" h, Current pattern, applied scrollwork, shaded ivory to dark brown ground 170.00

Mug

4½" h, blue-green grapes on sides, shaded brown ground w/branch handle and thumb rest, "Laughlin Art China" mark 23.00

4¾" h, blue decal of monk drinking from wine bottle, shaded cobalt ground, "Laughlin Art China" mark 35.00

Pitcher

5" h, squat shape, Current pattern ... 75.00

6¼" h

Rose blossom transfer 40.00

White Pets design, blue puppies, shaded blue and brown ground 8¼" d, lobed body, bunches of 45.00

green and red grapes and leaves, shaded brown ground, mkd 75.00

Plate, red and green grapes and leaves in center, shaded brown ground 12.00

Tray, 12" l, 8" w, White Pets design 75.00

Vase, 8⅜" h, 2 handles, White Pets design, white swans, blue-gray to pink shaded ground 95.00

BLACK TULIP DESIGN, SILVER TRIM, "WELLS CENTURY" MARK

Cup and Saucer	5.00
Dinner Plate	8.00
Fruit Bowl	6.00
Platter, 11½" l	12.00
Soup Bowl	8.00

BLUE WILLOW PATTERN

Cup and Saucer	3.00

Plate

9" d	9.00
10" d	10.00
Platter, 13½" l	35.00
Soup Bowl	6.00

CALEDONIA PATTERN

Soup Bowl	3.00

CALAROSE PATTERN

Bread and Butter Plate	2.00
Cup and Saucer	2.00
Salad Plate	3.00

CAMELIA PATTERN

Soup Plate	4.00

CARDINAL PATTERN

Bread and Butter Plate	3.00
Cereal Bowl	4.00
Dinner Plate	4.00
Salad Plate	3.00

CASHMERE PATTERN

Cereal Bowl	4.00
Cup and Saucer	5.00

Plate

6" d	5.00
8" sq	6.00
9¼" d	7.00
Soup Plate	8.00

Gravy Boat w/undertray, Calarose pattern, $24.00

CASUALSTONE PATTERN

Butter Dish	17.00
Dinner Plate	4.00

CENTURY SHAPE

Platter, 13½" l, 10" w, decal of black tulip	18.00

CHATEAU PATTERN

Bread and Butter Plate	2.00
Cup and Saucer	2.00
Dessert Plate	2.00
Gravy Boat	5.00
Platter	
11¼" l	4.00
13¼" l	6.00
Sauce Dish	2.00
Soup Bowl	3.00
Vegetable Bowl, 9¼" l	8.00

CHINESE BUDDHA PATTERN

Baker	9.00
Creamer	8.00
Dinner Plate	5.00
Platter, 11" l	15.00
Sugar Bowl	12.00

CLIVE PATTERN

Soup Plate	6.00

COLONIAL PATTERN, RED-BROWN FLORAL TRANSFERS, EMB BODY

Gravy Boat, "Laughlin China, Semi-Vitreous Colonial" mark	20.00
Vegetable Bowl, Cov, oval	24.00

COLONIAL KITCHEN PATTERN, SWING OR VIRGINIA ROSE SHAPE

Bowl, 5½" d	5.00
Bread and Butter Plate	3.00
Creamer	18.00
Cup and Saucer	4.00
Dinner plate	4.00
Fruit Dish	8.00
Salad Plate	12.00
Soup Plate	6.00
Sugar Bowl, Cov	25.00

CONCHITA PATTERN

Serving Dish, 13½" l, 8" w, 5 sections	55.00

Dinner Plate, Chateau pattern, $3.00

CURRIER AND IVES PATTERN

Creamer	10.00
Cup and Saucer	6.00
Gravy Boat	8.00
Luncheon Plate	6.00
Shakers, pr	10.00
Soup Bowl	9.00
Sugar Bowl	12.00
Vegetable Bowl, 8¾" d	15.00

COUNTESS PATTERN

Creamer	20.00
Plate, 10" d	8.00
Soup Plate	10.00
Sugar Bowl, Cov	30.00

DOGWOOD PATTERN, 1950

Cup and Saucer	3.00
Dinner Plate	4.00
Sauce Dish	3.00
Sugar Bowl	5.00

DOGWOOD PATTERN, RHYTHM SHAPE

Cup and Saucer	12.00
Dinner Plate	9.00
Fruit Bowl	8.00
Salad Plate	6.00
Serving Bowl, 9" d	16.00

DREAMLAND PATTERN

Milk Tankard	195.00
Vase, 3½" h	50.00

DRESDEN EGGSHELL PATTERN

Cup and Saucer	9.00
Dinner Plate	8.00
Soup Bowl	7.00

ENGLISH GARDEN PATTERN

Gravy Boat, w/undertray	28.00
Teapot, 4¾" h, green striping, Century shape	35.00

EPICURE PATTERN

Cup and Saucer	
Pink	16.00
Turquoise	16.00
White	16.00
Plate	
6¼" d	
Charcoal	8.00
Turquoise	8.00
8¼" d, pink	6.00
10" d	
Charcoal	8.00
Pink	8.00
Turquoise	12.00
White	12.00
Shakers, turquoise, pr	20.00
Soup Bowl, 6" d	
Turquoise	12.00
White	12.00

FIESTA

Ashtray	
Chartreuse	45.00
Cobalt	35.00
Ivory	40.00
Red	45.00

Turquoise	29.00
Yellow	26.00
Bowl	
7½" d, red	30.00
8" d, rimmed	
Blue	50.00
Cobalt	50.00
Light green	50.00
Bud Vase	
Cobalt	65.00
Red	65.00
Yellow	39.00
Candleholders, pr	
Bulb shape	
Ivory	47.00
Light green	60.00
Red	60.00
Yellow	47.00
Tripod shape	
Cobalt	225.00
Ivory	275.00
Carafe, yellow	135.00
Casserole, Cov, 8½" d	
Chartreuse	150.00
Cobalt	125.00
Yellow	55.00
Charger, 14" d	
Turquoise	30.00
Yellow	20.00
Chop Plate	
13" d	
Gray	40.00
Ivory	25.00
Red	31.00
Turquoise	25.00
Yellow	21.00
15" d	
Red	50.00
Yellow	32.00
Coffeepot	
Red	220.00
Rose	300.00

Turquoise	110.00
Yellow	95.00
Coffeepot, A.D., ivory	180.00
Compote, 12" d, ftd, yellow	90.00
Cream and Sugar	
Red creamer, yellow sugar, cobalt figure-eight tray	325.00
Yellow creamer, yellow sugar, cobalt figure-eight tray	225.00
Creamer, ring or stick handle	
Med green	45.00
Rose	22.00
Turquoise	12.00
Yellow	14.00
Cream Soup	
Chartreuse	35.00
Cobalt	48.00
Dark green	45.00
Gray	50.00
Ivory	38.00
Red	50.00
Turquoise	22.00
Yellow	36.00
Cup and Saucer	
Gray	45.00
Med green	42.00
Rose	32.00
Cup and Saucer, A.D.	
Cobalt	45.00
Ivory	45.00
Red	52.00
Turquoise	45.00
Yellow	45.00
Eggcup	
Green	25.00
Ivory	39.00
Red	65.00
Turquoise	25.00
Yellow	38.00
Fruit Bowl	
4¾" d	
Chartreuse	20.00
Cobalt	18.00
Ivory	14.00
Med green	350.00
Rose	22.00
Turquoise	14.00
Yellow	13.00
5½" d	
Gray	25.00
Ivory	17.00
Med green	48.00
Red	22.00
Turquoise	17.00
Yellow	17.00
Gravy Boat	
Chartreuse	45.00
Med green	175.00
Rose	35.00
Turquoise	350.00
Jelly Compote	
Ivory	40.00

Carafe, 10" h, Fiesta pattern, orange glaze, imp "Fiesta Made in USA" mark(A), $110.00

Jug, 2 pt
  Chartreuse 70.00
  Gray 80.00
  Ivory 50.00
  Med green 49.00
  Rose 75.00
Kitchen Kraft
Bowl, 10" d, chartreuse 70.00
Cake Plate, 10¾" d, decal of turkey,
  gold rim, set of 7 .... 175.00
Cake Server, light green 75.00
Casserole, Cov, med green 85.00
Jar, Cov
  Cobalt, large 275.00
  Yellow, large 235.00
  Yellow, small 250.00
Jug, Cov
  Cobalt 325.00
  Green 250.00
  Yellow 150.00
Pie Plate, 10" d, light green w/decal ... 40.00
Platter, 13" l, yellow 45.00
Shakers, red, pr 65.00
Stacking Set, refrigerator jars, yellow ... 55.00
Marmalade Jar, med green 125.00
Mixing Bowl
  #4, coral 65.00
  #6, light green 85.00
  #7, light green 150.00
Mug
  Chartreuse 45.00
  Gray 45.00
  Rose 40.00
  Turquoise 30.00
  Yellow 50.00
Mustard Jar
  Cobalt 140.00
  Yellow 100.00
Nappy
  4½" d
    Gray 30.00
    Ivory 30.00
    Rose 45.00
  5½" d
    Gray 30.00
    Ivory 39.00
    Rose 25.00
  8" d
    Cobalt 45.00
    Yellow 45.00
  8½" d
    Chartreuse 32.00
    Gray 36.00
    Med green 85.00
    Rose 35.00
    Yellow 27.00
  9½" d
    Red 50.00
    Turquoise 40.00
    Yellow 33.00
Onion-Soup Bowl, Cov
  Red 525.00

Turquoise 450.00
Yellow 245.00
Pitcher
  Disc, Juice
    Red 45.00
    Yellow 65.00
  Disc, Water
    Chartreuse 135.00
    Cobalt 75.00
    Gray 135.00
    Ivory 60.00
    Light green 95.00
    Med green 355.00
    Red 90.00
    Yellow 55.00
  Ice
    Ivory 60.00
    Red 100.00
    Yellow 75.00
Plate
  6½" d
    Chartreuse 4.50
    Cobalt 5.00
    Ivory 3.50

Water Pitcher, 8" h, Fiesta pattern,
turquoise glaze, "Fiesta, Made in USA"
mark(A), $93.00

Ice Water Pitcher, 6" h, Fiesta pattern,
light green glaze, imp "Fiesta USA"
mark(A), $45.00

Light green	6.00	Soup Plate		
Med green	10.00	Cobalt	32.00	
Red	5.00	Ivory	24.00	
Rose	5.00	Med green	24.00	
Turquoise	3.50	Red	39.00	
Yellow	3.00	Turquoise	24.00	
7" d		Yellow	20.00	
Cobalt	9.00	Sugar Bowl, yellow	10.00	
Gray	10.00	Sugar Bowl, Cov		
Ivory	6.00	Gray	30.00	
Med green	25.00	Light green	32.00	
Red	10.00	Red	595.00	
Turquoise	9.00	Turquoise	20.00	
Yellow	5.50	Syrup Pitcher		
9" d		Cobalt	225.00	
Chartreuse	13.00	Red	250.00	
Dark green	13.00	Turquoise	195.00	
Gray	16.00	Teapot, large		
Ivory	9.00	Cobalt	150.00	
Red	16.00	Green	125.00	
Rose	16.00	Light blue	60.00	
Turquoise	9.00	Teapot, med		
Yellow	8.00	Cobalt	75.00	
10⅜" d		Rose	235.00	
Chartreuse	34.00	Yellow	85.00	
Cobalt	22.00	Tumbler, juice		
Gray	35.00	Cobalt	26.00	
Ivory	22.00	Ivory	22.00	
Med green	39.00	Red	28.00	
Red	22.00	Yellow	20.00	
Rose	28.00	Tumbler, water		
Turquoise	22.00	Cobalt	22.00	
Yellow	18.00	Ivory	15.00	
Plate, Divided		Pink	45.00	
10½" d		Red	35.00	
Cobalt	30.00	Turquoise	15.00	
Ivory	20.00	Yellow	15.00	
Red	34.00	Vase		
Turquoise	21.00	8" h		
Yellow	20.00	Light green	350.00	
11½" d		Turquoise	350.00	
Cobalt	30.00	10" h		
Ivory	25.00	Cobalt	525.00	
Platter		Green	425.00	
12" d		Ivory	450.00	
Cobalt	25.00			
Turquoise	25.00			
13" d, turquoise	24.00			
Relish Tray				
Red	30.00			
Red, w/inserts	180.00			
Turquoise base, mixed colors	165.00			
Salt and Pepper				
Dark green	32.00			
Med green	80.00			
Red	35.00			
Yellow	14.00			
Sauceboat				
Chartreuse	37.00			
Ivory	28.00			
Turquoise	28.00			
Yellow	28.00			

Teapot, 7" h, Fiesta pattern, red glaze,
"Fiesta, Made in USA" mark(A), $190.00

12" h
Cobalt	495.00
Ivory	550.00
Turquoise	525.00

FLYING BIRDS PATTERN
Platter, 15" l	38.00

FORMAL PATTERN
Dessert Service, 4 cups and saucers, 4 dessert plates, creamer, sugar bowl	35.00

FOUR SEASONS PATTERN
Plate, 4" d, Winter	55.00

HACIENDA PATTERN, W/RED STRIPE
Cup and Saucer	20.00
Fruit Bowl	14.00

Plate
6" d	8.00
9" d	24.00
Platter	38.00

HARLEQUIN PATTERN
Ashtray
Rose	60.00
Turquoise	20.00
Bowl, 7" d, rose	25.00

Butter Dish, Cov, 1/2 lb
Rose	110.00
Yellow	55.00

Candleholder
Red, pr	250.00
Yellow, pr	150.00

Casserole, Cov
Dark green	115.00
Gray	125.00
Rose	85.00
Yellow	85.00

Creamer and Cov Sugar Bowl
Gray	10.00
Rose	10.00
Yellow	25.00

Creamer, Novelty
Maroon	48.00
Red	25.00
Rose	38.00
Yellow	25.00

Cream Soup
Chartreuse	28.00
Gray	28.00
Light green	28.00
Turquoise	18.00
Yellow	18.00
Cup and Saucer, med green	30.00

Cup and Saucer, A.D.
Light green	25.00
Maroon	65.00
Spruce	65.00
Turquoise	9.00
Yellow	9.00

Eggcup, Dbl
Chartreuse	28.00
Dark green	28.00
Gray	14.00
Maroon	22.00

Mauve	22.00
Spruce	22.00
Turquoise	14.00

Eggcup, Single
Light green	8.00
Maroon	25.00
Rose	25.00
Turquoise	10.00
Yellow	8.00

Figure
Donkey, maroon	85.00
Duck, maroon	50.00
Fish, spruce	95.00
Lamb, brown	25.00
Penguin, red	25.00

Gravy Boat
Gray	18.00
Rose	18.00

Jug, 22 oz
Gray	65.00
Red	50.00
Rose	48.00
Yellow	48.00
Marmalade Jar, turquoise	155.00

Nappy, 8 1/2" d
Gray	38.00
Maroon	38.00
Oatmeal Bowl, forest green	15.00
Pitcher, disc, juice, lemon yellow	40.00

Plate
6" d
Dark green	6.00
Gray	6.00
Med green	15.00
Red	4.00

7" d
Chartreuse	12.00
Med green	16.00
Red	7.00
Rose	7.00

9" d
Dark green	14.00
Gray	14.00
Maroon	14.00
Med green	22.00
10" d, gray	35.00

Platter
11" d
Maroon	24.00
Rose	18.00
Spruce	24.00

13" d
Light green	28.00
Turquoise	18.00
Yellow	18.00

Service Water Pitcher
Chartreuse	55.00
Maroon	85.00
Red	65.00
Rose	65.00
Spruce	65.00
Yellow	65.00

Spoon Rest, yellow	175.00

Teapot

Chartreuse	110.00
Gray	125.00

Tea Set, pot, creamer, sugar bowl, orange	95.00

Tumbler

Light green	48.00
Maroon	48.00
Yellow	35.00

Vegetable Bowl, oval

Light green	38.00
Maroon	38.00
Red	28.00
Rose	28.00
Spruce	38.00

HEMLOCK PATTERN, MAROON

Bowl

6" d	3.00
8" d	4.00
9" d	4.00
Cereal Bowl	2.00
Gravy Boat	4.00

Plate

6¼" d	2.00
7¼" d	2.00
9" d	3.00
10" d	3.00
Platter, 16" l	6.00
Soup Bowl	3.00
Sugar Bowl, Cov	5.00

HIGHLAND PLAID, YELLOW AND BLACK

Bread and Butter Plate	5.00
Cup and Saucer	4.00
Dinner Plate	6.00
Sauce Dish	4.00
Shakers, pr	8.00
Sugar Bowl, Cov	8.00

HISTORICAL AMERICA PATTERN

Chop Plate, 10" d	12.00
Dinner Plate	8.00
Soup Bowl	8.00

JUBILEE PATTERN

Bread and Butter Plate, cream beige	2.00

Casserole, Cov, shell pink	45.00
Coffeepot, cream beige	15.00
Creamer, cream beige	5.00
Dinner Plate, cream beige	7.00
Juice Set, 7 pieces, original box	725.00
Juice Tumbler, shell pink	75.00

Platter

11" l, mist gray	7.00
13" l, cream beige	10.00
Sauceboat, celadon green	10.00
Teapot, shell pink	10.00

KITCHEN KRAFT

Kitchen Bouquet pattern

Pie Baker, 9½" d	16.00
Platter, 12¾" l	16.00
Mixing Bowl, 10⅜" d, purple, red, and yellow tulips w/fencing	12.00
Teapot, 8½" h, pink roses	23.00

LADY ALICE PATTERN

Bowl, 5¾" d	4.00
Cereal Bowl	4.00
Cream and Sugar	20.00
Cup and Saucer	2.00
Eggcup	10.00

Plate

7" d	5.00
9" d	6.00

Platter

12" l	12.00
14" l	15.00

LADY GREENBRIAR PATTERN

Berry Bowl	2.00
Bread and Butter Plate	2.00
Dessert Plate	2.00
Dinner Plate	3.00
Soup Bowl	3.00
Sugar Bowl	6.00
Teapot	15.00

MARGARET ROSE PATTERN

Soup Bowl	6.00

MARIGOLD SHAPE

Platter

12½" l, multicolored decal of 2 period dancers, red marigolds on rim	10.00

Silver trim

10½" l	12.00
11½" l	14.00
12½" l	20.00

MEXICANA PATTERN, W/RED LINE, CENTURY SHAPE

Cup and Saucer	28.00
Fruit Bowl	14.00

Kitchen Kraft

Fork	65.00
Pie Lifter	65.00

Plate

6" d	8.00
7" d	16.00
9" d	24.00
10" d	48.00

Vegetable Bowl, Cov, 10½" H-H, 6" h,
Hudson shape, white(A), $25.00

Plate, 8¹/₂″ sq, Mexicana pattern, $10.00

Platter, 13¹/₄″ H-H	45.00
Soup Plate	28.00

OLD ENGLISH SCENE PATTERN

Gravy Boat	10.00
Relish Dish	2.00
Serving Bowl, 9″ d	5.00
Soup Bowl	6.00

PASTORAL PATTERN

Cake Plate	10.00
Cup and Saucer	10.00
Luncheon Plate	8.00

PATRICIAN PATTERN

Dinner Plate	5.00

PINK WILLOW PATTERN

Berry Bowl	2.00
Cereal Bowl	4.00
Dinner Plate	6.00
Salad Plate	3.00
Soup Bowl	4.00

PRISCILLA PATTERN

Berry Bowl	4.00
Bread and Butter Plate	4.00
Cake Plate	22.00
Casserole, Cov, 9″ d	12.00
Creamer	8.00
Cup and Saucer	11.00
Dessert Bowl	15.00
Dinner Plate	6.00
Gravy Boat, w/undertray	20.00
Pie Baker	4.00
Pitcher, 5¹/₂″ h	12.00
Platter	
11″ d	15.00
13³/₄″ l	15.00
Salad Plate	5.00
Soup Bowl	8.00
Sugar Bowl	12.00
Vegetable Bowl, 9¹/₄″ l	7.00

QUEEN ESTHER PATTERN

Berry Bowl	6.00
Bread and Butter Plate	2.00

Creamer	10.00
Dinner Plate	12.00
Salad Plate	2.00
Soup Plate	12.00
Sugar Bowl, Cov	12.00

RIVIERA PATTERN

Casserole, Cov	
Mauve Blue	95.00
Red	95.00
Yellow	85.00
Cream and Sugar, light green	55.00
Cup and Saucer, light green	24.00
Fruit Bowl, 5″ d	
Ivory	9.00
Mauve Blue	14.00
Red	14.00
Yellow	9.00
Gravy Boat	
Ivory	18.00
Light green	18.00
Jug, Cov	
Ivory	85.00
Light green	85.00
Jug, Open, mauve blue	70.00
Plate, 9″ d	
Light green	12.00
Mauve Blue	20.00
Red	8.00
Yellow	12.00
Platter, 11¹/₂″ d	
Oval well	
Ivory	32.00
Light green	28.00
Red	32.00
Yellow	28.00
Sq well, ivory	28.00
Shaker	
Light green	12.00
Red	14.00
Soup Plate, 8″ d, light green	24.00
Syrup, Cov, red	125.00
Teapot	
Ivory	120.00
Red	130.00
Tumbler	
Handle, green	50.00
Juice	
Ivory	45.00
Mauve	35.00
Yellow	35.00

RHYTHM ROSE PATTERN

Berry Bowl, Kitchen Kraft	1.00
Bread and Butter Plate, Kitchen Kraft	2.00
Cake Plate, 10¹/₂″ d	13.00
Casserole, Cov, 9″ d, Kitchen Kraft	9.00
Coffeepot, Kitchen Kraft	12.00
Creamer, Kitchen Kraft	2.00
Dinner Plate, Kitchen Kraft	4.00
Gravy Boat, turquoise	25.00
Mixing Bowl	
6¹/₄″ d	4.00

8¼" d	11.00
10" d	13.00
Pie Baker, Kitchen Kraft	5.00
Platter	
13" l	13.00
14" l, Kitchen Kraft	5.00
Salad Bowl, 9" d, Kitchen Kraft	5.00
Salad Plate, Kitchen Kraft	2.00
Soup Bowl, Kitchen Kraft	3.00
Sugar Bowl, Cov, Kitchen Kraft	3.00
Teapot, Kitchen Kraft	10.00
Water Pitcher, 5¾" h, Kitchen Kraft	8.00

ROYAL HARVEST PATTERN

Cup and Saucer	3.00
Dinner Plate	6.00

SERENADE PATTERN

Chop Plate, pink	20.00
Coupe Soup, blue	20.00
Creamer, pink	15.00
Cup and Saucer, blue	18.00
Gravy Boat, green	20.00
Plate, 7" d, pink	9.00

SPRINGTIME PATTERN

Bread and Butter Plate	2.00
Dinner Plate	3.00
Salad Plate	2.00
Soup Bowl	3.00

TULIP BASKET PATTERN

Cup and Saucer	7.00
Creamer	8.00
Dinner Plate	6.00
Soup Bowl	7.00
Sugar Bowl	12.00
Vegetable Bowl, 9" l	10.00

TURQUOISE PATTERN

Cereal Bowl	5.00
Nappy, 9" d	12.00
Platter, 11" l	12.00
Sugar Bowl, Cov	12.00

VIRGINIA ROSE SHAPE, ASSORTED DECALS

Bowl, 5" d	10.00
Creamer	5.00
Eggcup	18.00
Gravy Boat	10.00
Plate	
7" d	2.00
9" d	5.00
Platter	
11½" l	20.00
15" l	38.00
Serving Bowl, 8½" d	15.00
Soup Bowl	5.00

WELLS ART GLAZE

Creamer, rust	4.00
Cup and Saucer, rust	2.00
Dinner Plate, rust	16.00
Luncheon Plate, rust	3.00
Plate, 10" d, multicolored decal of Dutch girl w/tulips and Dutch boy w/sailboat, rust ground, pr	20.00

Platter, 15" l, rust, "Wells Art" mark	20.00
Salad Plate, rust	2.00
Syrup Jug, Cov, green, "Wells Art" mark	15.00
Tea Set, pot, creamer, sugar bowl, green	60.00

WHEAT PATTERN

Cup and Saucer	5.00
Dinner Plate	6.00
Teapot	15.00

WHITE ROSE PATTERN

Bread and Butter Plate	3.00
Creamer	8.00
Cup and Saucer	4.00
Dinner Plate	6.00
Platter	
11" d	12.00
13" d	15.00
Sauceboat	10.00
Sauce Dish	3.00
Serving Bowl	15.00
Soup Plate	7.00

MISCELLANEOUS

Wash Set, 3 piece, pitcher, 12½" h, bowl, 16" d, cov chamber pot, gold Greek key design on white ground	225.00

MAYER CHINA
BEAVER FALLS. PA
U. S. A.
SHASTA
160

MAYER CHINA COMPANY
Beaver Falls, Pennsylvania
1881–1985

History: Joseph Mayer came from England and organized Mayer Potteries Company, Ltd., with his brother in 1881. They later incorporated as Mayer China Company.

During its history, the company made a variety of products. Tea leaf white ironstone was an early ware. By the turn of the century, white granite, semi-porcelain, dinner sets, toilet sets, and odd dishes were made.

By 1915 mostly whitewares were being made for hotel, restaurant, and institutional use. Tablewares for home use were gradually discontinued.

Shenango China Company of New Castle, Pennsylvania, purchased Mayer China in 1964, both companies were then purchased by Interpace in 1968, and in 1979 Shenango was sold to Anchor Hocking Corporation. Mayer China took over Walker China Company in 1980, and closed it one year later. Interpace sold Mayer in 1979 to investors who subsequently sold it in 1985 to Syracuse China Company.

A wide variety of marks was used during the long history and various ownership changes of Mayer China Company.

CURTIS PATTERN
Plate, 7¼" d.. 3.00
KIRKWOOD PATTERN
Dinner Plate, 9" d.............................. 4.00
MONTICELLO PATTERN
Cup and Saucer 4.00
Dinner Plate 8.00
SHARON PATTERN
Dinner Plate, 9" d.............................. 4.00
THE DALTON PATTERN
Cup and Saucer 6.00
MISCELLANEOUS
Cup and Saucer, blue leaf and S-scroll
border 3.00
Gravy Boat, w/undertray, 3½" h, boat, 7" l, tray, 8½" l, white w/matte gold border 5.00
Plate
  Dinner
    Blue-green border w/thin white bands, made for American Export Lines 15.00
    Blue leaf and S-scroll border........ 5.00
  Salad, blue-green border w/thin white bands, made for American Export Lines 10.00
    Three sections, brown and turquoise star bursts 3.00
Pitcher, 4¾" h, bulbous shape, black oriental figures on green ground, black oriental characters on neck, "San Toy, Mayer, Beaver Falls, Pa." mark 180.00
Relish Tray, 9¼" l, 2 green inner bands, white ground, commercial ware... 4.00

Creamer, 3½" h, dark red and green "Georgian Bay Line" logo, "Mayer China, Beaver Falls, Pa., U.S.A." mark, $10.00

Sugar Bowl
  2¼" h, rect, white w/gold trim, commercial ware......................... 5.00
  Mauve band on rim and cov, white ground, commercial ware, "Mayer China, Beaver Falls, Pa. 454" mark 6.00

METLOX POTTERY
Manhattan Beach, California
1927–1989

History: T.C. Prouty and Willis, his son, established Metlox Pottery in Manhattan Beach, California, in 1927 and made ceramic outdoor signs. The sign business declined during the Depression, T.C. died in 1931, and Willis converted the plant to dinnerware production. The first line of dishes was called California Pottery and featured bright-colored glazes. Table and kitchenwares called Poppytrail were made in fifteen different colors for an eight-year period, starting in 1934. In 1936 the company's trademark became "Poppytrail," symbolic of the poppy, California's state flower. Talc, the major component of the body, and the metallic oxides used in the glazes were native to California.

In the late 1930s, Carl Romanelli, the first artware designer at Metlox, started Metlox Miniatures—small-scale animal figurines and other novelty pieces. Romanelli also designed Modern Masterpieces that included bookends, wall pockets, figural vases, figures, and such.

A very limited amount of pottery was made during World War II since the factory was converted to war production, but after the war dinnerware production resumed. Evan Shaw purchased the business from Willis Prouty in 1946 and introduced the first decorated dinnerware line. California Ivy in 1946 was the first hand-painted pattern. Numerous patterns followed through the prosperous fifties.

In 1958 Metlox purchased the trade name and dinnerware molds of Vernon Kilns and developed a separate Vernon Ware branch. Artwares continued in the fifties and sixties with matte-glazed pieces and American Royal Horses and Nostalgia, scale model carriages.

Shaw also brought the Disney line with him to Metlox from his American Pottery in Los Angeles, and Disney figures were made until 1956. During the sixties and seventies, the company made Poppets by Poppytrail—stoneware flower holders and planters—Colorstax—solid-color-glazed dinnerware—and numerous cookie jars.

Evan Shaw died in 1980 but his family remained involved in the company until it closed in 1989. Numerous marks were used on Metlox pieces.

Reference: Jack Chipman, *Collector's Encyclopedia of California Pottery,* Collector Books, 1992.

ANTIQUE GRAPE PATTERN
Bread and Butter Plate	4.00
Cup and Saucer	3.00
Dinner Plate	5.00
Salad Plate	3.00

AZTEC PATTERN
Bowl, 9½" d	18.00
Cereal Bowl	9.00
Cream and Sugar	53.00
Cup and Saucer	15.00
Dinner Plate	10.00
Fruit Bowl	10.00
Gravy Boat	40.00
Platter, 13" d	32.00
Shakers, pr	15.00
Soup Bowl	10.00
Vegetable Bowl, divided	25.00

BLUE VINTAGE PATTERN
Plate, 10½" d	10.00
Platter, 14" d	30.00

CALIFORNIA FRUIT PATTERN
Bowl	
6¼" d	4.00
8" d	9.00
10" d	12.00
Coffeepot	40.00
Creamer	5.00
Cup and Saucer	6.00
Pitcher, 9" h	40.00
Plate, 10½" d	7.00
Platter	
9¼" l	20.00
13" d	20.00
Salad Plate	3.50
Serving Bowl, 9" d	20.00
Teapot	40.00

CALIFORNIA IVY PATTERN
Creamer	14.00
Cup and Saucer	10.00
Dinner Plate	8.00
Eggcup	9.00
Gravy Boat	20.00
Marmalade Jar	20.00

Pitcher, 2½ qt	20.00
Salad Bowl	30.00
Shakers, pr	14.00
Teapot	45.00
Vase, 6¼" h	15.00

CAMELLIA PATTERN
Bowl, 6½" d, flanged	7.50
Bread and Butter Plate	7.00
Chop Plate	55.00
Cup and Saucer	24.00
Dinner Plate	15.00
Salad Plate	10.00
Soup Plate	18.00
Vegetable Bowl, 10" d	50.00

DELLA ROBBIA PATTERN
Butter Dish	22.00
Cup and Saucer	6.50
Dinner Plate	9.00

DESERT DAWN PATTERN
Bread and Butter Plate	4.00
Cup and Saucer	3.00
Dinner Plate	5.00
Salad Plate	3.00

FLORAL LACE PATTERN
Bread and Butter Plate	4.00
Cup and Saucer	3.00
Dinner Plate	5.00
Salad Plate	3.00

HAPPY TIME PATTERN
Bread and Butter Plate	4.00
Bread Tray	20.00
Canister Set, wood top, set of 4 graduated sizes	125.00
Cup and Saucer	8.00
Dinner Plate	5.00
Soup Bowl	8.00
Vegetable Bowl, round	12.00

HOMESTEAD PROVINCIAL PATTERN
Coffee Server, blue	55.00
Creamer	10.00
Match Holder	45.00
Pitcher, 14" h, figural rooster	325.00
Plate, 10" d	12.00
Sugar Bowl	15.00
Vegetable Bowl, divided	28.00

LA MANCHIA PATTERN
Cereal Bowl	2.00
Dinner Plate	3.00
Gravy Boat	4.00
Shakers, pr	4.00
Sugar Bowl, Cov	5.00

MEADOW ROSE PATTERN
Dinner Plate	12.00

MONTEREY PATTERN, VERNONWARE
Bread and Butter Plate	3.00
Creamer	6.00
Cup and Saucer	3.00
Dessert Plate	3.00
Dinner Plate	7.00
Salad Plate	5.00
Vegetable Bowl, 9½" l	9.00

PEACH BLOSSOM PATTERN

Plate, 10½" d	9.00

PROVINCIAL ROOSTER PATTERN

Berry Bowl	5.00
Bread and Butter Plate	5.00
Creamer	14.00
Cup and Saucer	7.00
Dinner Plate	5.00
Platter, 14" l	23.00
Salad Plate	5.00
Shakers, pr	15.00
Vegetable Bowl, divided	45.00

QUAIL RIDGE PATTERN

Berry Bowl	7.00
Bread and Butter Plate	6.00
Coffeepot	90.00
Creamer	25.00
Cup and Saucer	12.00
Dinner Plate	12.00
Mug	12.00
Salad Plate	10.00
Soup Plate	10.00

RED ROOSTER PATTERN

Berry Dish	5.00
Bowl	
10" d	20.00
11½" d	35.00
Bread and Butter Plate	7.00
Bread Dish	25.00
Butter Dish, ¼ lb	25.00
Canister	
Coffee	32.00
Flour	48.00
Sugar	44.00
Tea	48.00
Carafe, Cov	40.00
Casserole, Cov, figural rooster	120.00
Cereal Bowl	7.00
Chop Plate, 12" d	20.00
Coffeepot,	28.00
Condiment Set, 9 piece w/wooden wheel	125.00
Cream and Sugar	22.00
Cup and Saucer	8.00

Teapot, 11½" h, Provincial Rooster pattern, $65.00

Dinner Plate	12.00
Eggcup	15.00
Platter, 14" l	20.00
Salt and Pepper, figural	20.00
Vegetable Bowl, Cov, 10" d	30.00

ROYAL OAK PATTERN

Dinner Plate, 10¾" d	9.00

SCULPTURED DAISY PATTERN

Ashtray	6.00
Bowl	
6" d	4.00
7½" d	6.00
8" d, 2 handles	20.00
9" d	15.00
Butter Dish, ¼ lb	15.00
Celery Dish, 9½" l	15.00
Cream and Sugar	10.00
Cup and Saucer	7.00
Gravy Boat	20.00
Plate	
6¼" d	3.00
7½" d	5.00
10½" d	8.00
Platter	
11" d	18.00
13" d	15.00
15" d	20.00
Salad Bowl, 12" d	30.00
Salt and Pepper	10.00
Soup Plate	12.00
Sugar Bowl	5.00
Teapot	30.00
Tumbler	20.00
Vegetable Bowl, oval	12.00

SCULPTURED GRAPE PATTERN

Bowl	
6½" d	4.00
7½" d	5.00
Casserole, Cov	40.00
Cream and Sugar	10.00
Cup and Saucer	8.00
Pitcher	15.00
Plate	
6½" d	4.00
8" d	6.00
11" d	6.00
Platter	
13" d	12.00
14" d	25.00
Salt and Pepper	8.00
Vegetable Bowl	
8½" d	40.00
9½" d	50.00

SCULPTURED ZINNIA PATTERN

Bowl, 6" d	4.00
Cup and Saucer	7.00
Plate	
5" d	4.50
6" d	6.00
10" d	9.00
Platter, 13" d	15.00
Teapot	45.00

Vase, 9" h, white figure on front, flower on reverse, pink ground, "C. Romanelli" on base, $95.00

VERNON ROSE PATTERN, VERNONWARE

Bread and Butter Plate	2.00
Chop Plate, 12" d	8.00
Cup and Saucer	5.00
Salad Plate	2.00

WILD POPPY PATTERN

Cereal Bowl	5.00
Creamer	8.00
Cup and Saucer	6.00
Dinner Plate	7.00
Mug	7.00
Salad Plate	6.00
Sugar Bowl, Cov	10.00
Vegetable Bowl, 9" d	10.00

WOODLAND GOLD PATTERN

Bread and Butter Plate	2.50
Cereal Bowl	3.00
Dinner Plate	4.00
Fruit Bowl	3.00
Salad Plate	3.00

VASE, ROMANELLI

8" h, zodiac Taurus, ...	95.00
9" h, fan shape, nude and swan, blue .	125.00

the next year, decalcomania dinnerware was being produced and sold domestically. S.S. Kresge Company was one of the major customers for the open-stock dinnerwares.

When competition increased after the war, Kresge purchased the factory and mass-produced the dinnerwares to be sold in its stores. Mount Clemens operated as a subsidiary of Kresge and made semi-porcelain dinnerware to compete with Homer Laughlin's Fiesta. Dark green, blue, and pink pieces were made in patterns such as Flower Basket, Poppy, Robin, Rose Marie, Springtime, Exotic Bird, and Mildred, a later pattern made from 1934–1968.

The pottery was sold to David Chase in 1965, and the name was changed to Mount Clemens China Company one year later. During the 1970s there was another reorganization, and Mount Clemens was formed into a new company called Jamestown China, but the name was changed back to Mount Clemens in 1980.

The marks on the early pieces included the company's initials. Most later pieces were not marked although some had "U.S.A." in relief.

OLD MEXICO PATTERN

Cream and Sugar	12.00
Cup and Saucer	6.00
Dinner Plate	4.00
Soup Bowl	5.00
Vegetable Bowl	13.00

POPPY PATTERN

Platter	
9" l	5.00
10¼" l	5.00
13½" l	9.00
Soup Bowl	3.00

TOULON PATTERN

Butter Dish, Cov	12.00
Potato Bowl, Cov	15.00

MADE IN U.S.A.
535H
1935

MOUNT CLEMENS POTTERY COMPANY
Mt. Clemens, Michigan
1914–1987

History: A group of Michigan businessmen started Mount Clemens Pottery in 1914 and by

Soup Bowl, 8" d, Bluebirds design, $15.00

c1943

Shenandoah
PASTELS
MADE IN U.S.A.

Dinner Plate, 9" d, Far East pattern,
"Paden City Pottery Co." and chimney
mark, $4.00

PADEN CITY POTTERY
Sisterville, West Virginia
1914–1963

History: Paden City Pottery was started near Sisterville, West Virginia, in 1914 and made semi-porcelain dinnerware. The company perfected underglaze decals which would not change color in the glost firing. Bakserv, a 1931 kitchenware line, was made both in solid colors and with decals. The Shenandoah line had six different variations in solid colors and with decals that were intended to resemble hand painting.

The Elite shape from 1936 was plain and round with shell-like handles, finials, and feet. One year later shell-like embossing was added and the shape was called Shellcrest. The Caliente line from 1936 utilized bright colors on the Elite/Shellcrest shape. Decals also were used. A Blue Willow pattern was started in 1937. Sears sold the Nasturtium pattern about 1940. Highlight was designed by Russel Wright in 1951 and made in five colors for two years.

Paden City closed in 1963. A variety of backstamps was used.

AMERICAN BEAUTY PATTERN

Creamer	17.00
Gravy Boat	29.00
Platter, 13¾" l	29.00
Sugar Bowl, Cov	18.00
Teapot	38.00

CALIENTE PATTERN

Casserole, Cov, cobalt	12.00
Dinner Plate, cobalt	5.00
Mixing Bowl, 8½" d, yellow	8.00
Pitcher, orange	19.00
Serving Plate, 13" d, tangerine	18.00
Teapot, blue	30.00

COSMOS PATTERN, SHENANDOAH WARE

Bread and Butter Plate	6.00
Cup and Saucer	9.00
Dinner Plate	9.00
Salad Plate	5.00

COTTAGE ON THE HILL PATTERN

Platter, 11½" l	11.00

EDGEMORE PATTERN

Berry Bowl	1.00
Vegetable Bowl, 8¾" d	3.00

FAR EAST PATTERN

Cake Plate, 11¼" H-H	6.00
Creamer	5.00
Plate	
6" d	3.00
9" d	4.00
Soup Bowl	5.00

IVY PATTERN

Cup and Saucer	3.00
Dinner Plate	4.00
Salad Plate	3.00

JONQUIL PATTERN

Bread and Butter Plate	4.00
Cream and Sugar	12.00
Dinner Plate	5.00
Platter, 15⅞" l, Shenandoah Ware	15.00
Salad Plate	4.00
Teapot	15.00

MINION SHAPE

Dinner Plate, 9¼" sq, dark green or gray	6.00

MODERN ORCHID PATTERN

Cup and Saucer	6.00
Platter, 13¾" l	9.00
Salad Plate	15.00

NASTURTIUMS PATTERN, SHENANDOAH WARE

Platter, 13½" l	20.00

PADEN ROSE PATTERN

Cup and Saucer	5.00
Dinner Plate	10.00
Salad Plate	7.00

PATIO PATTERN

Dinner Plate	7.00

PINK ROSE PATTERN

Bread and Butter Plate	2.00
Cup and Saucer	2.00
Dinner Plate	6.00
Gravy Boat	5.00
Soup Bowl	5.00

POPPY PATTERN

Bread and Butter Plate	3.00

Teapot, 5¼" h, Red Rose pattern, $38.00

Cup and Saucer	5.00
Dinner Plate	6.00
Teapot	15.00
REGAL PATTERN	
Dinner Plate	8.00
SPINNING WHEEL PATTERN	
Bread and Butter	3.00
Cup and Saucer	4.00
Dinner plate	4.00
Fruit Bowl	3.00
MISCELLANEOUS	
Bowl, 9" d, multicolored decal of 1939 New York World's Fair, maroon rim w/gold drops	15.00
Cake Plate, 8" sq, multicolored florals in center and 4 sections of border	2.00
Relish Tray, 9½" l, Art Deco style flowers in center	12.00
Teapot, 7½" h, small blue flower w/black leaves on each side and under spout, imp body lines, blue line rims	30.00

ᑭOPE GOSSER
CHINA
MADE IN USA
ROSE POINT

CHINA
POPE-GOSSER
CHINA

c.1910

POPE-GOSSER CHINA COMPANY
Coshocton, Ohio
1902–1958

History: The Pope-Gosser China Company was organized in Coshocton, Ohio, in 1902 by Charles Gosser and Bentley Pope, who had worked at Trenton and Knowles, Taylor, and Knowles. The new company made a high-quality, highly vitrified translucent china body for vases and such.

Pope-Gosser won a silver medal for superior semi-porcelain at the 1904 Louisiana Purchase Exposition in St. Louis and also won other awards. Despite this recognition the wares were not profitable, and the firm switched production to dinnerware.

Pope-Gosser joined with eight companies in 1929 to form the American China Corporation. After the corporation broke up, Pope-Gosser was reorganized by Frank Judge in 1932 and continued to make semi-porcelain until it closed in 1958.

Rose. Point, used on a variety of bodies from 1934–1958, had a raised design of trailing roses in white. Covered pieces had a rose finial and decals were added in 1935. Steubenville Pottery bought the molds for Rosepoint when Pope-Gosser closed, and in 1959 Canonsburg acquired Steubenville's property. Rosepoint marked "Made by Steubenville" was manufactured at Canonsburg after 1959.

Pope-Gosser closed in 1958 due to foreign competition. A variety of marks was used.

BLUEBELL PATTERN	
Bread and Butter Plate	2.00
Creamer	5.00
Cup and Saucer	2.00
Dinner Plate	3.00
Soup Bowl	3.00
Sugar Bowl, Cov	8.00
Vegetable Bowl	10.00
MELROSE PATTERN	
Bread and Butter Plate	2.00
Cup and Saucer	2.00
Dinner Plate	4.00
ROSE POINT PATTERN	
Butter Dish, Cov	15.00
Cereal Bowl	4.00
Cup and Saucer	4.50
Teapot	15.00
SHARON PATTERN, FUTURA	
Bread and Butter Plate	2.00
Butter Dish, Cov	6.00
Creamer	3.00
Cup and Saucer	2.00
Dinner Plate	4.00
Gravy Boat	3.00
Platter, 12¾" l	12.00
Salad Plate	2.00

Gravy Boat, Bluebell pattern, $6.00

Soup Bowl	2.00
Sugar Bowl	4.00
Teapot	12.00
Vegetable Bowl	
9½" l, divided	10.00
11" d	8.00

MISCELLANEOUS

Bowl, 10¼" d, white and pink dogwood blossoms in center, 3 bunches of dogwood on border w/emb flower bunches, "POPE-GOSSER" and unicorn mark 32.00

Celery Dish, 8¾" l, gold overlay border, white ground, gold-line rim 5.00

Plate

8¼" d

Decal of mountainous lake scene, maroon 1909 calendar below, gold "Compliments of The State Bank of Florence, Florence, Wis." above, green luster border, gold rim, "POPE-GOSSER CHINA" and unicorn mark 25.00

Multicolored lighthouse in center, green luster border w/1910 calendar.. 10.00

9¾" d, multicolored decal of woman seated by lake w/bridges, tunnel, and forest, yellow border w/raised gold classical designs on rim, "Pope-Gosser" mark 35.00

Platter, 12½" l, border of pink roses w/winding thorny stems, gold accents, "Pope Gosser China" mark.... 12.00

Teapot, 6¼" h, multiple thin horiz platinum bands, "Pope Gosser China" mark.................................. 24.00

Vegetable Tureen, Cov, 12" H-H, wide and narrow gold banding, gold loop handles, gold loop knob, "Pope Gosser China" mark.............. 45.00

Plate, 6" d, multicolored floral border, raised ridge rim, "Pope-Gosser, Made in U.S.A., Sterling 14" mark, $6.00

DOGWOOD

ROYAL CHINA COMPANY
Sebring, Ohio
1933–1986

History: The Royal China Company took over the E.H. Sebring China Company plant in 1933. After the collapse of the American Chinaware Corporation conglomerate, the factory was not used for several years, but by 1939 it had been remodeled and was working again.

Royal China made semi-vitreous dinnerware, baking and cooking ware, tea sets, premiums, and artware. Some of the major patterns included: Bluebell, Blue and Pink Willow, and Royal Oven Ware—all from the 1940s; Old Curiosity Shop (1950s); and Colonial Homestead which was sold by Sears, Roebuck and Company (1950s through 1960s). One of Royal's most popular patterns was Currier and Ives which was introduced in 1949 and featured green or cobalt blue designs based on the artists' drawings.

Royal purchased the French-Saxon Company in 1964 and operated it as a subsidiary. The company also operated the W.S. George Pottery in East Palestine, Ohio, although Jeanette closed it after buying Royal China Company in 1969. There was a major fire at the Royal China plant in 1970, but the pottery was rebuilt. Both the Jeanette and Royal names were purchased by Coca-Cola Bottling Company of New York in 1976. Royal was sold again in 1981 to J. Corporation of Boston, which then sold it to Nordic Capitol of New York City in 1984. Through all these changes, the Royal name was kept and used on new lines. The last year of production was 1986.

Numerous marks were used during the long history of Royal China.

Reference: William C. Gates, Jr. and Dana E. Ormerod, *The East Liverpool, Ohio, Pottery District: Identification of Manufacturers and Marks,* The Society for Historical Archaeology, 1982.

BLUE POINT PATTERN

Plate, 10¼" d.......................................	8.00

BLUE WILLOW PATTERN

Cake Plate	15.00
Casserole, Cov	25.00
Cereal Bowl	5.00
Dinner Plate	6.00
Grill Plate	12.00
Pie Baker	35.00

Plate, 6" d	4.00
Salad Plate	4.00

BUCKS COUNTY PATTERN

Berry Dish	2.00

CHIPPENDALE PATTERN

Berry Bowl	2.00
Creamer	4.00
Cup and Saucer	6.00
Dinner Plate	5.00
Salad Plate	4.00
Soup Bowl	2.00
Sugar Bowl, Cov	4.00

COLONIAL HOMESTEAD PATTERN

Bread and Butter Plate	2.00
Cake Plate	16.00
Casserole	45.00
Cereal Bowl	6.00
Chop Plate	20.00
Cream and Sugar	18.00
Cup and Saucer	3.00
Dinner Plate	4.00
Gravy boat, w/liner	20.00
Platter	15.00
Salad Plate	3.00
Serving Bowl, 10" d	14.00
Soup Bowl	7.00
Teapot	55.00
Tidbit, 3 parts	24.00

CURRIER AND IVES PATTERN

Blue

Bread and Butter Plate	2.00
Cereal Bowl	8.00
Chop Plate	15.00
Chowder Mug	18.00
Coffee Mug	10.00
Cream and Sugar	12.00
Cup and Saucer	5.50
Dinner Plate	4.00
Gravy Boat	10.00
Luncheon Plate	3.50
Pie Baker	12.00
Platter, 13" l	25.00
Salad Plate	8.00

Cake Plate, 11¼" H-H, Colonial Homestead pattern, green, $16.00

Dinner Plate, 10" d, Currier and Ives, The Old Grist Mill pattern, blue, $4.00

Salt and Pepper	6.00
Serving Bowl	12.00
Soup Bowl	6.00
Teapot	48.00
Trivet	15.00

Pink

Creamer	15.00
Cup and Saucer	18.00
Dessert Bowl	8.00
Dinner Plate	12.00
Salad Plate	8.00
Soup Bowl	18.00

DAISY ANN PATTERN

Platter, 12½" d	12.00

IVY PATTERN

Creamer	2.00
Cup and Saucer	3.00
Sugar Bowl, Cov	4.00

MEMORY LANE PATTERN

Bread and Butter Plate	3.00
Casserole, Cov	45.00
Creamer and Cov Sugar Bowl	8.00
Cup and Saucer	6.00
Dinner Plate	5.00
Salad Plate	3.00
Soup Plate	4.00
Teapot	55.00
Vegetable Bowl	12.00

OLD CURIOSITY SHOP PATTERN

Cup and Saucer	4.00
Dinner Plate	4.00
Luncheon Plate	7.00
Teapot	55.00

ROBIN HOOD PATTERN

Bread and Butter Plate	2.00
Cup and Saucer	3.00
Dinner Plate	4.00

ROYAL SPLENDOR PATTERN

Berry Bowl	2.00
Bread and Butter Plate	2.00
Dinner Plate	4.00
Soup Bowl	3.00

SAPPHIRE PATTERN

Bread and Butter Plate	2.00
Casserole, Cov, 10¼" H-H	10.00
Cup and Saucer	3.00
Dinner Plate	6.00
Platter, 13¼" l	7.00
Salad Plate......................................	2.00
Soup Bowl	3.00
Vegetable Bowl, 8½" d.....................	6.00

STARGLOW PATTERN

Dinner Plate	3.00

SUNNY DAY PATTERN

Cup and Saucer	4.00
Dinner Plate	3.00

TULIP PATTERN

Berry Dish	3.00
Dessert Plate...................................	2.00
Platter, 11¼" l	7.00
Vegetable Bowl, 8½" d.....................	7.00

SALEM CHINA COMPANY
Salem, Ohio
1898–Present

History: Salem China Company was founded in 1898 in Salem, Ohio. First white granite ware was made, then earthenware, kitchen articles, and semi-porcelain. The company had financial problems, was purchased by F.A. Sebring in 1918, and was successful after that.

Many of the shapes and patterns were designed by Viktor Schreckengost during the 1930s and 1940s. The company made fine dinnerware until 1967, much of which was trimmed with 22K gold.

A wide variety of marks was used; some included a date code. In 1968 Salem became a sales and service organization.

CENTURY SHAPE

Plate, 7¼" d, multicolored floral center, lacy gold border	4.00
Service Plate, gold and ivory band......	12.00

DOMINION PATTERN, VICTORY SHAPE

Berry Bowl.......................................	2.00
Cup and Saucer	2.00
Dinner Plate	3.00
Salad Plate......................................	2.00

IMPERIAL PATTERN

Service Plate, gold and pink band.......	12.00

MANDARIN TRICORNE

Creamer...	4.00
Cup	2.00
Cup Plate...	6.00
Sugar Bowl, Cov	8.00

MINUET PATTERN

Dinner Plate	5.00

NORTH STAR PATTERN

Butter Dish	5.00
Cereal Bowl......................................	2.00
Cup and Saucer	2.00
Dessert Plate...................................	3.00
Dinner Plate	3.00
Fruit Dish	2.00
Gravy Boat	5.00
Salad Bowl	8.00
Salad Plate......................................	2.00
Shakers, pr......................................	5.00

PETIT POINT BASKET PATTERN

Cup and Saucer	3.00
Dinner Plate	4.00
Dessert Bowl	9.00
Dessert Plate, 6½" d	3.00
Salad Plate, 7¼" d	3.00
Serving Bowl, 8" d	9.00
Soup Bowl, 8½" d	7.00
Utility Bowl, 4¾" d...........................	5.00
Vegetable Bowl, 9" d	7.00

ROSEMARIE PATTERN

Dinner Plate	4.00

SHEFFIELD PATTERN

Casserole, Cov, 10¼" H-H	15.00

STREAMLINE PATTERN, SILVER BANDS

Cereal Bowl, 7" d	3.00
Creamer...	5.00
Dessert Plate, 6¼" d	3.00
Gravy Boat	5.00
Sugar Bowl, Cov	8.00

Service Plate, 10⅞" d, multicolored Godey print, ivory ground, maroon border w/gold overlay, "Imperial Salem China" mark, set of 6, $60.00

WILD ROSE PATTERN

Cake Plate 8.00

MISCELLANEOUS

Platter, 13½" l, Godey design, center w/2 women, one in purple and green, one in gray and blue, w/parasols, raised ribbed border, ear-shaped handles 18.00

SCAMMELL'S TRENTON CHINA

SCAMMELL CHINA COMPANY
Trenton, New Jersey
1924–1954

History: D. William Scammell worked with the Maddocks from Maddock Pottery Company in the Old Lamberton Works in 1902 and at one point bought out their interest in that facility. Eventually he purchased the remaining stock in Maddock Pottery Company and in 1924 formed the Scammell China Company to make hotel and railroad china.

In 1939 Lamberton China, a fine translucent product for home use, was introduced and made in a wide variety of ivory-toned tablewares. Decorations were molded, painted, modeled, gilded, and transfer printed with decals made by Scammell. Scenic blue china, made for the Baltimore and Ohio Railroad for about twenty-five years, showed "Cumberland Narrows," "Indian Creek," "Thomas Viaduct," "Potomac Valley," "Harper's Ferry," and such.

Scammell used a wide assortment of marks. Lamberton china pieces were marked with the words "Lamberton Ivory China Made in America" within a square.

DINNERWARE

Floral center, gold-banded rim

Cup and Saucer.............................. 3.00
Dinner Plate.................................. 5.00
Luncheon Plate 4.00
Salad Plate 3.00

Glasgow Rose pattern, bread and butter plate, 5½" d, salad plate, 7¼" d, luncheon plate, 9" d, dinner plate,

Dinner Set, 10 dinner plates, 10 luncheon plates, 10 bread and butter plates, 10 cups and saucers, Puritan pattern, "Lamberton" mark, $350.00

9½" d, "Ye Old Canoe Place Inn" logo, 41 piece (A)........................... 302.00

MISCELLANEOUS

Plate

7¼" d, portrait of Mark Twain and steamboat, black transfer, "Scammells Trenton China" mark 15.00

7⅝" d, "Dorling—Flora" mark 6.00

9" d

Gold Masonic emblem in center, gold "PUTMAN 338 OF THE CITY OF NEW YORK 1854–1929" on medium blue border, "Lamberton Scammell" mark............... 15.00

"Harper's Ferry, West Va.," blue transfer, "Scammell Lamberton" mark.............................. 80.00

10½" d, transfer scenes of Lafayette College, polychrome hanging swags and fleur-de-lys border, ivory ground, "Lamberton-Scammell" mark, set of 9(A) 112.00

11" d

"George Washington's Inauguration," blue transfer 100.00

Platter, 12¼" l, Alhambra pattern, tan ground, red band, "Lenape Scammell's Trenton China" mark, $6.00

"New York World's Fair—1939," cobalt transfer **65.00**
Platter, 15½" l, white ground, gold trim, raised border design, scalloped edge, "Scammell, East Liverpool Ohio Potteries" mark **10.00**
Soup Plate, 9" d, 5 blue crowns w/blue banners, white and yellow scattered designs, "Scammells Lamberton China" mark **6.00**

SEBRING POTTERY COMPANY
East Liverpool, Ohio
1881–1898
Sebring, Ohio
1898–1940s

History: The Sebring Pottery Company was formed when five Sebring brothers established a partnership with George Ashbaugh and Sampson Turnbull in 1887. The group purchased a plant, remodeled it, and made white granite ware. After two years, the brothers bought out their partners and added semi-vitreous porcelain production.

In 1893 the brothers leased the plant of the former East Palestine Pottery Company. In 1896 they built the Ohio China Company in East Palestine, gave that up two years later, and built a new pottery, called Klondike, in East Liverpool. Wares included plain and decorated semi-porcelain, ironstone dinner and toilet sets, commemorative plates, and accessory pieces.

The brothers laid out the town of Sebring, Ohio, and moved their East Liverpool operations there. Other potteries established by the family during the early 20th century included the Oliver China Company, Strong Manufacturing Company, Limoges China Company, Saxon China Company, E.H. Sebring China Company, and Sebring China Company.

During the early years of the 20th century, Sebring Pottery made numerous organizational changes, but continued to produce semi-vitreous dinnerware. In 1940 the company was absorbed by Limoges China Company which continued the Sebring China line until 1948. There were numerous marks used during the erratic history of Sebring Pottery.

Reference: William C. Gates, Jr. and Dana E. Ormerod, *The East Liverpool, Ohio, Pottery District: Identification of Manufacturers and Marks,* The Society for Historical Archaeology, 1982.

BRIAR ROSE PATTERN
Plate, 8" d.................................. **5.00**
CHANTILLY PATTERN
Bread and Butter Plate **8.00**
Cream and Sugar **15.00**
Cup and Saucer **12.00**
Dinner Plate **10.00**
Fruit Bowl................................. **8.00**
Jelly Dish **9.00**
Soup Bowl **10.00**
Vegetable Bowl **12.00**
FORTUNE PATTERN
Dinner Plate **10.00**
Luncheon Plate.............................. **3.00**
Platter, 12" l.............................. **12.00**
Salad Plate **6.00**
Vegetable Bowl, Cov, 9¼" d.............. **6.00**
SERENADE PATTERN
Bowl, 8¾" d, decal of 2 women in classical garden setting, lute player, horiz ribbed burgundy border w/gold floral overlay **35.00**
THE POPPY PATTERN
Plate, 9¼" d, "Sebring, The Poppy, Golden Maize" mark...................... **5.00**
VERMILLION ROSE PATTERN
Casserole, Cov................................... **8.00**
Chop Plate.. **8.00**
Vegetable Bowl, Cov **8.00**
MISCELLANEOUS
Bowl, 9¾" d, pink and white dogwood blossoms w/lily of the valley in center, shaded green luster ground w/gold overlay design, blue rim, "Sebring S-V" mark **8.00**

Cake Set, master plate, 9" sq, 4 plates, 6¼" sq, rust and yellow flowers, green leaves, yellow ground, "Golden Maize by Sebring, Reg U.S. Pat. Office 230442, July 13, 1921" mark, $48.00

Platter, 11⁵/₈" l, multicolored decal, white ground w/rose accents, sgd "Daudinian," "S.P. Co. S-V, Sebring, Ohio" mark, $32.00

Dish

    10¼" l, scalloped-shell shape w/curved handle at end, blue transfer of Grecian woman in room setting in center, pink ribbed border, sponged and lined gold rim, "The Sebring" mark **95.00**

    11½" d, 4 large lobes w/raised orange-red flower heads on shaded blue ground, purple chrysanthemums in center...........................   **25.00**

Platter, 14³/₈" l, decal of florals w/4 yellow arches in center and at ends, maroon border w/gold floral overlay, "Triumph Sebring Pottery Co., Royal Fortune, Maroon 40" mark **9.00**

Vegetable Bowl, Cov, 11¼" H-H, 6" h, gold "K" in center panel, pink florals w/blue ribbons, blue line, gold handles, rim, and finial, "Sebring China" mark...................................   **7.00**

NEW CASTLE, PA, U.S.A.
© INTERPACE
CH-35

MADE IN USA
CASTLETON
CHINA
REG. U.S. PAT. OFF.

SHENANGO POTTERY COMPANY/CASTLETON CHINA, INC.

New Castle, Pennsylvania

1901–Present

History: The Shenango China Company was incorporated in New Castle, Pennsylvania, in 1901 and made semi-vitreous hotel and home

dinnerware, and toilet sets. After financial difficulties, the firm reorganized as the Shenango Pottery Company. Additional problems led to a takeover, and the new management purchased the plant of New Castle Pottery Company and moved into those facilities in 1913.

Through the years of the Depression Shenango continued making hotel wares and railroad china. At the request of William Haviland from the Theodore Haviland Company of Limoges, France, in 1936, Shenango Pottery Company made wares using Haviland's formula, blocks, cases, decals and such. These were made until 1958 and were marketed with the trademark "Haviland, New York."

In 1939 the American representative for Rosenthal China of Germany, Louis Hellman, arranged for the American pottery to use Rosenthal shapes and patterns. In 1940 the first Castleton China based on Rosenthal designs was made by Castleton China, Inc. Shenango eventually purchased Castleton stock and took over the sales and manufacture of Castleton China in 1951, continuing to make a fine dinnerware line until c1970.

To create a fine china line with European craftsmanship and American technology, artists were hired to fashion contemporary designs, shapes, and decorations. During this period, Eva Zeisel designed the Castleton Museum shape—the first entirely hand-crafted, free-form modern shape in fine china.

In 1955 Mamie Eisenhower ordered gold service plates for the White House State Dining Room. Castleton also created a special design for Eisenhower's first birthday in the White House, and in 1968 a Castleton set by Shenango was made to be used by the Johnson administration at state dinners. Dinnerware sets also were made for foreign heads of state. During the 1950s Castleton made a series of game plates and a line of everyday china.

The name of the company was changed back to Shenango China, Inc., in 1954. Two years later the firm developed a "Fast-Fire" kiln which revolutionized the vitrified china industry by reducing the glost fire time to one hour and ten minutes from thirty-six to forty hours.

In 1959 Shenango bought Wallace China in California and operated it as a wholly owned subsidiary. Two years later the assets of Shenango were transferred to Shenango Ceramics, Inc., which was held by the Sobiloffs who had purchased all the shares in 1959. Mayer China Company of Beaver Falls, Pennsylvania, was purchased in 1964 and Wallace China was liquidated. In 1968 all assets of Shenango, including Castleton and Mayer, were sold by the Sobiloffs to Interpace Corporation which made Franciscan earthenware and fine china.

Shenango was taken over by Anchor Hocking Corporation in 1979, and hotel, restaurant, and institutional wares are still being made. Marks with "Castleton China" date from 1940–1968; "Interpace" from 1968–1979. Over the years, numerous other marks were used, including the Shenango Indian, the trademark of Shenango China.

CASTLETON
Bouquet pattern
Creamer and Cov Sugar Bowl 85.00
Caprice
Bread and Butter Plate 6.00
Cup and Saucer 12.00
Dinner Plate 12.00
Salad Plate 10.00
Castleton Rose pattern
Cream and Sugar 80.00
Gravy Boat 80.00
Platter, 15" l..................................... 125.00
Soup Plate 25.00
Vegetable Bowl
  Cov.. 150.00
  Oval... 65.00
Dolly Madison pattern
Cup and Saucer 18.00
Salad Plate 12.00
Essex pattern
Cup and Saucer 12.00
Dinner Plate 12.00
Fantasy pattern
Platter, 15" l..................................... 70.00
Gloria pattern
Bread and Butter Plate 7.00
Cup and Saucer 20.00
Cup and Saucer, A.D. 10.00
Dinner Plate 9.00
Fruit Dish.. 12.00
Salad Plate 12.00
Soup Bowl 12.50
Lace pattern
Cup and Saucer 25.00
Ma-Lin pattern
Bread and Butter Plate, 6" d................ 15.00
Dinner Plate 35.00
Cream Soup...................................... 35.00
Cup and Saucer 25.00
Salad Plate, 7" d 20.00
Phoenix pattern
Cup and Saucer 20.00
Regal pattern
Plate, 7³/₈" d...................................... 12.00
Regina pattern
Cup and Saucer 30.00
Dinner Plate 25.00
Royal pattern
Bread and Butter Plate 15.00
Cup and Saucer 18.00
Dinner Plate 20.00
Luncheon Plate.................................. 18.00
Salad Plate.. 16.00
Sunnyvale pattern
Bread and Butter Plate 10.00

Cream and Sugar 70.00
Cup and Saucer 25.00
Thistle pattern
Bread and Butter Plate 5.00
Creamer.. 8.00
Cup and Saucer 5.00
Dinner Plate 7.00
Platter, 14³/₄" l 25.00
Salad Plate.. 6.00
Sugar Bowl 12.00
Miscellaneous
Game Plate
  10¹/₂" d, etched, pheasant or quail,
    Richard Bishop, pr...................... 100.00
SHENANGO
Apple Blossom pattern
Cup and Saucer 2.00
Dinner Plate 3.00
Salad Plate.. 2.00
Howard Johnson pattern, Commercial ware, brick red logo
Plate
  Bread and Butter, 6¹/₂" d................ 15.00
  Dinner, 9" d 30.00
Navy china
Cup and Saucer, blue roped anchor and pinstripes, "Shenango China Co., Newcastle, Pa." mark 12.50
Dinner Plate 7.00
Soup Plate 7.00
Roselyn pattern
Grill Plate 20.00
Westward Ho pattern
Creamer.. 35.00
Cup and Saucer 35.00
Dinner Plate 50.00
Gravy Boat 40.00
Platter
  11¹/₂" l... 75.00
  13" l.. 85.00
Sugar Bowl 50.00

Plate, 8" d, lavender, blue, and green animals, white ground, "Shenango China USA" mark, $35.00

MISCELLANEOUS

Ashtray, 4¹/₂" d, Inca Ware, beige
   ground w/advertising...................... **20.00**
Cup and Saucer, Blue Willow pattern . **22.00**
Plate
   7" d, "Turf Catering Company," 2
     brown horses' heads on rim, tan
     ground, "Inca Ware, Shenango
     China, New Castle, Pa. U.S.A."
     mark... **4.00**
   7¹/₂" d, "Topsy's Eat With Their Fin-
     gers," black girl w/pigtails........... **380.00**
   8¹/₂" d, Blue Willow pattern **10.00**
   10³/₄" d, 3 sections, maroon Rose-
     lyn Castle, set of 4 .... **25.00**
Soap Dish, 8¹/₄" l, shell shape, white
   ironstone.. **20.00**

Blue Ridge
China
Hand Painted
Underglaze
Southern Potteries, Inc.
MADE IN U.S.A.

HAND PAINTED-UNDERGLAZE

Blue Ridge
MADE IN U.S.A.
SOUTHERN POTTERIES, INC.

SOUTHERN POTTERIES, INC./ BLUE RIDGE DINNERWARE

Erwin, Tennessee
1938–1957

History: Southern Potteries was incorporated in 1920 with E.J. Owens from the Owens China Company as president. Charles W. Foreman purchased the pottery in the early 1920s and introduced a technique of hand painting under the glaze. By 1938 Blue Ridge dinnerware was available with full freehand painting and the unique look of each piece was a great success since so many other companies used decal decorations.

Dinnerware imports were cut off during World War II and this allowed potteries in the United States to expand. The mid 1940s until the early 1950s were the peak years of production for Southern Potteries. After that, imports again became prominent and the growing popularity of plastics also interfered with pottery sales.

In 1951 Southern Potteries sold wares at major department stores and other retail outlets and made more hand-painted pieces than any other pottery in the United States. Most of the freehand painting was done by decorators who copied from over four hundred master patterns. Most lines were created by a chief designer, sometimes in conjunction with buyers from major department stores. Lena Watts was the chief Blue Ridge designer before moving to Stetson China Company.

There were eleven different shapes of Blue Ridge dinnerware, including Candlewick with a beaded edge, Colonial with fluted shapes, Piecrust with a crimped rim, Clinchfield with a wide, flat edge, and Trailway with wide, painted borders. The majority of patterns pictured assorted florals, fruits, farm scenes, roosters, leaves, peasant figures, and such. Some of the patterns were used on several different shapes. Patterns usually were numbered chronologically: 3000 numbers in the 1940s, 4000s in the 1950s. Most Blue Ridge patterns were not named at the factory, only numbered, and sometimes they acquired a name when they were advertised either by the pottery or the store that sold them. Many patterns were named by Betty and Bill Newbound in their book *Blue Ridge Dinnerware.*

A line of about forty pieces of vitreous specialty items, introduced about 1945, included decorative pitchers, shakers, creamers, sugar bowls, chocolate pots, teapots, vases, relishes, and character jugs. China was not used to make dinnerware sets. Teapots were made in both earthenware to match dinnerware and in china. A small line of ovenware also was made.

Premiums were made for Avon, Quaker Oats, Stanley Home Products, and also for trading-stamp companies and Montgomery Ward. During the mid 1950s a line of lamp bases was introduced, as were china character jugs portraying a Pioneer Woman, Daniel Boone, Paul Revere, and an Indian. Artist-signed pieces from the mid 1940s included scenic and wildlife plates and platters on earthenware blanks.

Labor costs continued to rise and the pottery business decreased. In the later years, when designs were stamped on the pottery and filled in by hand, sales declined. Southern Potteries tried cutting operating time in half, but eventually closed in 1957.

Nine different marks were used on Blue Ridge pottery, some concurrently. Some pieces have jobbers' marks from supermarkets and trading-stamp companies.

References: Winnie Keillor, *Dishes, What Else? Blue Ridge of Course!,* privately printed, 1983; Betty Newbound, *Southern Potteries, Inc. Blue Ridge Dinnerware,* Revised 3rd Edition, Collector Books, 1989, values updated 1993.

Collectors' Club: Blue Ridge Collectors Club, Phyllis Ledford, 245 Seater Road, Erwin, TN 37650-3925, dues $5.

Newsletter: National Blue Ridge Newsletter, Norma Lilly, 144 Highland Drive, Blountville, TN 37617-5404, bimonthly, $6.

Museum: Unicoi Heritage Museum, near Erwin, TN.

ANTIQUE #1 PATTERN
Pitcher, 5" h.. **75.00**
APPLE AND PEAR PATTERN
Divided bowl, 6 berry bowls **35.00**
APPLE JACK PATTERN
Tidbit tray, 3 tiers................................ **20.00**

AUTUMN APPLE PATTERN
Plate, 10½" d...................................... 14.00
AVON PATTERN
Salad Plate....................................... 15.00
BECKY PATTERN
Cup and Saucer, A.D. 25.00
BELLEMEADE PATTERN
Bowl, 9½" d 12.00
Creamer and Cov Sugar Bowl 18.00
Cup and Saucer 12.00
Dinner Plate 10.00
Fruit Bowl 16.00
Platter, 13" d.................................... 18.00
Soup Plate 10.00
BLOSSOM TIME PATTERN
Shakers, pr....................................... 35.00
BLUEBELL BOUQUET PATTERN
Dinner Plate 7.00
Platter, 15" d.................................... 16.00
BRITTANY PATTERN
Cup and Saucer, A.D. 50.00
BUTTERCUP PATTERN
Fruit Bowl, 6" d 8.00
CADENZA PATTERN
Creamer, pedestal type 9.00
CALAIS PATTERN
Berry Bowl.. 20.00
Cup and Saucer 25.00
Plate, 10" d...................................... 25.00
CALICO PATTERN
Cake Tray, maple leaf shape 40.00
Shakers, pr, blossom top 30.00
CAROL'S ROSES PATTERN
Cup and Saucer 4.00
Dinner Plate 6.00
CHANTICLEER PATTERN
Cup and Saucer 10.00
Dinner Plate 12.00
CHERRIES PATTERN
Cup and Saucer 5.00
Dinner Plate 5.00
Sauce Dish 3.00
Serving Bowl, 9½" d.......................... 12.00
Soup Bowl 5.00
CHERRY BOUNCE PATTERN
Dinner Plate 4.00
CHERRY COKE PATTERN
Berry Dish 3.00
Cup and Saucer 8.00
Dinner Plate 6.00
Teapot 98.00
CHINTZ PATTERN
Bonbon, flat shell.............................. 35.00
Chocolate Pot 158.00
Pitcher, 8¼" h, Milady shape.............. 100.00
CHRISTMAS TREE PATTERN
Cup and Saucer 45.00
Plate
  8" d.. 60.00
  10" d.. 65.00

COUNTRY FAIR PATTERN
Cup and Saucer 6.00
Salad Plate, 8½" d 6.00
CRAB APPLE PATTERN
Creamer and Cov Sugar Bowl 15.00
Plate
  9" d.. 8.00
  10" d.. 10.00
Teapot, Colonial shape 50.00
DAFFODIL PATTERN
Bowl, 6" d 8.00
Creamer.. 6.00
Cup and Saucer 4.00
Plate
  6" d.. 4.00
  10½" d.. 8.00
Sugar Bowl 12.00
DELTA DAISY PATTERN
Teapot, Colonial shape 50.00
DRESDEN DOLL PATTERN
Cup and Saucer 16.00
EMALEE PATTERN
Cup and Saucer, A.D. 25.00
FAIRMEADE FRUITS PATTERN
Eggcup.. 15.00
FALLING LEAVES PATTERN
Cake Plate, 12" d 22.00
Platter
  13½" d.. 14.00
  15½" d.. 18.00
FLIRT PATTERN
Soup bowl 6.00
FLO PATTERN
Vase, 9¼" h, ruffled top...................... 65.00
FLOUNCE PATTERN
Teapot, Colonial shape 50.00
FOLKLORE PATTERN
Plate
  7¼" d.. 3.00
  10⅜" d.. 4.00
Platter, 13½" d 6.00

Plate, 6¼" d, Crab Apple pattern,
green, red, and brown, $3.00

FRENCH PEASANT PATTERN

Bowl, oval	75.00
Celery, leaf shape	60.00
Chocolate Pot	295.00
Cream and Sugar	120.00
Cup and Saucer	60.00
Pitcher, 8¼" h, paneled body	350.00
Plate	
7" d	25.00
9¼" d	50.00
10" d	50.00
Platter	
11" d	189.00
13" d	115.00
15" l	195.00
Range Shaker	35.00
Salad Bowl	250.00
Vegetable Bowl	75.00

FRUIT FANTASY PATTERN

Bowl, 5¼" d	8.00
Butter Pat	15.00
Creamer	6.00
Cup and Saucer	10.00
Plate	
8" sq	7.00
9½" d	6.00
Platter, 15" l	18.00
Vegetable Bowl, 9¼" d	18.00

FRUIT SALAD PATTERN

Salad Plate, pears	28.00

GARDEN LANE PATTERN

Shakers, pr	35.00

GRANDMOTHER'S GARDEN PATTERN

Plate, 9½" d	6.00

GREENBRIAR PATTERN

Cream and Sugar	8.00
Cup and Saucer	7.00
Fruit Bowl	2.00
Gravy Boat	8.00
Plate	
6" d	4.00
9½" d	9.00

Plate, 9⅜" d, French Peasant pattern, $50.00

Platter	
11½" l	12.00
12½" l	14.00
Soup Bowl	4.00
Vegetable Bowl, 9" d	7.00

GREEN LANTERNS PATTERN

Dinner Plate	5.00

HILDA PATTERN

Dinner Plate	4.50
Gravy Underplate	5.00

HONOLULU PATTERN

Salad Plate, 8½" d	7.00

JUNE BOUQUET PATTERN

Vegetable Bowl, 9" d	16.00

JUNE BRIDE PATTERN

Cup and Saucer	6.00

JUNE ROSE PATTERN

Teapot, Colonial shape	110.00

KATE PATTERN

Teapot, Colonial shape	50.00

KISMET PATTERN

Teapot	55.00

LYONNAISE PATTERN

Plate, 6" d	10.00
Platter	95.00

MAGIC CARPET PATTERN

Cup and Saucer, A.D.	35.00

MARDI GRAS PATTERN

Fruit Bowl	4.00
Pie Baker	25.00
Plate	
6" d	4.00
9½" d	5.00
Sugar Bowl	6.00
Vegetable Bowl	8.00

MICKEY PATTERN

Plate, 10" d	7.00

MOUNTAIN IVY PATTERN

Creamer	3.00
Cup and Saucer	3.00
Dinner	6.00
Salad Plate	4.00
Sugar Bowl	5.00
Vegetable Bowl, 9" l	8.00

NOCTURNE PATTERN

Teapot, Colonial shape, yellow	85.00

NORMANDY PATTERN

Berry Bowl	12.00
Bowl	
9" d	45.00
9" l	45.00
Cereal Bowl, 6½" d	23.00
Cup and Saucer	25.00
Plate	
6" d	10.00
9" d	22.00
Platter, 11" l	22.00
Soup Plate	25.00

OAK LEAF PATTERN

Creamer	3.00

Dinner Plate	6.00
Luncheon Plate	3.00
Sugar Bowl	5.00
Vegetable Bowl, oval	8.00

ORCHARD GLORY PATTERN

Fruit Bowl	5.00
Sugar Bowl	5.00

PAPER ROSES PATTERN

Shakers, pr	40.00

PARTRIDGE BERRY PATTERN

Creamer	5.00

PETUNIA PATTERN

Plate, 10" d	7.00

POINSETTIA PATTERN

Creamer	8.00
Lug Soup Bowl	3.00
Soup Plate	3.50
Sugar Bowl	12.00

POM POM PATTERN

Creamer and Cov Sugar Bowl	35.00

QUAKER APPLE PATTERN

Cereal Bowl	5.00
Cup and Saucer	7.00
Plate	
6" d	7.00
7" d	8.00
Soup Plate	6.00

RED BARN PATTERN

Plate, 9" d	20.00

RIBBON PLAID PATTERN

Cereal Bowl	8.00

RIDGE DAISY PATTERN

Cigarette Set, box, 4 ashtrays	100.00
Party Plate and Cup	16.00
Relish Dish, 4 parts, top handle	50.00

ROCK ROSE PATTERN

Eggcup	18.00

ROSE MARIE PATTERN

Chocolate Set, pot, creamer, sugar bowl	235.00

RUSTIC PLAID PATTERN

Dinner Plate	6.00
Salad Plate, 6¼" d	4.00

SHOWGIRL PATTERN

Platter, 13" d	12.00

SPIDERWEB PATTERN

Cream and Sugar	20.00
Teapot	50.00

SPINDRIFT PATTERN

Pie Baker	15.00

SPRAY PATTERN

Bowl, 6" d	3.00
Cup and Saucer	5.00
Plate	
6" d	3.00
9¼" d	4.00

STANHOME IVY PATTERN

Bowl, 5¼" d	5.00
Cup and Saucer	3.00
Dinner Plate	5.00

STRAWBERRY SUNDAE PATTERN

Cup and Saucer	3.00
Dinner Plate	4.00

SUNFIRE PATTERN

Bread and Butter Plate	3.00
Cup and Saucer	5.00
Dinner Plate	4.00
Salad Plate	2.00

SUNGOLD #1

Creamer	8.00
Sugar Bowl	12.00

SUNGOLD #2

Eggcup	14.00

SUNNY PATTERN

Cereal Bowl	8.00

TULIP ROW PATTERN

Cup and Saucer, A.D.	25.00

VALLEY VIOLET PATTERN

Butter Pat	35.00
Cup and Saucer	20.00
Eggcup, Dbl	30.00
Shakers, pr	35.00
Sugar Bowl	40.00

VERNA PATTERN

Cake Tray, maple-leaf shape	40.00

VINTAGE PATTERN

Plate, 11½" d	28.00

WALTZ TIME PATTERN

Bowl, 9" d	10.00

WHIRLIGIG PATTERN

Bread and Butter Plate	5.00
Cake Plate	6.00
Soup Bowl	12.00

WILD CHERRY PATTERN

Cereal Bowl	4.00
Cup and Saucer	10.00
Plate	
9½" d	8.00
10½" d	9.00
Platter, 14" l	14.00
Sauce Dish	4.00
Soup Plate	8.00

*Plate, 9³⁄₈" d, Weathervane
pattern, $8.00*

WILD STRAWBERRY PATTERN

Creamer	10.00
Sugar Bowl	10.00

YELLOW NOCTURNE PATTERN

Cup and Saucer	6.00
Dinner Plate	8.00
Teapot	12.00

YELLOW ROSE PATTERN

Teapot, chevron handle	98.00

MISCELLANEOUS

Pitcher

6" h, figural chick, white	40.00
6¹/₂" h, Spiral Daisy pattern	65.00
7" h, Tralee Rose pattern, spiral	45.00

7¹/₂" h, Jane shape

Scatter pattern	88.00
Sculptured Fruit pattern	60.00

8³/₄" h

Betsy, figural girl	85.00
Rebecca, Whirl Rose pattern	195.00
Salt and Pepper Rooster, 4³/₄" h, hen, 4" h, yellow w/brown	120.00

Vase

8" h, boot shape, Gladys	95.00

9" h, ruffled

Calico pattern	110.00
Tapered shape, Delphine pattern	60.00

STETSON CHINA COMPANY
Lincoln, Illinois
1919–1966

History: Stetson, a family enterprise, started as a decorating and distributing company in Chicago, Illinois, in 1919. In the early years blanks were purchased from Mount Clemens Pottery. To make sure a steady supply of blanks was available, Stetson took over the Illinois China Company in Lincoln, Illinois, in 1946 and changed the name to the Stetson China Company.

Stetson China made large quantities of dinnerware with an outlined design that was filled in by hand. This resulted in a uniform pattern without using a decal. These hand-painted dinnerwares were very popular with the public and a wide assortment of patterns was sold in department and specialty stores. Dinnerware also was made for the Procter & Gamble Company to use as premiums. Earthenwares also were made, as well as premium orders decorated with decals for grocery stores.

Stetson eventually closed down since it could not compete with the inexpensive imports. Although several different marks were used, many pieces were not marked at all and have been confused with products of Southern Potteries.

DINNERWARE

Multicolored garden flowers in center, gold overlay inner border, brown outer border w/gold overlay

Creamer	3.00
Cream Soup	3.00
Dinner Plate	4.00
Platter, 13¹/₄" l	8.00
Salad Plate	3.00
Sugar Bowl	5.00
Vegetable Bowl, 8¹/₂" d	6.00

GOLDEN EMPRESS PATTERN

Plate, 10" d	12.00
Soup Bowl, 8" d	5.00

RIO PATTERN

Bread and Butter Plate	2.00
Creamer	3.00
Dinner Plate	5.00
Fruit Dish	3.00
Platter, 10³/₄" l	8.00
Soup Plate	5.00
Sugar Bowl	6.00
Vegetable Bowl, 8¹/₂" d	10.00

MISCELLANEOUS

Bowl, 9" d

Blue, yellow, pink, and black plaid design	18.00
Purple flower in center w/gold trim, gold rim	7.00
Cup and Saucer, large yellow flower	6.00
Mixing Bowls, 5¹/₂", 6", 7", 9¹/₄" d, gold floral overlay on ext, pink and blue floral bouquet on int and ext, Mt. Clemens blanks, set of 4	45.00

Platter, 11¹/₂" l, Rio pattern, dark pink flowers w/green and yellow leaves, brown stems, "Rio Stetson China Co." mark, $7.00

Plate
  6" d, center w/pink rose and blue forget-me-nots, inner gold geometric band, gold overlay border w/raised gold-outlined shaped rim **10.00**
  9¼" d, decal of Dutch woman holding buckets, canal and windmill in background, raised beaded rim **5.00**
  9½" d, yellow pear w/green leaves and brown stems in center, red dashes **8.00**
  10" d
    Period courting couple w/flute player in center, multicolored, gold lacy overlay border **12.00**
    Purple tulip, pink rose, and white magnolia w/green leaves, heavy gold geometric overlay border **12.00**

10⅜" d
  Green holly leaves w/red berries, 5 brown rectangles, gray streaked ground **7.00**
  Multicolored floral center, rust rim w/gold overlay, "Royal Stetson, Deluxe, 22K Gold" mark, set of 10 .... **50.00**
Dinner Plate
  Concentric pink rings border to rim **7.00**
  Large yellow flower on border..... **8.00**
Platter, 13½" l, stylized green leaves w/white stripes, brown dashes, gray ground **12.00**
Soup Bowl, 8¼" d, Dutch scene in center, lacy gold overlay border **3.00**
Tray, 11" l, oval, Mexican design in center... **5.00**
Vegetable Bowl, 9½" l, decal of garden flowers in center, cobalt border w/gold overlay **10.00**

Bread and Butter Plate, 6" d, Heritage Ware, hp yellow flower, green leaves, $2.00

Plate, 10" d, multicolored decal, gold trim, $10.00

Steubenville
ROSE DAWN
1931

STEUBENVILLE POTTERY COMPANY
Steubenville, Ohio
1879–1959

History: A group of citizens opened Steubenville Pottery in 1879 in Steubenville, Ohio, to make semi-vitreous dinner and toilet sets, cream-colored wares, granite ware, and semi-porcelain.

The company produced American Modern, the most popular dinnerware in America in its time. (See Russel Wright.) Another popular Steubenville pattern was Woodfield, a leaf pattern in solid colors of Salmon pink, Tropic, Dove gray, Rust, and Golden fawn. Steubenville was distributed to leading department stores in the United States.

The company experienced difficulties in the 1950s and closed in 1959. Canonsburg Pottery purchased Steubenville molds and continued to make some of the pottery.

A wide variety of marks was used.

ADAM ANTIQUE PATTERN

Butter Dish, Cov, 8¼" d	25.00
Cereal Bowl	10.00
Cup and Saucer	8.00
Eggcup	5.00
Plate, 7½" d, set of 6	60.00
Soup Plate, 8¼" d	8.00
Tea Set, breakfast, pot, creamer, sugar bowl	65.00

FAIRLANE PATTERN

Coffeepot	12.00
Cup and Saucer	5.00
Dinner Plate	4.00

HORIZON PATTERN

Bread and Butter Plate	3.00
Creamer	6.00
Gravy Boat	10.00
Sugar Bowl	8.00

MARFIELD PATTERN

Dish, 8½" d, w/handle, gray	6.00

PEACOCK GARDEN PATTERN

Cereal Bowl	2.00
Creamer	4.00
Cup and Saucer	2.00
Dessert Dish	2.00
Dinner Plate	3.00
Sugar Bowl, Cov	5.00
Teapot	15.00

WOODFIELD PATTERN

Cup and Saucer, gray, rose, or chartreuse	4.00
Dinner Plate, gray or chartreuse	3.00
Pitcher, chartreuse	25.00
Teapot, rust	25.00

Dessert Plate, 7³/₈" sq, multicolored florals, cobalt border w/gold overlay, "Steubenville USA" and fort mark, set of 4(A), $16.00

Tea and Toast Set, Woodfield pattern, blue-green, $10.00

MISCELLANEOUS

Game Platter, 15" l, multicolored elk in forest setting, yellow border	45.00
Pitcher, 2½" h, decal of Mexican man and woman on one side, house on reverse, cream ground, Trend shape	3.00
Plate, 9" d, center decal of woman w/large bonnet, 1910 calendar on border, "Steubenville China" mark	40.00

O.P.CO.
SYRACUSE
CHINA
1897–1920s

1895–1897

SYRACUSE CHINA/ONONDAGA POTTERY COMPANY

Syracuse, New York
1871–Present

History: In 1871 the Onondaga Pottery Company bought out Empire Pottery and changed its name to Onondaga. In 1966 it became the Syracuse China Company of Syracuse, New York. Onondaga made white granite ware with the coat of arms of New York as its mark. High-fired semi-vitreous wares were introduced in 1885 with an innovative guarantee against cracking and crazing.

"Imperial Geddo" from 1888 was a true vitrified china that was thin and translucent, and it won an award at the Columbian Exposition in 1893. Onondaga had developed a full line of china by 1891. In 1893 the company was making cream-colored white granite wares that were both plain and decorated, and dinner and toilet services. Semi-porcelain was made from 1886–1898.

The company continued to expand and added a new plant in 1921. It acquired Vandesa-Syracuse Ltd. of Quebec, a maker of hotel china, in 1959. In 1970 Syracuse discontinued chinaware for home use, having been forced out by the inexpensive imports. By the following year they were one of the largest producers of hotel, restaurant, airline, and commercial types of high-quality tablewares. All of the production was moved to one location in 1979 when it was no longer a privately owned company. In 1984 Syracuse purchased the Mayer China Company.

A date code was included on the wide variety of marks used.

ALCORA PATTERN

Dinner Plate	5.00

ARCADIA PATTERN

Bread and Butter Plate	6.00
Cup and Saucer	12.00
Dinner Plate	12.00
Salad Plate	10.00

BAROQUE PATTERN

Soup Plate	10.00

BOMBAY PATTERN

Chop Plate, 11" d	12.00
Coffeepot	35.00
Cream and Sugar	20.00
Cup and Saucer	12.00
Gravy Boat	22.00
Plate	
6¼" d	7.00
8" d	8.00
10" d	10.00
Platter	
12" d	22.00
16" d	25.00
Vegetable Bowl	
9" d	20.00
10" d	25.00

Dinner Plate, 8" d, yellow, green, and blue Arts and Crafts design, A. Robineau(A), $28.00

BRACELET PATTERN

Gravy Boat	13.00
Soup Plate, rimmed	28.00
Vegetable Bowl, Cov	125.00

BRIARCLIFF PATTERN

Bread and Butter Plate	6.00
Cup and Saucer	12.00
Dinner Plate	12.00
Salad Plate	9.00

BURMESE PATTERN

Cream and Sugar	30.00
Plate	
7" d	7.00
9½" d	10.00
Platter, 12" d	10.00
Relish Tray, 10" l	10.00

CANDLELIGHT PATTERN

Dinner Plate	10.00
Salad Plate	8.00

CELESTE PATTERN

Gravy Boat	80.00
Vegetable Bowl, 10" l	25.00

CHEVY CHASE PATTERN

Bread and Butter Plate	8.00
Cup and Saucer	12.00
Dinner Plate	12.00
Salad Plate	10.00

CLOVER PATTERN

Cereal Bowl, 5½" d	8.00
Cup and Saucer	12.00
Gravy Boat, w/attached undertray	20.00
Plate, 10" d	10.00
Platter	
12" d	15.00
14" d	20.00
Salad Plate, 8" d	8.00
Vegetable Bowl, 8" d	15.00

CORALBEL PATTERN

Bread and Butter Plate	7.00
Cup and Saucer	15.00
Dinner Plate	15.00
Soup Plate	24.00
Salad Plate	10.00
Vegetable Bowl, Cov	20.00

COVENTRY PATTERN

Bowl, 6¼" d	10.00
Bread and Butter Plate	5.00
Cream and Sugar	30.00
Cup and Saucer	15.00
Dinner Plate	20.00
Gravy Boat	50.00
Luncheon Plate	15.00
Platter	
12" d	26.00
14" d	55.00
Salad Plate	10.00
Soup Bowl	5.00
Vegetable Bowl	
Cov	60.00
Oval	35.00

DAWN PATTERN

Bread and Butter Plate	4.00
Cup and Saucer	8.00
Dinner Plate	5.00
Salad Plate	4.00

EDMONTON PATTERN

Bread and Butter Plate	8.00
Plate, 10" d	10.00
Sugar Bowl, Cov	15.00

FEDERAL PATTERN

Cup and Saucer	22.00

FORGET-ME-NOT PATTERN

Dinner Plate	18.00
Gravy Boat	55.00
Sugar Bowl	25.00

GARDENA PATTERN

Gravy Boat, w/attached undertray, "O.P. Co. Syracuse China" mark	22.00

GOV. CLINTON

Dinner Plate	18.00
Platter	
12" d	18.00
14" l	20.00
16" l	25.00

INDIAN TREE PATTERN

Bread and Butter Plate	5.00
Cup and Saucer	10.00
Dinner Plate	10.00
Salad Plate	8.00

JEFFERSON PATTERN

Bread and Butter Plate	15.00
Cup and Saucer	28.00
Dinner Plate	30.00
Salad Plate	18.00

LADY MARY PATTERN

Plate, 9" d	10.00
Platter, 14" l	25.00
Vegetable Bowl, oval, 10½" l	15.00

MEADOW BREEZE PATTERN

Cup and Saucer	25.00
Plate	
7" d	15.00
8" d	18.00

MELROSE PATTERN

Cup and Saucer	7.00
Dinner Plate	8.00
Luncheon Plate	8.00
Vegetable Bowl, oval	12.00

MONTICELLO PATTERN

Bread and Butter Plate	5.00
Cup and Saucer	10.00
Dinner Plate	10.00
Salad Plate	8.00

OLD COLONY PATTERN

Cup and Saucer	17.00
Plate	
8" d	12.00
8¾" d	12.00

OLD IVORY PATTERN

Berry Bowl, cobalt w/gold trim	20.00
Bread and Butter Plate	7.00
Cake Plate, 10" d	42.00
Cup and Saucer, A.D.	17.00
Dinner Plate	
9¾" d	15.00
10¼" d	15.00
Luncheon Plate, 8" d	10.00
Platter	
14" l, 10¼" w	30.00
16" l, 11½" w	40.00
Salad Plate, 7" d	9.00

ORCHARD PATTERN

Bread and Butter Plate	5.00
Cup and Saucer	10.00
Dinner Plate	15.00
Salad Plate	8.00

ORIENTAL PATTERN

Bread and Butter Plate	4.00
Cream and Sugar	25.00
Cup and Saucer	6.00
Dinner Plate, 9½" d	10.00
Luncheon Plate, 9" d	8.00
Platter	
11½" l, 9" w	25.00
13½" l, 10" w	35.00
16" l, 11½" w	50.00
Soup Plate	8.00

ORLEANS PATTERN

Bouillon Cup	5.00
Cream and Sugar	8.00
Gravy Boat	8.00
Platter	
12" d	12.00
14" d	15.00

PORTLAND PATTERN

Bread and Butter Plate	6.00
Cup and Saucer	8.00
Dinner Plate	8.00
Platter, 12" d	12.00

RIVIERA PATTERN

Bread and Butter Plate	6.00
Cup and Saucer	12.00
Plate, 12" d	25.00
Platter, 14" l, 10½" w	45.00
Salad Plate	10.00

ROMANCE PATTERN

Bread and Butter Plate	3.00
Cup and Saucer	5.00
Dinner Plate	4.00
Salad Plate	3.00

ROSALIE PATTERN

Bread and Butter Plate	10.00
Cup and Saucer	20.00
Fruit Bowl	12.00
Plate, 10" d	15.00
Salad Plate	14.00
Vegetable Bowl, oval	28.00

ROSE MARIE PATTERN

Bread and Butter Plate	6.00
Chocolate Set, pot, creamer, sugar bowl	169.00
Cup and Saucer	12.00
Dinner Plate	12.00
Salad Plate	9.00
Soup Plate	12.00

ROSLYN PATTERN

Bread and Butter Plate	3.00
Cup and Saucer	3.00
Luncheon Plate	4.00
Salad Plate	3.00

SELMA PATTERN

Cup and Saucer	15.00
Dinner Plate	12.00
Gravy Boat, w/attached underplate	45.00
Plate, 6" d	8.00
Salad Plate	10.00
Vegetable Bowl, oval	35.00

SERENE PATTERN

Cream and Sugar	10.00
Salad Plate	5.00

SHARON PATTERN

Bread and Butter Plate	15.00
Cup and Saucer	28.00
Dinner Plate	30.00
Salad Plate	18.00

SHERWOOD PATTERN

Bread and Butter Plate	15.00
Cup and Saucer	30.00
Dinner Plate	30.00
Salad Plate	18.00

SILHOUETTE FLIRTATION PATTERN

Bread and Butter Plate	6.00
Plate, 10½" d	15.00
Salad Plate, 8" d	10.00

STANSBURY PATTERN

Plate, 10" d	10.00
Platter, 12" l, 9" w	25.00
Salad Plate, 8" d	8.00
Soup Plate	10.00

SUNBRIGHT PATTERN

Teapot	75.00

SUZANNE PATTERN

Dinner Plate	30.00
Gravy Boat	85.00
Platter, 14" l	75.00

SYMPHONY PATTERN

Dinner Plate	15.00

TEMPLE BELLS PATTERN

Cream Soup, w/underplate	15.00

VICTORIA PATTERN

Plate, 10" d	15.00
Platter, 12" l, 9" w	35.00

WEBSTER PATTERN

Bread and Butter Plate	5.00
Cup and Saucer	10.00
Dinner Plate	10.00
Salad Plate	8.00

CHINA

c.1910

OVENPROOF
MADE IN USA

3366

1930s

TAYLOR, SMITH, AND TAYLOR
Chester, West Virginia
1901–1981

History: John Taylor and Charles Smith organized a company to make plain and decorated semi-porcelain in 1899, using the facilities of the Taylor, Smith, and Lee pottery. Taylor's sons joined the firm and a pottery was built in Chester, West Virginia. The name Taylor, Smith, and Taylor was retained even though the firm was managed by the Smith family.

The pottery was very successful and the facilities were enlarged many times. Semi-vitreous dinner and toilet sets were made along with wares for hotels and restaurants.

A very large variety of patterns, shapes, and designs was made. Two of the most popular lines were Lu-Ray and Vistosa from 1938. Lu-Ray came in soft solid colors of Windsor blue, Sharon pink, Surf green, Persian cream and Chatham gray. Vistosa was available in light green, cobalt blue, deep yellow, and mango red.

Cooking and oven wares were made in the 1960s. In 1972 the company was sold to the Anchor Hocking Corporation which closed it in 1981 due to a depressed market for dinnerwares. Many different marks were used.

Reference: William C. Gates, Jr. and Dana E. Ormerod, *The East Liverpool, Ohio, Pottery District: Identification of Manufacturers and Marks,* The Society for Historical Archaeology, 1982.

BREAK O'DAY PATTERN

Cake Server	8.00
Cereal Bowl	3.00
Creamer	5.00
Cup and Saucer	3.00
Dinner Plate	4.00
Salad Plate	2.00

COFFEE TREE PATTERN

Creamer	2.00

Cup and Saucer 3.00
Dinner Plate 2.00
Platter, 13¼" l 5.00
Soup Bowl 2.00
Sugar Bowl, Cov 3.00

CONVERSATION SHAPE

Plate, 10½" sq, daylily in center 3.00
Vegetable Bowl, 9" d, center w/orange lilies and green leaves, dark green border, "Taylor, Smith, and Taylor, Conversation, Designed By Walter Teague" mark 3.00

COURTING COUPLE PATTERN

Gravy Boat 27.00
Platter, 13¼" l 25.00
Vegetable Bowl, 9⅛" l 22.00

DAYLILY PATTERN

Dessert Bowl 4.00
Dinner Plate 6.00
Serving Bowl 15.00

DOGWOOD PATTERN

Berry Dish 2.00
Creamer... 3.00
Dinner Plate 3.00
Salad Plate.. 2.00
Soup Bowl 3.00
Sugar Bowl 4.00
Vegetable Bowl, 8¾" d...................... 6.00

EVER YOURS PATTERN

Berry Bowl 1.00
Bread and Butter Plate 2.00
Cup and Saucer 2.00
Dinner Plate 3.00
Salad Plate.. 2.00

LU-RAY PATTERN

Bowl, 8¾" d
   Sharon pink.................................. 18.00
   Surf green.................................... 10.00
   Windsor blue 10.00
Bread and Butter Plate, Sharon pink.... 3.00
Creamer, Windsor blue....................... 6.00
Cup and Saucer, A.D.
   Sharon pink.................................. 30.00
   Windsor blue 20.00
Eggcup, Sharon pink 14.00
Gravy Boat
   Sharon pink.................................. 10.00
   Surf green.................................... 22.00
Grill Plate
   Sharon Pink.................................. 45.00
   Surf green.................................... 50.00
Nut Dish, Sharon pink 75.00
Plate
   9½" d, Windsor blue...................... 4.00
   10" d
      Sharon pink 14.00
      Windsor blue............................ 14.00
Plate, divided, yellow 25.00
Platter, 13" d, Sharon pink 7.00
Sugar Bowl, Cov, Sharon pink 15.00
Teapot, Windsor blue 25.00

Tumbler
   Sharon pink.................................. 10.00
   Windsor blue 10.00
Vegetable Bowl, 9" d, Windsor blue ... 12.00

PARAMOUNT, IVORY PATTERN, FLORALS

Bread and Butter Plate 4.00
Creamer... 8.00
Cup and Saucer 5.00
Dinner Plate 8.00
Salad Plate.. 5.00
Sauceboat, w/attached undertray 12.00
Sugar Bowl 12.00
Vegetable Bowl, 10" l, rect 15.00

PASTORAL PATTERN

Bread and Butter Plate 5.00
Cup and Saucer 8.00
Soup Bowl 8.00

PETIT POINT BOUQUET PATTERN

Berry Dish 10.00
Bread and Butter Dish........................ 5.00
Cup and Saucer 3.00

REVEILLE PATTERN

Plate, 6¾" d...................................... 4.00

ROOSTER PATTERN

Bread and Butter Plate 3.00
Custard Cup....................................... 3.00
Dinner Plate 6.00
Fruit Dish... 3.00
Gravy Boat 20.00
Soup Bowl 4.00

SECOND SELECTION PATTERN

Dinner Plate 5.00

SILHOUETTE PATTERN

Butter Dish, Cov 150.00
Pretzel Jar, 6½" h.............................. 95.00
Salad Bowl, 8¾" d............................. 18.00
Salt and Pepper, 5" h 65.00

SUMMER ROSE PATTERN

Dinner Plate, 10" d............................ 5.00
Sauce Bowl, 5¼" d............................ 2.00

VISTOSA PATTERN

Chop Plate
   13" d... 13.00
   14½" d, yellow 17.00
Shakers, green, pr.............................. 14.00

MISCELLANEOUS

Ale Set, tankard, 14" h, 4 mugs, 4¾" h, decals of sad-eyed dogs, shaded brown ground 150.00

Cup and Saucer, Silhouette pattern, $28.00

Luncheon Plate, 8¼″ d, Summer Rose pattern, $3.00

Mug, 3½″ h, green shadow design of
grape bunches on sides **12.00**
Pitcher, 9″ h, w/ice lip, blue and green
garden flowers on sides in raised
gold-outlined panels, gold trim,
"Taylor, Smith & Lee" mark............ **45.00**
Pitcher and Bowl Set, pitcher, 11¾″ h,
bowl, 16″ d, white ironstone, raised
shield design on neck, flying horse
and "TST" mark............................... **150.00**
Plate
7″ d
    Black decal of B.P.O.E. elk, shaded
    purple border w/raised design,
    shaped rim, entwined "TST" mark   **28.00**
    Multicolored garden flowers on top,
    blue ground, shaped rim, sou-
    venir inscription on front **20.00**

UNIVERSAL POTTERIES, INC.
Cambridge, Ohio
1934–1976

History: Universal Potteries acquired the
Atlas-Globe Company in Cambridge, Ohio, in
1934 and made semi-porcelain dinnerware, bak-

ing dishes, and utilitarian kitchenwares, including refrigerator wares. Dinnerware production
continued until 1956, then stopped in favor of
floor and wall tile development. The name of the
company changed to the Oxford Tile Company
in 1956 and the factory closed in 1976.

Cat-Tail, from the 1930s–1940s, was a very
popular decal pattern that was used on a variety
of shapes. Calico Fruit from the 1940s was sold
in department and catalog stores. Ballerina from
the late 1940s–1950s originally came in four
solid colors: Periwinkle blue, Jade green, Jonquil
yellow, and Dove gray. Chartreuse and Forest
green were added in 1949. Designer Charles Co-
belle added five new patterns for the Ballerina
shape in 1950: Painted Desert, Mermaid, Passy,
Gloucester Fisherman, and The Fountain. In
1955 pink and charcoal were added as was the
Moss Rose pattern. Ballerina Mist was done in
blue-green with decals.

In 1937 Walter Kail Titze designed Upico,
one of the most extensive of Universal's shapes.
Dinnerwares and kitchenwares were made in
solid colors, with decals, and in combinations of
both.

Many other patterns and shapes were made
and elaborate marks were used.

Universal Promotions distributed Universal
Potteries products from 1937–1956. Other potteries made dinnerware and kitchenware for Universal Promotions after 1956, including Homer
Laughlin, Taylor, Smith, and Taylor, and Hull
Pottery—all of which used the Universal Ballerina marks.

BALLERINA PATTERN
Cream and Sugar **7.00**
Cup and Saucer **4.00**
Salt and Pepper.................................. **6.00**
Tray, 9¼″ l, periwinkle **3.00**
Utility Plate, 10⅛″ H-H, chartreuse **5.00**
BALLERINA MIST PATTERN
Berry Bowl.. **3.00**
Butter Dish, Cov **8.00**
Bread and Butter Plate **3.00**
Creamer and Cov Sugar Bowl **12.00**
Cup and Saucer **5.00**
Dinner Plate **4.00**
Salt and Pepper.................................. **10.00**
Soup Plate **4.00**
BALLERINA ROSE PATTERN
Dinner Plate, 10″ d........................... **3.00**
BITTERSWEET PATTERN
Casserole, Cov.................................. **15.00**
Soup Bowl **8.00**
CALICO FRUIT PATTERN
Bowl, 9″ d **25.00**
Bowl, Cov, 5″ d **20.00**
Cake Plate, 12¾″ H-H **18.00**
Creamer.. **6.00**
Custard Cup...................................... **5.00**
Water Jug **28.00**

CAMWOOD IVORY, FLORAL DECAL PATTERN
Cereal Bowl 2.50
Dinner Plate 3.50
Plate, 11½" d.................................... 4.00
CAT-TAIL PATTERN
Batter Jug 130.00
Bowl
  5" d.. 4.00
  9" d.. 13.00
  10" d.. 15.00
Cake Plate 12.00
Canteen Jug, 7½" h........................... 20.00
Casserole, Cov
  8¼" d... 25.00
  9" d.. 30.00
Cream and Sugar 17.00
Cup and Saucer
  Flat base...................................... 8.00
  Ftd base 8.00
Gravy Boat 13.00
Plate
  6" d.. 4.00
  10" d.. 10.00
Platter
  11½" d.. 13.00
  13" d.. 30.00
Refrigerator Set, canteen jug, 7½" h,
cov casserole, 8¼" d, 3 cov jars, 4",
5", 6" d.. 150.00
Shakers, pr....................................... 10.00
Soup Plate 8.00
DUTCH WINDMILL PATTERN
Bowl
  5¼" d... 5.00
  6¼" d... 8.00
  7½" d... 12.00
Bread and Butter Plate, 7¼" d............ 2.00
Cake Plate, 11¾" d 8.00
Cup and Saucer 5.00
Custard Cup...................................... 5.00
Dessert Plate, 6¼" d 2.00
Dinner Plate, 10¼" d 4.00
Pie Baker, 10" d................................ 15.00
Pie Plate, 9" d 6.00
Platter, 7½" l 9.00
Salad Plate, 7¼" d 2.00

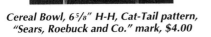
*Cereal Bowl, 6⅝" H-H, Cat-Tail pattern,
"Sears, Roebuck and Co." mark, $4.00*

FASCINATION PATTERN
Casserole, Cov, 10" H-H.................... 10.00
Plate, 9" d.. 4.00
HOLLAND ROSE PATTERN, OLD HOLLAND MARK
Berry Bowl.. 2.00
Cup and Saucer 4.00
Soup Bowl 4.00
HOLLYHOCKS PATTERN
Casserole, Cov.................................. 25.00
IRIS PATTERN
Casserole, Cov.................................. 10.00
Cup and Saucer 5.00
Dinner plate 5.00
Gravy Boat 6.00
Pie Baker 8.00
Water Jug.. 20.00
LARGO PATTERN
Cereal Bowl...................................... 2.00
Custard Cup...................................... 5.00
Mixing Bowl, 7½" d 10.00
Soup Bowl 8.00
LORELLA SHAPE
Bread and Butter Plate, yellow w/white bow and dashes.............. 2.00
Cup and Saucer, pink w/white bow and dashes 3.00
Dinner Plate, green w/white bow and dashes.................................. 3.00
Platter, 14" H-H, pink w/white bow and dashes.................................. 12.00
Salad Plate, green or pink w/white bow and dashes 2.00
MOSS ROSE PATTERN
Berry Bowl.. 2.00
Bread and Butter Plate 3.00
Creamer.. 6.00
Cup and Saucer 2.00
Dinner Plate 4.00
Soup Bowl 3.00
Sugar Bowl 10.00
Vegetable Bowl, 8¾" d...................... 10.00
MOUNT VERNON PATTERN
Pie Baker 15.00
Teapot 32.00
Tray, 9" l 12.00
RED POPPY PATTERN
Casserole, Cov, 9½" d 22.00
Grill Plate 5.00
Salt and Pepper, silver trim 9.00
REFRIGERATOR LINE, MONTGOMERY WARD, FLOWERED COV, BLUE BASE
Bowl, Cov
  4¾" d... 8.00
  6" d.. 9.00
  7" d.. 15.00
Shaker 12.00
UPICO PATTERN
Teapot, individual size, red................ 30.00
WOOD VINE PATTERN
Cup and Saucer 5.00

Canteen Refrigerator Jug, 7¹/₂" h, Zinnia pattern, $30.00

Mixing Bowl, 9¹/₄" d, orange-red roses and green leaves, 22K gold trim, $8.00

Dessert Plate, 6¹/₄" d	3.00
Dinner Plate	4.00

ZINNIA PATTERN

Casserole, Cov	14.00

MISCELLANEOUS

Ball Jug, w/ice lip, red glaze	18.00

RODEO PATTERN
MADE IN CALIF. USA
WALLACE CHINA

WALLACE CHINA COMPANY
Vernon, California
1931–1964

History: The Wallace China Company was founded in Vernon, California, in 1931 to make vitrified hotel china. Both plain and transfer-printed dinnerwares were produced for institutional use. During the 1930s and 1940s Willow design china was made in blue, green, brown, and red.

George Poxon brought his Poxon China designs to Wallace when he was hired by the company. In 1943 the M.C. Wentz Company of Pasadena commissioned Wallace to produce

hotel Barbecue Ware which became part of the Westward Ho housewares line.

Till Goodan, the well-known western artist, created three patterns: Rodeo, Boots and Saddle, and Pioneer Trails. His name is usually included somewhere in the design. He also designed the three-piece Little Buckaroo Chuck set for children and El Rancho and Longhorn for restaurants.

Shadowleaf, originally designed for restaurants, was available as an open-stock pattern as well. In 1959 Wallace became part of the Shenango China Company. Wallace closed in 1964. A variety of backstamps was used on Wallace pieces.

Reference: Jack Chipman, *Collector's Encyclopedia of California Pottery,* Collector Books, 1992.

BOOTS AND SADDLES PATTERN

Ashtray	45.00
Creamer...............................	45.00
Cup and Saucer	42.00
Plate	
7¹/₄" d...	28.00
9" d...	32.00
10¹/₂" d..	38.00
Shakers, pr	78.00
Sugar Bowl	50.00
Water Pitcher, disc	375.00

CHUCKWAGON PATTERN

Plate, 6¹/₄" d.....................................	35.00

DESERT WARE PATTERN

Dinner Plate, 9" d	12.00
Platter, 11¹/₄" l	13.00

EL RANCHO PATTERN

Bowl, 4³/₄" d	25.00
Cup and Saucer	75.00
Gravy Boat	65.00
Jam Jar, Cov, w/undertray	85.00
Mustard Jar, Cov, w/undertray	85.00
Pitcher, disc, "Last Frontier Village, Las Vegas, Nevada" advertising.......	275.00
Plate	
6" d...	45.00
7" d...	55.00
9¹/₂" d...	75.00
Platter, oval	90.00

KIT CARSON PATTERN

Ashtray	45.00
Cereal Bowl	22.00

LONGHORN PATTERN

Plate, 7¹/₄" d.....................................	25.00

PIONEER TRAILS PATTERN

Bowl, 9" d	100.00
Creamer and Cov Sugar bowl	100.00
Platter, 15" l, 10" w, oval..................	160.00
Vegetable Bowl	
Oval..	95.00
Round	95.00

RODEO PATTERN

Ashtray	45.00

Plate, 7" d, Rodeo pattern, brown shades, $44.00

Bowl
5¾" d	**70.00**
13" d	**800.00**
Chili Bowl	**85.00**
Chop Plate	**90.00**
Creamer	**20.00**
Cup and Saucer	**50.00**
Mug and Saucer	**95.00**
Plate	
9" d	**75.00**
10½" d	**90.00**
Platter, 15" d	**225.00**
Salt and Pepper	**60.00**
Vegetable Bowl	**50.00**
Water Pitcher	**495.00**

MISCELLANEOUS
Ashtray
Davy Crockett	**50.00**
Sam Houston	**80.00**
"Storz" advertising	**55.00**

RUSSEL WRIGHT
New York, New York
1936–1967

MFG. BY
STEUBENVILLE
c.1930s

History: In 1936 Russel Wright and his wife Mary joined with Irving Richards to create the Raymor Company. For a five-year period, Wright designed exclusively for Raymor, after which the Wrights sold the company to Richards and established their own design firm called Russel Wright Associates. Raymor continued to sell and distribute Wright designs plus many others.

When Russel Wright designed American Modern dinnerware in 1939, the shapes were so non-traditional and innovative that most of the Ohio River area potteries did not want to produce it. However, Steubenville Pottery in Ohio agreed to manufacture it if Mary and Russel Wright provided the financing. It was to be distributed exclusively by Raymor for a five-year period. From 1939–1959 it was the largest-selling dinnerware ever and necessitated several Steubenville expansions to keep up with the demand. American Modern won the American Designers Institute Award for the best ceramic design in 1941.

This strictly functional, amorphous-shaped dinnerware was sold in starter sets, fifty-three piece sets in other groupings, and as open stock. It was heavily advertised and mass produced for the middle class. Originally, the colors were Seafoam blue, Granite gray, Chartreuse, Curry, Coral, Bean brown, and white. In 1950 black Chutney and Cedar green were added, followed by Cantaloupe and Glacier blue in 1955. Bean brown was discontinued during World War II. The finish had a muted, soft glow with a textured feeling. A tremendous assortment of pieces was made, with new shapes being added all during the time of production. Several different marks were used.

Wright's next project after American Modern was an art pottery line for Bauer Pottery Company that was marketed by Raymor. Though there were twenty shapes involved and sixteen different glaze colors, there was a tremendous amount of difficulty with the glazes, and the line was only produced for about six months.

Iroquois Casual China by Russel Wright designed in 1946, was made by the Iroquois China Company and distributed by Garrison Products of New York City. Featuring oven-to-table pieces, this, too, became a best-selling dinnerware. Original colors were Sugar white, Lemon yellow, and Ice blue, followed by Nutmeg, Avocado yellow, and Parsley green. Lemon and Parsley were short-lived. The original shapes had a pinch style and a mottled glaze. Major design changes in 1951 gave Iroquois Casual a more polished look. By 1951 colors included Charcoal, Ripe apricot, Pink Sherbet, Lettuce green, Oyster, Cantaloupe, Aqua, Brick red, and Forest green. Not all items were made in all colors and buyers mixed pieces. Iroquois was restyled again in 1959 and sold in forty-five piece sets.

Russel Wright designed solid-color institutional dinnerware for Sterling China Company in 1949. Ivy green, Straw yellow, Suede gray, Cedar brown, white, and Shell pink pieces were made and decorated with customers' logos and such.

Paden City Pottery Company manufactured Highlight and the Russel Wright design was marketed by Justin Tharaud. Original colors were Blueberry, Nutmeg, Pepper, and Citron, and later white and dark green. At first it had a soft matte glaze, and later a high gloss finish. This design was more sophisticated than American Modern and Iroquois Casual, but due to struggles between Wright and the marketer, it was only produced until the mid 1950s.

The first patterned line by Wright was White Clover for the Harker Pottery Company. It had a silk-screened engraved-like decoration and was made in Meadow green, Golden spice, Coral sand, and Charcoal from 1951–1955.

In 1955 Wright designed an oriental-inspired line for Knowles in the Esquire shape. The naturalistic designs were made in beige, white, pink, yellow, and blue in a matte finish with an underglaze rubber-stamped pattern and an overglaze gold stamping. Pattern names, such as Seeds, Grass, Queen Anne's Lace, Snow Flower, Botanica, and Solar, were marked on the bottom with a gold backstamp. This lower-priced line was designed for stores such as Sears, Roebuck and Company and Montgomery Ward, and for premium stamp companies, but it was not successful and was discontinued in 1962.

Russel Wright used numerous marks on his dinnerwares designed for Steubenville, Harker, Iroquois, Paden City, Sterling, and Knowles, and on his art pottery for Bauer. He closed his studio in 1967.

References: Ann Kerr, *Collectors' Encyclopedia of Russel Wright Designs,* Collector Books, 1990; ———, *Russel Wright Dinnerware,* Collector Books, 1985.

BAUER

Ashtray, gray ext, aqua int, #8	250.00
Bowl, 6³/₄" d, 2¹/₂" h, tan.....................	150.00
Corsage Vase, 5" h, gunmetal, #3	300.00
Vase	
5" h	
Cinnamon	275.00
Ovoid shape, yellow glaze	300.00
Tan glaze...............................	225.00
8¹/₂" h, pillow shape, rust	295.00
10³/₄" h, flattened cylinder shape, matte terra-cotta glaze(A)............	398.00

HARKER, WHITE CLOVER

Ashtray, Charcoal	25.00
Bread and Butter	
Charcoal	3.00
Golden spice...............................	3.00
Meadow green	3.00
Cereal Bowl, Meadow green..............	8.00
Clock, Coral sand ..:..........................	85.00
Creamer	
Charcoal	20.00
Meadow green	12.00

Cup and Saucer	
Charcoal	14.00
Meadow green	12.00
Dinner Plate, 10¹/₂" d	
Charcoal	20.00
Golden spice.................................	5.00
Meadow green	8.00
Fruit Bowl, Charcoal.........................	8.00
Platter, 13¹/₄" d, Charcoal	25.00
Salt and Pepper	
Charcoal	22.00
Meadow green	20.00
Soup Bowl, Charcoal	10.00
Vegetable Bowl, 8" d, Charcoal..........	25.00
Water Pitcher, Meadow green	55.00

IROQUOIS, CASUAL

Beverage Pitcher, Mustard gold	85.00
Butter Dish, Cov	
Lemon yellow	95.00
Lettuce green	60.00
Pink sherbet	65.00
Carafe	
Ice blue......................................	125.00
Nutmeg..	75.00
Sugar white	175.00
Casserole, Cov	
Nutmeg..	28.00
Pink sherbet, w/Charcoal cov..........	15.00
Cereal Bowl, 5¹/₄" d, redesigned, Ripe apricot	7.50
Coffee Cup and Saucer	
Lemon Yellow	24.00
Sugar white	18.00
Creamer, redesigned, Sugar white.......	12.00
Cup and Saucer	
Avocado yellow	8.00
Cantaloupe..................................	15.00
Lemon yellow	12.00
Oyster..	10.00
Ripe apricot	8.00
Cup and Saucer, redesigned, Cantaloupe....................................	20.00
Dessert Bowl, 4³/₄" d, redesigned, Ripe apricot	8.00
Dish, Cov, 10" d, divided, Ice blue	25.00
Fruit Bowl, Nutmeg	3.00
Mug, 13 oz	
Ice blue......................................	35.00
Nutmeg..	65.00
Mug, redesigned	
Lettuce green	55.00
Pink sherbet	60.00
Plate	
6¹/₂" d	
Avocado yellow	4.00
Cantaloupe...............................	2.00
Charcoal	2.00
Nutmeg....................................	2.00
10" d	
Avocado yellow	6.00
Cantaloupe...............................	16.00
Ice blue	4.00
Lemon yellow............................	8.00

Nutmeg	4.00
Pink sherbet, redesigned	6.00
Ripe apricot	6.00
Turquoise (aqua), redesigned	16.00
Platter, 12¾" l	
Avocado yellow	18.00
Ice blue	8.00
Ripe apricot	18.00
Salad Plate, 7½" d, redesigned	
Mustard gold	5.00
Ripe apricot	8.00
Shakers	
Lettuce green	12.00
Pink sherbet	12.00
Soup Bowl, Ice blue	3.00
Stacking Creamer	
Cantaloupe	20.00
Charcoal	6.00
Ice blue	5.00
Lettuce green	9.00
Nutmeg	5.00
Sugar white	29.00
Stacking Sugar	
Cantaloupe	20.00
Charcoal	6.00
Ice blue	5.00
Lettuce green	9.00
Sugar white	29.00
Tea cup and Saucer	
Avocado yellow	6.00
Ice blue	6.00
Nutmeg	7.00
Tea cup, redesigned, ice blue	4.00
Teapot, redesigned	
Lemon yellow	85.00
Sugar white	145.00
Vegetable Bowl, 8" d	
Cantaloupe	36.00
Lettuce green	18.00
Nutmeg	8.00
Pink sherbet	8.00
Vegetable Bowl, divided	
Parsley green	40.00

EDWIN KNOWLES, GRASSES PATTERN

Bowl, Cov, 8" d	25.00
Bread and Butter Plate	3.00
Cup and Saucer	12.00
Dinner Plate	10.00
Salad Plate	10.00
Sugar Bowl	22.50
Water Pitcher, 9½" h	55.00

PADEN CITY, HIGHLIGHT

Bowl	
6½" d, white	14.00
7" d, white	14.00
Bread and Butter Plate, white	5.00
Charger, 15" d	
Blueberry	55.00
Pepper	55.00
Creamer, White	14.00
Dinner Plate, White	10.00
Platter, 13½" d, Nutmeg	25.00
Salad Plate, White	8.00

Fruit Bowl, 12" l, Edwin Knowles,
Grasses pattern, blue and gold
lines, "Russel Wright by Knowles USA"
mark, $45.00

STERLING

Ashtray, Suede gray	65.00
Coffee Bottle, Cov, Cedar brown	95.00
Cream Pitcher, Straw yellow	6.00
Cup and Saucer, Cedar brown	12.00
Teapot, Cedar brown	40.00
Water Pitcher, redesigned, two-tone ...	95.00

STEUBENVILLE, AMERICAN MODERN

Baker, 10¾" l	
Chartreuse	10.00
Seafoam blue	10.00
Butter, Cov, Granite gray	130.00
Carafe	
Bean brown	200.00
Coral	120.00
Casserole, Cov, coral	45.00
Celery Tray, 13" l	
Black Chutney	40.00
Coral	15.00
Seafoam blue	12.00
Chop Plate	
Black Chutney	25.00
Granite gray	12.00
White	8.00
Coffeepot, A.D.	
Black Chutney	95.00
Seafoam blue	40.00
White	130.00
Cream and Sugar, Coral	15.00
Cup and Saucer, A.D.	
Black Chutney	6.00
Chartreuse	12.00
Coral	12.00
Granite gray	12.00
Seafoam blue	13.00
Fruit Bowl, Bean brown	15.00
Gravy Boat, Coral	13.00
Lug Fruit, Seafoam blue	5.00
Lug Soup	
Black Chutney	20.00
Coral	5.00
Seafoam blue	5.00
White	30.00
Pickle Dish, w/liner	

Chartreuse......................................	8.00
Seafoam blue	8.00

Plate
6" d

Bean brown...............................	5.00
Black chutney............................	2.00
Cedar green..............................	3.00
Seafoam blue............................	3.00

10" d

Black chutney............................	4.00
Chartreuse	5.00
Coral	12.00
Granite gray	4.00
Seafoam blue............................	5.00

Platter

Black chutney	20.00
Granite gray	12.00
Ramekin, Cov, Black chutney	165.00
Refrigerator Jar, Seafoam blue............	125.00

Salad Bowl, 11" d

Cedar green	60.00
Granite gray	55.00

Salad Fork and Spoon

Coral	75.00
Seafoam blue	85.00

Salad Plate, 8" d

Bean brown	15.00
Cedar green	60.00
Chartreuse...................................	4.00
Granite gray	4.00
Soup Bowl, Glacier blue....................	20.00
Sugar Bowl, Cov, chartreuse	6.00

Teapot, 5¹/₂" h, 9¹/₂" l, Steubenville
American Modern, Seafoam
blue(A), $50.00

Teapot

Bean brown	55.00
Coral..	45.00
Granite gray	45.00

Vegetable Bowl, 10" d

Coral	12.00
Seafoam blue	20.00

Vegetable Bowl, divided

Cedar green	45.00
Granite gray	60.00

Water Pitcher

Bean brown	90.00
Black Chutney...............................	55.00
Chartreuse....................................	75.00
Coral..	75.00
Granite gray	90.00

GENERAL MANUFACTURERS

This heading contains the largest group of companies. Dinnerware, novelties, figures, planters, vases, and the like were all part of extensive lines from many of these prolific companies. Those that produced specialized lines, such as art pottery, will be found in the appropriate category.

ABINGDON USA

ABINGDON POTTERY
Abingdon, Illinois
1934–1950

History: The Abingdon Sanitary Manufacturing Company began in 1908 and made china plumbing fixtures. By 1934 Abingdon Pottery had started to produce art pottery using the same equipment and material used for plumbing fixtures, a true white vitreous porcelain. Domestic and English clays were used for the high-fired china bodies.

Many skilled modelers worked on the numerous decorative and utilitarian designs made at the manufactory. Ralph Nelson, Joe Pica, and Harley Stegall created more than one thousand designs for Abingdon during its short history. Regular gloss, crazed, mottled, crystalline, iridescent, and matte glazes, plus unusual textures, were used. New colors and glazes were introduced every spring and fall during the seventeen-year history.

Art pottery production was expanded in 1945, and the company name was changed to Abingdon Potteries, Inc. Controlling stock was sold to Briggs Manufacturing Company of Detroit in 1947, and three years later art pottery production was discontinued. The company reverted to producing sanitary wares, the art ware lines were sold to Haeger Pottery, and molds were sold to Pigeon Forge Pottery and were later used by Western Stoneware of Monmouth, Illinois.

A tremendous variety of pieces in a wide range of colors were modeled, including cookie jars, teapots, lamps, figurines, bookends, pitchers, vases, candleholders, flowerpots, small animals, and much more. Shades of blue, red, yellow, pink, green, brown, and gray were used on the hand-decorated examples. A total of 149 colors were produced. Blanks also were sold to other companies for decoration.

Almost all pieces of Abingdon pottery were marked, usually in blue underglaze. Some paper labels were also used.

Reference: Norma Rehl, *Abingdon Pottery*, Milford, New Jersey, privately printed, 1981.

Collectors' Club: Abingdon Pottery Collectors, Mrs. Elaine Westover, RR1, Abingdon, IL 61410, $5.00 per year, quarterly newsletter.

Museums: Abingdon City Library, IL; Illinois State Museum, Bloomington, IL.

Bookend, 6¾" h, figural horse's head, black, #441, pr................................	**50.00**
Candleholder, 5" h, dbl, scalloped, pink, #575	**55.00**
Console Set, center bowl, 11¼" l, 2 dbl-armed candlesticks, 4¼" h, yellow-green glaze	**27.00**
Cornucopia	
4¾" h, 8½" l, blue	**25.00**
7" h, green, #565	**15.00**
8" l, pink, #569	**15.00**
Dish, 12" l, figural open leaf, rolled handle, med blue glaze, stamped mark	**12.00**
Figure	
4½" h, pouter pigeon, white, #388 .	**65.00**
5" h, goose	
Blue, #571.................................	**30.00**
Yellow	**18.00**
7" h	
Kneeling nude, pink, #3903	**175.00**
Peacock, white, #416	**38.00**
Flower Boat, 13" l, 4" w, fern leaf, gloss green, #426	**85.00**

*Figure, 10" h, mist green glaze, imp
mark, pr, $85.00*

*Vase, 8" h, light blue glaze, #538,
$48.00*

Flowerpot, 5" h, antique white, #151..	**45.00**
Flower holder, 5½" h, fern leaf, gloss	
green, #434....................................	**48.00**
Planter	
4¾" h, 9" l, rect, fan shape w/raised	
bow at base, dark green glaze,	
#484..	**14.00**
6½" h, Mexican and cactus, hand	
decorated, #616D	**55.00**
7¼" h, raised sailing ship, imp rope	
handles, sea green glaze..............	**18.00**
Shakers, Little Bo Peep, pr	**40.00**
Tea Tile, 5" sq, Coolie, white #401	**65.00**
Vase	
3½" h, whatnot, beige, #A2	**65.00**
4¾" h, 11" l, dbl cornucopia shape,	
med blue glaze............................	**20.00**
5" h, flower holder, blue, #491	**18.00**
5½" h	
Box, white, #402	**65.00**
Classic, blue, #140	**35.00**

6" h	
Beta, blue, #110	**35.00**
Rope, beige, #324	**25.00**
7" h, flattened oval shape, emb sail-	
ing ship on sides, ball-column	
handles, med blue glaze, #494....	**20.00**
9" h, quilted top, rope twist han-	
dles, white, #599	**10.00**
9½" h	
Coolie, matte white glaze, #308 ..	**35.00**
Peach glaze, #101	**35.00**
10" h	
Art Deco style, dusty rose, #114 ..	**25.00**
Beta, maroon, #102	**58.00**
10¾" h, raised stiff leaves on sides,	
2 small scroll handles, peach	
glaze	**25.00**
11" h	
Draped, blue glaze, #557	**35.00**
Lung shape, turquoise, #302........	**145.00**
Swirl, blue, #514	**22.00**

*Vase, 7" h, hp green cactus, blue
and red striped clothing, white
ground, $65.00*

Vase, 10" h, peach glaze, #117, $50.00

15" h
Fern Leaf, matte white, #433 .... **185.00**
Volute, white, #412 .... **165.00**

after
1904

ANCHOR POTTERY
Trenton, New Jersey
1884–1927

History: Israel Lacey purchased a plant from the Joseph Moore Pottery estate and renamed it Anchor Pottery. James Norris operated the facility producing cream-colored, white granite, and semi-porcelain wares. Both dinnerwares and toilet sets were made.

After a succession of managers, the plant closed in 1927 and was taken over by Fulper Pottery Company of Flemington, New Jersey.

Bowl, 8¾" d, 3 small bunches of pink and yellow roses, brown leaves, ext vert ribbing **17.00**
Mug, 5¼" h, decal of monk w/violin, shaded brown ground **35.00**
Pitcher
3½" h, pink and purple hibiscus and green leaves, green base, gold spattered rim, mkd **3.00**
7" h, brown "ICE WATER" on side, white raised leaf and document ground **50.00**

Wash Set, pitcher, 12" h, bowl, 16" d, toothbrush holder, cov soap dish, shaving mug, hot water pitcher, cold water pitcher w/bowl, yellow and purple pansies, gold trim, mkd, $595.00

J.A. BAUER POTTERY
Los Angeles, California
1909–1962

History: John Andrew Bauer founded a pottery company in 1909 in Los Angeles, California, with workers from his Paducah Pottery in Kentucky. He started production with a line of quality flowerpots made from California adobe clay. Stonewares were manufactured as soon as suitable clays were found. Bauer made whiskey jugs, water coolers, covered jars, butter churns, and such, but flowerpots were the mainstay during the first two decades.

Bauer's art pottery line of vases and flower bowls with matte green glazes won a Bronze Medal at the 1915 Panama-California Exhibition in San Diego. Bauer's son-in-law, Watson Bockmon, and the Bernheim family bought the pottery in 1922. During the Depression Bockmon bought out the Bernheims and incorporated as the J.A. Bauer Pottery Company, Inc.

In the early 1930s, Victor Houser developed new opaque colors of green, light blue, and yellow which were used for plain pieces as well as those with ring designs. The pots, vases, and stoneware dishes were appropriate for use both indoors and out. Additional colors were added over the years.

The Bauer company purchased the Batchelder tile factory in 1932 and used it as a second plant. Additional lines, such as Art Moderne style Monterey, were introduced in 1934.

Slip-cast vases, planters, jardinieres, candlesticks, flower bowls, and figurines were called Cal-Art. They were usually marked in the mold and were made in satin-matte and regular finishes in the mid 1930s.

During World War II, La Linda was developed with pastel colors and leadless glazes and it became a big seller. After the war and the end of restrictions, Ring-Ware was redesigned with streamlined contours and new contemporary colors.

Monterey Moderne, new in 1948, used a contemporary style to compete with Russel Wright designs. Herb Brusche's lines, Contempo and Al Fresco, were produced by Bauer in the 1950s. Bauer's dinnerwares were practical and unembellished and pleased the general buying public.

Bauer also introduced special pottery for

florists and gardeners, including vases, bowls, planters, sand jars, urns, bird baths, and jardinieres. The loss of key employees in the 1950s along with competition from inexpensive Japanese ceramic imports caused the Bauer pottery to close in the early 1960s.

Bauer pottery used a great many different marks, most of which were impressed on the bottom of pieces.

References: Jack Chipman, *Collector's Encyclopedia of California Pottery,* Collector Books, 1992; —— and Judy Stangler, *The Complete Collectors Guide to Bauer Pottery,* Jo-Books, 1982.

ARTWARE

Bulb Bowl, 6" d, blue, Fred Johnson design	75.00
Horn of Plenty, 6½" h, yellow, Cal-Art	35.00
Plate, 7" d, hp Dutch design, black	15.00
Vase	
6" h, fan shape, Matte Carlton design	
Orange	70.00
Yellow	70.00
8" h, yellow, Fred Johnson design	45.00

BRUSCHE MODERN WARE

Bowl, 5" d, chartreuse	5.00
Cup and Saucer	
Chartreuse	6.00
Pink speckle	10.00
Plate, chartreuse	
6" d	4.00
8" d	6.00
10" d	6.00
Tidbit Set, 3 piece, chartreuse	25.00

FLORIST AND GARDEN WARE

Bowl, 16" l, 8" w, pumpkin, speckled ivory	25.00

LA LINDA PATTERN

Casserole, Cov, 1 qt, green, copper holder	75.00
Creamer, gloss burgundy	25.00
Pie Plate, 10½" d, green, copper holder	35.00
Salt and Pepper, gloss burgundy	50.00
Sugar Bowl, Cov	
Brown	25.00
Gloss light green	30.00
Tumbler, matte green	17.50

MONTEREY MODERN PATTERN

Butter Dish, Cov, yellow	65.00
Creamer, miniature, turquoise blue	20.00
Gravy Boat, Chinese yellow	30.00
Platter, 18" l, maroon	55.00
Tidbit Set, 3 tiers, chartreuse	25.00

PREMIUM LINE

Mixing Bowl	
#12, green	25.00
#16, brown	22.00
#30, pink	20.00

RING WARE

Baking Dish, Cov	
Dark blue	25.00
Green	20.00
Yellow	20.00
Bowl	
9" d, green	30.00
9½" d, Chinese yellow	22.00
14" d, green	165.00
Butter Dish, orange-red	50.00
Candleholder, spool, cobalt, pr	38.00
Carafe, 8" h, cobalt, metal lid, raffia-wrapped handle	65.00
Cereal Bowl, 4½" d	
Blue	18.00
Gray	18.00
Chop Plate	
13" d, yellow	45.00
14" d, burgundy	50.00
Creamer, green	15.00
Cup and Saucer, cobalt	20.00
Mixing Bowl	
#12, yellow	35.00
#36, red	17.50
Pie Baker, cobalt	35.00
Pitcher	
4½" h, yellow	25.00
6" h, orange	45.00
Plate	
6" d, green	7.00
9" d	
Gray	20.00
Green	20.00
Yellow	20.00
Salad Bowl, ftd, ivory	40.00
Tumbler	
6 oz, wood handle, red	18.00
12-oz size, maroon	21.00
Vase	
6" h, green	35.00
9" h, green	50.00
10" h, orange	85.00
#30, pink	20.00

Pitcher, 5¼" h, Ring ware, dark blue, $45.00

STONEWARE
Bean pot, 6" h, tab handles, gloss rust
   glaze, #3 .... **225.00**
Vase
   11" h, Venus, white glaze **75.00**
   13¾" h, Art Deco style, fan shape,
     gloss turquoise glaze, pr **95.00**

1890   1886

EDWIN BENNETT POTTERY
Baltimore, Maryland
1844–1936

History: Edwin Bennett founded his pottery in 1844 in Baltimore, Maryland, to manufacture high-quality commercial pottery wares. Teapots, the most important items in the Bennett line, were made in porcelain, whiteware, majolica, and Rockingham. Bennett also made yellowware, caneware, flint enamel, and queensware. By 1848 his works were in demand, and he sent for his brother William to assist him.

Charles Coxon joined the Bennett brothers in 1850. Most of his designs were made in Rockingham ware and included shaving mugs, ale pitchers, water coolers, chamber pots, teapots, and his most famous piece, a ten-sided pot with the words "Rebekah at the Well" below the figure of a woman.

During the post–Civil War expansion period, Bennett introduced a line of white earthenware for both dinner and toilet sets. Some were produced with embossed flower or wheat motifs, while others were decorated with transfer printed in a variety of designs. He also used these whiteware bodies for spatterware and spongeware pieces. After 1876 much of the whiteware was marked with a variety of backstamps, including some initials. Bennett also experimented with parian wares and American Belleek tea sets.

After the Chicago Exposition of 1893, where the company received a medal of commendation, artwares were introduced. Henry Brunt was responsible for the firm's art pottery lines.

Brubensul ware, an earthenware line, was introduced in 1894. Mostly pedestals and jardinieres were made with majolica-type glazes in browns, greens, blues, and oranges which flowed together when fired. Pieces were usually marked with paper labels.

Albion ware was introduced in 1895 as an oriental-style slip-painted underglaze ware predominately in greens with a transparent glaze. It was marked with the Bennett and Albion names in addition to the date and artist's cipher.

The pottery company continued to expand in the early part of the 20th century. In place of artwares, production centered on pottery for everyday use. Yellowware called Bennett Bakeware was the primary line along with Bennett S-V, a double-glazed whiteware. These pieces were produced by simple overglazed stenciling or hand-painted designs.

George Bauer, who became general manager during the 1920s, realized that something other than the usual decal-decorated white or cream-colored dinnerwares was needed. To tempt buyers during the Depression, he introduced color—at first in pastel tones, and then in more intense hues. In addition, decals, when used, tended to dominate the plates.

Bauer contributed three patents for pottery making that allowed for significant changes in methods of decoration. In the first patent dated September 1931, Bauer introduced a pliable metal stencil for adding color to pottery examples. On some pieces, the stencil was used to block color applications, and on others it provided the outline for decoration. Stenciled patterns, including flowers, vines, figures, polka dots, and checks, were used on cake services, canister sets, salt boxes, pie plates, and dinnerwares.

Bauer's other patents were utilized at Harker Pottery which he joined in 1939, though some incised and encrusted cameo examples were made before Bennett closed and before the 1941 patent was granted.

The Edwin Bennett Pottery Company filed for bankruptcy in 1936 due to the economic climate.

Museums: Maryland Historical Society Museum, Baltimore, MD; Museum of History and Technology, Smithsonian Institution, Washington DC.

Bowl, 7" d, 4" h, white ironstone,
   raised scalloped design **17.00**
Platter, 10" l, purple, orange, and yellow flower clusters on border, green
   lined rim **25.00**
Syrup Pitcher, Cov
   6¼" h, faience, morning glory de-

Bowl, 6" h, 11³/₄" d, white, "E.B.P. Co.
Semi-Granite" mark, $40.00

sign on sides, albino, "Bennett's
Patent" mark................................ **175.00**
8" h, maroon crane standing in
rushes, gray ground, pewter lid.... **145.00**
Birds on branches design, pewter
lid, dtd 1878................................ **85.00**
Vase
6³/₄" h, 5³/₄" w, 2 handles and feet,
pillow shape, seated man
w/camel on front, desert scene on
reverse, gloss green ground, incised "E. Bennett Pottery Co.,
1896, Albion, KB" mark(A) **1650.00**
8¹/₂" h, 8" w, pillow shape, brown,
green, and cream Arabian man
on horse, green ground, "Albion,
E. Bennett Pottery Co., 1896, KB"
mark(A) **1100.00**

E. & L.P. NORTON
BENNINGTON VT.
c1861

THE BENNINGTON POTTERIES
Bennington, Vermont

NORTON POTTERY, 1793–1894
History: Captain John Norton established
Norton Pottery in Bennington, Vermont, where
he first made earthenwares for kitchen use. Numerous family members continued to join the
firm throughout its history.

In 1815 gray stoneware production was
added, and in 1823 salt-glazed stonewares were
made with brushwork replacing the incised and
impressed decorations. Stonewares from this period were marked with the Norton name and the
town of Bennington. The mark was impressed
and usually had cobalt rubbed into the letters to
color them. Through the years there were various
changes in the mark, but the Norton name was
always included.

From the 1850s through the 1880s Norton
family members remained in control of the pottery. Slip-trailed decorations were used on the
Norton salt-glazed stonewares depicting birds,
florals, pine trees, and deer. The mark used from
1861–1881, "E. and L.P. Norton, Bennington,
VT," was the most common mark and used for
the longest period of time including the era of increased production immediately following the
Civil War. Norton only marked stonewares.

Rockingham production probably started
about 1841. Solid-brown examples were made
for several years, and then by 1849 mottled
brown pieces were made. Hound-handled pitchers, the most desirable pieces made in Rockingham glaze, came in four different sizes.

FENTON POTTERY, c1835–1858
History: Christopher Webber Fenton leased
an area of the Norton Pottery about 1835. After
he married Julius Norton's sister, he became partners with Norton from 1843–1847. During this
period Norton and Fenton made stoneware
crocks, jugs, and six-sided brown pitchers in at
least four sizes, in different designs, and with a
variety of handles. These pieces were impressed
"Norton and Fenton, Bennington, VT." The partnership also produced Rockingham-glazed goblets, pitchers, tea and coffeepots, sugar bowls,
relish dishes, covered butter dishes, and an assortment of bowls and bakers.

After the short-lived partnership with Norton,
Fenton worked on his own to refine the coloring
process for Rockingham ware. He sprinkled
metallic oxides on the transparent glaze used on
the bisque ware and obtained tones of blue, yellow, and orange that blended with the brown
color on Rockingham pieces. He called this variation Flint enamel and patented it in 1849.

Fenton made Toby bottles in Rockingham,
Flint enamel, and graniteware. Five different
Toby pitchers and several varieties of Toby snuff
jars were made in Rockingham and Flint enamel.
Standing poodles holding baskets of fruit in their
mouths were made in brown Rockingham, Flint
enamel, graniteware, and parian. Cow creamers,
door knobs, soap dishes, teapots, and seated
dogs in the form of inkwells and paperweights
also were produced. Parian pieces, difficult
to identify as Bennington products, included a

large variety of vases and pitchers, as well as statues.

Fenton was considered one of the greatest potters of his time. Despite his short-lived pottery operation, he managed to produce graniteware, brown Rockingham, Flint enamel, slip-covered redwares, and scroddled ware made with variegated clays to resemble veined marble. He was the first potter working in America to make parian ware and some of these pieces were sent for exhibit to the Crystal Palace Fair in New York City.

In 1853 Fenton incorporated as the United States Pottery Company. At other times during its existence, the pottery was called Fenton's Works, or Lyman, Fenton and Company. Despite the tremendous variety and size of production, the Fenton factory closed in 1858 due to a combination of increased costs, poor marketing techniques, and financial instability caused by the approaching Civil War.

About one-fifth of Fenton pieces were marked. He adopted an oval impressed mark: "Lyman, Fenton & Co./Fenton's Enamel/Bennington, VT/Patented 1849." Four variations of this mark were used on the Rockingham and Flint enamel pieces, including Toby bottles.

References: Richard Carter Barret, *Bennington Pottery and Porcelain,* Bonanza Books, 1958; ———, *How to Identify Bennington Pottery,* Stephen Greene Press, 1964; Laura Woodside Watkins, *Early New England Potters and Their Wares,* Harvard University Press, 1950.

Museums: Bennington Museum, VT; Brooklyn Museum, NY; Museum of Ceramics, East Liverpool, OH; National Museum of American History, Smithsonian Institution, Washington, DC; Shelburne Museum, VT; Wadsworth Atheneum, Hartford, CT.

POTTERY AND PORCELAIN

Bottle, 10³/₄" h, figural Toby, Rockingham glaze, imp "Lyman Fenton & Co., Bennington, Vt." mark(A) **715.00**

Bowl, 3³/₄" d, 1⁵/₈" h, brown and tan Flint enamel glaze, unmkd **195.00**

Candlestick, 8³/₈" h, Rockingham glaze, pr(A) **370.00**

Cuspidor
8" d
  Diamond pattern, scroddled ware(A) **550.00**
  Flint enamel glaze **65.00**
10" d, Rockingham glaze, imp "Lyman Fenton & Co., Bennington, Vt." mark **75.00**

Figure
7¹/₂" h, standing lion w/paw on ball, Rockingham glaze, attributed to Lyman Fenton & Co., Bennington, Vt., chips and hairlines(A) **1760.00**
8" h, standing poodle, Rockingham

glaze w/coleslaw fur, attributed to Lyman, Fenton & Co., pr(A) **11,000.00**

Flask
5¹/₄" h, book shape, Flint enamel glaze, imp "Ladies Suffering G"(A) **412.00**
7" h, figural boot/stopper, Flint enamel glaze(A) **35.00**

Flowerpot, 4¹/₂" h, Flint enamel glaze, attributed to Lyman, Fenton & Co., cracked(A) **715.00**

Hand Vase, 6¹/₂" h, Flint enamel glaze, attributed to Lyman Fenton & Co., mid 19th C(A) **275.00**

Pitcher
7" h
  Climbing Ivy pattern, smear glaze(A) **90.00**
  Molded Grape pattern, Rockingham glaze, "Lyman R. Fenton East Bennington Vt." mark, repaired(A) **165.00**
7¹/₄" h, Flint enamel glaze, attributed to Lyman Fenton & Co., c1850, chip on spout................... **275.00**

Flask, 5¹/₂" h, brown Rockingham glaze(A), $90.00

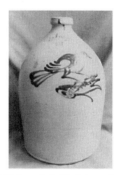

Jug, 15" h, cobalt bird, imp "J. AND E. NORTON, BENNINGTON, VERMONT," 2 gallon size(A), $375.00

7³/₄″ h, Sunflower pattern, smear glaze, "U.S. Pottery ribbon, #12" mark(A) **182.00**

8¹/₄″ h, Pond Lily design

Blue and white, "U.S. Pottery ribbon, #14″ mark(A) **110.00**

Smear glaze, "U.S. Pottery ribbon, #14″ mark(A) **165.00**

9¹/₄″ h, Leaf and Flower design, smear glaze, raised "Fenton Works" mark(A) **275.00**

10″ h, alternate ribbed body, Flint enamel glaze(A) **935.00**

10¹/₄″ h, blue and white Paul and Virginia pattern, "U.S. Pottery ribbon, #10″ mark(A) **220.00**

11″ h, Daffodil pattern, smear glaze(A) **135.00**

12¹/₂″ h, Flint enamel glaze, attributed to Lyman Fenton & Co.(A) ... **825.00**

Pitkin, Cov, 6¹/₄″ h, ribbed body, Rockingham glaze(A) **990.00**

Sugar Bowl, 9″ h, domed cov, Flint enamel glaze, imp "Lyman, Fenton 1849 Bennington Vt." mark............. **875.00**

Syrup Pitcher, Cov, 7¹/₄″ h, Spinning Wheel pattern, white glaze, c1850.. **225.00**

Toby Jug, 5⁷/₈″ h, Rockingham glaze, Fenton mark....................................... **450.00**

Tulip Vase, 9″ h, Flint enamel glaze, attributed to Lyman Fenton & Co.(A) **385.00**

STONEWARE

Churn, 17¹/₂″ h, ovoid shape, cobalt slip stylized flower, imp "E. Norton & Co. Bennington, Vt. 4″ mark on neck, chips and flakes(A)................. **165.00**

Crock

7″ h, cobalt painted oak leaf, imp "E & LP NORTON BENNINGTON VT." mark, one gallon, hairlines **250.00**

7¹/₄″ h, straight sides

Brushed cobalt leaf design, imp label "E. & L.P. Norton, Bennington, Vt."(A) **154.00**

Albany slip, imp "NORTON & CO. BENNINGTON VT." mark, one gallon, c1880(A) **44.00**

9″ h, cobalt quill stylized floral design, imp label "E. & L.P. Norton, Bennington, Vt. 2″ mark, chips and hairlines(A) **110.00**

10¹/₂″ h, cobalt slip feather design, imp "E. & L.P. Norton, Bennington, Vt. 3″ mark(A)...................... **225.00**

12¹/₂″ h, cobalt floral design, imp "E. & L.P. NORTON, BENNINGTON" mark(A) **95.00**

13″ h, cobalt bird on branch w/dots below, imp "E. & L.P. NORTON, BENNINGTON, VT." mark, cobalt "6″ **585.00**

Jar

10¹/₂″ h, ovoid shape, imp label

"Julius Norton, Bennington, Vt. 2″ mark, w/blue accents(A)......... **50.00**

12³/₄″ h

Cobalt slip floral design, imp "J. Norton & Co., Bennington, Vt." mark(A)...................................... **745.00**

Ovoid shape, cobalt brushed floral design, imp circ "Norton & Fenton, Bennington, Vt." mark(A)...................................... **385.00**

13¹/₄″ h, cobalt quill design of buildings, fences, and rooster, imp "J. & E. Norton, Bennington, Vt. 3″ mark, old repair(A) **797.00**

Jar, Cov, 12″ h, ovoid shape, blue dbl handles, imp blue L. NORTON 2″ mark, c1830(A) **242.00**

Jug

10¹/₂″ h, cobalt slip stylized flower, imp "J. & E. Norton, Bennington" mark(A) **357.00**

11¹/₄″ h, cobalt quill bird on branch, imp "J. & E. Norton, Bennington, Vt." mark(A) **385.00**

12³/₄″ h, cobalt slip floral design, imp label "E. & L.P. Norton, Bennington, Vt. 2″ mark(A)............... **407.00**

13″ h, cobalt brushed floral design, "Norton & Fenton, East Bennington, Vt. 2″ mark(A) **275.00**

18″ h, cobalt slip stylized floral design, pebbly glaze imp label "J. Norton, Bennington, Vt. 4″(A) **545.00**

Pitcher

11¹/₄″ h, brown Albany slip, imp label "E. Norton & Co., Bennington, Vt."(A) **302.00**

12¹/₂″ h, cobalt quill bird on branch design, imp label "F. & E. Norton, Bennington, Vt.," repaired(A)....... **200.00**

Whiskey Jug

11¹/₂″ h, cobalt abstract flower, imp "E. & L.P. NORTON/BENNINGTON, VT." mark, 1 gallon, c1861–81(A) **187.00**

12³/₄″ h, cobalt painted bird on branch, imp "J. & E. Norton VT. 1¹/₂″ mark(A)............................. **4125.00**

13¹/₄″ h, cobalt painted jumping deer, imp "NORTON & FENTON, EAST BENNINGTON, VT. 2″ mark, c1845(A) **550.00**

14″ h

Blue abstract floral design, imp "JULIUS NORTON BENNINGTON, VT.2″ mark, repaired handle **150.00**

Cobalt cabbage rose, imp "J. NORTON & CO. BENNINGTON VT. 2″ mark, c1859...................... **275.00**

Ovoid shape, 3 blue flowers, imp "L. NORTON & SON BENNINGTON 2″ mark, spider crack(A).......... **132.00**

15¹/₂″ h, ovoid shape, blue flower

design, imp "L. NORTON & SON/BENNINGTON" mark 2 gallon, c1833–38(A).............................. **412.00**

Brayton Laguna
1927

BRAYTON LAGUNA POTTERY
South Laguna Beach, California
1927–1968

History: Durlin E. Brayton started his pottery in the late 1920s by working at home making handcrafted earthenware dinnerwares in mixed colors. Pieces were press molded by hand and dipped in a series of opaque glazes in colors like rose, strawberry pink, eggplant, jade green, lettuce green, chartreuse, old gold, burnt orange, lemon yellow, silky black, and white.

In addition to regular place settings, serving pieces such as teapots, pitchers, and large bowls were made by Brayton. He also made flowerpots, vases, tea tiles, wall plates, and figurines in limited quantities.

Working with his second wife, Webb, the business was expanded into a commercial facility. It was licensed by Walt Disney from 1938–1940 to produce ceramic figures of the Disney characters. Birds, animals, and human figures also were made in a variety of finishes, along with planters, vases, ashtrays, candleholders, cookie jars, salt and pepper shakers, and other household items.

The first outside designer to work for Brayton Laguna was H.S. Anderson, a Swedish woodcarver who was responsible for humorous figurines and groups, such as the English hunter with fox and hounds, the hillbilly shotgun wedding set, and the popular purple cow, bull, and calf family.

Eventually more than twenty-five designers worked at the pottery making hand-decorated figurines. By the end of World War II, it was a major ceramics supplier to retail outlets all over the United States and in many foreign countries, since imports were limited during the war. After the war, cheaper Japanese and Italian imports again flooded the market, and Brayton Laguna's business declined. With the deaths of Webb in 1948 and Durlin Brayton in 1951, sales continued to slide and the pottery closed in 1968.

Various marks were used on Brayton Laguna pieces, though some pieces were not marked due to their small size.

Reference: Jack Chipman, *Collector's Encyclopedia of California Pottery*, Collector Books, 1992.

Figure, 6½" h, 11" l, purple body, white horns, black tail and feet, $150.00

Canister, Dutch boy and girl **165.00**
Figure
  6½" h, girl w/bonnet, holding bouquet of flowers, blue shades **35.00**
  7½" h, 2 ducks, turquoise crackle glaze **45.00**
  8" h
    Dutch boy, blue shades **35.00**
    Man and woman in 1890s nightshirts **40.00**
    Sally, white pinafore, yellow dress w/blue spots, brown hair . **34.00**
  9" h, Gay Nineties lady **95.00**
  13" h, giraffe, green........................ **55.00**
  13" l, panther, red glaze **75.00**
  Shotgun Wedding, multicolored, c1938, set of 6 .... **450.00**
Flower Holder, 6¾" h, Sally **15.00**
Planter, 8" h, lady w/basket, white...... **65.00**
Salt and Pepper
  5" h, black peasants **25.00**
  Calico cat and dog **40.00**
  Mammy and chef **70.00**
  Peruvian couple **150.00**
Vase, 14" h, figural blackamoor, polychrome turban **250.00**
Wall Pocket, 24" h, figural blackamoor, pr **110.00**

BRUSH-MCCOY POTTERY COMPANY
Roseville and Zanesville, Ohio

(see J.W. McCoy in General Manufacturers section)

Ashtray, 6½" d, dbl figural frog, natural colors 50.00

Bank

2½" h, 4½" l, figural pig, blue onyx ... 75.00

Billy Possum, brown glaze 225.00

Bowl, 5" d, Amaryllis Kolorkraft, blue glaze, #011 .... 32.00

Candleholder, 3" h, blue majolica, pr . 30.00

Cherry pattern

Casserole, Cov 35.00

Shakers, pr 16.00

Fern Dish, 7" l, Woodland, green #93 ... 35.00

Eggcup, 2¼" h, Fannie Farmer chicken, yellow and red 37.50

Jardiniere, 6½" h, blended green and olive glaze, #242 .... 35.00

Jug, 7½" h, Olympia corn design 325.00

Lawn Ornament, 10" l, figural frog, natural colors, #486D 158.00

Mug

4½" h, Art Glazed Dutch, cream w/brown and green, #348 .... 35.00

Davy Crockett, dark brown 15.00

Pitcher

6" h, corn line, shape #44 .... 45.00

7" h, stoneware, blue and white Dutch boy and girl kissing w/windmill 100.00

10½" h, majolica, log cabin and folk dancing, tan 200.00

Planter

5½" h

6" l, bear on log, brown shades, gold trim, #205 .... 28.00

7½" l, dove on bowl, multicolored, #802 .... 15.00

Dancing girls, multicolored 12.00

7" l, figural turtle, brown and cream 15.00

10" l, rect, stepped shape, ftd, turquoise glaze, imp "BRUSH 23" mark 20.00

12" l, sailboat, tan and red 45.00

Pot, 2½" h, Rockcraft, gray, #801 .... 18.00

Salt and Pepper, cream ground w/pink clover, green leaves, #K1, K2 .... 18.00

Spittoon, 7" h, Loy-Nel-Art, florals on brown ground 65.00

Urn, 6" h, brown onyx 9.00

Vase

4" h

Majolica, green 50.00

Zuniart swastika pattern 110.00

5" h

Art Vellum, mottled green 30.00

Brown onyx 22.00

Green onyx, swan handles 29.00

6" h

Amaryllis, majolica finish, mkd ... 55.00

Brown onyx 25.00

Peach Bloom, Ivotint, #0192, c1929 .... 95.00

7" h

Amaryllis, glossy 18.00

Loy-Nel-Art, dbl handles, cherries design, olive-brown shading 125.00

8" h

Blue onyx 25.00

Brown onyx 25.00

Green onyx 20.00

King Tut pattern 250.00

Loy-Nel-Art, daisies design 85.00

Narrow base tapered to wide body, imp vert lines, gray ext, turquoise int 20.00

8½" h, Jewel, #042 .... 395.00

9" h

Flecked tan glaze 50.00

Moderne kolorkraft, blue glaze 50.00

9¼" h, bulbous base w/2 small handles, tapered neck w/emb tulip heads, matte white ext, turquoise int 20.00

14" h, Loy-Nel-Art, orange and green foliage 275.00

Wall Pocket, bucking horse, tan, brown, and green 85.00

Mug, 4⅝" h, raised dancing figures, brown and green shading over yellow ground, "Brushware" mark, $40.00

BUFFALO POTTERY
Buffalo, New York

(see Buffalo Pottery history in Art Pottery section)

ALBINO WARE

Mug, 4¼" h, windmill and boat scene, sgd "R. Smart," dtd 1913 .... 875.00

Plate, 10" d, sailboat scene 500.00

Platter, 13⅝" l, 10⅜" w, windmill
and boat scene, sgd "R. Smart," dtd
1911 .... **1650.00**
Tankard, 7" h, sailing scene, sgd "Harris" **300.00**

BONREA PATTERN
Butter Dish, Cov **25.00**

WILLOW WARE
Bowl, 8" l, 6½" w, dtd 1916 .... **25.00**
Butter Tub, dtd 1916 .... **35.00**
Cream Soup **10.00**
Cup and Saucer, gaudy willow **80.00**
Cup and Saucer, A.D. **14.00**
Pitcher
2¾" h, semi-vitreous, dtd 1909(A)... **66.00**
4⅞" h, gilt accents, dtd 1907(A)...... **82.00**
5¼" h, gaudy willow **75.00**
6½" h, dtd 1908(A) **130.00**
Plate
8¼" d, gaudy willow, dtd 1908 .... **90.00**
9" d **60.00**
10" d, gaudy willow **100.00**
Platter
10½" l, dtd 1911 .... **60.00**
12" l, dtd 1916 .... **85.00**
13" l **75.00**
17" l, 12" w, dtd 1922 .... **150.00**
Sugar Bowl, dtd 1911 .... **70.00**

MISCELLANEOUS
Chamber Pot, 10½" d, applied handles, roses design on white **125.00**
Charger, Rouge Ware
11½" d, "Morgan's Road Coach
Tavern" **350.00**
12" d, "Breakfast at the Three Pigeons" **595.00**
Chocolate Pot, 11" h, floral decoration, gold accents **80.00**
Fish Set, platter, 15" l, 11" w, 6 plates,
9" d, multicolored fish on each,
artist sgd **295.00**
Jug
6" h
Blue-green ducks in flight, gold
trim, mkd **325.00**
"Landing of Roger Williams,"
multicolored, dtd 1906 .... **495.00**
"The Buffalo Hunt," dark green
top, gold handle **325.00**
Whaling City, brown transfer **850.00**
6¼" h, "Cinderella," brown transfer
w/red, green, and yellow enamel
accents, eagle mark(A) **412.00**
6½" h, Dutch design **345.00**
7" h, "Whirl of Town," butterscotch
luster **495.00**
7½" h, George Washington, blue
transfer, gold trim **395.00**
8" h, brown, green, and blue Robin
Hood on front, bow and stag on
reverse, c1906 .... **550.00**

9" h
Blue printed sailors' busts on
front, lighthouse on rocky
shore on reverse, nautical border, "Marine Jug, 1907, 1414"
mark(A) **495.00**
Gloriana design, blue transfer,
dtd 1907 .... **475.00**
9¼" h, blue printed Bon Homme
Richard designs, "John Paul
Jones" inside spout, dtd 1907(A).. **660.00**
Milk Pitcher, 6" h, chrysanthemum
design **90.00**
Pitcher
5" h, pink and light green florals **35.00**
8" h, pink and yellow roses, gold
trim **85.00**
Plate
7½" d
"B & M Smelter, Great Falls,
Montana," blue-green transfer.. **95.00**
"Statue of Liberty," green transfer. **95.00**
9¼" d
Cobalt stamped Arts and Crafts
style roses, stamped "BUFFALO
POTTERY CO." mark(A) **77.00**
"Dr. Syntax Disputing His Bill
with the Landlady," blue transfer, dtd 1906 .... **275.00**
Grouse, green transfer, dtd
1908(A) **93.00**
Wild ducks breaking cover, green
transfer, dtd 1908(A) **93.00**
10" d
"Independence Hall," blue transfer **25.00**
"Niagara Falls," blue transfer,
c1907 .... **35.00**
"The White House," blue-green
transfer **45.00**

Jug, 9¼" h, Marine, blue transfer,
blue "Buffalo Pottery" mark, dtd
1900, $675.00

Platter, 14" l, 11" w, "The Buffalo
Hunt," dark green border, scalloped
rim w/gold **300.00**
Plaque, 9" d, "The Gunner," blue-
green w/gold rim **60.00**
Serving Plate, 11¼" H-H, green and
red geometric border, Roycroft orb
on face, mkd(A).............................. **412.00**
Tumbler, 4½", h, flared rim, blue
scrolls and flowers on white ground,
set of 6 .... **295.00**
Vase, 4" h, Multifleure, Blue Lune **95.00**
Wash Set
   5 piece, pitcher, bowl, chamber
   pot, toothbrush holder, soap dish,
   chrysanthemum pattern **375.00**
   6 piece, pitcher, 12" h, bowl, 17" d,
   pitcher, 7½" h, cov soap dish,
   5½" d, mug, 3¾" h, toothbrush
   holder, 4¾" h, purple and yellow
   roses w/green leaves, gilt trim,
   molded handles and lips, purple
   "Buffalo Pottery" mark, c1910 ..... **495.00**

CATALINA
MADE IN
U. S. A.
POTTERY
1937–1942

CATALINA ISLAND POTTERY
Avalon, California
1927–1942

History: William Wrigley, Jr., owned Catalina
Island and in 1927 started a tile plant there to use
its plentiful clay deposits. After several years
Harold Johnson joined the business and was responsible for many designs and glazes used on
colored ornamental pottery.

The company received an award for its extensive tile work on the Catalina Casino, which was
completed in 1929. Then the firm shifted its attention to using the native brown-burning clay to
slip cast souvenir items, vases, flower bowls,
lamps, candleholders, and other decorative accessories.

Virgil Haldeman became ceramic engineer in
1930, and he made outstanding and unusual
glazes. Colors such as mandarin yellow, Catalina
blue, Descanso green, Toyon red, turquoise,
Pearly white, Seafoam, and Monterey brown
were utilized. Spanish-style wrought-iron frames
and stands were made for scenic tile panels and
decorative wall plates that came in Moorish patterns, Spanish galleons, and undersea garden designs.

A wide variety of glazes was used on the

tablewares that were introduced about 1930.
Three basic dinnerware designs, plus numerous
serving pieces, were sold all over the country. In
1936 a new dinner service with a raised rope
border in satin-finish pastel colors was introduced.

Because the local brown clay was very brittle
and broke easily, a new white burning clay was
brought in from Lincoln, California, in 1932, but
this proved to be quite costly. In 1937 the
Catalina molds and designs were sold to
Gladding, McBean in Los Angeles, and that company continued to make the Catalina line from
1937 until 1941.

A number of versions of "Catalina" or
"Catalina Island" were used to mark the original
Catalina pieces, which are more desirable especially if made with the brown clay. Some paper
labels also were used. "Catalina Pottery" was
used by Gladding, McBean to mark its Catalina
pottery line.

References: Jack Chipman, *Collector's Encyclopedia of California Pottery,* Collector Books,
1982; Steven and Aisha Hoefs, *Catalina Island
Pottery Collectors Guide,* privately printed,
1993; Tile Heritage Foundation, *Catalina Tile of
the Magic Isle,* 1993.

DINNERWARE
Bowl, 14" l, oval, scalloped edge,
pedestal base, matte green glaze **175.00**
Chop Plate, 13" d, rope border, blue
glaze **110.00**
Coaster, 4" d, Catalina blue glaze **20.00**
Coffee Mug, Catalina blue glaze **35.00**
Coffee Set, server, 10½" h, 6 handled
mugs, green glaze **250.00**
Cup and Saucer, matte green glaze **35.00**
Plate
   6¼" d, rolled edge, Catalina blue
   glaze **24.00**
   7" d, ivory glaze............................. **13.00**
   10" d
      Mandarin yellow glaze **22.50**
      Smooth edge, matte green glaze .. **25.00**
   10½" d, scalloped edge, Catalina
   blue glaze................................... **35.00**
   12" d, scalloped, green glaze **32.00**
Platter
   13" d, turquoise glaze **75.00**
   14½" d, smooth edge, matte blue
   glaze **85.00**
Tumbler
   2¾" h, matte green glaze **18.00**
   4" h, orange glaze **15.00**
Duotone
Plate, blue and white
   6" d.. **15.00**
   8½" d.. **17.50**
Rancho, Gladding McBean mark
Bowl, 5" d **15.00**

Plate, 7" d.. **14.00**
Platter, 14" d....................................... **18.00**
MISCELLANEOUS
Ashtray
  3³/₄" h, figural standing bear, cream
    glaze **195.00**
  4" h, figural sleeping Mexican,
    green glaze................................. **250.00**
  5³/₄" d, figural cowboy hat, yellow
    glaze **28.00**
Bookend
  4¹/₂" h, figural frog, Pearly white, pr **2200.00**
  5" h, figural seated monk w/book,
    green glaze, c1932, pr **1000.00**
Bowl
  8¹/₂" d, shell shape, gold.................. **65.00**
  9" d, toyon red, white clay **75.00**
  9³/₄" sq, white ext, turquoise int....... **35.00**
  11¹/₂" d, fluted, orange glaze **250.00**
  14" d, green ext, yellow int **35.00**
  15" l, 9¹/₂" w, white ext, turquoise
    int.. **46.00**
Bud Vase, 5" h, flared, beige glaze **55.00**
Candleholder
  4" h, pedestal base, flared rim, pink
    glaze, #606, pr **120.00**
  4¹/₂" h, eggcup shape, Manchu yel-
    low, pr.. **150.00**
Carafe
  7" h, wooden handle, gloss yellow
    glaze **38.00**
  Toyon red **65.00**
Charger
  12¹/₂" d, green, yellow, and blue
    painted banjo player, ivory
    ground, red clay body, stamped
    "CATALINA" mark(A) **440.00**
  14" d, green, yellow, and orange
    galleon on sky blue ground, red
    clay body, restored back,
    stamped "CATALINA" mark(A) **440.00**
Cigarette Box, 4³/₄" l, horse's head,
  white glaze **500.00**
Creamer, 2³/₄" h, matte blue glaze,
  imp mark **60.00**
Decanter, 7¹/₂" h, bulbous shape,
  gloss yellow glaze **95.00**
Dish, 14" d, shell shape, scalloped
  edge, white glaze **150.00**
Plate
  10¹/₂" d, multicolored kissing par-
    rots, black ground........................ **850.00**
  14" d, Submarine Garden pattern.... **2000.00**
Platter
  14" d, scalloped, matte blue glaze .. **95.00**
  16" l, 12" w, rooster design **60.00**
Sugar Bowl, 2³/₄" h, matte blue glaze .. **60.00**
Vase
  4¹/₂" h
    Oxblood glaze, Gladding
    McBean **55.00**

Relief of hotel and palms, brown
  glaze, mkd **28.00**
5" h
  Fluted, yellow ext, burgundy int .. **38.00**
  Matte green glaze **110.00**
  Stepped shoulder, 2 small sq han-
    dles, clay body, imp mark........ **300.00**
5³/₄" h
  Nautilus-shell shape, white ext,
    salmon int............................... **75.00**
  Oxblood glaze, Gladding
    McBean **150.00**
6" h
  Cuspidor shape, periwinkle blue
    glaze(A) **175.00**
  Flared rim, caramel glaze w/crys-
    tals, "Catalina Pottery" mark **265.00**
  Flared shape, blue glaze, red clay **125.00**
  Oval shape, gloss blue glaze,
    #509 .... **17.00**
  7" h, flared shape, white ext, blue
    int... **45.00**
7¹/₂" h
  Bulbous shape, tan and brown
    streaks.................................... **75.00**
  Shell shape, cream ext, salmon
    pink int, "Gladding McBean"
    mark **38.00**
7³/₄" h, conch-shell shape, cream
  ext, salmon pink int **50.00**
8" h
  Pedestal base, flared to 4 corners,
    scalloped rim, blue glaze **75.00**
  Yellow, green, and blue glaze **75.00**
  9" h, oxblood red glaze, Gladding
    McBean mark **165.00**
  9¹/₂" h, matte aqua pebbled glaze
    ext, white int, "Catalina Pottery"
    mark... **245.00**
10¹/₄" h
  Oxblood glaze, Gladding
    McBean **175.00**

Vase, 5¹/₂" h, tan glaze, ridged
base, "Catalina Island, #839"
mark, pr, $225.00

*Vase, 7¹/₂" h, white ext, peach int,
"Catalina Pottery, Made in
U.S.A." mark, Gladding, McBean,
c1937–1942, $45.00*

Trumpet shape, fluted, ftd, matte green finish	**95.00**
10¹/₂" h, light blue glaze	**185.00**
12" h, trumpet shape, fluted body, ftd, tan ground, rust accents	**125.00**
13¹/₂" h, fluted body, orange glaze, mkd	**600.00**
15¹/₂" h, tapered base, flared rim, dbl handles, matte blue glaze, mkd	**350.00**
17" h, Floriform, red glaze	**195.00**

MOTHER GOOSE
HAYNES
Ware
Decoration
No. 510

HAYNES
BALtº
1900-1904
or later

CLIFTON
HHB
DECOR'B.

CHESAPEAKE POTTERY/ D.F. HAYNES AND SON COMPANY
Baltimore, Maryland
1880–1914

History: Chesapeake Pottery was started in 1880 by Henry and Isaac Broughman and John Tunstall. In 1882 D.F. Haynes and Company purchased the plant, expanded it, and in 1887 sold it to Edwin Bennett. After a few years, he sold the works to his son and David Haynes, and it was renamed Haynes, Bennett and Company. When Bennett retired in 1895, Frank Haynes joined the firm and it became D.F. Haynes and Son in 1896.

The company made semi-porcelain toilet sets, dishes, jardinieres, and novelties. Majolica was made between 1881 and 1890. The company's first majolica dinner pattern was Clifton. Avalon Faience was a more elegant design based on French faience. Both of these patterns had off-white backgrounds, new to American majolica. A third faience design was Real Ivory.

Parian and white granite ware were made after 1895. Products included jugs, lamps, vases, and clocks.

An assortment of marks was used. In 1914 American Sugar Refining Company bought the facility and pottery making was discontinued.

Reference: Marilyn G. Karmason with Joan B. Stacke, *Majolica*, Harry Abrams, 1989.

Museum: Peale Museum, Baltimore, MD.

Bowl, 4³/₄" h, 8¹/₄" d, ftd, faience, raised berries, yellow flowers, green leaves, cream pebbly ground, "CLIFTON" and half moon mark	**135.00**
Charger, 13" d, portrait bust of Spotted Wolf, mkd	**175.00**
Cream Pitcher, 5¹/₄" h, turquoise raised leaves and spotted berries, gold bow under spout, "Avalon Faience" mark	**85.00**
Compote, 5³/₄" h, faience, blackberry pattern, turquoise outlined leaves, gold trim, cream pebbly ground, Avalon	**150.00**
Jardiniere	
6¹/₄" h, rust and green ground w/gold trim, lions'-head handles	**75.00**
7¹/₂" h, Lotus Ware design, 3 handles, sgd "S.E. Wells"	**50.00**

*Beverage Set, pitcher, 6¹/₂" h, 6 mugs,
5" h, black company crest, brown and
tan shades, hairlines, "Haynes Baltimore" mark(A), $100.00*

Lemonade Bowl, 12" d, ftd, faience,
blackberry design, Avalon mark **185.00**
Pitcher
3½" h, faience, berry design,
"Avalon Faience, Balto." mark..... **45.00**
4⅞" h, faience, red raspberries,
Avalon mark **75.00**
5" h
Faience, center band of raised red
outlined leaves and berries,
fretwork above and below,
beaded neck **65.00**
Gainsborough Decoration pat-
tern, "Haynes" mark................ **45.00**
Holland Sunset pattern, "Haynes"
mark **50.00**
6¾" h, faience, red strawberries,
Avalon mark.............................. **150.00**
7¼" h, Gainsborough Decoration
pattern, "Haynes" mark **15.00**
7½" h, Severn Ware, silver and gold
flowers, foliage, and butterfly,
gloss sand ground, branch handle, incised bands at top and
base(A) **1045.00**
10¼" h, faience, dark red oak
leaves, cream ground, dark red
raised base, hound face handle,
"Avalon Faience, Balto." mark..... **98.00**
Planter, 4½" h, 7½" d, Holland Sunset pattern, 4 green feet, "Haynes"
mark **75.00**
Plate
8" d, faience
Molded green and gold leaves
and flowers, cream ground,
Avalon mark **25.00**
Red leaves, gold berries, cream
pebbly ground, Avalon mark.... **75.00**

9" d
Faience, red "Chew Rose Leaf
Fine Cut" on front, raised pink
flowers and green leaves,
cream pebbly ground, Avalon.. **575.00**
White ironstone.......................... **2.00**
Relish Dish, 8" l, faience, grapes design, "Avalon Balto." mark **55.00**
Toothbrush Holder, 5" h, faience,
gold floral design, white ground,
"Haynes" mark............................... **65.00**
Vase
4⅜" h, faience, red buttercup de-
sign, Avalon **75.00**
5" h, faience, brown outlined
branches.................................... **75.00**
5¾" h, faience, chrysanthemums,
Avalon mark.............................. **85.00**

COLONIAL POTTERY
East Liverpool, Ohio
1903–1929

History: The Colonial Pottery Company was
formed in East Liverpool, Ohio, in 1903 when
East Liverpool Potteries Company dissolved.
Ironstone and semi-porcelain toilet sets, dinnerwares, and hotel and restaurant wares were
made. Many examples had gold trim. Several different marks were used until the firm closed in
1929.

Bowl, 10" d, multicolored garden
flowers in center, raised ribbon and
bows on inner border, scattered
flowers and gold drops on rim......... **12.00**

Vase, 8½" h, Gainsborough Decoration,
yellow, green, and cream, "Haynes"
mark, $15.00

Bowl, 9⅝" d, brick red and black
pagoda in center, raised shaded blue
border, gold sprigs, "The Colonial"
mark, $20.00

Chamber Pot, Cov, white ground, gold outlined curlicues and swirls, fancy handle w/gold trim, c1920, mkd **40.00**
Mug, 5¼" h, multicolored decal of tavern scene, shaded brown ground **75.00**
Plate
   9¼" d, calendar, pink roses between green decal, 1909, "The Colonial" mark **30.00**
   9⅝" d, brown bulldog decal, gold "Compliments of Henry Grantman," raised scroll border, gold wavy rim **12.00**
   10¼" d, decal of Indiana's largest department store, "Compliments Fall 1909 Kaufmann and Wolf" ... **15.00**
Platter
   13¼" l, center w/2 birds in water, raised scalloped border w/gold floral trim **10.00**
   13½" l, decal of strutting pheasant in forest scene, raised beaded band on border, gold-dusted shaped rim, "Colonial" and eagle head mark **50.00**

c.1892 and later

c.1890

DRESDEN POTTERY COMPANY
East Liverpool, Ohio
1875–1927

History: In 1875 Brunt, Bloor, Martin and Company operated at the Dresden Pottery Works in East Liverpool, Ohio, making white ironstone, gold-decorated wares, tablewares, tea sets, toilet wares, spittoons, toys, and hotel ware. A local labor dispute in 1882 forced the company to sell out to the Potter's Co-Operative Company— formed by a group of potters in response to the labor problems. The cooperative, headed by H.A. McNicol, used the Dresden Pottery Works' facility to make dinnerware, tea sets, sanitary wares, and hotel china until 1925 when a new corporation, Dresden Pottery Company, took over. Dresden made semi-vitreous dinnerware, hotel china, and plain and decorated specialty wares for two years, and then disbanded. A variety of marks was used.

Reference: William C. Gates, Jr. and Dana E. Ormerod, *The East Liverpool, Ohio Pottery District: Identification of Manufacturers and Marks,* The Society for Historical Archaeology, 1982.

Berry Bowl, single bluebird w/rose on border w/blue stripe, semi-vitreous ware, "Potters Co-Operative" mark, set of 4 .... **8.00**
Bowl
   9¼" d, pink and white poppies w/gray-green leaves in center, gold band on rim w/gold-drop inner band **10.00**
   10" d, garden flowers in center, yellow border shaded to brown rim w/raised design, "NAOMI" and banner mark **25.00**
   10½" d, apples and grapes in center, pink border w/gold trim, semi-vitreous ware, "Potter's Co-operative" mark **16.00**
   12¼" d, center w/large pink and gold-brown roses, pink shaded border w/raised design, "PERFECT" and ribbon mark **12.00**
Cake Plate, 10¼" H-H, decal of fruit in center, med blue border w/raised design, "Potters Co-Operative" mark **10.00**
Charger, 12¾" d, black, rose, and green pagoda and bridge, oriental scene in center, black and yellow floral and scroll border, "Dresden China" mark **28.00**
Chocolate Pot, 9¼" h
   Decal of 2 Dutch men on one side, 2 Dutch children on reverse, blue striped borders **50.00**
   Large yellow roses w/green leaves and stems, dark brown ground shading to cream **55.00**
Pitcher
   8" h, "Yale," peach base, raised gold-outlined triangles on shoulder, raised gold-outlined neck **120.00**
   8½" h, white ironstone, "Potters Co-Operative" mark **35.00**
Plate
   6⅝" d
      Advertising, multicolored scene of man and woman holding hands in muffler, gold "Compliments of George D. Williams, The Leading Grocer, 721 State St., Erie, Pa," gold banded border, white ground... **14.00**
      Bunch of cherries in center, brown to blue-green shaded ground, gold rim, "Dresden China" mark **12.00**
      Gibson girl and man leaning on

rail, Capital building in background, "Sight Seeing" in corner, gold rim, sgd "Christy" 35.00

7 1/2" d

Multicolored decal of different game fish, gold overlay designed rim, "Dresden" and wreath mark, set of 5 .... 55.00

Open roses in center, advertising on front, 1910 calendar border 25.00

Turquoise transfer of "Seaside Hotel—Pavilion—Corpus Christi, Texas," gold line and rim, "Dresden China" mark...... 45.00

8 1/4" d, large pink rose in center, 1909 calendar leaves on border w/holly leaves and berries, gold line rim, gold "Compliments of A. Gerstenkorn, General Merchant, Prices To Please The People, Crete, Ill.," Brunt mark................ 38.00

9 1/4" d

Bust of woman in blue gown in center, 4 pink roses on border, gold outlined shaped rim, advertising on reverse 38.00

Gibson girl in center w/blond hair, purple hat and feather, white fur piece, floral border, "Wm. Brunt Pottery Co., East Liverpool, Oh." mark 60.00

9 1/2" d

Hanging plums and foliage, shaded purple ground, gold rim, "Dresden China" mark...... 12.00

Multicolored decal of Gypsy woman in center, 3 roses on border, "Compliments of Lipfoski, Palatine, Ill." on front...... 32.00

Three large pink roses w/green leaves and thorny stems, shaded lustered pea green 15-sided border............................ 18.00

10 1/4" d, decal of purple, pink, and orange roses in center, shadow ground, dbl gold striped rim 7.00

10 1/2" d

Courtship scene, gold border....... 10.00

Orange, purple, and dark pink roses in center, gilt border........ 17.50

Platter, 13" l, red, white, and pink open roses in center, shaped gold rim w/gold spatter, "Dresden, Semi-Porcelain" mark 35.00

Soap Dish, 5 3/8" h, 5" w, hanging, white ironstone, "Dresden China Warranted" mark........................... 75.00

Wash Set, 5 piece

Pitcher, 10 3/4" h, bowl, 15 3/4" d, small pitcher, cov circ dish, toothbrush holder, lime green base w/gold outlined raised flow-

Plate, 10 1/2" d, brown transfer, gold line and rim, $125.00

ers, "Dresden Semi-Porcelain" mark.. 250.00

Pitcher, 12" h, bowl, 15 3/4" d, cov soap dish, small pitcher, toothbrush holder, scattered dark pink roses, gold dusted borders, "Dresden China" and wreath mark....... 250.00

E. L. P. Co.

E. L. P. CO.
WACO CHINA

EAST LIVERPOOL POTTERY COMPANY
1894–1901

EAST LIVERPOOL POTTERIES COMPANY
East Liverpool, Ohio
1901–1907

History: John and Robert Hall, along with Monroe Patterson, established the East Liverpool Pottery Company in Ohio in 1894. For the first two years the firm made plain and decorated ironstone china, then semi-vitreous porcelain.

It was one of the six potteries that formed the East Liverpool Potteries Company in 1901 to compete with the larger pottery producers. The other potteries were Globe Pottery Company, Wallace and Chetwynd, East End Pottery Company, and George C. Murphy Pottery Company, all from East Liverpool, and United States Pottery Company from Wellsville, Ohio. They used variations of the same mark.

In 1903 the Halls broke away and started Hall China Company. The others also left the merger and returned to their individual operations except for Globe and United States Pottery which maintained East Liverpool Potteries until 1907. United States Pottery continued alone under the East Liverpool Potteries name and made semi-vitreous tableware, hotel ware, and toilet ware in Wellsville. One of its dinnerware lines was Elpco. In 1936 the firm became Purinton Pottery Company.

Reference: William C. Gates, Jr. and Dana E. Ormerod, *The East Liverpool, Ohio, Pottery District: Identification of Manufacturers and Marks,* The Society for Historical Archaeology, 1982.

Museum: Museum of Ceramics at East Liverpool, OH.

Cracker Jar, 6¼" h, scattered open violets, gold outlined raised swirls on body, shaped knob, "WACO" mark ...   50.00

Cream and Sugar, white semi-porcelain, raised scroll design, vert ribbing, "WACO" mark 15.00

Gravy Boat, 8½" l, scattered chrysanthemums and leaves, blue transfer, white body w/raised design, "WACO" mark 16.00

Jardiniere, 4½" h, 12¾" l, scattered purple-red dogwood pattern, semi-vitreous ware, "East Liverpool Potteries" mark......................................   55.00

Milk Pitcher, 9" h, white semi-porcelain, raised scroll design, vert ribbing, "WACO" mark 20.00

Mug, 4¾" h, monk reading newspaper on front, green ground, gold rim, "E.L.P.C." and shield mark 45.00

Cracker Jar, 7" h, pink flowers, small blue flowers, green leaves, white ground, "EAST LIVERPOOL POTTERIES" mark, $60.00

Pitcher

6" h, decal of boy and cat, "GOOD LUCK" on front, mkd 35.00

7" h, red and white hibiscus w/green leaves, shaded green borders w/raised curlicues, gold trim, flowers on int, "E.L.P.CO." and shield mark 50.00

9" h, w/ice lip, blue-green ground, gold outlined raised curlicues on body, gold "Geo. Rost." on sides, "WACO" mark 75.00

Pitcher and Bowl, pitcher, 12" h, bowl, 15" d, white ironstone, raised curlicues on base, raised panels on neck, "EAST LIVERPOOL POTTERIES CO." mark 130.00

Platter, 13½" d, multicolored center decal of 2 Dutch women and child, molded border, white shaded to dark green ground 40.00

FLORENCE CERAMICS
Pasadena, California
1939–1964

History: Florence Ward started working with clay in 1939 in Pasadena, California, as therapy after the death of one of her sons. While her husband and other son were busy with the war, she started Florence Ceramics in her garage workshop. She molded and cast figurines and hand decorated them with hand-made flowers. Twice yearly she introduced new semi-porcelain figures—ladies, men, and figural groups. After the war her family joined her in the business and a modern factory was built.

The Florence Collection included reproductions of historical couples in period costumes, fictional characters, European royalty, and subjects from paintings. Lace decoration was used on figurines and some were incorporated into lamps. Less-expensive figural vases and children in period attire were made, as well as busts, wall plaques, wall pockets, vases, smoking sets, picture frames, clock frames, candleholders, and a large assortment of birds.

In 1956 sculptor Betty Davenport Ford designed a line of modeled, bisque-finished animal figures, including highly stylized rabbits, dogs, cats, doves, and squirrels. These were made for only two years.

Names were usually incised in the base of figures when possible, or paper labels were used. The company name also was ink stamped.

After Florence's husband died in 1964, production was stopped, and the company was sold to Scripto Corporation, which retained the Florence name but made advertising specialty ware such as mugs, cups, and ashtrays. In 1977 all production was stopped.

Reference: Jack Chipman, *Collector's Encyclopedia of California Pottery,* Collector Books, 1992.

Figure

6" h

Oriental boy and girl, white w/gold trim, pr	75.00
Sue, yellow	50.00

6¼" h, Jim

Rose, gold trim	65.00
White, gold trim	58.00

6½" h, Jim.. 98.00

7" h

8" l, Catherine, seated	115.00
Bust of oriental man and woman, pr	90.00

7½" h

Gentleman, top hat, turquoise waistcoat	85.00
Melanie	55.00
Rebecca, seated	95.00
Sarah, green	55.00
Storybook Time	300.00

8" h

Amelia	110.00
Chinaman, black and white	20.00
Grace, blue	75.00
Lillian, pink	90.00
Linda Lou, pink	75.00
Shirley, blue	85.00
Sue Ellen, pink	75.00

Figure, 9" h, Charmaine, green w/magenta trim, $85.00

8¼" h, Garry, salmon, pink, black, and white, gold trim	95.00

8½" h

Abigail, tan and dark green	95.00
Annebel	140.00
Annette	125.00
Dutch girl holding baskets	65.00
Jennifer	130.00

8¾" h, Sherri.. 150.00

9" h

Birthday Girl	125.00
Madeline	120.00
Scarlet	75.00
Yvonna	140.00

9½" h

Claudia	95.00
Owl, natural colors	300.00
Vivian, w/parasol, purple shading	140.00

10" h

Bust of boy or girl, mottled sq base, white glaze, pr	65.00
Leading Man	150.00
Marie Antoinette, white	125.00
Oriental female dancer	125.00
Prima Donna	150.00

11" h

Ava	125.00
Bust of boy or girl, irid finish, pr	300.00

12" h

Louis XV, white w/pink, blue, and gold	250.00
Madame Pompadour, white	225.00
Pinky and Blue Boy, pr	595.00

Flower Holder

7" h, figure of girl holding skirt	38.00
8¼" h, lantern boy or girl, green, pr	110.00

Planter, 5¾" h, figural lady, pink 35.00

Wall Plaque

7" h, bust of blond woman w/dark brown bonnet, brown ribbon on neck, shaped shaded brown rim, pierced for hanging	55.00
7¼" h, bust of woman in burgundy bonnet, gold trim, gray border	55.00

Ashtray, 6½" l, white and yellow rose w/green leaves, shaded green ground w/gold trim, "Florence, Pasadena, California" mark, $15.00

FRANKOMA POTTERY

FRANKOMA

FRANKOMA POTTERY
Sapulpa, Oklahoma
1933–Present

History: In 1933 John Frank established a small studio in his home in Norman, Oklahoma, to make pottery. He left his teaching position at the University of Oklahoma in 1936 and moved to Sapulpa, Oklahoma, and set up a small factory utilizing the local red-brown clay. Frank developed the once-fired process in which the clay body and colored glazes were fused. Many designs reflected the local heritage of the Southwest Indians and native flora and fauna.

Working with J.W. Daugherty, John developed the Rutile art glazes that were characteristic of Frankoma ware. Colors, chosen to reflect the hues found in the Southwestern landscape, were given names such as Prairie green, Desert gold, Woodland moss, Peach glow, Terra-Cotta rose, Clay blue, and White sand. The red of the earthenware clay body showed through the glaze, producing a mottled effect. Green, gold, and black were introduced first in 1933 and are still in use. The other colors were added over a period of years. The pottery started with the production of sculptures. A number of fine artists created figures such as Seated Figure, Seated Indian Bowlmaker, Red Irish Setter, Indian Head, Phoebe, and Afro Girl and Man. Ray Murray was one of the most prolific artists and was responsible for Indian Chief, Fan Dancer, Mountain Girl, and numerous others.

Due to a series of setbacks, the company switched production to dinnerwares and collectibles series, although a separate sculpture catalog was reintroduced in 1972 and discontinued after 1974.

Mayan-Aztec dinnerware was inspired by the American Indian tribes of the Southwest. It was made from 1936–1938 in pitchers, Toby mugs, and coffee mugs. In 1948 it was made in full sets in Desert gold and Bronze green. Wagon Wheel was made in 1948, as was Plainsman, which became the largest dinnerware line in Frankoma production. Lazybones came in 1953, and Westward in 1962 was the last new pattern made.

Miniature ceramic Christmas cards, started in 1944 by John and his wife, Grace Lee, were sent out every year and were designed as ashtrays, pitchers, trays, and such. Grace Lee continued them after she remarried in 1975. She also designed the Madonna plaques in rubbed bisque— a chocolate brown matte rub with a stain instead of glaze. Grace Madonna was done in 1977 and Madonna of Love came out in 1978.

John Frank created a line of Christmas plates that were marked "First Issue." He made them from 1965 until his death in 1973, and then the designs were done by his daughter Joniece. Different biblical scenes were pictured in low relief with a white semi-translucent glaze known as Della Robbia. This type of finish allowed the red underglaze to show.

Numerous collectible lines were made at Frankoma. Teenagers of the Bible was introduced in 1972, political mugs were made for the National Republican Woman's Club from 1968 until 1979, and Bicentennial Plates started in 1972 with the history of the American Revolution. Other series included Conestoga Wagon, done in a pale soft blue, Oklahoma Wildlife Federation plates (1972), a bottle vase series (1969), and Toby mugs (1976).

Additional pieces made at Frankoma included bookends, vases, wind bells, bowls, trivets, canisters, salt and pepper sets, and Will Rogers plaques.

A series of marks was used over the years, and most pieces were marked. Stock numbers were also used on most pieces.

In 1983 the pottery was destroyed by fire and rebuilt.

References: Phyllis and Tom Bess, *Frankoma Pottery,* privately printed, 1983; Susan N. Cox, *The Collector's Guide to Frankoma Pottery, Book Two,* Page One Publications, 1982; Donna Frank, *Clay in the Master's Hands,* Vantage Press, 1977.

MAYAN-AZTEC PATTERN
Bowl, 8½" d, green	25.00
Cereal Bowl, 7X	3.00
Mug, 7C, set of 6	18.00
Pitcher, 9" h, brown	20.00
Salad Plate, 7G	3.00
Teapot, green	52.00

PLAINSMAN PATTERN
Gravy Boat, 3½" h, 8" w, dbl spout, center handle, Prairie green	28.00
Plate	
7" d	4.00
10" d	6.00
Soup Bowl	3.00

POLITICAL MUG
Democratic	
1976, Freedom red	25.00
Republican	
1968, White sand	85.00

Political Mug, Republican, 1968, white sand, $85.00

1969, "NIXON-AGNEW," red ext, white int	85.00
1970, blue ext, white int	50.00
1972, green ext, white int	25.00
1978, blue-green	85.00
1979, brown	85.00

WAGON WHEEL PATTERN

Bowl, 10" d, green	12.00
Cream and Sugar, green	22.00
Cup and Saucer, green	9.00
Lazy Susan, green, #94FC	69.00
Pitcher	
7" h, green	45.00
2 qt, #94-D	20.00
Plate	
6½" d	5.00
10" d	8.00
Teapot, 5½" h, brown and tan	30.00
Vase, 6¾" h, prairie green, imp "FRANKOMA 94" mark	20.00

WESTWIND PATTERN

Chocolate Set, tray, 10½" d, server, 7" h, 4 mugs, 4½" h, mottled green w/brown trim	69.00

MISCELLANEOUS

Bookend	
6" h, charger horse, Onyx black, Ada clay, #420, pr	195.00

7" h, Dreamer Girl, Prairie green, pr	250.00
Bowl, 8" d, black glaze, #238	65.00
Candleholder, 3" h, Dusty rose, Ada clay, #307, pr	50.00
Ewer, 8" h, red ext, brown int	25.00
Figure	
6" h, Mountain Girl, Prairie green, Ada clay	190.00
7" h, seated Puma, buff glaze, Ada clay, sgd "Taylor"	200.00
8" l, lying Puma, gloss black finish	20.00
12" h, matte brown finish	
Indian maiden	16.00
Mare and colt	12.00
Jug, 11" h, 2 handles, ribbed, Moss green glaze	55.00
Mask	
Comedy, 7" h	12.00
Tragedy, 9" h	13.00
Planter, 8" h, swan, Prairie green	12.00
Salt and Pepper	
3" h, figural tepees, Forest green, #47H	12.00

Honey Pot, 5¼" h, tan w/brown accents, imp "FRANKOMA #803 6J" mark, $10.00

Teapot, tan body, brown accents, imp "FRANKOMA #1020" mark, $12.00

Vase, 8" h, Prairie green, $45.00

4⅝" h, shaded brown ground,
unmkd **20.00**
Vase
5½" h, figural flower girl, #700 .... **35.00**
7¼" h, desert scene, tan finish, mkd **30.00**
7½" h, pillow shape, cactus design,
tan, #4 .... **40.00**
10" h, leaf handle, brown, #71 .... **45.00**
12" h, bottle shape, red w/black,
white int, #V-3 .... **45.00**
13" h, black and terra-cotta, #V-13 . **50.00**

GALENA POTTERY
Galena, Illinois, Area
1843–1899

History: The pottery from the Galena area of Illinois and southern Wisconsin was a redware with a lead glaze similar to that of New England. Some pieces of this utilitarian pottery had a rough texture, some were smooth and glossy, others had splotches or spots in reds, greens, browns, and yellows.

In 1843 D.A. Sachett and Company established a pottery in Galena, followed by Alfred Suckett who soon added other sites. There were several different owners over the next thirty years, but eventually Andrew Jennings controlled the potteries until their demise.

Galena pottery was also made in several locations in Elizabeth, Illinois, where the wares were characterized by thin walls, some unglazed examples, and some applied mold work. Potters in Mineral Point, Wisconsin, made utilitarian glazed redwares and several types of complex roof tiles.

Galena pots were wheel thrown, partially dried, glazed, and then fired once to be ready for market. Each piece was distinctive. No two were exactly alike in coloring, some had grooved lines, and some had sawtooth or cogwheel decorations. The best parts of the Galena pots were the top edges which had larger and heavier edge moldings than found on pieces from other potteries. The only decorative color features were the occasional spots or the effects of dipping halfway into cream-colored slip. Most pieces were not marked except with numbers to indicate the capacity of a specific piece.

Utilitarian pieces included jars and pots for preserves, butter, soap, dye, lard, meats, oils, milk, dough, honey, apple butter, and such. There were pitchers, serving bowls, bottles, colanders, flowerpots, and dogs. Tiles for drainage, chimney collars, and roof tiles also were made to meet local needs. All the Galena area potteries used the same red clay and glazes during their fifty-or-so years of production. Preserve jars were the most common items made, and these were glazed both inside and out.

Reference: Wayne B. Horney, *Pottery of the Galena Area*, privately printed, 1965.

Collectors' Club: Collectors of Illinois Pottery and Stoneware, David McGuire, 1527 East Converse Street, Springfield, IL 62703, $15 per year, newsletter.

Bowl, 9½" d, 6¼" h, stacking rim,
dark green glaze w/orange spots(A) . **165.00**
Crock
9¾" h, bulbous lip, greenish glaze
w/orange spots, imp "2," hair-
lines(A) **50.00**
11¼" h, greenish glaze w/amber
spots and black flecks, red clay
imp "3"(A) **165.00**
12¾" h, ovoid shape, tooled lines,
dark green-orange glaze, incised
"2"(A) **65.00**
13" h, green and red mottled glaze . **475.00**
2 gallon, red and green mottled
glaze, drain holes in base, c1840 **300.00**
Figure
9" h, seated dog, dark brown glaze,
red clay, chip on tail(A) **770.00**
11½" h, dog w/tricorne, dark glaze . **650.00**
Flowerpot, 9" d, 5⅜" h, attached
saucer, hanging type, applied stars,
unglazed(A) **55.00**
Jar
3½" h, amber glaze, red clay(A) **60.00**
4¼" h, olive brown glaze, red clay,
chips on lip(A) **30.00**
5¾" h
Cream slip drip over dark amber
glaze, red clay, chips(A) **225.00**
Greenish glaze, brown flecks,
chips(A) **55.00**
6" h, light greenish amber glaze
w/olive spots, chips(A) **115.00**
6¾" h, greenish glaze w/amber
spots(A) **225.00**
7¼" h, bulbous lip, gray-green
glaze w/orange spots and brown
flecks(A) **50.00**
8" h, greenish orange glaze, rim
chips(A) **110.00**
8½" h, two-tone orange glaze
w/yellow slip(A) **20.00**
8¾" h, sloping shoulder, flared lip,
greenish orange glaze w/brown
sponging(A) **85.00**
9" h, cream top, orange bottom **400.00**
9½" h, ovoid shape, green glaze
w/orange spattered spots **625.00**
10" h, two-tone green glaze w/or-
ange spots, tooled band, bulbous
lip, imp "2," hairlines(A) **165.00**
10¾" h, greenish glaze w/amber
spots(A) **165.00**
12¾" h, gloss amber glaze, imp "4,"
chips and hairline(A) **45.00**
13" h, barrel shape, bulbous lip,
tooled line and shoulder detail,
greenish orange glaze(A) **35.00**

Jar, 10 1/2" h, honey glaze w/green splashes, $260.00

13 1/2" h
Bulbous lip, applied handles, greenish orange glaze w/brown flecks, imp "3"(A) 30.00
Ovoid shape, greenish glaze w/orange spots, incised "5"(A) . 75.00
Jar, Cov, 7 1/2" h, dark green glaze 130.00
Jug
6" h, flared lip, applied handle, brown flecked glaze(A) 60.00
6 1/4" h, sloping shoulder w/tooled line, applied strap handle, mottled greenish orange glaze(A) 165.00
9 1/2" h, ovoid shape, greenish amber glaze w/orange spots(A) 192.00
10" h, ovoid shape
Orange glaze 375.00
Tooled lip, strap handle, green glaze, chips(A) 25.00
10 1/4" h, bulbous lip, strap handle, greenish orange glaze w/orange spots, chips(A) 50.00
10 1/2" h, ovoid shape, strap handle, mottled orange and green glaze w/brown flecks, chips(A) 385.00
10 3/4" h, applied strap handle, gloss green glaze w/orange spots, hairlines(A) 220.00
11 3/4" h, ovoid shape, green-amber glaze w/brown flecks, strap handle(A) 121.00
12 1/2" h, ovoid shape, light green splashed glaze w/orange spots 1100.00
Milk Bowl, 10 1/4" d, 3 3/8" h, mottled greenish glaze w/orange spots, tooled lid, chips(A) 395.00
Pitcher, 5 1/2" h, side spout, applied strap handle, tooled line on shoulder, mottled greenish orange glaze(A) 255.00
Preserving Jar
7 1/4" h, ridge at flared lip, greenish

glaze w/orange spots and brown flecks, chip(A) 250.00
7 7/8" h, shiny greenish glaze w/orange spots, lip chips(A) 135.00
8" h, orange glaze(A) 45.00
8 1/4" h, Cov, orange glaze w/green spots(A) 35.00
8 1/2" h
Bulbous lip and tooled shoulder, greenish orange glaze(A) 18.00
Orange glaze w/2 shades of yellow slip(A) 40.00
10" h, Cov, green glaze w/orange spots(A) 110.00
10 1/2" h, line at shoulder, bulbous lip, mottled yellowish tan glaze(A) 165.00
Flared lip, greenish amber glaze w/green spots and brown flecks(A) 65.00

MADE IN
U. S. A.

FRANCISCAN
WARE
+ + +
MADE IN U.S.A.

GLADDING, MCBEAN AND COMPANY/FRANCISCAN CERAMICS
Glendale and Los Angeles, California
1875–1984

History: Charles Gladding, Peter McBean, and George Chambers founded the Gladding, McBean Company in 1875. Using clay from Placer County, California, the firm made ornamental terra-cotta and other building materials. Through rapid expansion, it became one of the largest manufacturers of clay products in the western United States by 1926.

Tropico Pottery which had been making terra-cotta garden pottery and tiles since 1904 was acquired by Gladding, McBean in 1923 as its Glendale plant, and was expanded. This facility was known for its tiles all over the country.

The company patented a one-fire talc body known as Malinite in 1928 and used this as the base for their earthenware pieces beginning in 1934. ["Franciscan," symbolic of California, was the trade name used by the company.] The El Patio design was made in twenty colors and over one hundred three shapes from 1934–1954. The Coronado line was made from 1936–1956 in fifteen colors and more than sixty shapes. These were initially sold with four place settings packaged together and in designated starter sets, a marketing technique which was exceptionally popular with brides.

In 1937 the initial hand-painted Franciscan pattern on the El Patio shape was called Padua and had six color combinations and thirty-two shapes. Other decorated dinnerware lines included Del Mar and Mango in 1937, and Hawthorne in 1938. Apple in 1940, Desert Rose in 1942, and Ivy in 1948, with border designs embossed in the mold, were hand tinted by decorators. Desert Rose was the most popular underglaze dinnerware pattern.

Gladding, McBean purchased the Catalina line and molds in 1937 and continued production of Catalina Rancho until 1941. The company also produced an extensive line of artware vases and bowls with various glaze combinations that were marketed as Catalina Art Pottery.

The oxblood glaze created by ceramic engineer Max Compton was used on Chinese-style shapes for Angelino ware from 1938–1942 and was produced in periwinkle blue, light bronze, and satin ivory.

A new vitrified body for hotel china was developed in 1939 and used the following year for Franciscan Fine China. The Masterpiece China line made from 1941–1979 featured over one hundred sixty-five decorative patterns on nine basic shapes. Informal china called Discovery was made in a medium weight by a series of designers from 1958–1975.

Competition from fine-quality inexpensive Japanese china began in the 1950s, and the company eventually stopped china production in 1979, though the earthenware lines were continued. Due to declining sales, Gladding, McBean sold its Franciscan plant in 1962 to Lock Joint Pipe Company which became Interpace Corporation in 1968.

New patterns continued to be developed in the 1960s and 1970s, including Tulip Time, Pebble Beach, and Hacienda, to name a few. Kaleidoscope was produced in solid-color glazes. Wall, floor, and decorative tiles continued to be made until 1982.

Franciscan ceramics were sold to Josiah Wedgwood and Sons Ltd. of England in 1979. Production was stopped in Los Angeles in 1984 although the wares continued to be made in England.

A tremendous variety of marks was used during the years of production.

References: Jack Chipman, *Collector's Encyclopedia of California Pottery*, Collector Books, 1992; Delleen Enge, *Franciscan Ware*, Collector Books, 1981.

FRANCISCAN
Apple pattern
Ashtray **15.00**

Berry Bowl...	**9.00**
Bowl, 8¼" d	**35.00**
Butter Dish, Cov	**15.00**
Casserole, Cov..................................	**65.00**
Cereal Bowl	**10.00**
Chop Plate	
12½" d...	**50.00**
14" d...	**55.00**
Comport	**75.00**
Cream and Sugar	**25.00**
Cup and Saucer	**7.00**
Gravy Boat	**30.00**
Mug, 4" h	**20.00**
Pickle Tray, 10½" l............................	**30.00**
Pitcher, Ice Lip..................................	**110.00**
Plate	
6½" d...	**10.00**
8½" d...	**15.00**
9½" d...	**20.00**
11" d...	**38.00**
Platter	
12½" d...	**38.00**
14" l...	**50.00**
Relish Tray, 3 parts	**40.00**
Salad Plate.......................................	**5.00**
Salt and Pepper Mill, wood top and base	**450.00**
Soup Bowl, 8" d, flat.........................	**15.00**
Soup Tureen	**300.00**
Spoon Rest..	**12.00**
Sugar Bowl	**6.00**
Teapot	**75.00**
Tile	**25.00**
Tumbler, 5½" h	**25.00**
Turkey Platter, 18" l	**150.00**
Vegetable Bowl	
Cov	**65.00**
Divided, 10¾" l	**48.00**
Water Pitcher, w/6 tumblers	**275.00**
Arcadia Green pattern	
Cup and Saucer	**10.00**
Dinner Plate	**9.00**
Salad Plate.......................................	**9.00**

Dinner Plate, 10" d, Apple pattern, $28.00

Autumn Leaves pattern

Cup and Saucer	8.00
Plate	
6" d	2.00
9" d	5.00
Platter	
11" d	13.00
13½" d	14.00
16½" l	15.00
Shakers, pr	81.00
Soup Bowl	10.00
Sugar Bowl	5.00
Vegetable Bowl, divided	15.00

Bouquet pattern

Cereal Bowl	9.00
Dinner Plate	12.00
Platter, 14" d	30.00
Salad Plate	9.00

Cafe Royal pattern

Bud Vase	95.00
Cereal Bowl, 6" d	15.00
Cup and Saucer	18.00
Plate	
8" d	18.00
10" d	20.00
Platter, 14½" l	45.00

California Poppy pattern

Cream and Sugar	10.00
Cup and Saucer	10.00
Dessert Plate	5.00
Dinner Plate	8.00
Jam Jar, Cov	12.00
Salad Plate	5.00

Claremont pattern

Dinner Plate	20.00

Cloud Nine pattern

Bread and Butter Plate	3.00
Dinner Plate	4.00

Coronado pattern

Bowl	
7¾" d, ivory satin	7.00
8" d, coral satin	10.00
Chocolate Set, pot, A.D. cups and saucers, turquoise gloss glaze	90.00
Chop Plate	
Blue satin	15.00
Ivory satin	24.00
Compote, 7" d, coral satin	12.00
Cream and Sugar, ivory satin	10.00
Creamer	
Maroon gloss	14.00
Yellow satin	8.00
Cream Soup, yellow gloss	15.00
Cup and Saucer	
Ivory satin	5.00
Yellow satin	8.00
Gravy Boat, coral satin	25.00
Plate	
6½" d	
Ivory satin	2.00
Yellow satin	3.50
7½" d, yellow satin	3.00
8½" d	

Gray satin	10.00
Ivory satin	6.00
Yellow satin	5.00
9⅜" d	
Gray satin	12.00
Ivory satin	6.00
10½" d	
Coral gloss	15.00
Ivory satin	10.00
Platter	
13" l	
Ivory satin	15.00
Yellow satin	18.00
15½" l, turquoise gloss	20.00
Relish Dish, 9" l, ivory satin	15.00
Salad Bowl, coral satin	30.00
Soup Plate, yellow gloss	15.00
Sugar Bowl, yellow satin	8.00
Teapot	
Coral satin	35.00
Ivory satin	16.00
Yellow gloss	20.00
Vase	
8½" h, turquoise gloss, #156	22.00
10" h, apple green gloss	45.00

Cosmopolitan pattern

Coffeepot	45.00

Desert Rose pattern

Bowl	
5" d	6.00
6" d	6.00
9" d	45.00
10½" d	65.00
Butter Pat	4.00
Candlestick, 3" h, pr	75.00
Casserole, Cov	15.00
Celery Dish, 11" l	10.00
Cereal Bowl	7.00
Chop Plate, 14" d	45.00
Coffeepot	110.00
Cream and Sugar	22.00
Cup and Saucer	25.00
Dinner Bell	110.00
Eggcup	9.00
Fruit Bowl	10.00
Gravy Boat	35.00
Marmalade Jar	80.00
Mug	
Large	30.00
Small	25.00
Plate	
6" d	5.00
8" d	7.50
10½" d	15.00
10¾" d, divided	70.00
Platter	
11½" d	45.00
12½" d	25.00
14" l	40.00
Relish Dish, 12" l, 3 parts	60.00
Salad Bowl, 10½" d	70.00
Sauce Dish	5.00
Shakers, 6" h, pr	38.00

Gravy Boat, 4" h, 8¹/₂" l, Desert Rose pattern, $35.00

Water Jug, 7¹/₂" h, El Patio pattern, orange glaze, Franciscan, $33.00

Soup Plate	12.00
Tea Canister	125.00
Teapot	75.00
Tile	22.00
Tray, 11" d, 3 parts	30.00
Tumbler	24.00
Vegetable Bowl	
9" d	36.00
Divided, 10³/₄" d	48.00
Water Pitcher, 9" h	45.00

Eldorado pattern, gold and gray

Cream and Sugar	18.00
Cup and Saucer	10.00
Fruit Plate, 6" d	5.00
Plate	
6" d	7.00
10" d	8.00
Salt and Pepper	8.00

El Patio pattern

Casserole, Cov	35.00
Cereal Bowl	12.00
Chop Plate	25.00
Coffee Server, Amber Glo	20.00
Cream and Sugar	21.00
Cup and Saucer, A.D.	30.00
Dinner Plate, 10¹/₂" d, lime green	10.00
Gravy, w/attached undertray, light blue-gray	15.00
Onion Soup	10.00
Salad Bowl, 11" d	20.00
Shakers, pr	18.00

Fresh Fruit pattern

Dinner Plate	14.00
Platter, 14" l	38.00
Tile	28.00

Haciendas pattern

Bread and Butter Plate	2.00
Cup and Saucer	3.00
Dinner Plate	4.00
Salad Plate	3.00

Heritage pattern

Bread and Butter Plate	7.00
Dinner Plate	10.00

Indigo pattern

Dinner Plate	3.00

Ivy pattern

Bowl	
4" d	10.00

6" d	13.50
8" d	10.00
Bread and Butter Plate	5.00
Cereal Bowl, 6" d	12.00
Creamer	20.00
Cup and Saucer	18.50
Gravy Boat	20.00
Plate	
6¹/₂" d	9.00
9¹/₂" d	16.00
10¹/₂" d	18.00
11" d	24.50
Relish Dish	20.00
Salad Plate, 6¹/₂" d	10.00
Sandwich Plate, 14" l, w/cup	15.00
Serving Dish, 10¹/₂" l	10.00
Soup Plate, 8¹/₂" d	21.00
Soup Tureen	150.00
Sugar Bowl, Cov	30.00
Teapot	95.00
Tumbler	30.00
Vegetable Bowl	
8" d	20.00
9" d	30.00

Jamoca pattern

Bread and Butter Plate	3.00
Cup and Saucer	8.00
Dinner Plate	5.00
Salad Plate	4.00
Sugar Bowl, Cov	12.00

Madiera pattern

Bowl, 7¹/₄" d	6.00
Butter Dish	25.00
Creamer	7.00
Cup and Saucer	6.00
Dinner Plate	7.00
Luncheon Plate	6.00
Platter, 13¹/₂" l	25.00
Salad Plate	5.00
Shakers, pr	10.00
Vegetable Bowl, Cov	35.00

Mariposa pattern

Bread and Butter Plate	18.00
Coffeepot	32.00

Creamer..............................	**18.00**
Cup and Saucer	**22.00**
Dinner Plate	**20.00**
Salad Plate....................................	**18.00**

Meadow Rose pattern

Creamer..............................	**15.00**
Cup and Saucer	**12.00**
Dinner Plate	**12.00**
Platter, 14" l...................................	**38.00**
Sugar Bowl	**20.00**

Metropolitan pattern

Tea Set, pot, creamer, cov sugar bowl, aqua ext, white int	**75.00**

Midnight Mist pattern

Bread and Butter Plate	**5.00**
Platter, 13" d...................................	**70.00**

Montecito pattern

Creamer..............................	**8.00**
Cup and Saucer	**6.00**
Dessert Plate....................................	**5.00**
Dinner Plate	**6.00**
Salad Plate....................................	**4.00**
Sugar Bowl	**12.00**

Oasis pattern

Bread and Butter Plate	**6.00**
Cup and Saucer	**7.50**
Dinner Plate	**8.00**

October pattern

Baking Dish	
8" sq	**95.00**
13" l, 9" w...................................	**120.00**
Butter Dish, Cov	**30.00**
Cereal Bowl	**10.00**
Creamer and Cov Sugar Bowl	**50.00**
Cup and Saucer	**25.00**
Fruit Dish....................................	**5.00**
Gravy Boat	**30.00**
Mug, 7 oz	**22.00**
Plate	
8" d....................................	**18.00**
10" d....................................	**25.00**
Platter, 14" d....................................	**65.00**
Shakers, pr....................................	**20.00**
Teapot	**85.00**

Palomar pattern

Plate, 10½" d, yellow rim	**15.00**

Patio pattern

Cup and Saucer	
Burgundy	**5.00**
Yellow	**5.00**
Dinner Plate, 8" sq, yellow	**6.00**

Pebble Beach pattern

Bread and Butter Plate	**3.00**
Cup and Saucer	**5.00**
Dinner Plate	**6.00**
Salad Plate....................................	**4.00**

Platinum Band pattern

Cup and Saucer	**10.00**

Renaissance pattern

Platter, 15¾" l	**35.00**

Sea Sculptures

Cereal Bowl, white	**10.00**

Dinner Plate, sand	**14.00**
Salad Plate, sand................................	**10.00**

Sierra pattern

Cup and Saucer	**25.00**
Plate, 6½" d....................................	**12.00**

Starburst pattern

Ashtray, oval....................................	**65.00**
Bowl, 8" d, divided............................	**8.00**
Bread and Butter Plate	**2.00**
Cup and Saucer	**6.00**
Fruit Bowl....................................	**12.00**
Gravy Boat, w/ladle	**75.00**
Mustard, Cov	**95.00**
Oil and Vinegar, pr............................	**125.00**
Plate, 10" d	**4.00**
Platter	
13" l....................................	**45.00**
15" l....................................	**30.00**
Relish, 3 parts	**65.00**
Salad Plate	**3.00**
Salt and Pepper................................	**60.00**
Tea Set, pot, creamer, sugar bowl, wide gold bands and handles	**145.00**

Sycamore pattern

Bread and Butter Plate	**2.00**
Creamer....................................	**3.00**
Dinner Plate	**4.00**
Platter, 13" d....................................	**4.00**

Tiempo pattern

Butter Dish, Cov, tan	**40.00**
Tumbler, charcoal	**35.00**
Water Pitcher, taupe	**30.00**

Tuliptime pattern

Bread and Butter Plate	**3.00**
Cup and Saucer	**5.00**
Dinner Plate	**5.00**
Salad Plate....................................	**4.00**

Wheat pattern

Chop Plate, 13" d	**57.00**
Cream and Sugar	**10.00**

Wildflower pattern

Platter, 14" l....................................	**100.00**
Salad Plate....................................	**75.00**
Water Pitcher....................................	**175.00**

Woodlore pattern

Open Server, 18" l.............................	**12.00**
Platter, 13" d....................................	**13.00**

MISCELLANEOUS

Figure, 12" h, bust of young girl, ivory satin glaze.....................................	**32.00**
Vase	
5½" h, globe shape, 2 handles, brown glaze, mkd........................	**45.00**
6" h, shell shape, ivory ext, coral int, #C-351	**45.00**
6¼" h, bulbous shape, matte white ext, gloss turquoise int	**20.00**
12" h	
Avalon artware, ivory ext, turquoise int, #C-30	**150.00**
Triangle shape, turquoise ext, coral int, #C-267.....................	**150.00**

Tulip shape, oatmeal-colored
glaze, #C-338 .... **100.00**

J-71

Gonder
U S A

GONDER CERAMIC ARTS, INC.
South Zanesville, Ohio
1941–1957

History: Lawton Gonder purchased the former Zane Pottery Company after Florence Pottery burned in 1941. He started working with many of the Rum Rill molds he had purchased and brought with him from Florence where he had been manager.

After World War II, Gonder was able to make a higher-priced art pottery, and he hired excellent sculptors and artists to design his pieces. Gonder is also known for numerous pottery making innovations such as Flambe glazes for commercial use, Gold Crackle glaze, and crackle glazes which duplicated old Chinese patterns. He also developed Volcanic Glazes, the unusual effects of which were created by melting one glaze over another.

With the increasing demands for pottery after the war, Gonder twice added to his building in 1946 and opened Elgee Pottery, a separate plant to make ceramic lamp bases. It operated for eight years before being destroyed by fire, after which another addition was made to the South Zanesville facility and all operations moved there.

When foreign imports started to hurt the pottery business, Gonder converted to the production of ceramic tile in 1955. Two years later he sold the company to Allied Tile Company but continued to work as a consultant before he retired.

Gonder made art pottery figures, such as elephants, cats, and panthers, in addition to an assortment of vases and ginger jars with Chinese glazes and shapes. Other glazes used were Mother-of-Pearl, Coral, Ebony Green, Royal Purple, Wine Brown, and Red Flambe. Gold Crackle was used on figures as well as vases.

Additionally, he made cookie jars, candleholders, bookends, ewers, ashtrays, planters, and figural lamp bases. During the early 1950s, Gonder designed La Gonda, a line of dinnerware with square-shaped pieces and handles shaped like the letter G.

Many Gonder pieces had a double glaze with a pink interior. Most pieces were marked "GONDER" or "GONDER USA" in a variety of ways and were numbered. Some pieces also had paper labels.

Reference: Ron Hoopes, *The Collector's Guide and History of Gonder Pottery*, L-W Books, 1992.

Collectors' Club: Gonder Collectors, P.O. Box 4263, N. Myrtle Beach, SC 29597, quarterly newsletter, $8 per year.

Basket, 9" h, white glaze, #H-39 .... **20.00**
Candleholder, green ext, pink int, #E-
14, pr **20.00**
Ewer, 13½" h, figural seashell, starfish
on base, apple green, #508 .... **48.00**
Figure
5½" h, kneeling coolie, yellow marbleized finish, #547 .... **25.00**
13" h, standing female, magenta, pr **75.00**
14" h, Oriental man and woman,
red-brown pr, ... **75.00**
14½" h, female figure carrying rod,
molded base, green glaze **25.00**
15" l, reclining panther, amber,
#217 .... **115.00**
19" l, reclining panther, yellow
w/brown streaks, #210 .... **105.00**
21" h, rooster, red **70.00**
Lamp, 13" h, stork design, streaked
brown glaze **195.00**
Pitcher
8" h, green, #H-73 .... **10.00**
8½" h, bulbous paneled shape,
mottled yellow glaze **18.00**
11" h, overlapping design, dbl loop
handles, green glaze, #J-69 .... **16.00**
Planter
4½" h, sq shape, magenta w/white
drip, pr **8.00**
5" h, figural swan, gold crackle finish **22.00**
13" l, figural gondola, yellow and
pink **25.00**
15" l, figural panther, amber, #237 . **75.00**
Vase
7¼" h, chartreuse ext, pink int **12.00**
7½" h, flat open flower, gold
crackle glaze, #E-3 .... **95.00**
8" h
Figural swan, green, #J-31 .... **29.00**
Rect shape, emb vert leaves, reddish glaze, #402 .... **24.00**
Ribbed body, scalloped flared
rim, 2 handles, mottled gray
ext, salmon int, paper label **20.00**
Tiger lily, olive green glaze, #H-
79 .... **25.00**
8½" h, leaf mold
Brown shades, #H-69 .... **25.00**
Irid yellow glaze, loop handle,
#H-77 .... **40.00**
8¾" h, bulbous body, narrow
shoulder, flared rim, green glaze,
#120 .... **28.00**
9" h, molded overlapping leaves

*Vase, 9 1/4" h, gray w/brown splashes,
peach int, imp "GONDER #H-69"
mark, $20.00*

*Vase, 9 3/4" h, mustard yellow ext, peach
int, imp mark, $65.00*

Mustard ext, salmon int, #78	**18.00**
Turquoise, #H-68	**20.00**
9 1/2" h, pearl gray ext, pink int.........	**24.00**
10" h, figural doe's head, turquoise, #518...	**75.00**

1941

HAEGER POTTERY
Dundee and Macomb, Illinois
1871–Present

History: For four generations, Haeger Pottery has remained a family owned business with products characterized by lustrous glazes, bright colors, or soft, glowing pastels. The company was started in 1871 by David Haeger in Dundee, Illinois, to make bricks and tiles. Edmund, his son, took over in 1900 and in 1914 introduced the first piece of art pottery—the Classic Greek Vase Design #1. Edmund built a complete working ceramic factory for exhibit at the 1934 Chicago World's Fair.

Dinnerwares, made as early as 1919, consisted of hexagonal plates, salad bowls with matching plates, and mayonnaise bowls. An assortment of tea wares was made, along with children's feeding bowls, plates, and mugs. From 1929–1933 Haeger dinnerwares were done in blue, yellow, and green.

Joseph Estes, Edmund's son-in-law, became general manager in 1938 and expanded and diversified the product line. The Royal Haeger line of artwares and lamp bases was introduced during his tenure and was designed by Royal Arden Hickman, chief designer from 1938–1944. A wide variety of finishes were used on Royal Haeger pieces, including brilliant high-gloss glazes in a large color spectrum. A tremendous variety of Royal Haeger pieces were made to fill the huge demand—pitchers, vases, figurines, planters, lamps, candleholders, jardinieres, bowls, leaf plates, ashtrays, and such. The panther, a popular figure from 1941, came in three sizes in a high-gloss ebony finish. Some pieces were decorated with "stick ups"—small handmade flowers and leaves applied with liquid slip.

In 1939 the Royal Haeger Lamp Company was established to produce a wide variety of lamps, and this enterprise proved very successful. Royal Haeger figurines were used for the lamp bases with the styling carried through in the design of the lamp shades and finials. Hickman also designed many of these details. Lamps were made at the Dundee location from 1939–1969, when production moved to Macomb after Haeger took over the Western stoneware plant. Both figural and non-figural lamps and TV lamps were made.

Eric Olsen became the chief designer for the Haeger Potteries, Inc., in 1947 and stayed until 1972. During that time he designed ninety percent of the Haeger artware and lamps and his creations were lifelike and graceful. The Studio Haeger line was introduced in 1947 with a variety of different finishes. One of Olsen's most famous designs was the ebony and Haeger red bull introduced in 1955.

Joseph Estes became president of the pottery in 1954. The Royal Garden Flower line was designed by Elsa Ken Haeger and made from 1954–1963. The body, called "porceramic," resembled porcelain more than pottery and had soft matte finishes and muted glazes. Vases, planters, low bowls, candlesticks, figurines, and jardinieres were made.

In 1979, the fourth generation of the family took over at Haeger. Nicholas became president of Royal Haeger Lamp Company in Macomb, and Alexandra became president of Haeger Potteries of Dundee. By 1984 Nicholas was president of Haeger Potteries of Macomb, and Alexandra was president of Haeger Industries, Inc., and was on the Board of Directors.

Rare examples of Royal Haeger include the Portable Electric Fountains from 1941, a line of music boxes, and clocks.

The first piece of Royal Haeger done by Royal Hickman was numbered "R-1." Numbers were then assigned to subsequent designs in chronological order, so the lower the number, the older the design. A wide variety of other marks was used in conjunction with the numbering system, and lamps often had a paper label as the only identifier. Pieces from the Studio Haeger line were marked with a number prefixed with an "S;" Royal Garden Flower pieces had an "RG" prefix and a number.

Reference: Lee Garman and Doris Frizzell, *Collecting Royal Haeger*, Collector Books, 1989.
Museum: Haeger Museum, Dundee, IL.

Gladiola Vase, 10¼" h, blue glaze, "#R-453 Royal Haeger" mark, $38.00

Bookend, 5" h, lily, olive and tan, #R-1144, pr	**38.00**
Bowl, 12" d, Daisy, mauve and blue...	**30.00**
Console Set, tiger, 11" h, #R-313, tigress, 11" h, #R-314, rect planter, 10½" l, #R-282, amber glaze	**165.00**
Figure	
10" h, garden girl by pool, pink and brown shading, #3679	**25.00**
12" h, bullfighter, ruby red glaze, #6343, pr	**55.00**
16" h, Egyptian cat, glass eyes, orange finish	**85.00**
16½" h, gypsy girl, white w/green accents, #R-1224	**30.00**
Flower Frog, 10" h, nude riding fish, olive green	**48.00**
Flowerpot, 6½" h, crisscross basket weave design, rose glaze, #512-S	**15.00**
Pitcher	
7½" h, ewer shape, dark green base shaded to yellow middle, #RG92	**3.00**
8½" h, raised yellow and orange star patterns, matte brown ground, "Royal Haeger" mark	**15.00**
9" h, ewer shape, raised bluish sandy swirls, blue-green glaze, "ROYAL HAEGER RG82" mark	**15.00**
Planter	
6½" h, rect, molded overlapping leaves, pinecone handles, brown ext, turquoise int, c1940	**12.00**
24" l, mermaid, white w/gold brush, #505	**120.00**

Vase	
7½" h, figural dbl conch shells, pink and blue, #R-322	**18.00**
8" h, figural cornucopia with nude, mauve with turquoise, #R-426	**25.00**
9" h	
Gazelle, chartreuse finish, #3398-y	**15.00**
Leaping sailfish, green, #R-271	**125.00**
Organic, 4 buttresses, frosted matte green glaze	**250.00**
9½" h, smooth orange crackled glaze	**90.00**
10" h	
Barber bottle shape, matte gold finish	**40.00**
Sphere w/3 plumes, mauve w/blue-green accents, #R-281	**50.00**
10½" h, cream figure of ballerina standing next to brown open flower, #3531	**28.00**

Planter, 7⅝" h, yellow glaze, "#R-182 Royal Haeger USA" mark, $13.00

12" h

Figural horse's head, green, #R-
857, pr **25.00**
Orange-peel finish, mkd **45.00**
15" h, running deer, honey brown
glaze, #R-706 .... **25.00**

HULL POTTERY COMPANY
Crooksville, Ohio
1905–1986

History: A.E. Hull, William A. Watts, and J.D. Young left the Globe Stoneware Company and founded the A.E. Hull Pottery Company in 1905 and concentrated on stonewares. They purchased the Acme Pottery Company of Crooksville, a semi-porcelain dinnerware firm.

Hull made artwares, lamp bases, novelties, blue-banded and Zane Grey kitchenwares, lusterwares, and stoneware products that were sold to gift shops and florists all over the country. The very popular Hull Art, in matte and high gloss finishes, was molded in relief and decorated in bright colors.

From 1921–1929 Hull imported earthenware china and pottery from Europe. In 1927 the company started making tiles in matte, gloss, and stippled finishes, but discontinued them in 1933 since they were too expensive to make profitably.

A.E. Hull, Jr., who took over the pottery in 1930 when his father died, made stoneware, kitchenware, garden ware and florist ware. In 1937 he left to manage the Shawnee Pottery Company, and Gerald Watts, William's son took over. From 1937–1944 shaving mugs and other toiletry items were made for Shulton.

Art pottery lines at Hull from the late 1930s included Tulip, Orchid, Calla Lily, Thistle, and Pinecone. Matte art pottery wares continued to flourish during the 1940s with patterns such as Iris, Dogwood, Poppy, Rose, Magnolia, Wildflower, Water Lily, Granada, Bowknot, and Woodland. Two high gloss lines from the period were Rosella and Magnolia. Many of these art lines were marked with a decorator's number and/or letter.

Kitchenware and novelty items were made in the early 1940s, including the 1943 Red Riding Hood cookie jar blanks designed by Louise Bauer. These pieces were sent to the Royal China

and Novelty Company of Chicago for decoration.

A major fire struck the plant in 1950. J.B. Hull took over in 1952 when the new plant was built and changed the name to The Hull Pottery Company. Louise Bauer was the designer for many of the art lines at Hull. New lines included Parchment and Pine, Sunglow, Ebb Tide, Classic, Blossom Flite, Butterfly, Serenade, Royal Woodland, and Fiesta.

Numerous novelty items, including swans, banks, dogs, and cats, as well as kitchenwares were made in the 1950s. In the 1960s, the focus changed from art lines to House 'n Garden serving ware that was made until the factory closed, and Crestone, a casual serving ware in turquoise with a white edge.

After J.B. Hull died in 1978 several different presidents were involved with the company which continued to produce dinnerware lines such as Heartland, Blue Belle, the Ridge Collection, and House 'n Garden. The factory closed in 1986, unable to survive union strikes and competition from inexpensive foreign-made wares.

A wide assortment of marks was used on the different types of Hull pieces. Paper labels also were used.

References: Barbara L. Burke, *A Guide to Hull Pottery Company: The Dinnerware Lines,* Collector Books, 1993; Pamela Coates, *Hull,* privately printed, 1974; Joan Gray Hull, *Hull, The Heavenly Pottery,* 2nd edition, privately printed, 1992; Brenda Roberts, *The Collectors Encyclopedia of Hull Pottery,* Collector Books, 1981, 1993 value update; *Ultimate Encyclopedia of Hull Pottery* and *The Companion Guide to Ultimate Encyclopedia of Hull Pottery,* Walsworth Publishing, 1992; Mark E. Supnick, *Collecting Hull Pottery's Little Red Riding Hood: A Pictorial Reference and Price Guide,* L-W Books, 1989.

Collectors' Club: Dan and Kimberly Pfaff, 466 Foreston Place, Webster Groves, MO 63119, $20 per year, monthly newsletter.

Newsletter: Barbara Burke, 4213 Sandhurst Drive, Orlando, FL 32817, *Hull Dinnerware Collectors Newsletter,* $10 per year, bimonthly.

APPLE PATTERN

Grease Jar	**15.00**
Salt and Pepper...................................	**14.00**

BOUQUET PATTERN

Cream and Sugar	**50.00**
Grease Jar	**35.00**
Milk Pitcher, 32 oz	**35.00**
Mixing Bowl	
7½" d..	**30.00**
9½" d..	**35.00**
Salt and Pepper...................................	**48.00**

CENTENNIAL PATTERN

Bean Pot	**100.00**
Sugar Bowl	**50.00**

CRESCENT PATTERN

Casserole, Cov, #B-7	**14.00**
Creamer, 4¹/₂" h, #B-14	**12.00**
Sugar Bowl, 4¹/₄" h, #B-15	**20.00**

CRESTONE PATTERN

Casserole, Cov, turquoise and white, #57	**50.00**

EARLY ART STONEWARE

Vase

7" h, #40	**60.00**
8" h, #26	**60.00**

FLORAL

Casserole, Cov, 7¹/₂" d, #42	**40.00**
Grease Jar, Cov, #43	**30.00**

Mixing Bowl

6" d	**15.00**
7" d	**15.00**
8" d	**20.00**
9" d	**25.00**
Shakers, pr, #44	**25.00**

HOUSE 'N GARDEN

Bean Pot, 2-qt size	**15.00**

Bowl

5¹/₄" d	**1.00**
7" d	**15.00**
8" d, w/pour spout	**20.00**
Butter Dish	**10.00**
Coffeepot	**25.00**
Cream Pitcher	**10.00**
Cruets, oil and vinegar, brown	**35.00**
Gingerbread Man Plate, 10" d, gray	**20.00**

Mug

5" h	**5.00**
6¹/₄" h	**5.00**

Plate

6" d	**1.00**
10" d	**1.50**
Salad Bowl, 10" d	**30.00**

Salt and Pepper

Barrel	**10.00**
Mushroom	**10.00**
Serving Dish, 7" d	**1.00**
Soup Bowl, 6¹/₂" d	**2.00**
Sugar Bowl	**5.00**
Teapot, mirror brown	**20.00**
Vinegar and Oil Cruets	**20.00**

LITTLE RED RIDING HOOD

Bank

Hanging	**2350.00**
Standing, 7" h	**595.00**
Batter Pitcher, 6¹/₂" h	**340.00**
Butter, Cov	**279.00**

Canister

Coffee	**650.00**
Flour	**525.00**
Salt	**1000.00**
Sugar	**650.00**
Cracker Jar	**475.00**

Creamer

Pour through head	**275.00**

Creamer, 5" h, Little Red Riding Hood, tab handle, $275.00

Side pour	**125.00**
Tab handle	**275.00**
Dresser Jar	**625.00**
Grease Jar, flower w/gold trim	**1800.00**
Hanging Match Holder	**625.00**
Lamp	**2400.00**
Milk Pitcher, 8" h	**235.00**

Salt and Pepper

3¹/₂" h	**45.00**
5¹/₂" h	**75.00**
Spice Jar, Nutmeg	**385.00**
String Holder	**2400.00**

Sugar Bowl

Crawling	**250.00**
Side pour	**125.00**
Teapot	**245.00**
Wall Pocket	**400.00**

STONEWARE, UTILITY

Bake Dish, 8" d, blue and green bands, #106	**40.00**
Bowl, 7" d, Nuline	**5.00**

Canister, raised wheat design

3¹/₂" h, pepper, blue	**59.00**

6¹/₂" h

Rice, green	**69.00**
Sugar, green	**69.00**
Casserole, Cov, 7¹/₂" d, blue, Nuline, #B13	**50.00**
Custard Cup, 2" h, blue and green bands, #114	**20.00**
Jar, Cov, 6" h, blue and green bands, #110	**75.00**

Mixing Bowl, blue and green bands

6" d, #100	**25.00**
8" d, #100	**40.00**
9" d, #100	**50.00**
Pretzel Jar, Cov, 9¹/₂" h, #492	**200.00**
Salt Box, 6" h, blue and green bands, #111	**125.00**
Stein, 6¹/₂" h, #492	**35.00**
Tankard, 9¹/₂" h, #492	**175.00**

MISCELLANEOUS

Clock, Bluebird design, Sessions movement	**225.00**

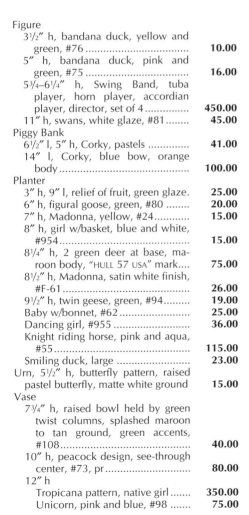

Planter, 6 1/4" h, cream ground w/pink and olive green accents, #80, $24.00

c. 1878–1885

1890s

KNOWLES, TAYLOR, AND KNOWLES
East Liverpool, Ohio
1870–1929

History: Isaac Watts Knowles started his business in 1854. It was incorporated in 1870 as Knowles, Taylor, and Knowles when John N. Taylor, his son-in-law, and Homer S. Knowles, his son joined the company. In the 1860s and early 1870s, yellow earthenware and Rockingham wares were made. White ironstone for hotel china was introduced in 1872, and the other wares were discontinued. Ironstone tea sets, dinner services, toilet wares, cooking wares, accessories, and pitchers were made.

In 1888 a new plant was built to make porcelain. Joshua Poole, a Belleek manager from Ireland, supervised the production of the thin, creamy, eggshell porcelain based on the Irish examples. This was the first pottery in the midwest to make the Belleek porcelains. After only nine months, the factory burned and had to be rebuilt. When the new factory was ready, the management decided not to return to the production of Belleek, but rather to make a new translucent bone china body to compete with the Belleek being made at the Trenton, New Jersey, firms. The new line was Lotus Ware—an excellent-quality porcelain comparable to English and European products. The white Lotus Ware body was adorned with flowers, leaves, filigree, and lacelike decorations, all done entirely by hand. Colored bodies, such as olive and celadon green, also were used. Patterns had names such as Arcanian, Cremonian, Etruscan, Parmian, Thebian, and Umbrian. A wide assortment of this very ornamental, delicate ware was made before the handwork proved to be too expensive and the product was discontinued in 1897. Production of semi-porcelain continued, however, and hotel china, hospital wares, and electrical porcelains were made. The firm continued through several managerial changes before business declined in the mid 1920s and the doors were closed in 1929.

A wide variety of marks was used by Knowles, Taylor, and Knowles. Many Lotus Ware pieces had the company's initials with a star and crescent shape printed inside a circle and "Lotus Ware" printed underneath.

Figure

3 1/2" h, bandana duck, yellow and green, #76	10.00
5" h, bandana duck, pink and green, #75	16.00
5 3/4–6 1/4" h, Swing Band, tuba player, horn player, accordian player, director, set of 4	450.00
11" h, swans, white glaze, #81	45.00

Piggy Bank

6 1/2" l, 5" h, Corky, pastels	41.00
14" l, Corky, blue bow, orange body	100.00

Planter

3" h, 9" l, relief of fruit, green glaze	25.00
6" h, figural goose, green, #80	20.00
7" h, Madonna, yellow, #24	15.00
8" h, girl w/basket, blue and white, #954	15.00
8 1/4" h, 2 green deer at base, maroon body, "HULL 57 USA" mark	75.00
8 1/2" h, Madonna, satin white finish, #F-61	26.00
9 1/2" h, twin geese, green, #94	19.00
Baby w/bonnet, #62	25.00
Dancing girl, #955	36.00
Knight riding horse, pink and aqua, #55	115.00
Smiling duck, large	23.00

Urn, 5 1/2" h, butterfly pattern, raised pastel butterfly, matte white ground | 15.00

Vase

7 3/4" h, raised bowl held by green twist columns, splashed maroon to tan ground, green accents, #108	40.00
10" h, peacock design, see-through center, #73, pr	80.00
12" h	
Tropicana pattern, native girl	350.00
Unicorn, pink and blue, #98	75.00

References: Mary Frank Gaston, *American Belleek,* Collector Books, 1984; William C. Gates, Jr. and Dana E. Ormerod, *The East Liverpool, Ohio, Pottery District: Identification of Manufacturers and Marks,* The Society for Historical Archaeology, 1982.

Museums: Museum of Ceramics at East Liverpool, OH; National Museum of History and Technology, Smithsonian Institution, Washington, DC.

DINNERWARE
Bluebirds pattern
Platter

14" l	10.00
16¾" l	36.00

Oriental flowers in basket, rust rim

Creamer	7.00
Dinner Plate, 9½" d	8.00
Fruit Bowl, 6" d	6.00
Luncheon Plate	8.00

LOTUS WARE
Bowl

3¾" h, fluted design, raised beaded decoration, white, "KTK Lotus Ware" mark(A)	58.00
4¼" h, ovoid shape, matte pink glaze shaded to white, raised gilt flowering branches, copper-gilt jeweled medallions at ends, pink int, "KTK Lotus Ware" mark(A)	357.00
4½" h	
Fishnet pattern, ruffled beaded rim, white, "KTK Lotus Ware" mark(A)	275.00
Raised molded turquoise and gilt flowers and prunus on branches, ruffled beaded rim, "KTK Lotus Ware" mark(A)	275.00
5¼" h, ruffled rim, white, "KTK Lotus Ware" mark(A)	50.00

Rose Bowl, 4½" h, 6½" w, purple and blue flowers w/green stems, shaded tan ground, gold handles, "KTK Lotus Ware" mark(A), $395.00

9" w, 5" h, floral design, twig handles	1300.00

Bud Vase

6" h, applied scroll handles at neck, fluted rim, light green and white applied floral and leaf design, dark green ground, "KTK Lotus Ware" mark(A)	1045.00
7½" h, small applied loop handles, light green applied leaves and flowers, dark green ground, "KTK Lotus Ware" mark(A)	990.00
9¾" h, petal foot, applied scrolling handles, applied white and green flower and leaf design, dark green ground, "KTK Lotus Ware" mark(A)	1760.00
Creamer, 3" h, fishnet pattern	250.00

Ewer

6" h, matte yellow ground, gilt and pink flowers, raised gilt leaf scrolls on neck(A)	182.00
9" h, child's portrait on one side, ships in harbor on reverse, mkd	675.00
9½" h	
Purple, blue, and pink flowers sprigs w/gilt leaves, "KTK Lotus Ware" mark(A)	385.00
White applied flowers and leaves, light green ground, "KTK Lotus Ware" mark(A)	1210.00
Pitcher, 6¾" h, tapered baluster shape, molded fluted design, molded chrysanthemums pattern on rim, scrolled handle, white, "KTK Lotus Ware" mark(A)	165.00
Potpourri Jar, 7½" h, raised reticulated scrolling gadroons, beaded rim and foot, white, "KTK Lotus Ware" mark(A)	880.00
Teapot, 8½" h, tapered shape, pastel painted floral sprays w/gilt accents, white ground, "KTK Lotus Ware" mark(A)	247.00

Tea Set, pot, creamer, sugar bowl

Blue, purple, and green painted wildflowers, white ground, gilt accents, "KTK Lotus Ware" mark(A)	495.00
Fishnet pattern w/red and yellow roses, mkd	750.00
Urn, 15" h, ewer shape, pedestal base, applied handles, raised jewel design, white(A)	4620.00

Vase

4¼" h, bowl shape, reticulated medallions, white(A)	358.00
7" h, multicolored prunus blossom design	950.00
7½" h, bowl shape, ruffled rim, applied chains, white(A)	1100.00

8" h, figural lily w/leaf base, white, "KTK China" mark(A)................. **412.00**

8¼" h

Dbl-gourd shape, applied stepped handles, pink and white flowers w/green leaves, gilt accents, raised gilt border, white ground, "KTK Lotus Ware" mark(A).................................. **385.00**

Flask shape, applied scroll handles, white applied floral design, light green ground, "KTK Lotus Ware" mark(A)............... **1045.00**

MISCELLANEOUS

Creamer and Cov Sugar Bowl, pink and blue flowers, gilt accents, matte finish, "KT & K China" mark(A) **110.00**

Ewer, 10¼" h, globular shape w/tapered neck and petal-shaped rim, applied gilt arched handles, matte turquoise glaze w/gilt accents, "KTK China" mark(A) **1100.00**

Figure, 7¼" l, modeled head of boxer dog, white ironstone(A) **330.00**

Jardiniere, 7¼" h, yellow roses, white ground, scrolled gilt rim and trim, mkd **85.00**

Pitcher

5½" h, squat shape, molded leaf body, turquoise glaze, branch handle, sponged gold rim **15.00**

6" h, ironstone, printed sprays of red and blue flowers w/green leaves on sides, light tan ground.. **35.00**

6½" h, bulbous shape, turquoise, gold rim, int, and handle **45.00**

9" h

Bust of pug in center, shaded brown ground, gold rim, c1906 **90.00**

White opaque body, "K-T-K, S-V" mark **95.00**

Plate

8" d

Center portrait of brunette woman in blue gown, red poppy in hair, blue-green irid border, "1904 Pittsburg Commandery No. 1 Triannual San Francisco California" on reverse, "K-T-K Semi-Vitreous Porcelain" mark **125.00**

Multicolored pheasants, cobalt and gold border, "Pittsburg Commandery 27th Triannual 1898" on reverse **45.00**

8¼" d, center decal of globe and "THE GREAT WAR" w/flags and gold "COMPLIMENTS OF OLYMPIA CANDY CO., KALAMAZOO, MICH.," 1920 calendar leaves on border w/crests of allies.. **30.00**

9¾" d, pointer dog in center, ducks and flower border **35.00**

Shaving Mug, 3¾" h, pink open flowers w/green outlined leaves, vert ribbed neck, "IOWA" mark **18.00**

Syrup Pitcher, 8¼" h, pewter lid, fan-shaped pastel designs w/butterflies.. **65.00**

Teapot, 8½" h, tapered form, gilt outlined leaves w/colored wildflowers, gilt handle, "KTK China" mark(A).... **110.00**

Wash Set

2 piece, white ironstone, pitcher, 9½" h, bowl, 16½" d **100.00**

5 piece

Semi-vitreous ware, pitcher, 11½" h, bowl, 16¼" d, cov soap dish, mug, toothbrush holder, white lobed body, molded leaves at neck, gold dusted rim and handle, "K-T-K, S-V" mark **350.00**

White ironstone, pitcher, 9" h, bowl, 15¼" d, cov chamber pot, cov soap dish, small pitcher, maroon center band outlined w/black stripes **450.00**

Whiskey Jug, maroon "Spring Lake, Handmade, Sour Mash, Bourbon," white ground.................................. **89.00**

LENOX

LENOX

BELLEEK

LENOX, INC.

Trenton, New Jersey

1889–Present

History: Jonathan Coxon, Sr., and Walter Scott Lenox founded the Ceramic Art Company in Trenton, New Jersey, in 1889 after they had both worked at Ott and Brewer. Lenox had apprenticed there and at Willets and had been art director at Ott and Brewer. They worked together until Lenox bought out his partner in 1894 and became sole owner. The Ceramic Art Company made table items, vases, thimbles, inkstands, and parasol handles.

At first Lenox concentrated on Belleek wares and imported two potters from Ireland. Americans were purchasing their fine china from European firms since there was nothing comparable being made in America, and Lenox was anxious to improve American ceramics to compete with or exceed these imports. Despite blindness and paralysis which occurred in 1895, Lenox continued to work every day along with Harry Brown, who assisted in all phases of the company. In 1906, the company's name was changed to Lenox, Inc.

Lenox discovered that superior table services could be made from Belleek ware. Mostly ornamental wares had been made up to that time. From 1889–1918 the main production of Lenox was decorative pieces, but when dinnerware exceeded sales of decorative pieces, it became the mainstay of Lenox production.

Tiffany and Company in New York displayed Lenox's first complete set of dinnerware in 1917. In that year, President Wilson ordered a seventeen hundred piece dinner set designed by Frank G. Holmes for the White House. Other presidential sets were made for Franklin Delano Roosevelt in 1932, Harry S. Truman in 1951, and Ronald Reagan in 1981.

The company was well established by the time Lenox died in 1920. Several important patterns had been introduced before his death, including Lenox Tradition in 1914 and Autumn China in 1919. William Morley, a noted artist, designed beautiful plates with landscapes, birds, horses, ships, game, and flowers. Most were done in a hand-painted series of twelve.

By the 1930s, Lenox, Inc., was a major force in the American market, making translucent ivory-toned fine china, translucent fine white bone china, and a casual line with the strength of stoneware. Frank Holmes, another Lenox designer, was responsible for modern styles on ivory grounds.

During World War II when imports from Europe were cut off, Lenox continued to expand and supply fine China for the growing American market. Major expansion took place during the 1960s when Lenox acquired companies which produced silver, crystal, and casual wares. Additional plants were built in North Carolina in the 1980s and 1991 and today there is a new plant in Pomona, New Jersey.

Lenox continued to introduce new patterns all during its history, using only 24-karat gold and platinum for the trims. A line of figurines, as well as Toby mugs, ring boxes, salt and pepper shakers, cosmetic bottles, and lamp bases, were made by Lenox.

Originally palette marks were used which were followed by wreath marks.

References: Mary Frank Gaston, *American*

Belleek, Collector Books, 1984; Richard E. Morin, *Lenox Collectibles,* Sixty Ninth Street Zoo, 1993.

CERAMIC ART COMPANY, BELLEEK

Bud Vase
  6" h, round base, narrow neck, Art Nouveau style florals and swirling ribbons, lemon yellow, tan, and light green, palette mark **345.00**
  6½" h, portrait bust of period woman w/bonnet, shaded green ground, gold int, "CAC" palette and "Belleek" mark **350.00**
  10" h, black spiderwebs w/yellow, pink, blue, and orange butterflies, pearlized ground **245.00**
Cider Pitcher, 6½" h, purple blueberries, green and blue ground, palette mark **175.00**
Coffee Set, pot, creamer, sugar bowl, sterling silver overlay, c1921, "Lenox Belleek" mark **2900.00**
Cream and Sugar, Art Nouveau floral panels, marbleized base, Lenox Belleek **195.00**
Creamer, 4" h, light pink w/gold-paste florals, lavender palette mark, c1889–1906 .... **75.00**
Cup and Saucer, Engagement pattern, rust color **75.00**
Cup and Saucer, A.D., vert fluted body, gold-paste flowers, gold ring handle **85.00**
Ewer, 14" h, tankard shape, monk reading, green ground **395.00**
Inkwell, 4½" h, painted flowers, CAC Belleek **275.00**
Lemonade Pitcher, 6¼" h, painted peaches on branches, med green ground, raised gold dots on sq handle, artist sgd, green "L," palette, and "Belleek" mark **410.00**

Bowl, 5⅛" h, 8" d, Ceramic Art Company, Belleek, blue and pink flowers, "L Belleek" palette mark, $190.00

Mug
5" h, barrel shape, hp nut pods and
leaves, "CAC" palette mark **145.00**
5¹/₂" h, hp fruits and leaves, "CAC
Belleek" mark **125.00**
6" h, apples and leaves in colors,
"CAC Belleek" mark, c1906 .... **95.00**
Pitcher, 8" h, pockmarked body,
scrolled feet, beaded handle(A) **50.00**
Salt, hp roses, gold trim, ruffled rim,
"Lenox Belleek" palette mark, pr **110.00**
Stein, 7¹/₂" h, monk design, brown
shades, sterling lid, "CAC Lenox"
mark **325.00**
Sugar Shaker, 7" h, hex, green mythical
birds, gold trim, green palette mark. **195.00**
Tankard, 14¹/₂" h, orange to yellow
trumpet flowers, shaded green
ground **300.00**
Vase
4¹/₂" h, squat bulbous shape, hp
nasturtiums, cream ground **125.00**
8" h, bluebirds and berries design,
sgd "N. Frances," c1906, green
"Lenox palette" mark **295.00**
10" h
Black spiderwebs w/yellow, pink,
blue, and orange butterflies,
pearlized ground, c1906–24 .... **225.00**
Cherry blossoms on trailing vines,
3 medallions of young girls,
pale green ground, gold rim
and foot w/lotus flowers and
pink beading, palette mark **295.00**
10¹/₂" h
Magenta roses w/green leaves,
cream top ground, green
shaded base, matte gold int,
c1889–1906 .... **395.00**
Orange flower heads on shoul-
der, shaded reddish ground,
c1895 .... **395.00**
11¹/₂" h, cylinder shape, painted
green, yellow, and red stylized
flowers, ivory ground, stamped
palette mark(A) **192.00**
12" h, hp deer scene, transition
mark **350.00**
12¹/₂" h, pastel pink and yellow
roses, pedestal base, slender
neck, flared top, 2 gold handles at
neck, c1889 .... **325.00**
18" h
Dancing lady w/cherubs, ornate
gold handles **550.00**
Painted poinsettias **635.00**
Wine Jug, 5¹/₂" h, portrait of cavalier
on front, toast on reverse, artist sgd . **395.00**
LENOX
Alden pattern
Cup and Saucer **15.00**
Dinner Plate **15.00**

*Vase, 12" h, Ceramic Art Company,
Belleek, HP orange poppies, shaded
green ground, pearl luster handles and
base, gold rim, c1896–1906, green
palette mark, $495.00*

Amethyst pattern
Bread and Butter Plate **12.00**
Salad Plate **18.00**
Annapolis pattern
Dinner Plate **30.00**
Salad Plate **25.00**
Antoinette pattern
Bread and Butter Plate **16.00**
Cup and Saucer **45.00**
Dinner Plate **25.00**
April pattern
Cup and Saucer **36.00**
Ashtray, 8¹/₂" sq, ivory **26.00**
Autumn pattern
Bread and Butter **10.00**
Chop Plate **125.00**
Cream Soup **75.00**
Cup and Saucer **22.50**
Cup and Saucer, A.D. **50.00**
Dinner Plate **12.00**
Platter, 16" l **150.00**
Vegetable Bowl **90.00**
Barclay pattern
Bread and Butter Plate **23.00**
Beacon Hill pattern
Cup and Saucer **38.00**
Dinner Plate **30.00**
Bellaire pattern
Cream Soup, w/underplate **25.00**
Bellevue Maroon pattern
Bread and Butter Plate **12.00**
Cup and Saucer **12.00**
Dinner Plate **18.00**
Salad Plate **15.00**
Belvidere pattern
Bread and Butter Plate **22.00**
Chop Plate **85.00**
Cream and Sugar, gold mark **55.00**

Cup and Saucer	30.00
Dinner Plate	25.00
Salad Plate	23.00

Blue Ridge pattern

Bread and Butter Plate	12.00
Cup and Saucer	38.00

Blue Royale pattern

Gravy Boat	95.00

Blue Tree pattern

Bread and Butter Plate	28.00
Chop Plate	185.00
Cup and Saucer	48.00
Dinner Plate	27.00
Fruit Bowl	35.00
Salad plate	35.00
Vegetable Bowl, oval	110.00

Brandy Wine pattern

Cup and Saucer	38.00
Dinner Plate	30.00

Brookdale pattern

Creamer	28.00
Dinner Plate	15.00

Burlington pattern

Chop Plate	115.00
Salad Plate	23.00

Carolina pattern

Bread and Butter Plate	10.00
Cup and Saucer	24.00
Salad Plate	12.00

Castle Garden pattern

Bread and Butter Plate	11.00

Celeste pattern

Bread and Butter Plate	12.00
Cup and Saucer	29.00
Dinner Plate	27.00
Salad Plate	16.00
Vegetable Bowl, oval	79.00

Chateau pattern

Cup and Saucer	35.00
Dinner Plate	29.00

Cinderella pattern

Cup and Saucer	10.00
Dinner Plate	12.00
Plate	
6½" d	5.00
8" d	6.00
Soup Plate	10.00

Clarion pattern

Cup and Saucer	22.00

Colonnade pattern

Cup and Saucer	15.00
Vegetable Bowl, oval	35.00

Coquette pattern

Dinner Plate	29.00
Salad Plate	12.00

Country Floral pattern

Dinner Plate	18.00
Salad Plate	12.00

Countryside

Dinner Plate	12.00

Cretan pattern

Bread and Butter Plate	4.00

Dinner Plate	10.00
Salad Plate	6.00

Courtland pattern

Bread and Butter Plate	12.00
Cream and Sugar	100.00
Cup and Saucer	32.00
Salad Plate	20.00
Vegetable Bowl, oval	70.00

Daybreak pattern

Bread and Butter Plate	13.00
Cup and Saucer	29.00
Dinner Plate	22.00
Salad Plate	16.00

Desert Morn pattern

Cup and Saucer	28.00

Empress pattern

Bread and Butter Plate	16.00

Eternal pattern

Bread and Butter Plate(A)	4.00
Cup and Saucer (A)	3.00
Dinner Plate(A)	8.00
Salad Plate(A)	5.00
Vegetable Bowl, oval	48.00

Festival pattern

Dinner Plate	20.00

Fireflower pattern

Cup and Saucer	12.00

Firesong pattern

Cream and Sugar	75.00
Cup and Saucer	20.00

Flirtation pattern

Chop Plate, 12¾" d	45.00
Cup and Saucer	30.00
Dinner Plate	15.00
Platter, 13¾" l	50.00
Vegetable Bowl, oval	75.00

Forever pattern

Cup and Saucer	20.00
Dinner Plate	16.00

Fountain pattern

Dinner Plate	25.00

Gaylord pattern

Bread and Butter Plate	14.00
Salad Plate	17.00
Ginger Jar, 6" h, ribbed body and cov, pink glaze, cream knob, green wreath mark	85.00

Golden Blossom pattern

Plate, 10½" d	16.00

Golden Gate pattern

Casserole, Cov	150.00
Chop Plate	65.00
Fruit Dish	16.00

Golden Mood pattern

Dinner Plate	35.00

Golden Wreath pattern

Bread and Butter Plate	12.00
Cup and Saucer	32.00
Dinner Plate	29.00
Vegetable Bowl, 8⅜" l, oval	45.00

Harvest R441 pattern

Bread and Butter Plate	4.00

Chop Plate, 12¾" d 22.00
Cream Soup 12.00
Cup and Saucer 10.00
Cup and Saucer, A.D. 7.50
Dinner Plate 10.00
Plate, 8½" d 6.00
Heiress pattern
Bread and Butter Plate 10.00
Cup and Saucer 18.00
Dinner Plate 18.00
Helmsley pattern
Bread and Butter Plate 14.00
Dinner Plate 20.00
Salad Plate 17.00
Holly pattern
Plate, 13" d 135.00
Interlude pattern
Cereal Bowl 15.00
Cup and Saucer 25.00
Dinner Plate 25.00
Salad Plate 15.00
Kingsley pattern
Cup and Saucer 25.00
Dinner Plate 20.00
Vegetable Bowl, Cov 95.00
Lacepoint pattern
Cup and Saucer 15.00
Dinner plate 15.00
Plate, 6½" d 10.00
Lenox Rose pattern
Bread and Butter Plate 8.00
Cake Plate, 11" d, handle, green
    mark 55.00
Coffeepot 135.00
Cup and Saucer 22.00
Dinner Plate 18.00
Fruit Bowl 18.00
Gravy Boat 65.00
Platter, 13" l 70.00
Salad Plate 18.00
Vase, 6¾" h, 2 handles, green mark ... 85.00
Vegetable Bowl 45.00
Lotus Garden pattern
Bowl, 10" l 15.00
Bread and Butter Plate 7.00
Cup and Saucer 10.00
Dinner Plate 8.00
Platter, 16" d 20.00
Salad Plate 7.00
Mandarin pattern
Tea Service, pot, creamer, sugar, 6
    cups and saucers, 6 ice cream
    plates, 6 cake plates 650.00
Mansfield pattern
Bread and Butter Plate 15.00
Chop Plate 89.00
Cup and Saucer 30.00
Dinner Plate 27.00
Salad Plate 18.00
Vegetable Bowl, oval 59.00
Mayflowers pattern
Bread and Butter Plate 16.00

Cup and Saucer 39.00
Dinner Plate 29.00
Salad Plate 19.00
Meadow Song
Cup and Saucer 29.00
Dinner Plate 35.00
Medley pattern
Bread and Butter Plate 14.00
Cup and Saucer 32.00
Dinner Plate 29.00
Salad Plate 19.00
Melissa
Cup and Saucer 20.00
Meredith pattern
Bread and Butter 6.00
Vegetable Bowl, oval 35.00
Mid Summer pattern
Cup and Saucer 32.00
Dinner Plate 28.00
Ming pattern
Bread and Butter 10.00
Chop Plate 60.00
Creamer 50.00
Cream Soup 25.00
Cup and Saucer 30.00
Cup and Saucer, A.D. 20.00
Dessert Plate 35.00
Dish, Pedestal
    5" d 35.00
    9" d 45.00
Luncheon Plate 35.00
Platter, 13" d 65.00
Salad Plate 15.00
Salt and Pepper 20.00
Vegetable Bowl, oval 15.00
Monteray pattern
Cup and Saucer 9.00
Dinner Plate 10.00
Moonspun pattern
Bread and Butter Plate 10.00
Cup and Saucer 32.00
Dinner Plate 20.00
Salad Plate 14.00
Vegetable Bowl
    Oval 75.00
    Round 85.00
Montclair pattern
Bread and Butter Plate 10.00
Cup and Saucer 30.00
Dinner Plate 22.00
Salad Plate 15.00
Monticello pattern
Plate
    9" d 24.00
    10¼" d 29.00
Olympia
Gold pattern
    Bread and Butter Plate 19.00
    Compote 29.00
    Cup and Saucer 30.00
    Dinner Plate 30.00
    Salad Plate 24.00

Vegetable Bowl, oval	89.00
Water Pitcher	89.00
Platinum, Cup and Saucer	30.00

Oxford pattern
Soup Bowl	10.00

Pavlova pattern
Bread and Butter Plate	10.00
Cup and Saucer	15.00
Dinner Plate	12.00
Salad Plate	10.00

Peachtree pattern
Creamer	35.00
Cup and Saucer	30.00
Dinner Plate	25.00
Fruit Bowl	15.00
Vegetable Bowl, 9½" l, oval	45.00

Pine pattern
Bread and Butter Plate	20.00
Cup and Saucer	35.00
Dinner Plate	30.00
Fruit Bowl	24.00
Salad Plate	24.00

Plum Blossom pattern
Dinner Plate	27.00

Priscilla pattern
Bread and Butter Plate	22.00
Gravy Boat	50.00
Salad Plate	25.00

Quakertown pattern
Sugar Bowl	24.00

Rapture pattern
Bread and Butter	12.00
Cup and Saucer	25.00
Dinner Plate	25.00
Salad Plate	15.00

Renaissance pattern
Plate, 7" d	24.00

Rhodora pattern
Bread and Butter Plate	15.00
Cup and Saucer	25.00
Dinner Plate	25.00
Salad Plate	20.00

Rocail pattern
Soup Plate, red	20.00

Roselyn pattern
Cup and Saucer	25.00
Dinner Plate	25.00
Platter	
13" d	95.00
16" l	125.00
Vegetable Bowl	65.00

Sachet pattern
Cup and Saucer	40.00

Sandpiper pattern
Bread and Butter Plate	5.00

Shalimar pattern
Cup and Saucer	30.00
Dinner Plate	29.00

Silhouette pattern
Creamer	26.00
Cup and Saucer	18.00

Snowflower pattern
Cake Plate	6.00
Cup and Saucer	8.00
Dinner Plate	6.00

Springdale pattern
Dinner Plate	22.00

Springtime pattern
Cup and Saucer, A.D.	18.00

Stanford pattern
Cream Soup	20.00

Tuscany pattern
Bread and Butter Plate	30.00
Cup and Saucer	59.00
Salad Plate	39.00

Tuxedo pattern
Cream Soup	35.00
Cup and Saucer	40.00
Dinner Plate	38.00
Salad Plate	10.00
Vegetable Bowl, oval, 8½" l	50.00

Weatherly pattern
Cream and Sugar	95.00
Cup and Saucer	35.00
Dinner Plate	30.00
Vegetable Bowl, open	95.00

Westbury pattern
Gravy Boat	50.00

Westchester pattern
Cup and Saucer	35.00
Soup Plate	30.00

Westwind pattern
Bread and Butter	12.00
Cup and Saucer	25.00
Dinner Plate	25.00
Gravy Boat	145.00
Salad Plate	15.00
Vegetable Bowl, oval	95.00

Wheat pattern
Bread and Butter Plate	20.00
Cereal Bowl	22.00
Cup and Saucer	25.00
Dinner Plate	25.00
Salad Plate	20.00
Vegetable Bowl, oval	50.00

Windsong pattern
Bread and Butter Plate	17.00
Creamer	48.50
Cup and Saucer	44.50
Dinner Plate	28.50
Salad Plate	17.50

Wyndcrest pattern
Bread and Butter Plate	16.00
Cup and Saucer	38.00
Dinner Plate	32.00
Salad Plate	18.00

#B-368-A
Salad Plate	15.00

#X-305-263, gray rim w/gold outline
Plate, 10½" d	15.00

MISCELLANEOUS

Bud Vase, 8¼" h, bulbous base, flared

fluted neck, large pink rose w/gold leaves, gold band at waist and base, gold wreath mark 38.00

Candlestick, 9" h, hp mottled gray, green, and mauve shades, gold trim, green palette mark, pr 85.00

Cup and Saucer, ivory w/heavy acid-etched silver overlay, green wreath mark 85.00

Cup and Saucer, A.D.
Band of emb gold on rim of cup and saucer, set of 6 .... 150.00
Cherub in clouds design, gold handle and trim, for Marshall Field, green wreath mark 75.00

Dish, 9" l, molded leaf shape, ivory(A) 44.00

Dresser Box, 4" w, kidney shape, violets and buttercups design 65.00

Figure
4³/₄" h, penguin, coral glaze 185.00
8¹/₂" h
Breakfast at Tiffany's 125.00
Female bust w/cascading hair, white glaze 245.00
First Waltz 115.00
12" l, swan, ivory glaze, green mark 55.00

Lamp Base, 12" h, tassle-type handles, white leaves, green ground, green mark 95.00

Pitcher, 7" h, stylized bird of paradise, blue mark....................................... 34.00

Planter, 6³/₄" h, figural swan, ivory, gold wreath mark 88.00

Relish Tray, 11" H-H, raised leaves and grain on int, gold outlined handles, white 45.00

Tea Service, teapot, creamer, cov sugar bowl, 5 cups and saucers, Art Nouveau style sterling silver floral and stem overlay 750.00

Tray, 10¹/₂" l, leaf shape w/ring handle, silver trim 30.00

Vase
4" h, gloss cobalt ground, Art Nouveau style fan-shaped silver overlay, brown mark(A) 121.00
6" h, raised floral design, green body, green mark 55.00
7" l, basket shape, applied silver trim, c1930................................. 95.00
7¹/₂" h
Emb shells top and base, thin white chain handles, pr............ 400.00
Floral transfers, gold trim, blue wreath mark.............................. 80.00
8" h, trumpet shape, blue base w/band of flowers on base and inner rim, ivory ground, gold trim, green mark 115.00
8¹/₂" h, emb leaf design, ivory(A) 40.00
9" h, fluted tapered body, sawtooth rim, ivory body, gold rim(A) 20.00
10" h
Cylinder shape, 2 enameled birds 188.00
Iris motif, white ground, green wreath mark.............................. 120.00
Pedestal base, flared body, scalloped rim, white wheat-type flowers, pink ground, green mark 115.00
White relief of classical scene of columns, steps, and trees, green ground, green mark 165.00
11" h
Saxony, flowers and bird design, pr.. 295.00
Urn shape, gold swan handles, pr 165.00

PROMENADE
BURGUNDY T-S284 C.D.
WARRANTED 22K GOLD

c.1915-1925

Candy Dish, 6" h, ivory, gold trim, gold wreath mark, $100.00

LIMOGES CHINA COMPANY
1900–1949

AMERICAN LIMOGES CHINA COMPANY
Sebring, Ohio
1949–1955

History: In 1900 Frank and Frederick Sebring organized the Sterling China Company in Sebring, Ohio, and manufactured porcelain dinnerware and tea, chocolate, salad, fruit, and soup sets similar to the European wares made for the American market.

The name was changed to Limoges China Company. After a huge fire, porcelain was discontinued, and only semi-vitreous china was made in a wide variety of decalcomania patterns. After a dispute with the Limoges China Company of France concerning overuse of the Limoges name, the firm became known as the American Limoges China Company in 1949.

Limoges completely revolutionized the pottery industry with the development of the tunnel kiln which replaced the beehive type. Viktor Schreckengost was an important designer for Limoges. A wide variety of marks was used before the company closed in 1955.

CANDLE GLOW PATTERN
Cream and Sugar 25.00
CHATEAU FRANCE PATTERN
Plate, 7¼" d, chateau in trees, gold
  lacy overlay border, scalloped rim
  w/raised design 2.00
FEDERAL, CORAL PINK PATTERN, CANDLELIGHT
Bread and Butter Plate 2.00
Creamer.. 3.00
Cup and Saucer 3.00
Dinner Plate 5.00
Gravy Boat 4.00
Luncheon Plate................................... 2.00
Salad Plate.. 2.00
Shakers, pr.. 5.00
Sugar Bowl, Cov 6.00
Vegetable Bowl, 8¾" d........................ 10.00
GREY BLOSSOM PATTERN
Plate, 9¼" d, "American Limoges"
  mark 8.00
LITTLE RED RIDING HOOD PATTERN
Berry Bowl... 5.00
Bread and Butter Plate 5.00
Cup and Saucer 20.00
Dinner Plate 15.00
NEW PRINCESS PATTERN, CANDLELIGHT
Cup and Saucer 3.00
Dinner Plate 4.00
Salad Plate.. 3.00
ROYAL IMPERIAL PATTERN, CANDLELIGHT
Bread and Butter Plate 2.00
Creamer.. 3.00
Cup and Saucer 2.00
Dinner Plate 3.00
Gravy Boat, w/undertray 5.00
Soup Bowl 3.00
Salad Plate.. 2.00
Sauce Dish 2.00
Sugar Bowl, Cov 5.00
Vegetable Bowl, Cov 10.00
TRIUMPH SHAPE
China D'Or pattern
Berry Bowl... 3.00

Bread and Butter Plate 2.00
Casserole, Cov, 9¼" d 12.00
Chop Plate, 10" d 8.00
Dinner Plate 4.00
Salad Plate.. 3.00
Soup Plate 5.00
Posey Shop pattern
Berry Bowl... 2.00
Bread and Butter Plate 2.00
Creamer.. 3.00
Cup and Saucer 2.00
Dinner Plate 5.00
Platter, 12" H-H 10.00
Salad Plate.. 2.00
Sugar Bowl, Cov 5.00
Vegetable Bowl 8.00
Starflower pattern
Cream and Sugar 14.00
The Pansy pattern
Bread and Butter Plate 2.00
Creamer.. 3.00
Cup and Saucer 3.00
Dinner Plate 3.00
Fruit Dish.. 2.00
Vermillion Rose, Belvediere
Bread and Butter Plate 1.00
Casserole, Cov.................................... 5.00
Cereal Bowl.. 2.00
Chop Plate.. 3.00
Dinner Plate 2.00
Salad Plate.. 1.00
Shakers, pr.. 2.00
Sugar Bowl, Cov 2.00
Miscellaneous
Bowl, 8¾" d, multicolored garden
  flowers in center, ringed yellow border 5.00
Creamer, garden flowers on side,
  "Oslo-Pink" mark 3.00
Plate
  9½" d, decal of multicolored stylized garden flowers, dark yellow
    border w/rings, "American Limoges Triumph Everglades Yellow
    Vista" mark, set of 5 .... 25.00
Platter, 13¼" d, black flower grouping
  in center, pink border, "American
  Limoges, Yorktown-T, Karen" mark. 5.00
Sugar Bowl, Cov, garden flowers on
  side, "Oslo-Green" mark................ 3.00
Vegetable Bowl, Cov, 9½" H-H, garden flowers, "Cotillion-Blue" mark.. 12.00
Vegetable Bowl, oval, multicolored
  floral center, "Sweden-Blue" mark .. 5.00
Wild Rose pattern
Bread and Butter Plate 2.00
Butter Dish 12.00
Creamer.. 6.00
Cup and Saucer 4.00
Dessert Plate 2.00
Dinner Plate 4.00

Fruit Dish.. 2.00
Gravy Boat 12.00
Platter
   11³/₄" l.. 15.00
   15" l.. 18.00
Soup Bowl 3.00
Sugar Bowl, Cov 8.00
MISCELLANEOUS
Bowl
   8¹/₄" d, tan flowers in center on blue
     ground, scattered yellow and
     brown flowers w/gold overlay
     border, "Candlelight Limoges, Vi-
     enna" mark.................................. 4.00
   9¹/₄" d, strawberries in center, scal-
     loped blue border w/raised pan-
     els, gold trim 48.00
   9¹/₂" d, decal of grapes and leaves
     in center, pea green border
     w/gold bellflower overlay 35.00
Cake Set, pitcher, 6¹/₂" h, master plate,
   9¹/₂" d, 4 cake plates, 8" d, 4 cups
   and saucers, creamer, rust, yellow,
   and magenta flowers w/green and
   black leaves in center, raised chartreuse border w/gold trim, "Emerald
   Glow" mark 69.00
Game Set, platter, 14¹/₄" l, 6 plates, 9"
   d, multicolored decals of forest animals, lustered med green borders,
   gold rim, "Limoges China" mark 225.00
Plate
   7" d, 10-sided, decal of 2 Dutch
     children and "Souvenir of Port
     Clyde, Maine," raised cobalt bor-
     der w/gold flower overlay 32.00
   7¹/₂" d, 3 red and green pears
     w/blossoms and branch in center,
     lustered yellow-green border w/8
     dark red geometric drops, "Limo-
     ges China" mark 17.00

Soup Plate, 7¹/₂" d, Bluebird pattern,
"Limoges USA China Co." mark, $12.00

Cake Plate, 10³/₄" H-H, Sweden
Blue, "American Limoges Triumph"
mark, $5.00

8" d
   Decal of "The Seven Castles,"
     yellow lustered border w/black
     Indian designs......................... 15.00
   Ten-sided, 2 deer in brown and
     green forest setting w/autumn
     leaves, raised design on border
     w/gold trim, white ground,
     "Limoges China Co." mark....... 15.00
8¹/₄" d
   Basket-weave border w/small
     pink roses and trailing green
     vines, "Limoges China" mark ... 14.00
   Three pink roses w/green leaves,
     flowing blue border w/gold
     drape overlay, shaped rim,
     "Limoges China" mark 15.00
8³/₄" sq, multicolored decal of
   Charles Lindbergh's flight and
   bust, yellow ground, "Limoges
   China" mark 35.00
9" d, blue and green bouquet in
   center, flowing blue border, 12-
   sided, "Limoges China" mark....... 14.00
10" d
   Light and dark purple grapes, pea
     green shadow ground, shaded
     pink border w/raised scrolling,
     scalloped rim, "Limoges
     China" mark 6.00
   Old Dutch, Magenta tulips in
     center, raised border 8.00
Tray
   10³/₄" H-H, scene of French
     chateau, and man pulling horse
     and cart, cream ground w/ribbed
     border and gilt, "LeMaitre" on
     front 15.00
   11¹/₂" l, orange-red single rose
     w/brown leaves, raised vert
     ribbed border, "American Limo-
     ges Victory" mark 5.00

MADDOCK POTTERY COMPANY
1893–1923
THOMAS MADDOCK AND SONS
1882–1929
JOHN MADDOCK AND SONS
1895–1929
Trenton, New Jersey

Cracker Jar, 8" h, pink, red, and yellow roses, shaded green ground, gold trim, "62 Annual Banquet Chester Lodge No. 236 F & A 917 Thursday Evening Dec. 1-1910" inside cov, "N.J. Pottery Trenton, Maddock's & Son 1910" and "Thomas Maddock Sons Co. Trenton, N.J." mark, $110.00

History: Three separate Maddock family potteries were operating at approximately the same time in Trenton, New Jersey.

The Maddock Pottery Company operated from 1893–1923 in the old Lamberton Works that eventually became the home of Scammell China Company. White granite dinner sets, toilet sets, and plain and decorated odd dishes were made, as well as Lamberton China, for hotels.

Thomas Maddock and Sons operated from 1882–1929. Thomas Maddock had worked with Astbury from 1875–1882, but then took his sons in as his partners. The company made white earthenware, sanitary ware, decorated ware, and souvenir and fraternal pieces. After purchasing Glasgow Pottery in 1900 American China was made.

John Maddock and Sons operated from 1895–1929 and made sanitary ware, sanitary specialties, and plumbers' ware.

A wide variety of marks was used by all three potteries.

Chamber Pot, pink roses w/gold trim, stoneware, "Maddock Lamberton" mark 95.00
Cream Pitcher, 4³/₄" h, vert fluted base, center gold band, single pink rose under spout, band of pink roses on rim, gold trimmed shaped handle 10.00
Ewer, 11" h, black transfer of bust in turban, "Herrmann Lodge No. 125, F.A.M.," blue shaded ground, gold inner rim, "Maddock, Trenton" mark 175.00
Pitcher, 7¹/₄" h, scattered multicolored florals on sides, light tan ground, scalloped and raised gold rim, "Maddock's Lamberton Works, Royal Porcelain" mark 55.00
Plate, 9³/₄" d, blue w/gold trim, Masonic emblem 25.00

Tankard, 12" h, cobalt w/silver trim, Masonic emblem, dtd 1913 .... **175.00**

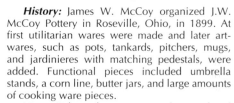

J.W. MCCOY
1899–1911
BRUSH MCCOY
1911–1918
NELSON MCCOY
1910–1990
Roseville and Zanesville, Ohio

History: James W. McCoy organized J.W. McCoy Pottery in Roseville, Ohio, in 1899. At first utilitarian wares were made and later artwares, such as pots, tankards, pitchers, mugs, and jardinieres with matching pedestals, were added. Functional pieces included umbrella stands, a corn line, butter jars, and large amounts of cooking ware pieces.

Mount Pelee, a lava-type ware that was hand molded mostly in iridescent black, was first made in 1902. After a fire in 1903, different art lines were emphasized. Olympia and Rosewood were brown glazed with some diagonal orange streaks, Green Matt dates from 1906, and Loy-Nel-Art from 1908 was a brown ware with underglaze slip decoration similar to work done at Weller. Renaissance was a brown-glazed ware with a flowing poppy in the Art Nouveau style.

Albert Cusick from Avon Faience began to

work for the factory in 1908. His designs became the principal influence for more than thirty-five years, starting with the Corn line of pitchers, mugs, and jars.

George S. Brush was appointed general manager in 1909 after experience at Owens Pottery from 1901–1905 and at his own Brush Pottery in 1907. He had acquired the molds of Union Pottery to make general kitchen wares, bowls, stoneware, and art pottery pieces, but after fire destroyed Brush Pottery, he joined McCoy.

In 1911 the J.W. McCoy Pottery name was changed to the Brush McCoy Pottery Company and many lines of artware and utilitarian wares were made. The following year Brush McCoy purchased the A. Radford Pottery molds and equipment. The expanded operations necessitated a move to Zanesville where the concentration was on artwares while the Roseville site continued the manufacture of utilitarian wares. Navarre, with incised Art Nouveau figures, was made for the Henri Deux line in matte green and white in 1912. Other lines included Venetian, Basket Weave, and Green Woodland. Sylvan and Old Egypt were introduced in 1915.

Moss Green was made in 1915, while Vogue and Bon-Ton were made in 1916. After the Zanesville pottery burned in 1918, all work was continued at the enlarged Roseville plant where a huge number of lines were made.

Stoneware art lines produced from 1923–1928 at Brush McCoy's Roseville plant included Jetwood, Jewel, Florastone, Zuni-art, Panelart, Kracklekraft, King Tut, and Stone Kraft. These were basically unglazed but had applied squeeze-bag glaze decorations.

In 1925 the name of the factory was changed to the Brush Pottery Company. During the 1930s, the company made planters, ashtrays, cookie jars, and an assortment of novelties. Brush Pottery had several different owners from 1978 until it closed in 1982.

NELSON MCCOY

History: Nelson McCoy, backed by his father J.W., established the Nelson McCoy Sanitary Stoneware Company in 1910 to manufacture utilitarian pieces such as jugs, churns, and crocks. By the mid 1920s, he expanded into molded artwares such as vases, jardinieres with matching pedestals, and pots.

In 1933 the name was changed to Nelson McCoy Pottery. During the early 1940s, kitchenwares, tablewares, garden and florist ware, vases, industrial artware, cooking utensils, and heavy dinnerwares were made, as well as numerous novelties, including over two hundred varieties of cookie jars.

After Nelson died in 1945, the firm remained in the family. The company was purchased by Mount Clemens Pottery in 1967 and a series of ownership changes followed. Nelson McCoy, Jr., the fourth generation in the family to be involved

with pottery making, left the company in 1981. More changes followed and the plant finally closed in 1990.

Most of the McCoy pieces were not marked, except the impressed "Loy-Nel-Art" pieces and some others marked "McCoy." "MITUSA," (Made in the United States of America) was the trademark used for ten years after being registered in 1915 and it was stamped on the bottom of the Brush McCoy wares. Very few other pieces of Brush McCoy were marked. A variety of marks was used by Brush and Nelson McCoy potteries.

References: Sharon and Bob Huxford, *The Collectors Encyclopedia of McCoy Pottery,* Collector Books, 1993 value update; ———, *The Collectors Encyclopedia of Brush McCoy Pottery,* Collector Books, 1978; Martha and Steve Sanford, *The Guide to Brush McCoy Pottery,* privately printed 1982.

Newsletter: *Our McCoy Matters,* Kathy Lynch, c/o McCoy Publications, P.O. Box 14255, Parkville, MO 64152, $24. bimonthly.

Museum: Zanesville Art Center, OH.

Additional Listings: See Cookie Jars in the Utilitarian section.

BROCADE PATTERN

Bud Vase, 7¼" h, green	**6.00**
Vase, 7¼" h, blue and black	**13.00**

EL RANCHO PATTERN

Casserole	**85.00**
Coffee Mug	**40.00**
Coffeepot	**95.00**
Ice Tea Server	**75.00**
Soup Tureen	**45.00**

FLORASTONE

Vase, 12" h	**95.00**

SPRINGWOOD PATTERN

Bowl, 3½" h, 6" d, ftd, green w/white flowers	**8.00**

MISCELLANEOUS

Bank	
Figural eagle w/spread wings, natural colors	**27.00**
Sailor w/seabag, Seaman's Bank For Saving, white and blue	**48.00**
Seated sad dog w/barrel, gray base..	**35.00**
Bean Pot, 3" h, 3-ftd, black	**6.00**
Bookend, brown, green, red, and yellow, pr	**30.00**
Candlestick, molded leaves design, orchid glazed finish, pr	**18.00**
Cream and Sugar, Elsie and Elmer	**50.00**
Creamer, 5" h, emb water lily motif, brown, #124	**18.00**
Figure	
16" l, panther, black glaze	**125.00**
Wishing well, light brown base, green top	**7.00**
Jardiniere	
3¼" h, lime green	**8.00**

Celery Vase, 5³/₄" h, gloss pink glaze, pr, $38.00

3¹/₂" h, holly motif, green, "Nelson McCoy Pottery Co." mark **14.00**
Lamp Base, figural cowboy boots, brown **25.00**
Mug
  5" h, springer spaniel design, sgd **25.00**
Buccaneer
  Brown **18.00**
  Green **15.00**
Pitcher
  6" h, sailfish, blue glaze **60.00**
  9¹/₂" h, emb grapes and leaves motif, rustic glaze **24.00**
Planter
  2" h, 10" l, candleholder in center, yellow w/green, hairline **9.00**
  3" h, 8" l, figural Dutch shoe, yellow **8.00**
  7" h
    Figural wishing well, brown shades **7.00**
    Kitten, gold trim **50.00**
    Triple lily, yellow flowers w/green leaves, brown base **22.00**
  Basket, dbl overhead handles, cream ground, black accents **28.00**
  Bird dog, black and white, brown base **60.00**
  Chinese man with wheelbarrow, yellow glaze w/black accents **11.00**
  Dbl shells, dark green finish **10.00**
  Panther, green finish **18.00**
  Pelican, turquoise finish **16.00**
  Quail, red-brown and green accents **25.00**
  Shell Dish, loop handle, peach finish **9.00**
  Spinning waterwheel, brown shades **8.00**
  Swan, pink, #4 .... **20.00**
Planting Dish
  3" h
  9" l, fluted edge, yellow w/green trim **5.00**
  11" l, gray w/green trim **15.00**

5" h, 12¹/₂" l, pink flower, blue-black base **21.00**
Shakers, figural nested cabbages, pr.... **40.00**
Sprinkler, figural turtle, green finish **15.00**
Tankard, buccaneer, brown finish **59.00**
Tea Set, pot, creamer, sugar bowl, Pine Cone pattern, green finish **40.00**
Vase
  4" h, Sylvan, green **35.00**
  8" h, grapes design, rustic glaze **10.00**
  8³/₄" h, mission style, matte green glaze **30.00**
  9" h, figural swan, red w/black accents, black int **35.00**
  14" h, leaves and circles design, matte white glaze **125.00**
  Basket, molded overlapping leaves w/berries, green, brown, and red . **23.00**
Figural
  Fawn, green, #7 .... **25.00**
  Uncle Sam, green, c1943 .... **25.00**
  Pitcher, ewer shape, relief of grapes and leaves, dark pink finish **18.00**
Wall Pocket
  Apple **30.00**
  Banana.. **65.00**
  Bellows **65.00**
  Birdbath **35.00**
  Lily, turquoise, #8 .... **28.00**
  Mexican man, white **20.00**
  Pear **25.00**
Umbrella
  Black **25.00**
  Gold.. **45.00**

c.1905-1920

D.E. MCNICOL POTTERY COMPANY

East Liverpool, Ohio; Clarksburg, West Virginia
1892–1954

History: In 1892 in East Liverpool, Ohio, the D.E. McNicol Pottery was formed from the former McNicol, Burton and Company. The first products were yellowware, Rockingham, and white ironstone called semi-granite. In 1902 a second plant for Rockingham and yellowware was added, and the original plant continued making ironstone.

A new plant was built in Clarksburg, West Virginia, in 1914 and another in East Liverpool five years later. Production was expanded to include hotel, dinner, and toilet wares in semi-granite, semi-porcelain, and cream colors. The company continued to make yellowware until 1927.

Another specialty of McNicol was calendar and souvenir plates in a wide array of styles and decorative motifs. The West Virginia plant specialized in white and decorated vitrified china for hotels, railroads, hospitals, and restaurants.

McNicol consolidated its operations in 1929 by closing the East Liverpool plants and concentrating on vitrified china in Clarksburg until 1954 when all production ceased. Numerous marks were used.

Bowl
   7¹/₂" d, multicolored decal of woman in tan dress w/red sash, holding bowl of apples, scattered floral rim, "Souvenir of St. Joseph, Michigan" **28.00**
   9¹/₄" d, white and pink hibiscus, gold lacy design on border, green lustered shaded floral ground **18.00**
   12" d, white rose in center w/small pink roses, lustered pea green shaped rim **7.00**
Chamber Pot, 6¹/₂" h, 9" d, tan spatter **65.00**
Grill Plate, 9¹/₂" d, 2 green inner bands, commercial ware, "McNicol China, Clarksburg, W. Va." mark **5.00**
Milk Pitcher, 4¹/₄" h, white ironstone, "McNicol, Clarksburg, W. Va." mark **5.00**
Pitcher and Bowl, pitcher, 11¹/₂" h, bowl, 16¹/₂" d, white ironstone w/raised sculpture design, "D.E. McNicol, Clarksburg, W. Va." mark **160.00**
Plate
   7¹/₂" d, oriental harbor scene in cen-

ter, flowered border, green transfer, commercial ware................... **5.00**
   8" d, decal of male and female moose in forest setting, yellow border, dark brown shaped rim w/raised dots **8.00**
8¹/₄" d
Decal of multicolored swimming trout, lustered gold-yellow dashes on border, lustered green shaped rim, "Compliments Kimball Bros. Briggsville, Wi." on front, "D.E. McNicol, East Liverpool, Ohio" mark **8.00**
Multicolored scene of Panama Canal and American flag in center, 1915 calendar, inner gold drop band, lustered orange-yellow border.................. **45.00**
Two multicolored shorebirds at water's edge, gold "J.C. Miller Furniture Co., Furniture and Undertaking, Elgin, Texas" on front, green rim, "D.E. McNicol, East Liverpool" mark **35.00**
9" d
Calendar, multicolored pears in center, gold "16th Anniversary W.J. Paynter, Baker & Grocer," 1909 calendar on border, "McNicol Carnation" mark **35.00**
Fox hunter and shepherd in center, scalloped rim w/gold trim, "Compliments of the Season" on front, "McNicol Carnation" mark **20.00**
White ground, green striped rim, commercial ware **9.50**
9¹/₄" d
Decal of woman in green gown w/purple sash, arm touching flowered branch, shaped rim, "Grossvater Beer" on reverse.... **28.00**

Chamber Pot, 9¹/₂" h, 10¹/₂" d, white ironstone, black "Warrented, Royal Seal, D.E. Mc N. P. Co. Liverpool" mark, $45.00

Plate, 8¹/₂" d, black, brown, and white birds, yellow-green ground, gilt trim and advertising, "D.E. McNicol East Liverpool, Ohio" mark, $40.00

Pink carnations in blue bowl in center w/1917 calendar surround, "Compliments of O.O. Russel, Latty, Ohio," gold overlay border 15.00

Three groups of white and pink roses w/green leaves, shaped gold rim 5.00

9³/₄" d, F.O.E. emblem and eagle, blue decal 15.00

10" d

F.O.E. emblem, blue decal, white ground 10.00

Molded int handles, white and pink poppies w/green leaves in center, shaded green to brown molded border 10.00

Red-brown oak leaves, white ground, "McNicol Carnation" mark 12.00

10¹/₄" d, 3 sections, blue willow design 18.00

Relish Dish, 8¹/₄" l, seal of North West Lion's Athletic Club, maroon and black striped border, "McNicol Vitrified China, Albert Pick" mark 7.00

Teapot, 5" h, Touraine pattern, blue flowers, gold rim and trim, white ground, mkd, $28.00

Cream Pitcher, 4" h, band of green stylized leaves on shoulder, gold trim, crackle glaze 6.00

Pitcher and Bowl, pitcher, 13" h, bowl, 17¹/₂" d, Victorian style pink and magenta roses w/green leaves, gold-outlined raised white leaves on base, gold trim, marked 265.00

Plate, 9¹/₈" d, blue, yellow, and red floral border, yellow-outlined rim, crackle glaze, 3 chimney mark 4.00

Platter, 14¹/₂" l, bouquet of wildflowers in center, scattered floral border 14.00

Shaving Mug, 3¹/₂" h, wide and narrow gold horiz banding 18.00

Tray, 12⁵/₈" l, orchids in center w/advertising, blue banded rim 10.00

MERCER POTTERY
Trenton, New Jersey
1868–1930s

History: The Mercer Pottery was incorporated in 1868 in Trenton, New Jersey, with James Moses as head of the company and Jonathan Coxon as manager. Ironstone, semi-vitreous, and semi-porcelain wares were made. By the 1900s, the products included porcelain and white granite dinner sets, toilet sets, sanitary wares, and druggist supplies.

Some of the pieces made at Mercer Pottery were marked with a double shield and were interchangeable with identically shaped and marked pieces from International Potteries. A globe mark was impressed on Mercer's white granite ware.

Butter Drain, Cov, 8¹/₂" H-H, Touraine pattern, green lace border, gilt trim, white ground 12.00

MONMOUTH
POTTERY CO.
MONMOUTH, ILL.

MONMOUTH POTTERY
Monmouth, Illinois
1893–1906

History: In 1893 banker William Hanna and his associates established Monmouth Pottery Company in Monmouth, Illinois, to make stonewares. The plant had major fires in 1897 and 1905.

Monmouth stoneware pieces were usually straight sided and salt glazed or slipped in Albany or Bristol finishes. Frequently the only decoration was the stenciled capacity numbers within a circular motif. Not all examples were plain. Blue-sponged water coolers, crocks, and pitchers also were made, as well as miniature crocks, jugs, chickens, pigs, dogs, and cows. Some miniatures were sponged while others were Bristol glazed or had the Albany slip finish. A large selection of other utilitarian wares were produced, including crocks, milk bowls, butter jars, churns, jugs, preserve jars, tobacco jars, cuspidors, and chamber pots.

The maple leaf was used as the company logo along with several other marks during the thirteen years of operation. Many pieces were marked "MONMOUTH POTTERY CO. MONMOUTH, ILL."

In 1906 a merger took place with six other companies and the facility became Plant One of Western Stoneware. Production continued on many of the same items but the Monmouth Pottery logo was no longer used.

Reference: Jim Martin and Bette Cooper, *Monmouth-Western Stoneware,* Wallace-Homestead, 1983.

Collectors' Club: Collectors of Illinois Pottery and Stoneware, David McGuire, 1527 East Converse Street, Springfield, IL 62703, $15 per year, newsletter.

Vase, 11¹/₂" h, silver-green glaze, "Monmouth Pottery, Monmouth, Il." sticker, c1937, $165.00

Crock, 6 gallon, blue label, c1900, $69.00

Vase, 8" h, matte turquoise glaze, "U.S.A. Monmouth Pottery, Monmouth, Il." paper label, pr, $75.00

Casserole, Cov, 8³/₄" d, yellow stylized flowers w/blue centers and blue flowers w/yellow centers	**20.00**
Figure, 3" h, 7¹/₂" l, standing pig, brown Albany slip glaze, emb "MONMOUTH POTTERY CO MONMOUTH, ILL," c1880–1900(A)	**715.00**
Jug, 7¹/₂" h, white clay w/brown glaze, "Monmouth Pottery Co., Monmouth, Ill." mark, chips(A)	**440.00**
Planter, 6¹/₂" h, 8¹/₂" l, brick surface pattern, turquoise glaze	**35.00**
Vase	
9" h, Aztec, brown glaze	**95.00**
Matte olive green finish w/silver specks, horiz ribbing	**85.00**

MORTENS STUDIO
Chicago, Illinois
1937–1956

History: Oscar Mortens came from Sweden and made detailed animal figures that were distributed through Mortens Studio, a firm he co-founded with Gunnar Thelin, an expert in glazes. Artists were hired to produce the Royal Designs line that included more than two hundred dogs, over one hundred horses, and a variety of other animals in lesser quantities. Wires were embedded in a plaster type material to support the weight of the figure. Bookends and wall plaques also were made.

Examples were marked "Copyright by the Mortens Studio" in ink or with a decal.

Figure	
3" h	
Boxer pup, sitting, #823	**65.00**

English bulldog pup, cream and
black, #832 .... 75.00
3¼" h
Bassett hound, standing, black
and white w/tan, #878 .... 95.00
Cocker spaniel pup, sitting
Black, #820 .... 85.00
Cream and red, #820 .... 60.00
Dalmatian pup, sitting, #812 .... 70.00
3½" h
Boston bullterrier pup, black and
white, #838 .... 75.00
Chihuahua pup, sitting, black and
tan, #865 .... 60.00
Dachshund, red, "I am a Dachs-
hund" sticker, #866B 85.00
German shepherd pup, cream
and black, #844 .... 75.00
Wirehaired terrier, sitting 50.00
4" h, 5" l, pug, standing, buff, chip
on ear, #738 .... 100.00
4¼" h, beagle 45.00
4½" h
Boxer, sitting, #794 .... 65.00
Cocker spaniel, charcoal 50.00
4¾" h
Airedale, standing, black and tan,
#741 .... 95.00
French poodle, cream, #772 .... 95.00
5" h
Cocker spaniel, standing, brown
spots, #763A 85.00
Dalmatian, sitting 65.00
Springer spaniel, red spots,
#721A..................................... 90.00
5½" h
Chihuahua, black and tan, #777B   85.00
Wirehaired terrier, standing 50.00
5¾" h, collie, sitting, tan and
cream, #791 .... 95.00
6"
H, collie, standing, tan and
cream, #759A 125.00

*Figure, 4½" h, Pekingese, brown
shades, "Copyright By The Morten Studios" sticker, $159.00*

L, chinchilla Persian cat, cream,
#912 .... 100.00
6½" h
Boxer, sitting, fawn, #780 .... 76.00
German shepherd
Sitting, gray and black, #756.... 95.00
Standing, tan and black, #755.. 100.00
Pointer, cream and black spots,
crazed, #847 .... 95.00
6¾" h, greyhound, standing, black,
#757... 100.00
7" h, horse, 3 feet on ground, ears
back, gray, #705 .... 125.00
7⅛" l, boxer, lying down, fawn,
#781... 65.00
7½" h, Great Dane, sitting, fawn,
#750B 85.00
8½" h, rearing palomino horse........ 75.00

NEW GENEVA AND GREENSBORO POTTERY

Fayette County, Pennsylvania
1849–1917
Greene County, Pennsylvania
1810–early 20th century

History: Greensboro, in Greene County, and
New Geneva, in Fayette County, were two Pennsylvania towns that were opposite each other. In
about 1810 Alexander and James Vance became
the first Greensboro potters to make redware
covered with brown slip. Later they used a white
clay to make gray stonewares. Many other
stoneware potters worked in the area, some of
whom also made salt-glazed products. In 1849
George Debolt and Harry Atchison were working
in New Geneva and by 1860 there were numerous others, such as James Hamilton who is
known for his pumps and forty- to fifty-gallon
jugs.

During the early years at New Geneva and
Greensboro, potters used freehand and cut-and-
stenciled designs of birds, leaves, flowers, vines,
plants, and fruit, as well as straight and curved
lines. Painting was done either before or after the
glaze. Blue was the most popular color for un-
derglazing, while enamels were used for over-
glazing. Some pieces were neither decorated nor
signed.

An assortment of vases, canning jars, whiskey
jugs, milk pitchers, water pitchers, doorstops,
flowerpots, banks, and six- to twenty-gallon
crocks were made. With the coming of the age of
glass, the pottery business slowly declined.

Reference: Dr. Carmen A. Guappone, *New Geneva and Greensboro Pottery, Illustrated and Priced,* Guappones' Publishers, 1975.

Bank, 5" h, dark brown slip floral design, tanware(A) **363.00**
Churn, 18¾" h, tooled surface, amber and brown slip w/stenciled design, chips(A) **149.00**
Jar
  10¼" h, cobalt "New Geneva" label and florals(A) **110.00**
  11¾" h, cobalt stenciled and freehand "Williams and Reppert, Greensboro, Pa. 2," chips(A) **225.00**
  12¼" h, cobalt stenciled and freehand "Hamilton & Jones, Greensboro, Pa. 2"(A) **137.00**
  13¾" h, ovoid shape, cobalt stenciled and freehand "Hamilton & Jones, Greensboro, Pa. 3"(A) **330.00**
  14" h, cobalt stenciled and freehand label "R.T. Williams, Manufacturer, New Geneva, Pa. 3"(A).. **248.00**
  15" h, cobalt stenciled "Jas Hamilton & Co, Greensboro, Pa 4" on front(A) **181.00**
  15½" h, cobalt and freehand label "C.L. Williams & Co., Successors to R.T. Williams Manufacturers of Stoneware, New Geneva, Pa. 5," hairlines(A) **220.00**
  16" h, applied handles, cobalt stenciled "Hamilton and Jones, Greensboro, Pa. 5" on front, chips(A) **143.00**

Jar, 16½" h, blue HP floral and stencil design, 6 gallon, repaired cracked base, c1860–70, Greensboro(A), $2860.00.
Photograph courtesy of Harmer Rooke Galleries, New York, NY

  16½" h, cobalt stenciled and freehand "Williams & Reppert, Greensboro, Pa." on front, stains and chips(A) **160.00**
  18" h, 3 bands of brushed cobalt stylized leaves, imp label "Boughner, Greensboro, Pa. 8"(A) **850.00**
  18½" h, brushed cobalt floral design, imp "Hamilton, Greensboro, Pa. 8" on front, cracked(A) **852.00**
  20½" h, stenciled and freehand cobalt "Williams and Reppert, Greensboro, Pa. 10" and eagle(A) **1100.00**
Jug
  7½" h, dark brown slip and stenciled "S.T. Suit, Suitland, Maryland, 1869, Whiskey", tanware(A) **385.00**
  10" h, red clay w/brown slip, stenciled "M.C.R., M.C Russell, Maysville, Ky."(A) **192.00**
  11" h, cobalt stenciled "Hamilton & Jones, Greensboro Pa." on front(A) **247.00**
  11¾" h, cobalt stenciled "T.F. Reppert, Greensboro, Pa."(A) **72.00**
Flowerpot, 4⅞" h, attached base, two-tone brown Albany slip and unglazed tan clay, finger-crimped lips, hole in base(A) **192.00**
Pitcher
  5½" h, dark brown slip floral design, tan ground(A) **385.00**
  6" h, dark brown slip floral and leaf design, tanware **440.00**
Preserving Jar
  8" h, cobalt stenciled "Greensboro" and pear label on front, chips(A).. **154.00**
  8½" h, blue "A. Conrad, New Geneva, Pa" on front(A) **220.00**
  9¼" h, cobalt brushed lines, stenciled "New Geneva Pottery" label, chips(A) **280.00**
  9½" h
    Blue stenciled "Geneva Pottery," cobalt wavy lines(A) **200.00**
    Cobalt stenciled "A. Conrad, New Geneva, Pa." on front(A).. **275.00**
  10" h
    Cobalt stenciled
      "Hamilton & Co, Greensboro, Pa" on front(A) **187.00**
      "Jas. Hamilton & Co., Greensboro, Pa." and rose on front(A) **247.00**
    Cobalt stenciled and freehand "Hamilton & Jones, Greensboro, Pa." on front, hairlines(A) **154.00**
  13½" h, dbl handles, stenciled "JAS. HAMILTON & CO. GREENSBORO PA. 3" and leaf design, salt glaze, c1860–70(A) **330.00**

ZANESVILLE, OHIO
U S A

OHIO POTTERY
1900–1923

FRAUNFELTER CHINA COMPANY
1923–1939
Zanesville, Ohio

History: Ohio Pottery operated in Zanesville, Ohio, from 1900–1923. Hotel ware was made, as well as hard-paste dinnerware from 1918–1920 and kitchenwares, which were introduced c1915.

Fraunfelter China Company took over in 1923 and also purchased American China Products Company of Chesterton, Indiana. Dinnerware in both plants was made until Fraunfelter died in 1925 and the Chesterton plant was closed.

Both Ohio and Fraunfelter sold large quantities of blanks for decoration since not many other firms made European-quality porcelains at competitive prices. Fraunfelter closed during the Depression, then reorganized, reopened, and closed again in 1939.

A wide variety of marks was used.

Casserole, Cov
7¼" d, Art Deco motif on lid **55.00**
8½" d, purple grape bunches w/leaves, yellow ground, "Fraunfelter China" mark **45.00**
Coffeepot, 7½" h, Drip-o-lator, white stepped-back shoulder w/band of multicolored florals, "Enterprise Aluminum Company Fraunfelter" mark **32.00**

Coffeepot, 7½" h, beige glaze, Drip-O-lator, "The Enterprise Aluminum Co., Fraunfelter China" mark, $32.00

Coffee Set, urn, 14½" h, creamer, sugar bowl, Royal Rochester pattern, band of multicolored garden flowers, tan ground, matte gold rim, metal fittings **75.00**
Teapot
5" h, vert ribbed body and cov, med brown glaze, "Fraunfelter China" mark **22.00**
6½" h, large stylized yellow rose w/purple center, multicolored leaves and small purple flowers on sides, vert fluted body, silver trim, "Fraunfelter China" mark **45.00**
Vase, 6" h, variegated rose and purple luster decoration **270.00**

c.1885

OTT AND BREWER
Trenton, New Jersey
1863–1892

History: Etruria Pottery was established by Joseph Ott and others. In 1865 John Brewer joined the firm and the name became Ott and Brewer. Until 1875 mostly white granite and cream-colored wares were made.

Isaac Broome, the first American artist to work in parian, was employed at Ott and Brewer from 1873–1878. He did portrait busts of historical figures, the most famous of which was Cleopatra. He is best known for his pair of parian baseball vases, made in 1876 and displayed at the Centennial Exposition.

In 1882 William Bromley, Jr., William, his father, and John, his brother, came from the Belleek factory in Ireland to Ott and Brewer where they perfected an American Belleek formula utilizing native clays. Many Irish patterns were copied and Ott and Brewer became known for tete-a-tete sets that were as delicate as their Irish Belleek counterparts.

Royal Worcester type designs also were used on the Belleek body as were oriental metallic designs in dark colors on matte grounds.

In 1892 Ott and Brewer sold to C. Cook and Company, and the Bromleys went to work for Willets Manufacturing Company. Ott and Brewer used five different marks on their Belleek porcelains.

Reference: Mary Frank Gaston, *American Belleek,* Collector Books, 1984.

Museum: New Jersey State Museum, Trenton, NJ.

SWASTIKA
KERAMOS

OWEN CHINA
MINE RVA
32 7A

Creamer

3" h, Belleek, pink and brown flowers and leaves, Tridacna body	225.00
4½" h, Belleek, cylinder shape, gold florals, gold-trimmed handle	75.00
Cup and Saucer, Belleek, eggshell body, wishbone handle, gold-paste florals	135.00
Egg Holder, Belleek, pedestal base, dolphin finial, gold-paste flowers and sponged gold trim	950.00
Mug, 5½" h, Belleek, shaded cobalt swallows, black "When Swallows Homeward Fly"	185.00
Pitcher, 6½" h, Belleek, horn shape w/branch handle, gold-paste flowers, brown bark base	850.00
Sugar Bowl, Cov, 4" h, Belleek, pink and brown flowers, Tridacna body	275.00
Tray, 14" w, Belleek, cockleshell shape	975.00
Vase, 11" h, hp multicolored overglaze colors	350.00
Wash Set, partial, pitcher, 7" h, bowl, 15" d, chamber pot, 8¼" d, 5¼" h, cov soap dish, cov slop jar, mauve and tan orchid design w/gold-paste orchids, raised panels w/shell designs, ribbed handles w/gold trim, white ground	550.00

Dish, Cov, 9" d, Belleek, matte olive and brown oak leaves, matte gold trim, white ground, "Ott & Brewer Belleek" mark, $750.00

OWENS CHINA COMPANY/MINERVA
Minerva, Ohio
1906–1932

History: Owens China Company was founded by Ted Owens in Minerva, Ohio, in 1906. The local clay was used to make semiporcelain, hotel china, and tea and dinner services with underglaze and overglaze decorations.

Swastika Keramos was first exhibited in 1906 and made for a few years thereafter. This art pottery line was distinguished by bronze, brass, and copper metallic lusters and scenic decorations on a white clay body.

Despite its success, the company could not survive the economic hardships caused by the Depression. Some Swastika Keramos pieces were marked with an in-mold raised seal; others were unmarked.

ART POTTERY

Ewer, 10" h, large green leaves on red-gold ground, metallic glaze, "Swastika Keramos" mark	475.00
Mug, 4½" h, raised grapes and vines, matte green finish	150.00
Vase	
5" h, green, pink, green, and brown luster on gold floral, attrib. to John Lesell, Swastika Keramos	325.00
5⅞" h, red, gold, and green drip design, "Swastika Keramos" mark	425.00
8" h	
Gold filigree design	200.00
Two handles, green swirling design on rough white ground, "Swastika Keramos" mark(A)	100.00
10½" h, green luster leaves, matte gold luster finish, "Swastika Keramos" mark	1250.00
12" h, 2 handles, coralene opalescent glaze w/emerald green drops on gold ground	200.00

GENERAL LINE

Ewer, 11¾" h, bust of black-haired woman in blue gown w/sunflower in hair, raised body swirls, shaded brown ground, figural foo dog handle, "Owens Minerva" mark	130.00
Plate	
8¼" d, decal of bust of brown-	

Lemonade Set, pitcher, 6" h, 6 cups,
4³/₄" h, red cherries and green leaves,
brown to cream shaded ground, "helmet
Owens Minerva" mark, $125.00

haired woman w/daisy in hair,
blue gown on shoulders, raised
shaped aqua-shaded rim **48.00**
9" d, maroon 1906 calendar w/mul-
ticolored pastoral scenes, shaped
beaded rim, gold "Compliments
of George Spatz, 304 High
Street," "Owens Minerva" mark ... **24.00**

Pennsbury Pottery Morrisville Pa.

PENNSBURY POTTERY
Morrisville, Pennsylvania
1950–1970

History: Pennsbury Pottery was started by
Henry and Lee Below, German immigrants who
were both associated with Stangl Pottery in Trenton, New Jersey, before founding their own pottery in 1950.

The first products at Pennsbury were birds,
similar in many respects to those made by Stangl,
though fewer varieties were made. The largest
birds were the rooster and the hen; the rarest,
those done in all white or ivory glaze. Birds were
made until the mid 1950s in a variety of color
combinations and were numbered.

Slick-chick, another Pennsbury product, was
a small bird perched on top of a hollowed out
gourd. Slick-bunny also was made. These pieces
were not always marked.

The finish on Pennsbury's earthenware required two high-temperature firings. The background colors varied from a light tan to a dark
brown.

The first Pennsbury dinnerware line was the
Black Rooster, followed by Red Rooster, and

then the Folkart line in brown finish. Folkart
made on white with cobalt blue decorations was
called Blue Dowry. During the 1960s, the Folkart
name was changed to Brown Dowry. Another
pattern was Toleware which was dark brown
with red and white fruit. When made in white
with a blue ground and blue fruit decoration, it
was called Delft Toleware. Hex was made in two
versions: one had small heartlike designs between teardrops and the other, Pennsylvania
Hex, had no hearts.

The most popular and sought after Pennsbury
products were decorative pieces, especially ashtrays and hanging plaques, with clever sayings
on them. Other popular pieces were those with
Amish designs, figures, and scenes. These artware examples were made in a small number of
shapes, not complete sets, but there were quite a
few Amish-decorated lines. Other desirable
pieces included Barber shop Quartet, Gay
Nineties, Eagle, and Fisherman.

A Christmas plate, Stumar Angel, was made
only in 1970. Additional Christmas merchandise
was made on a commissioned basis.

A limited number of pieces were molded in
high relief instead of being decorated with
carved designs. Railroad plaques and trays featured different locomotives, and Ships detailed
eight sailing ships. During the early 1950s,
Pennsbury made commemorative merchandise
that customers ordered for Christmas and wed-
dings, such as ashtrays, beer mugs, coasters, etc.
Associations and businesses also ordered pieces
for their groups. The company made a wide variety of novelties in the form of bread plates, oil
and vinegar bottles with sayings, pottery pie
pans, banks, salt and pepper shakers, tiles, figural
candleholders, and the like.

After Henry died, Lee and Ernst, her son, operated the pottery until the late 1960s when sales
decreased due to the heavy competition from
less expensive European and Japanese imports.
In 1970 the owners were forced to file for bank-
rupty and production ceased. The pottery was
destroyed by fire in 1971.

The earliest decorated pieces were signed by
hand. Some marks were hand incised or
stamped, and some pieces were not marked at
all.

Reference: Lucile Henzke, *Pennsbury Pot-*
tery, Schiffer Publishing, 1990.

AMISH
Ashtray, 5" d **25.00**
Coffee Mug, 3¹/₄" h **35.00**
Creamer, 2" h, Amish lady's head **22.00**
Oil and Vinegar, Amish heads **135.00**
Pitcher
  2¹/₂" h, pr, man and woman **30.00**
  4" h **25.00**
BARBERSHOP QUARTET PATTERN
Coaster, 5" d

"Horowitz" 30.00
"Schultz"...................................... 30.00
Pretzel Bowl, 12" l, 8" w..................... 65.00
BLACK ROOSTER PATTERN
Butter Dish, 4" h 40.00
Cake Stand, 11" d 65.00
Canister, 8" h, tea 86.00
Casserole, Cov 20.00
Cup and Saucer 25.00
Fruit Bowl, 5" d 25.00
Plate, 10" d.. 33.00
Salad Bowl, 6¼" d............................ 35.00
Soup Bowl, 6½" d, ruffled edge 35.00
Soup Tureen, ladle and stand, #1163.. 150.00
Wall Pocket 42.00
DUTCH TALK
Bowl, 9" d 125.00
EAGLE PATTERN
Beer Mug, 5" h 35.00
Pitcher, 5¼" h 32.00
Pretzel Bowl, 11" l, 8" w.................... 85.00
HARVEST
Tile, 6" sq 40.00
HEX PATTERN
Creamer.. 15.00
Pitcher, 4" h.................................... 25.00
Plate
  8" d... 30.00
  10" d... 33.00
RED ROOSTER PATTERN
Candleholder, 5" d 40.00
Cream and Sugar 30.00
Cup and Saucer 25.00
Pitcher
  4" h.. 30.00
  6" h.. 40.00
Plate, 10" d.................................... 34.00
Soup Bowl, ruffled edge, 6¼" d 35.00
Vegetable Dish, divided...................... 49.00
SWEET ADELINE
Mug, 4½" h 29.00
MISCELLANEOUS
Ashtray
  "Doylestown Trust" 25.00
  "Outen The Light" 25.00
  "Such Schmootzers"........................ 25.00
Figure
  3" h
    Redstart, #113, natural colors 110.00
    Wren, #109
      Natural colors 85.00
      White.. 75.00
  3½" h
    Hummingbird, white, #119 .... 125.00
    Nuthatch, natural colors, #110 .... 110.00
  4" h
    Audubon warbler, natural colors,
      #122 .... 150.00
    Bluebird, natural colors, #103 ..... 140.00
  5½" h, "Slick Chick," yellow and
    green 28.00

Pitcher, 4" h, tan ground, pr, $55.00

10" h, standing hen, cream and
  brown.. 250.00
12" h, hen and rooster, brown, tan,
  and ivory, pr...................................... 650.00
Mug, 5" h, "Swallow the Insult"......... 45.00
Pie Pan
  9" d
    "Harvest"................................... 80.00
    "Picking Apples" 75.00
    "Walking to Homestead"............. 80.00
Plaque
  4" d
    "Outen the Light" 25.00
    "Such Schmootzers" 25.00
    "What Giffs" 32.00
  6" d
    Amish couple courting 35.00
    Amish farm scene 35.00
  9½" l, 7" h
    Lafayette train, Baltimore and
      Ohio 80.00
    Tiger train, Pennsylvania 80.00
Wall Plate, 11½" d, "Scarce Family" .. 119.00

PFALTZGRAFF POTTERY COMPANY
York, Pennsylvania
1811–Present

History: German immigrant George Pfaltz-graff and other members of his family made red-ware and stoneware for well over one hundred years in York, Pennsylvania. Pfaltzgraff is one of the oldest pottery makers in the United States and the entire family has been involved in the production of stoneware and related products.

Crocks, jugs, pots, and such were made from 1811–1913. Food storage was the primary purpose for these gray salt-glazed and blue decorated stoneware pieces. Red clay flowerpots were made from 1913–1942 after which the company returned to stoneware production. Art pottery was made from 1931–1937 and kitchenwares were introduced in the 1930s. A very popular group of character mugs and tumblers marked "Muggsie" were made in the 1940s. The line included Derby Dan, Cockeyed Charlie, Handsome Herman, Flirty Girty, Myrtle, Sleepy Sam, Pickled Pete, Burnie, and others.

Pfaltzgraff first made dinnerware in 1940 and eventually the plants were expanded to meet the production needs for these useful and decorative lines. Patterns included Gourmet, Heritage, Yorktowne, and Village.

Utilitarian pieces made by the company included mixing bowls, custard cups, planters, cookie jars, ashtrays, and other kitchenwares.

The trademark was a castle outlining a variety of different marks.

Pitcher, 8¹/₂" h, brown spatter on gloss yellow ground, $15.00

AMERICA PATTERN
Cup and Saucer	8.00
Plate	
7" d	8.00
10¹/₄" d	15.00

GOURMET PATTERN
Bowl, 5¹/₂" d	9.00
Cup and Saucer	12.00
Plate, 10" d	15.00
Snack Tray, 11¹/₂" l, 9" w	12.00

HERITAGE PATTERN
Coffeepot, 8³/₄" h	25.00
Tureen, 9" h	25.00

TEA ROSE PATTERN
Dinner Plate	5.00
Soup Plate	5.00
Vegetable Bowl, 9" d	12.00

VILLAGE PATTERN
Bread and Butter Plate	2.00
Coffeepot	30.00
Cup and Saucer	3.00
Dinner Plate	4.00
Salad Plate	3.00
Soup Bowl	5.00
Tureen, w/ladle	65.00

MISCELLANEOUS
Cigar Jar, 6³/₄" h, Handy Harry	350.00
Flowerpot, 3³/₄" h, attached saucer, gloss yellow glaze	10.00
Mug, 3" h, Muggsie	
Flirty Girty	65.00
Handsome Herman	25.00
Jigger	35.00
Nick	25.00
Planter	
3¹/₂" h, ball shape, pink glaze	25.00
6" h, Art Deco style, turquoise glaze	40.00
Sprinkler Bottle, Myrtle	125.00

Pitcher, 9¹/₄" h, Seafoam blue base, white top, $20.00

Vase	
3¹/₂" h, burnt orange w/crystals	65.00
7" h, Art Deco design, orange glaze	65.00
12" h, handles, orange glaze	60.00
14" h, matte green glaze, #175	175.00

PICKARD CHINA
Chicago and Antioch, Illinois
1894–Present

History: Pickard China was a decorating firm founded by Wilder Pickard in Chicago in 1894.

Many artists from The Art Institute of Chicago hand painted china blanks made by other companies, primarily European firms.

By 1908 Pickard made more than one thousand shapes and designs, such as fruits, florals, birds, portraits, and scenes. Vases, tablewares, dresser sets, tea sets, and dessert sets all were made. Figural-type patterns included Dutch Decoration on a bisque-like surface and Praying Mohammedan on vases and framed wall plaques. Designs included Cornflower Conventional from 1908, Aura Argenta Linear in gold and silver from 1910, and Pink Enamel Flower. The number of tea sets, hot chocolate sets, and after-dinner coffee services increased in 1910.

Gold-encrusted and gold-etched china were introduced in 1911 and became Pickard's most popular lines. Patterns included Bordure Antique, Honeysuckle, Deserted Garden, Antique Chinese Enamels, Encrusted Linear, and Italian Garden. Gold-decorated wares are still being made.

A 1913 allover scenic design called Wildwood was awarded first prize at the Chicago Ceramic Exhibition that year. Four new patterns from 1916 were Secret Garden, Columbine, Rosabelle, and Mauresque. Many top artists who worked at Pickard from 1905–1919 signed their works. Edward S. Challinor, noted for his floral, fruit, bird, and scenic designs, came to Pickard in 1902 and remained there until his death in 1952.

After World War I, the concentration on gold-encrusted and etched pieces continued. The designs were transferred to a specially prepared tissue paper by means of a press and then transferred to the china. In 1925 the company incorporated as Pickard Studios. Mostly Bavarian blanks were used after the war. A pattern of fine gold lines resembling snowflakes also was used in the 1920s.

Around 1935, after Wilder's son Austin joined the firm, a formula to make china was developed and the company built a plant in Antioch, Illinois. By 1938 a completely vitrified, translucent, thin, light product with excellent glaze was being manufactured. The first china both made and decorated at Pickard was introduced at Marshall Field in Chicago in 1938.

The name of the company was changed to Pickard, Inc., and by 1941 the entire operation had moved from Chicago to Antioch. The firm obtained fuel oil during World War II by making china for the Navy.

During the transition period from 1942–1952 when Challinor was art director, simpler dinnerware patterns were becoming a larger part of the business. Although various forms of gold decoration were still used, decalcomania from Challinor originals were employed. Some hand-painted patterns also were made, including Botany, Chinese Seasons, Bouquet, Field Flowers, Aurora, Challinor Rose, and Camellia. A large quantity of allover gold-etched art pieces was still made for coffee sets, cake plates, bonbon dishes, vases, salts and peppers, ashtrays, and cigarette boxes.

After Challinor died in 1952, the amount of hand painting decreased because the costs were exceptionally high and qualified artists were difficult to find. New designs in 1955 included Gossamer, Blue Skies, and Silver Twilight. Austin's son Pete joined the business and designed new shapes and decorations, including Crescent, a popular modern pattern. Monogrammed ware was brought back along with a new art line called Accent that was decorated with gold or platinum.

Pickard started producing limited edition commemorative plates and bells in 1970. The following year the company was selected by the U.S. Department of State to make official china for use in embassies and diplomatic missions.

When Pickard worked only as a decorating firm, two marks may be found: one for Pickard and one for the company that made the china blanks. In 1920 the backstamp included the words "Pickard Etched China" in a black border. In 1925 the first lion trademark appeared. A variety of marks was used when Pickard made its own china.

References: Sharon Darling, *Chicago Ceramics and Glass: An Illustrated History from 1871 to 1933,* Chicago Historical Society, 1979; Dorothy Pickard Platt, *The Story of Pickard,* privately printed, 1970.

Collectors' Club: Pickard Collectors' Club, Alicia Miller, 300 E. Grove Street, Bloomington, IL 61701, $20 per year, quarterly newsletter.

Berry Bowl, 5¾" d, blackberries and
  leaves on int, set of 6(A) **121.00**
Bowl
  7" d, 2 handles, fruit design w/gold
    trim on rim, sgd "Topin" **150.00**
  8" d, trefoil shape, 3 handles, gold-
    outlined red poppies and green
    leaves on int and ext w/heavy
    gilding, sgd "Leach"(A) **247.00**
  9¼" d, 4¾" h, ftd, Modern Conven-
    tional design, Hessler **285.00**
  9¾" d
    Landscape and bird design,
      gilded molded rim, sgd "E.
      Challinor"(A).......................... **302.00**
    Strawberries and white flowers,
      gold scalloped border, artist
      sgd... **185.00**
  10½" l, 9⅝" w, open handles, cher-
    ries and blueberries outlined
    by scrolls, yellow and rose pastel
    shading, scalloped rim,
    c1898–1906 .... **275.00**
Cake Plate
  10½" d, open gold handles, Desert
    Garden pattern, black circles

w/gold, multicolored fruit on shaded ground, c1912 .... **180.00**

10¾" d, painted violets, heavy gilded trim, sgd "Fisher"(A) **275.00**

11" d
Italian Garden design, sgd "Yeschek" **245.00**
Night landscape scene, sgd "Marker"(A)............................ **247.00**
Oriental bird, butterflies, and flowers, gilded border and handles, sgd "Klein"(A) **66.00**

Candy Dish, 7" l, 4-ftd, gold scalloped rim, int w/cerise-rose scrolls and cherry clusters and leaves on shaded brown ground, light yellow ext w/cherry clusters and leaves, sgd "Vokral" **185.00**

Celery Tray, 14" l, 6⅝" w, yellow and purple grapes w/green, blue, and yellow leaves on cream ground, gold edge w/maroon design, sgd "Challinor"...................................... **225.00**

Chamberstick, painted roses and ribbons, gilded border and handle, sgd "H. Reury"(A)................................ **275.00**

Chocolate Pot, 9¼" h, red, lime, and yellow grape clusters, dark green, purple, and red shaded ground, gold trim, gold-trimmed loop handle, scalloped pedestal base, sgd "Vokral" **435.00**

Chocolate Set
3 piece
Pot, 8½" h, cov sugar bowl, creamer, overall gilding, panels of bowls of fruit, sgd "Vokral"(A) **275.00**
Pot, 10½" h, cov sugar bowl, creamer, flowers on white ground w/silver overlay(A) **605.00**
4 piece, pot, cov sugar bowl, creamer, tray, Desert Garden pattern, fruit design, gilded trim, sgd(A) **440.00**
7 piece, pot, 6 cups and saucers, painted fruit design, gilded accents and trim, sgd "Osborne"(A). **770.00**

Coffeepot, 6¾" h, night landscape scene, gilded spout, handle, and finial, sgd "Marker"(A).................... **495.00**

Coffee Set, pot, 8½" h, creamer, sugar bowl, 3⅓" h, hp yellow and pink roses, gilded trim, sgd "C. Marker" .. **450.00**

Cologne Bottle, 5" h, pink roses, blue florals, gilded trim, gold ball stopper, c1915 .... **165.00**

Console Set, fruit bowl, 11" d, 5¾" h, ftd, 2 handles, 2 candlesticks, 8¾" h, overall gilding w/roses, sgd "E. Challinor"(A)................................... **577.00**

Cookie Stand, 7" d, 2½" h, white

lilies, gold stems, raised gold tulips and stems, gilded trim and rim, sgd "Yeschek" **195.00**

Cream and Sugar, boat shape, chrysanthemum-type flowers, gilded trim, c1905 .... **95.00**

Creamer and Cov Sugar Bowl, hp plums and grapes, sgd "Marker" **175.00**

Cup and Saucer
Brocade pattern, raised white pattern, silver rim **13.00**
Light pink poppies and daisies, heavy gilding, sgd "Faladik"(A) **75.00**
Stylized orange trees w/heavy gilding, sgd "E. Tolpin"(A) **55.00**

Cup and Saucer, A.D.
Daffodil pattern, sgd "Challinor" **85.00**
Golden Rose pattern **45.00**
Overall gold................................. **13.00**

Dinnerware
Grandeur pattern
Bread and Butter Plate **6.00**
Cup and Saucer **8.00**
Dinner Plate **8.00**
Salad Plate................................ **7.00**
Victoria pattern
Bread and Butter Plate **10.00**
Dinner Plate **20.00**
Salad Plate................................ **14.00**

Dish, 10¼" l, 3¼" h, shell shape, molded handle and gilded rim, painted acorns and leaves, sgd "J. Nessy"(A) **220.00**

Dresser Tray, 15½" l, Italian Garden pattern, gilded border and handle, sgd "Gasper"(A) **302.00**

Flask, 10¾" h, gold-outlined ears of corn, burgundy ground(A) **605.00**

Fruit Bowl, 9½" d
4" h, 3-ftd, white lilies and green leaves, heavy gilding, sgd "Fisher"(A).................................. **220.00**
4¼" h, scalloped rim and foot, gilded abstract pattern on ext, red cherries and green leaves on int, gilded foot, sgd "O. Goess"(A)..... **302.00**

Hat Pin Holder, 5" h, painted yellow flowers, gilded top, sgd "Beutlich"(A) **275.00**

Humidor, 5¼" h, gilded and decorated w/poppies and daisies, sgd "Gasper"(A)...................................... **1017.00**

Jar, gilded cov, panel of flowers on mottled blue ground(A) **385.00**

Lemonade Pitcher
6¾" h
Painted red currants and leaves, gilded and painted rim, gilt handle, sgd "Reau"(A)............. **275.00**
Red poppies and green leaves, gilded rim and handle, sgd "N.R. Gifford"(A) **330.00**

7¼" h, gilded w/panels of enameled mixed flowers, sgd "E. Tolpin"(A) **522.00**

Mug

5" h, Venetian canal scene of fishing boats and Santa Maria Della Salute, irid luster ground, gilded rim, sgd "A. Comyn"(A) **990.00**

6" h, strawberries and foliage design, gold-trimmed handle, artist sgd, c1910 .... **90.00**

Nappy, 6" d, center w/blackberries and blossoms, gilded trim, scalloped rim, sgd "J. Gottlieb" **135.00**

Nut Bowl, 8" d, 3" h, gilded and scalloped rim, painted nuts, sgd "Vokral"(A) **132.00**

Pitcher

7½" h, gold, green, blue, yellow, and lilac water lilies in water, gloss glaze ext, rainbow irid int, sgd "Leroy," c1905–10 .... **595.00**

8" h, large poinsettias on sides, gilded trim, large loop handle, sgd "Gasper" **285.00**

10" h, red currants design, sgd "Reau," c1905 .... **450.00**

13¾" h, tankard shape, painted friar peeling turnip at table w/beer stein, gilded handle, sgd "P. Gasper"(A) **880.00**

14" h, tankard shape, metallic grapes and vine leaves, gilded rim and handle, sgd "Hessler"(A) **385.00**

15" h, tankard shape, Falstaff holding jug of ale, sgd "P. Gasper"(A). **1540.00**

Plate

7⅝" d, acorns and leaves in center, rose and light green ground, scalloped gold border, sgd "Wright" .. **75.00**

7¾" d, gooseberries on yellow and red-brown ground **75.00**

Pitcher, 4¼" h, bluish and mahogany irises, blue and green trim, gilt handle and rim, Limoges blank, artist sgd, $245.00

8" d

Scenic design, vellum finish, sgd "HLG" **160.00**

Western landscape, pastel colors, sgd "Marker" **95.00**

8½" d

Hp sweet pea flowers, gilded scalloped rim **65.00**

Scenic Yosemite design, sgd "Marker" **195.00**

8¾" d

Red carnations design, artist sgd, c1905 .... **185.00**

Three large sprays of irid green, violet, and salmon leaves, buds, and flowers, border w/red and gold tracery leaf and flower groups, sgd "F. James"... **105.00**

9" d, pastel lilies w/enamel, luster, and gilded accents, sgd "Yeshek" **165.00**

9⅛" d, painted peaches, gilded and molded border, sgd "S. Heap"(A). **99.00**

9½" d, painted poppies, sgd "Reury" **75.00**

10¾" d, painted garden and flowers, heavy gilded border, sgd "E. Challinor"(A) **137.00**

12½" d, painted roses, gilded border, sgd "Seidel"(A) **275.00**

Platter, 12½" d, landscape and bird decoration, heavy gilding, sgd "E. Challinor"(A) **412.00**

Powder Box, 6¼" d, white rose w/ornamental gilding, sgd "A. Motzfeldt"(A) **412.00**

Relish Tray, 9½" l, floral design in colors **75.00**

Sauce Dish, 6½" l, w/underplate, leaf shape, gilded w/red poppies and green leaves, sgd "Wagner"(A) **302.00**

Sugar Caster, 4½" h, Aura Argenta Linear pattern, gold and silver stylized berries, sgd "Hess"(A) **165.00**

Sugar Cube Dish, 8" l, stylized flowers and gilding(A) **44.00**

Syrup Jug, w/underplate, painted white lilies and green leaves, heavy gilded trim, sgd "Yeschek"(A) **275.00**

Tea Service, pot, creamer, sugar bowl, 10 cups and saucers, overall gilding, flower-decorated borders, sgd "Reau"(A) **770.00**

Tea Set

3 piece, pot, cov sugar bowl, creamer, roses and gold ribbon design, gilded rims, bases, handles, and finials, sgd "C. Hahn"(A) **605.00**

4 piece, pot, creamer, sugar bowl, cake plate, pink apple blossoms and green leaves, gilded trim, artist sgd(A) **522.00**

Tray

10" l, 5" w, "Golden Melody," cardinal and holly transfer............... **75.00**

11¼" d, orange irid cherries and green leaves on dark green ground, heavy gilded trim(A) **220.00**

Vase

5½" h, 3-ftd, gulls, meadow, and stream decoration, sgd "E. Challinor"(A) **385.00**

6½" h, palm trees and moonlit water, artist sgd **310.00**

7" h, red poppies on maroon ground, wide gold irid band, narrow gilded band on rim and base(A) **220.00**

7¼" h, Venetian canal w/boats, irid luster ground, gilded rim, sgd "N.R. Gifford"(A) **660.00**

7⅝" h, Art Nouveau, yellow flowers w/green and maroon leaves, black ground, gilded trim, sgd "Gifford," c1895–98 .... **325.00**

8" h, fluted top, stylized poinsettias, gilded trim, pearlized ground, artist sgd **215.00**

8½" h, yellow roses and green leaves, blue ground, gold collar, gold base band, sgd "Challinor," c1905–10 .... **425.00**

8¾" h, 2 handles, scenic panel and peacock, heavy gilding, sgd "E. Challinor"(A) **495.00**

9¼" h, gilded base and rim, painted lady w/flowing robes, sgd "Grane"(A) **2420.00**

10" h

Garden scene, matte finish, sgd "Marker" **475.00**

Yosemite pattern, mountain landscape scene, gilded rim and handles, sgd "Marker"(A) **605.00**

10½" h

Orange and brown mountain landscape w/stag(A) **1430.00**

Trumpet shape, painted daisies and carnations, gilded rim and base, sgd "E. Challinor"(A) **467.00**

10¾" h, gold neck, red-outlined leaves, gold-outlined irid green and blue fronds and stems, cerise, orange, and yellow poppy-type flowers under neck, sgd "Shoner" **445.00**

12" h, 2 handles, overall gilding, panel of lady w/basket of flowers, sgd "F. Cirnacty"(A) **935.00**

12½" h, 9¼" w, ovoid shape, 2 ring handles, ftd, Deserted Garden pattern, painted fruits w/gilding, sgd "Yeschek"(A) **1485.00**

13" h, painted tulips, gilded rim and base, sgd "C. Hahn"(A) **795.00**

13¾" h, dbl handles, painted pink carnations, gilded rim, base, and handles, sgd "Reau"(A) **715.00**

19¾" h, painted nude female w/long blond hair and blackbird, gilded handles, neck, and base, sgd "Grane"(A) **3740.00**

Water Pitcher

10" h, hex, Antique Chinese Enamel pattern, heavy gilding, sgd "E. Tolpin"(A).................................. **357.00**

10¼" h, melon ribbed, purple grapes and green leaves, heavy gilding, sgd "Seidel"(A) **247.00**

Whiskey Set, jug, 2 tumblers, tray, Pickard tartan w/crest of rampant lion, heavy gilding, sgd "A. Passovy"(A) **1430.00**

RED-CLIFF IRONSTONE
MADE IN USA

RED CLIFF POTTERY
Chicago, Illinois
1950–1980

RED-CLIFF
IRONSTONE
MADE IN U.S.A.

History: Red Cliff Pottery in Chicago, Illinois, distributed and decorated old-fashioned ironstone pieces. In the 1950s and 1960s, original pieces of English Tea Leaf ironstone were copied by Hall China for distribution by Red Cliff. All the pieces were clearly marked. The Walker China Company of Bedford Heights, Ohio, made some of the flatware Tea Leaf pieces for Red Cliff, but all the hollowware and molded pieces were made by Hall.

Chocolate Pot, 11" h, white ironstone, flattened panel shape w/gooseneck spout, raised leaf design **65.00**

Creamer, 5" h, white ironstone, raised puffy leaves on body, mkd **15.00**

Pitcher, 6¾" h, white ironstone, paneled.. **45.00**

Sugar Bowl, 5½" h, white ironstone, raised puffy leaves on body, fancy handles, mkd **20.00**

Tea Leaf pattern

Cup and Saucer.............................. **20.00**

Plate, 8¼" d **7.50**

Teapot, 9¾" h, white ironstone, molded grapes and vines on spout and at handle terminal **18.00**

Tray, 12½" l, rect, white ironstone, raised grape clusters on border, branch handles, mkd.................... **20.00**

Sauceboat, 10" l, white, mkd, $45.00

Tureen, oct, white ironstone
  3³/₄" h, 11³/₄" H-H, raised scalloped
  design................................... **90.00**
  Fruit finial
  Soup
    11¹/₄" h **165.00**
    14" h, w/ladle and undertray,
    branch handles.................... **195.00**
  Vegetable, 8¹/₄" h.................... **50.00**

RED WING
UNION STONEWARE
RED WING, MINN
U.S.A.

RED WING POTTERY
Red Wing, Minnesota
1877–1967

History: The Red Wing Stoneware Company operated in Red Wing, Minnesota, from 1877–1906. David Hallum, who originally used the Goodhue clay for utilitarian stonewares, was the chief engineer. The clay was a light tan-gray that retained its color when fired. Decorators at the Red Wing area potteries used the slip-cup method rather than brushes to embellish the utilitarian stoneware pieces. Various types of glazes were used, such as salt and Bristol, and Albany slip coated the inside of the crocks. The earlier pieces had more complicated designs on cruder pieces. By 1888, when stoneware crocks were used to store everything, Red Wing was the largest American producer of these products and its wares had heavy, rounded rims, ear handles, and salt glaze that was uniform in color and smoothness. The butterfly was the first trademark and the leaf the second one. Not all pieces were marked, but the words "Red Wing Stoneware Company" were stamped on the front of some crocks.

Water jars, crocks in all sizes, meat jars with covers, butter jars, churns, and the like were decorated with drawings of animals, flowers, birds, or geometric designs in a blue color made from cobalt oxide. The front of fruit jars, honey jars,

cheese crocks, mixing bowls, whiskey jugs, and druggists' chemical jugs often had a square or picture advertising a company's name and address.

MINNESOTA STONEWARE COMPANY, 1883–1906: This company used a pressing mold to mark its stonewares with raised letters in a circle or double circle. The early examples have the words "Red Wing" after "Minnesota Stoneware." "Minn." was added to the mark when the firm started to ship its products out of state.

NORTH STAR STONEWARE COMPANY, 1892–1896: This company, which only operated on its own for four years, used a star on the bottom of all the early pieces. Some examples were marked "North" in the star points.

UNION STONEWARE COMPANY, 1894–1906: This business was formed as a selling agency for three large potteries: Red Wing, North Star, and Minnesota Stoneware. North Star was bought out by the other two companies in 1896.

RED WING UNION STONEWARE COMPANY, 1906–1936: In 1906 Union Stoneware became the merged production company of Red Wing, North Star, and Minnesota Stoneware. In 1912 a red wing was added to the trademark. During the late 1920s, stoneware vases, flowerpots, bread crocks, pitchers, jardinieres, and mugs were made using a "brushware" technique.

RED WING POTTERIES, INC, 1936–1967: In 1936 the legal name of the merged company became Red Wing Potteries, Inc. Stonewares were discontinued in 1947, but from the late 1930s until the factory closed in 1967, approximately 84 different dinnerware patterns were made. The most popular hand-painted lines were Bob White (1956) and Round Up (1958). Solid-color dinnerwares also were in demand. Foreign competition, a decaying physical plant, and a labor strike caused Red Wing to close its doors.

See also Red Wing Pottery/Rum Rill Pottery in the Art Pottery section.

References: Stan Bougie and David Newkirk, *Red Wing Dinnerwares,* privately printed, 1981; Dan and Gail DePasquale, *Red Wing Collectibles,* Collector Books, 1986; ———, *Red Wing Stoneware,* Collector Books, 1983; Bonnie Tefft, *Red Wing Potters and Their Wares,* Locust Enterprises, 1981; Lyndon C. Viel, *The Clay Giants: The Stoneware of Red Wing, Goodhue County, Minnesota,* Book 3, Wallace-Homestead, 1987.

Collectors' Club: Red Wing Collectors' Society, Inc., Ken and Dee Dee Gorgan, P.O. Box 124, Neosho, WI 53059, $15 per year, bimonthly newsletter.

Museums: Goodhue County Historical Society Museum, Red Wing, MN; Kenosha Public Museum, WI.

ARDENNES PATTERN
Cream and Sugar, dubonnet **20.00**

Plate, 6" d	5.00
Teapot, dubonnet	25.00

BOB WHITE PATTERN

Beverage Server	65.00
Bowl	
6½" d	10.00
9" d, handled	25.00
Bread Tray, 24" l, 5" w	75.00
Casserole	
2 qt	38.00
3 qt, stick handles	25.00
Creamer	12.00
Cup and Saucer	10.00
Gravy Boat	45.00
Hors d'oeuvres Bird	32.00
Lazy Susan, 14" d, metal stand	75.00
Pitcher	
7" h	18.00
12" h	16.00
Plate	
6½" d	6.00
7½" d	9.00
8" d	7.00
10½" d	11.00
Platter	
20" d	45.00
Small	10.00
Relish Tray, 12" d, 3 parts	22.00
Salad Bowl, 12" d	35.00
Shakers, pr	24.00
Sugar Bowl, Cov	15.00
Teapot	49.00
Vegetable Bowl, divided	20.00
Vinegar and Oil	250.00
Water Cooler	250.00
Water Pitcher	45.00

BRITTANY PATTERN

Buffet Bowl	30.00
Cream Soup, Cov	11.00
Shakers, pr	10.00
Sugar Bowl, Cov	12.00
Teacup and Saucer	10.00

BROCADE PATTERN

Cereal Bowl	4.00
Cup and Saucer	5.00
Fruit Bowl	3.00
Plate, 7" d	3.00
Platter, 13" d	10.00

CAPISTRANO PATTERN

Bread Tray, sage green	20.00
Butter Dish, Cov, sage green	20.00
Casserole, Cov, sage green	30.00
Celery Dish, sage green	11.00
Creamer	
Gray	9.00
Sage green	9.00
Cup and Saucer, sage green	9.00
Fruit Dish	5.00
Gravy Boat, gray	12.00
Plate	
6½" d	4.00

Divided Tray, 13¾" l, Capistrano pattern, $22.00

7½" d	6.00
10½" d	8.00
11" d	8.00
Platter, 15" d, sage green	20.00
Salt and Pepper, sage green	9.00
Soup Plate	7.00
Sugar Bowl, Cov, sage green	15.00
Vegetable Bowl, divided	10.00
Water Pitcher	
Gray	25.00
Sage green	25.00

CHERRIES BAND

Pitcher	
6" h	175.00
8½" h, blue-gray, S. Dakota advertising	275.00

CHRYSANTHEMUM PATTERN

Cup and Saucer	5.00

COUNTRY GARDEN PATTERN

Cereal Bowl	3.00
Creamer	8.00
Cup and Saucer	6.00
Gravy Boat	8.00
Plate, 10½" d	9.00
Salad Plate	5.00
Sugar Bowl, Cov	8.00

CRAZY RHYTHM PATTERN

Fruit Dish w/handle	6.00

DAISY CHAIN PATTERN

Plate, 6" d	5.00

DAMASK PATTERN

Cream and Sugar	15.00
Cup and Saucer	5.00
Gravy Boat, Cov	10.00
Plate	
7" d	3.00
10" d	4.00

DESERT SUN PATTERN

Cup and Saucer	10.00
Fruit Dish	6.00
Plate	
6" d	4.00
7" d	5.00
10" d	8.00

DRIFTWOOD PATTERN

Plate, 6½" d	4.00

EBB TIDE PATTERN
Casserole, Cov 20.00
Plate, 7" d 7.00

FLIGHT PATTERN
Platter, 13" d 45.00
Vegetable Bowl, divided 40.00

FONDOSA PATTERN
Custard Cup, pastel blue 8.00
Relish Tray, pink 17.00
Shakers, yellow, pr 10.00

FRUITS PATTERN
Plate, 7½" d 5.00

GOLDEN VIKING PATTERN
Cup and Saucer 9.00
Plate
    6½" d 5.00
    10½" d 8.00

HAMM'S BEER DESIGNS
Mug, Hamm's Krug Klub, dark brown
    glaze 55.00
Pitcher, deer, trees, and lake 275.00
Salad Bowl, large, deer, trees, and
    lake 270.00

HEARTHSIDE PATTERN
Plate, 6½" d 6.00

HEARTHSTONE ORANGE PATTERN
Cereal Bowl 5.00
Cream and Sugar 11.00
Cup and Saucer 9.00
Dinner Plate 7.00
Salad Plate 4.00
Salt and Pepper 6.00

IRIS PATTERN
Cup and Saucer 8.00
Plate
    6½" d 4.00
    7½" d 5.00
    10½" d 8.00

KASHMIR PATTERN
Cereal Bowl 5.00
Plate
    6" d 4.00
    7" d 5.00
    10" d 7.00

LEXINGTON ROSE PATTERN
Casserole, Cov 17.00
Cup and Saucer 8.00
Plate, 6½" d 4.00

LOTUS PATTERN
Chop Plate 10.00
Creamer, metallic brown 5.00
Cream Soup, metallic brown 4.00
Cup and Saucer 8.00
Nappy 10.00
Plate
    6½" d 4.00
    10½" d 8.00
Relish Dish 12.00
Sugar Bowl, Cov, metallic brown 7.00
Water Pitcher, metallic brown 15.00

LUTE SONG PATTERN
Butter Dish, Cov 35.00
Cup and Saucer 7.00
Dinner Plate 5.00
Plate, 7" d 5.00
Vegetable Bowl, divided 7.00

MAGNOLIA PATTERN
Chop Plate 8.00
Creamer, chartreuse 2.00
Cream Soup, Cov 5.00
Cup and Saucer 3.00
Hostess Set, 10½", 7½" d, w/alu-
    minum rod 9.00
Nappy 6.00
Plate, chartreuse
    6½" d 2.00
    7½" d 3.00
    10½" d 6.00
Sugar Bowl, Cov 6.00
Tidbit set, 2 tiers, 7½" d, 10½" d 9.00

MERRILEAF PATTERN
Bread Tray 28.00
Cup and Saucer 10.00
Gravy Boat, Cov 20.00
Salt and Pepper 12.00
Vegetable Bowl, divided 15.00

MONMARTE PATTERN
Vegetable Bowl, divided 10.00

MORNING GLORY PATTERN
Plate, 6½" d, pink 4.00

NORMANDY PATTERN
Creamer and Cov Sugar Bowl 18.00
Gravy Boat, w/attached tray 12.00
Plate
    6" d 5.00
    7" d 5.00
    10" d 7.00
Salt and Pepper 7.00
Teapot 30.00

OOMPH PATTERN
Creamer 10.00
Cup and Saucer 8.00
Shakers, pr 8.00
Sugar Bowl, Cov 10.00

ORLEANS PATTERN
Cream and Sugar 22.00
Dinner Plate 8.00
Shakers, pr 10.00
Soup Bowl, Cov 14.00
Teapot 38.00

PEPE PATTERN
Cup and Saucer 7.00
Gravy Boat, Cov 13.00
Platter, 13" d 13.00
Vegetable Bowl 9.00

PINK SPICE PATTERN
Plate
    6½" d 4.00
    7½" d 6.00
    10½" d 9.00

PLUM BLOSSOM PATTERN

Creamer, brown metallic 10.00

POMPEII PATTERN

Butter Dish, Cov 10.00
Cereal Bowl 6.00
Cup and Saucer 9.00
Plate, 6" d 4.00

PROVINCIAL WARE

Bean Pot, #22 .... 10.00
Casserole, Cov, 3 qt 10.00

RANDOM HARVEST PATTERN

Plate
  6½" d.. 6.00
  8½" d.. 7.00
Sugar Bowl, Cov 10.00
Teapot 20.00

REED PATTERN

Creamer, orange 8.00
Mixing Bowl
  5" d
    Orange 9.00
    Russet 11.00
  6" d, turquoise 9.00

RED WING ROSE PATTERN

Dinner Plate 5.00
Sugar Bowl, Cov 9.00

ROUNDUP PATTERN

Bowl, 12" d 125.00
Casserole
  Large 195.00
  Small 130.00
Chafing Dish..................................... 195.00
Creamer.. 30.00
Cup and Saucer 40.00
Mustard Jar 35.00
Salad Bowl, 9½" d 80.00
Salad Plate 18.00
Soup Bowl 35.00
Sugar Bowl, Cov 65.00

SAFFRON WARE

Bean Pot, Cov 50.00
Bowl
  7" d, blue and rust sponging, mkd... 98.00
  8" d, "Wolf & Jagow, Lomira, Wi."
    advertising.................................. 175.00
  9½" d, fluted paneled sides, rust
    and blue sponging on yel-
    lowware, #6 .... 150.00
Casserole, Cov, 8¾" d, brown and
  white rings 135.00

SMART SET PATTERN

Bowl, 9" d 32.00
Butter Warmer, Cov 22.00
Casserole, Cov, w/wire stand, 2 qt 95.00
Coffee Cup and Saucer 10.00
Plate
  6½" d.. 4.00
  7½" d.. 5.00
Platter, 20" l..................................... 25.00
Salt and Pepper................................. 20.00
Teapot 275.00

STONEWARE

Bean Pot, 2 small handles, dark brown
  top, gray base................................. 100.00
Beater Jar,½ gallon, "Stanhope, Ia."
  advertising 88.00
Bowl
  5" d, Greek key pattern 60.00
  6" d, paneled, red and blue spong-
    ing... 70.00
  7" d
    Blue, rust, and cream sponging.... 68.00
    Grayline 120.00
  8" d, grayline w/advertising............. 95.00
Buttermilk Feeder 75.00
Casserole, Cov, 8¼" d, sponge band .. 150.00
Chicken Drinking Fount, "Klondike,
  Des Moines, Ia" on front, 1 qt, Red
  Wing Union mark 95.00
Chicken Feeder, Ko-Rec style 125.00
Crock
  9½" h, black elephant-ear leaves
    and "2" on front 50.00
  10" h
    Red wing, "2" and blue oval "Red
      Wing Union Stoneware Co.,
      Red Wing, Mn." on front,
      c1906 .... 53.00
    Two black birch leaves and "2"
      on front, c1900 .... 50.00
  11" h, blue target and "3" on front .. 125.00
  15¼" h, dbl wire handles, red wing,
    "8," and blue "Red Wing Union
    Stoneware Co.," on front 98.00
  22½" h, cobalt quill design of 2
    leaves and "20"(A)..................... 165.00
  25¼" h, red wing, "25" and blue
    oval "Red Wing Union
    Stoneware, Red Wing Mn." on
    front 148.00
Jug
  9¾" h, raised "Microbe Killer, Wm.
    Radams" on shoulder, 1 gallon.... 350.00
  16½" h, red wing and "3" on front.. 58.00
  18" h, red wing, "4," and blue oval
    "Red Wing Union Stoneware Co.,
    Red Wing, Mn." on front 60.00
  18½" h, red wing, "5," and blue
    oval "Red Wing Union
    Stoneware, Red Wing, Mn." on
    front 70.00
  Miniature
    "Jones Bros. Blue Grass Belle
      Vinegar, Louisville, Ky".......... 295.00
Milk Pitcher, 8" h, light gray w/dark
  blue edging, crimped lip, logo on
  front 235.00
Mixing Bowl, 7" d, "Cap," blue spong-
  ing, white ground............................ 100.00
Pitcher, 9" h, brown glazed grape de-
  sign, rickrack border, waffle ground
  "RED WING NORTH STAR STONEWARE"
  mark 85.00

Preserving Jar
"Mason Fruit Jar,"
    1 qt, Red Wing Union, c1899 ...... **95.00**
    2 qt, mkd **200.00**
Safety Valve, ½ gallon **90.00**
Refrigerator Jar, 4¾" h **175.00**
Water Cooler, 5 gallon, w/bubbler and
    lid **450.00**
Whiskey Jug, 17¾" h, stenciled "RED
    WING/UNION STONEWARE CO. RED WING
    MINN, 5," large wing, cream Bristol
    glaze, c1890(A) **66.00**

TAMPICO PATTERN
Bowl, 5¼" d **6.00**
Creamer **7.00**
Cup and Saucer **14.00**
Fruit Bowl **7.00**
Plate
    8" d **8.00**
    11½" d **8.00**
Relish Tray, 13" l, divided **22.00**
Sugar Bowl **7.00**
Water Pitcher **25.00**

TIP TOE PATTERN
Platter, 13" l **12.00**

TOWN AND COUNTRY PATTERN
Cereal Bowl, light green **5.00**
Creamer
    Forest green **6.00**
    White **8.00**
Cup and Saucer, rust **6.00**
Plate
    6½" d
        Metallic brown **3.00**
        Rust **3.00**
    8" d, rust **3.00**
    10½" d, rust **5.00**
Relish Tray, 7" l, peach **4.00**

TURTLE DOVE PATTERN
Plate
    7" d **4.00**
    10" d **7.00**

TWO STEP PATTERN
Platter, 13" l, beige **13.00**

VILLAGE GREEN PATTERN
Bean Pot **25.00**
Beverage Pitcher **15.00**
Bread and Butter Plate **2.00**
Butter Dish **18.00**
Casserole, Cov **12.00**
Cream and Sugar **20.00**
Mug **9.00**
Plate, 7½" d **3.00**
Platter, 13" d **10.00**

MISCELLANEOUS
Figure
    11" h, multicolored standing cow-
    boy or cowgirl, #B1415 and
    B1414, pr **250.00**
Sand Jar, 15½" h, green brushed deer . **1500.00**
Water Pitcher, 7½" h, molded body

Jug, red wing, blue marks, 4
gallon, $100.00

swirls, yellow glaze, imp "RED WING
U.S.A. #735" mark **35.00**

PEEK·A·BOO
Van Tellingen
©

REGAL CHINA CORPORATION
Antioch, Illinois
1938–Present

History: Regal China Corporation of Antioch,
Illinois, was founded in 1938 and bought by
Royal China and Novelty Company, a distributing and sales organization, in the 1940s as the
manufacturer for its contract and premium business.

Snuggle Hugs, in shapes such as bunnies,
bears, pigs, Dutch Boys and Girls, were designed
by Ruth Van Tellingen Bendel in 1948. She also
designed the pajama-clad Peek-a-Boo bears in
large and small shaker sets and cookie jars. Regal
was responsible for much of the decorating done
on Hull Pottery's Red Riding Hood collection.

At the present time, Regal produces on a contract basis only and has not sold to the retail trade
since 1968. Products made for other companies
included a cookie jar for Quaker Oats in 1976, a
milk pitcher for Ovaltine, a ship decanter and
coffee mug for Old Spice in 1983, lamp bases for
Lamplight Farms, pieces for Marshall Burns, and
vases for Soovia Janis in 1985. Regal is currently
a wholly owned subsidiary of Jim Beam Distil-
leries and makes the Jim Beam bottles.

Regal marks include the name of the product.

OLD MACDONALD PATTERN
Butter Dish, cow **195.00**

Canister

Cereal	225.00
Flour	225.00
Peanuts	350.00
Potato Chips	275.00
Sugar	195.00
Tea	50.00

Creamer, rooster	30.00
Grease Jar, pig	145.00
Milk Pitcher, cow's head	165.00

Salt and Pepper

Boy and girl	125.00
Churn	45.00
Feed Sack	175.00
Goat w/red sack	110.00
Spice Containers, allspice, cloves, ginger, nutmeg, and pepper	425.00
Teapot, duck	275.00

VAN TELLINGEN DESIGNS

Salt and Pepper

Black boy and dog

Gray	48.00
Tan	50.00
Brown bears	12.00
Ducks	24.00

Canister, 7¹/₂" h, "Old MacDonald Farm," red base, $150.00

Salt and Pepper, 3³/₄" h, yellow, Van Tellingen, $16.00

Dutch boy and girl	25.00
Mary and yellow lamb	30.00

Pink

Bears	25.00
Rabbits	25.00
Sailor and mermaid	65.00
Yellow rabbits	25.00

R.R.P. Co.
ROSEVILLE OHIO
1500—
U.S.A.

ROBINSON-RANSBOTTOM POTTERY
Roseville, Ohio
1901–Present

History: Frank Ransbottom purchased the Oval Ware and Brick Company in Roseville, Ohio, with his three brothers. It was called the Ransbottom Brothers Pottery for eight years and produced stoneware jars.

By 1920 it merged with Robinson Clay Products. Since stoneware jars were declining in popularity, production was shifted to garden wares, such as planters, urns, and bird baths—still made today along with crocks, water coolers, milk churns, and water pitchers.

Old Colony was made from the mid 1930s until 1940, while Rustic Ware was made from the mid 1930s until the 1960s. Both functional and decorative pieces, hand decorated under the glaze in various color combinations, were sold under the Crown Pottery brand.

Other wares were jardinieres, flowerpots, figurines, vases, teapots, plates, casseroles, baby-shoe planters, and commemorative cups and mugs. About twenty-five different cookie jars were made, with the figural ones being the most desirable. Both stoneware and white-bodied character cookie jars were available into the 1960s, but the whiteware jars were discontinued due to high-production costs.

Much of the pottery was marked. Most examples include "R.R.P.Co., Roseville, O." or some variation of that mark. Some also had the five-point crown symbol in several variations. Paper labels also were used.

Reference: "R.R.P.Co.—Roseville's Other Pottery Survives," *Antique Weekly*, July 20, 1992.

Museum: The Pot Shop, Roseville, OH.

Ashtray, 9" sq, aqua ground, tan splashed border, imp mark **9.00**

Beater Jar, 6½" h, brown sponging on yellow ground, stamped mark **34.00**

Bowl
7" d, molded overlapping waves w/dimples and smooth surfaces, ivory surface **5.00**
9" d, blue and maroon drip glaze **24.00**

Bowl, Cov, 9" d, vert fluted base, raised band of kitchen utensils against brick wall, fluted cov, teal blue glaze **38.00**

Flowerpot, 5" h, raised leaf surface, green and shaded tan ground **10.00**

Jardiniere, 9" h, multicolored blended glaze **24.00**

Jardiniere and Pedestal, 31" h, raised yellow flower heads w/brown centers, wraparound vines, pink ground **100.00**

Pitcher
4¼" h, yellow body w/imp brown waffle panels, horiz ringed base .. **5.00**
5½" h, hex w/raised diamond design, salmon glaze, imp mark **15.00**
6" h
Gray ground, 2 wide blue bands on base, stamped mark **27.00**
Raised yellow waffle pattern on sides, pale yellow ground, mkd **20.00**
Red petaled flowers w/blue centers, green leaves and stems, ivory ground **15.00**
7½" h, gloss dark brown body, sand and cream drip on top and handle, imp mark **16.00**
8½" h, monk pattern **65.00**

Planter, 3½" h, 6½" d, bowl shape, blue-green mottled glaze **20.00**

Vase
5⅞" h, cornucopia shape, matte white glaze **10.00**
8" h
Leaves in relief, white glaze **22.00**

Planter, 4" h, 5½" l, mottled brown dog, mottled green base, imp "R.R.P. Co. Roseville, Ohio No. 1302-41 USA" mark, $15.00

Oval base, tapered body to flared top, flattened oval shape, vert lines in center, yellow glaze, imp "R.R.P. Co." mark **5.00**

1900-1908

SEVRES CHINA COMPANY
East Liverpool, Ohio
1900–1908

History: In 1900 a group of men purchased the former Sebring Pottery and it became the Sevres China Company. It made semi-porcelain dinnerware, hotel ware, and toilet and tea sets. The company did not do well, and several of the original owners dropped out.

J.R. Warner joined the group in 1908 and changed the name of the company to Warner-Keffer China Company, but the pottery closed in 1911. Various marks included a fleur-de-lis with names such as Geneva, Berlin, Melton, and Sevres underneath. Hotel china was marked as such.

Bowl
10¾" d, single tab handle, 6 pink roses on border, raised beaded rim, mkd **6.00**
12" d, center w/green and red leaves and flowers, sawtooth rim w/raised design **7.00**

Charger, 11⅞" d, Royal Meissen Ware, scattered red and orange garden flowers, inner gold band, green border, gold rim **20.00**

Pitcher, 7" h, figural seated owl, matte med brown glaze **125.00**

Plate
6¾" d, center w/3 cherries hanging from branch, shaped rim w/alternating yellow-green and green shading...................................... **9.00**
8" d, 1909 calendar in center, pink roses on border........................... **15.00**
9" d, standing Dutch boy in center, scattered purple flowers on border.. **25.00**
9⅜" d, decal of cherries hanging from branch, raised design on rim w/lime green and yellow shading **18.00**
9¾" d, decal of 2 Dutch children in center, 4 bunches of pink dogwood blossoms on border **68.00**

Pitcher, 8³/₄" h, multicolored decal, blue-green shading, gold trim, mkd, $75.00

10" d, bunches of red rasberries, raised basket-weave border, gold speckled rim	10.00
10¹/₄" d, 3 bunches of pink and white roses w/green leaves, gold overlay border w/raised molding .	9.00
10³/₄" d, decal of deer in forest in center, border w/gold overlay, shaped rim	5.00
Sugar Bowl, 5³/₄" h, wishbone handles, small pink roses w/green sprays, gold trim	24.00

SHAWNEE POTTERY
Zanesville, Ohio
1937–1961

History: Addis E. Hull, Jr., came from the Hull Pottery Company of Crooksville, Ohio, and with Robert C. Shilling and some others started the Shawnee Pottery Company in 1937. Its name was taken from an Indian tribe that inhabited the area and the company trademark was the Shawnee Indian with an arrowhead.

Shawnee manufactured earthenware products that were inexpensive, but were of high quality. The firm acquired the American Encaustic Tile Company plant in Zanesville. Both kitchen and utilitarian wares were made along with decorative art pottery pieces, such as ashtrays, bookends, trays, paperweights, wall pockets, jardinieres, and lamp bases.

Overglaze and underglaze decorations were done in varying textures and both in bright and pastel colors. By utilizing new methods of drying the pottery, Shawnee's unique glazing method required only one firing. This greatly reduced costs while producing a good product.

From 1937–1942 Shawnee supplied inexpensive decorated pottery for stores such as Kresge, Kress, Woolworth, and Sears, Roebuck and Company. Mostly flowerpots, dishes, vases, and figurines were made for these chains. Dinnerware and kitchenware, called the Valencia line, was also made for Sears and a free set was given with any refrigerator purchase.

Rudy Ganz was hired by Shawnee in 1938, and he designed some of the most popular cookie jars, such as Jack and Jill, Sailor Boy, Smiley, and Puss'n Boots.

Decorative pottery was made for Rum Rill from that company's own designs and premiums were made for such companies as Procter & Gamble. During the war, production of consumer goods slowed down since the factory was mainly used for war contracts.

In 1945 Robert Heckman joined Shawnee as a designer. His green and yellow King Corn line was a huge success. He also introduced a Pennsylvania Dutch line of small figurines, salt and pepper sets, planters, and vases.

After Hull left Shawnee in 1950, Albert P. Braid became president. There were financial losses during the early 1950s when the market was flooded with novelty pottery. When John Bonistall took over in 1954, he changed the emphasis of the company from kitchenware to decorative items. He introduced new lines and sales increased. To cut costs, he eliminated hand decorating and substituted the spray-gun method of decoration. Kenwood Ceramics, a new division Bonistall introduced, made kitchenwares. The glaze on King Corn was changed to a darker green and a lighter yellow and the line, renamed Queen Corn, was sold in prepackaged sets. Touche was one of the most successful art lines; others included Liana, Chantilly, Petit Point, Cameo, Fairywood, Fernwood, and Elegance. Shawnee became one of the largest and most successful potteries in the country under Bonistall's management. When it closed in 1961, Bonistall purchased the molds and started Terrace Ceramics in Marietta, Ohio.

Many Shawnee pieces were marked with a number only, but some were marked with a number and "U.S.A." Different ranges of numbers were used on different lines and paper labels also were used.

References: Dolores Simon, *Shawnee Pottery*, Collector Books, 1977; Jim and Bev Mangus, *Shawnee Pottery*, Collector Books, 1994; Mark E. Supnick, *Collecting Shawnee Pottery*, L-W Books, 1989; Duane and Janice Vanderbilt,

The Collector's Guide to Shawnee Pottery, Collector Books, 1992.

Museum: Har-Ber Village, near Grove, OK.

Collectors' Club: Shawnee Pottery Collectors, Dept. NR, P.O. Box 713, New Smyrna Beach, FL 32170-0713, Pam Curran, Newsletter Editor, *Exclusively Shawnee,* $25 per year, monthly.

KING CORN

Butter Dish, Cov	36.00
Casserole, 1½ qt.	50.00
Cereal Bowl	45.00
Coffee Pitcher	75.00
Creamer	25.00
Cup and Saucer	40.00
Fruit Bowl	40.00
Mixing Bowl	
5" d	6.00
6" d	9.00
6¾" d, #94	32.00
9" d, #95	35.00
Mug	30.00
Plate	
#68	100.00
#92	35.00
#93	39.00

Pitcher, 4¾" h, King Corn, green and yellow, $70.00

Salt and Pepper, 5½" h, King Corn, green and yellow, $30.00

Platter, 12" l	45.00
Relish Dish	28.00
Sugar Bowl, Cov	28.00
Teapot	
#65	135.00
#75	55.00
Vegetable Bowl, 9" d	60.00

LOBSTER DESIGN

Casserole	
2 qt	30.00
Med, #902	18.00
Shakers, pr	24.00
Sugar Bowl	26.00

QUEEN CORN

Butter Dish, #72	60.00
Mug	35.00
Pitcher	25.00
Plate, #68	30.00
Sugar Bowl	35.00
Teapot	58.00

VALENCIA PATTERN

Teapot, 8 cup	69.00

WHITE CORN

Creamer and Sugar Bowl	65.00
Pitcher	50.00
Salt and Pepper	
Large	25.00
Small	20.00
Sugar Shaker	25.00

MISCELLANEOUS

Bud Vase	
8" h, handled, blue, "USA #1178" mark	8.00
Leaf shape, blue and yellow, #1125	6.00
Canister, Fernware, blue	55.00
Casserole, Sundial pattern, pink top, black base, med size, #902	45.00
Creamer	
Elephant, pink ears	25.00
Pig	
Blue scarf, yellow ground	60.00
Gold trim	35.00
Peach flower	60.00
Puss'n Boots	
Green and yellow	75.00
Pink ribbon	45.00
Figure, Pekingese, small	50.00
Lamp Base	
Champ the dog, blue, brown, and white	15.00
Oriental couple	55.00
Pie bird	
Bennie the Baker	125.00
Pink bird	30.00
Pitcher	
Bo Peep	
Blue bonnet	85.00
Peach ruffles	75.00
Small size, #47	89.00
Chanticleer	55.00

Charlie	65.00
Flower and fern, blue-green	15.00
Fruit, yellow ground, "Shawnee #80" mark	68.00
Gold trim	150.00
Smiley pig	
Clover	195.00
Peach flower	95.00
Gold trim	525.00
Red flower	150.00
Planter	
4" h, 4" w	
Cockatiel, multicolored w/gold trim, #523	8.00
Figural butterfly, #524	13.00
5½" h, watering can w/emb flowers, dark rose	13.00
6" h, girl w/basket of flowers, #616	18.00
Baby shoe, blue	8.00
Bowl type w/ivy	15.00
Boy at stump, multicolored, "USA #533" mark	10.00
Boy w/chicken, yellow, brown, and white, #645	28.00
Bridge, brown and yellow, "SHAWNEE #756" mark	20.00
Canopy bed, white and blue, #734	75.00
Cat w/saxophone, yellow and brown, #729	45.00
Cherub, multicolored, "USA #536" mark	8.00
Cov wagon, 6" h, 9½" l, green	20.00
Donkey w/cart, blue and brown, "USA #538" mark	8.00
Elephant, #759	12.00
Elf on shoe, white w/gold trim, #765	10.00
Figural fawn	
Turquoise and black	12.00
White w/green base, #624	10.00
Gazelle, blue and tan, #613	16.00
Globe, blue-green and brown	20.00
High-heeled shoe, turquoise	11.00
Hound and pekingese, green and brown, #611	8.00
Hound w/jug, brown and green, #610	12.00
Lamp and stump, chartreuse and black, #737	18.00
Oriental	
W/book, multicolored, "USA #574" mark	8.00
W/cart, multicolored, #539	8.00
Piano, green, #528	24.00
Pup on shoe, brown	9.00
Seated donkey w/basket, red and gray, #671	18.00
Standing doe and fawn, yellow w/red base, #669	16.00
Truck cab, dark red, #680	15.00
Two orientals w/basket, green, #537	6.00
Windmill, green and white w/gold trim, "SHAWNEE #715" mark	20.00

Wishing well w/2 Dutch children, green, #710	25.00
Woman in chair w/flowers, multicolored, "USA #616" mark	15.00
Salt Box, Fernware, green	38.00
Salt and Pepper	
Large	
Daisy	35.00
Chanticleer	30.00
Fernware, green	28.00
Fruit, #8	22.00
Mugsey, blue trim	80.00
Swiss children, w/gold	95.00
Sunflowers	39.00
Winnie and Smiley	
Clover bud	90.00
Green scarf	65.00
Small	
Chanticleer	30.00
Cottages	250.00
Ducks	35.00
Farmer Pigs	30.00
Flowerpots, gold trim	20.00
Milk cans	12.00
Mugsey	45.00
Owls	15.00
w/gold trim	50.00
Puss 'N Boots	32.00
Smiley, peach bibs	40.00
Wheelbarrows	18.00
Sugar Bowl Cookie Cottage, #8	16.00
Teapot	
Elephant, yellow	115.00
Emb flower, green	25.00
Flower, blue	36.00
Granny Ann	
Coral apron	80.00
Gold trim	175.00
Green apron	115.00
Pennsylvania Dutch	125.00
Snowflake, blue	
Med	45.00
Small	35.00
Tom Tom the Piper's Son, blue tie	75.00
Vase	
7" h, hand, cream	17.00

Salt and Pepper, 5½" h, Dutch boy and girl, blue trim, cream ground, $72.00

*Vase, 11¼" h, peach textured surface,
white ground, cream int, imp "Shawnee
USA" mark, $48.00*

7½" h, emb wheat design, #1258 ...	10.00
9" h, cream w/pink flower and green leaves, #1289	15.00
Bulbous shape w/flowers, blue, "SHAWNEE #827" mark	20.00
Dove, yellow, #829	18.00
Leaf, blue-green, #823	24.00
Philodendron leaves, green, "SHAWNEE #805" mark	15.00
Pineapple, white, "SHAWNEE #839" mark..	15.00
Swan, maroon w/gold trim, #806	12.00
Wall Pocket	
Birds and birdhouse, blue and purple, #830....................................	15.00
Grandfather clock, blue and white, #1261...	28.00
Mantel clock, #530	18.00
Sunflower.......................................	6.00

c1947

SPAULDING CHINA COMPANY
Sebring, Ohio
1942–1957

History: The Spaulding China Company began production in 1942 in Sebring, Ohio, under the direction of Morris Feinberg as president. Its motto, "gift shop merchandise at chain store prices," emphasized its concern for design and quality. Eighty-five percent of the production was Royal Copley merchandise which was sold

in chain stores. Woolworth was the biggest customer.

Colors were applied with an air brush on mass-produced Royal Copley pieces, such as figurines of all kinds, planters, vases, and wall planters. The first items in the line were bud vases and pitchers with decals of pink and blue flowers on a cream ground. More birds were made than any other single shape since they were the biggest sellers. Other very successful pieces were piggy banks, roosters, large ducks, and oriental boy and girl wall pockets. Tony Priolo was the primary artist for the Spaulding firm.

Pieces made for the Royal Windsor and Spaulding lines were very similar in design to the Royal Copley examples. Royal Windsor and Spaulding were sold to jobbers and distributors who then sold the articles to department stores, florists, and gift shops. Planters made for the florist trade included the Books of Remembrance pieces. Lamp bases were made under the Spaulding label.

During the mid 1950s there was strong competition from the inexpensive Japanese imports that were flooding the U.S. market. With ever-increasing labor costs driving the prices for U.S. goods higher, Feinberg retired in 1957 and operations at the Sebring plant ceased. Orders continued to be filled for two years by the China Craft Company.

Many Spaulding items were marked with either a green or gold stamp, and some were marked with raised letters. Most only had paper labels.

Reference: Leslie C. and Marjorie A. Wolfe, *Royal Copley and More about Royal Copley,* Collector Books, 1992.

Collectors' Newsletter: Barbara Burke, 4213 Sandhurst Drive, Orlando, FL 32817, *The Copley Connection,* $10 per year, bimonthly.

ROYAL COPLEY LINE

Ashtray, 5" d, bird perched on rim......	20.00
Bank	
4½" h, pig, pink	40.00
6" h, pig, pink	35.00
6¼" h, bow tie pig, blue body.........	20.00
7½" h	
Pig, "For My Mink" on chest........	45.00
Rooster, "Chicken Feed" on base, multicolored	38.00
Figure	
5" h	
Kingfisher, extended wings, red ...	15.00
Skylark	
Blue and white........................	10.00
Blue and yellow	10.00
Sparrow, blue	18.00
5½" h, hen, black and white, green base...	45.00
6¼" h, seated cocker spaniel	15.00

7¼" h
Cockatoo, chartreuse 27.00
Hen, black and white 60.00
7½" h, oriental boy or girl, red, pr... 30.00
8" h
Cat, black 38.00
Dancing girl
Dark blue bodice, red skirt....... 38.00
Light blue bodice, yellow skirt,
red hat................................ 48.00
Seated cocker spaniel 18.00
Titmouse, multicolored............... 15.00
Pitcher, 8" h
Blown-out fruit on sides, med blue
ground.. 38.00
Floral Beauty, blown-out blue flow-
ers, red body 25.00
Planter
4" h, Wilder leaf design, white and
black, gold trim 12.00
4½" h
Brown bear cub on brown and
green log................................. 18.50
Harmony, red and tan 6.00
5¼" h, cat and tub 15.00
5¾" h
Cream and brown bear sitting on
green log................................. 12.50
Dog pulling "Flyer" wagon, mul-
ticolored 30.00
6" h
Elf and tree stump, red hat, green
clothes, gold trim 25.00
Figural fish, yellow and black 40.00
Gray cat clinging to side of tree ... 19.00
Peter Rabbit, multicolored 25.00
6¼" h, figural angel, blue, gray, and
yellow 15.00
6½" h, reclining poodle, pink 40.00
7" h
Dog w/suitcase, brown shades..... 28.00
Wheelbarrow girl, light green
dress, red hat, dark green
wheelbarrow........................... 17.00

Planter, 6¼" h, green jacket, brown
hair, Royal Copley, $12.00

Planter, 7½" h, multicolored, Royal
Copley, $32.00

Planter, 7¾" h, green jacket, light green
pants, yellow hat, yellow basket, Royal
Copley, $10.00

7½" h
Cat w/cello, brown shades and
white 40.00
Deer and fawn, brown glaze 32.00
Oriental child w/bamboo planter,
black, white, and tan 30.00
7¾" h
Dog and mailbox, tan and brown
shades...................................... 15.00
Rooster w/high tail, black, red,
yellow, and green 22.00
8" h
Angel, blue................................. 15.00
Bear w/lollipop, white and black . 22.00
Bird on birdhouse, multicolored .. 45.00
Blackamoor
Prince 28.00
Princess 35.00
Deer on stump, brown shades 16.00
Kitten and birdhouse, multicol-
ored 35.00
Pirate, red scarf........................... 32.00
Rooster and wheelbarrow, multi-
colored 40.00
Teddy bear, brown 18.00
White bear cub climbing tan and
green tree stump 22.50

8¼" h, brown cat w/ball of yellow yarn	22.50
9" h, gazelle's head, gold outlined	9.00

Smoker's Set, cigarette holder, 3" h, 2 ashtrays, 2" h, figural seated mallards 45.00

Vase
6" h, flared shape, decal of Lord's Prayer 35.00
6¼" h, brown figural horse's head, black mane 15.00
6½" h
Kitten on stump 15.00
Stylized ram's head, brown shading 25.00
7" h, pink dogwood, blue-green ground.. 20.00
7½" h, philodendron, cream w/green leaves, brown base 8.00
8¼" h, Dogwood, brown and white 30.00
8½" h, figural mare's and colt's heads 15.00

Wall Pocket
5¾" h, apples and leaves design 20.00
7" d, figural hat, rose ground 25.00

ROYAL WINDSOR LINE
Figure
5¾" h, mallard w/bent head............ 4.50
6¾", 8½" h, Gadwell hen and drake, "A.D. Priolo" mark, pr....... 48.00
Planter, 7" h, white standing poodle, black planter 22.00

MISCELLANEOUS
Creamer
4¼" h, figural pig, pink 18.00
4½" h, figural chick, yellow and red... 10.00
Figure
4" h, pheasants, natural colors, pr ... 35.00

Vase, 8½" h, green leaves, tan crackle ground, black base, Royal Copley, $9.00

7" h, standing pheasant, orange-red glaze	18.00
7⅜" h, parakeets, dbl, blue	35.00

TULIP

STANGL POTTERY/FULPER POTTERY
Flemington and Trenton, New Jersey
1929–1978

See also Hill/Fulper in the Art Pottery section.

History: In 1926 Fulper purchased the Anchor\Pottery in Trenton, New Jersey, where dinnerwares were made. The Flemington Pottery burned in 1929 and manufacturing moved temporarily to Trenton while Flemington was rebuilt at a different site. Martin Stangl acquired Fulper in 1929.

Both art pottery and dinnerwares were made, but by the late 1930s the concentration was on dinnerware, low cost artware, and utilitarian pieces. Colonial and Americana were the most popular shapes. In 1942 the white body was replaced with red and slip was hand carved to reveal the colored clay underneath. Artists hand painted with bright colors under the glaze and between the carved lines.

During World War II Fulper Pottery curtailed its regular lines due to a shortage of raw materials. Inspired by Audubon prints of American birds, Stangl decided to produce a line of pottery birds with fine clay bodies. Auguste Jacob designed and created the models for the molds and various decorators painted the birds in high-gloss glazes. Twelve different porcelain birds, more elaborate than the pottery ones, were made with intricate decorations, lifelike colors, finely molded details, and more leaves and flowers. By 1978 when production of these figures was discontinued, over one hundred varieties had been produced.

Other company lines included Kiddieware, made from c1942 until the 1970s, which featured hand-painted, hand-carved subjects such as nursery rhymes and wild-west themes. Dinnerwares included Indian Summer, Maize-Ware, and more than fifty other patterns introduced between 1942 and 1968. In the late 1950s a popular art line called Antique Gold was made by hand brushing 22-karat gold over matte green glaze. Granada Gold was gold over turquoise, Black gold was brushed over black, and Platinum was a silver-brushed finish.

Martin Stangl died in 1972 and Frank Wheaton, Jr., bought the pottery. When he sold out to Pfaltzgraff Pottery Company in 1978, production was stopped and the Flemington location was used as an outlet shop for Pfaltzgraff products.

Each of the bird figures was signed on the bottom with the decorator's initials, marked with a model number, "Stangl Pottery," and an "F" under the glaze if decorated at Flemington. Paper tags also were used to identify the species and the labels included both the Fulper and Stangl names until about 1955 when the company name was changed to Stangl. Many other Stangl items, with the exception of the dinnerwares, had an impressed mark in the mold with "Stangl" or "Stangl USA" and a shape number.

References: Harvey Duke, *Stangl Pottery,* Wallace-Homestead, 1993; Joan Dworkin and Martha Horman, *A Guide to Stangl Pottery Birds,* Willow Pond Books, Inc. 1977; Norma Rehl, *The Collectors Handbook of Stangl Pottery,* Democrat Press, 1982.

Collectors' Club: Stangl Bird Collectors Association, Jim Davidson, P.O. Box 419, Ringoes, NJ 08551, $25 per year, quarterly newsletter.

AMBER GLO PATTERN

Bowl, 8" d	6.00
Coffeepot	35.00
Coffee Server	45.00
Dinner Plate	12.00
Pickle Dish	9.00
Teapot	30.00

APPLE DELIGHT PATTERN

Cup and Saucer	5.00
Luncheon Plate	8.00
Mug	14.00

BACHELOR BUTTON PATTERN

Lug Soup Bowl, 5½" d	6.00

BITTERSWEET PATTERN

Bowl

5½" d	6.00
6¼" d	7.00
Bread and Butter Plate	6.00
Cream and Sugar	15.00
Cup and Saucer	10.00
Plate, 10" d	8.00
Salad Plate	8.00
Shakers, pr	4.00
Sugar Bowl	12.00

BLUEBELL PATTERN

Creamer	10.00
Cup and Saucer	8.00
Dinner Plate	10.00
Teapot	25.00

BLUEBERRY PATTERN

Bread and Butter Plate	3.00
Cereal Bowl	12.00
Chop Plate, 12½" d	12.00
Cream and Sugar	12.00

Cup and Saucer	12.00
Dinner Plate	10.00
Gravy Boat	12.00
Salad Plate	5.00

BLUE DAISY PATTERN

Plate, 8" d	6.50

CARIBBEAN PATTERN

Bowl, 9" d	34.00

COLONIAL PATTERN

Candleholder, yellow, pr	25.00
Syrup Pitcher, Cov, aqua	40.00

COLONIAL ROSE PATTERN

Cup and Saucer	8.00

Plate

6" d	5.00
10" d	16.00

CORNUCOPIA

7¼" h, gold, #5065	20.00
Black Gold, #5065	18.00

COUNTRY GARDENS PATTERN

Cereal Bowl	5.00
Cup and Saucer	12.00
Gravy Boat	15.00

Plate

5" d	7.00
9" d	5.00
Server, 3 tiers	38.00
Vegetable Bowl, 8" d	25.00

COUNTRY LIFE PATTERN

Creamer	15.00
Plate, 6" d	9.00

DAISY PATTERN

Plate, 8" d	4.00

FESTIVAL PATTERN

Chop Plate	22.00

FIGURAL BIRD

2½" h, Nuthatch, #3593	39.00

3" h

Kentucky Warbler, #3598	55.00
Rufous Hummingbird, #3585	80.00

3¼" h

Indigo Bunting, #3589	90.00
Orioles, #3402	55.00

3½" h

Allen Hummingbird, #3634	115.00
Blackpoll Warbler, #3810	160.00
Wilson Warbler, #3597	55.00
Wren, #3401	65.00
4⅛" h, Golden-crowned Kinglet, #3848	110.00
4¼" h, Cerulean Warbler, #3456	75.00

4½" h

Blue-Headed Vireo, #3448	75.00
Carolina Wren, #3590	95.00
Reiffer's Hummingbird, #3628	125.00

4¾ h

Gray Cardinal, #3596	85.00
Parula Warbler, #3583	55.00
5" H, Prothonotary Warbler, #3447	85.00
5½" h, Bird of Paradise, #3408	85.00
6" h, Cockatoo, pink, #3405	65.00

6¼" h, Red-headed Woodpecker,
#3751 .... 265.00
6½" h, Cardinal, #3444 .... 65.00
7" h
Hen, yellow, #3446 .... 150.00
Parakeets, dbl, #3582D 200.00
8" h, Wrens, dbl, #3401D 100.00
8½" h
Bluebirds, dbl, #3276D 185.00
Woodpeckers, dbl, #3752D 180.00
9" h
Flying duck, teal blue, #3443 .... 250.00
Rooster, #3445 .... 175.00
Key West Quail Dove, #3453 .... 225.00
9½" h, Cockatoos, dbl, #3405D 74.00
10¼" h, Bluejay w/leaf, #3716 .... 525.00

FROSTED FRUIT PATTERN
Sugar Bowl 18.00

FRUIT PATTERN
Cup and Saucer 9.00
Gravy Boat 15.00
Sugar Bowl, Cov 15.00

FRUIT AND FLOWERS PATTERN
Platter, 13½" d 40.00
Salad Bowl, 10" d 30.00

GARDEN FLOWER PATTERN
Cigarette Box 40.00
Dinner Plate 12.00

GOLDEN BLOSSOM PATTERN
Bowl, divided, 11" l 24.00
Chop Plate 20.00
Cream and Sugar 22.00
Cup and Saucer 12.00
Eggcup 10.00
Fruit Cup 7.00
Mug 14.00
Vegetable Bowl, divided 15.00

GOLDEN GRAPES PATTERN
Bowl, 6" d 10.00

GOLDEN HARVEST PATTERN
Bowl, 10" d 15.00
Creamer 7.00
Cup and Saucer 7.00
Dinner Plate 8.00
Gravy Boat 14.00
Pitcher 20.00
Plate, 6" d 3.00
Sugar Bowl 10.00

KUMQUAT PATTERN
Chop Plate, 12" d 30.00
Salad Bowl, 10" d 25.00

LYRIC PATTERN
Pitcher, 11" h 85.00

MAGNOLIA PATTERN
Breakfast Set, master bowl, 4 small
bowls, 4 cups and saucers, 8 plates,
creamer, sugar bowl 200.00
Butter Dish 5.00
Chop Plate, 12½" d 10.00
Cream and Sugar 10.00
Cup and Saucer 8.00

Fruit Dish 6.00
Plate
6" d 3.00
9" d 4.00

MEDITERRANEAN PATTERN
Tea Service, pot, cov sugar bowl,
creamer, 4 cups and saucers 95.00

NEWPORT PATTERN
Plate, 10" d, hp, blue ship w/white
sails, #3333 .... 25.00

ORCHARD SONG PATTERN
Cup and Saucer 8.00
Plate, 10" d 7.00
Server, center handle 10.00

PETITE FLOWERS PATTERN
Bowl, 6" d 10.00

RAINBOW WARE
Bowl, 5" d 55.00
Candlestick, 2 birds in branches,
#1389, pr 175.00
Console Bowl, 13" d, w/pelican
flower frog 225.00

ROOSTER PATTERN
Cereal Bowl 28.00
Salad Bowl, 10" d 35.00

SCROLL PATTERN
Bowl, 10" l, tangerine, #3042 .... 35.00

STARFLOWER PATTERN
Bowl, 5⅝" d 7.00
Cream and Sugar 10.00
Cup and Saucer 8.00
Plate
6" d 3.00
8" d 7.00
10" d 10.00
Relish Dish 6.00

TERRA ROSE DESIGN
Basket, 9½" h, mauve shades 60.00

THISTLE PATTERN
Bowl, 4" d, crimped 5.00
Casserole, individual 7.00

Plate, 6" d, Rooster pattern, orange and
black rooster, red and mustard bands,
brown border, yellow ground, pierced
for hanging, $15.00

Chop Plate, 12" d	10.00
Coffeepot	45.00
Cup and Saucer	11.00
Eggcup	4.00
Gravy Boat	22.00
Plate	
6" d	5.00
8" d	4.00
9" d	5.00
10" d	5.00
Salt and Pepper	6.00
Sauce Dish, 5½" d	3.00
Serving Plate, handled	14.00
Vegetable Bowl	
8" d	8.00
9½" d	10.00
Teapot	45.00

TIGER LILY PATTERN

Sugar Bowl, individual	10.00

TOWN AND COUNTRY PATTERN

Coffee Set, pot, creamer, sugar bowl, blue	75.00
Dinner Plate, blue	6.00
Flowerpot, yellow	15.00
Mug, blue, set of 4	60.00
Toothbrush Holder, brown	30.00
Shakers, pr	20.00
Soup Bowl, blue	20.00

TULIP PATTERN

Bean Pot, 6 qt	55.00
Cup and Saucer	8.00
Pitcher, 4½" h	12.00
Plate	
6" d	6.00
9" d	13.00
11" d	22.00
Tea Set, pot, creamer, sugar bowl	65.00

WILD ROSE PATTERN

Butter Dish	8.00
Cereal Dish	3.00
Cream and Sugar	8.00
Cup and Saucer	5.00
Gravy Boat	8.00

Plate	
6" d	2.00
8" d	3.00
9" d	5.00
Teapot	35.00

MISCELLANEOUS

Ashtray	
5½" d, shell shape, Antique Gold finish	10.00
10" l, oval, Canada geese	45.00
Bank, 4" h, figural pig, tulip design	250.00
Basket, 14" d, 7½" h, leaf shape, blue glaze, Terra Rose, #3427	85.00
Bud Vase, 6½" h, Antique Gold finish	28.00
Candleholder, 2" h, Antique Gold finish	12.00
Candy Dish, Cov, 5½" l, Antique Gold finish, #3676	28.00
Figure	
Elephant, 3" h, ivory white glaze	125.00
Flowerpot, 6¼" h, w/saucer, fluted body, yellow glaze, #1261	9.00
Pin Tray, 7" l	
4" w, med blue	12.00
7" w, divided, silver green	18.00
Pitcher	
8" h, thrown, aqua glaze, #3214	78.00

Ashtray, 11" l, natural colors, grayish ground, $25.00

Plate, 9" d, Tulip pattern, blue, $13.00

Figure, 9" h, Redstarts, #3490D, $225.00

11¼" h, Granada Gold, #4055 .... **55.00**
16" h, Granada Gold, #4055 .... **95.00**
Planter
1½" h, pig, med blue glaze, #1745 . **25.00**
9" l, 4" w, aqua glaze, #3227 .... **35.00**
11" l, center over-handle, mauve
glaze, #3253 .... **85.00**
Salt and Pepper
Hen and rooster, natural colors **125.00**
Stoby Jug
Archie, mustachioed man w/hat **175.00**
Preacher.. **275.00**
Vase
5" h, Tulip, Terra Rose **45.00**
7" h, 2 handles, matte tangerine ext,
green int, #3105 .... **46.00**
7¼" h, dbl handles, Granada Gold,
#3103 .... **68.00**
7½" h, scalloped green ext w/loops,
tan int, "#3568 Terra Rose" mark . **18.00**
7¾" h, Granada Gold, #2041 .... **20.00**
8" h
Ball shape, matte green glaze,
#1909 .... **75.00**
Urn shape, sq base, scroll han-
dles, Caribbean, #2041 .... **20.00**
10" h
Bellflower design, orange glaze ... **175.00**
Figural overlapping leaves, purple
glaze, "Terra Rose Stangl" mark **50.00**
13" h
Figural horse's head, blue flambe,
white trim, #3611, "STANGL
TERRA ROSE MADE IN TRENTON,
U.S.A." mark **675.00**
Urn shape, Pebblestone pattern,
#3993 .... **135.00**
Wig Stand, 10½" h, brunette **150.00**

MADE IN U.S.A.

CHINA

STERLING CHINA COMPANY
East Liverpool (Wellsville), Ohio
1917–Present

History: In 1917 a group of men founded the Sterling China Company in the former Patterson Brothers pottery in Wellsville, Ohio, and made vitreous hotel china. The factory had numerous additions, and the product line continued to ex-

pand. During World War II Sterling supplied most of the dinnerware used by the United States Armed Forces.

Sterling used a wide variety of primarily traditional decorations on its hotel ware. The company's commercial china was used by airlines, hotels, restaurants, railroads, and steamship companies. By 1949 it was one of the three largest producers of vitrified hotel and restaurant china in the world.

After World War II and until 1950 Sterling had a non-traditional line of streamlined tableware designed by Russel Wright in Ivy green, Straw yellow, Suede gray, and Cedar brown. (See Russel Wright.) The company continued to expand. From 1951–1976 it operated a plant in Puerto Rico and made Caribe China. In 1954 Sterling absorbed the Scammell China Company that now produces the Lamberton China line.

A wide variety of marks was used by Sterling for its commercial wares. Though its pottery was actually in Wellsville, Sterling preferred the East Liverpool address and used it to identify the company.

DESERT TAN PATTERN
Dinner Plate **8.00**
Luncheon Plate **6.00**
GOLDEN MAIZE PATTERN
Tea Set, teapot, 5¼" h, creamer, and
sugar bowl **42.00**
MISCELLANEOUS
Cake Plate, 6¼" sq, red and pink roses
in center, raised blue and gilt bor-
der, set of 4 .... **20.00**
Mug, 4¼" h, shaded brown decal of
monk drawing ale into mug from
keg on cream ground, dark brown
base and rim, "Sterling China" and
crown mark...................................... **28.00**
Pitcher
6¼" h, hp red poppies on shaded
brown to cream ground, "Sterling
China," crown, and "American
Pottery Co." mark **19.00**
9" h, paneled, Dutch boy and girl
on front, 3 Dutch children on re-
verse, green bands, gold rim **45.00**
11" h, gold "Best in Ohio,
Wellsville Water" on side **75.00**
Plate
8½" d, pale purple grapes w/green
and red leaves in center, pale
blue border w/gold grape overlay,
"Best Wishes, Dent Blue, Fife
Lake, Fancy Grocer" on front....... **7.00**
9" d
Calendar, multicolored mountain
scene in center, 1909 calendar
on border, gold "Compliments
of Weingartner & Co. Palo
Alto, Cal" **29.00**

Tray, 9¹/₂" l, red floral border, "Vitrified China, Sterling China, East Liverpool, Ohio, U.S.A." mark, $4.00

Oct, 3 flying ducks in marsh setting, gold overlay inner border, yellow to blue-green shaded outer border	**20.00**
9¹/₄" d	
Bust of woman w/purple flowers in hair, holding bunch of purple flowers, gold overlay border	**30.00**
Tan, brown, and mustard stylized leaves, scalloped border, "Sterling China Vitrified China, East Liverpool, Ohio" mark	**3.00**
Platter	
12³/₄" l, band of multicolored galleons on border, waves at each end	**24.00**
21" l, multicolored fish in center, purple irid border, scalloped rim, black edge	**85.00**
Sugar Bowl, Cov, band of multicolored galleons on border	**12.00**

1868

**Thompson's
Old Liverpool
Ware**

T H | OM
P S | ON

c.1910–1930s

C.C. THOMPSON POTTERY COMPANY
East Liverpool, Ohio
1868–1938

History: The company was started under the name Thompson and Herbert in 1868. The partners built a small pottery to make Rockingham and yellow Queensware. Two years later, Herbert was bought out, the name became C.C. Thompson and Company, and the firm was expanded.

It made a wide variety of pieces in cream-colored ware and continued to make the same pieces in Rockingham and yellowware, except for the toilet sets. In 1899 it incorporated as C.C. Thompson Pottery Company and added white ironstone toilet and dinnerware products.

In 1917 yellowware, Rockingham, and cream-colored ware were phased out in favor of semi-porcelain dinnerware. Production stopped in 1938 due to poor business conditions.

A wide variety of marks was used on the wares.

Museum: Museum of Ceramics at East Liverpool, OH.

Bowl	
9" d,	
Exotic bird and foliage in center, vert ribbing, gold rose overlay on border, straight-sided rim	**5.00**
Large pink and yellow roses in center, lustered green border w/gold-lined rim	**10.00**
Pink, yellow, and white roses w/green foliage in center, vert ribbed border w/yellow to pea green shading, shaped rim, mkd	**18.00**
Spanish sailing ship in center, shaded pea green border, "Lawndale Tea and Coffee" on front	**8.00**
9¹/₄" d	
Pink and yellow roses in center, shaded pink ground, gold floral band, floral buds on border	**5.00**
Purple and white flowers and rose in center, gold roses on inner border, lustered yellow rim	**8.00**
Butter Dish, 9" H-H, oct cov, blue and pink garden flowers w/blue outline,	

Bowl, 9¹/₂" d, multicolored garden flowers, irid green border w/gold floral overlay, shadow leaves on int, mkd, $5.00

round base w/oct insert, vert fluting
w/gold trim **26.00**
Plate
9¼" d
Iron red chrysanthemums w/black
leaves, shaded pink border
w/raised design **8.00**
Roses in center, med blue border
w/raised design **8.00**
Spanish galleon in center, pink
border w/raised design **8.00**
10" d, decal of purple and green
grapes w/winding tendrils and
leaves, gold band on rim, artist
sgd **12.00**
Platter, 13¼" l, orange poppies
w/green leaves suspended from border, raised shell design on border,
silver-lined shaped rim, "Old
Heather Ware" mark **10.00**
Sauce Dish, 5¼" d, multicolored
pears in center, lustered green border, "Francis Thompson" mark, set
of 6 .... **12.00**

TRENTON POTTERIES COMPANY
Trenton, New Jersey
1892–1969

History: In 1892 five individual Trenton operations joined together to form Trenton Potteries
Company. Crescent, Delaware, Empire, Enterprise, and Equitable Pottery Companies combined their resources, but continued to operate
separately after the merger.

For the most part, four of the companies
made vitreous china sanitary wares, while Equitable made more tablewares and other items for
hospitals. The companies experimented with
making porcelain sanitary wares like those which
had to be imported from England. A new plant
called Ideal Pottery was constructed to make
porcelain bathtubs. With the addition of the tunnel kiln in 1922, operations to produce sanitary
wares were greatly improved. Slip casting was
also substituted for pressing clay into molds.

In 1924 Crane obtained a controlling interest
in Trenton Potteries and continued the operation
until fires in 1967 and 1969 caused the facility to
close down.

The French artist Lucien Boullemier was responsible for the beautifully decorated urns
made by Empire Pottery that were exhibited at
the Louisiana Purchase Exposition in St. Louis in
1904. His paintings on the porcelain were ex-
quisite; four different craftsmen worked on the
urns.

From the mid 1930s until sometime after
World War II, some art pottery, mostly for florist
shops, was produced by TEPECO and fired in the
same kilns as the sanitary wares. The same pastel
colors used for the sanitary wares—pale green,
yellow, blue, pink, off-white, dark red-brown,
and charcoal—were found on thick-walled, usually undecorated wares. Shapes were both Art
Deco and classic in design. Vases, planters, wall
pockets, flowerpots, centerpiece bowls, console
sets, bud vases, rose bowls, candleholders, ashtrays, and umbrella stands were made. Many of
the forms were made in varying sizes and shapes.
Some of the ashtrays were made for advertising
and promotional purposes. A stamped mark was
used on all the wares.

Reference: Dr. M.W. Lerner, "The Art Pottery
of the Trenton Potteries Company," *The Antique
Trader Weekly Annual of Articles,* Volume XV,
1983.

Museums: Brooklyn Museum, NY; City of
Trenton Museum, NJ; New Jersey State Museum,
Newark, NJ.

Console Set, bowl, 10" d, 2 candlesticks, 3½" h, dark brown glaze,
"TRENTON TEPECO" mark **75.00**
Planter, 5" h, 7" w, fan shape, vert
panels, aqua glaze, "TRENTON TE-
PECO" mark **12.00**
Vase
5½" h, ball shape, turquoise glaze .. **50.00**
5⅝" h, narrow base, bulbous body,
light blue glaze, "TRENTON TEPECO"
mark **35.00**
5¾" h, ball shape, 3 horiz rings at
center, yellow glaze, "TRENTON TE-
PECO" mark **58.00**

Vase, 6¼" h, aqua glaze, "TRENTON TE-
PECO" mark, $20.00

Vase, 10" h, off-white glaze, mkd(A), $60.00

6" h
  Bulbous shape, 3 bands in center,
    maroon ground, pr **85.00**
  Shell shape, maroon glaze **20.00**
7" h, trumpet shape, med blue
  glaze, "TRENTON TEPECO" mark **18.00**

William Ellis Tucker
China Manufacturer
Philadelphia
1828

WILLIAM ELLIS TUCKER
Philadelphia, Pennsylvania
1826–1838

History: William Ellis Tucker opened his factory in 1826 in Philadelphia, Pennsylvania. At first he worked with John Bird and made decorative and useful Queen's ware in the classical shapes of the Empire style. Many designs were copied from English and French porcelains.

Tucker was the first to use American subject matter on porcelain and his designs included views of Philadelphia, patriotic heroes, and President Jackson. Tucker made porcelains for Jackson's White House and for the Philadelphia elite, some with black, sepia, or polychrome scenes. Many pieces were unmarked to resemble unmarked French porcelains. A wide variety of shapes was made, such as spill vases, ornate urns, twelve different pitcher forms, fruit baskets, tea sets, paneled cups, plates, platters, and bowls. Floral and botanical motifs were used on later Tucker porcelains. Many examples had gold trim and gilded ormolu handles.

In 1828 Thomas Hulme became a partner due to Tucker's financial problems, but the two men did not stay together for long. Tucker's brother Thomas became an apprentice employee in 1828 and eventually became chief decorator. In 1831 Judge Hemphill became a partner.

After William Tucker died in 1832, Hemphill kept Thomas on as plant superintendent until 1837. When Hemphill sold the factory, Thomas leased the operation for about six months, but he was unable to successfully compete with tariff-free imported goods, and closed the factory in 1838.

Museums: Brooklyn Museum, NY; Henry Ford Museum, Dearborn, MI; Metropolitan Museum of Art, New York, NY: Philadelphia Museum of Art, PA; William Penn Memorial Museum, Harrisburg, PA.

Cup and Saucer, sepia painted Italianate landscape, gilt rim, chipped.. **175.00**
Pitcher, 8½" h, multicolored garden flowers on base, center gold band, gold scroll and leaf design on throat, shaped handle **2500.00**
Plate
  6⅛" d, 4 pink and green rosebud sprigs, 3 gilt leaf sprigs, gilt rim.... **150.00**
  6¼" d, sepia painted Italianate landscape in center, gilt rim, hairline, pr(A) **330.00**
Soup Plate, 8¾" d, Wheat pattern, gilt floral border **225.00**
Teapot
  8½" h, landscape scene, repaired(A)
  .... **275.00**
  9" h, baluster shape, bouquet of garden flowers w/green leaves on side, wide gold band on shoulder, rim, cov, and feet, gold pointed knob, gold striped handle and spout **4500.00**
Vase, trumpet shape, center band of red roses and garden flowers between gold bands, scattered gold leaves on base, gold rim and foot
  6½" h.. **2800.00**
  7" h... **3500.00**

Teapot, 11" h, Spider pattern, gold design, $2850.00

*Jar, stoneware, blue markings,
5 gallon, $39.00*

UHL POTTERY
Huntingburg, Indiana
1849–1944

History: Louis and August Uhl founded Uhl Pottery in Evansville, Indiana, in 1849 when they came to America from Germany. In 1908 the company moved to Huntingburg.

An extensive line of utilitarian wares was made including crocks in sizes ranging from one-quarter to sixty gallons, churns and covers, milk pans, mixing bowls, drinking jars, covered casseroles, bean pots, canister sets, 6-cup drip coffeemakers, bud vases, and piggy banks.

Wren houses were made in terra-cotta or glazed dull colors; frogs and turtles were glazed. Birdbaths, flowerpots, and sundials were made for outdoor use.

Despite its extensive line, the company was unable to compete with foreign markets and it closed in 1949. Some pieces were marked "Uhl Pottery, Huntingburg, Ind."

Reference: Earl F. McCurdy and Jane A. McCurdy, *A Collectors' Guide and History to Uhl Pottery,* Ohio Valley Books, 1988.

Collectors' Club: Uhl Collectors Society, Tom Uebelhor, 233 E. Timberlin Lane, Huntingburg, IN 47542, $10 per year, bimonthly newsletter.

Bean Pot, blue	190.00
Bowl, 11½" d, horiz ribbing, red-brown ext, gray int	75.00
Casserole, Cov, 7½" d, blue, mkd	22.00
Crock	
4¾" h, gray salt-glaze finish	25.00
10¾" h, blue "UHL POTTERY," acorn, and "3" on front	65.00
Figure, frog, brown and green accents	
6" l, unmkd(A)	605.00
9" l, "UHL POTTERY CO. HUNTINGBURG IND" mark(A)	990.00
Flowerpot and Saucer, 4¾" h, horiz rings, blue glaze, "Uhl Pottery Co. Huntington, Ind." mark	45.00
Jar, acorn shape, 2 gallon	45.00
Jug, 19¾" h, blue "UHL POTTERY," acorn, and "5" on front	50.00
Mug	
2½" h, barrel shape, brown glaze	60.00
4" h, tan glaze	8.00

Pitcher	
5½" h, simulated barrel staves w/metal hoops, blue glaze	85.00
7¼" h, narrow base and top, wide waist, dark red ext, gray int	75.00
8" h, bulbous shape, blue	185.00
1 gallon, blue and white sponging	429.00
Planter, 3¾" h, half-ball shape w/architectural feet, dark red ext	45.00
Storage Jar, 5" h, mauve ext, white int, "Uhl Pottery Co. Huntington, Ind" mark	45.00
Vase	
2½" h, 5" l, figural shoe, brown	75.00
5" h, flared top, blue glaze	50.00
7" h, bulbous base, narrow neck, flared rim, gray glaze, blue ink mark	45.00
8" h, trumpet shape, gray crackle glaze, blue ink mark	10.00
8¼" h, trumpet shape w/rolled rim	
Gloss med blue glaze	120.00
Smooth matte gray glaze, #123	38.00

1879–1891

UNION PORCELAIN WORKS
Greenpoint, Brooklyn, New York
1861–1904

History: Thomas Smith purchased the Boch Brothers Pottery in 1861 in the Greenpoint section of Brooklyn, New York, and established the

Union Porcelain Company. After first concentrating on porcelain house trimmings, he made utilitarian wares such as pitchers, spittoons, bowls, shaving mugs, cups and saucers for coffee, tea, and chocolate, and heavy oval dishes.

Smith had studied hard-paste porcelain making in France and Union Porcelain Works was the first American pottery to produce a true hard-paste porcelain. He utilized the underglaze method of decoration on his pitchers, tete-a-tete tea sets, vases, and such. In 1874 Karl Muller became artistic director at Union and created sculptures for the Philadelphia Centennial International Exhibition in 1876. His Century vase, considered the finest example of American ceramics at the Centennial, detailed the progress of America through its first century. Muller also made pedestals, statues, and vases with plant and animal motifs or classical designs.

The company used a variety of marks on its wares.

Museums: Brooklyn Museum, NY; Henry Ford Museum and Greenfield Village, Dearborn, MI; Metropolitan Museum of Art, New York, NY.

Cream and Sugar, floral design, light
blue ground **100.00**
Match Holder, 3¹/₄" h, blue-outlined
white base, cone-shaped holder
w/brown striking surface, "Union
Porcelain, Greenpoint, N.Y." and
bird's head w/snake marks **110.00**
Oyster Plate
8" l, 6¹/₂" w, molded shells, gold
and white, pr **350.00**
8¹/₄" d, 6 raised wells w/painted
crayfish and sea creatures, brown
coral ground, gold Greek key rim,
set of 4 .... **1350.00**
Pitcher, 10¹/₂" h, white cameo of fight-

Vase, 8¹/₂" h, gloss white glaze,
unmkd, $875.00

ing men at card game and gift of king to gentleman, Wedgwood blue ground, figural tusked-animal spout, shaped ferret handle, stamped "UPW, Union Porcelain Works, Green Point, NY, 12, 85" mark (A).. **4400.00**
Tray, 17³/₄" d, enamel and gilt period dancing scene in center, band of multicolored florals on inner border, gilt rim, inscribed "U.P.W." mark **3850.00**
Vase, 12¹/₄" h, orange-red and yellow-coral w/scattered flowers on black ground, white shoulder w/red, yellow, and brown flowers and green leaves, modeled brown monkey handles, restored hairline, mkd **5500.00**

VERNON KILNS
MADE IN
U.S.A.
CALIFORNIA

SALAMINA
Designed by
Rockwell Kent
VERNON KILNS
MADE IN USA

Designed by
WALT DISNEY
Copyright 1940
VERNON KILNS
Made in U.S.A.

VERNON KILNS
Vernon, California
1931–1958

History: Fay Bennison purchased the Poxon China Company in 1931 and changed its name to Vernon Kilns. During the early years of the company, an artware department was established and vases, bowls, candlesticks, and figurines were made along with dinnerwares. Due to economic problems, the artware line was discontinued in 1937.

Vernon Kilns employed many famous and gifted artists and became a leader in the dinnerware market. Gale Turnbull was hired as art director in 1936 and created the Ultra shape for solid-color dinnerware. Rockwell Kent transfer printed designs onto this shape for patterns such as Salamina, Our America (regional scenes of America), and Moby Dick (ships and scenes from the novel). Don Blanding also used the Ultra shape for his tropical floral and fish designs, such as Lei Lani, one of the most popular Vernon patterns.

The company contracted with Walt Disney to

make figures based on characters in *Fantasia, Dumbo,* and *The Reluctant Dragon. Fantasia* figurines were made from actual models used in the production of the film, and vases, bowls, and a dinnerware pattern also were based on *Fantasia* themes. All of these pieces were marked.

The Coronado shape was used in 1938 for solid-color premium ware. The Melinda shape was designed by Royal Arden Hickman in 1942 and was used for fourteen different patterns, including solid-color Native California and traditional English look-alike patterns. The San Fernando shape was used for Early Days and P.F.D., both transfer-printed patterns. The hand-painted Organdie and Brown-Eyed Susan were very popular patterns during the war years. Many variations of the brown-and-yellow-plaid Organdie line were sold in later years.

In the mid 1940s, San Marino, representing a complete change from earlier shapes, was used for three solid-color, drip-glazed lines—Casual California, California Shadows, and California Originals. Chatelaine, a square-shaped pattern with embossed leaf corners and leaf handles and finials, was made in four solid colors in 1953. Anytime shape, designed by Eliot House in 1955, was used for nine different patterns. A large variety of shapes was used on the lightweight dinnerwares that were made until 1958 and sold in department, jewelry, and gift stores.

Vernon Kilns was a pioneer in the transfer-printing process. All sorts of commemoratives sold well, as did French opera reproductions and the Bit Series. Almost every possible subject found its way onto souvenir plates and collectors have identified more than one thousand different ones. Dinnerware shapes were used to make the ten-and-one-half-inch diameter souvenir plates.

After World War II, the United States was flooded with imports from Japan, England, and Scandinavia. Edward Fischer took over Vernon Kilns when Fay Bennison retired in 1955, but ever-increasing costs and the continuing foreign competition forced the pottery to close in 1958. Metlox Potteries bought the Vernon Kilns molds, modified some shapes, and continued to make some patterns for several years, using both Vernon backstamps and "by Metlox."

Almost all of the Vernon Kilns pieces were marked, and some were artist signed.

References: Jack Chipman, *Collector's Encyclopedia of California Pottery,* Collector Books, 1992; Bess Gedney Christensen, "Souvenir Plates from Vernon Kilns," *The Antique Trader Weekly,* June 3, 1992; Maxine Feek Nelson, *Collectible Vernon Kilns,* Collector Books, 1994; ———, *Versatile Vernon Kilns, An Illustrated Value Guide, Book II,* Collector Books, 1983.

Newsletter: Vernon Views, P.O. Box 945, Scottsdale, AZ 85252, Pat Faux Editor, quarterly, $10 per year.

ART POTTERY

Flower Bowl, 10½" d, turquoise, #135	65.00
Planter, figural white bird, 8" l, #134 ..	25.00

BARKWOOD PATTERN

Creamer	10.00
Sugar Bowl, Cov	12.00
Vegetable Bowl, 9" d	8.00

BITS OF OLD NEW ENGLAND SERIES

Plate, 8½" d

"Haying"	20.00
"The Cove"	20.00

BITS OF THE OLD SOUTH SERIES

Plate, 8½" d, "Cypress Swamp"	22.00

BITS OF THE OLD WEST SERIES

Plate, 8½" d, "The Fleecing"	18.50

BROWN-EYED SUSAN PATTERN

Butter Dish, ¼ lb	40.00
Chop Plate, 12" d	20.00
Dinner Plate, 10" d	15.00
Teapot	45.00

CALICO PATTERN

Syrup Pitcher	50.00

CALIFORNIA SHADOWS PATTERN

Cup and Saucer, cocoa brown	4.00
Dinner Plate, cocoa brown	6.00
Platter, 13½" l, cocoa brown	12.00

CHINTZ PATTERN

Creamer	20.00
Plate, 10" d	9.00
Shakers, pr	18.00
Sugar Bowl	25.00
Teapot	110.00

CORAL REEF

Bread and Butter	25.00
Chop Plate, 12" d	45.00
Coffeepot, 6 cup	150.00
Cup and Saucer	55.00

Plate

9¾" d, swimming fish, maroon transfer	25.00
10½" d, brown transfer	85.00

DELORES PATTERN

Creamer	8.00
Gravy Boat	8.00

Teapot, 7" h, Brown Eyed Susan pattern, $45.00

Plate, 10¼″ d....................................	**14.00**
Shakers, pr......................................	**10.00**
Sugar Bowl, Cov	**12.00**
Teapot	**28.00**

EARLY CALIFORNIA PATTERN

Ashtray, turquoise...........................	**8.00**
Berry Dish, brown	**3.00**
Bread and Butter Plate, brown	**3.00**
Casserole, Cov, turquoise	**22.00**
Cup and Saucer, red	**6.00**
Eggcup	
Tan	**12.00**
Teal blue.................................	**10.00**

GINGHAM PATTERN

Bonbon, 3 tiers	**20.00**
Bowl, 5″ d	**8.00**
Bread and Butter Plate	**3.00**
Chop Plate......................................	**11.00**
Coffee Server	**12.00**
Creamer	
Large	**8.00**
Small......................................	**7.00**
Cup and Saucer	**10.00**
Cup and Saucer, oversized	**150.00**
Dinner Plate	**8.00**
Fruit Bowl, 5½″ d	**6.00**
Gravy Boat	**6.00**
Lug Soup	**8.00**
Mixing Bowl	
5″ d	**8.00**
6″ d	**8.00**
7″ d	**9.00**
8″ d	**9.00**
9″ d	**10.00**
Pitcher	
1 qt, green and yellow plaid, green	
border	**35.00**
2 qt	**20.00**
Platter, oval	
12″ l......................................	**15.00**
14″ l......................................	**20.00**
Shakers, pr......................................	**12.00**
Soup Plate	**5.00**
Sugar Bowl, Cov	**10.00**
Syrup Jug	**10.00**
Teapot	**24.00**
Tumbler...	**10.00**
Vegetable Bowl	
9″ d, open	**15.00**
11½″ l, divided	**20.00**

HAWAIIAN FLOWERS PATTERN

Chop Plate, 12″ d	
Blue transfer..............................	**65.00**
Brown transfer............................	**28.00**
Coffeepot, blue transfer......................	**125.00**
Plate, 9½″ d, blue transfer	**15.00**

HEAVENLY DAYS PATTERN

Serving Bowl, divided........................	**18.00**

HIBISCUS PATTERN

Tureen, w/undertray, brown transfer	
w/hand tinting.............................	**325.00**

HOMESPUN PATTERN

Casserole, Cov..................................	**25.00**
Cereal Bowl.....................................	**9.00**
Chop Plate, 12″ d	**12.00**
Creamer..	**7.00**
Cup and Saucer	**10.00**
Eggcup	**12.00**
Gravy Boat	**18.00**
Jug, 5″ h...	**15.00**
Lug Soup	**9.00**
Mixing Bowl	
5″ d	**8.00**
6″ d	**8.00**
8″ d	**10.00**
9″ d	**12.00**
Plate	
6″ d	**3.00**
7″ d	**8.00**
9½″ d	**10.00**
Pitcher, 8½″ h	**18.00**
Shakers, pr......................................	**8.00**
Sugar Bowl, Cov	**8.00**
Vegetable Server, divided	**19.00**

HONOLULU PATTERN

Berry Bowl.......................................	**12.00**
Cup and Saucer, hp yellow flowers,	
blue transfer	**30.00**

IMPERIAL PATTERN

Bowl, 9″ d, "Show Stopper," white	
sgraffito on ebony ground, gray	
swirls	**30.00**

LEI LANI PATTERN

Berry Bowl, maroon transfer, hp ac-	
cents	**12.00**
Chop Plate, 12″ d	**45.00**
Cup and Saucer	**10.00**
Cup and Saucer, oversized, San	
Marino shape	**55.00**
Plate	
6″ d	**10.00**
9″ d, maroon transfer, hp ac-	
cents	**20.00**

LINDA PATTERN

Bowl, 5″ d	**5.00**
Bread and Butter Plate	**3.00**
Butter Dish	**8.00**
Chop Plate, 12″ d	**12.00**
Gravy Boat	**10.00**
Luncheon Plate	**6.00**
Plate, 9″ d	**8.00**
Shakers, pr......................................	**8.00**

MAYFLOWER PATTERN

Berry Bowl.......................................	**6.00**
Bowl, 9″ d	**12.00**
Butter Dish, ¼ lb	**45.00**
Creamer..	**20.00**
Gravy Boat	**45.00**
Plate, 10″ d.....................................	**12.00**
Shakers, pr......................................	**30.00**
Sugar Bowl	**20.00**
Teapot	**75.00**

MODERN CALIFORNIA PATTERN

A.D. creamer, cov sugar bowl, and
tray, orchid 40.00
Chowder Bowl, Cov, ivory 25.00

NATIVE CALIFORNIA PATTERN

Bread and Butter Plate
    Blue 12.00
    Green.. 18.00
Chop Plate, 14" d, yellow 30.00
Shakers, yellow, pr 16.00

ORGANDIE PATTERN

Berry Dish 3.00
Bowl
    5½" d.. 4.00
    9" d.. 20.00
Carafe... 20.00
Cereal Bowl 2.00
Chop Plate, 12" d 8.00
Coaster, 4" d.................................... 3.00
Coffee Server 25.00
Cov Creamer and Sugar Bowl 15.00
Cup and Saucer 4.00
Dessert Bowl 4.00
Individual Baker 5.00
Mug.. 17.00
Plate
    6½" d.. 2.00
    7½" d.. 3.00
    9" d.. 10.00
    10" d.. 5.00
Platter
    10" l... 12.00
    13" l... 20.00
Shakers, pr 12.00
Syrup Jug, 5" h 8.00
Tumbler... 18.00

RAFFIA PATTERN

Creamer and Cov Sugar Bowl 14.00
Cup and Saucer, green and brown 7.00
Dinner Plate 7.00
Salt and Pepper................................. 10.00

ROCKWELL KENT DESIGNS

Moby Dick pattern
    Bowl, tab handles, walnut brown 15.00
    Chop Plate, 17" d, walnut brown 280.00
    Cream and Sugar, walnut brown 40.00
    Cup and Saucer, walnut brown 35.00
    Dinner Plate, walnut brown............. 35.00
    Fruit Bowl, walnut brown 10.00
    Gravy Boat, walnut brown 24.00
    Salad Plate, 7" d, walnut brown........ 22.00
    Salt and Pepper, walnut brown 40.00
    Soup Plate, walnut brown 18.00

OUR AMERICA PATTERN

Chop Plate, 13" d, brown 195.00
Plate, 10" d...................................... 60.00

SALAMINA PATTERN

Charger, 16½" d, kneeling Salam-
    ina(A) 220.00
Creamer.. 58.00
Lug Soup 40.00

Plate
    6½" d, Salamina sitting at ocean 30.00
    10½" d, kneeling Salamina 50.00

SOUVENIR PLATE, 10½" D

Franklin Roosevelt, scenes of Warm
    Springs, Ga., and Little White
    House, blue transfer 40.00
General MacArthur, blue transfer........ 30.00
Pennsylvania Turnpike, blue transfer .. 10.00
Seattle, green transfer........................ 15.00
State of Alabama............................... 20.00
State of Georgia 15.00
Will Rogers, maroon transfer.............. 35.00

TAM O' SHANTER PATTERN

Butter Dish, ¼ lb 15.00
Pitcher, 1 qt 12.00
Plate
    6½" d.. 3.00
    9½" d.. 3.00
    10½" d.. 4.00
Serving Bowl, divided........................ 18.00
Shakers, pr 16.00
Teapot 45.00
Vegetable Bowl, Cov, dbl handles 55.00

TICKLED PINK PATTERN

Bread and Butter Plate 2.25
Butter Dish 6.00
Casserole 14.00
Cup and Saucer 5.50
Dinner Plate 8.00
Gravy Boat 14.00
Pitcher, 4" h..................................... 22.00
Salad Plate 3.50
Shakers, pr 7.00

TWEED PATTERN

Teapot 38.00

ULTRA CALIFORNIA PATTERN

Creamer, pink................................... 14.00
Mixing Bowl
    6" d, ivory 18.00
    7" d, light blue 20.00
    8" d, yellow 22.00

*Souvenir Plate, 10¼" d, U.S. Marine
Corps, tan and brown, c1940s, $65.00*

9" d
Aqua	**27.00**
Light green	**30.00**
Plate, 7½" d, pink	**9.00**

WALT DISNEY DESIGNS
Bowl
6½" d, Satyr, white ext, turquoise int, #124	**125.00**
10½" d, Sprite, light green, #125	**350.00**

12" d
Raised-wing nymph design Pink ext, white int, #122	**225.00**
Pistachio	**250.00**
12" l, 7" w, rect, mushroom, pink, #120	**125.00**

Figure
4½" h
Black baby Pegasus, #19	**4350.00**
Satyr bull, white w/painted design	**395.00**
Baby Wheem, yellow hair, blue jacket, red kerchief, #37	**360.00**
Shakers, Hop Low mushroom, mkd, pr	**145.00**

Vase
5½" h, Fantasia, Gold Fish, pink	**195.00**
10" h, relief of Diana, Goddess of the moon, gloss white glaze, c1940, mkd(A)	**275.00**

WINCHESTER 73 PATTERN
Chop Plate, 14" d, rifle in center	**195.00**
Creamer	**30.00**
Eggcup	**35.00**
Sugar Bowl	**40.00**

MISCELLANEOUS
Coffee Set, carafe, 6 cups and saucers, pomegranate, Harry Bird	**175.00**
Vase, 5" h, sphere shape, white, sgd "May and Vieve Hamilton"	**100.00**

Rosemeade
NORTH DAKOTA

WAHPETON POTTERY COMPANY
Wahpeton, North Dakota
1940–1961

History: Laura Taylor and Robert Hughes established the Wahpeton Pottery Company in Wahpeton, North Dakota, in 1940. Laura designed the original models for the pottery they called Rosemeade. The pieces were hand modeled in North Dakota clay, plaster molds were made, and then the pieces were slip cast.

Rosemeade pottery was successful from the start, and there were huge demands for the pieces made there. After several years, Laura and Robert married, moved their factory, and soon built an addition. Howard Lewis came from the

Niloak Pottery and joined them as plant manager and partner in 1944. He was responsible for formulation of the glazes and also introduced the swirl clay from Niloak.

Laura's designs were inspired by her surroundings in North Dakota, and she experimented with colors, for instance, mixing red and amber to make harvest gold. She excelled in designing birds, animals, and other wildlife, especially pheasants and mallards. She made nineteen different designs of pheasants, the first one in 1942. Animal-shaped salt and pepper sets were quite popular. High gloss glazes, dark bronze, and softly shaded matte finishes were used on bookends, tea bells, vases, candleholders, creamer and sugar sets, planters, plaques, miniatures, figurines, ashtrays, TV lamps, and commemorative wares. Over two hundred designs of Rosemeade pottery were made, and many pieces included advertisments.

In 1956 Howard Lewis sold his interest to the Hughes, and Joe McLaughlin came from Red Wing. Laura died in 1959, and the factory closed in 1961.

Most Rosemeade examples have a paper sticker and/or are marked "ROSEMEADE" in black or blue lettering. Paper stickers include the wild prairie rose and "ROSEMEADE".

Reference: Shirley L. Sampson and Irene J. Harris, *Beautiful Rosemeade*, privately printed, 1986.

Collectors' Club: North Dakota Pottery Collectors Society, Sandy Short, Box 14, Beach, ND, 58621, $10 per year.

Museum: Richland County Historical Museum, Wahpeton, ND.

Ashtray
Rust, "Montana, The Treasure State"	**40.00**
Standing chicken, white w/red comb	**125.00**

Bank, figural
Grizzly bear, black	**450.00**

Hippopotamus
Gold	**500.00**
Rose	**500.00**

Bell
4½" h, hp peacock design	**185.00**
Pink flamingo handle, green base	**95.00**
Bookend, figural dog, red glaze	**139.00**
Bowl, 4½" d, multicolored swirl design	**100.00**
Bud Vase, 7½" h, chartreuse glaze	**20.00**
Candy Dish, 7" l, 3" h, hand thrown and pinched, matte white glaze	**45.00**
Cranberry Jar, figural turkey, natural colors	**125.00**
Cream and Sugar, figural turkey	**130.00**

Figure
Elephant, light blue	**35.00**
Horse, pink	**45.00**

Howling coyote, tan and gray	150.00
Indian god of Peace, white	175.00
Mountain goat, white	200.00
Pheasant, large, natural colors	290.00
Figure, Miniature	
Buffalo	66.00
Gophers, pr	20.00
Seals, pr	20.00
Florist's Vase, 8" h, raised cattail design, blue	20.00
Flower Frog	
Bird on log	22.00
Figural fish	28.00
Frog, blue and tan, stamped "North Dakota"	35.00
Heron, tan and white	45.00
Hors D'oeuvre, 4" h, figural pheasant, 4-compartment tray, green	45.00
Jam Jar, barrel, white	110.00
Juice Set, pitcher, 4" h, 4 tumblers, 3⅝" h, dark blue	75.00
Mug	
Duck decal	45.00
Wheat, beige	60.00
Paperweight, 2¾" d, 2½" h, elephant design, gloss blue glaze	150.00
Pitcher, 5¼" h, twisted handle, matte mauve glaze	45.00
Planter	
4" h, deer and log	30.00
5" h, figural	
Elephant, blue glaze	40.00
Kangaroo	55.00
Swan, blue	10.00
Donkey and tree, dark brown	75.00
Dove, cream	200.00
Kangaroo, cream and blue-green	95.00
Pony, pink glaze	75.00
Raised grapes and leaves, rect, light green	75.00
Seated doe, blue and rose	50.00
Plaque, trout	130.00
Salt and Pepper	
Bell peppers, dark green	30.00
Bloodhounds, brown	30.00
Bluegill fish	250.00

Bobwhites	30.00
Brussel sprouts, light green	40.00
Cattle, rust	150.00
Chickens, white	37.00
Chows, blue	30.00
Corn	30.00
Cucumbers, green	30.00
Dogs' Heads	18.00
Dolphins	30.00
Donkeys' heads	30.00
Dutch mills, blue	65.00
Egyptian, priest and wolf's head	125.00
Flamingos	75.00
Flickertails, tan	35.00
Golden pheasants	50.00
Gophers	45.00
Greyhounds	30.00
Kangaroos, matte white w/rose feet .	140.00
Mallard ducks	45.00
Mice, gray	20.00
Miniature	
Elephants	30.00
Skunks	25.00
Ox Heads, "Souvenir Harrison, Ark," rust	60.00
Pelicans, rust	65.00
Pheasants	
Golden	120.00
Tails down	60.00
Prairie Roses	35.00
Raccoons	75.00
Roadrunners, gray shades	95.00
Quail	35.00
Setters, tan and white	40.00
Sunfish	150.00
Swans, black	85.00
Tulips, rose and green	30.00
Windmills	200.00
Spoon Rest	
Horse's head, blue w/black mane ...	55.00
Pansy	45.00
Rose	45.00
Water lily	45.00
Sprinkler Can, emb rabbit on side, dark brown	55.00
Television Lamp, horse, black glaze ...	490.00

Flower Frog and Bowl, 7½" h, 8½" l, tan figure, light green bowl, $135.00

Watering Can, 4¼" h, pink, "Rosemeade" mark, $65.00

Vase
  5" h
    Cylinder shape, wheat design,
      light blue glaze 55.00
    Flared top, painted florals, "AK"
      mark 500.00
  6½" h, figural boot, matte blue
    glaze 50.00
  7½" h, emb wheat design, brown ...   45.00
Figural
  Doe and tree trunk, blue and rose   30.00
  Lovebirds, green and cream.........   30.00
Swan
  Black glaze 20.00
  Bronze metallic glaze 50.00
Wall Pocket
  Doe, rose and blue, pr 75.00
  Moon and maid, cream glaze.........   25.00

IOGA

c.1905-1920

WARWICK CHINA COMPANY
Wheeling, West Virginia
1887–1951

History: The Warwick China Manufacturing
Company was incorporated in 1887 in Wheeling, West Virginia, and continued operating until
1951. Vitreous china was its specialty, and it was
one of the first American companies to produce
these wares.

A wide assortment of pieces was made, including jardinieres, clocks, umbrella stands,
dresser sets, shaving mugs, bowls, dinnerware
sets, platters, pitcher and bowl sets, garden ornaments, and other decorative and utilitarian items.
Pieces were either hand painted or decorated
with decals. Many lines pictured florals, frater-
nal-order emblems, Indians, monks, and such.

At the height of its production, Warwick
made over ten thousand sets of dinnerware per
month. After 1912 hotel china was made and
some bone china was made after 1940.

Style names were impressed in the base of a
piece. Hand-painted letters, usually in red, indicated finish or coloring. A number, also usually
in red, indicated the type of decoration used.
There were at least forty-seven different backstamps used on Warwick examples. "IOGA" appeared on some early wares.

Reference: Donald C. Hoffmann, Jr., *Why
Not Warwick,* privately printed, 1975.
  Collectors' Club: Warwick China Collectors'
Club, Don Hoffmann, 1291 N. Elmwood Drive,
Aurora, IL 60506.

Beer Pitcher
  7⅝" h, decal bust of monk, brown
    shades, gold rim, "IOGA" mark 75.00
  10½" h, decal of B.P.O.E. elk,
    brown tints, sq handle, "IOGA"
    mark......................................   175.00
Beer Set, pitcher, 10½" h, 6 mugs,
  4½" h
    Dickens-type characters on mugs,
      bust of monk on pitcher, shaded
      brown ground............................   1600.00
    Monks scene, "IOGA" mark 475.00
Bowl
  8" d, 4" h, red poinsettia, shaded
    brown ground, "IOGA" mark........   60.00
  9" d, Flow Blue, floral design 125.00
Bowl, Cov, 6" d, 2 handles, white and
  pink roses, green ground, "IOGA"
  mark 85.00
Bud Vase, 8¾" h, rose design, "IOGA"
  helmet mark.....................................   125.00
Candy Dish, 6" l, leaf shape, floral de-
  sign, gold trim, mkd 20.00
Chateau pattern
  Cup and Saucer............................   10.00
  Gravy Boat.....................................   20.00
  Vegetable Bowl, Cov.....................   30.00
Chocolate Pot
  7½" h, cherries design 55.00
  9¼" h, Flow Blue pansy design 985.00
  11" h, floral design, twist-off lid 165.00
Chocolate Set, pot, 10¾" h, 5 cups
  and saucers, wild roses and daisies
  design, emb and gold trim, scal-
  loped bases 245.00
Cuspidor 8" d, floral decoration,
  "IOGA" mark 70.00

*Chamber Pot, 5¾" h, 9¼" d, pink
cherubs w/yellow, magenta, and green
flowers and leaves, gold trim, "Warwick
Semi-Porcelain" mark(A), $75.00*

Dinnerware, Platter, 15" l, raised matte gold ribbed border design, scalloped rim, green helmet mark ...   45.00

Dresser Tray, 10" l, 6" w, fluted, small blue and yellow flowers, pale blue and yellow ground, black "Warwick China" mark..................................   30.00

Gravy Boat, w/underplate, green flowers, white ground, mkd 12.00

Mug, 4½" h

Decal of B.P.O.E. elk, brown tones .   78.00

Decal of Indian portrait, brown glaze 90.00

Decal of poppies, brown ground.....   65.00

Decal of sailor's head, red ground, "IOGA" mark..............................   50.00

Pitcher

7½" h, large multicolored flowers, brown-toned ground, "IOGA" mark...............................   70.00

9½" h, poppies design, "IOGA" mark   120.00

Plate

8¼" d, swimming fish decal...........   50.00

9½" d

Decal of monk drinking ale, brown tones, "IOGA" mark........   65.00

Indian design in colors 100.00

10" d, coach scene, yellow and gold bands.............................   95.00

Platter, 14" H-H, shaded pink roses w/green leaves, raised handles w/gilt trim 47.00

Spirit Jug, 6" h, Dickens-type character w/guitar, shaded brown ground..   95.00

Syrup Pitcher, 4" h, orange poppies, spring lid, black "WARWICK CHINA" mark 85.00

Tankard, 13" h, monk design, "IOGA" mark 185.00

Tray, 11¼" H-H, scattered bunches of pink and red roses, gold rim, open handles 22.00

Urn, 10" h, bust of woman w/ruffled neckline, blue hair-ribbon, brown ground, "IOGA" mark 152.00

Vase

4¾" h, pinecone design, shaded brown ground, "IOGA" mark........   35.00

8" h

Bulbous base, tall tapered neck, girl w/floral hat, shaded tan to brown ground, "IOGA" mark 125.00

Pillow shape, brunette child, white bonnet, "IOGA" mark.......   145.00

9" h

8" w, bulbous shape, portrait bust of young woman, "IOGA" mark .   250.00

Two handles, sea gulls on white ground 225.00

9½" h, bulbous oval base, narrow neck, flared rim w/gold outline, 2 tapered loop handles from body

Vase, 10½" h, multicolored portrait, shaded brown ground, "IOGA" mark, $110.00

to neck, open red flower w/green leaves, shaded brown ground, "IOGA" mark..............................   155.00

10" h

Bulbous shape, twig handles, poinsettias design.....................   145.00

Narcissus, ring handles, white sea gulls 100.00

10½" h

Multicolored flowers, "IOGA" mark 120.00

Portrait of woman w/black hair, yellow sunflower, blue drape, brown ground, twig handles 175.00

Red roses on blue-green ground ..   90.00

Two standing cranes in colors, white ground 195.00

11½" h, flower design, tan and brown ground, white int, gold trim 150.00

WATT POTTERY COMPANY
Crooksville, Ohio
1922–1965

History: After working at Ransbottom Brothers Pottery until 1921, W.J. Watt purchased the Globe Stoneware Company in Crooksville, Ohio, and renamed it the Watt Pottery Company. The company was run by Watt, his sons, and other family members. From 1922–1935 the company made stoneware containers in the form of jars, jugs, Dutch pots, milk pans, preserve jars, and mixing bowls. At first all pieces were done on the potter's wheel; later they used a "jar machine."

In 1925 Watt diversified its production and made jardinieres, chicken waterers, mixing bowls, and churns with dashers. When a tunnel kiln was added, capacity increased to over fifteen thousand pieces daily.

By the mid 1930s the firm discontinued stonewares and made plaster molds for new items. Banded Watt ware, introduced in the late 1930s, had a cream-colored ground with various colored bands. One of the earliest combinations featured blue and white bands. The pattern was used for kitchenwares of all types: mixing bowls, cookie jars, covered casseroles, pie plates, bean pots, pitchers, salt and pepper shakers, spaghetti bowls, cream and sugar sets, mugs, grease jars, etc. In the 1940s the banded mixing bowls were made in graduated sizes.

The Pansy pattern, made in 1950, was Watt's first attempt at hand-painted pottery and featured a small flower with a yellow center and green leaves on rose-colored clay. Many variations were made including Raised Pansy, Cut-leaf Pansy, and Cross Hatch. No two pieces were exactly alike since each one was hand painted.

The Apple series, introduced in 1952 and made for ten years, was the best-selling pattern and is the most sought after today. Deep red apples with green leaves were set against a cream ground. Variations included Reduced Decoration Apple, Open Apple, and Double Apple. Some of these pieces were ordered as grocery and hardware store premiums for sales promotions.

Several variations of the Starflower series from the early 1950s were used for dinnerwares. The most popular one had a deep red starflower with green leaves. Two versions of the Tulip series were made in the mid 1950s. Standard Tulip had deep green leaves, one large royal blue tulip, and one deep red tulip. Dutch Tulip had a cobalt blue tulip, green and red leaves, and a folk art style.

Other series from that period included Cherry and Tear Drop or American Red Bud. The 1955 Rooster series showed a crowing rooster that was outlined in black, had green and red feathers, and was standing in grass. American Foliage series from 1959 featured brown leaves on brown stems.

During the late 1950s the Morning Glory series was produced with an embossed lattice design and raised morning glories and leaves in several color combinations. In addition to all the regular series, many pieces of Watt Pottery were made in a wide variety of color schemes and designs.

Marks varied during the years of Watt production. Due to a lack of uniformity, it is difficult to date pieces by their backstamps. Most pieces had a circular impression on the bottom, some had a number corresponding to the mold number, and others were not marked at all.

References: Dave and Sue Morris, *Watt Pottery—An Identification and Value Guide,* Collector Books, 1993; William I. Watt, *Watt Collectibles,* 2nd Edition, privately printed, 1989.

Collectors' Club: Watt Pottery Collectors USA, Dennis Thompson, Box 26067, Fairview, OH 44126, quarterly newsletter *Sproutings,* $12 per year.

Newsletter: *Watt's News,* Dave and Sue Morris, P.O. Box 708, Mason City, IA 50401, quarterly, $10 per year.

APPLE PATTERN

Baking Dish, 5½" h, 8½" d, #96	**45.00**
Bean Pot, 6½" h, #76	
Dbl apple(A)	**775.00**
Single apple	**95.00**
Bowl	
4" d, #04	**75.00**
5" d, #05	
Dbl apple	**200.00**
Single apple,	**35.00**
6" d, #6	**40.00**
6½" d, reduced apple, #75	**65.00**
7" d,	**35.00**
8½" d, ribbed, #8	**45.00**
8¾" d, #601	**85.00**
9" d, ribbed, #9	**75.00**
9½" d, #73	**85.00**
13" d, open apple, #39	**1000.00**
Bowl, Cov	
8½" d	
5½" h, #96	**35.00**
6½" h, #67	**45.00**
8¾" d, 6½" h, #601	**130.00**
Canister	
Coffee, 7" h, #82	**325.00**
Flour, 8" h, #81	**325.00**
10½" h, domed top, #91(A)	**2300.00**
Casserole, Cov	
5" d, tab handle	**225.00**
6½" d, #601	**115.00**
7½" l, stick handle, #18	**195.00**
Cereal Bowl, 5½" d, #74	**35.00**
Cream Pitcher, 4½" h, #62	**45.00**
Dinner Plate, 10" d(A)	**650.00**
Grease Jar, 5½" h, #01	**250.00**
Ice Bucket, 7¼" h, w/lid	**195.00**
Mug, 3¾" h, #121	**200.00**
Pie Plate, 9" d, w/advertising	**150.00**
Pitcher	
5½" h, #15	**35.00**
6½" h, #16	
"Smiths Farm Products" advertising	**75.00**
Three-leaf variety	**115.00**

Refrigerator Pitcher, 8" h, Apple pattern, #69, $285.00

Mixing Bowl, 4" h, 7" d, Kitch-N-Queen pattern, #7, $24.00

8" h, #17
Ice lip 150.00
No ice lip 135.00
Platter, 15" d, #31(A) 650.00
Salad Bowl, 9½" d, #73 .... 65.00
Spaghetti Bowl, 13" d, 2-leaf variety,
#39 .... 225.00
Teapot, 5¾" h, #505 .... 985.00

AUTUMN FOLIAGE PATTERN
Bowl, 8½" d, #65 .... 55.00
Mug, 3¾" h, #121 .... 225.00
Pitcher, 5½" h, w/advertising 45.00
Vinegar and Oil, 7" h, #126 .... 350.00

BASKETWEAVE
Bowl, 9½" d, green, #102 .... 20.00
Casserole, Cov, 8½" d, brown, #128 .. 40.00

CABIN ART
Milk Pitcher, 6½" h 35.00

CHERRIES PATTERN
Bowl
7" d, #7 .... 50.00
8" d, #8 .... 60.00
Casserole, Cov, 9" d, #3/19 .... 75.00
Pitcher, 5½" h, #15 .... 60.00
Spaghetti Bowl, 13" d 105.00

DUTCH TULIP PATTERN
Bowl, 8½" d, #65 .... 75.00
Casserole, Cov, 4" h, 8" l, #18 .... 185.00
Creamer, 4½" h, #62 .... 120.00
Pitcher, 8" h, ice lip, #17 .... 85.00

EAGLE PATTERN
Bowl, 9½" d, #73 .... 70.00

ESMOND
Canister Set, 4 sections w/wood base.. 265.00

EVENBAKE
Pitcher, 7" h, blue and white bands 55.00

HEIRLOOM
Mug, 5¼" h, dark brown, #806 .... 60.00

KATHY KALE
Bean Pot 30.00
Bowl, 5½" d 90.00

KITCH-N-QUEEN
Casserole, Cov, 8¾" d 55.00
Nested bowls, #5, 6, 7, 8, 9, 10, 12,
14 .... 350.00
Pitcher, 8" h, #17 .... 95.00

KLA HAM'RD
Casserole, Cov 65.00
Pitcher, 7" h 65.00

LEAF PATTERN
Coffee Canister, 5" h, wood lid 189.00
Flour Canister, 6" h 200.00

ORCHARD WARE
Carafe w/electric warmer, brown
glaze, #132 .... 389.00

MORNING GLORY, QUILTED
Pitcher, 8" h, ice lip, yellow ground,
#96 .... 450.00
Sugar Bowl, 4¼" h #98 .... 210.00

PANSY PATTERN
Bowl
11" d, 2½" h, cut-leaf variety 90.00
13" d, #39 .... 75.00
Casserole, Cov, 7½" l, w/handle
Cut-leaf variety 46.00
Raised pansy design 195.00
Pizza Plate, 15" d, crosshatched
pansy 275.00
Plate
6½" d, bull's-eye center 45.00
10" d 40.00
Platter, 15" d, cut-leaf variety 95.00
Spaghetti Bowl
13" d, cut-leaf variety 70.00
15" d, bull's-eye center 85.00

PEEDEECO
Bean Pot, Cov, 6⅓" h 60.00

RIO ROSE
Luncheon Plate, set of 6 .... 90.00
Spaghetti Bowl, 8" d 30.00

ROOSTER PATTERN
Casserole, Cov, 10½" l, oval, #86(A) .. 1400.00
Creamer, 4½" h, #62 .... 65.00

Pitcher, 6¹/₂" h, Rooster pattern,
#16, $165.00

Pitcher
  5¹/₂" h, #15
    Plain 65.00
    w/advertising 85.00
  8" h, sq, #69 .... 225.00
Roaster, Cov, 10" d, #86 .... 389.00
SLEEPING MEXICAN DESIGN
Bowl, 5¹/₂" d 35.00
STARFLOWER PATTERN
Bowl, 5" d, #5 .... 60.00
Canister set, sugar, flour, 8¹/₂" h, cof-
  fee, tea, 7" h(A) 1500.00
Casserole, 7¹/₂" l, stick handle, #18..... 100.00
Creamer, 4¹/₂" h, #62 .... 30.00
Ice Bucket, 7¹/₄" h 185.00
Mug, 4¹/₂" h, #501 .... 125.00
Pitcher
  5¹/₂" h, #15................................... 15.00
  6¹/₂" h, #16................................... 60.00
    Green on brown 125.00
Platter, 15" d
  Green flower on brown ground 95.00
  #31 .... 135.00
Refrigerator Pitcher, 8" h, no ice lip,
  #17 .... 175.00
Salt and Pepper, 4" h, barrel shape 140.00
Spaghetti Bowl, 13" d 35.00
Tumbler, 4" h, #56 .... 300.00
TEAR DROP PATTERN
Bean Pot, Cov, 6¹/₂" h, #76 .... 95.00
Bean Server, 3¹/₂" h, #75 .... 18.00
Bowl, 7" d, #66 .... 300.00
Bowls, Nested, #5, 5" d, #6, 6" d, #7,
  7" d 70.00
Cheese Crock, 8" h, #80 .... 300.00
Pitcher, 5¹/₂" h, #15 .... 55.00
Refrigerator Pitcher, 8" h, #69 .... 175.00
TULIP PATTERN
Bowl
  7¹/₂" d... 65.00
  8¹/₂" d, #65..................................... 80.00
  10¹/₂" d, #85................................... 180.00
Casserole, Cov, 5¹/₂" h, 7³/₄" d, #600 .. 129.00
Cheese Crock, 8" h, #80 .... 775.00

Pitcher
  8" h, ice lip, #17 .... 289.00
  8¹/₂" h, refrigerator, #69(A) 625.00
WHITE DAISY PATTERN
Casserole, 3³/₄" h, 7¹/₂" l, stick handle . 125.00
Mixing Bowl, 7" d, #7 .... 40.00
Plate, 8¹/₂" d..................................... 75.00
MISCELLANEOUS
Dog Dish, 7" d, green glaze 40.00
Goodies Jar
  8¹/₂" h, #59(A) 470.00
  9¹/₂" h, #72(A) 475.00

WESTERN STONEWARE (INCLUDING MACOMB AND WEIR)
Monmouth, Illinois
1906–Present

History: Western Stoneware Company was
formed in 1906 in Monmouth, Illinois, when
seven companies merged: Monmouth Pottery,
Weir Pottery, Macomb Pottery, Macomb
Stoneware, D. Cultertson Stoneware (from White
Hall, Illinois), Clinton Stoneware (from Missouri),
and Fort Dodge Stoneware (from Iowa). Plants
were identified by number—one to seven. Pieces
were marked with the stenciled logo: the maple
leaf, "WESTERN STONEWARE COMPANY", and the
plant number.

By 1924 Western was producing more than
two hundred twenty-five different sizes and varieties of stoneware containers, including milk
pans, jugs, jars, churns, preserve jars, butter jars,
and flowerpots. Items necessary for dairy production and food and liquid preparation and storage
all were made. Some were made by hand and
some in molds. Western Stoneware's products
were sold through jobbers and salesmen.

By the 1920s glass fruit jars began to replace
stoneware storage containers since glass cost less
to produce, was easier to transport, and weighed
less. Dairies also used less stoneware and tin
containers became readily available. Experiencing labor and financial problems and a divided
management, Western realigned its plants again
in 1926. Plant One made the Maple Leaf brand
of standard kitchen and pantry utilitarian items, ·
the Colonial design items, and Westko chicken
waterers. Plant Two was used for the new artware line that was made for a twenty-year period
starting in 1926 under the Monmouth Pottery

label. Lines such as Burnt Wood Effect—brown brushware patterns that included Egyptian designs—and the blue-and-green Dull Finish were used for fern dishes, jardinieres, ashtrays, candleholders, bowls, and lamps. Bright Finish—black, green, blue mottled, gray, lavender, yellow, and blue—was used on lamp bases, bowls, pitchers, bookends, candleholders, vases, urns, wall pockets, and cigarette holders. Many of these pieces had paper labels. Westko garden pottery also was made at Plant Three in Macomb.

Western Stoneware was also the last maker of Old Sleepy Eye items, but referred to the line as Indian Head, rather than using the chief's name. Before production stopped in 1937, pitchers in five sizes, steins in two sizes, a sugar bowl, hot plate or trivet, jar, bowl, three sizes of mugs and a vase were made, although not all shapes were made every year. Though cobalt blue on white was the most common combination, brown on white, green on white, and brown on yellow also were available, as were solid colors. In 1952 the molds were redesigned and steins were made in chestnut brown for one year. Very limited numbers of board-of-director steins were made from 1968–1973 and mugs were made for the Old Sleepy Collectors Club of America, Inc. from 1976–1981. (See Old Sleepy Eye in the Utilitarian Section)

During the 1940s and 1950s there were frequent changes of ownership at Western and the focus was shifted to premium items in 1956. The Marcrest premium line, made for the Marshall Burns Company of Chicago, included ovenproof stoneware in a wide assortment of pieces. During the period, Eva Zeisel designed a collectible line of stonewares for Western.

Additional changes in ownership occurred in the 1960s and 1970s and in 1985 the company ceased operations. Local residents formed a group to take over and renamed the company De Novo Ceramics Ltd. It is still in business making stonewares and earthenwares.

MACOMB POTTERY, MACOMB, ILLINOIS, 1880–1906

History: Macomb Pottery Company was incorporated in 1880. It was one of the potteries in the 1906 Western Stoneware merger. Macomb's products, mass-produced Bristol or Albany slip-glazed wares that were typical of the area, included butter crocks in many sizes, jars up to thirty gallons in size, jugs from one-pint to fifteen-gallon sizes, a patented stone mason jar, umbrella stands, match safes, animals, cuspidors, pudding pans, churns, bean pots, flowerpots with saucers, and jardinieres. The stenciled or embossed mark included the words "MACOMB POTTERY CO. MACOMB, ILL."

WEIR POTTERY, MONMOUTH, ILLINOIS, 1899–1905

History: Banker William Weir incorporated Weir Pottery in Monmouth, Illinois, in 1899 and died two years later. In 1902 the pottery had a major fire, but was rebuilt immediately.

In 1903 Weir Pottery received a contract to produce 500,000 pieces of cast stoneware mugs, vases, bowls, and butter crocks for premiums that would be given away by the Sleepy Eye Milling Company of Sleepy Eye, Minnesota. These pieces were glazed in Flemish blue and gray and had the bust of a Sioux Indian chief. They were marked "Old Sleepy Eye." Pitchers with the chief's profile also were made. (See Old Sleepy Eye in the Utilitarian section)

One million patented Weir Seal Jars, stoneware fruit jars with bail tops, were produced for the H.J. Heinz Company. Cruets for various companies, jugs, and butter crocks also were made.

The logo for the company was "WEIR POTTERY CO." stamped within a circle. Weir was sold in 1905 and consolidated into the Western Stoneware Company in 1906, becoming Plant Number Two.

Reference: Jim Martin and Bette Cooper, *Monmouth-Western Stoneware,* Wallace-Homestead, 1983.

Collectors' Club: Collectors of Illinois Pottery and Stoneware, David McGuire, 1527 East Converse Street, Springfield, IL 62703, $15 per year, newsletter.

MACOMB STONEWARE

Churn, 12" h, salt glaze, blue stenciled "MCCOMB POTTERY CO-2-MACOMB, ILL"(A) **110.00**

Crock, 11½" h, blue "Maccomb Pottery Co., Maccomb, Ill" and "4" on front **80.00**

Preserve Jar, 5½" h, salt glaze, imp "MC COMB STONEWARE CO. MC COMB, ILL.," press molded, pint **150.00**

WEIR POTTERY

Fruit Jar
9" h, white glaze, metal closure,

Canning Jar, 9" h, amber top, white base, imp "WEIR POTTERY, PAT MARCH 1, 1892" on lid, $50.00

"Weir, Pat. April 16, 1901" mark
on lid... 55.00
9½" h, metal snap lock, white base,
amber top and lid, Weir #2 .... 75.00
Horseradish Jar, ½ pint, brown top,
advertising 85.00
Storage Jar
8¼" h, white glaze, 1 pint.............. 60.00
8½" h, salt Bristol glaze, emb "THE
WEIR PAT MARCH" on lid, wire bail,
1 qt(A) 55.00
8¾" h, metal snap lock, white
glaze, original preserving label,
"Pat. Date March 4, 1882, April
18, 1891" 72.00

WESTERN STONEWARE
Brushware
Bowl, 7" d, 2" h, c1912 .... 17.00
Eva Zeisel design
Red rooster w/blue florals
Cup and Saucer............................... 20.00
Dinner Plate.................................... 12.00
Salad Plate 10.00
Stoneware
Bowl, 9" d, blue and brown sponging. 80.00
Butter Milk Feeder, 1 gallon................ 135.00
Crock
9½" h, blue "leaf and Western
Stoneware, Monmouth, Ill, and
2" on front, blue tall leaves on re-
verse... 50.00
10½" h, blue leaf and "Western
Stoneware, Monmouth, Ill and 3"
on front, blue tall leaves on re-
verse... 50.00
13" h, cobalt flowers on reverse, 1
gallon 45.00
20½" h, blue "15 and Western
Stoneware" on front..................... 40.00
Jug
12" h, brown top, gray base, #1 ...... 17.00
14" h, brown top, gray base, #2 ...... 20.00
Brown top, #3 .... 85.00
Poultry Waterer, inverted gallon-jug
shape w/base 95.00

Jar, Cov, amber top, gray base, blue
label, 4 gallon size, c1915, $75.00

Water Fount, 14" h, cobalt maple leaf
with "Western Stoneware, Monmouth" and "5" at top, calla lilies
on front, metal spout, wire handles . 195.00
Miscellaneous
Mug, 4¾" h, tan ground, imp leaf and
"U.S.A." mark 5.50
Vase, 8" h, trumpet shape, leaves in
relief, green to white shaded glaze,
blue "Western Stoneware, Mon-
mouth, Ill" mark............................. 25.00

LA BELLE
CHINA

WHEELING POTTERY COMPANY
Wheeling, West Virginia
1879–1909

History: The Wheeling Pottery Company was
organized in 1879 in Wheeling, West Virginia, to
make plain and decorated white granite ware. In
1887 the management formed a second company called La Belle Pottery that made plain and
decorated Adamantine China and utilitarian
wares. Two years later the two companies joined
together.

In 1903 Wheeling Potteries Company was organized by combining Wheeling, La Belle, and
Riverside Pottery Company (all Wheeling, West
Virginia, firms) and Avon Potteries of Tiltonsville,
Ohio. Riverside made sanitary wares, Avon
made artwares, and each factory continued making semi-porcelain, sanitary ware, artware,
and/or utilitarian pieces. Products included Flow
Blue wares, tankards, Virginia Girl plates,
cracker jars, children's items, and a full line of
dinnerware. In 1909 the name was changed to
Wheeling Sanitary Manufacturing Company. The
company went into receivership and was reorganized to make sanitary ware.

A variety of marks was used.

Asparagus Tray, Flow Blue, "LaBelle"
mark 65.00
Banana Bowl, 13" l, Flow Blue 250.00
Biscuit Jar, Flow Blue......................... 295.00
Bowl
9" d, 2" h, Flow Blue...................... 125.00
10¼" d, center w/green grapes and
leaves, tab-shaped border w/gold
accents, "W.P LaBelle" mark 32.00
Butter Dish, Cov, Flow Blue, "LaBelle"
mark 250.00
Butter Pat, Flow Blue, "LaBelle" mark . 45.00
Cake Plate, 10" d, Flow Blue 120.00

Celery Tray, 13 1/2" l, Flow Blue........... **110.00**

Cereal Bowl, Flow Blue **95.00**

Charger

    12 7/8" d, Flow Blue **225.00**

    13" d, floral design **175.00**

    14 1/4" d, hp bust of young woman, cobalt border, "Wheeling Pottery" mark................................. **225.00**

Chocolate Pot, Flow Blue **800.00**

Chop Plate, 11 1/2" d, Flow Blue........... **135.00**

Creamer and Cov Sugar Bowl, Flow Blue **200.00**

Cup and Saucer, Flow Blue, "LaBelle" mark **55.00**

Gravy Boat, w/attached undertray, Flow Blue....................................... **195.00**

Pitcher

    6 1/4" h, Flow Blue, dolphin handle, "LaBelle" mark **235.00**

    6 1/2" h, floral design..................... **375.00**

    7 1/2" h, raised red flowers w/green leaves, sponged gold rim and handle, "Wheeling Pottery" mark **55.00**

Plate, Flow Blue

    6" d.. **45.00**

    8 3/4" d, molded design w/gold trim, "LaBelle" mark **80.00**

    9 1/2" d.. **95.00**

    10 1/4" d, multicolored bust of brunette woman, dark green border w/raised design, "LaBelle" mark **65.00**

Platter

    12" l, 8 3/4" w, Flow Blue.................. **150.00**

    14 5/8" l, 10 5/8" w, Flow Blue **325.00**

    17" l, 12 1/2" w, brown turkey transfer, Flow Blue border w/gold clover overlay, "LaBelle" mark **575.00**

    17 1/2" l, 14" w, floral design **375.00**

    18" l, Flow Blue, "LaBelle" mark..... **495.00**

Serving Bowl, 12" l, 9 1/2" w, Flow Blue, flower-shaped handles, gold tracery, "La Belle" mark **200.00**

Charger, 11 1/2" d, LaBelle pattern, Flow Blue, gold trim, "WP LaBelle" mark, $225.00

Syrup Pitcher, w/undertray, Flow Blue pattern, "LaBelle" mark **595.00**

Tray, 9 1/2" l, 8 1/2" w, Flow Blue **170.00**

Vegetable Bowl, Flow Blue

    9 1/2" l, 9" w **165.00**

    10" l, 7" w..................................... **125.00**

Vase, 17" h, iris and hibiscus design in colors, mkd **80.00**

Wash Set, pitcher, 11" h, bowl, 15" d, pitcher, 7" h, cov soap dish, 5 1/2" d, vase, 5 1/2" h, blue florals w/tan and green leaves, gilt trim, molded handles, scalloped rims, "Wheeling Pottery" mark **295.00**

WHITE'S POTTERY
Utica, New York
1834–1910

History: Noah White was the first in his family to make pottery in Utica, New York, in 1834. At first he made stoneware at Addington Pottery. In 1839 he bought out Addington and another factory and joined with Nicholas, his son, and two other potters and made wares marked "N. White."

Another son joined the company in 1843. The pottery had a variety of names as family members came and went. From 1850–1870 wares were marked "White Utica" or "White's Utica." Noah died in 1865 and additional name changes followed. From 1876–1882, the mark was "Whites, Utica, N.Y."

By 1907 stoneware production ended. White Pottery, Inc., was the last name used and that company closed in 1910.

Crock

    6 3/4" h, brushed cobalt leaf design, imp label "N.A. White & Son, Utica, N.Y.," hairlines(A) **192.00**

    7" h, cobalt slip bird looking backward, imp label "White's Utica," hairlines(A) **400.00**

    9" h

        Ovoid shape, cobalt slip bird on branch design, imp label "White's Utica," hairlines(A) **313.00**

    10 1/2" h, cobalt quill bird on branch, imp label "Whites Utica, N.Y. 3," glaze flakes(A) **330.00**

    11 1/4" h, dbl handles, cobalt painted bird on flower, imp "N.A. White & SON UTICA, N.Y. 4," salt glaze, c1870(A) **660.00**

    11 1/2" h, cobalt quill long-tailed bird

Crock, 9" h, cobalt flower, imp "N.A.
WHITE AND SON, UTICA, NEW YORK," 2 gal-
lon(A), $215.00

looking backward, imp "WHITES
UTICA"(A) 105.00
Jug
11½" h, ovoid shape, brushed blue
line design, imp label "N. White,
Utica"(A) 220.00
13" h, ovoid shape, blue runny ab-
stract flower, imp "N. WHITE.
UTICA," salt glaze, 3 gallon,
c1850(A) 253.00
13½" h, cobalt quill bird on branch,
imp "WHITES, UTICA 2," chips(A) 330.00
14" h, brushed cobalt flower design, imp "N.A. WHITE & SON,
UTICA, N.Y. 2"(A) 302.00
Cobalt stylized tree design, "N.
WHITE. UTICA," ¾ gallon 185.00
Whiskey Jug
11¾" h, blue painted fir tree, imp
"WHITES UTICA," salt glaze, 1 gal-
lon, c1890 .... 175.00
13¾" h, large blue dbl flower de-
sign, imp "WHITE'S BINGHAMPTON
2," salt glaze, chip on base,
c1870(A) 264.00

BELLEEK

WILLETS
1890s

OPAQUE

PORCELAIN
1884–c.1890

WILLETS MANUFACTURING COMPANY

Trenton, New Jersey
1879–1909

History: The three Willet brothers, Joseph,
Daniel, and Edmund, purchased the Excelsior

Pottery in Trenton, New Jersey, and changed its
name to Willets Manufacturing Company in
1879. The plant was enlarged several times since
a wide variety of wares was made, including sanitary, earthenware, opaque china, white granite,
white and decorated pottery, art porcelain, and
decorated dinner and toilet sets.

Walter Scott Lenox, formerly at Ott and
Brewer, became head of decorating at Willets in
1884. Willets began making hard porcelain in
1886, as suggested by Lenox, and when William
Bromley, Sr., came to Willets from Ott and
Brewer in 1887, he brought his formula for
Belleek porcelains.

Willet's Belleek, called Art Porcelaine, was
first made in 1887 and resembled its Irish forerunner. The Belleek examples at Willets were exceptionally graceful and delicate. A group of outstanding decorators designed woven baskets,
oval picture or mirror frames with tiny naturalistic flowers in high relief, and other fine pieces.
Each item was a unique, handmade work of art.
Most Belleek was marked.

Belleek production was suspended for a short
time in 1888 due to harsh economic times in the
United States. Lenox resigned, and the factory
was reorganized. In the early 1890s, Belleek production was resumed, but there was increasing
competition from other firms making American
Belleek. Willets also made porcelains with a variety of backgrounds, ormolu, and gilding.

In 1909 the company went into receivership
and was reorganized as the New Jersey Pottery
Company. The printed mark on Belleek porcelain was a twisted serpent with the word "WIL-
LETS" below or above. Many different red,
brown, black, blue, and green marks were used
on other products.

Reference: Mary Frank Gaston, *American
Belleek,* Collector Books, 1984.

Museums: Newark Museum, NJ; New Jersey
State Museum, Trenton, NJ.

A.D. Set, Belleek, coffeepot, creamer,
cov sugar bowl, 4 ftd cups, hp crest
of Princeton University, gold trim,
one cup damaged, c1889 .... 995.00
Bowl
3½" d, Belleek, overall gold and
blue flowers 35.00
5¼" d, Belleek, 3 toes, pearl luster
w/green and gold trim 42.00
7½" sq, Belleek, hp flowers and
berries 250.00
8¾" d, Belleek, ruffled, painted
roses, artist sgd 295.00
Chalice, 11" h, Belleek, monk smok-
ing cigar 650.00
Charger, 10½" d, Belleek, gold,
bronze, and enamel floral center,
scalloped rim 185.00
Chocolate Cup and Saucer, Belleek,

Humidor, 7" h, Belleek, med brown,
"Willets Belleek" mark, $290.00

gold "W" and trim, purple design,
gilt dragon handle 37.00
Clock, 13½" h, Belleek, hp flowers
and scrolls....................................... 650.00
Cream and Sugar, Belleek, silver over-
lay.. 250.00
Creamer, 3¾" h, Belleek, scalloped
body, gold rope-twist handle, gold-
paste flowers and leaves.................. 190.00
Cup and Saucer, A.D., groups of gar-
den flowers separated by radiating
brown branches 95.00
Mug, Belleek
3¾" h, band of cards, chips, dice,
pipes, and bottle w/snake, "Zeke"
on handle 195.00
5¾" h, Belleek, enamel bust of St.
Bernard dog, dragon handle,
"G.Y. Houghton"(A) 415.00
6" h, figural lizard handle, white 100.00
7" h, foliage design on upper sec-
tion, dark green lower section 175.00
Platter, 16½" l, blue-green Princess
pattern, Globe, "W.M.Co." and
"Princess" mark............................. 5.00
Salt, Belleek, gold enameled ext
w/blue flowers, white int................ 39.00
Sugar Bowl, Cov, 6¾" h, blue Rosalie
pattern 80.00
Tankard, 6" h, Belleek, design of peli-
can and trees at sunset, gilt dragon
handle.. 375.00
Tea Set, Belleek, pot, 4¼" h, creamer,
cov sugar bowl, flat cylinder shape,
wide wishbone handles, flared
knobs, white 325.00
Vase, Belleek
2¾" h, pearlized, blue stylized
flowers, gold trim 145.00
7" h, flattened ball shape w/rolled
rim, white water lilies w/yellow
centers and green stems, large
green pads, shaded green to tan
ground, snake mark 145.00

10" h,
Painted violets design, mkd 200.00
Roses and light green leaves, dark
green ground 275.00
13½" h, hp poppies design 285.00
14" h, tapered shape w/narrow
neck, painted flowers 325.00
15" h, lilacs design........................ 350.00

WINFIELD POTTERY
Pasadena, California
1929–1962

History: Winfield Pottery was originally
founded as a school and studio by Lesley Winfield Sample in Pasadena, California, in 1929.
Cast porcelain vases and bowls were made in
both opaque and transparent glazes in a variety
of colors.

Designer Margaret Gabriel created utilitarian
dinnerware pieces, including the first square-
shaped dinnerware in the United States in 1937.
Her hand-painted patterns included Bamboo in
1937, Tulip, Avocado, and Geranium in 1938,
and Citrus in 1939.

When Sample died in 1939, Margaret and
Arthur Gabriel took over Winfield, expanding
production and building a new factory. Additional dinnerware patterns were Yellow Flower,
Weed, Acorn, and Fallow. Tyrus Wong created
dinnerware patterns in the 1940s and 1950s and
also used oriental motifs on large plates. Other
artwares included glazed vases, low flower
bowls, candleholders, and planters.

In 1946 American Ceramic Products of Santa
Monica assisted with the tremendous backlog of
dinnerware orders that had built up during World
War II. "Winfield China" was used by the Santa
Monica firm on the expanded line, while Winfield Pottery used the trademark "Gabriel Porcelain."

A group of investors incorporated Winfield in
1947 after the Gabriels retired. In the mid 1950s
Douglas Gabriel became the sole owner. With
the influx of imported china, production slowed
down until the plant closed in 1962.

Winfield marks usually include an incised
shape number.

Reference: Jack Chipman, *Collector's Encyclopedia of California Pottery,* Collector Books,
1992.

BLUE BAMBOO PATTERN
Ashtray 3.00
Creamer.. 4.00

BLUE SPRUCE PATTERN
Bread and Butter Plate 3.00
Cup and Saucer 5.00
Dinner Plate 5.00
Salad Plate 4.00

DESERT DAWN PATTERN
Bread and Butter Plate 3.00
Butter Dish, Cov 17.00
Coffeepot 30.00
Cream and Sugar 20.00
Cup and Saucer 5.00
Dinner Plate 5.00
Salad Plate 3.00

GREEN BAMBOO PATTERN
Plate
  6" d, "Winfield" mark 4.00
  10½" d 6.00

TIGER IRIS PATTERN
Nappy, 5" d 3.00
Plate, 10½" d 6.00
Platter, 14" d 12.00

WILLOW PATTERN, BLUE GROUND
Bread and Butter Plate 5.00
Cup and Saucer 5.00

Dish, 10⅛" sq, turquoise w/brown splashed rim, imp "306 Pasadena" mark, $15.00

Dinner Plate 8.00
Salad Plate 5.00
MISCELLANEOUS
Plate, 7" d, Bird of Paradise design 10.00
Vase, 7" h, raised iris design, cobalt,
  dtd 1929 .... 195.00

UTILITARIAN WARE

The categories listed in this section are generic in nature. They include collectible objects made by any number of manufacturers (for example, cookie jars and railroad china) and are listed here by type rather than by company.

ACOMA

Marie
+
Sartano

AMERICAN INDIAN POTTERY
Arizona, Colorado, New Mexico, South Carolina
1600–Present

History: Areas in New Mexico and the southwestern United States have an uninterrupted history of pottery production, from the historic period of about 1600 until the present time.

Pottery was very important to the Pueblo Indians who made utilitarian pottery for cooking, storage, and gathering, and made other pieces for ceremonial and trading purposes. Bowls were made in a wide assortment of sizes, with the dough bowl being the largest. Jars also came in many sizes; the large storage jars were used for grain. Water jars, canteens, pitchers, and other pieces all served everyday needs, while ceremonial vessels and effigy figures were for special events.

No two pieces of pottery were alike and the Pueblos did not use a potter's wheel. The clay was rolled into ropes that were coiled to build up walls. Shaping and thinning was accomplished with a piece of gourd for a scraper. The body surface was rough and was usually covered with a fine red or white clay slip. Many decorations were black or dark colors that were made by adding powdered manganese or iron to the boiled juice of plants. Shaped and decorated pieces were set out on a sheet metal or rock framework and covered with slabs of dried cow dung or slow burning fuel which was then lit. The fire was smothered if the final pottery was supposed to be black. If not, the fire produced shades of cream, tan, red, orange, or yellow. Several hours were needed for firing.

For the most part, pottery was made by women, but some men worked on pots too. A variety of decorations was used including feathers, star patterns, floral motifs, volutes, clouds, circles, suns, and animals, to name a few. Each pueblo area used the ceramic materials that were available in its own group of villages. Each type of pottery had a two-part name signifying the form and decoration characterized by the geographical area of distribution and the time of manufacture. There were great varieties in types, sizes, colors, and designs from the various pottery areas.

By about 1900, pottery production was on the decline, except for ceremonial pieces and limited utilitarian items, because it was not necessary to make cooking and eating pieces that were available in the Anglo world. During the 20th century, there was a revival of pottery making and new types and styles were developed. The Pueblos did not repeat pottery styles from earlier periods. The specific area in which a piece was made can be determined by identifying the tempering material used. Each of the six pueblos used a particular temper (the neutral ingredient added to the clay).

Many pueblos incorporated the "ceremonial" line break in their pottery decorations, although there is not a definite reason for this break. Encircling black lines framed decorative motifs and a small interruption in the framing lines was called a break. Many forms of feather shapes were symbolic, such as round capped feathers, series of feathers, and split feathers. At different times and in different areas, black or red rims were used.

In the northern Tewa pueblos of Picuris and Taos, pottery was mostly utilitarian in nature. The other northern pueblos of San Juan and Santa Clara made unpainted red and black wares. In about 1850 Santa Clara used a sculpted bear paw trademark on jars in sets of three or more. They also made the wedding vase which was a double-spouted jar with connecting handles.

The southern Tewa villages specialized in

painted pottery. The most famous of these areas is the San Ildefonso pueblo. From 1760–1880 the standard style on large simple storage jars was Powhoge Polychrome—black-painted geometric motifs on cream slip. Water jugs were more common than bowls. For a time pottery making declined, but the coming of the railroad revitalized the tourist trade about 1880. San Ildefonso Polychrome and other attractive red-and-black decorated pottery was made in response to the renewed interest.

Maria Martinez and Julian, her husband, became famous in 1918 for their black wares. They were very prolific and their popular pieces had a deep glossy black background with matte-black decorations, often a stylized feather design. They also made polychrome pieces as a result of Julian's experimentation with colors.

Other southern villages included Tesuque pueblo, where pottery was made until c1910, and Nambe pueblo where painted pottery was produced. In the northeast Keres pueblos, the Cochiti used ceremonial symbols on its pottery, and the Santo Domingo used naturalistic decorations. There were six pueblos in the central area: Zia, Santa Ana, Jemez, San Felipe, Isleta, and Sandia—all making an assortment of pottery.

The Acoma, Laguna, and Zuni were the only potters who tempered clay with finely crushed shards of pottery. Nearly every broken pottery piece was saved by these New Mexican pueblos for re-use in this way. Red banding was not used on Acoma or Laguna pottery. In 1850 McCarthys Polychrome had bird and floral motifs, while Acoma Polychrome, from the turn of the century, had geometric decorations. Laguna Polychrome decorations mostly followed Acoma traditions, but were less intricate and bolder. Zuni Polychrome, made from about 1850, had sunflowers, deer with a red arrow from the mouth to the heart, birds, and butterflies.

The Hopi villages in Arizona made pottery that was different from that of the Pueblos. Hopi pieces were yellow with mottled orange tones, had motifs that were painted on a polished paste rather than slip, and had flat or convex bases. A new school of pottery started by Nampeyo and her family about 1900 (and still in existence) revived the ancient Sikyatki polychrome style. The Hopi still make pottery for their own use, as well as to sell.

North American Indians did not use a potter's wheel to make their wares. They used a paddle and anvil to thin and compress coils or used the tools to form pieces without coils. Some northern Plains Indians also used this method. In addition, pieces were modeled or molded in a basket.

The Catawba Indians from Rock Hill, South Carolina, were the most active pottery makers of the eastern tribes. They made tablewares, vases, pitchers, and flowerpots with non-characteristic designs and forms and sold the wares to support themselves in the 1900s. They used the coil method and open pit firing and their blackwares were similar to those made by the San Ildefonso pueblo.

Several tribes comprise the Colorado River Division of the Yuman group. Early Yuman pottery had less decoration than the Pueblo wares. Mojave made painted wares with the paddle and anvil coil method.

References: John W. Barry, *American Indian Pottery,* Books Americana, Revised Edition, 1984; Kenneth M. Chapman, *The Pottery of Santo Domingo Pueblo,* University of New Mexico Press, 1977; ———, *The Pottery of San Ildefonso Pueblo,* University of New Mexico Press, 1970; Rick Dillingham, *Acoma and Laguna Pottery,* School of American Research Press, 1993; Larry Frank and Francis H. Harlow, *Historic Pottery of the Pueblo Indians 1600–1880,* Schiffer Publishing, Ltd., 1990; Betty LeFree, *Santa Clara Pottery Today,* University of New Mexico Press, 1975; Susan Peterson, *Maria Martinez, Five Generations of Potters,* Smithsonian Institution Press, 1978.

Museums: Arizona State Museum, Tucson, AZ; Denver Art Museum, CO; El Pueblo Museum, Pueblo, CO; Heard Museum of Primitive Art and Anthropology, Phoenix, AZ; Koshare Indian Museum, La Junta, CO; Milwaukee Public Museum, WI; Museum of the American Indian, Heye Foundation, New York, NY; Museum of New Mexico, Santa Fe, NM; National Museum of the American Indian, Smithsonian Institution, Washington, DC; San Diego Museum of Man, CA; Southwest Museum, Los Angeles, CA; University of Arizona Museum of Art, Tucson, AZ.

NORTHWEST
Pipe, 3¼" h, 7" l, Argillite panel, rect form, pierced and incised totem designs, Haida(A) **1430.00**

PLAINS AND SOUTHEASTERN
Bowl
   3" h, frog effigy, reddish wash, Arkansas mounds, c1800 .... **650.00**
   10" d, fish effigy, red wash, Mississippian **625.00**
Cooking Vessel, 5" h, Ohio burial ground(A) **75.00**
Jar, 4½" h, 5½" d, globular shape, effigy, 2 lizards on shoulder, Mississippian(A) **192.00**
Pitcher, 7" h, 7" d, effigy, figural dog handle, black diamonds on white, c1100, Colorado **1500.00**
Pot
   3⅛" h, 5½" H-H, 2 small branch handles, brown-gray clay, Mississippian **325.00**
   3¾" h, 5¼" d, 4 small ring handles for rope on rim, brown-gray clay, Mississippian **375.00**

Bowl, 10″ d, 6½″ h, Plains and South-eastern, cat serpent effigy, red wash on yellow clay, Chickasawba site, Mico County, Arkansas, c900–1100AD, $625.00

5¾″ h, bulbous body, flared top, gray clay, Mississippian **250.00**

6¾″ h, bulbous body, gray clay, Mississippian **285.00**

7¼″ h, bulbous body, cylinder neck, reddish circ designs **125.00**

Water Bottle, 8″ h, gray clay, Mississippian **475.00**

SOUTHWESTERN

Bowl

5¾″ d, 6″ h, black geometric design on cream slip ground, red-brown base, Jemez(A) **72.00**

6″ d, red and brown birds on tan ground, Hopi(A) **150.00**

7½″ d, 2½″ h, orange and brown kachina on int, polished light yellow ground, ext lug, Hopi(A) **1650.00**

9¼″ d, 4″ h, black-outlined crosses, gray-ivory slip on red clay body, red-painted flat base and int, restored, Santa Ana(A) **330.00**

9½″ d, 4½″ h, black geometric design on cream, red slip bottom, central starburst int, Santo Domingo(A) **660.00**

10½″ d, carved thunderbirds on int, sgd "Juanita Wo-een," Pueblo(A) . **302.00**

12″ d, 2½″ h, in-curved rim, dark umber design outlined in white on polished orange slip ground, frog mark, holes in rim, Hopi(A) .. **770.00**

16½″ d, int w/black designs of conc circles, triangles, blocks, and "hand" device, ext w/3 black linear bands, triangles, lines and dots, clay slip ground on bisque body, vert crack and chips, early 14th C(A) **3850.00**

Candlestick, 5¼″ h, carved redware, Santa Clara, pr **250.00**

Canteen

5⅛″ h, umber bird design, Acoma(A) **35.00**

7″ h, black turtle on polished red ground, lug restored, Maricopa(A) **220.00**

8″ d, brown geometric design w/red slip on white ground, twisted handles, Pueblo(A) **202.00**

Compote, 5″ d, black swirls on red ground, Maricopa(A) **206.00**

Cup

4½″ h, figural moccasin, red and brown geometric slip design, Pueblo(A) **90.00**

5″ h, figural human head and torso w/painted features, Pueblo(A) **85.00**

Dough Bowl, 14½″ d, 6½″ h, black teardrops, brown and brick red circles and slashes, dark brick red int, c1900, Zia **4350.00**

Figure, 10¼″ h, hollow body of standing man w/hat, hands on hips, incised features, red clay w/black and red accents on cream slip ground, Zuni(A).. **880.00**

Jar

3⅝″ h, 4½″ d, blackware, gunmetal sheen w/feather design, sgd "Marie & Sartano"(A) **522.00**

4¾″ h, 8⅜″ d, squat-shoulder shape, red ochre and umber geometric design on creamy orange slip, ear of corn mark, Hopi(A) **220.00**

5¼″ h, 9″ d, dark brown and red stylized checkered geometrics and butterflies, yellow-orange painted ground, sgd "Grace Chapella," Hopi(A) **357.00**

5½″ h, 7½″ d, blackware, matte black painted frieze of winged geometric devices on shoulder, sgd "Marie and Julian," San Ildefonso(A) **1760.00**

5⅞″ h, matte black water serpent, "Avanyu" on shoulder, black polished body, inscribed "Anna," San Ildefonso(A) **550.00**

6½″ h, 8″ d, black leaf and triangle design w/spirit line on buff, red base, Santo Domingo(A) **288.00**

6¾″ h, 4″ d, cylinder shape, brick red, tan, and black geometrics, Hopi... **465.00**

7″ h

9½″ d, black Gila monsters and etched geometric design on black ground, sgd "Olivia Lopez Quezada," Pueblo(A)..... **330.00**

Flat base, cream-white slip on white clay body, 4 relief-modeled frogs, black and red-orange accents, rim cracks, Zuni(A) **770.00**

7¼″ h, ivory slip on white clay body, red and black painted

Jar, 9" h, 9" d, Southwestern, poly-chromed, Trios/Zia, c1880, $5600.00

Jar, 10½" h, Southwestern, polychrome heart line deer and geometrics, "W. Garcia Acoma, New Mexico" mark(A), $165.00

crosshatched scrolls and geometrics and 3 "heart-line" deer, crack in base, Zuni(A) **1450.00**

7⅜" h, 8¾" d, black design on cream-buff slip over red slip bottom, Santo Domingo(A) **302.00**

9" h, indented base, cream slip w/red and black swagged and banded decoration, San Ildefonso(A) **1430.00**

9⅛" h, 12½" d, umber geometric design w/red ochre on white slip, band break, bottle bottom, late 19th C, Zia(A) **2580.00**

9¼" h, ivory slip on red clay body, black and red painted bisected and scrolled foliate devices, red banded base and inner lip, indented base, slip wear, Zia(A) **935.00**

9½" h

6" d, cylinder shape, brick red leaping fish, black geometrics, light brown smear ground, Hopi **850.00**

10" d, red ochre and black geometric on cream slip, redware bottle bottom w/red stripe, San Ildefonso(A) **1400.00**

10" h

Black body, claw handles, Santa Clara(A) **52.00**

Umber and red ochre thunderbird design on creamy orange slip, ear of corn mark, Hopi, pr(A) ... **585.00**

10½" h, 8" d, black leaf design on cream, age lines, Santo Domingo(A)............................... **357.00**

11" h, 11" d, black, carved rain serpent design on upper half, Santa Clara(A) **385.00**

11¼" h

Black-painted tree and ovals on cream slip ground on red clay body, brick red base and inner lip, Santo Domingo(A) **2460.00**

Flared form w/indented base, black hatched, checkered, and stepped geometric design w/bats on white slip ground, white clay body, Acoma(A) **6050.00**

11½" h, tan clay w/red slip eagle, crosses, rain, and geometric designs, back handle, Pueblo(A) **275.00**

21" h, 22½" d, blackware, flat base, indented bear paw, Santa Clara Pueblo(A) **7700.00**

23¾" h, 3 bands of stylized and scrolling forms, terra-cotta and black on beige ground, Pueblo **2800.00**

Olla

9" d, 9" h, polychrome, black birds, orange band on base, off-white ground, c1900, Cochiti............... **2350.00**

9½" h, indented base, red, black, and orange arched panels w/floral motifs and bird figure, pink slip ground on red clay, Zia(A) **2310.00**

10" d, 12" h, dark red-brown trim, striated white-gray ground, c1890, Zuni................................. **6400.00**

11" d, 10" h, red and brown polychrome geometric design, scalloped rim, Acoma Pueblo(A) **1850.00**

11½" d, 11" h, brick red flowers, black stems and leaves, black zigzags, striated black and white ground, c1890, Zia...................... **4850.00**

13" d, 11" h, orange zigzags, black geometrics, streaked white ground, c1910, Acoma/Laguna.... **3750.00**

Pitcher, 5¾" h, black-outlined brick red open flower under lip, black leaves, tan ground, Pueblo **45.00**

Plate

4½" d, black feather design on black, sgd "Marie and Julian," San Ildefonso(A) **110.00**

Olla, 11" h, Southwestern, black and burnt orange on cream slip, San Ildefonso, unmkd(A), $1210.00

Pot, 6¹/₂" h, Southwestern, black polished carved geometrics, Legoria Tafoya, "Ste. Clara Pueblo" mark(A), $275.00

Pitcher, 7¹/₂" h, Southwestern, black birds w/stylized flowers on cream slip, Santo Domingo(A), $200.00

10¹/₄" d, matte black geometric design on black gloss ground, inscribed "Susana," San Ildefonso(A) 302.00

11" d, doe and fawns, red, sgd "Reycita," Santa Clara(A) 206.00

12¹/₂" d, water serpent, Avanyu design, Santa Clara(A) 110.00

Pot, 6" h, 6" d, handled, natural clay w/cream slip ground, red and brown slip deer and heart-line design, Pueblo(A) 387.00

Seed Jar

9¹/₄" d, 4¹/₂" h, black lightning scroll motif in 4 sections, orange ground, Hopi(A) 440.00

10" d, dark red and brown conc swagged devices, pointed brown band on neck, light orange clay body, Hopi(A).............................. 522.00

Vase

9¹/₂" h, prayer feather design, Hopi(A) 275.00

14" h, 8" d, cylinder shape, poly-

chrome red and dark brown stylized bird and faces on tan ground, flying ant mark on base, Hopi(A) 1100.00

Water Jar

6¹/₂" h, 7³/₄" d, red, ochre, and umber bird and floral design on polished white slip ground, 4-lobed concave base, Acoma, c1900(A) 685.00

9³/₄" h, 12" d, ochre and umber geometrics and lines on creamy tan slip ground, wide base band, concave bottle bottom, late 19th C(A)... 1100.00

10¹/₈" h, 11" d, umber, dark and light ochre swirled geometrics on white slip body, concave base, Acoma, 1900(A) 8580.00

11" h, 11¹/₂" d, dark and light ochre and umber flowers and geometrics on white slip ground, concave bottle base, c1900(A) 3120.00

Wedding Jar, 6¹/₄" h, dbl spout, umber and red ochre avian design on cream slip, hairline, Acoma(A) 85.00

CHILDREN'S WARE
c1850–1950s

History: Numerous American manufacturers made miniature versions of their products for children to use in play. Dishes to use for feeding babies also were made.

Manufacturers decorated pieces with animal themes, nursery rhymes, fairy tales, children's activities, and the artwork of famous illustrators such as Kate Greenaway. Knowles, Taylor, and Knowles, East Liverpool China, Buffalo Pottery, Florence Cook Pottery, Harker, Homer Laughlin, Canonsburg, Salem China, Southern Potteries, Warwick, Smith Phillips, and Roseville were some of the makers. There were also many unmarked sets.

American production of children's ware reached a peak during World War II before the less-costly Japanese imports became available. After the war, production declined, and many of the firms went out of business.

References: Doris Lechler, *Children's Glass Dishes, China, and Furniture,* Collector Books, 1983 values, Volume II 1986, updated 1991; Lorraine May Punchard, *Child's Play,* published by author, 1982; Margaret and Kenn Whitmyer, *Collector's Encyclopedia of Children's Dishes: An Illustrated Value Guide,* Collector Books, 1993.

Collectors' Clubs: Children's Things Collectors Society, Linda Martin, P.O. Box 983, Durant, IA 52747, CTCS Newsletter; Toy Dish Collectors Club, Anna Green, P.O. Box 92, Effort, PA 18330, $25 for quarterly newsletter.

Newsletter: *The Tiny Times,* Abbie Kelly, P.O. Box 351, Camillus, NY 13031.

Museum: Margaret Woodbury Strong Museum, Rochester, NY

Creamer, 3⅝" h, yellow chicks, green band, black striping, cream ground, Roseville, $115.00

Bowl
    6" d, multicolored decal of Dutch boy in cart pulled by hobbyhorse on int, ext w/multicolored Dutch children, tan ground, Syracuse mark **28.00**
    7½" d, Campbell Kids, Buffalo Pottery **65.00**
Cereal Bowl
    5½" d, standing rabbit, Roseville..... **90.00**
    6" d, sitting puppy, Roseville **50.00**
Creamer
    3" h, side pour, chicks on center band, Roseville **115.00**
    3½" h
        Little girl w/bonnet, Roseville **135.00**
        Sitting puppy, Roseville **95.00**
        Splashing duck decal, Zona, Weller.................................... **155.00**
        Standing rabbit pattern, Roseville(A)............................. **50.00**
Cup
    Bo Peep's lamb, Stangl Kiddieware . **55.00**
    Old Mother Hubbard's Cupboard, Stangl Kiddieware...................... **26.00**
Cup and Saucer
    2" h, 5" d, band of rabbit's heads, #7, Roseville............................... **179.00**
    Roosevelt Bear, hairline, "Buffalo Pottery" mark **225.00**

Dish, 3 sections
    7½" d, each section w/child and calico animal, yellow ground, Crown Pottery **30.00**
    9¾" d, decal of Little Miss Muffet, Shenango China **35.00**
    10¼" l
        Kitten Capers, Stangl Kiddieware . **35.00**
        Mealtime Special, Stangl Kiddieware.................................. **40.00**
    Multicolored decal of children in each section, ABC rim, 24K gold trim, "Salem China" mark **16.00**
Eggcup, 3½" h, standing rabbit pattern, Roseville **50.00**
Juvenile Dish
    6" d, decal of horse and puppies in center, rolled gold geometric border, D.E. McNicol **55.00**
    6½" d, green and orange standing rabbits, Roseville(A).................... **50.00**
    7¾" d
        Decal of Baby Bunting on log in center, cats and children in background, rolled rim w/gold "BABY'S PLATE," and "KUNZMANN-ESSER, HOUSE FURNISHER," Trenle Pottery mark **98.00**

Feeding Dish, 10¼" l, Our Barnyard Friends, multicolored Stangl Kiddieware, $50.00

Campbell Kids, c1913, Buffalo Pottery 70.00

8" d

Decal of "Baby Bunting Takes a Hoe" in center, gold overlay border, "D.E. McNicol" mark... 60.00

Ducks, Roseville 80.00

Multicolored decal of irises in center, rolled edge w/blue alphabet, "D.E. McNicol" mark .. 55.00

Nursery rhyme decal, Roseville ... 125.00

Standing rabbits on border, Roseville 125.00

9¼" H-H, decal of girl seated on stool feeding teddy bear in high chair, "I Go Here Says the Fork" and "I Go Here Says the Spoon" on each handle, "My Own Plate, Division of International Silver Co., Homer Laughlin" mark........ 45.00

Figural clown w/mug, blue, Hankscraft 75.00

Plate

6" d, multicolored decal of Little Bo Peep, "Souvenir of Groton, N.Y.," semi-vitreous porcelain, Knowles, Taylor, and Knowles 26.00

7" d, decal of black cow jumping over moon, red dish and gold spoon, red rim, "Salem China" mark...................................... 20.00

7½" d, Rabbit pattern, med blue, Dedham(A) 413.00

8" d, decal of children w/geese, Roseville 135.00

8¼" d, decals of children, lamb, and chicken, Buffalo Pottery 65.00

Tea Service

11 piece, teapot, cov sugar bowl, creamer, 4 tea plates, 4 cups and saucers

Blue Delft-type transfers on white

Tea Service, 11-piece, pot, creamer, sugar bowl, 4 cups and saucers, 4 cake plates, blue transfers, white ground, "Semi-Vitreous Edwin M. Knowles, China, Made in U-SA 43-8" mark, $145.00

ground, "E.L.P. Co. China" mark 225.00

Violets and butterflies, emb designs, eagle and "Columbia" mark 255.00

12 piece

Teapot, cov sugar bowl, creamer, 4 tea plates, 4 cups and saucers, oval cake tray w/handles, Sunday Best pattern, bands of roses, Edwin Knowles, c1910 .... 145.00

Teapot, cov sugar bowl, creamer, waste bowl, 4 tea plates, 4 cups and saucers, small blue flowers, c1890, Knowles, Taylor, and Knowles 225.00

Tureen, w/ladle, oct shape, branch handles, grape finial, white ironstone, Red Cliff.............................. 65.00

CHINA CO.
HAND DECORATED
22 KT. GOLD
U.S.A.

COOKIE JARS
1920s–Present

History: Ceramic cookie jars, usually made of earthenware, were manufactured by a tremendous number of potteries from the 1920s until the present time, though the peak production years were from the 1940s to the 1970s. Nelson McCoy from Roseville, Ohio, and American Bisque Company from Williamstown, West Virginia, were the two biggest cookie jar producers.

There were five primary methods of decoration: glaze, paint, glaze and paint combination, glaze and transfer combination, and a mixture of all three elements. The glaze finish, whether matte or glossy, was the most durable. Cold-paint decoration—painting that was not fired—deteriorated easily since it was either applied directly to the bisque body or on top of the glaze. Transfers were fired-on decals applied over the glaze, and these also could be damaged by frequent use.

By the late 1930s, McCoy made over three hundred varieties of cookie jars. The first jars were a plain bean-pot shape and in 1939 the first figural Mammy with cauliflowers was introduced. McCoy jars were characterized by very detailed mold features, hand-painted details on top of the glaze, the use of decals, frequent use of fruit and vegetable designs, and a canister shape. Most of the company's cookie jars were marked.

American Bisque was second to McCoy in the numbers of jars made from 1937–1973. Important examples included the Flintstone group, Olive Oyl, and Popeye. American Bisque jars also showed a lot of molded and decorated details. Most were glazed by air brushing, very few solid-color jars were made, and jars frequently had a wedge on the bottom to aid in firing. Most pieces were marked "U.S.A.," and sometimes a number was included. Paper labels also were used.

The Abingdon Pottery Company from Abingdon, Illinois, made twenty-two designs from 1939–1950—the first was Little Old Lady, both in solid colors and with decorations. The company used an ink-stamped "Abingdon USA" mark, plus an impressed serial number.

Don and Russ Winton made many cookie jars for Brush Pottery Company of Roseville, Ohio. The first ones were made of stoneware and were decorated with simple leaves and flowers. From the mid 1940s until 1971 they designed jars shaped like people, animals, fruits, and vegetables.

California Originals, a Torrance firm, made animal-shaped cookie jars and was licensed by Walt Disney, Walter Lantz, DC Comics, Muppets, and other such companies to produce character cookie jars.

Hall China Company from East Liverpool, Ohio, made mostly canister-shaped jars as accessories to its dinnerware and kitchen utility lines. Eva Ziesel designed some of the jars and hers were marked "Hall's Superior Quality Kitchen Ware Made in USA." That backstamp was one of the many marks the company used on its cookie jars.

The Hull Pottery Company of Crooksville, Ohio, is best known for Little Red Riding Hood objects. Though Hull owned the patent rights as of 1943, much of the Red Riding Hood collection was made by Regal China of Antioch, Illinois. In addition to cookie jars, there were spice jars, sugar bowls, creamers, match safes, salt and pepper shakers, planters, mugs, canisters, butter dishes, teapots, cracker jars, and milk pitchers. Sometimes Little Red Riding Hood's basket is open, on other products it is closed. Most pieces have impressed, ink-stamped, or a gold stamped mark.

Metlox Potteries from Manhattan Beach, California, made a wide assortment of cookie jars from 1947 until 1989. Many were made under the name "Poppytrail of California." From 1939–1944 designer Rudy Gantz made Smiley Pig, Winnie Pig, Sailor Boy, Jack and Jill, and

other such cookie jars for Shawnee Pottery Company of Zanesville, Ohio. Shawnee molds were bought by Terrace Ceramics in 1961 and then McNicol China Company of Clarksburg, West Virginia, used them. From 1935–1975 Robinson-Ransbottom Pottery Company of Roseville, Ohio, made cookie jars similar to those being made by American Bisque. Twin Winton of Pasadena, California, made cookie jars with a wood-tone matte glaze finish in 1951. After moving to San Juan Capistrano in 1964, the company made an eighteen-jar Collectors' Series consisting of an owl, Raggedy Ann, Andy, donkey, etc. In 1977, the business, including the molds, was sold to Treasure Craft. Now located in Compton, California, and owned by Pfaltzgraff Pottery Company since 1988, Treasure Craft is one of the American potteries still making large quantities of cookie jars.

The numerous other companies that made cookie jars include Bauer, California Cleminsons, DeForest, Fredericksburg Art Pottery Company, Frankoma, Gladding, McBean and Company, Haeger Potteries, Inc., Pearl China Company, Pennsbury Pottery, Pfaltzgraff Pottery, Purinton Pottery Company, Red Wing Pottery, and Cronin China Company, to name a few.

Advertising cookie jars were used to promote products and were sometimes offered as premiums or made under license to publicize certain logos. Many decorating companies bought bisque cookie jars from potteries and then applied glaze, paint, transfers, or combinations of these decorating methods. The jars were sold through individual marketing departments or through a distributor.

Black Americana cookie jars are highly collectible today. Brayton Laguna Pottery Company, Pearl China, Mosaic Tile Company, and Fielder and Fielder all made mammys. Studio artists designed cookie jar series, such as Carol Gifford's Watermelon Mammy. Rick Wisecarver made thirty-two molds from 1983–1991 in Roseville, Ohio, using black and country themes. These were all signed on the back.

References: Harold Nichols, *McCoy Cookie Jars: From The First To The Latest,* Nichols Publishing, 1987; Fred and Joyce Herndon Roerig, *Collector's Encyclopedia of Cookie Jars,* Collector Books, 1991; ———, *Collector's Encyclopedia of Cookie Jars, Book Two,* Collector Books, 1993; Mike Schneider, *The Complete Cookie Jar Book,* Schiffer Publishing, 1991; Ermagene Westfall, *An Illustrated Value Guide to Cookie Jars,* Collector Books, 1983; ———, *An Illustrated Value Guide to Cookie Jars, Book II,* Collector Books, 1993.

Newsletters: *Cookie Jarrin,* Joyce Roerig, editor, R.R. Box 504, Walterboro, SC 29488, $19.95, bimonthly; *Crazed Over Cookie Jars,* Maureen Saxby, P.O. Box 254, Savanna, IL 61074.

Museum: The Cookie Jar Museum, Lemont, IL.

ABINGDON

Clock, green trim	150.00
Cookie Girl w/braids	95.00
Hobbyhorse	250.00
Humpty Dumpty	300.00
Jack-in-the-Box	750.00
Jack-O'-Lantern	265.00
Lil' Old Lady	
Green glaze	135.00
White glaze	235.00
Little Miss Muffet	375.00
Money Sack	65.00
Pineapple	75.00
Train Engine	125.00
Wigwam	950.00
Windmill	425.00

AMERICAN BISQUE

After School Cookies	45.00
Bear w/indented spots	59.00
Blackboard Hobo	275.00
Boots	115.00
Boy Pig	70.00
Casper the Ghost(A)	715.00
Cat in basket	35.00
Cat on beehive	35.00
Cheerleader, w/flasher	275.00
Chick w/blue-checkered vest	50.00
Churn Boy	80.00
Coffeepot	40.00
Cookie Truck, yellow lid	85.00
Davy Crockett in woods	850.00
Deer in forest	100.00
Dino	1450.00
Dutch Girl	45.00
Elephant w/baseball cap, yellow	125.00
Fred Flintstone, Dino, golf bag and flag on lid(A)	1210.00
Granny	80.00
Kittens w/yarn	55.00
Liberty Bell	50.00
Olive Oyl(A)	1400.00
Paddle Boat	295.00
Pig	
Patch	65.00
Straw hat	79.00
Pinky Lee	595.00
Polka Dot Mammy	1560.00
Poodle, maroon and black	98.00
Popeye	725.00
Rubble House	1200.00
Seal on igloo	180.00
Sandman Cookies, w/flasher(A)	225.00
Sea Bag	175.00
Sailor Elephant	95.00
Schoolhouse w/bell	70.00
Spaceship(A)	200.00
Squirrel w/top hat	150.00
Swee' Pea(A)	4000.00
Toothache Dog	725.00

Tortoise and Hare, w/flasher	850.00
Tugboat	225.00
Umbrella Kids	350.00
Wilma on telephone	1500.00
Yarn Doll	80.00
Yogi Bear	325.00

BAUER

Hp Dutch boy and girl, flowers and strawberries, "Sugar 'N Spice 'N Everything Nice," wood lid	200.00
Ring-ware, yellow	95.00

BRAYTON LAGUNA

Fish	825.00
Grandma w/bonnet	725.00
Gypsy Woman	
Floral top	645.00
Plaid top	645.00
Mammy, yellow	1250.00
Matilda	450.00
Plaid Dog	400.00
Provincial Woman	1395.00
Yellow Plaid Pig	595.00

BRUSH

Angel	975.00
Bear, brown	125.00
Circus Horse	
Brown and green	1245.00
Green, brown, and white	995.00
White, pink, and blue	775.00
Cow, purple	1425.00
Davy Crockett(A)	225.00
Elephant w/ice cream cone(A)	350.00
Formal Pig	135.00
Granny	
Green dress	450.00
Polka dot dress	450.00
Happy Squirrel	170.00
Harpo Marx	1150.00
Humpty Dumpty w/beanie	275.00
Little Boy Blue(A)	900.00
Little Red Riding Hood(A)	1050.00
Owl, yellow	135.00
Panda, black and white	395.00
Pumpkin w/lock on door	325.00
Puppy Police	750.00
Sitting Pig	495.00
Squirrel on log	65.00
Stylized	
Cat(A)	425.00
Owl	415.00
Teddy Bear, feet together	200.00

CALIFORNIA ORIGINALS

Big Bird	75.00
Cookie Monster	65.00
Elf Schoolhouse	69.00
Humpty Dumpty	125.00
Koala Bear	205.00
Mickey Mouse on drum	195.00
Oscar the Grouch	125.00
Pillsbury Doughboy	45.00
Platypus Duck	175.00

Santa Claus	525.00
Superman	350.00
Tortoise and Hare	35.00
Winnie the Pooh	125.00
Wonder Woman, brown tones	475.00
Woody Woodpecker	450.00

CROOKSVILLE

Taverne pattern	40.00

DEFOREST

Fortune Cookies	75.00
Halo Boy(A)	825.00
Nun	350.00
Sailor Monkey, yellow hat	225.00

DORANNE OF CALIFORNIA

Cat w/bow tie, tan	65.00
Cow Over Moon, green	175.00
Cupcake	40.00
Graduate Owl	79.00
Lunch Box, blue	60.00
Seal	50.00
Shaggy Dog, brown	40.00

ENESCO

Betsy Ross	165.00
Betty Boop	395.00
Cinderella	250.00
Garfield Cat	65.00
Mickey Mouse w/leather ears	375.00
Snow White	775.00

FITZ AND FLOYD

Aunt Jemima	300.00
Bunny Hollow	100.00
Catherine the Great	110.00
Cookie Factory	115.00
Domesticat	100.00
Haunted House	125.00
Hermoine Heifer	100.00
Keebler's Elf	235.00
Mother Rabbit	100.00
Pig and scarf	40.00
Polka Dot Witch	300.00
Prunella Pig	100.00
Queen of Hearts	130.00
Santa Claus	125.00

GLADDING, MCBEAN, FRANCISCAN

Apple pattern	175.00

GONDER

Pirate	1495.00

HALL

Blue Blossom, banded	225.00
Clover pattern	85.00
Jewel Tea(A)	125.00

HARKER

Cameoware, pink	45.00

HULL

Apple	25.00
Barefoot Boy(A)	190.00
Bouquet pattern	120.00
Gingerbread Boy	
Gray	85.00
White	125.00

Little Red Riding Hood	
Closed basket	230.00
Open basket	240.00
W/gold stars on apron	375.00

LANE

Cowboy	795.00
Indian	1195.00

MADDUX

Humpty Dumpty	225.00

MCCOY

Animal Crackers(A)	35.00
Asparagus	30.00
Banana	129.00
Barn, pink	350.00
Baseball Boy	195.00
Bean Pot	25.00
Bear	35.00
Bear and Beehive	45.00
Bobbie Baker	35.00
Caboose	165.00
Cauliflower Mammy	950.00
Christmas Tree(A)	500.00
Circus Horse	240.00
Coffee Grinder	20.00
Coke Can	48.00
Coalby Cat	350.00
Cookie Cabin Bank	78.00
Cookie Wagon	75.00
Cookstove	
Black	35.00
White	25.00
Duck on basket	42.00
Engine	165.00
Davy Crockett	550.00
Drum	45.00
Ear of Corn	185.00
Elephant	
Split trunk	275.00
Whole trunk	150.00
Football Boy	195.00
Freddie Gleep, green	650.00
Frontier Family	25.00

Clown bust, McCoy, red, blue, and green, white body, $55.00

*Indian Chief, McCoy, dark brown,
"McCoy USA" mark(A), $150.00*

Hamm's Bear	200.00
Honey Bear	54.00
Honeycomb	30.00
Kangaroo, blue(A)	200.00
Keebler Tree House	48.00
Leprechaun, red	2300.00
Lunch Box	30.00
Mack Dog	55.00
Mammy	
Aqua dress	650.00
Brown dress	250.00
White dress	125.00
Mother Goose	90.00
Nabisco Barnum's Animals	295.00
Picnic Basket	43.00
Potato Basket	35.00
Puppy w/sign	50.00
Raggedy Ann	85.00
Sad Clown	75.00
Silver Treasure Chest	90.00
Smiley Face	18.00
Snoopy on doghouse	245.00
Stagecoach	1000.00
Tepee	300.00
Teddy and friend w/box	40.00
Thinking Puppy	25.00
Touring Car	78.00
Traffic Light	40.00
Turkey	225.00
W.C. Fields	145.00
Winking Pig	350.00
Wishing Well	25.00
World Globe, cold paint(A)	325.00
Wren House	115.00

METLOX

Bear	50.00
Cabbage and Rabbit	65.00
Chicken	55.00
Cookie Bear	445.00
Cow, purple, white and yellow flowers, butterfly	750.00
Fido Dog	75.00

Francine Duck	75.00
Lion	180.00
Mammy w/yellow trim(A)	700.00
Mouse	75.00
Penguin	55.00
Pineapple	75.00
Pretty Ann	65.00
Puddles	65.00
Raccoon	100.00
Raggedy Andy	100.00
Raggedy Ann	125.00
Roller Bear	80.00
Sir Francis Drake	35.00
Slenderella Pig	75.00
Squirrel on pinecone	65.00
Topsey, blue and white polka dots	395.00

MISCELLANEOUS

Angel Cook(A)	400.00
Cinderella, blond hair	295.00
Corn, Terrace Ceramics	65.00
Home Sweet Home, Clay Art	45.00
Indian Chief	195.00
Nestle's Tollhouse	85.00
Mr. Peanut	45.00
Pig figural, brown glaze, early 20th C(A)	308.00
Stagecoach, Sierra Vista(A)	250.00
Wizard of Oz, Clay Art	59.00

MOSAIC TILE

Mammy, yellow dress	595.00

MORTON

Ozark Hillbilly	65.00

NORTH DAKOTA SCHOOL OF MINES

Aunt Susan	5200.00
Duck	165.00
Farm animals	1200.00

PEARL CHINA

Chef	545.00
Mammy	89.00
Watermelon Mammy	7300.00

PENNSBURY

Harvest	160.00

*Woody Woodpecker, red, white, and
tan, $350.00*

PFALTZGRAFF

Cookie Cop	425.00
Derby Dan	275.00

POPPYTRAIL, METLOX

Asparagus	40.00
Cookie House	20.00

POTTERY GUILD

Apple, white irid	35.00
Dutch Boy	60.00
Dutch Girl	79.00
Elsie the Cow	265.00
Little Red Riding Hood	135.00
Tomato, white irid	45.00

PURINTON

Howdy Doody	350.00
Rooster	300.00

RED WING

Chef Pierre

Blue	95.00
Green	180.00
Speckled pink and black	165.00
Dutch Girl, blue	75.00
Jack Frost, short version	425.00
King of Tarts, turquoise	600.00

Monk

Beige	85.00
Blue	70.00
Green	140.00
Pineapple	79.00

REGAL

Churn Boy	295.00
Davy Crockett(A)	850.00
Diaper Pin Pig	385.00
Dutch Girl, peach trim	495.00
Goldilocks	350.00
Hobbyhorse	255.00
Hubert	1200.00
Kraft T Bear	155.00
Little Red Riding Hood	300.00
Majorette	450.00
Old MacDonald Barn	300.00
Oriental Lady	365.00
Peek-A-Boo	1100.00

Quaker Oats, Regal, multi-colored, $120.00

Rocking Horse	250.00
Toby Cookies	795.00

ROBINSON RANSBOTTOM

Chef	210.00
Frosty the Snowman	695.00
Hi Diddle Diddle	225.00
Hootie Owl	80.00
Jocko Ape	325.00
Peter Peter Pumpkin Eater	110.00
Preacher	85.00
Sailor	275.00

Sheriff Pig

Green hat	90.00
Yellow hat	90.00
Snowman	825.00
Soldier	295.00
Whale	950.00
Wise Bird	55.00

ROSEVILLE

Clematis	150.00
Freesia, brown, shape #4	250.00

SHAWNEE

Bank

Smiley Pig

Butterscotch base	295.00
Chocolate base	650.00

Chef Pierre, Red Wing, yellow, $45.00

Smiley Pig, Shawnee, yellow bib, $125.00

Winnie Pig
    Butterscotch base 295.00
    Chocolate base 295.00
Bo Peep, blue bonnet 90.00
Dutch Boy
    Decals and gold trim 300.00
    Striped pants 150.00
Dutch Girl, yellow dress, cold paint ... 150.00
Elephant, pink................................. 110.00
Happy, crisscross pants...................... 150.00
King Corn 149.00
Lucky, gold trim and decals(A)............ 575.00
Mugsey 350.00
Owl, gold 295.00
Puss 'N Boots................................... 150.00
    Decals and gold trim 350.00
Queen Corn..................................... 195.00
Sailor Boy 130.00
Smiley Pig
    Blue bib 195.00
    Blue bib, gold trim 225.00
    Green scarf 110.00
    Pink scarf and flower...................... 200.00
    Shamrocks 190.00
    Yellow bib, gold, and decals 595.00
Winking Owl 110.00
Winnie Pig
    Blue collar and flower.................... 200.00
    Peach color 225.00

STARNES
Bear on blocks 385.00
Froggy Goes a Courtin' 475.00
Pirate on chest 500.00
Rag Doll 235.00

TREASURE CRAFT
Adobe House.................................... 44.00
Aladdin's Lamp................................. 59.00
Carousel 46.00
Dalmatian w/glass bowl..................... 49.00
Disney Bulldog Cafe 59.00
Fish.. 49.00
Genie 59.00
Hobo.. 35.00
Lighthouse 49.00
Mrs. Potts 60.00
Nana 60.00
Pickup Truck, red 325.00
Spice 49.00
Sugar 49.00
Toucan 45.00
Watering Can 39.00

TWIN WINTON
Cable Cookie Car 125.00
Cookie Counter 95.00
Cookie Shack................................... 130.00
Elephant Sailor................................. 55.00
Gunfighter Rabbit 130.00
Squirrel, cream 60.00
Walrus(A) 360.00

VANDOR
Beethoven Piano............................... 59.00

Betty Boop
    Figural head 140.00
    Standing.. 825.00
Cowboy 60.00
Crocagator 59.00
Fred Flintstone 159.00
    W/Pebbles..................................... 165.00
Howdy Doody................................... 295.00
Jukebox 135.00
Mona Lisa 50.00
Popeye 500.00
Radio 49.00

WALT DISNEY
Big Al 120.00
Donald Duck, sitting(A) 125.00
Dumbo(A).. 155.00
Lollipop Jar...................................... 175.00
Mickey/Minnie turnabout(A) 85.00
Mickey Mouse w/drum(A).................. 135.00
Pluto(A).. 160.00
Tigger(A)... 145.00

WATT
Apple/pear, wire handle 200.00
Esmond, wood lid, brown 125.00
Happy/Sad face 950.00
Pansy, raised.................................... 150.00
Policeman(A) 1400.00
Starflower, #21 .... 175.00
Tulip
    #80 .... 325.00
    #503 .... 415.00

WELLER
Mammy 3750.00

OLD SLEEPY EYE STONEWARE AND POTTERY
Monmouth, Illinois

WEIR POTTERY COMPANY 1899–1905

WESTERN STONEWARE COMPANY 1906–1937

History: Sleepy Eye, Minnesota, and the Sleepy Eye Milling Company were named for the Sioux Indian chief from Brown County. In business from 1883–1921, the Sleepy Eye Milling Company used the Indian's bust as its advertising trademark. Premiums given away by this company were made by the Weir Pottery Company and Western Stoneware Company in Monmouth, Illinois.

The Weir Pottery Company was the original manufacturer of the Old Sleepy Eye premiums: the butter crock, bowl, tankard, and vase made from 1899–1905 in the molded Flemish blue and gray stoneware. Weir received a contract to make 500,000 pieces of this stoneware. The vase pictured the trademark head used by Sleepy Eye Milling Company and had "Old Sleepy Eye" embossed under the bust. The reverse side had the cattails, dragonfly, and frog. The background texture of the vase resembled an orange peel, but the salt crock, tankard, and bowl had a smooth finish. Pieces were put into sacks of flour as premiums until the government made the company stop that practice. A cobalt and white pitcher with the Indian's head was also made.

In 1906 seven potteries, including Weir, merged to form the Western Stoneware Company. Western was the last producer of Sleepy Eye premiums from 1906–1937. Pitchers were made by Western Stoneware in cobalt blue and white in five sizes: half-pint, pint, quart, half-gallon, and gallon. These pieces all had the same shape and were decorated on one side with a profile of the Indian in a war bonnet. Wigwams, trees, or a crouching Indian were pictured on the reverse side.

Until 1937 Western also made steins in two sizes, a sugar bowl, hot plate or trivet, jar, bowl, vase, and three sizes of mugs. In addition to blue on white, these pieces were made using brown on white, green on white, brown on yellow, and also in some solid colors. Many pieces were unmarked, but some had a diamond-shaped backstamp with "WSCO Monmouth, Illinois" in blue or black under the glaze.

In 1952 molds were redesigned and steins were made in two sizes. The Indian head was still molded on the handle and the scene on one side resembled the earlier steins, but the Indian profile was changed on the reissued pieces and the glaze was chestnut brown. The pieces were marked with a raised maple leaf and "W" rather than an embossed "Old Sleepy Eye."

Commemorative steins in blue and buff colors were made by Western from 1968–1973 for members of the Board of Directors and other dignitaries but were not available to the general public.

References: Jim Martin and Bette Cooper, *Monmouth-Western Stoneware,* Wallace-Homestead, 1983; Elinor Meugniot, *Old Sleepy Eye,* Delos L. Hill and Ozella I. Hill, 1979.

Collectors' Club: Old Sleepy Eye Collectors' Club of America, Inc. P.O. Box 12, Monmouth, IL 61462, $10 per year, quarterly newsletter.

Butter Bowl, 5" h, 6¼" d, stoneware, Weir Pottery	525.00
Creamer	
Blue and gray	229.00
Blue and white	150.00

Mug, cobalt and white	
4½" h	195.00
4¾" h	175.00
Pitcher	
4" h	
Blue rim(A)	470.00
Cobalt and blue, #1	180.00
5¼" h	
Blue rim(A)	790.00
Plain rim, "Monmouth Pottery" mark	195.00
6½" h	
Blue and white	200.00
Cobalt and gray, #3, unmkd	175.00
7" h	135.00
8" h	
Blue rim(A)	325.00
Cobalt and white, Western Stoneware	100.00
8½" h, green to brown shading, repaired	600.00
9" h	
Blue rim	600.00
Plain rim	195.00
Salt Bowl, 6½" d	450.00

Pitcher, 6½" h, tan and cobalt, #3, $275.00

Stein, 7¾" h, gray stoneware, blue design, Monmouth Pottery, $795.00

Stein
  5¹/₂" h, brown glaze, 22 oz, Western
    Stoneware **500.00**
  7³/₄" h
    Brown and white **1350.00**
    Brown glaze, 40 oz, Western
    Stoneware **500.00**
    Dark green(A) **3600.00**
    Flemish blue on gray **500.00**
  Sugar Bowl, 3¹/₄" h, 3¹/₂" d, cobalt and
    white(A) **325.00**
Vase
  8¹/₂" h, cylinder shape
    Brown and gold.......................... **625.00**
    Indian and cattails **375.00**
    Matte green glaze(A)................... **500.00**
  9" h
    Cattail, brown on yellow **850.00**
    Flemish blue on gray **375.00**

RAILROAD CHINA
19th and 20th Centuries

History: China made for railroad dining cars was usually a basic, heavyweight, institutional-grade ware that was also used for hospitals and restaurants. There were an endless variety of sizes, shapes, and patterns that were selected by each railroad. Pieces usually had heavy rolled edges, stout bottom rims, and were thick. Colorful company heralds were used to identify the railroad. Dining car china was also used as a promotional or advertising item to create interest in the railroad.

Initially, dining car china came from England and France, but the American manufacturers soon took over. More than sixty different factories made railroad china at one time or another. Many railroads did not have patterns specifically designed for them, but would take a stock pattern from a manufacturer and customize it to suit their needs by placing the railroad's name or logo on the surface. Usually, the additional transfer pattern was placed below the border and toward the top of the article, but sometimes the border design was interrupted by a railroad's name, or the logo was placed in the center of a piece. Some pieces can be identified only by a backstamp that includes a railroad company's name.

One of the most prolific manufacturers of railroad china was Buffalo China and that company marked many pieces with the date that the pattern was designed or copyrighted. In 1932 Buffalo created a set to celebrate the bicentennial of George Washington's birthday. The Chessie cat pattern was made for the Sportsman line of the Chesapeake and Ohio Railroad, one of Buffalo's largest clients. Other Buffalo patterns included Flora of the South, Susquehanna, DeWitt Clinton, and Platinum Blue.

Syracuse China, started as Onondaga Pottery in the 1870s, was a major manufacturer of railroad dining car china. Adobe, Mimbreno, Chuck Wagon, DeWitt Clinton, Stampede, Berkshire, Chessie, Silhouette, Glory of the West, Wild Rose, were just a few of the numerous patterns made.

Hall China made many serving pieces for railroads. Some of the patterns made by Shenango China in New Castle, Pennsylvania, another major manufacturer, were McKinley, Flambeau, El Reno, Yellowstone, Mountain Laurel, and Feather River.

Some additional companies involved with railroad china production were Sterling, Warwick, Lenox, Scammell, McNicol, Homer Laughlin, Fraunfelter, Iroquois, Mayer, and Knowles, Taylor, and Knowles.

References: Stanley L. Baker, *Railroad Collectibles: An Illustrated Value Guide,* Fourth Edition, Collector Books, 1990; Douglas W. McIntyre, *The Official Guide to Railroad Dining Car China,* privately printed, 1990.

Collectors' Clubs: Railroadiana Collectors Association, Inc., Joe Mazanek, 795 Aspen Drive, Buffalo Grove, Il 60089, $15 per year, quarterly newsletter, *The Express; Key, Lock and Lantern,* P.O. Box 15, Spencerport, NY, quarterly newsletter.

Museums: Baltimore and Ohio Railroad, Baltimore, MD; California State Railroad Museum, Sacramento, CA; Charleston Railroad Artifacts Museum, SC; Mid-Continent Railway Historical Society, North Freedom, WI; Museum of Transportation, Boston, MA; National Museum of Transport, St. Louis, MO; National Railroad Museum, Green Bay, WI; New York Museum of Transportation, Albany, NY.

ALASKA
McKinley pattern, black logo and border, yellow-green stripes
Plate, 5" d(A) **137.00**
ATCHISON, TOPEKA, AND SANTA FE
Adobe pattern, red-brown logo, tan base
Dinner Plate **50.00**
Platter, 9" l, 7" w **95.00**
Ramekin **45.00**
Bleeding Blue pattern
Dinner Plate(A) **180.00**
Mimbreno pattern, shaded red-brown design, brown stripe
Butter Pat.. **45.00**
Plate, 7" d(A) **50.00**
Sauce Dish **70.00**
Poppy pattern
Cup, "Syracuse China" mark.............. **26.50**
Plate, 10" d.. **30.00**

ATLANTA AND WEST POINT
Montgomery pattern, red floral rim
Dinner Plate, divided, McNicol mark .   **100.00**

ATLANTIC COAST LINE
Carolina pattern, gray stripes
Butter Pat(A) **18.00**
Eggcup(A) **27.00**
Plate, 7½" d(A) **18.00**
Flora of the South pattern, red and yellow flowers, green leaves, light green stripe
Butter Pat...   **89.00**
Plate, 8" d(A) **100.00**
Platter
  9" l(A) **66.00**
  10" l(A) **88.00**
  12" l(A) **100.00**
Palmetto pattern, red-orange and green logo, green border
Bowl, 6" l(A) **77.00**
Platter, 12" l(A) **44.00**

BALTIMORE AND OHIO
Capital pattern, gold logo, black and gold band
Bowl
  6" d(A) **22.00**
  8" d(A) **22.00**
  10" d, backstamped **95.00**
Gravy Boat(A) **77.00**
Ice Cream Dish(A) **44.00**
Platter, 13½" d **175.00**
Centenary pattern
Bouillon Cup **95.00**
Butter Pat, Shenango mark.................   **45.00**
Divided Plate, 10½" d, "Lamberton" mark **160.00**
Plate
  7" d(A) **33.00**
  8" d(A) **55.00**
Soup Plate, 9¼" d.............................   **115.00**
Derby pattern, blue design
Bowl
  6½" l(A) **33.00**
  10" d(A) **44.00**

BOSTON AND ALBANY
Berkshire pattern
Compote(A) **313.00**

CHESAPEAKE AND OHIO
Chessie pattern, black logo, blue and yellow stripes
Ashtray, 3½" d, Syracuse mark **55.00**
Fast Flying Virginia pattern, med blue letters
Bowl, 7" d(A)......................................   **440.00**
George Washington pattern
Ashtray, multicolored portrait **100.00**
Cup and Saucer(A)..............................   **100.00**
Service Plate, multicolored portrait, gold decorated border, Buffalo Pottery **595.00**
Soup Plate, 9" d(A)............................   **88.00**
Silhouette pattern, black silhouette of gazebo
Cup and Saucer, A.D. Syracuse mark..   **60.00**

CHICAGO, BURLINGTON & QUINCY
Aristocrat pattern, gold and black center logo, gold and black Greek key border
Cereal Bowl, 6" d, c1927..................   **175.00**
Violets and Daisies pattern
Butter Pat **35.00**
Cup and Saucer(A)..............................   **143.00**
Fruit Plate, 4¾" d..............................   **18.00**
Plate
  7¼" d...   **20.00**
  9" d **30.00**
Platter, 16" l(A)..................................   **88.00**
CHICAGO, MILWAUKEE, PUGET SOUND
Puget pattern, green design, white ground
Platter, 13½" l, 9¼" w......................   **195.00**
CHICAGO, MILWAUKEE, ST. PAUL & PACIFIC
Hiawatha pattern, blue w/gray highlights
Bowl, 4" d(A)......................................   **232.00**
La Crosse pattern, green stripes
Platter, 11½" l, 8" w.........................   **30.00**
Olympian pattern, gold logo
Cup and Saucer, Lenox.......................   **95.00**
Peacock pattern, multicolored peacock and flowers, blue stripe
Cup, A.D., set of 6 ....   **75.00**
Plate, 7½" d(A)..................................   **40.00**
Sauce Dish, 5" d **15.00**
The Traveler pattern, flying geese, pink w/black accents, Syracuse mark
Dinner Plate **95.00**
Platter, 8" l..   **50.00**

DENVER AND RIO GRANDE WESTERN
Prospector pattern
Celery Dish, 10" l, blue design of prospector...   **95.00**
Cereal Bowl **40.00**
Cup and Saucer **150.00**
Cup and Saucer, A.D. **295.00**
Dinner Plate, 9" d **100.00**
Platter
  7" l...   **55.00**
  9½" l...   **65.00**
  11½" l...   **75.00**
Salad Bowl **40.00**

ERIE
Starucca pattern, blue logo
Eggcup(A) **44.00**
Susquehanna pattern, blue and orange logo, blue and orange border
Relish Tray, 10" l(A)...........................   **145.00**

FLORIDA EAST COAST
Carolina pattern, gray stripes
Butter Pat, c1926 ....   **12.00**

GREAT NORTHERN
Empire pattern, brown floral band, tan ground
Butter Pat...   **14.00**
Creamer...   **14.00**
Glory of the West pattern, green and gray shades
Dinner Plate(A) **145.00**

Mountain and Flowers pattern, multicolored flowers

Bowl

6" d(A)	37.00
8" d(A)	**44.00**

Plate

5" d(A)	20.00
7" d(A)	20.00

Platter

7" l(A)	33.00
9¹/₂" l(A)	**44.00**

MAINE CENTRAL

Bar Harbor pattern

Platter, 8" l(A) 330.00

Kennebec pattern, black logo, red and black rim stripes

Platter, oval 250.00

MINNEAPOLIS, ST. PAUL, AND SAULT STE MARIE

Logan pattern, brown, orange, blue, and yellow flower band

Dinner Plate(A) 66.00

MISSOURI, KANSAS, AND TEXAS

Alamo pattern, orange-brown center

Service Plate, 10¹/₂" d, blue rim, Buffalo mark.......................... 550.00

MISSOURI PACIFIC

Bismark pattern, black and orange rim stripes

Dinner Plate, crazing, Iroquois mark... **165.00**

Cobalt Blue pattern, gold buzz-saw logo, blue ground

Ashtray, Hall china 65.00

Eagle pattern

Plate

6¹/₂" d, black logo	45.00
9" d, black logo	75.00

St. Albans pattern, blue and orange flowers, green leaves, green stripes

Plate, 7" d, Syracuse mark, c1915....... 25.00

State Capitals pattern

Service Plate

Diesel locomotive in center, floral border, multicolored	295.00
Steam locomotive in center, floral border, multicolored	235.00

NEW YORK CENTRAL

DeWitt Clinton pattern, light blue, gray, and brown train, floral border

Plate

7¹/₂" d(A)	18.00
9" d(A)	55.00

Platter

9" l(A)	25.00
12¹/₂" l, 8¹/₂" w	60.00

Hudson pattern, light green and tan border

Platter, 11" l, 7¹/₂" w 95.00

Mercury pattern, dark brown design

Platter, 9" l(A) 27.00

Vanderbilt pattern, green and red geometric band, gold leaf on rim

Bowl, 5" sq(A)................................. 30.00

Plate, 7⁵/₈" d, DeWitt Clinton pattern, New York Central black train, blue, gray, and white border, "Buffalo China, Made For New York Central Lines" mark, $35.00

Milk pitcher	95.00
Soup Plate, 10" d(A).........................	20.00

NEW YORK, NEW HAVEN AND HARTFORD

Indian Tree pattern, multicolored design, black and brown border

Plate

6" d(A)	27.00
8" d(A)	33.00
9" d(A)	55.00

Merchants pattern, red map, blue-gray train, white and gray stripes

Plate, 8¹/₂" d(A) 82.00

Platinum Blue pattern, white design, blue base

Bowl, 9" l(A)	12.00
Butter Pat(A)	50.00
Cup and Saucer(A)	77.00
Plate, 7" d(A)	18.00
Platter, 8" l(A)	33.00
Relish Tray, 10" l(A)	27.00

NICKEL PLATE ROAD

Ft. Wayne pattern

Platter, 11¹/₂" l, 7³/₄" w, "Buffalo China" mark................................. 180.00

NORFOLK AND WESTERN

Bristol pattern, green wreath, brown-outlined green leaves, green stripes

Bowl, 7¹/₂" l, oval(A) 66.00

Cavalier pattern, green design, brown border

Bowl, 5¹/₂" d(A).................................. 35.00

NORTHERN PACIFIC

Monad pattern, red and black logo, green, orange, and light green stripes

Bowl, 6" d(A) 33.00

Plate

6" d(A)	27.00
7" d(A)	55.00

PENNSYLVANIA RAILROAD

Allegheny pattern, multicolored design, gold stripes

Cup and Saucer, A.D.(A).................... 935.00

Broadway pattern, red, brown, and green pattern, brown stripes

Bouillon.................................... 35.00

Gotham pattern, orange-brown design, ivory base

Service Plate(A)............................... 55.00

Keystone pattern, red design

Bowl, Oval
   6" d(A) 25.00
   7" d(A) 20.00
Butter Pat(A) 55.00
Plate
   5" d(A) 25.00
   6" d(A) 20.00
Platter, 9½" l(A) 66.00

Mountain Laurel pattern, pink-outlined white flowers, green leaves, brown stems, green border

Plate
   7¼" d... 25.00
   9½" d... 48.00
Soup Bowl, 7½" d, backstamped........ 85.00

Purple Laurel pattern, purple, blue, and yellow band, red-brown stripes

Bowl, 6" d(A) 20.00
Butter Pat... 65.00
Grapefruit Dish.............................. 25.00
Ice Cream Dish............................... 45.00
Oatmeal Dish 45.00
Relish Tray, 9" l(A)........................... 66.00
Soup Plate 45.00

PITTSBURGH AND LAKE ERIE

Youngstown pattern, green logo, green and brown stripes

Plate, 7" d(A) 110.00

PULLMAN

Calumet pattern, black logo, red and black stripes

Butter Pat... 60.00

Indian Tree pattern, multicolored, brown and green border

Bowl, 5" d(A) 55.00
Plate
   6¾" d... 75.00
   12¼" d, 4-sections.......................... 225.00
Platter, 10" d(A) 82.00

READING RAILROAD

Bound Brook pattern, green zigzag rim

Platter, 12" l, 8½" w, mkd................. 250.00

Stotesbury pattern, multicolored design, blue and gray stripes

Relish Tray, 10" l(A)........................... 247.00

SOUTHERN

Piedmont pattern, green and brown stripes

Cup and Saucer(A)............................. 110.00

SOUTHERN PACIFIC

Prairie Mountain Wildflowers pattern, red, yellow, and blue flowers, black stripe

Bowl, 6" d, unmkd............................ 35.00
Plate
   7" d... 34.00
   9½" d... 38.00

Sunset pattern, multicolored logo, green stripe, white blossoms, green leaves

Bowl, 7" d(A)..................................... 70.00

SOUTHERN RAILWAY

Peach Blossom pattern, brown, orange, and white logo, orange and blue stripes

Celery Dish, 12" l 135.00
Platter, 10" l(A) 33.00
Soup Bowl, 9" d................................. 125.00

UNION PACIFIC

Challenger pattern

Plate, 5" d(A) 20.00

Desert Flower pattern, green and brown leaves, shaded green ground

Cereal Bowl...................................... 32.00
Dinner Plate 75.00
Platter, 12" l(A) 44.00
Salad Plate.. 35.00
Soup Bowl, Cov................................ 65.00
Soup Plate 35.00

Harriman Blue pattern

Bowl
   6" d(A) 22.00
   7" l(A) 25.00
Fruit plate, 6" d................................. 25.00
Plate, 7" d(A) 27.00
Platter
   12½" l, 8¾" w 75.00
   15" l.. 125.00

New Challenger pattern, red-outlined blue letters, red stripes

Plate, 9½" d, Syracuse mark 70.00
Platter, 8" d...................................... 40.00

Portland Rose pattern, red roses, green leaves, ivory ground

Cereal Bowl, backstamped 345.00

Winged Streamliner pattern, rust transfer, gold stripe

Bouillon.. 24.00
Butter Pat... 25.00
Cereal Bowl 35.00
Cup and Saucer 20.00
Platter, 11½" d 45.00
Soup Bowl 45.00

Plate, 10½" d, iron red train, Union Pacific, "Scammell Trenton China" mark, $30.00

WABASH
Toledo pattern, white w/black rim
Sauce Dish, 4¾" d, "WABASH, The
   Stearnes Co." mark......................... **45.00**
Wabash pattern, maroon letters
Bowl
   5" d(A) **77.00**
   6" d(A) **88.00**
   7" d(A) **99.00**
Cup and Saucer(A)............................. **324.00**
Plate, 7½" d(A) **132.00**

REDWARE
East, Midwest, South
17th Century–early 20th Century

History: Redware was made in all the colonies for use in food preparation and for all types of storage vessels. Most redware was thrown on a wheel; handles and spouts were formed separately and then attached. Pie plates and platters were drape molded. Not many pieces were made by press molding or slip casting.

Redware pieces were seldom marked. A tremendous variety of forms was produced by American redware potters and similar shapes were made over long periods of time in many different areas. The vast majority of pieces were not decorated at all but had a basic glaze of lead and silica which fired to a clear, shiny finish. Glazes were applied by dipping, pouring, or painting. The bottoms and sometimes the rims were left unfinished since they were fused together in the kiln.

A colorless glaze was used most of the time, but three basic pigments also were used. Iron oxide produced a range of browns, copper oxide produced green, and manganese dioxide resulted in brown to jet black finishes. Some pieces were completely covered with colored glaze, others were partially decorated with a sponged or brushed glaze.

White slip was either trailed or brushed on pieces as a decorative element or as a background for additional decoration. Sgraffito decorated pieces were covered with thick white slip through which designs were scratched to reveal the redware body underneath. Green, yellow, brown, or black were used to highlight the pieces.

Most decorations were done freehand, but sometimes paper patterns were used. Decorated pieces usually were intended for display or gifts. Since redware was very fragile, most pieces were sold in the immediate area where they were made. Some early redware pieces were dated and signed by the potters.

During the 18th and 19th centuries, most redware was made to meet domestic needs. Tablewares included bowls in many sizes, platters, porringers, cups, mugs, beakers, goblets, and serving dishes, such as compotes, bread baskets, divided vegetable bowls, tureens, and cake stands. Trivets, eggcups, teapots, coffeepots, sugar bowls, salts, pitchers in sizes from ½-pint creamers to 2-gallon ciders, puzzle jugs, and beer pitchers were all made. Cooking and baking utensils included bean pots, stew pots, pipkins in 1-pint to 1-gallon sizes, pudding pans, bakers, nappies, roasting pans and skillets, pie plates, cake and jelly molds, milk pans, cream and butter pots, and churns.

Jugs, jars, pots, and crocks were made for food and drink storage along with water coolers, flasks, and bottles. Pitchers and wash bowls, barber bowls, shaving mugs, soap dishes, spittoons, chamber pots, bedpans, pap boats, and hot water bottles also were made in redware, along with fat lamps, candlesticks, fishing lamps, candle molds, match holders, toys, and miniatures including salesmens' samples. Some figural pieces were made for mantel decorations. By 1900 flowerpots, decorative terra-cotta for builders, and many novelty items were made for promotional purposes.

Redware products became the standard since pewter was expensive and difficult to get, and wood was hard to clean, but gradually glass, tin, and iron replaced redware storage vessels, utilitarian pieces, and dishes. By the mid 19th century, European imports replaced redware dishes and, at a later time, American ironstone was another alternative.

The majority of the early New England redware potters came from Massachusetts where they followed the British traditions. The other eastern states of New Hampshire, Vermont, Connecticut, Rhode Island, and Maine all had potters working on redwares. In New York State redwares were made from the 1650s until 1942.

Pennsylvania became the most important American redware center. From the 17th until the 20th centuries, the region's designs showed the English and German influences and many of the artistic sgraffito pieces were marked. North Carolina was well known for redware pottery, and limited amounts were made in other mid-Atlantic states. Some redwares were made in the midwest, but very little came from the south and west.

References: William C. Ketchum, Jr. *American Redware,* Henry Holt and Company, 1991; Kevin McConnell, *Redware: America's Folk Art Pottery,* Schiffer Publishing, 1988.

Museums: Bennington Museum, VT; Brooklyn Museum, NY; Henry Ford Museum and Greenfield Village, Dearborn, MI; Henry Frances du Pont Winterthur Museum, DE; Shelburne Museum, VT; Wadsworth Atheneum, Hartford, CT.

Apple Butter Jar, 6½" h, ribbed strap
   handle, dark amber glaze w/brown
   flecks(A) **82.00**

Bank

3" h, 3¹/4" d, orange shape and color **175.00**

3¹/4" h, bullet shape, incised "Pass Me Not," med brown glaze w/dark splotches, incised "1882" on base.. **85.00**

4" h, applied cutouts of children and flowers, orange glaze(A) **302.00**

4¹/4" h, narrow neck, flared lip, overall floral design, multicolored glaze, red, yellow, and green flowing slip(A) **88.00**

4³/4" h, painted woodland scene w/cabin and bridge(A) **302.00**

12" h, cylinder shape, applied hen and chicks **540.00**

Bean Pot, Cov, 6" h, 6¹/2" d, dark brown glaze at top, unglazed base **60.00**

Bedpan, 14¹/2" l, brushed black design on rim(A)...................................... **10.00**

Bowl

7⁷/8" d, yellow slip w/sgraffito bird and floral design and green splashes, coggled rim(A) **687.00**

10" d, 4" h, brown sponged glaze, chips(A) **95.00**

12¹/2" d, 2¹/2" h, sgraffito design of eagle, flowers, and "1827"(A) **412.00**

14¹/2" d, tapered body, unglazed ext, red glazed int w/brown mottled rim(A) **962.00**

Candle Sconce, 5³/8" h, shield back, loop handle, clear glaze(A) **550.00**

Candlestick, 2³/4" h, dark brown glaze(A)... **33.00**

Chamber Pot, 6¹/2" d, ribbed strap handle, dark amber glaze w/black splotches(A)................................... **203.00**

Charger, 13" d, yellow slip "Indian Bitters"(A)................................... **3300.00**

Cup, 3⁵/8" h, 2 ribbed strap handles, mottled greenish glaze w/brown accents, chips and hairline(A) **137.00**

Cuspidor, 2" h, 3³/4" d, applied tooled floral design, "A.L.S. Manufactured, St. Jobs, Ohio" on base(A) **50.00**

Dish

5" d, yellow slip free-form design, coggled rim(A) **357.00**

6" d, slip designs of 2 yellow lines and dots, coggled rim(A).............. **165.00**

7" d, brown sponged glaze w/flecks(A)................................... **247.00**

11¹/4" d, green wash w/slip decoration(A) **1980.00**

11¹/2" d, yellow slip dots, notched rim(A)... **1045.00**

11¹/2" l, oblong shape, dark green glaze w/orange spots(A).............. **275.00**

Figure, 10¹/4" h, chest of drawers, yellow slip w/brown speckles, incised "Annie Marie Marsden 1884" on back(A) **825.00**

Flask, 7¹/4" h, ovoid shape w/small lipped neck, brown Albany slip glaze, pint(A)................................. **121.00**

Flowerpot, attached saucer

4¹/4" h, yellow slip w/brown sponging, hairlines(A) **71.00**

5¹/2" h, finger-crimped rim, tooled foliage band, greenish amber glaze, chips **135.00**

Herb Pot, 4¹/4" h, brown splotches on ochre ground(A) **522.00**

Jar

3¹/2" h, 4¹/2" d, greenish orange spotted glaze(A)......................... **192.00**

4³/8" h, ovoid shape, orange glaze w/green accents, flakes(A) **125.00**

5¹/2" h, ovoid shape, dark red glaze, brown splotches(A)..................... **55.00**

6" h

8¹/2" d, Cov, brown and white swirled slip, tooled wavy line, blue accents(A) **236.00**

Squat shape, strap handle, dark brown glaze(A) **65.00**

7¹/2" h, incised wavy line on rim, mottled greenish brown glaze, imp "Winchester, Va." on bottom(A) **330.00**

7⁵/8" h, greenish glaze, imp label "S.H. Sonner, Strasburg, Va. 1," rim chips(A).............................. **50.00**

8" h, dark brown glaze(A) **21.00**

8¹/4" h

Tooled band, brown flecked glaze(A) **77.00**

Yellow slip w/reddish flecks(A) **225.00**

9³/8" h, ovoid shape, applied handles, tooled ribbed shoulder, clear glaze w/brown splotches(A) **165.00**

9¹/2" h

Glazed with manganese splotches(A) **522.00**

Ovoid shape, brown-green glaze w/brown flecks, imp "A. Wilcox, West Bloomfield." label, hairlines(A) **545.00**

11¹/4" h, Cov, squat shape, 2 small handles, incised wavy and straight lines, tobacco-decorated(A) **440.00**

12¹/2" h, ovoid shape, dark brown mottled glaze, chips(A) **50.00**

13¹/4" h, Cov, tobacco-decorated(A) **620.00**

14¹/4" h, ovoid shape w/applied handles, dark brown glaze, incised straight and wavy lines(A) ... **182.00**

Jug

4¹/4" h, incised house on bottom, grayish brown glaze(A) **17.00**

4¾" h, grotesque, brown glaze w/white teeth, "Brown's Pottery, Arden, N.C."(A) **225.00**

6⅝" h, ovoid shape w/ribbed strap handle, hairline(A) **165.00**

6¾" h, strap handle, tooled lines on shoulder, green glaze w/red highlights(A) **82.00**

7" h
Applied strap handle, brown splotches(A) **94.00**
Ovoid shape, mustard glaze, dtd 1888 .... **80.00**

8" h
Ovoid shape, ribbed strap handle, dark brown glaze, chips(A) **104.00**
Pinched spout, ribbon-loop body, applied handle, yellowware glaze **90.00**

14¼" h, green glaze w/amber spots, hairlines(A) **440.00**

Loaf Pan
11⅞" l, 8-sided, yellow slip chains and stars on border(A) **797.00**
12⅝" l, yellow slip squiggles(A) **1480.00**

Milk Pan
9" d, 3" h, greenish amber glaze w/white slip(A) **247.00**
16" d, 4" h, glazed int(A) **104.00**

Mold, Turk's Head
6¼" d, fluted w/scalloped rim, green glaze w/amber spots and brown splotches(A) **94.00**
7½" d, reddish glaze w/brown flakes, white and dark brown slip on rim(A) **61.00**
9" d, swirling flutes, brown sponged rim(A) **45.00**
11¾" l, fish, amber and brown glaze, chips(A) **110.00**

Mug
3¾" h, brown speckled glaze(A) **25.00**
5" h, rust colored glaze **42.00**

Pie Plate
7¼" d, puddle of yellow slip in center, coggled rim, chips(A) **137.00**
8" d, green and brown 3-line design, coggled rim, chips and hairline(A) **1100.00**
9" d, 3 yellow slip wavy lines, coggled rim, chips on rim(A) **467.00**
9⅝" d, scattered 3 yellow slip lines, coggled rim(A) **385.00**
10¾" d, closely spaced groups of 3 yellow slip lines, coggled rim, chips and wear(A) **250.00**
10⅞" d, incised distelfink, stylized flowers, German inscription, and "1786," mottled red glaze, coggled rim(A) **192.00**
11" d
Coggled rim(A) **18.00**

Green, yellow, and brown slip decoration **245.00**
11½" d, yellow slip crossed-lines design, chips(A) **137.00**

Pitcher
2½" h, tobacco-decorated(A) **240.00**
6" h, copper luster stylized snakes in fauna, black ground, cracks at handle **375.00**
6½" h, pear shape, strap handle, black mottled and tooled ext, tan int, c1820 .... **395.00**
6¾" h, white slip w/marbleized red, brown, and green(A) **50.00**
6⅞" h, white slip w/brown spotted glaze(A) **10.00**
7¾" h, ovoid shape, strap handle, light green slip w/brown splotches(A) **250.00**
8" h, molded stylized floral design w/cherub heads, hound handle, dark brown glaze, imp "National Sellers, Upper Hanover, Pa." on base, worn glaze and chips(A) **192.00**
8½" h, applied rose design, black glaze(A) **110.00**
9" h, brown glaze(A) **17.00**
11¾" h, tobacco-decorated(A) **1430.00**

Plaque, 6¾" h, molded polychromed rooster(A) **214.00**

Plate
7½" d, slip design, coggled edge..... **45.00**
10¼" d, geometric design in yellow slip and green and brown glaze, orange ground(A) **220.00**

Posset Pot, ribbed strap handle, small pouring spout, brown splotches(A) .. **225.00**

Preserve Jar
4⅝" h, mottled green and brown designs(A) **935.00**
6½" h, ovoid shape, brown Albany slip(A) **25.00**
7" h, ovoid shape, yellow glaze(A) .. **45.00**

Trencher, 13¾" l, 9⅝" w, yellow slip
decoration, rim chips, $2475.00

8½" h, clear glaze w/brown splotches and flecks(A) **181.00**

Salt, 2" h, 3" d, ftd, greenish brown mottled glaze(A) **55.00**

Shaving Mug, 4¼" h, dark brown glaze, strap handle, chips and hairline(A) **77.00**

Stew Pot, 8½" h, ribbed body, green glaze **725.00**

Sugar Bowl, Cov, 5¾" h, rope-twist handles w/tooling, dark brown fleck glaze(A) **192.00**

Teapot, 4¾" h, black metallic glaze(A) **40.00**

Vase
   5" h, yellow slip and leaf-shaped sgraffito designs, attributed to Bucks County, Penna.(A) **258.00**
   6¼" h, greenish brown glaze w/orange spots(A) **25.00**

SPONGEWARE
New Jersey and Midwest
c1850s–1960s

History: Spongeware is a decorating technique probably first used on whiteware. At various times it was applied to earthenware and yellowware and to stoneware that had been covered with opaque white Bristol slip. Sponged stoneware bodies tended to be simpler than sponged earthenware examples.

The mottled effect of spongeware decoration varies from object to object. Much of the decoration seems to be randomly placed blotches or dots, but some pieces show repeats of a specific shape or pattern. Sometimes the decoration appears to form a net pattern, is arranged in rows, or is combined with solid-color bands.

Blue-sponged white earthenware was made in New Jersey, Pennsylvania, and Ohio as early as c1850. International Pottery Company and Etruria Pottery from New Jersey were among the early companies that sponged white earthenwares. James Bennett was probably the earliest Ohio maker of blue-sponged wares. By the time spongeware was being made in larger quantities, in the 1880–1940s, potteries were using stoneware and yellowware clay bodies and producing mostly utilitarian pieces.

Red Wing, Minnesota, was a popular area for stoneware production and Minnesota Stoneware, the first regional company to produce these wares, used a white Bristol slip glaze to cover bail-handled jugs and pipkins marked with the company name. When Minnesota Stoneware merged with Red Wing Union Stoneware Company in 1906, spittoons, covered chamber pots, covered slop jars, umbrella stands, and other objects were added to the line. The merged businesses continued to make sponged designs on marked pieces until 1936, using several color combinations—blue on white, brown on white, and red and blue on white.

During the early 1930s sponged designs were used on yellowware pieces, such as pitchers, mixing bowls, covered bowls, casseroles, baking dishes, bean pots, butter crocks with tops, beater jars, and small handled jugs. Sponge colors were blue or brown on white, red and blue on white, and brown and green on yellow. A variety of marks was used such as "RED WING SAFFRON WARE," "RED WING OVENWARE," "RED-WING U.S.A.," and "MADE IN REDWING." From 1936 until 1967 the company name was Red Wing Potteries and it continued to make spongewares until after World War II. A large amount of advertising spongewares was made.

The Western Stoneware Company in Monmouth was the largest Illinois stoneware producer from 1910–1940, but it made less spongeware than Red Wing and its pieces were heavier and cruder. Sponged water coolers, mixing bowls, and spittoons, were marked "WESTERN STONEWARE CO." or "WESTERN STONEWARE COMPANY/MONMOUTH, ILLINOIS."

From 1893 until 1906 when it was purchased by Western, Monmouth Pottery made marked spongeware water coolers in two- to ten-gallon sizes and miniature water coolers.

Many smaller makers produced spongeware at various times in their histories. Fulper Pottery in Flemington, New Jersey, made stoneware pitchers, spittoons, vases, and jardinieres designed by J.M. Stangl. Stangl still makes sponged pieces on a white earthenware body. Robinson-Ransbottom still produces spongeware in Ohio.

A tremendous assortment of spongeware utilitarian pieces was made, with bowls being the most common. Mixing bowls in many sizes, as well as "shoulder bowls" and nappies ranging in sizes from 4"–12" in diameter, were made. Capped bowls were often used for advertising premiums.

Pitchers in a variety of sizes and shapes were made, with allover blue sponging being the most popular. Storage vessels, such as shoulder jugs, bail-handled jugs, water coolers, covered butter crocks, and kitchen storage jars, also were made. Cooking utensils included pie plates from six to twelve inches in diameter, custard cups, beater jars, colanders, measuring cups, funnels, casseroles, bean pots, and stew pans. Tablewares included plates, mugs, teapots, mush cups and saucers, platters, gravy boats, and covered sugar bowls. Toilet sets, cuspidors, umbrella stands, vases, and jardinieres all were made in spongeware, as were miniatures used for gift items and advertising.

References: William C. Ketchum, Jr. *American Country Pottery, Yellowware and Spongeware,* Alfred A. Knopf, 1987; Kevin McConnell, *Spongeware and Spatterware,* Schiffer Publishing, 1990; Earl F. and Ada Robacker, *Spatterware and Sponge,* A.S. Barnes & Co. 1978.

Bowl

    5" d, tan and brown sponging **45.00**

    5½" d

        Blue, orange, and gray sponging..   **65.00**

        Rust, blue, and cream sponging...   **26.00**

    6" d

        Blue sponging, white ground **149.00**

        Green, brown, and cream spong-

           ing **45.00**

    7" d, blue sponging

        Pouring spout, yellowware body,

           wire bale(A) **137.00**

        White ground **145.00**

    7" l, oval, ironstone, blue sponged

        int, c1850 ....   **195.00**

    7½" d, green and yellow sponging..   **70.00**

    7¾" d, blue sponging, yellowware

        body(A) **38.00**

    8" d

        Brown, tan, and green sponging ..   **60.00**

        Ribbed, blue sponging, white

           ground, white scalloped band

           at middle **165.00**

    8¼" d, 2¾" h, blue sponging, gilt

        trim, yellowware body(A) **159.00**

    8½" d, blue sponging, yellowware

        body...   **110.00**

    9" d

        5" h, brown sponging on cream...   **22.00**

        Raised design on ext, green,

           brown, and tan sponging **95.00**

    9½" d

        5" h, red, cream, and blue spong-

           ing **175.00**

        Brown, blue, and cream spong-

           ing, "Wisconsin Big Store" on

           int...   **195.00**

    9¾" d, 5" h, rust and blue on

        cream **135.00**

    10" d, blue sponging, white ground   **165.00**

    10¼" d, shouldered, bail handle,

        blue sponging, white ground **185.00**

    11½" d, blue sponging, white

        ground, white band at middle......   **345.00**

Creamer, 4" h, blue sponging, yel-

    lowware body(A)............................   **71.00**

Cup and Saucer, oversized, blue

    sponging, white ground, chip on

    table ring(A) **60.00**

Custard Cup, brown sponging, yel-

    lowware body, crazing, set of 6(A) ..   **38.00**

Milk Bowl, 9" d, 3" h, blue sponging,

    white ground.................................   **165.00**

Milk Pitcher, 5" h, blue and rust

    sponging **275.00**

Mixing Bowl, 14" d

    6¼" h, turned rim, blue sponging,

        white ground **275.00**

    6½" h, turned rim, blue sponging,

        cream ground **225.00**

Pie Plate, 9" d

    Blue sponging, white ground...........   **85.00**

    Brown and cream sponging.............   **100.00**

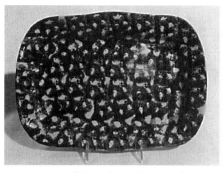

Tray, 13½" l, 10" w, blue sponging,
white ground, late 19th C, $315.00

Pitcher

    4½" h, molded ribs, brown and

        green sponging, black advertising

        transfer(A)..................................   **55.00**

    4¾" h, molded Gothic arch design,

        brown sponging, yellowware

        body(A) **38.00**

    5" h, rust and green sponging........   **80.00**

    5½" h, white clay w/black spong-

        ing(A) **22.00**

    7⅝" h, molded hunt scenes, blue

        and white sponging(A).................   **550.00**

    8¼" h, blue and white sponging,

        blue-stripes in center **220.00**

    9¼" h, stoneware, blue sponging,

        white ground **485.00**

    9½" h

        Emb lattice, vines, roses, and

           scrolls, cream and tan sponging

           w/blue accents.........................   **400.00**

        Red, green, and blue panels **225.00**

Salt and Pepper, green, yellow, and

    tan sponging, white ground.............   **125.00**

Teapot

    7¼" h, olive green and white

        sponging, chips on lid **290.00**

    Blue sponging, white ground...........   **565.00**

STONEWARE

Most of the United States
1630s–Present

History: Traditional stoneware had a ceramic body made of certain clays that became vitrified when fired, were non-porous and non-absorbent, and were exceptionally strong. A glaze was not required to make pieces watertight, but surfaces were very coarse and gritty. Most pieces were salt glazed to make the surface smoother and the result was a transparent, shiny, pebbled finish that resembled orange peel. Salt glazing was the norm in the northeast and midwest through the 19th century.

Albany slip, an alternative glaze used by 1800, was made by mixing dark brown, finely grained clay and water. This method produced a smooth, opaque brown-colored glaze used to cover both the inside and outside of a piece, or just the inside with a salt-glazed exterior.

Alkaline glaze, used in the southeastern United States, produced a drippy olive or brown finish that was smoother and more uniform. Bristol glaze produced a white opaque finish that copied porcelain and white earthenwares. Started in the 1880s, this glaze provided a base for spongewares or was combined with Albany slip for brown-white wares.

The earliest stoneware examples prior to c1800 were based on the English and German traditions brought to America by the potters. Before the late 1800s, stoneware was thrown on the potter's wheel and handles and spouts were applied separately. Eventually, slip casting dominated stoneware production, but press molding and drape molding also were used.

Since stonewares were designed with strict utilitarian purposes in mind, the forms were rather simple and limited in range. From the 18th through the 19th centuries, the shapes of the basic bowls, jugs, mugs, pots, chamber pots, and such remained the same. Ovoid forms eventually were replaced by straight-sided examples.

Decoration was achieved in several different ways on the utilitarian stoneware examples. Before 1840, most designs were scratched into the surface prior to firing. The incised decoration was then filled in with cobalt blue or manganese brown. Sometimes designs were stamped or impressed with a coggle wheel. Applied decorations were attached elements that were either hand shaped or formed in a press mold. Freehand slip decoration was usually done in cobalt blue and some manganese. Prior to 1850 decorations were simple squiggles, tulips, trees, and such.

After 1850 stylized birds, animals, humans, houses, ships, and scenes were used. Stencil decoration, in use c1870, pictured florals, figurals, and geometrics, such as circles, stars, and diamonds, along with the name of the pottery company.

Slip-trailed decorations in cobalt blue on salt-glazed stonewares were primarily found in New England at Bennington, Vermont, and in the Hudson River and Erie Canal areas of New York State. Brushed or painted cobalt blue decorations were indigenous to western Pennsylvania and Ohio.

Most stoneware containers were made to be used to store foods and liquids and therefore were extremely durable. Variously shaped jugs from 1/2-pint to 20-gallon sizes were made, as were jars, pots for cream, crocks for preserving and storing, tobacco humidors, and water coolers. Bottles held beer and soft drinks, flasks were made in pint and half-pint sizes, and canteens in

pint and quart sizes often were used for advertising.

Prior to 1850 most potters made simple mugs, but some larger mugs and steins had pewter lids. Goblets, glasses, and pitchers in one-pint to two-gallon sizes were made. Few tablewares were made, although punch bowls, covered and footed sugar bowls, salts, and bowls in 1/2-gallon to five-gallon sizes were available. Bean pots usually were brown and are still being made today. Teapots also were brown glazed. Household and dairy items, such as churns and mortars, inkwells and bottles, chamber pots, spittoons, and hot-water bottles were made. Flowerpots and urns appeared after the 1860s. Toys, banks, whistles, and miniatures were made along with mantle pieces, doorstops, figural dogs, lions, and face jugs.

Vermont was one of the most important centers for stonewares. The Norton factory (see Bennington) and the Farrar family made significant contributions. Many of the nation's earliest potters settled in New York since there were good sources for clay there. In Utica Noah White, with his sons and grandsons, made stonewares from 1838–1907 and these are highly collectible today. (See White's Pottery in the General Manufacturers' section.)

In 1828 in New Jersey, David and John Henderson made the first successful American molded stonewares at the Jersey City Pottery. Their pitchers, spittoons, and soap dishes were marked. Abraham Fulper and one of his sons made blue-decorated stonewares in 1860.

There was a vast stoneware industry in Pennsylvania, while Yorktown, Virginia, had one of the nation's earlier stoneware kilns. In the early 1900s, much blue and white utilitarian stoneware was made in a number of Ohio Valley potteries such as Brush-McCoy, Nelson McCoy, Burley, Uhl, and Logan. Many other areas of Ohio had significant stoneware production, as did North and South Carolina, and the midwestern states, especially Red Wing, Minnesota. (See Red Wing in the General Manufacturers' section.)

Many manufacturers of blue and white stonewares left no records and pieces frequently cannot be identified by maker.

References: Georgeanna H. Greer, *American Stonewares: The Art and Craft of Utilitarian Potters,* Schiffer Publishing Ltd. 1981; Edith Harbin, *Blue and White Stoneware Pottery Crockery: Identification and Value Guide,* Collector Books, 1977; Kathryn McNerney, *Blue and White Stoneware,* Collector Books, 1991, values updated; Don and Carol Raycraft, *Country Stoneware and Pottery,* Collector Books, 1985; _____ , *Collector's Guide to Country Stoneware and Pottery,* 2nd Series, Collector Books, 1990.

Collectors' Club: Blue and White Pottery Club, 224 12th Street, N.W., Cedar Rapids, IA 52405, $12 per year, newsletter.

Museums: Bennington Museum, VT; Brooklyn Museum, NY; DAR Museum, Washington, DC; Henry Ford Museum and Greenfield Village, Dearborn, MI; Henry Francis du Pont Winterthur Museum, DE; Museum of Ceramics at East Liverpool, OH; Shelburne Museum, VT.

Bank
   3" h, figural Noah's Ark, green glaze, chip on roof(A) **60.00**
   4³/₄" h, figural jug, light pink glaze(A) **82.00**
Bowl
   9" d, gray alkaline glaze, early 20th C(A) **143.00**
   9¹/₂" d, daisy on waffle design, blue and white **100.00**
   10¹/₂" d, 3¹/₂" h, leaf spray on int, incised "LASET UNS ESSAN AUS DEASER SCHESEL SNETZ UND SPECK 1809" on ext, light green speckled glaze over white slip, c1809, Pennsylvania(A) **2640.00**
   11" d, 6" h, dbl handles, blue stylized leaf and strawberry design, imp blue "JOHN B PEWTRESS 2," salt glaze, c1840, chips(A) **3190.00**
Butter Crock, 12" d, brushed cobalt floral design, imp "1¹/₂," hairlines(A) **413.00**
Churn
   11¹/₂" h, dbl handles, imp "P. SCHAEFER POTTERY 85.89 CLAY ST. GREENPOINT/1¹/₂," white Bristol glaze, chips and hairlines, mismatched lid(A) **100.00**
   13¹/₄" h, cov, dbl handles, blue abstract florals, imp "L. LEHMAN & CO. WEST 12 ST. N.Y.," salt glaze, 2 gallon, chips and hairlines(A) **198.00**
   15³/₄" h, dbl handles, light blue flower, imp "CLARK & LUNDY TROY," salt glaze, c1860 .... **450.00**
   16" h, dbl handles, imp "GEO. W. DOANE LOUISVILLE KY/4," incised clipper ship and script "HOMEWARD BOUND," salt glaze, c1850(A) **3080.00**
   16¹/₂" h, dbl handles, blue swan w/ wreath and "4," imp "HARTS FULTON," salt glaze, hairlines, c1860(A) **1980.00**
   17" h, dbl lug handles, Albany slip glaze w/salt, 4 gallon, Texas(A).... **1045.00**
Colander, 11¹/₂" d, 5³/₄" h, brown Albany slip, late 19th C(A) **220.00**
Cooler
   11³/₈" h, blue abstract plant design, imp "GATE CITY WATER COOLER. PATENTED MAY 25TH 1886/6," salt glaze, hairlines,1¹/₂ gallon(A) **132.00**
   13¹/₂" h, cobalt flowers on front and

rear, cobalt top bands, salt glaze, 2 gallon, c1830–60(A) **1210.00**
   23¹/₄" h, incised cobalt foliage, branches, "x," and "A.B. Lake Hopewell, Ohio," wooden plug and spigot, chips, repaired handle(A) **8360.00**
Creamer, 3⁷/₈" h, dark brown Albany slip glaze w/sgraffito "Emma" under spout(A) **44.00**
Crock
   7¹/₂" h, dbl handles, imp "BOSTON," red-brown salt glaze surface, c1820(A) **440.00**
   8¹/₂" h, 12¹/₄" d, cobalt quill script label "Mrs. Jane Henderson, Springfield, Ohio," hairline(A) **357.00**
   9" h, dbl handles, cobalt
     Chicken eating corn and "N.Y. 2.", salt glaze, 2 gallon(A) **495.00**
     Foliage design **100.00**
     Slip tulip design **375.00**
   9¹/₂" h, imp "Cross Bros, Sterling, Pa. 2," brushed cobalt slip flower(A) **150.00**
   11¹/₄" h, cobalt quill polka dot floral design, imp "4," hairlines(A) **82.00**
   11³/₄" h, ovoid shape, dbl handles, blue incised seed pod on front, "1823" on reverse, salt glaze, 3 gallons, c1823(A) **1265.00**
   12³/₄" h, ovoid shape, cobalt brushed floral design and "2"(A).. **225.00**
   13¹/₄" h
     Applied handles, cobalt bird on branch, imp "cobalt 5", imp "EVAN R. JONES, PITTSTON, PA" **1750.00**
     Dbl handles, imp blue "GOODWIN & WEBSTER," salt glaze, c1840(A) **187.00**
   13³/₄" h, applied handles, cobalt quill "6 Butter 1870"(A) **385.00**
Cuspidor
   4" h, 8" d, Leon slip glaze, dark olive, early 20th C, Meyer(A) **935.00**
   8¹/₂" d, gray salt glaze w/brown accents, chips(A) **55.00**
Door Stop, 2¹/₂" h, 7¹/₂" l, figural sleeping dog, blue glaze, Hyssong Pottery, c1890(A) **143.00**
Figure, 6¹/₄" h, seated dog, white body, green spots, clear glaze, Ohio(A) **770.00**
Ginger Jar, 7¹/₄" h, brown slip glaze, c1850(A) **100.00**
Harvest Jug, 8¹/₂" d, gray salt glaze w/blue accents and black drip(A) **154.00**
Inkwell, 3⁵/₈" d, gray salt glaze(A) **60.00**
Jar
   5³/₄" h, incised wavy lines w/cobalt accents, brownish gray salt glaze, chipped base(A) **335.00**

7" h, ovoid shape, blue encircling florals, imp "H.O. SMITH ALEXA, D.C.", salt glaze, 1 qt, c1845(A).... **2310.00**

8½" h, ovoid shape, 2 applied handles, cobalt brushed foliage design(A) **159.00**

9½" h, ovoid shape, gray and brown glaze, imp "Boston 1804"(A)..................................... **1210.00**

10⅛" h, dbl handles, blue incised profile of colonial man's head w/ruffled shirt, 1 gallon, c1790(A) **6875.00**

11" h, ovoid shape, dbl handles, cobalt floral design and "1798," salt glaze, hairlines(A)................. **1605.00**

11¼" h, ovoid shape
  Cobalt brushed floral design and "2," chips on base(A) **100.00**
  Incised cobalt bird and 2 flowers, imp "I. SEYMOUR TROY," 1 gallon, salt glaze(A) **1100.00**

12" h
  Imp rouletted design on neck and shoulder, blue incised bowknot on front, imp blue "S. AMBOY.N.JERSEY," 2 gallon, c1800, hairlines(A)................... **2420.00**
  Overall green glaze, unmkd........ **65.00**

12¼" h, blue wreath and "1866," imp "C. HART & SON. SHERBURNE 3," salt glaze, chips on lip(A)............. **330.00**

12½" h, ovoid shape, dbl handles, incised man-in-the-moon on front, stylized rain clouds on reverse, salt glaze, 2 gallon, c1820(A) **1100.00**

13" h, dbl loop handles
  Incised blue swag and tassle design, imp "COMMERAWS STONEWARE/N. YORK CORLEARS HOOK," salt glaze, 3 gallon(A) ... **4125.00**
  Scalloped looped circles, imp "C.CROLIUS MANUFACTURER NEW-YORK," salt-glaze ext, brown int, 1 gallon(A) **1320.00**

13½" h, ovoid shape, applied handles, brushed cobalt flowers, imp "L. Minier 4," old chips(A) **247.00**

14¼" h, ovoid shape, brushed cobalt tulips, cobalt label "A. Black, Confluence, Pa.," gray salt glaze, chips on handles(A) **1210.00**

15¼" h
  Incised blue "Hanna & Co. Snuff," imp "4"(A) **330.00**
  Ovoid shape, cobalt brushed floral design, imp "J. Swank & Co. Johnstown, Pa. 4"(A) **175.00**

16" h, ovoid shape, applied handles, brushed cobalt floral design and "6"(A) **82.00**

16¼" h, ovoid shape, imp "J. Rambo 9"(A)............................... **55.00**

Jug
9" h
  Grotesque figural face, dark brown alkaline glaze, sgd "LANIER MEADERS"(A) **1870.00**
  Ovoid shape, imp "CHARLESTOWN" on shoulder, ochre drip at top, salt glaze finish, ½ gallon, c1830(A)................................. **297.00**

9¼" h, ovoid shape, reeded neck, imp "GOODALE/STEADMAN," salt glaze, ½ gallon(A) **77.00**

9¾" h, wide mouth, dark brown Albany slip, imp "B"(A) **33.00**

10¾" h, stenciled "WM. RADAM'S/MI-CROBE KILLER NO.1," Bristol glaze, c1890(A) **187.00**

11½" h, cobalt slip foliage design, imp label "L.W. Fenton, Ft. Lounsberg, Vt."(A) **192.00**

12" h, cobalt quilled "M.J. Madden, Rondout, N.Y."(A) **150.00**

12¾" h, imp "J. & S. Hart, Oswego Falls.," cobalt brushed "2"(A) **275.00**

13" h, ovoid shape, strap handle, gray glaze w/amber highlights, manganese brown on lip(A) **165.00**

13¼" h, imp "H. Purdy 2," brushed cobalt flower(A) **525.00**

13½" h, cobalt quill polka-dot bird, imp "2"(A) **412.00**

14" h, beehive shape, blue circled "Hayner Lock Box 290 Dayton, Ohio," "E.S. & B." on base **138.00**

14¼" h, ovoid shape
  Cobalt stenciled and painted "James Hamilton & Co., Greensboro, Pa. 2"(A) **525.00**
  Single flower and leaves and "2" in cobalt quill design(A) **275.00**
  Stylized cobalt slip floral design,

Jug, amber top, brown decoration, 5 gallon, $135.00

imp "O.L. & A.K. Ballard, Burlington, Vt. 2"(A) **290.00**

14½" h, ovoid shape, tooled lines and imp "Boston," ribbed strap handle, brown and gray salt glaze(A) **698.00**

15" h, ovoid shape, brown salt glaze(A) **110.00**

16¼" h, ovoid shape, cobalt brushed floral design, imp "W.E. Welding, Brantford 3"(A) **385.00**

18¾" h, dbl ear handles, imp "Westerwater and Lambright," cobalt brushed tree on front, wings on reverse(A) **215.00**

Match Safe, 3⅝" h, unglazed terra-cotta, bowl on pedestal base, roulette design, Meyer(A) **99.00**

Meat Tenderizer, 9½" h, wooden handle, "Pat'd Dec 25, 1877"(A).......... **70.00**

Milk Crock

7⅞" h, imp "W.H. Crisman Strasbourg.," "1" in dotted circle, salt glaze, c1860(A) **66.00**

10⅛" h, cobalt "2" and squiggly lines, hairline crack, c1820(A) **121.00**

Mug

3¼" h, bark-textured surface, Albany brown slip glaze(A) **275.00**

4½" h, imp "N.E. SMITH LAWLEY, ALA," brown Albany slip(A) **77.00**

5" h, Leon slip glaze, mustard w/green accents, Meyer(A) **143.00**

Pitcher

6" h, brown basket weave w/grapes and leaves **85.00**

7¾" h, brown Albany slip, incised zigzag band and sgraffito "Made by John Fowler, Dec. 20th, 1867"(A)...................................... **65.00**

8" h, black glaze w/applied "Minnie"(A) **265.00**

9" h, grape on waffle design, blue and white **175.00**

Plate, 10" d, Leon slip glaze, green, Meyer Pottery(A) **440.00**

Preserving Jar

8" h, brown Albany slip glaze, c1870(A) **37.00**

9½" h

Cobalt brushed design on shoulder, matte tan finish, red-brown Albany glazed int, chips(A) **35.00**

Stenciled and freehand cobalt "Weyman & Bro., Pittsburgh, Pa."(A) **412.00**

Vert cobalt squiggles from shoulder(A)...................................... **175.00**

10" h, cobalt

Brushed florals on shoulder(A)..... **115.00**

Stenciled "A.P. Donaghho, Parkersburg, W. Va."(A) **35.00**

Salt Crock, 3½" h, 6½" d, raised tan waffle ground, cobalt sunflower heads at base, cobalt "SALT" on front, cobalt rippled border **95.00**

Storage Jar

8¾" h, imp "U. KENDALL'S FACTORY, CIN." in circle, brown salt glaze, 1 gallon(A)...................................... **121.00**

8⅞" h, brown Albany slip glaze, c1880(A) **33.00**

9¾" h, brown salt glaze, c1850(A) .. **50.00**

10⅛" h, imp "BOSTON," ochre top and base, salt glaze,½ gallon, c1810(A) **440.00**

16" h, 4 sprays of blue flowers, dtd 1833/3 CMS, salt glaze, c1833(A) **440.00**

Whiskey Jug

9¾" h, imp "1809 PAUL.CUSHMAN.S STONEWARE.WEST OF ALBANY.GOAL. HALF.A.MILE.WEST," tan salt glaze, ½ gallon, cracks(A)...................... **3300.00**

11" h, imp blue "EATON & STOUT and 1821," 1 gallon, salt glaze(A)....... **1375.00**

11¼" h, blue scalloped design, imp oval "C.CROLIUS MANUFACTURER NEW-YORK," salt glaze, 1 gallon(A) **935.00**

11½" h, ovoid shape, blue leaf design, imp "S. BREWER NEW LONDON 1," salt glaze, c1850(A) **242.00**

12¼" h, ovoid shape, blue script "J.F." in cartouche w/rope border, imp "BOSTON," salt glaze, 1 gallon, c1793–97, handle hairline(A) **3300.00**

15½" h, imp "D.GOODALE.HARTFORD," salt glaze, 2 gallon, c1840(A) **165.00**

16" h, ovoid shape, imp "CHARLESTOWN GGG.", brown-tan salt glaze, 3 gallon, c1830(A) **357.00**

J & JG LOW
PATENT
ART TILE WORKS
CHELSEA MASS USA
COPYRIGHT 1881 BY
J & JG LOW

TILES   A.E.T.Co.

Eastern Half of United States and California

c1870s–Present

History: American tilemaking increased in importance after Philadelphia's Centennial Exposition of 1876 where the numerous European decorative ceramics that were displayed provided the impetus for American tilemakers to develop their own designs.

The majority of the tile factories were in the eastern half of the United States since ample clay was available there. Several companies were located in California. At least one hundred firms made art pottery tiles. Some factories made tiles along with their art pottery lines, while others concentrated on tiles and made small amounts of art pottery.

Some early art tiles were machine manufactured by large potteries, but the Arts and Crafts movement at the turn of the century placed the emphasis on handcrafted art. Tiles were then pressed and decorated by hand.

J. & J.G. LOW ART TILE WORKS, CHELSEA, MASSACHUSETTS, 1877–1907: The first important American art tile factory was the Low Art Tile Works founded by John Gardner Low in Chelsea, Massachusetts, in 1877. His colored, transparent-glazed tiles had Victorian themes—his favorite motifs being pastoral scenes, mythological subjects, and nymphs.

Three methods of tile production were used at Low Art. At first a dust process was used in which powdered clay was die-pressed onto a solid clay backing, resulting in sharp, heavily embossed designs. Artists undercut the designs with hand tools to give a crisp appearance. A second technique involved pressing leaves and flowers into the wet clay, leaving a delicate, life-like impression. Some tiles were made with designs hand cut into the tiles themselves, resulting in a high-relief picture. The most common sizes were six-by-six and four-by-four inches, but a variety of other sizes were also made. Low Art won many awards for its tiles.

Arthur Osborne, an Englishman, worked at Low Art from 1879–1893 and was known for his "plastic sketches"—low-relief pictures using clay instead of oil paint. These featured farm scenes, animals, birds, monks, cupids, and women on tiles up to 18 inches long. They were signed "AO" on the face of the sketch. Osborne also made other types of tiles in a variety of motifs.

Starting in c1882, Low Art made pottery and tile-decorated objects, such as clock cases, ewers, fireplace mantels, planters, inkwells, and flower holders. Low Art even made soda fountains starting in 1899. Brass objects incorporating tiles included candlesticks, boxes, paperweights, lamps, and trivets. Tiles were made in a wide variety of colors, but green and brown earth tones were the most prevalent.

BEAVER FALLS TILE COMPANY, BEAVER FALLS, PENNSYLVANIA, 1886–1927: Beaver Falls Tile Company was organized by Francis Walker in 1886 and made tiles in the Victorian style. Many tiles depicted busts of men, women, and children and classical scenes. Numerous tiles were used for stove decorations. Isaac Broome was a major sculptor-ceramist who worked for Beaver Falls in 1890 after leaving Ott and Brewer. He also made large panels of The Muses and a famous twelve-inch tile of George Washington.

AMERICAN ENCAUSTIC TILE COMPANY, ZANESVILLE, OHIO, 1875–1935: American Encaustic Tile Company was in an ideal location in Zanesville, Ohio, where there were plenty of clay deposits. By the early 1920s it was the largest tile company in the world and made a tremendous variety. Victorian-style motifs were used under clear, colored high glazes for some pieces, but hand-cut, hand-finished, unglazed terra-cotta tiles also were made, mostly by Herman Mueller, who later formed his own company in Trenton, New Jersey. American Encaustic also used the cloisonné technique in which designs were usually die stamped into a tile, leaving thin walls between the sections. These depressions were filled in with colored glazes.

Floor tiles were American Encaustic's first product. Frederick Rhead was hired as a designer in 1917. In the 1920s the company made faience tiles, but all sorts of decorative tiles were made using a wide variety of techniques. Novelties, souvenir plaques, and commemorative pieces also were made.

American Encaustic closed in 1935, and several years later reopened as Shawnee Pottery.

MOSAIC TILE COMPANY, ZANESVILLE, OHIO, 1894–1967: Mosaic Tile was started in 1894 by Karl Langenbeck and Herman Mueller from American Encaustic. At first the company made floor tiles such as Florentine Mosaic which had a dull finish and was inlaid with an assortment of colored clays. Langenbeck and Mueller left the firm in 1903, and William Shinnick became manager in 1907. The company added several branch offices and employed numerous artists.

Faience wall tiles were made in pastel colors in 1918. Ceramic mosaic, white wall tiles, and fireplace tiles were also made. Numerous commemorative tiles and plaques depicting famous people and events were manufactured, along with souvenir pieces. Some tiles had molded figures, similar to Wedgwood Jasperware, in a variety of shapes. Many different decorating techniques were used, including embossing, impressing, and decals.

UNITED STATES ENCAUSTIC TILE COMPANY, INDIANAPOLIS, INDIANA, 1877–1939: United States Encaustic Tile Company made floor, wall, and fireplace tiles in three finishes: unglazed, matte, or glazed in bright colors. Relief tiles were made in three- or six-section panels.

MORAVIAN POTTERY AND TILE WORKS, DOYLESTOWN, PENNSYLVANIA, 1877–PRESENT: Henry Chapman Mercer's earliest tiles were Moravian-inspired pieces made for floors, fireplaces, walls, ceilings, and large decorative panels. Mercer designs were inspired by medieval motifs, Indians, plants, animals, tapestries, and architectural finds. Mercer used a variety of decorating techniques, including brocade tiles which were done in high relief with irregular shapes which were often set into concrete. Some examples were unglazed, some were glazed in matte or shiny finish. His tiles were often cut into the shape of the figure instead of squares.

GRUEBY POTTERY, BOSTON, MASSACHU-SETTS (SEE GRUEBY IN THE ART POTTERY SEC-TION FOR HISTORY): The Grueby Pottery was the best of the Arts and Crafts tilemakers. The cloisonné technique was utilized to make tiles for fireplaces and bathrooms. A wide assortment of designs, such as tulips, castles, and landscapes, were die stamped on the tile and then glazed by hand. Most of the tiles were designed by Addison B. Le Boutillier.

ROOKWOOD POTTERY, CINCINNATI, OHIO (SEE ROOKWOOD IN THE ART POTTERY SECTION FOR HISTORY): Rookwood Pottery made faience tiles intended for exterior garden use or to be set into walls. Most of the tiles were large and heavily embossed.

References: Ralph and Terry Kovel, *Kovels' American Art Pottery*, Crown, 1993; Cleota Reed, *Henry Chapman Mercer and The Moravian Pottery and Tile Works*, University of Pennsylvania Press, 1989.

Collectors' Club: Tile Heritage Foundation, Box 1850, Healdsburg, CA 95448, quarterly bulletin, *Flash Point.*

Museums: Chrysler Museum, Norfolk, VA; Mercer Museum, Doylestown, PA; Museum of History and Technology, Smithsonian Institution, Washington, DC; Newark Museum, NJ.

TILES

3" sq
Ellipses in circle, green, terra-cotta, and brown, unmkd	**65.00**
Raised green leaf, cream ground, "Pewabic Detroit" mark	**75.00**
Scarab design, irid finish, Pewabic	**110.00**

3³⁄₄" sq, black-outlined and pink, blue, brown, white, and gray, incised "Corner North Bennet and Salem Streets," "51.5.11 S.E.G. RB" mark(A) ... **385.00**

4" sq
Bisque, morning glory design, Matt Morgan	**15.00**
Blue and orange geometric design, Grueby	**110.00**
Blue and yellow cross, unmkd	**100.00**
Brown-painted sailing ships w/white sails, blue and green sea, Marblehead(A)	**330.00**
Cardinal in tree, red, brown, and green, American Encaustic	**55.00**
Light blue geometric design, gloss black ground, Grueby	**50.00**
Molded relief of Love, Music,	

Beauty, or Industry, red clay, set of 4, imp "Grueby Boston" mark(A) ... **467.00**
Multicolored castle landscape, Grueby, set of 6 ... **450.00**
Pink-outlined celadon green relief of frog w/crown, Rookwood, dtd 1910(A) ... **110.00**
Pisces, cutout design, brown, chips on rim, Moravian ... **38.00**
Red clay w/stylized yellow, blue, and white blossoms, Grueby(A) ... **175.00**
Sky blue banner w/"A.E. Tile Works, April 19, 1892" and woman's face ... **90.00**

4¹⁄₄" sq
Brown gloss raised Pisces, Moravian	**40.00**
Circ geometric design, red-brown, Low Art Tile	**25.00**
Matte green, brown, and blue fountain and garden scene, unmkd(A)	**165.00**
Portrait bust of young woman w/hat, clear caramel glaze, Trent Tile Co.(A)	**49.00**

4¹⁄₂" l, 6" h, yellow and green raised chamberstick, "Grueby Tile" at top, matte green ground(A) ... **990.00**

4¹⁄₂" sq
Blue and buff zigzag design, Low Art Tile mark	**85.00**
Conc circles, teal blue glaze, Low Art Tile mark	**35.00**

5¹⁄₄" d
Blue basket w/pink and yellow flowers, white ground, California Faience mark(A)	**247.00**
Matte brown, blue and red peacock, gloss turquoise border, California Faience mark(A)	**467.00**

5¹⁄₂" sq
Bust of man in Dutch Renaissance

Brown, red, and white ship, 5" sq, green and blue sea, matte and gloss ground, California Faience(A), $330.00

style clothes, clear olive glaze, Beaver Falls(A) 220.00

Cloisonné-style sailing ship, blue and brown matte and gloss glazes, California Faience(A) 275.00

Profile bust of man w/ruffled collar, clear brown glaze, stamped "J. & J.G. Low" mark(A) 357.00

5¾" d

Blue, white, and green floral design, "NC, JM, W, A.M. & DA74" mark, Newcomb College....................... 850.00

Polychrome bouquet, matte blue ground, Whitford(A) 100.00

5¾" sq

Cloisonné-type matte mustard and brown Spanish galleon w/gloss turquoise accents, California Faience mark(A) 1430.00

Relief of matte purple, turquoise, and pink flower blossoms, Rookwood(A) 1100.00

6" sq

Art Deco style silver deer, black ground, silver grill in corners, American Encaustic 125.00

Beige and cobalt mermaid w/mirror, Grueby 225.00

Bisque, stylized azaleas, Matt Morgan 25.00

Blue and green landscape of trees and hills, signed "M.R.," Grueby(A)................................ 495.00

Brown and green trees, blue ground, Grueby(A)...................... 1045.00

Bust of Martha and George Washington, taupe glaze, Beaver Falls Tile Co., pr(A) 715.00

Cherub and cornucopia, Grueby 650.00

Cloisonné

Brown and ochre turtle under green wreath, mottled brown ground, sgd "E.A.," Grueby(A)... 605.00

Flying sea gulls over waves, matte green ground, corner chips, Grueby 195.00

Multicolored fruit and flowers in basket, matte blue ground, Marblehead(A) 715.00

Violet and beige almond-shaped pattern, green and orange abstract ground, Grueby(A) 220.00

Cream design of boy w/discs, gloss black ground 175.00

Egyptian Revival style raised tulip in matte rose on green ground, Owens....................................... 125.00

Faience, blue and white peasant man at table, woman w/flowers, dog on cliff, American Encaustic . 65.00

Gloss green glazed bust of baby

boy, framed, American Encaustic(A) 110.00

Lavender flowers w/green leaves in blue vase, white and blue border, Marblehead 200.00

Matte tan, red, and blue ship on waves, corner chip, Morasque..... 200.00

Multicolored horses, chip, Grueby .. 400.00

Red raised Cupid w/bow and "EROS," matte black ground, Grueby(A)................................... 165.00

Rust-orange and brown house w/gray roof, green grass and trees, blue-gray sky, Marblehead(A) 1760.00

Tan clay w/matte blue grapes, green leaves, brown branches on beige ground, Grueby(A)...................... 82.00

Tropical fish design, gloss finish, American Encaustic mark 65.00

Two blue, yellow, and green macaws perched on brown basket w/flowers, cream ground, cracks, Marblehead(A)................ 275.00

Yellow tulip and green leaves, green ground, Grueby 450.00

6⅛" sq

Incised woodland scene in green shades, Marblehead(A) 385.00

Raised geometric and teardrop design, fans in corners, brown shades, "J. & J. G. Low Chelsea Mass" mark 35.00

7" sq, red tulip w/green leaves, matte green ground, Grueby(A)............... 660.00

7½" sq, profile bust of woman w/long braid, clear blue glaze, stamped "American Encaustic Tile Co." mark(A) 935.00

7¾" sq, emb lion figure, organic matte brown glaze, Wheatley(A) 247.00

8" sq

Incised landscape w/tree at river,

Gloss green seaweed, beige ground, 6½" sq, Pewabic(A), $308.00

*Molded matte green and blue flower
head, 9" sq, Rookwood(A), $115.00*

matte blue glaze on bisque body,
Batchelder(A)............................ **220.00**
Sailing ship in 6 colors, Grueby **1250.00**
8½" h, 5½" w, black and white bust
of President Harding(A) **135.00**
8¾" h, 5¾" w, gray, black, and white
bust of Theodore Roosevelt, J.H.
Barrett and Co.(A) **385.00**
12" l, 6" h, red, green, and brown
semi-matte stone bridge, cottage,
and ducks, Richmond **100.00**
12" sq
Blue, green, and yellow geometric
design, Wheatley........................ **300.00**
Cloisonné-type tall ship on blue-
green sea, tan and beige sky, chip
on corner, Rookwood.................. **800.00**
17½" l, 11½" h, Autumn, nymphs
making harvest offering, light green
gloss glaze, American Encaustic(A) . **1540.00**
19" h, 9" w, classical portrait scene,
green glaze, Low Art Tile mark(A) ... **1320.00**
23½" l, 13¾" h, oval, relief of Cupid
w/blue and yellow flowers and
green foliage, burgundy ground,
"ROOKWOOD FAIENCE, 9375DD, USA"
mark(A) **880.00**
TILE FRAME
29⅝" l, 23¾" h, ivory Greek key pattern on light green ground, set of 14,
imp "Owens" mark(A) **660.00**
TILE PICTURE
6" sq
Set of 3, red clay w/white water lily
blossom, green leaves, dark green
ground, imp "Grueby Boston"
mark(A) **1100.00**
Set of 16, molded cattails and water
plants, gloss green glaze, "A.E.
Tile Co. Limited" mark(A) **825.00**
6" w, 3" h, set of 6, red clay body,
matte green, white, and black Greek

key pattern, central design of
"Kelsey Ranch Lexington Supplying
Waldorf Lunches," imp "Grueby
Tile Boston" mark(A) **660.00**
8" h, 40" l, center tile w/beige and
brown schooner on blue ground, 4
tiles w/seagulls and blue ground,
Grueby.. **2500.00**

YELLOWWARE
East and Midwest
1830–Present

History: Yellowware was imported to America from England in the 1820s. Pieces were made
from heavy earthenware clays that fired to varying shades of yellow when coated with a clear alkaline glaze. Yellowware was quite durable and
eventually replaced redware as a kitchen pottery
since it was less fragile.

Peak years of production for yellowware occurred between the 1860s and 1870s. More than
eighty American potteries produced yellowware
between 1830 and 1900, several of them still do
so. Yellowwares were eventually replaced by
whitewares and decorated porcelains.

Very little yellowware was marked, although
some pieces did have impressed marks. The first
pieces were made on the potter's wheel, but by
the late 1830s molded pieces were made by slip
casting, press molding, or drape molding. Handles were manually applied.

Most of the clays were found in Ohio and
New Jersey, and one of the first firms to make
utilitarian yellowwares was David and James
Henderson's Jersey City Pottery Company. Potters were brought there from England between
1828 and 1833. Bennett Pottery in Baltimore was
another important early yellowware maker.

The most common form of yellowware decoration was white, brown, or blue banding. Other
decorations included horizontal stripes in one or
several colors, sponge or mocha designs, and
Rockingham glaze. The most desirable decoration found on teapots was Rebekah-at-the-Well,
which was made by many different potteries.
Dog and lion figurals also were made in the
Rockingham-glazed yellowwares.

There were a tremendous number of forms
used for yellowwares, most were utilitarian in nature. Mixing bowls, made to nest together, came
in sizes ranging from three to seventeen inches in
diameter. Pitchers came in an endless variety of
sizes and shapes, nappies ranged from three to
thirteen inches. Pie plates, custard cups, tobacco
jars, soap holders, covered storage jars, rolling
pins, meat tenderizers, pepper pots, snuff boxes,
and such were all found in yellowware. All types
of food molds were made, from the miniature
candy and chocolate types to cornbread, jelly,

and Turk's-Head molds. Batter bowls had a lipped edge and ranged in size from seven to fifteen inches in diameter. Much advertising and promotional ware also was made.

Ohio was a major source of yellowware production, with East Liverpool the most important center. Many potters got their start there, such as Bennett, Harker, Goodwin, and William Brunt. By 1853 there were eleven different potteries in East Liverpool, all making utilitarian pieces, such as chamberpots, milk pans, butter tubs, mugs, flowerpots, pitchers, and bowls. Cincinnati also had a concentration of potters producing yellowwares.

During the 20th century, the Robinson-Ransbottom Pottery started yellowware production which continues to the present day, and both Hull and Red Wing made yellowwares as part of their production lines. Additional potteries producing yellowwares were found in New Jersey, Vermont, Pennsylvania, Maryland, and Illinois.

References: John Gallo, *Nineteenth and Twentieth Century Yellowware*, Heritage Press, 1985; William C. Ketchum, Jr. *American Country Pottery: Yellowware and Spongeware*, Alfred A. Knopf, 1987; Joan Leibowitz, *Yellowware: The Transitional Ceramic*, Schiffer Publishing, 1985; Lisa S. McAllister and John L. Michel, *Collecting Yellowware*, Collector Books, 1992.

Museums: Bennington Museum, VT; Henry Ford Museum and Greenfield Village, Dearborn, MI; Museum of Ceramics, East Liverpool, OH.

Baking Dish, 10" l, oval, applied game
  birds and vines, glazed int, stains
  and chips(A) **50.00**
Beater Jar, 5½" h, 3 brown stripes **75.00**
Bowl
  4½" d, pink and blue banding **12.00**
  5" d
    Molded foliage scrolls(A) **35.00**
    Raised columns and classical
      drops, med yellow **85.00**
  5¼" d, molded leaf and branch de-
    sign, light yellow **79.00**
  5⅜" d, blue and white stripes(A) **33.00**
  6" d
    Girl w/sprinkling can design **45.00**
    Molded slip-decorated med blue
      stripe, c1900–30 .... **38.00**
  6½" d, 2 white stripes in 2 brown
    stripes **75.00**
  7¼" d, 4 blue bands **49.00**
  8" d, brown center band **35.00**
  8¼" d
    Molded foliage scrolls, green and
      brown speckled glaze(A) **44.00**
    Molded slip-decorated blue
      bands, c1900–30 .... **49.00**
  9½" d
    Molded ridges, brown and green
      spatter(A) **55.00**

Two white stripes in 2 brown
    stripes **85.00**
  10" d, blue stripes **35.00**
  11" d
    Brown, white, and green earth-
      worm design, East Liverpool,
      Ohio, stains(A) **687.00**
    Cobalt bands **35.00**
  11½" d, 2 white stripes in 2 brown
    stripes **145.00**
  12" d
    Brown and blue bands **30.00**
    Two white stripes in 2 brown
      stripes **165.00**
  13½" d, white stripes(A) **60.00**
  14" d
    Brown banding **75.00**
    Molded rim w/"Sharpes War-
      ranted fireproof" label(A) **93.00**
    Two white stripes in 2 brown
      stripes **195.00**
  15½" d, blue band and white
    stripes, hairlines(A) **137.00**
  17" d, 2 white stripes in 2 brown
    stripes **285.00**
Bud Vase, 7¼" h, paneled(A) **38.00**
Butter Crock, 4" h
  4¾" h, molded staves, light blue
    glaze(A) **315.00**
  7¼" d, brown and white stripes,
    ribbed base **125.00**
Chamber Pot, 1⅞" h, 2⅝" d, white
  band w/dark brown stripes(A) **44.00**
Colander, 9½" d, 4½" h, white int
  glaze, molded ext(A) **116.00**
Creamer
  3¼" h, blue bands(A) **93.00**
  4¼" h, molded tavern scenes and
    vining, brown drip glaze(A) **15.00**
Dish, 5¾" d, brown Rockingham
  sponging(A) **50.00**
Figure
  5" h, seated dog w/basket in mouth,
    clear greenish glaze(A) **247.00**
  6" h, bust of Franklin, brown runny
    glaze(A) **33.00**

*Pitcher, 6½" h, blue stripe,
cream lines, slip decorated,
c1900–30, $145.00*

10" l, recumbent lion on rect base,
brown details, chips, Ohio(A) **440.00**

Jug, 8¼" h, applied ribbon handle,
redware int **110.00**

Medallion, 6¼" h, oval, white molded
bust of Washington(A) **253.00**

Mold, 3¾" l, 3½" w, ear of corn(A) **82.00**

Mug

   3" h, Rockingham glaze, chips(A).... **93.00**

   3¾" h, white center band w/2
   brown bands(A) **115.00**

   3⅞" h, ribbed strap handle, white
   band(A) **137.00**

   4⅝" h, blue bands, imp "100%
   Buckeye Pure" **69.00**

Pie Plate, Rockingham glaze

   9" d **165.00**

   10" d **175.00**

Pitcher

   2" h, emb bands(A) **70.00**

   4¾" h, slip-decorated brown stripe,
   corrugated bottom, c1910 .... **68.00**

6¼" h, molded shoulder and neck
detail, blue spotted glaze(A) **40.00**

6½" h

   Emb swastikas, brown and blue
   sponging, stains and chips(A) ... **115.00**

   Figural man's head w/tricorne,
   cobalt drip on yellowware
   body **60.00**

9" h, rose and lattice pattern **175.00**

Plate, 9½" d, emb rim design, set of
4(A) **330.00**

Preserving Jar, 8¼" h(A) **132.00**

Pudding Mold, 3" d, black stenciled
flower sprig, paneled ext,
c1880–90, Morton Pottery **58.00**

Rolling Pin, 15" l, turned wood han-
dles(A) **192.00**

Salt, 2⅜" h, ftd, brown and white
stripes(A) **110.00**

Shaker, 4⅜" h, blue, brown, and
white stripes(A) **385.00**

Washboard **595.00**

APPENDIX

Auction Houses

The following auction houses cooperated with us by providing complimentary subscriptions to their catalogues for all ceramics auctions. Their cooperation is appreciated greatly. Without this help, it would have been impossible to produce this price guide.

Butterfield and Butterfield
7601 Sunset Boulevard
Los Angeles, CA 40046

William Doyle Galleries
175 East 87th Street
New York, NY 10028

Dunning Auction Service
755 Church Road
Elgin, IL 60121

Garth's Auction, Inc.
2690 Stratford Road
P.O. Box 369
Delaware, OH 43015

Gene Harris Auction Center
203 So. 18th Avenue
P.O. Box 476
Marshalltown, IA 50158

Willis Henry Auctions
22 Main Street
Marshfield, MA 02059

Leslie Hindman Auctioneers
215 W. Ohio Street
Chicago, IL 60610

Joy Luke Auction Gallery
300 E. Grove Street
Bloomington, IL 61701

Phillips Auction Gallery
406 East 79th Street
New York, NY 10021

David Rago Arts and Crafts
17 South Main Street
Lambertville, NJ 08530

Harmer Rooke Galleries
32 East 57th Street
New York, NY 10022

Robert W. Skinner, Inc.
The Hermitage on the Garden 63 Park Plaza
Boston, MA 02116

Robert W. Skinner, Inc.
Bolton Gallery
Route 117
Bolton, MA 01740

Smith and Jones, Inc.
12 Clark Lane
Sudbury, MA 01776

John Toomey Gallery
818 North Boulevard
Oak Park, IL 60301

Don Treadway Gallery
2029 Madison Road
Cincinnati, OH 45208

Wolf's Auction Gallery
1239 West 6th Street
Cleveland, OH 44113

Additional American auction houses which hold auctions that include American pottery and porcelain.

Christie's
502 Park Avenue
New York, NY 10022

Christie's East
219 East 67 Street
New York, NY 10021

Du Mouchelles
409 E. Jefferson Avenue
Detroit, MI 48226

Sotheby's
1334 York Avenue
New York, NY 10021

Museums

Museums listed here have large general collections of American ceramics.

Art Museum, Princeton, NJ
Bennington Museum, VT
Brooklyn Museum, NY
Cincinnati Art Museum, OH
Cooper Hewitt Museum, New York, NY
DAR Museum, Washington, DC
Everson Museum of Art, Syracuse, NY
Henry Ford Museum and Greenfield Village, Dearborn, MI

Henry Francis duPont Winterthur Museum, DE
Jones Museum of Glass and Ceramics, Douglas Hill, ME
Los Angeles County Museum of Art, CA
Mint Museum of Art, Charlotte, NC
Museum of Ceramic Art at Alfred University, NY
Museum of Ceramics, East Liverpool, OH
New Orleans Museum of Art, LA
Oakland Museum, CA
Philadelphia Museum of Art, PA
Yale University Art Gallery, New Haven, CT
Zanesville Art Center, OH

Photo Credits

We wish to thank all those dealers and collectors who permitted us to photograph their American ceramics. Unfortunately, we are unable to identify the sources for all of our pictures; nevertheless we appreciate all of those people who have contributed to this price guide.

Colorado: Philomena, Hygiene. Florida: Clark and Vicki McLean, Tampa; Streety's, Sarasota.

Illinois: Barbara's Keepsakes, Richmond; J. Begani, Melrose Park; Gladys and Donald Breed, Naperville; Chez Therese Antiques, Chicago; Cobblestone Antiques, Arlington Heights; Collage Antiques, Arlington Heights; Collectable Memories, Grayslake; The Collector's Choice, Wilmington; Collector's Cove, Rockford; Bill and Helen Duncanson, Pekin; Essence of Yesteryear; Gallery 23, Chicago; Grape and Cable Antiques, Lombard; Hidden Treasures, Decatur; Tony Jandacek, La Grange Park; Edward Joseph, Chicago; K & M Antiques, Beardstown; Lockport Antique Associates, Lockport; Longfield's Keep, Evergreen Park; Mid Century, Chicago; 1905 Emporium Mall, Richmond; The Oak Peddlers, Elmhurst; Odell's Antiques, Highland Park; Partners in Time Antiques, Champaign; Peddle Horse Antiques and Collectibles, Des Plaines; Pumpkin Patch Antiques and Gallery, Chicago; Raymond's Antiques, Highland Park; Red Bandana, Chicago; Remembered Treasures, Palatine; Carrie Richmond Antiques, Inc. Barrington; Brandon Smith, Peoria; Somewhere in Time, Sycamore; Stimson's Antiques, St. Charles; Through the Looking Glass, Arlington Heights; Travers Family, Glen Ellyn; Treasures and Pleasures, St. Charles; V.J. Antiques, Downers Grove; Volo Antique Mall, Volo; Yesterday's Treasures, Wadsworth.

Indiana: The Antique Market, Michigan City. Iowa: Mark Bassett, Nevada; Larsen's Collectibles, Hampton; The Mansion, Spencer; St. John Antiques, Le Grand.

Michigan: Flo-Blue Shoppe, Birmingham; Fregeau Farm, St. Clair Shores; Golden Era Antiques, Farmington Hills; "Good Old Stuff," Elaine Brooks, Mt. Clemens; Harley's Antique Mall, Jackson; Historic House Antique Mall, Watervliet; Pottery Plus, Deb Honeycutt, Buchanan; Patricia Schuman, Royal Oak; Denney L. Tracy, Ann Arbor; Trade Winds Antiques, Watervliet.

Minnesota: Bomar Antiques and Collectibles, St. Paul; Brass Bed Antiques, Duluth; Steve Schoneck, Newport. New Jersey: Main Street Antique Center, Flemington; Richard Rupert, Woodbridge. New York: Historical Design Collection, Inc. New York City.

Ohio: Betty Blair, Jackson; Due's Collectibles, Maple Heights; J & V Antiques and Collectibles, Lorain; Leffler's Antiques, Toledo; Mainstreet Antiques, Columbiana; Jim and Cindy Naus, Toledo; Old World Antiques, Columbiana; Philomeno's Antiques and Collectibles, Columbiana; Show Tyme Antiques, Findlay; Bunny Walker, Bucyrus.

Oklahoma: Colonial Antiques, Tulsa. Pennsylvania: Antique Gallery, Philadelphia; Consign Mart at the Barn, Cresco; Richard A. Wagner, Sewickley.

Tennessee: Wade and Stephanie Anderton, Winchester. Wisconsin: Jan's Journeys Antiques, Twin Lakes; Joker's Wild, Madison; Nicol Knappen, Madison; Pipsqueak and Me, Janesville; Ed Ratliff, Milwaukee; Timeless Treasures, Milwaukee.

Publications

The American Art Pottery Association
Jean Oberkirsch, Membership
125 East Rose
St. Louis, MO 63119

American Pottery Journal
P.O. Box 14255
Parkville, MO 64152

Arts and Crafts Quarterly
9 South Main Street
Lambertville, NJ 08530

Ceramics Monthly
1609 Northwest Boulevard
Columbus, OH 43212

Pottery Lovers Newsletter
Pat and Ted Sallaz
4969 Hundson Drive
Stow, OH 44224

The Daze
10271 State Road, Box 57
Otisville, MI 48463

GLOSSARY

Applied Design: Ornamentation that is attached to the body or ground.

Architectural Form: The use of structural themes in the design of a piece of pottery. This type of design was used quite frequently during the Art Deco period and in art pottery.

Baluster Shape: Bulbous middle with a flared top and base.

Belleek: An eggshell-thin decorative porcelain. It was manufactured at several locations in the U.S. such as Lenox, Willets, and Knowles, Taylor, Knowles. It was influenced by the porcelain from Ireland.

Bisque: The unglazed initially fired porcelain or pottery body.

Cold Paint: The use of non-fired color to accent or decorate. Cold paint was used fairly extensively on cookie jars, although it easily wears off.

Crazing: Numerous surface cracks in the glaze resulting from the different shrinking patterns of the glaze and the body.

Crystalline Glaze: The recrystallization of particles during the cooling period, resulting in a lustered sheen to the surface.

Decalcomania: The application of a lithographed print to a glazed or an unglazed surface prior to glazing.

Earthenware: A lightly fired pottery which is often covered with a glaze to seal its porous surface.

Engobe: A French term for slip.

Faience: A French term for tin-glazed earthenware, synonymous with majolica. The term was used by several American manufacturers to describe their products.

Flint Enamel Glaze: A hard-surfaced mottled glaze frequently found on Bennington pottery.

Glaze: A glass coating applied to seal a porous body, rendering it non-porous.

Glost Firing: A second firing used to fuse the glaze over the bisque body.

Granite Ware: A form of stoneware with a speckled appearance.

Ground: The basic body on which decorations are applied.

Ironstone: An opaque white vitrified china designed for utilitarian purposes. It often contains iron slag for strength.

Jigger: A device in which plastic clay is shaped in a turning mold, often mounted on a potter's wheel; the mold forms exterior of vessel, while a template cuts interior contour.

Olla: A wide-mouthed bulbous pot.

Overlay: The application of a surface or over-glaze decoration, most often found on colored borders. The overlay is frequently a fine gold lattice treatment.

Porcelain: A highly vitrified ceramic ware with varying degrees of transluscency, depending on thickness.

Pottery: A generic term that includes earthenware, clay, and stoneware products, but generally excludes hard-paste ceramics such as porcelain.

Redware: Low fired, porous pottery used for utilitarian purposes.

Relief Design: The raised design that projects from the ground or body.

Rockingham Glaze: Brown glaze with orange, blue, and yellow mottling, associated with the Bennington potteries.

Sagger: A case composed of fire clay used to surround and protect objects during the firing process.

Salt Glaze: The application of salt during the firing of the glaze which produces an orange-peel-type or finely textured finish.

Sang-De-Boeuf Glaze: A splotchy, ox blood red glaze. The color is obtained from reduced copper oxide and was used in American and European art pottery.

Semi-Porcelain: A type of porcelain that does not reach vitrification associated with true high-fired porcelain. The body is somewhat duller in appearance than the smooth glossy body of true porcelain.

Semi-Vitreous: See Semi-Porcelain.

Sgraffito: The incision of a design through a layer of colored slip exposing the underlying red clay body.

Shaped Rim: A decorative technique whereby the rim has a regular or irregular pattern rather than a smooth outline.

Slip Cup: A small hollow cuplike device with tubes that are often made from turkey-feather quills or reeds; colored slip is trailed or dribbled through the tubes to create decorative patterns on a ceramic surface.

Slip Decoration: The use of liquid clay to produce a raised design on the body or ground. The slip is usually decorated with colored glazes.

Sponging: The application of color or glaze by dabbing with a sponge to produce a mottled effect.

Squeeze-Bag: A decorative technique whereby liquid clay or slip is applied to a body in a manner similar to that used in cake decorating.

Stoneware: A refined, partially vitrified pottery that results in a strong, non-porous body.

Terra-Cotta: An unglazed, lightly fired, reddish earthenware.

Transfer Printing: The application on a ceramic body of a metallic oxide design by means of a tissue print. Printing can be found under and over a glazed surface.

Vitreous: The fusion of ingredients at a high temperature, resulting in a strong, glassy body or surface.

Additional glossary terms can be found in the following books: Louise Ade Boger, *The Dictionary of World Pottery and Porcelain,* Scribners, 1971; George Savage and Harold Newman, *An Illustrated Dictionary of Ceramics,* Van Nostrand Reinhold Company, 1974.

BIBLIOGRAPHY

The following is a listing of general reference books on American ceramics that the reader may find useful. A list of marks books is also included.

Art Pottery References

Paul Evans, *Art Pottery of the United States*, Feingold and Lewis Publishing Corp., 1987.

Lucile Henzke, *Art Pottery of America*, Schiffer Publishing, Ltd, 1982.

Ralph and Terry Kovel, *Kovels' American Art Pottery: The Collector's Guide to Makers, Marks, and Factory Histories*, Crown, 1993.

General Ceramics References

Edwin Atlee Barber, *The Pottery and Porcelain of The United States and Marks of American Potters*, Feingold and Lewis, 1976.

Jo Cunningham, *Collector's Encyclopedia of American Dinnerware*, Collector Books, 1982, 1992 Value Update.

Ellen and Bert Denker, *The Warner Collector's Guide to North American Pottery and Porcelain*, Main Street Press, 1982.

Harvey Duke, *The Official Identification and Price Guide to Pottery and Porcelain*, Seventh Edition, House of Collectibles, 1989.

Alice Cooney Frelinghuysen, *American Porcelain 1770–1920*, Metropolitan Museum of Art, 1989.

Harold F. Guilland, *Early American Folk Pottery*, Chilton Book Company, 1971.

Lois Lehner, *Complete Book of American Kitchen and Dinner Wares*, Wallace-Homestead, 1980.

Elaine Levin, *The History of American Ceramics 1607 to the Present*, Harry N. Abrams, 1988.

Barbara Perry, editor, *American Ceramics*, Rizzoli International Publications, 1989.

Marks References

Gerald DeBolt, *Debolt's Dictionary of Whitewares and Porcelain: American Pottery Marks*, Collector Books, 1993.

William C. Gates and Dana E. Ormerod, *The East Liverpool, Ohio Pottery District: Identification of Manufacturers and Marks*, The Society for Historical Archaeology, 1982.

Lois Lehner, *Encyclopedia of U.S. Marks on Pottery, Porcelain and Clay*, Collector Books, 1988.

Resource Directory

David J. Maloney, Jr., *Maloney's Antiques and Collectibles Resource Directory 1994–1995*, Wallace-Homestead, 1993.

INDEX